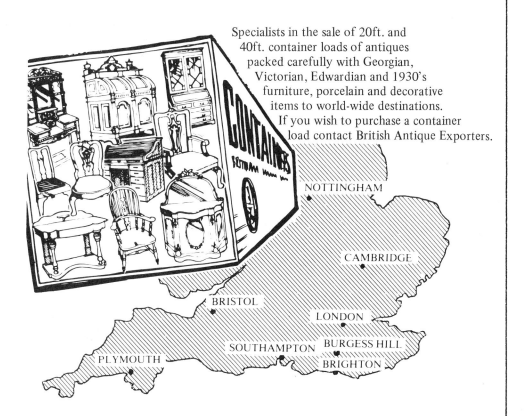

The publishers wish to express their sincere thanks to the following for their involvement and assistance in the production of this volume:

KAREN DOUGLASS (Art Editor)
JANICE MONCRIEFF (Assistant Editor)
ANNETTE CURTIS
SALLY DALGLIESH
TANYA FAIRBAIRN
FRANK BURRELL
ROBERT NISBET
LOUISE SIMPSON
JONN DUNLOP
EILEEN BURRELL
SARAH RITCHIE
MACDONALD GREEN
LISA JONES
ALAN KIDD

ISBN 0-86248-110-4

THE

LYLE

OFFICIAL

ANTIQUES

REVIEW 1989

COMPILED & EDITED BY
TONY CURTIS

INTRODUCTION

This year over 100,000 Antique Dealers and Collectors will make full and profitable use of their Lyle Official Antiques Review. They know that only in this one volume will they find the widest possible variety of goods — illustrated, described and given a current market value to assist them to BUY RIGHT AND SELL RIGHT throughout the year of issue.

They know, too, that by building a collection of these immensely valuable volumes year by year, they will equip themselves with an unparalleled reference library of facts, figures and illustrations which, properly used, cannot fail to help them keep one step ahead of the market.

In its nineteen years of publication, Lyle has gone from strength to strength and has become without doubt the pre-eminent book of reference for the antique trade throughout the world. Each of its fact filled pages are packed with precisely the kind of profitable information the professional Dealer needs — including descriptions, illustrations and values of thousands and thousands of individual items carefully selected to give a representative picture of the current market in antiques and collectibles — and remember all values are prices actually paid, based on accurate sales records in the twelve months prior to publication from the best established and most highly respected auction houses and retail outlets in Europe and America.

This is THE book for the Professional Antiques Dealer. 'The Lyle Book' — we've even heard it called 'The Dealer's Bible'.

Compiled and published afresh each year, the Lyle Official Antiques Review is the most comprehensive up-to-date antiques price guide available. THIS COULD BE YOUR WISEST INVESTMENT OF THE YEAR!

Tony Curtis

Printed by A. Wheaton & Co. Ltd., Exeter, Devon.
Bound by Dorstel Press, Harlow, Essex.

CONTENTS

Advertising Signs 66
American Indian Art 69
Arms & Armour 74
    Badges 78
    Daggers 84
    Flasks 88
    Fuchi-Kashira 89
    Helmets 90
    Medals 97
    Pistols 106
    Rifles 112
    Swords 116
    Tsubas 122
Autograph Letters & Documents 126
Automatons 129
Barometers 130
Books 134
Bronze 137
Buckets 152
Caddies & Boxes 154
Cameras 164
Chandeliers 170
China 172
    American 172
    Arita 178
    Berlin 180
    Bow 182
    British 184
    Canton 192
    Cardew, Michael 193
    Chelsea 194
    Chinese 196
    Clarice Cliff 197
    Coalport 198
    Copeland 199
    Coper, Hans 200
    Delft 201

Derby 202
Doulton 204
Earthenware 210
European 212
Famille Rose 213
French 214
German 216
Goldscheider 220
Goss 221
Imari 222
Italian 226
Japanese 232
Kangxi 235
Leach 236
Liverpool 238
Lowestoft 239
Lustre 239
Martinware 239
Mason's 240
Meissen 241
Ming 248
Minton 249
Moorcroft 253
Parian 253
Paris 254
Rie, Lucie 256
Rockingham 258
Rookwood 258
Royal Dux 260
Satsuma 261
Sevres 262
Spode 265
Staffordshire 266
Stoneware 272
Terracotta 277
Vienna 278
Wedgwood 279

Whieldon 282
Worcester 283
Clocks & Watches 289
Bracket Clocks 289
Carriage Clocks 294
Clock Sets 298
Lantern Clocks 299
Longcase Clocks 300
Mantel Clocks 308
Wall Clocks 318
Watches 320
Wristwatches 326
Copper & Brass 332
Corkscrews 336
Costume 340
Dolls 342
Enamel 348
Fans 350
Furniture 352
Beds 352
Bookcases 354
Bureau Bookcases 359
Bureaux 362
Cabinets 367
Canterburys 372
Chairs, Dining 374
Easy 384
Elbow 390
Chests-of-Drawers 400
Chests-on-Chests 406
Chests-on-Stands 408
Chiffoniers 410
Commodes & Pot Cupboards 411
Commode Chests 412
Corner Cupboards 414
Cupboards 416
Davenports 418
Display Cabinets 420
Dressers 422
Dumbwaiters 424
Kneehole Desks 425
Lowboys 429
Screens 430
Secretaires 433

Secretaire Bookcases 434
Settees & Couches 436
Sideboards 442
Stands 446
Stools 450
Suites 454
Tables 456
Card & Tea Tables 456
Centre Tables 462
Console Tables 466
Dining Tables 468
Dressing Tables 470
Drop-Leaf Tables 472
Gateleg Tables 473
Large Tables 474
Occasional Tables 476
Pembroke Tables 484
Side Tables 486
Sofa Tables 490
Workboxes & Games Tables 492
Writing Tables & Desks 494
Trunks & Coffers 500
Wardrobes & Armoires 504
Washstands 506
Whatnots 507
Wine Coolers 508
Glass 510
Beakers 510
Bottles 510
Bowls 511
Candlesticks 513
Decanters 514
Dishes 515
Drinking Sets 516
Goblets 517
Jugs 521
Miscellaneous Glass 522
Paperweights 524
Scent Bottles 530
Stained Glass 532
Tumblers 533
Vases 534
Wine Glasses 542
Gold 544

H.M.S. Invincible 546
Inros 550
Instruments 552
Iron & Steel 560
Ivory 562
Jewellery 566
Lamps 570
Marble 572
Miniatures 576
Mirrors 577
Miscellaneous 584
Model Ships 590
Model Trains 592
Models 594
Money Banks 595
Motoring Items 596
Musical Boxes & Polyphones 604
Musical Instruments 609
Napoleonic Memorabilia 614
Netsuke 620
Paper Money 628
Pewter 630
Photographs 632
Pianos 634
Portrait Miniatures 636
Prints 640
Quilts 649
Railwayana 650
Rock 'n' Roll 655
Rugs 658
Samplers 666
Share Certificates 668
Shoes 669
Silver 670
    Baskets 670
    Bowls 672
    Boxes 674
    Candelabra 676
    Candlesticks 678
    Casters 680
    Centrepieces 681
    Chambersticks 682
    Chocolate Pots 682
    Cigarette Cases 683

Claret Jugs 683
Coasters 684
Coffee Pots 685
Cream Jugs 687
Cruets 687
Cups 688
Dishes 690
Flatware 692
Goblets 694
Inkstands 695
Jugs 696
Miscellaneous Silver 697
Mugs 700
Mustards 700
Pomanders 701
Porringers 701
Salts 702
Sauceboats 703
Snuff Boxes 703
Tankards 704
Tea & Coffee Sets 706
Tea Caddies 710
Tea Kettles 711
Teapots 712
Trays & Salvers 714
Tureens 716
Urns 717
Vases 718
Vinaigrettes 719
Wine Coolers 720
Wine Funnels 721
Wine Labels 722
Wine Tasters 723
Snuff Bottles 724
Space Toys 730
Tapestries 732
Textiles 734
Titanic Memorabilia 738
Toys 740
Transport 756
Travel Posters 763
Weathervanes 770
Wine 772
Wood 776

Acknowledgements

Abridge Auction Rooms, Market Place, Abridge, Essex RM4 1UA
Anderson & Garland, Anderson House, Market Street, Newcastle-upon-Tyne NE1 6XA
Bagshaws, 17 High Street, Uttoxeter
Ball & Percival, 132 Lord Street, Southport, Merseyside PR9 0AE
Banks & Silvers, Fine Art Dept, 66 Foregate Street, Worcester
Barbers Fine Art Auctioneers, Smarts Heath Road, Mayford, Woking, Surrey
Bearnes , Rainbow, Avenue Road, Torquay TQ2 5TG, Devon
Bermondsey Antique Market, Tower Bridge Road, London
Biddle and Webb, Ladywood Middleway, Birmingham, West Midlands B16 0PP
Blackhorse Agencies, Ambrose, 149 High Road, Loughton, Essex IG10 4LZ
Bloomsbury Book Auctions, 3 & 4 Hardwick Street, London EC1R HRY
Boardman — Fine Art Auctioneers, Station Road Corner, Haverhill, Suffolk CB9 0EY
Bonhams, Montpelier Galleries, Montpelier Street, Knightsbridge, London SW7 1HH
Bracketts, 27-29 High Street, Tunbridge Wells TN1 1UU, Kent
British Antique Exporters, 206 London Road, Burgess Hill, West Sussex RH15 9RX
Broader & Spencer, 18 Quay Road, Bridlington, East Yorkshire YO15 2AP
Brown & Merry, 41 High Street, Tring, Herts HP23 5AB
Wm. H. Brown, Westgate Hall, Grantham, Lincs NG31 6LT
Lawrence Butler & Co., Butler House, 86 High Street, Hythe, Kent CT21 5AJ
Capes Dunn and Co., The Auction Galleries, 38 Charles Street, Manchester, Lancashire M1 7DB
Chancellors Hollingsworth, 31 High Street, Ascot, Berkshire SL5 7HG
Christie's, Cornelis Schuystraat 57, 1071 JG, Amsterdam
Christie's (International) S.A., 8 Place De La Talonwerie, 1204 Geneva
Christie's (Hong Kong) Ltd., 3607 Edinburgh Tower, 15 Queens Road, Hong Kong
Christie's, 8 King Street, St James's, London SW1Y 6QT
Christie's (Monaco) S.A.M., Park Palace, 98000 Monte Carlo
Christie's, 502 Park Avenue, New York, NY 10022
Christie's, 219 East 67th Street, New York, NY 10021
Christie's Scotland, 164-166 Bath Street, Glasgow, Scotland G2 4TG
Christie's South Kensington Ltd., 85 Old Brompton Road, London SW7 3LD
Chrystals Auctions, Unit 32, Spring Valley Industrial Estate, Braddan, Isle of Man
Coles, Knapp & Kennedy, Georgian Rooms, Ross-on-Wye, Herefordshire HR9 5HL
Bruce D. Collins, Fine Arts Gallery, Box 113, Denmark, Maine
Cooper Hirst, Goldlay House, Parkway, Chelmsford, Essex CM2 7PR
County Group, 102 High Street, Tenterden TN30 6AU, Kent
Dacre, Son and Hartley, 1-5 The Grove, Ilkley, West Yorkshire LS29 8HS
Dee & Atkinson, The Exchange Saleroom, Driffield YO25 7LJ, North Humberside
Dickinson, Davy & Markham, New Saleroom, Elwes Street, Brigg, DN20 8JH, North Humberside
Dreweatt Neate, Donnington Priory, Donnington, Newbury, Berkshire RG13 2JE
Du Mouchelles Art Galleries Co., 409 E. Jefferson Avenue, Detroit, Michigan 48226
Hy Duke & Son, Fine Art Salerooms, Weymouth Avenue, Dorchester DT1 1DG
Peter Eley, Western House, 98-100 High Street, Sidmouth, Devon EX10 8EF
Elliott & Green, Emsworth Road, Lymington, Hampshire SO41 9BL
R. H. Ellis and Sons, 44/46 High Street, Worthing, West Sussex BN11 1LL
Fellows and Sons, Bedford House, 88 Hagley Road, Edgbaston, Birmingham, West Midlands
John D. Fleming & Co., 8 Fore Street, Dulverton, Somerset TA22 9EX
John Francis, S.O.F.A.A., Chartered Surveyors, Curiosity Sale Rooms, King Street, Carmarthen
Geering & Colyer, 22/26 High Street, Tunbridge Wells, Kent TN1 1XA
Glendining's, Blenstock House, 7 Blenheim Street, New Bond Street, London W1Y 9LD
Goss & Crested China Co., 62 Murray Road, Horndean, Hants PO8 9JL
Andrew Grant, St Mark's House, St Mark's Close, Cherry Orchard, Worcester WR5 3DJ
Graves, Son & Pilcher, 71 Church Road, Hove, East Sussex BN3 2GL
W. R. J. Greenslade & Co., 13 Hammet Street, Taunton, Somerset TA1 1RN
Hamptons Fine Art, 93 High Street, Godalming, Surrey
Giles Haywood, The Auction House, St John's Road, Stourbridge DY8 1EW, West Midlands
Harvey's Auctions Ltd., 14-18 Neal Street, London WC2H 9LZ
Hetheringtons Nationwide, The Amersham Auction Rooms, 125 Station Road, Amersham, Bucks
Andrew Hilditch and Son Ltd., 19 The Square, Sandbach, Cheshire CW11 0AT
Hobbs & Chambers, 'At the Sign of the Bell', Market Place, Cirencester, Gloucestershire
Hobbs Parker, Romney House, Ashford Market, Ashford, Kent TN23 1PG
Holloways, 49 Parsons Street, Banbury, Oxfordshire OX16 8PF

Edgar Horn, Auction Galleries, 46/50 South Street, Eastbourne, BN21 4XB
Jacobs & Hunt, Lavant Street, Petersfield, Hampshire GU32 3EF
Kent Sales, Giffords, Holmesdale Road, Dartford, Kent
G. A. Key, Aylsham Salerooms, Palmers Lane, Aylsham, Norfolk NR11 6EH
King & Chasemore, West Street, Midhurst, West Sussex GU29 9NG
Lacy Scott (Fine Art Dept.), 10 Risbygate Street, Bury St. Edmunds, Suffolk IP33 3AA
Lalonde Fine Art, 71 Oakfield Road, Clifton, Bristol, Avon BS8 2BE
Lambert & Foster, The Auction Sale Rooms, 102 High Street, Tenterden, Kent
W. H. Lane & Son, Fine Art Auctioneer & Valuers, 64 Morrab Road, Penzance Cornwall
Langlois Ltd., Westaway Rooms, Don Street, St Helier, Jersey, Channel Islands
Lawrence Fine Art, South Street, Crewkerne TA18 8AB, Somerset
Lawrence's, Fine Art Auctioneers, Norfolk House, 80 High Street, Bletchingley, Surrey
David Lay, The Penzance Auction House, Alverton, Penzance, Cornwall TR18 4RE
Lewes Auction Rooms, 56 High Street, Lewes
Locke & England, Walton House, 11 The Parade, Leamington Spa
Lots Road Chelsea Auction Galleries, 71 Lots Road, Chelsea, London SW10 0RN
R. K. Lucas & Son, 9 Victoria Place, Haverfordwest, SA61 2JX
Lyon & Turnbull, 51 George Street, Edinburgh, Midlothian, Scotland
Mallams, Fine Art Auctioneers, 24 St Michaels Street, Oxford, Oxfordshire
Michael G. Matthews, The Devon Fine Art Auction House, Dowel Street, Honiton, Devon
McKenna's Auctioneers & Valuers, Bank Salerooms, Harris Court, Clitheroe, Lancashire
Miller & Company, Lemon Quay Auction Rooms, Truro, Cornwall TR1 2LW
Moore, Allen & Innocent, 33 Castle Street, Cirencester, Gloucestershire GL7 1QD
Morphets, 4-6 Albert Street, Harrogate, North Yorkshire HG1 1JL
Neales of Nottingham, 192 Mansfield Road, Nottingham, Nottinghamshire NG1 3HX
D. M. Nesbit & Co., 7 Clarendon Road, Southsea, Hampshire PO5 2ED
James Norwich Auctions Ltd., Head Office, 33 Timberhill, Norwich, Norfolk NR1 3LA
Olivers, 23/24 Market Hill, Sudbury, CO10 6EN
Onslow's Auctioneers, 14-16 Carroun Road, London SW8 1JT
Osmond, Tricks, Regent Street, Auction Rooms, Clifton, Bristol, Avon BS8 4HG
Outhwaite & Litherland, "Kingsway Galleries", Fontenoy Street, Liverpool, Merseyside L3 2BE
J. R. Parkinson Son & Hamer Auctions, The Auction Room, Rochdale Road, Bury, Lancashire
Parsons, Welch & Cowell, The Argyle Salerooms, Argyle Road, Sevenoaks, Kent
Phillips, 65 George Street, Edinburgh EH2 2JL
Phillips, 207 Bath Street, Glasgow G2 4DH
Phillips, Blenstock House, 7 Blenheim Street, New Bond Street, London W1Y 0AS
Phillips New York, 406 East 79th Street, New York, NY 10021
Phillips, The Old House, Station Road, Knowle, Solihull, West Midlands B93 0HT
Prudential Fine Art Auctioneers, 5 Woodcote Close, Kingston Upon Thames, Surrey KT2 5LZ
Prudential Fine Art Auctioneers, Trinity House, 114 Northenden Road, Sale, Manchester
Reeds Rains Prudential, Trinity House, 114 Northenden Road, Manchester M33 3HD
Rendells, Stone Park, Ashburton, Devon TQ13 7RH
Ernest R. De Rome, 12 New John Street, Westgate, Bradford BD1 2QY
Russell, Baldwin & Bright, The Fine Art Saleroom, Ryelands Road, Leominster HR6 8JG
Sandoe Luce Panes, Wotton Auction Rooms, Wotton-Under-Edge, Gloucestershire GL12 7EB
Sentry Box Military Antiques, 2 Market Street, Brighton, Sussex
Robt. W. Skinner Inc., Bolton Gallery, Route 117, Bolton, Massachusetts
Southgate Antique Auction Rooms, Rear of Town Hall, Green Lanes, Palmers Green, London N13
Henry Spencer & Sons, 20 The Square, Retford, Notts. DN22 6DJ
St John Vaughan with John Hogbin, 8 Queen Street, Deal, Kent CT14 6ET
David Stanley Auctions, Stordan Grange, Osgathorpe, Leicestershire LE12 9SR
G. E. Sworder & Sons, Northgate End Salerooms, 15 Northgate End, Bishops Stortford, Herts
Louis Taylor & Sons, Percy Street, Hanley, Stoke-on-Trent, Staffordshire ST1 1NF
Tiffen King Nicholson, 12 Lowther Street, Carlisle, Cumbria CA3 8DA
Duncan Vincent, Fine Art & Chattel Auctioneers, 105 London Street, Reading RG1 4LF
Wallis and Wallis, West Street Auction Galleries, West Street, Lewes, East Sussex BN7 2NJ
Warners, Wm. H. Brown, The Warner Auction Rooms, 16/18 Halford Street, Leicester LE1 1JB
Warren & Wignall Ltd., The Mill, Earnshaw Bridge, Leyland Lane, Leyland PR5 3PH
J. M. Welch & Son, Old Town Hall, Great Dunmow, Essex CM6 1AU
Wellington Salerooms, Mantle Street, Wellington, Somerset TA21 8AR
Peter Wilson Fine Art Auctioneers, Victoria Gallery, Market Street, Nantwich, Cheshire
Woolley and Wallis, The Castle Auction Mart, Salisbury, Wiltshire SP1 3SU
H. C. Wolton & Son, 6 Whiting Street, Bury St Edmunds, Suffolk IP33 1PB
Worsfolds Auction Galleries, 40 Station Road West, Canterbury, Kent
Wright-Manley, Beeston Sales Centre, Beeston Castle Smithfield, Tarporley, Cheshire

PERIODS

MONARCHS

Period	Date	Monarch	Date
TUDOR PERIOD	1485 - 1603	HENRY 1V	1399 - 1413
ELIZABETHAN PERIOD	1558 - 1603	HENRY V	1413 - 1422
INIGO JONES	1572 - 1652	HENRY V1	1422 - 1461
JACOBEAN PERIOD	1603 - 1688	EDWARD 1V	1461 - 1483
STUART PERIOD	1603 - 1714	EDWARD V	1483 - 1483
A. C. BOULLE	1642 - 1732	RICHARD 111	1483 - 1485
LOUIS X1V PERIOD	1643 - 1715	HENRY V11	1485 - 1509
GRINLING GIBBONS	1648 - 1726	HENRY V111	1509 - 1547
CROMWELLIAN PERIOD	1649 - 1660	EDWARD V1	1547 - 1553
CAROLEAN PERIOD	1660 - 1685	MARY	1553 - 1558
WILLIAM KENT	1684 - 1748	ELIZABETH	1558 - 1603
WILLIAM & MARY PERIOD	1689 - 1702	JAMES 1	1603 - 1625
QUEEN ANNE PERIOD	1702 - 1714	CHARLES 1	1625 - 1649
GEORGIAN PERIOD	1714 - 1820	COMMONWEALTH	1649 - 1660
T. CHIPPENDALE	1715 - 1762	CHARLES 11	1660 - 1685
LOUIS XV PERIOD	1723 - 1774	JAMES 11	1685 - 1689
A. HEPPLEWHITE	1727 - 1788	WILLIAM & MARY	1689 - 1695
ADAM PERIOD	1728 - 1792	WILLIAM 111	1695 - 1702
ANGELICA KAUFMANN	1741 - 1807	ANNE	1702 - 1714
T. SHERATON	1751 - 1806	GEORGE 1	1714 - 1727
LOUIS XV1	1774 - 1793	GEORGE 11	1727 - 1760
T. SHEARER	(circa) 1780	GEORGE 111	1760 - 1820
REGENCY PERIOD	1800 - 1830	GEORGE 1V	1820 - 1830
EMPIRE PERIOD	1804 - 1815	WILLIAM 1V	1830 - 1837
VICTORIAN PERIOD	1837 - 1901	VICTORIA	1837 - 1901
EDWARDIAN PERIOD	1901 - 1910	EDWARD V11	1901 - 1910

SILVER MARKS

Birmingham
Chester
Dublin
Edinburgh
Exeter
Glasgow
London
Newcastle
Sheffield
York

Example for 1850

	B	C	D	Ed	Ex	G	L	N	S	Y
1700										A
1701	A									B
1702	B									C
1703	C									D
1704	D									
1705	E									F
1706	F									G
1707	G									
1708	H									
1709	I									
1710	K									
1711	L									
1712	M									
1713	N									
1714	O									
1715	P									
1716	Q									
1717	R									
1718	S									
1719	T									
1720	U									
1721	V									
1722	W									
1723	X									
1724	Y									
1725	Z									
1726	A									
1727	B									
1728	C					S				
1729	D									
1730	E									

	B	C	D	Ed	Ex	G	L	N	S	Y
1731	F	L	B	J		Q	L			
1732	G	M	C	h		R	M			
1733	H	N	D	i		S	N			
1734	J	O	E	K	S	T	O			
1735	K	P	F	l		V	P			
1736	L	Q	G	m		a	Q			
1737	M	R	K			b	R			
1738	N	S	J	O		c	S			
1739	O	T	K	P		d	T			
1740	P	U	L	q		e	A			
1741	Q	W	M	r		f	B			
1742	R	W	N	S		g	C			
1743	S	X	O		S	h	D			
1744	T		P	u		i	E			
1745	U	Y	Q	w		K	F			
1746	V	Z	R	x		l	G			
1747	W	A	S	y	S	m	H			
1748	X	B	T	Z		n	I			
1749	Y	C	U	A		o	K			
1750	Z	D	V	B		p	L			
1751	a	E	W	C		q	M			
1752	b	F	X	D		r	N			
1753	c	G	Y	y		s	O			
1754	d	H	Z	E		t	P			
1755	e		A	G		u	Q			
1756	f		B	H	S	A	R			
1757	G	I	C	I		B	S			
1758	h	K	D	K	S	C			
1759	i	L	E	L			A			
1760	k	M	F	M		E	B			
1761	l	N	G	N		F				
1762	m	O	H	O		G				
1763	n	P	J	P	E	H				
1764	o	Q	K	Q		J				
1765	P	R	L	R		K				
1766	Q	S	M	S		L				
1767	R	T	N	T		M				
1768	S	U	O	U		N				
1769	T	W	P	W		O	G			
1770	T	X	Q	X		P	D			
1771	U	Y	R	Y		Q	E			
1772	V	Z	S	Z		R	F			
1773	A	W	A	A	A	S	S	G		
1774	B	X	B	B	B	T	H	F		

Year	B	C	D	Ed	Ex	G	L	N	S	Y
1775	C	Y	C		C		U	I		
1776	D	a	d		D	O	A	K	R	
1777	E	b	E		E		b	L	h	
1778	F	C	F	Z	F		C	M		C
1779	G	d	g		G		d	N	A	D
1780	H	e	H	A	H		e	O	Z	E
1781	I	f	I	B		I	f	P		F
1782	K	g	K	C			g	Q	G	G
1783	L	h	L	D	K	S	h	R	B	H
1784	M	i	M	E	L		i	S	I	J
1785	N	k	N	F	M	S	k	T	K	K
1786	O	l	O	G	N		l	U	R	L
1787	P	m	P	H	O		m	W	T	A
1788	Q	n	Q	H			n	X	W	B
1789	R	O	R	IJ			O	Y	M	C
1790	S	P	S	K	T	S	p	Z	L	d
1791	T	q	T	L	f		q	A	U	e
1792	U	r	U	M	U		r	B	U	f
1793	V	S	W	N	u		S	C	G	g
1794	W	t	X	O	W		t	D	H	h
1795	X	u	Y	P	X	S	u	E	q	i
1796	Y	V	Z	Q	y		A	F	Z	k
1797	Z	A	A	R			B	G	X	L
1798	a	B	B	S	B		C	H	V	M
1799	b	C	C	T	c		D	I	E	N
1800	c	D	D	U	D	S	E	K	N	O
1801	d	E	E	V	E		F	L	H	P
1802	e	F	F	W	F		G	M	M	Q
1803	f	G	G	X	G		H	N	F	R
1804	g	H	H	Y	H		I	O	G	S
1805	h	I	I	Z	I		K	P	B	T
1806	i	K	K	a	K		L	Q	A	U
1807	J	L	L	b	L		M	R	S	V
1808	k	M	M	c	M		N	S	P	W
1809	l	N	N	d	N		O	T	K	X
1810	m	O	O	e	O		P	U	L	Y
1811	n	P	P	f	P		Q	W	C	Z
1812	O	Q	Q	g	Q		R	X	D	a
1813	P	R	R	h	R		S	Y	R	b
1814	Q	S	S	i	S		T	Z	W	c
1815	r	T	T	j	T		U	A	O	d
1816	S	U	U	k	U		a	B	T	e
1817	t	V	W	l	a		b	C	X	f
1818	u	A	X	m	b		C	D	I	g
1819	V	B	Y	n	c	A	d	E	V	h
1820	W	C	Z	d	d	B	e	F	Q	i
1821	X	D	A	e	e	C	f	G	Y	k
1822	y	D	B	q	d	D	g	H	Z	l
1823	Z	E	C	r	e	E	h	I	U	m
1824	A	F	D	h	h	F	i	K	A	n
1825	B	G	E	t	i	G	k	L	b	o
1826	C	H	F	u	h	H	l	M	C	q
1827	D	I	G	v	l	I	m	N	d	q
1828	E	K	H	w	m	J	n	O	e	r
1829	F	L	I	x	n	K	O	P	f	s
1830	G	M	K	y	O	L	P	Q	g	t
1831	H	N	L	z	P	M	q	R	h	u
1832	I	O	M	A	q	N	r	S	k	v
1833	K	P	N	S	r	O	S	T	l	w
1834	L	Q	O	C	s	P	t	U	m	r
1835	M	R	P	D	t	Q	U	W	P	
1836	A	S	Q	E	U	R	A	X		z
1837	D	T	R	f	A	S	B	Y	r	A
1838	P	U	S	G	B	T	C	Z	S	B
1839	Q	A	T	H	C	U	D	A	t	C
1840	R	B	U	J	D	V	E	B	U	D
1841	S	C	V	K	E	W	f	C	V	E
1842	T	D	W	L	f	X	G	D	X	F
1843	U	E	X	M		Y	H	E	Z	G
1844	W	f	Y	N	O	Z	J	F	A	H
1845		G	Z	O	J	A	K	G	B	I
1846		h	a	P	K	B	L	H	C	K
1847		J	b	Q	c	C	M	I	D	L
1848	Z	K	C	R	M	D	N	J	E	M
1849	A	L	d	S	C	E	O	K	F	N
1850	B	M	e	T	d	F	P	L	G	O
1851	C	N	f	U	D	G	Q	M	H	P
1852	D	O	g	U	G	H	R	N	I	Q
1853	E	P	h	W	R	I	S	O	K	R
1854	F	Q	j	X	S	J	T	P	L	S
1855	G	R	k	Y	U	K	U	Q	M	T
1856	H	S	l	Z	L	L	L	R	N	U
1857	I	T	m	A	A	M	b	S	O	
1858	J	U	n	B	B	N	c	T	P	
1859	K	V	O	C	C	O	d	U	R	
1860	L	W	P	D	D	P	e	W	S	
1861	M	X	Q	E	E	Q	f	X	T	
1862	N	Y	T	F	F	R	g	Y	U	
1863	O	Z	S	G	G	S	h	Z	V	
1864	P	a	t	H	H	T	i	a	w	

16

	B	C	D	Ed	Ex	G	L	N	S	Y
1865	Q	b	u	i	I		R	b		X
1866	R	c	v	K	K		c	C		Y
1867	S	d	w	L	L		m	d		Z
1868	T	e	x	M	M	I	n	e		A
1869	U	f	y	N	N		o	f		B
1870	V	g	z	O	O		p	g		C
1871	W	h	A	P	P	A	q	h		D
1872	X	i	B	Q	Q	B	r	i		E
1873	Y	k	C	R	R	C	s	k		F
1874	Z	l	D	S	S	D	t	l		G
1875	a	m	E	T	T	E	u	m		H
1876	b	n	F	U	U	F	a	n		J
1877	c	o	G	V	A	G	b	o		K
1878	d	p	H	W	B	H	c	p		L
1879	e	q	I	X	C	I	d	q		M
1880	f	r	K	Y	D	J	e	r		N
1881	g	s	L	Z	E	K	f	s		O
1882	h	t	M	a	F	L	g	t	U	P
1883	i	u	N	b		M	h	u		Q
1884	k	A	O	c		N	i			R
1885	l	B	P	d		O	k			S
1886	m	C	Q	e		P	l			T
1887	n	D	R	f		Q	m			U
1888	o	E	S	g		R	n			V
1889	p	F	T	h		S	o			W
1890	q	G	U	i		T	p			X
1891	r	H	V	k		U	q			Y
1892	s	I	W	l		V	r			Z
1893	t	K	X	m		W	s			a
1894	u	L	Y	n		X	t			b
1895	v	M	Z	o		Y	u			c
1896	w	N	A	p		Z	a			d
1897	x	O	B	q		A	b			e
1898	y	P	C	r		B	c			f
1899	z	Q	D	s		C	d			g
1900	a	R	E	t		D	e			h
1901	b	A	F	u		E	f			i
1902	c	B	G	w		F	g			k
1903	d	C	H	r		G	h			l
1904	e	D	H	n		H	i			m
1905	f	E	K	z		I	k			n
1906	g	F	L	A		J	l			o
1907	h	G	M	B		K	m			p
1908	i	H	N	C		L	n			q
1909	k	J	O	D		M	o			r
1910	l	K	P	E		N	p			S
1911	m	L	Q	F		O	q			t
1912	n	M	R	G		P	r			u
1913	o	N	S	H		Q	s			v
1914	p	O	T			R	t			w
1915	q	P	U	K		S	u			x
1916	r	Q	A	L		T	a			y
1917	s	R	b	M		U	b			z
1918	t	S	C	N		V	c			a
1919	u	T	D	O		W	d			b
1920	v	U	e	P		X	e			c
1921	w	V	F	Q		Y	f			d
1922	x	W	S	R		Z	g			e
1923	y	X	h			a	h			f
1924	z	Y	I	T		b	i			g
1925	A	Z	B	U		C	k			h
1926	B	a	C	V		d	l			i
1927	C	b	m	W		e	m			k
1928	D	C	n	X		f	n			l
1929	E	P	O	Y		g	o			m
1930	F	e	P	Z		h	p			n
1931	G	ff		A		i	q			o
1932	H	G	Q	B		j	r			p
1933	J	H	R	C		k	S			q
1934	K	J	S	D		l	t			r
1935	L	K	T	E		m	u			S
1936	M	L	U			n	A			t
1937	N	m	V	G		O	B			u
1938	O	n	W	H		P	C			v
1939	P		X	J		Q	D			w
1940	Q	P	X	K		r	E			X
1941	R	Q	Z	L		S	F			y
1942	S	R	A			t	G			Z
1943	T	S	B	u		u	H			A
1944	U	C	C			v	I			B
1945	V	D	D	F		W	K			C
1946	W	E	E			X	L			D
1947	X	w	F	R		Y	M			E
1948	Y	X	G			Z	N			F
1949	Z	Y	H	J		A				G
1950	A	z	I			B	P			H
1951	B	A	J			C	Q			I
1952	C	B	K			D	R			K
1953	D	C	L			E	S			L
1954	E	D	M			F	T			M

17

CHINA MARKS

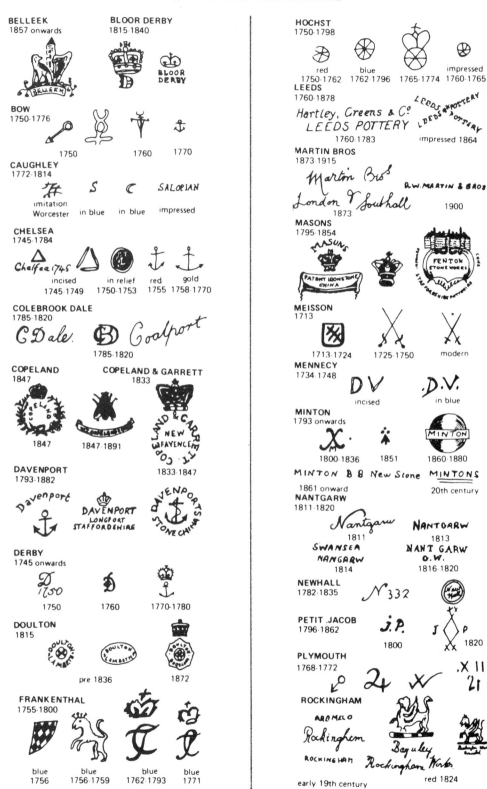

BELLEEK
1857 onwards

BLOOR DERBY
1815-1840

BLOOR DERBY

BOW
1750-1776

1750   1760   1770

CAUGHLEY
1772-1814

imitation   in blue   in blue   SALOPIAN
Worcester   impressed

CHELSEA
1745-1784

Chelsea 1745   incised   in relief   red   gold
                    1745-1749   1750-1753   1755   1758-1770

COLEBROOK DALE
1785-1820

CDale.   Coalport
              1785-1820

COPELAND
1847

COPELAND & GARRETT
1833

1847   1847-1891   NEW FAYENCE   1833-1847

DAVENPORT
1793-1882

Davenport   DAVENPORT
                 LONGPORT
                 STAFFORDSHIRE   DAVENPORTS
                                      STONE CHINA

DERBY
1745 onwards

1750   1760   1770-1780

DOULTON
1815

pre 1836   1872

FRANKENTHAL
1755-1800

blue   blue   blue   blue
1756   1756-1759   1762-1793   1771

HOCHST
1750-1798

red   blue   impressed
1750-1762 1762-1796   1765-1774 1760-1765

LEEDS
1760-1878

Hartley, Greens & Co
LEEDS POTTERY
1760-1783

LEEDS POTTERY
LEEDS POTTERY
impressed 1864

MARTIN BROS
1873-1915

Martin Bros
London & Southall
1873

R.W.MARTIN & BROS
1900

MASONS
1795-1854

MASONS
PATENT IRONSTONE
CHINA

FENTON
STONE WORKS

MEISSON
1713

1713-1724   1725-1750   modern

MENNECY
1734-1748

DV   .D.V.
incised   in blue

MINTON
1793 onwards

1800-1836   1851   MINTON
                             1860-1880

MINTON B B New Stone   MINTONS
1861 onward   20th century

NANTGARW
1811-1820

Nantgarw   NANTGARW
1811   1813

SWANSEA   NANT GARW
NANGARW   O.W.
1814   1816-1820

NEWHALL
1782-1835

N 332   Naw Hall

PETIT JACOB
1796-1862

J.P.   J   P
1800   XX   1820

PLYMOUTH
1768-1772

2⊥   .X 11
             '21

ROCKINGHAM

ARD MELO
Rockingham
ROCKINGHAM

Baguley
Rockingham Works.
red 1824

early 19th century

18

CHINA MARKS

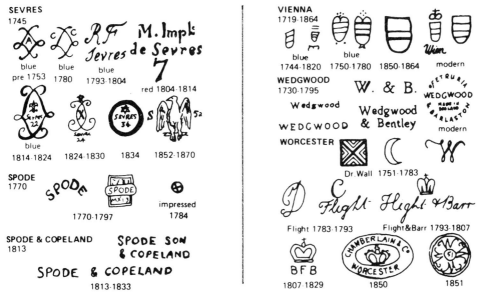

RECOGNITION & DATING

Obviously the task of committing every china mark to memory is one which will be outside the scope of most collectors and, indeed, most dealers too. For this reason, the following simple guides may prove to be of some assistance in determining the approximate date of a piece without having recourse to long, and frequently involved, lists of the marks used by various manufacturers over the years.

Any piece bearing the words 'English Bone China' or simply 'Bone China' is a product of the twentieth century and the words 'Made in England' also suggest twentieth century manufacture, though they could relate to pieces dating from 1875 onwards.

The word 'England' stamped on a piece suggests compliance with the McKinley Tariff Act of America, 1891 which required all imports to America to bear the name of the country of origin.

In 1862, the Trade Mark Act became law. Any piece bearing the words 'Trade Mark' therefore, can be assumed to date from 1862 onward.

Following the law relating to companies of limited liability, the word Limited or its abbreviations appears after 1860, though more commonly on pieces dating from 1885 onwards.

When a piece bears a pattern number or name, it can be assumed to date no earlier than about 1810.

Royal Arms incorporated into a small mark indicates a date after 1800.

During the mid 19th century the word 'Royal' was commonly added to the Manufacturer's name or trade name and, consequently, pieces bearing this word can usually be placed after 1850.

CHAIR BACKS

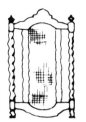

1660
Charles II.

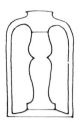

1705
Queen Anne.

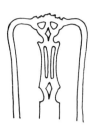

1745
Chippendale.

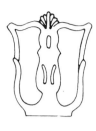

1745
Chippendale.

1750
Georgian.

1750
Hepplewhite.

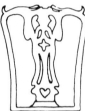

1750
Chippendale.

1760
French Rococo.

1760
Gothic.

1760
Splat back.

1770
Chippendale
ladder back.

1785
Windsor
wheel back.

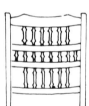

1785
Lancashire
spindle back.

1785
Lancashire
ladder back.

1790
Shield and
feathers.

1795
Shield back.

1795
Hepplewhite.

1795
Hepplewhite
camel back.

1795
Hepplewhite.

1810
Late Georgian
bar back.

CHAIR BACKS

1810
Thomas Hope
'X' frame.

1810
Regency
rope back.

1815
Regency.

1815
Regency
cane back.

1820
Regency.

1820
Empire.

1820
Regency
bar back.

1825
Regency
bar back.

1830
Regency
bar back.

1830
Bar back.

1830
William IV
bar back.

1830
William IV.

1835
Lath back.

1840
Victorian
balloon back.

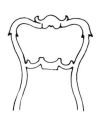

1845
Victorian.

1845
Victorian
bar back.

1850
Victorian.

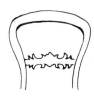

1860
Victorian.

1870
Victorian.

1875
Cane back.

LEGS

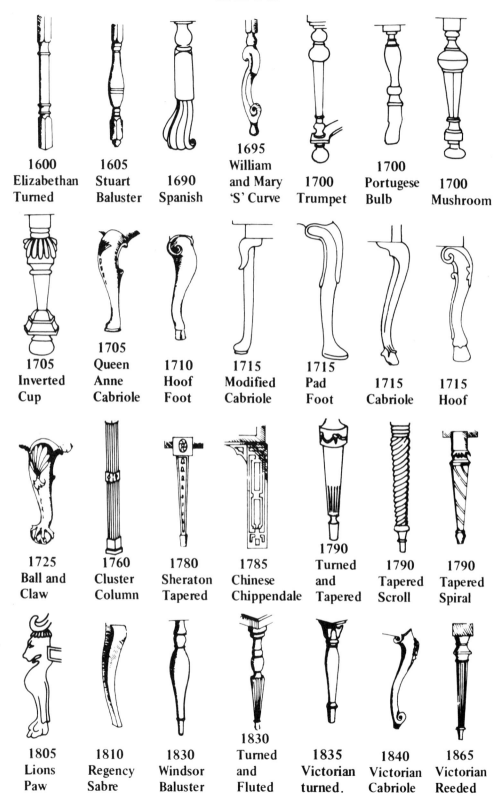

1600 Elizabethan Turned

1605 Stuart Baluster

1690 Spanish

1695 William and Mary 'S' Curve

1700 Trumpet

1700 Portugese Bulb

1700 Mushroom

1705 Inverted Cup

1705 Queen Anne Cabriole

1710 Hoof Foot

1715 Modified Cabriole

1715 Pad Foot

1715 Cabriole

1715 Hoof

1725 Ball and Claw

1760 Cluster Column

1780 Sheraton Tapered

1785 Chinese Chippendale

1790 Turned and Tapered

1790 Tapered Scroll

1790 Tapered Spiral

1805 Lions Paw

1810 Regency Sabre

1830 Windsor Baluster

1830 Turned and Fluted

1835 Victorian turned.

1840 Victorian Cabriole

1865 Victorian Reeded

FEET

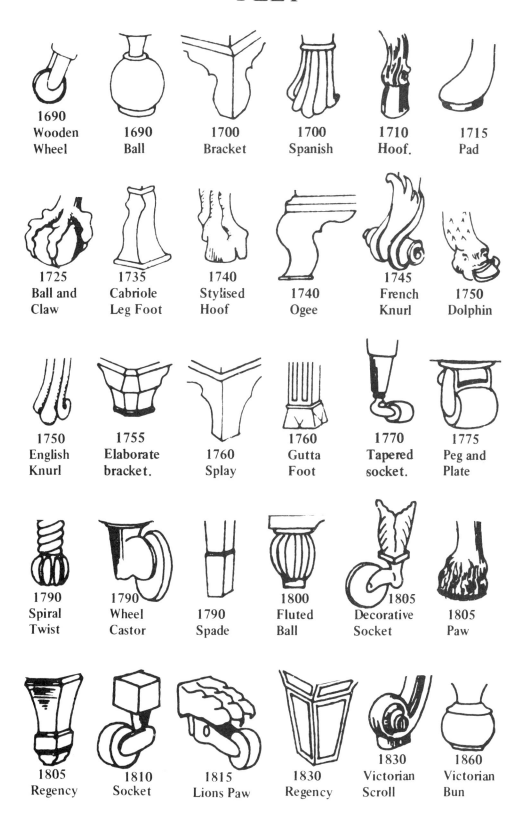

1690 Wooden Wheel

1690 Ball

1700 Bracket

1700 Spanish

1710 Hoof.

1715 Pad

1725 Ball and Claw

1735 Cabriole Leg Foot

1740 Stylised Hoof

1740 Ogee

1745 French Knurl

1750 Dolphin

1750 English Knurl

1755 Elaborate bracket.

1760 Splay

1760 Gutta Foot

1770 Tapered socket.

1775 Peg and Plate

1790 Spiral Twist

1790 Wheel Castor

1790 Spade

1800 Fluted Ball

1805 Decorative Socket

1805 Paw

1805 Regency

1810 Socket

1815 Lions Paw

1830 Regency

1830 Victorian Scroll

1860 Victorian Bun

23

HANDLES

1550
Tudor
drop.

1560
Early
Stuart
loop.

1570
Early
Stuart
loop.

1620
Early
Stuart
loop.

1660
Stuart
drop.

1680
Stuart
drop.

1690
William &
Mary solid
backplate.

1700
William &
Mary split
tail.

1700
Queen Anne
solid back-
plate.

1705
Queen Anne
ring.

1710
Queen Anne
loop.

1720
Early
Georgian
pierced.

1720
Early
Georgian
brass drop.

1730
Cut away
backplate.

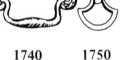

1740
Georgian
plain brass
loop.

1750
Georgian
shield drop.

1755
French
style.

1760
Rococo
style.

1765
Chinese
style.

1770
Georgian
ring.

1780
Late Georgian
stamped.

1790
Late Georgian
stamped.

1810
Regency
knob.

1820
Regency
lions mask.

1825
Campaign.

1840
Early
Victorian
porcelain.

1850
Victorian
reeded.

1880
Porcelain or
wood knob.

1890
Late Victorian
loop.

1910
Art
Nouveau.

✱ a Victorian milk bottle worth £150
✱ a model aeroplane worth £1,200
✱ a walking stick worth £4,000

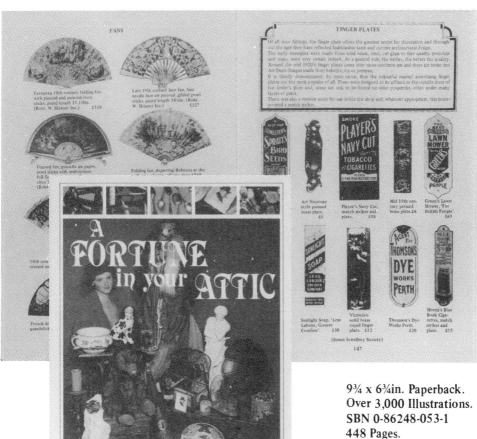

9¾ x 6¾in. Paperback.
Over 3,000 Illustrations.
SBN 0-86248-053-1
448 Pages.

The purpose of 'A Fortune in your Attic' is to take a detailed look at just the type of article that has been pushed under the stairs, stuck in the garage or stashed away in the loft, for with a little research and a bit of good luck you really could have A FORTUNE IN YOUR ATTIC.

✱ SURPRISED

check out over 3000 more amazing money-making facts

PEDIMENTS

1690
Swell frieze.

1700
Queen Anne.

1705
Double arch.

1705
Queen Anne.

1710
Triple arch.

1715
Broken circular.

1720
Cavetto.

1730
Swan neck.

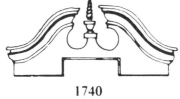

1740
Banner top.

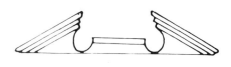

1740
Broken arch

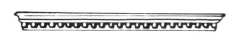

1750
Dentil cornice.

1755
Fret cut.

26

REGISTRY OF DESIGNS

BELOW ARE ILLUSTRATED THE TWO FORM OF 'REGISTRY OF DESIGN' MARK USED BETWEEN THE YEARS OF 1842 to 1883.

DATE AND LETTER CODE USED 1842 to 1883

EXAMPLE: An article produced between 1842 and 1867 would bear the following marks. (Example for the 12th of November 1852).

CLASS OF GOODS
YEAR
MONTH — DAY
BUNDLE

EXAMPLE: An article produced between 1868 and 1883 would bear the following marks. (Example the 22nd of October 1875).

CLASS OF GOODS
DAY
BUNDLE — YEAR
MONTH

1842	X	63	G
43	H	64	N
44	C	65	W
45	A	66	Q
46	I	67	T
47	F	68	X
48	U	69	H
49	S	70	O
50	V	71	A
51	P	72	I
52	D	73	F
53	Y	74	U
54	J	75	S
55	E	76	V
56	L	77	P
57	K	78	D
58	B	79	Y
59	M	80	J
60	Z	81	E
61	R	82	L
62	O	83	K

January	C	July	I
February	G	August	R
March	W	September	D
April	H	October	B
May	E	November	K
June	M	December	A

CHINESE DYNASTIES   REIGN PERIODS

Shang	1766 – 1123BC
Zhou	1122 – 249BC
Warring States	403 – 221BC
Qin	221 – 207BC
Han	206BC – AD220
6 Dynasties	317 – 589
Sui	590 – 618
Tang	618 – 906
5 Dynasties	907 – 960
Liao	907 – 1125
Song	960 – 1279
Jin	1115 – 1234
Yuan	1260 – 1368
Ming	1368 – 1644
Qing	1644 – 1911

MING

Hongwu	1368 – 1398	Hongzhi	1488 – 1505
Jianwen	1399 – 1402	Zhengde	1506 – 1521
Yongle	1403 – 1424	Jiajing	1522 – 1566
Hongxi	1425	Longqing	1567 – 1572
Xuande	1426 – 1435	Wanli	1573 – 1620
Zhengtong	1436 – 1449	Taichang	1620
Jingtai	1450 – 1456	Tianqi	1621 – 1627
Tianshun	1457 – 1464	Chongzheng	1628 – 1644
Chenghua	1465 – 1487		

QING

Shunzhi	1644 – 1662	Daoguang	1821 – 1850
Kangxi	1662 – 1722	Xianfeng	1851 – 1861
Yongzheng	1723 – 1735	Tongzhi	1862 – 1874
Qianlong	1736 – 1795	Guangxu	1875 – 1908
Jiali	1796 – 1820	Xuantong	1908 – 1911

9¾ x 6¾in. Paperback.
Over 3,000 Illustrations.
SBN 0-86248-047-7
448 Pages

This volume deals with the question — 'Just pieces of paper!' or valuable collectibles. We throw away today's newspaper or the empty soap powder packet without a second thought, light the fire with last week's comic and drop the used bus ticket in the waste bin. Yet the passing of a few years gives all these items a nostalgic fascination and in many cases a real monetary value.

✳ FASCINATING

check out over 3000 more amazing money-making facts

THERE ARE A GREAT MANY ANTIQUE SHIPPERS IN BRITAIN

but few, if any, who are as quality conscious as Norman Lefton, Chairman and Managing Director of British Antique Exporters Ltd. of Burgess Hill, Nr. Brighton, Sussex. Over twenty-five years' experience of shipping goods to all parts of the globe have confirmed his original belief that the way to build clients' confidence in his services is to supply them only with goods which are in first class saleable condition. To this end, he employs a cottage industry staff of over 50, from highly skilled antique restorers, polishers and packers to representative buyers and executives. Through their knowledgeable hands passes each piece of furniture before it leaves the B.A.E. warehouses, ensuring that the overseas buyer will only receive the best and most saleable merchandise for their particular market. This attention to detail is obvious on a visit to the Burgess Hill showrooms where potential customers can view what must be the most varied assortment of Georgian, Victorian, Edwardian and 1930s furniture in the UK. One cannot fail to be impressed by, not only the varied range of merchandise, but also the fact that each piece is in showroom condition awaiting shipment.

BRITISH ANTIQUE EXPORTERS LTD

SCHOOL CLOSE
QUEEN ELIZABETH AVENUE
BURGESS HILL
WEST SUSSEX, RH15 9RX, ENGLAND
Telex 87688   Fax 2014

Member of L.A.P.A.D.A.
Guild of Master Craftsmen

Telephone BURGESS HILL (044 46) 45577

As one would expect, packing is considered somewhat of an art at B.A.E. and the manager in charge of the works ensures that each piece will reach its final destination in the condition a customer would wish. B.A.E. set a very high standard and, as a further means of improving each container load, their customer/container liaison dept. invites each customer to return detailed information on the saleability of each piece in the container, thereby ensuring successful future shipments. This feedback of information is the all important factor which guarantees the profitability of future containers. "By this method" Mr. Lefton explains, "we have established that an average £7500 container will immediately it is unpacked at its final destination realise in the region of £10000 to £14000 for our clients selling the goods on a quick wholesale turnover basis". When visiting the warehouses various container loads can be seen in the course of completion. The intending buyer can then judge for himself which type of container load would be best suited to his market. In an average 20-foot container B.A.E. put approximately 75 to 150 pieces carefully selected to suit the particular destination. There are always at least 10 outstanding or unusual items in each shipment, but every piece included looks as though it has something special about it.

Based at Burgess Hill, 7 miles from Brighton and 39 miles from London on a direct rail link, (only 40 minutes journey), the Company is ideally situated to ship containers to all parts of the world. The showrooms, restoration and packing departments are open to overseas buyers and no visit to purchase antiques for re-sale in other countries is complete without a visit to their Burgess Hill premises where a welcome is always found.

ANTIQUE DEALERS POCKET BOOK

At last! Instant recognition and dating of thousands of antiques is possible – with this clear and comprehensive pocket manual from the world's foremost publisher of antiques reference books. There is more information to the square inch in this book than in any you can buy, whether you are a dealer, collector, or merely interested in identifying your own family heirlooms. Here are over 3,500 clear illustrations, not only of expensive objects but especially of the day-to-day items (many less than 100 years old but still of value) which make up the bulk of the antiques market. The Antique Dealers Pocket Book is a must for everyone interested in antiques – and an education in itself.

ISBN 0-86248-062-0
256 Pages
Size 8 x 5½in. Hardback
Over 3,500 clear illustrations

JUST
£3·95

Monarchs, Chinese Dynasties, Periods, Registry of Designs, China Marks, Handles, Pediments, Legs, Feet, Chair Backs, Silver Marks, Barometers, Bronze, Caddies & Boxes, Cameras, Cane Handles, Carved Wood, China, Clocks, Cloisonne, Copper & Brass, Dolls, Enamel, Fans, Furniture, Glass, Gold, Horn, Inros, Instruments, Iron & Steel, Ivory, Jade, Jewellery, Lamps, Lead, Marble, Mirrors, Model Ships, Model Trains, Money Banks, Musical Boxes, Netsuke, Quilts, Rugs, Samplers, Seals, Shibayama, Tsubas.

ANTIQUES
REVIEW

Anyone who has bought good antique furniture over the past twenty years should be congratulating themselves now because a recent review of prices since 1968 reveals that furniture is the best investment they could ever have made, outpacing property and shares. In fact it shows a greater rise in value than houses in the South East – and everyone knows what has happened to them! Furniture has also outpaced the Stock Exchange FT Price Index, even when 4 per cent per annum is added to allow for dividends.

According to the review, antique furniture has proved to be twice as good an investment as shares and its value has grown steadily by more than three times the inflation rate over the period covered.

To be even more specific the figures indicate that its value has risen on average

A George I walnut stool, the rectangular top upholstered in gros and petit point floral needlework, 26in. wide. (Christie's)
$15,752 £8,800

by 2,100 per cent over 20 years but during the same period, the Retail Price Index only rose by 511 per cent; in the same period the middle range house has risen by 1,000 per cent and share prices by 500 per cent.

It would seem that good furniture is also crash proof, for the October 1987 Stock Exchange debacle made little impression on its upward rise. Add to that comforting thought the fact that to own good furniture is to enhance your life and, unlike a house, you can take your furniture with you wherever you go.

It is also encouraging for antiques' enthusiasts to know that this steady rise in value looks set to continue as good pieces become rarer and more people become conscious of their potential. Top quality pieces are already becoming difficult to find and prices in America are higher than in Europe but that situation will soon level out

A George I walnut bachelor's chest with two short and three long graduated drawers, 30in. wide. (Christie's) **$30,294 £18,700**

for, since the turn of the year, European prices have been steadily catching up.

Although all antique furniture has gone up, not every category changes in value at the same rate. Regency, early mahogany and country furniture have fared particularly well but oak had a period of doldrums in 1986, though that is now over and its prices are on the rise again. Walnut too was slow to take off but is recovering strongly. Furniture from later periods is slowest of all to show dramatic rises though rarities and 'one off' pieces always sell well.

A table of prices for nine categories of antique furniture was analysed by computer at the beginning of 1988 for the Antique Collectors' Club. This analysis reveals that, starting in 1968 with a price base rate of 100, early Victorian dining chairs now stand at 1286 and whatnots at 1455. The appreciation is even more dramatic when Regency furniture is considered for, from the same 1968 base, a bergere chair stands at 7167 and a library table at 2615. The rise is also

A William IV burr yew davenport, the sliding top fitted with a pen drawer. (Christie's)   **$11,278 £6,380**

significantly shown in early mahogany for a George II card table stands at 2099 and a bureau of the same period at 4000. When this is translated into hard cash it means that a Victorian walnut davenport that cost £55 in 1968 commands a price in the region of £1,600 and a bergere armchair that cost £30 will sell for around £2,000 today. Experts are predicting that the next area to investigate for a good profit is oak furniture from the 17th century which is ready for a revival after a period of slump.

During the year under review however trade generally has been strong and good prices have been recorded across the board for all pieces of high quality English furniture but especially from those of the Georgian period. For example, a George II carved gilt wood mirror soared to £28,000; good George II open sided armchairs now fetch around £5,000 each and Phillips recently sold a George III mahogany two-stage serving table for £8,800 and a George III mahogany extending dining table for £13,500. The escalation in price for such desirable items has been noticed all over the country. In a rural saleroom at Newton Stewart in Scotland a Georgian dining table

An early Georgian walnut bureau, the cross-banded sloping front enclosing a fitted interior, 39½in. wide. (Christie's)

$9,345 £5,280

and six chairs was knocked down for £11,000 in the early summer of 1988. It is not only Georgian furniture that is going up and up. Victorian pieces have been showing increased activity and there is also a headlong rush to snap up good Edwardian pieces. Examples of high quality Edwardian furniture, especially signed pieces, have now broken the £10,000 barrier. Phillips sold a pair of satinwood marquetry semi circular side tables of mid 19th century style for £13,000; Victorian copies of earlier furniture have also been making good money as was seen by a reproduction Carlton House desk which sold for £8,000.

It is also interesting that Japanese buyers, who previously left furniture well alone, have recently turned their attention to Art Deco and modern pieces which go well with their Art Deco and Art Nouveau glass and their beloved Impressionist pictures in interior decorating schemes. Interest in 20th century pieces was further sharpened with the New York dispersal by Sotheby's of the Andy Warhol collection in the spring of 1988. Warhol collected across the board

A rare Gustav Stickley oak 'Eastwood' chair with three horizontal back splats, circa 1902. (Robt. W. Skinner Inc.) **$28,000 £16,666**

but he was a discriminating buyer of Art Deco furniture which he tracked down in Parisian flea markets before it was universally popular. He was particularly fond of pieces in exotic woods such as his galuchat and sycamore console table made by Pierre Legrain in the 1920's. Warhol was also an avid collector of pieces by Gustav Stickley who is one of the continually rising

A Regency mahogany Carlton House desk with balustraded three-quarter gallery, 61½in. wide. (Christie's) **$213,840 £132,000**

An early Victorian oak centre table with circular Roman micro-mosaic table top inlaid with a circular vista of St. Peters Square.
(Christie's) **$78,760 £44,000**

William IV parcel-gilt painted and oak cabinet on stand , 43in. wide , painted with the arms of the Duke of Westminster.
(Christie's) **$15,262 £8,250**

A George III mahogany open armchair in the manner of Thomas Chippendale.
(Christie's) **$42,735 £23,100**

A William IV mahogany pedestal bookcase with architectural pediment, 3ft. 3in. wide.
(Greenslade & Co.) **$1,320 £750**

An early 18th century japanned and decorated cabinet on a carved and silvered stand, 1.18m. wide. (Phillips) **$9,840 £6,000**

stars of the furniture world. Even a waste paper basket by Stickley can fetch four figures now. Other recent prices to ponder over include the $90,000 paid for a bench seat in typical fluid style by French Art Nouveau designer Hector Guimard, who was also responsible for the Parisian Metro entrance signs; and a lovely carved fruitwood mirror created by Emile Galle which sold for $90,000 at a sale held by Sotheby's in Monaco.

Of course, the star of Charles Rennie Mackintosh is still riding high. Almost any of his white lacquered chairs will fetch around £20,000 and even less decorative pieces like a fairly battered oak chair that once did duty in Miss Cranston's Glasgow tearoom cost its new owner £5,000 last year.

Modernist furniture, dating from 1930 to the end of the Second World War, looks set to be the next trendy craze. This area is dominated by Italian, Scandinavian and American designers and look out for chairs by Charles Voysey and anything by

American furniture designer Betty Joel, one of whose wardrobes changed hands for what is already regarded as the modest price of £600 during the period reviewed.

A laburnum bureau with fitted oak interior above four graduated long drawers. (Christie's) **$5,907 £3,300**

A fine painted and decorated poplar blanket chest, Western Pennsylvania, circa 1820, 40½in. wide. (Robt. W. Skinner Inc.)
$27,000 £16,071

An Ernest Gimson walnut bureau cabinet on stand, circa 1906, 99.5cm. wide. (Christie's)
$16,830 £11,000

A small attractive shaped back Bergere settee. (Jacobs & Hunt) $1,026 £580

George I burr walnut secretaire tallboy, the lower drawer centred by a sunburst, 42¼in. wide. (Christie's) $29,535 £16,500

An Irish George III mahogany wine waiter of rectangular shape, on cabriole legs. (Christie's) $13,783 £7,700

A fine 19th century satinwood cabinet in the French style finely inlaid with paterae, harebells, ribbon and berried foliage, 2ft. 9in. wide. (Warners, William H. Brown)
$4,800 £3,000

One of a pair of early Victorian rosewood open armchairs with cartouche shaped buttoned padded backs. (Christie's)
$11,654 £7,150

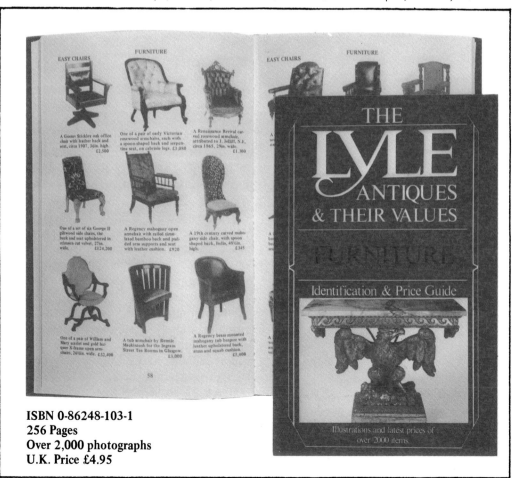

ISBN 0-86248-103-1
256 Pages
Over 2,000 photographs
U.K. Price £4.95

A pair of 19th century rosewood armchairs with shaped legs. (John Hogbin & Son)
$3,772 £2,300

A Sidney Barnsley walnut bookcase on two stepped trestle ends, 106.8cm. wide. (Christie's) **$11,781 £7,700**

Any analysis of activities in the antiques world during the last year would not be complete without detailing the effects of the Stock Market crash in mid October, '87.

In the beginning, it had the effect of driving investors out of stocks and shares into 'safer' investments, especially the best quality antiques. But they were discriminating and played safe, buying only what was secure and not being prepared to speculate until their nerves settled down. All of the big three auction houses noted that the middle range sales were worst affected by the economic uncertainty and it took several months before speculative activity recommenced. Return it did however and by spring '88, all of the big three houses reported good returns. Christie's showed the highest percentage increase at 23 per cent; Phillips are closing on them fast with a 23 per cent improvement on their year's figures and Sotheby's were only up three per cent but that was explained by their staggeringly successful year in 1986-87. The fact that they improved on it at all was an excellent sign.

A George IV mahogany bow fronted chest of three short and three long drawers, 4ft. 2in. wide. (Greenslade & Co.) $565 £320

19th. century mahogany bow fronted sideboard on square tapering supports with spade feet, 5ft. wide. (Greenslade & Co.) $3,700 £2,100

A Regency oak and parcel-gilt sofa attributed to George Bullock. (Christie's)

$106,920 £66,000

ISBN 0-86248-105-8
256 Pages
Over 2,000 photographs
U.K. Price £4.95

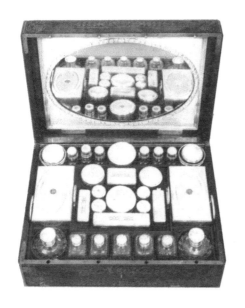

*An Anglo French silver mounted dressing
table set contained in a brass inlaid rosewood
case by G. Rawlings 1821 and P. Blazuiere,
Paris 1819-38. (Christie's)$25,740 £14,300*

Apart from top quality furniture, silver, and, because of 'knock on' effect, good plate as well, showed increased activity after the October uncertainty when it attracted the highest following for several years. Some of the prices paid were notable – for example, a set of three West Country silver casters by Gabriel Felling of Bruton, Somerset, sold by Phillips for £32,000. Even more impressive was the £533,823 ($907,500) paid at Christie's in New York for a silver gilt soup tureen that once belonged to Napoleon's mother. This tureen, by Jean Baptiste Claude Odiot, doubled Christie's estimate and broke all sale room records.

*An Exposition 'Navajo' vase set with stones
by Tiffany and Co., New York, 1900, 89ozs.
(Christie's) $44,000 £26,602*

When Sotheby's held their sale on the premises at Tyninghame, East Lothian, the home of the Earl of Haddington, a silver dessert service made by William Chawner in 1827, sold for four times its estimate at £52,800. The enthusiasm for silver and plate extended into the range of more modern pieces as well because Phillips secured £1,500 for a tea and coffee set designed by Harold Stabler and made by Ogden and Sons of Birmingham in 1936.

*A fine set of three Queen Anne silver casters
by Thomas Bolton, Dublin 1708, 36oz.
10dwt. (Woolley & Wallis)$23,100 £14,000*

A fine large black and white jade snuff bottle, superbly carved in the manner known as Suzhou School, 18th century. (Christie's) **$50,820 £30,800**

Webb cameo glass animal portrait vase signed G. Woodall below the scene and Thomas Webb & Son on the base, 8in. high. (Robt. W. Skinner Inc.) **$19,000 £10,100**

A Mount Washington magnum pink dahlia weight, 4¼in. diameter. (Christie's) **$28,600 £16,342**

THE
LYLE
ANTIQUES
& THEIR VALUES

GLASS

Identification & Price Guide

Illustrations and latest prices of over 2000 items.

ISBN 0-86248-107-4
256 Pages
Over 2,000 photographs
U.K. Price £4.95

A Galle carved acid etched triple overlay landscape vase, 50.5cm. high. (Christie's) **$10,824 £6,600**

An Almeric Walter pate-de-verre goblet,
designed by Henri Berge, 6¼in. high.
(Anderson & Garland) $1,595   £900

'Tete de Belier' a Lalique car mascot moulded
as a rams head with impressed signature R.
Lalique, France. (Christie's) $27,060 £16,500

Because of the strong Japanese interest
there has been a marked increase in prices
paid for Art Nouveau and Art Deco glass.
It was a Japanese collector who paid £60,500
for a Galle overlay purple and blue vase and
£20,900 for a bronze mounted Galle
"verrerie parlante" vase at Christie's. Prices
continue to rise throughout the glass field.
A Lalique car mascot, priced at around
£6,000 two years ago, now fetches over
£12,000. A James Couper and Sons
"Clutha" vase designed by Christopher
Dresser sold for £1,600 at Phillips. Prices are
also increasing rapidly for Orrefors glass.
This Swedish company celebrated the 75th
anniversary of its foundation by Johan
Ekman in 1988 and at a commemorative sale
held in Stockholm, prices paid for the
Orrefors products broke all records.

A rare Almeric Walter pate-de-verre paperweight , designed by H. Berge, 8cm. high.
(Christie's) $15,334   £9,350

An Almeric Walter pate-de-verre two handled
mortar pattern vase, designed by Henri
Berge, 5in. high. (Anderson & Garland)
                           $1,858 £1,050

An Art Deco shaped rectangular leaded
stained glass panel by Jacques Gruber,
70.2cm. wide. (Christie's) $5,772 £3,520

A rare hand painted tinplate four seater open tourer steam car by Doll & Co., circa 1924. (Christie's) **$5,750 £3,080**

It is interesting that Japanese buyers, strong now in glass, modern furniture, prints and Impressionist pictures, have expanded into dolls as well and overtaken Americans as chief buyers of antique dolls. It was a Japanese collector who paid £12,650 for a Bru doll accompanied by a trunk of doll's clothes at Phillips in London. At the same sale a Pettit Dumontier bisque headed doll made £6,000 and a late 19th century Noah's Ark with a full complement of animals made £3,200. Steiff bears hold their prices but there has been no great leap forward for them recently.

'The Royal Horse Artillery' in Service Dress with peaked caps and khaki uniform, by Britain's, set 318. (Phillips) **$10,725 £6,500**

A Leopold Lambert, musical automaton doll 'The Flower Seller', 19½in. high. (Lawrence Fine Art) **$6,265 £3,500**

Bing tinplate clockwork omnibus with driver, finished in cream and maroon, circa 1911. (Phillips)   **$15,900 £8,500**

'Answer-game', a Japanese battery operated robot with flashing eyes by Ichida, 1960's. (Christie's)   **$2,494 £1,334**

An Edwardian articulated silver teddy bear pin cushion, Birmingham 1908, by H.V. Pithey & Co. (Lawrence Fine Art) **$826 £462**

In the toy world, interest and prices have remained high for tin plate toys and automata. A turn of the century Bing limousine, which cost 5/- when it was new, can now sell for around £8,000. Buses with advertising slogans painted on their sides can cost even more. This year another limousine made by Bing's rival Marklin, sold for £18,700. Tin plate toys were turned out in large numbers by German manufacturers from the last half of the 19th century and names to look for include Bing, Marklin, Hess, Carette, Lehmann, Fleichmann, Gunthermann, Bub and Tipp. French makers like Andre Citroen and Jouets en Paris (J.E.P.) are also commanding high prices. British tin plate toy makers mainly worked in the 20th century and they include Brimtoy, Chad Valley, Mettoy and Triang.

That old favourite Dinky cars have escalated in price over the past year because of the news that the company is going into production again in the Far East. This has spurred collectors on in their search for earlier models. The company began producing toy cars and vans in 1934 and a Pickford's van from that year when it cost sixpence will sell now for around £500. Vans or buses with advertising slogans are most highly priced and pre-war rarities change hands for prices in excess of £1,000.

A fine mahogany and brass bi-unial magic lantern with triple rack telescopic brass bound lenses by Walter Tyler. (Christie's)
$1,200 £715

A rare William & Mary wooden doll, circa 1690 with rouged cheeks, 12½in. high. (Phillips) **$38,880 £24,000**

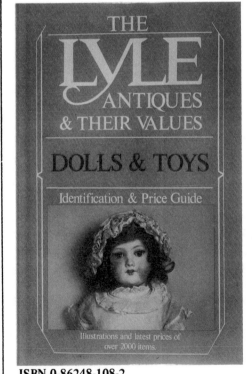

Roger Berdou original 54mm. mounted figure entitled 'Garde Imperiale Tartares Lithuaniens Trompette 1812' (Phillips) **$297 £180**

An extremely rare Honus Wagner T206 Series baseball card. (Phillips) $18,000 £10,150

Like toys, cigarette cards have long ago shaken off the tag of being a childish interest for they are fetching astonishing prices. Phillips sold a set of 25 Globe cigarette cards of French actresses for £5,500 and outdid even that by auctioning a rare set of Taddy's Clowns and Circus Artistes for £15,500. In New York they achieved the price of $18,000 for one Sweet Caporal card depicting Honus Wagner, a legendary baseball player who is thought to have been the greatest shortstop of all time. He played in the National League, Louisville, between 1897 and 1917.

Part of a rare set of twenty five Globe Cigarette cards of French actresses. (Phillips)
$9,900 £5,500

Part of a set of twenty 'Clowns & Circus Artistes' cigarette cards by Taddy & Co. (Phillips) $24,800 £15,500

Great Britain 1842 'The Queens Own' printed pictorial envelope used in Edinburgh to 'The Hon. Lady Dunfermline'. (Phillips)   **$10,500 £6,000**

A needlework sampler probably New Jersey made by Anna Braddock, aged 14, 1826. (Robt. W. Skinner Inc.)   **$38,000 £22,619**

A gramophone with the 'Gramophone Co. Maiden Lane, London' label, together with four 7in. diameter single sided E. Berliner records, circa 1900-10.
(Hobbs & Chambers) $1,600   £1,000

A silvered bronze mantel clock by Edgar Brandt, 30.6cm. high. (Christie's)
$5,050   £3,080

A pair of early 17th century gentleman's mule slippers. (Phillips) $14,700   £8,400

Mid 19th century Swiss gilt metal automaton, with three singing birds in a cage, 21in. high. (Christie's) $3,300   £1,885

An important Steinway style 'C' parlour concert grand piano, together with a duet stool . (Christie's) $66,000   £37,714

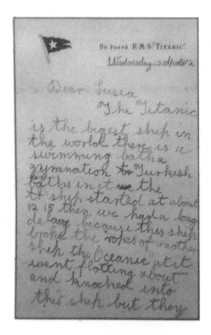

R.M.S. Titanic — A little girls letter written
on 'On Board R.M.S. Titanic' headed paper
dated Wednesday 10th April 1912 by
Eileen Lenox-Conyngham. (Phillips)
$2,880 £1,600

A Zanzibar Government 10 rupees note,
1928. (Phillips)   **$2,025 £1,250**

A needlework memorial sampler 'Mary Ann
Flanders' aged 10, 1815, New Hampshire.
(Robt. W. Skinner Inc.)   **$10,000 £5,617**

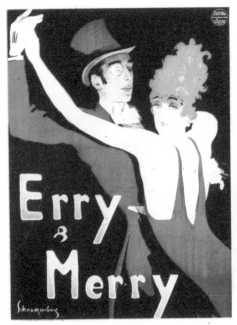

A Walter Schnackenberg poster entitled
'Erry & Merry', lithograph in colours,
50in. x 37½in. (Christie's) **$7,788 £4,400**

An example of the first Christmas card sent
to Henry Cole by William Makepeace
Thakeray. (Phillips)   **$4,775 £2,500**

A fine pair of French 19th century bronze busts of a Nubian man and woman, signed C.H. Cordier 1848, 83cm. and 79cm. high. (Christie's)   **$166,980 £101,200**

Herez carpet, the terracotta field with green palmette pendant indigo medallion with all over angular design, 3.76m. x 2.78m. (Phillips)   **$8,200 £5,000**

*A 19th century Stockmann painted
papier mache snuff box, 3¾in. diam.
(Hobbs & Chambers) $726   £440*

*A sextant by Lilley & Son, London, in a
mahogany case. (Greenslade & Co.)
$550   £310*

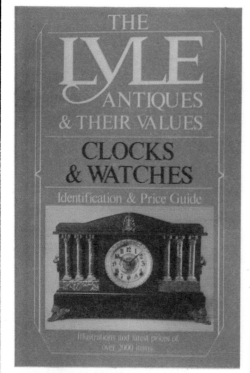

*An unusual 19th century Davenport cased
sewing machine by S. Davis & Co. (Phillips)
$2,080 £1,300*

An impressive English Delft wassail bowl and cover; on a domed circular foot, 51cm. high. (Phillips) $18,150 £11,000

A Royal Doulton 'George Washington Bicentenary' limited edition jug by Noke and Fenton, 10¾in. high. (Christie's)
$7,000 £3,960

An early 18th century terracotta bust of Van Dyke, on a moulded plinth, 31in. high. (Woolley & Wallis) $6,600 £3,500

One of a pair of Minton vases painted with robins perched on holly branches. (Greenslade & Co.) $525 £300

A large and early Wemyss model of a pig, 44cm. long. (Phillips) **$5,900 £3,200**

An important Dutch Delft plate painted in blue by Frederick van Frytom, late 17th century. (Phillips) **$10,675 £5,800**

Royal Doulton figure entitled 'Dreamland' designed by L. Harradine issued 1931-38 4¾in. high. (Abridge Auctions) **$1,750 £1,000**

A Worcester plate from The Duke of Gloucester service, gold crescent mark, circa 1775, 22.5cm. diameter. (Christie's) **$23,595 £14,300**

An exceptionally rare and important Bottger stoneware teapot and cover after a model by Irminger, circa 1710-15. (Phillips) **$60,750 £33,000**

A Royal Worcester blue-ground three-piece garniture, decorated by Thomas Bott, the largest 16in. high. (Christie's) $8,250 £4,714

China and porcelain remained fairly steady with top prices being paid for the more unusual or top quality items. Phillips recreated the 18th century "porcelain fever" for armorial pieces when they held a sale of the Bullivant collection in which a pair of water jugs with covers, painted with the crest of the Jervis family of Darlaston sold for £18,000. A set of nine soup plates, Yongzheng, bearing the crest of the Cock family, made £12,000. This armorial porcelain was very popular in the late 18th century with the families of rich aristocrats and wealthy merchants who ordered their pieces from Canton and the cargoes were brought back by East Indiamen.

Doulton remains strong and big money interest is extending into lesser priced areas as well now. For example, a two handled loving cup painted with a picture of Captain Cook sold for £1,550 at Phillips.

Delftware, Staffordshire saltglaze, Minton Majolica and Chelsea porcelain are all much sought after with strong American interest pushing up the prices. Christie's recently sold a Delftware bottle dating from around 1618 for £52,800, five times its estimate.

A Minton majolica garden seat modelled as a crouching monkey holding a yellow pomegranite with green foliage in one hand, circa 1870. (Christie's) $12,512 £7,150

A Worcester yellow-ground honeycomb moulded oval dish, circa 1765, 30cm. wide. (Christie's) $23,100 £13,200

A Whieldon tortoiseshell coffee pot and cover of baluster shape with domed cover, circa 1760. (Phillips) $8,010 £4,500

Whieldon teapot in the form of a bear, its head forming the cover, 15cm. high, circa 1750. (Phillips) $87,500 £50,000

A Continental pottery centrepiece modelled as a vintage car with a lady passenger and a gentleman passenger in Edwardian dress, signed W. Lachner, 1906, 17½in. long. (Christie's) $14,600 £8,250

A bottle vase by Hans Coper, the oviform body with short cylindrical neck, circa 1958, 65.2cm. high. (Christie's) $23,760   £13,200

*'The Wandering Minstrel', a limited edition
loving cup by Royal Doulton, designed by
Noke and Fenton, issued 1934.
(Abridge Auctions)* $350 £200

*A Royal Doulton figure entitled 'Perfect
Pair', HN581, designed by L. Harradine,
issued 1923-1938, 6¾in. high.
(Abridge Auctions)* $785 £450

ISBN 0-86248 106-6
256 Pages
Over 2,000 photographs
U.K. Price £4.95

A Regency tortoiseshell tea caddy. (Hetheringtons Nationwide) $704 £440

'The Butterfly Dancer', an unusual painted
bronze and ivory figure cast and carved from
a model by Demetre Chiparus, 43cm. high.
(Phillips) $33,300 £18,000

Travel poster, P.S.N.C. to South America by
Kenneth Shoesmith. (Onslow's) $341 £220

A Guild of Handicrafts silver and enamel
brooch designed by C. R. Ashbee, 1907.
(Christie's) $16,230 £9,900

19th century needlework carpet with geometric squares filled with flower heads and foliage. (Christie's)   **$17,622 £9,900**

An extremely rare drawing by Michael Jackson in blue ball point pen entitled 'Your Girlfriend' 18cm. x 11.5cm. (Phillips)
$1,870 £1,000

One of the interesting developments of the past year has been the rise in interest for the clothing and belongings of famous people. The world gasped when Charlie Chaplin's hat and the cane which he used in his film "The Great Dictator" was sold by Christie's for £82,500. His boots went to a Swiss museum for £38,500. A cap, decorated by pop star Boy George with buttons, badges and safety pins, changed hands at Phillips for £2,200. Sotheby's sold Rene Magritte's bowler hat, the one that appeared in several of his paintings, for £16,500 and that price

Charlie Chaplin's bowler hat and cane with
accompanying letter of authenticity .
(Christie's) $157,575   £82,500

A superb pair of Michael Jackson's purple
lace up dancing shoes heavily studded with
purple glass stones. (Phillips)$7,480 £4,000

A skin tight 'shimmy' dress of black silk satin
with a low V-neck, designed by Orry Kelly
and worn by Marilyn Monroe in 'Some Like
It Hot'. (Christie's) $37,000 £19,800

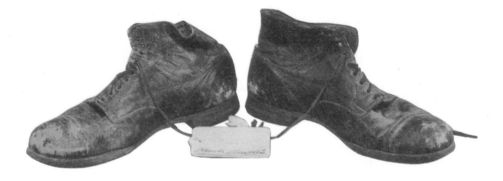

Charlie Chaplin's pair of worn leather laced working boots. (Christie's)$73,535 £38,500

was as surreal as any of the painter's pictures because the estimate had been only £1,000. At Christie's, the straw hat Fred Astaire wore in "The Ziegfield Follies" made £3,410; a shirt worn by John Wayne in one of his cowboy epics made £2,420 and, best of all, the black dress that Marilyn Monroe wore in "Some Like It Hot" sold for an astonishing £19,800.

The garden has taken over from the fitted kitchen and luxury bathroom as chief preoccupation of up-market decorators with the result that garden statuary and artefacts have rocketed in price. Lead garden urns can now change hands at £4,000 a pair; statues have trebled their prices and are still rising; Edwardian and Victorian cast iron chairs and settees, especially' the ones with embossed fern backs, are conservatively priced at around £400 a chair. This is sure to be an area where there will be increased activity in the future for all the big auction houses are turning their attention towards the garden.

Another field that is fairly new and rising rapidly is Judaica. A pair of Torah finials dating from 1712 and the work of Samuel Edlin of London sold by Sotheby's for £50,000 this year and Phillips sold a rare 18th century Dutch Sabbath lamp in the shape of a star for £30,000.

All in all, the attraction of antiques and the past shows no signs of fading. In fact nostalgia for bygone days is increasing through all sections of society and BBC television's "Antiques Roadshow" has soared to a position immediately after the soaps in the table of viewing figures. Over 14 million people switch on to watch it every week.

The attraction of the past was demonstrated when the contents of an old pharmacy in the village of Chatteris, Cambridgeshire, was sold recently and hundreds of people turned out for the sale and the viewing. The shop belonged to Hedley Dwelly who inherited it from his father in 1940. Mr Dwelly senior had taken over the 18th century shop in 1911 and changed little but his son was an even greater conservationist, retaining everything as it was in 1940 when his father died. As a result it was a time capsule and Phillips auctioned its contents to enthusiasts for £19,000.

Dwelly's Pharmacy, 33 Park Street, Chatteris, Cambridgeshire. (Phillips) **$34,300 £19,000**

THE **LYLE** OFFICIAL ARTS REVIEW 1989

The Price Guide to Paintings

Tony Curtis

U.K. Price £14.95

Thousands of artists are listed alphabetically with more than 2,000 illustrations of their work, and also included are details of the medium in which they worked, titles of their pictures which have been sold during the past year and the most important of all, a comprehensive record of the prices actually paid not only nationwide but at auctions throughout Europe, Canada, America, and Australia.

ANTIQUES
REVIEW 1989

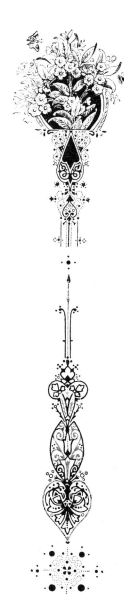

THE Lyle Official Antiques Review is compiled and published with completely fresh information annually, enabling you to begin each new year with an up-to-date knowledge of the current trends, together with the verified values of antiques of all descriptions.

We have endeavoured to obtain a balance between the more expensive collector's items and those which, although not in their true sense antiques, are handled daily by the antiques trade.

The illustrations and prices in the following sections have been arranged to make it easy for the reader to assess the period and value of all items with speed.

You will find illustrations for almost every category of antique and curio, together with a corresponding price collated during the last twelve months, from the auction rooms and retail outlets of the major trading countries.

When dealing with the more popular trade pieces, in some instances, a calculation of an average price has been estimated from the varying accounts researched.

As regards prices, when 'one of a pair' is given in the description the price quoted is for a pair and so that we can make maximum use of the available space it is generally considered that one illustration is sufficient.

It will be noted that in some descriptions taken directly from sales catalogues originating from many different countries, terms such as bureau, secretary and davenport are used in a broader sense than is customary, but in all cases the term used is self explanatory.

65

Tizer 'The Appetizer'. (Street
Jewellery) $75 £40

Milkmaid Brand Milk. (Street Jewellery) $370 £200

Monsters. (Street Jewellery) $230 £125

Rowntree's Pastilles. (Street Jewellery)
$100 £55

'Black Cat' Virginia Cigarettes. (Street Jewellery)
$325 £175

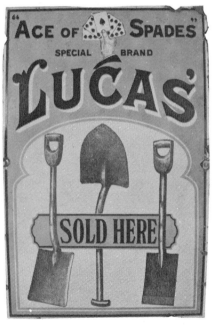

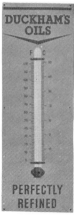

Lucas 'Ace of Spades'. (Street Jewellery)   Duckham's Oils. (Street   Komo Metal Paste. (Street
$275 £150   Jewellery) $140 £75   Jewellery) $275 £150

Hall's Distemper. (Street Jewellery) $220 £120

Martini. (Street Jewellery)
$160 £85

Nestle's Milk. (Street Jewellery)
$140 £75

Singer Sewing Machines.
(Street Jewellery)
$175 £95

'Matchless' metal polish. (Street
Jewellery) $465 £250

Belga Vander Elst. (Street
Jewellery) $120 £65

Player's 'Drumhead' cigarettes.
(Street Jewellery) $185 £100

Shell. (Street Jewellery) $75 £40

Anti-Laria Sparkling Wine. (Street
Jewellery) $140 £75

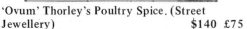

'Ovum' Thorley's Poultry Spice. (Street
Jewellery) $140 £75

'Redgate' Table Waters. (Street Jewellery)
                              $110 £60

Van Houtens Cocoa. (Street Jewellery)
          $160 £85

Phipp's 'Diamond Ale'. (Street
Jewellery) $200 £110

Fry's Pure Breakfast Cocoa.
(Street Jewellery) $160 £85

Taylor's Depository. (Street
Jewellery) $370 £200

Drink Coca Cola. (Street
Jewellery) $140 £75

Mazawattee Tea. (Street Jewellery)
          $220 £120

Nectar Tea. (Street Jewellery)
          $130 £70

Veno's 'Cough Cure'. (Street
Jewellery) $140 £75

Sunlight 'Guarantee of Purity.
(Street Jewellery) $700 £375

Ogden's 'Coolie Cut Plug'. (Street Jewellery) $140 £75

Colman's Starch. (Street
Jewellery) $85 £45

A Navajo silver and turquoise Concho belt, hand-hammered silver, comprised of seven oval conchos and six butterflies. (Robt. W. Skinner Inc.) $1,600 £898

Plains beaded and fringed hide pipebag, Sioux/Arapaho, 1880's, 23½in. long. (Robt. W. Skinner Inc.) $1,400 £786

California coiled basketry bowl, Pomo gift basket, oval, 10½in. long, 4in. high. (Robt. W. Skinner Inc.)
$1,200 £674

A North American Plains Indian leather drawstring purse with blue and white bead decoration. (Phillips) $151 £85

A Navajo silver Concho belt, comprised of nine open-centre conchos and a repoussed buckle. (Robt. W. Skinner Inc.) $750 £421

A Navajo silver Concho belt, comprised of seven oval conchos, six butterflies and open centre buckle. (Robt. W. Skinner Inc.)
$1,600 £898

Two Cascades/Plateau imbricated coiled baskets, Klikitat, 19th century, 10¼in. and 7¼in. high. (Robt. W. Skinner Inc.) $1,300 £730

Plains beaded hide cradle cover, Sioux, 1880's, 19in. long. (Robt. W. Skinner Inc.) $1,500 £842

Northwest Coast polychrome wood totemic carving, 19th century, cedar, 29½in. high. (Robt. W. Skinner Inc.) $2,300 £1,292

Northwest Coast polychrome wood rattle, cedar, carved in two sections and joined with square metal nails, 11¼in. long. (Robt. W. Skinner Inc.) $350 £196

Plains polychrome and fringed hide doll, Northern, 1880's, 18½in. high. (Robt. W. Skinner Inc.) $1,800 £1,011

California coiled basketry bowl, Pomo, diam. 12in., 5¾in. high. (Robt. W. Skinner Inc.) $500 £280

Nez Perce twined cornhusk bag, 13½ x 18in. (Robt. W. Skinner Inc.) $475 £266

Southwestern polychrome pottery jar, San Ildefonso, black on red, Powhoge Period, 12½in. diam. (Robt. W. Skinner Inc.) $1,100 £617

Hopi polychrome wood Kachina doll, early 20th century, 'Topsy', 7¾in. high. (Robt. W. Skinner Inc.) $425 £238

Tlingit twined spruce root rattle top basket, 5¼in. diam. (Robt. W. Skinner Inc.) $500 £280

Hopi polychrome wood Kachina doll, 'Ang-ak-China', early 20th century, 9in. high. (Robt. W. Skinner Inc.) $425 £238

Tonita Pena, (Quah Ah), (San Ildefonso), Winter Dancers, tempera on white paper, signed, 5¾ x 6¾in. (Robt. W. Skinner Inc.) $550 £308

Hopi polychrome wood Kachina doll, 'Bule Mana', early 20th century, 13in. high. (Robt. W. Skinner Inc.) $1,000 £561

Tonita Pena, (Quah Ah), (San Ildefonso), Ceremonial Dancers, tempera on white paper, signed, 5½ x 7in. (Robt. W. Skinner Inc.) $325 £182

Hopi polychrome wood Kachina doll, possibly the clown figure, 'Piptuka', early 20th century, 8½in. high. (Robt. W. Skinner Inc.) $900 £505

Richard Martinez, (Opa Mu Nu), (San Ildefonso), Bonnet Dancer, tempera on white paper, signed, 10½ x 12¾in. (Robt. W. Skinner Inc.) $650 £365

Nez Perce twined cornhusk bag, false embroidered in homespun wool and natural grass, 19 x 24in. (Robt. W. Skinner Inc.) $400 £224

Southwestern polychrome pottery jar, Zia, 14in. diam. (Robt. W. Skinner Inc.) $2,100 £1,179

Nez Perce twined cornhusk bag, false embroidered in natural dyed cornhusk and grass, 19½ x 26in. (Robt. W. Skinner Inc.) $475 £266

Plains beaded and fringed hide doll, Northern, 1880's, 13½in. high. (Robt. W. Skinner Inc.) $1,600 £898

Jimmy Toddy (Beatien Yazz), (Little No Shirt), (Navajo), Running Antelope, circa 1940, tempera on white paper, signed, 14 x 15½in. (Robt. W. Skinner Inc.) $375 £210

Great Lakes beaded cloth bandolier bag, early 20th century, 42in. long. (Robt. W. Skinner Inc.) $600 £337

Southwestern coiled basketry bowl, Pima, 16in. diam. (Robt. W. Skinner Inc.) $850 £477

An Indian-style covered woven basket, 1916, 8¼in. high, 10½in. diam. (Robt. W. Skinner Inc.) $450 £267

California coiled basketry tray, Pomo gift basket, with cotton twine and shell disc handle. (Robt. W. Skinner Inc.) $1,200 £674

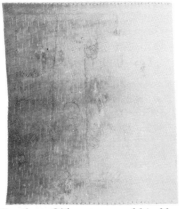

Southern Ojibwa engraved birchbark instruction scroll, Mide Ghost Lodge Menominee, 67in. long. (Robt. W. Skinner Inc.) $1,300 £730

Late 19th century Hopi polychrome wood Kachina doll, possibly 'Qoia', a Navajo singer, 16½in. high. (Robt. W. Skinner Inc.) $4,000 £2,247

Navajo fringed Germantown rug, woven on a bright red ground in navy-blue, dark red, pink, white and green, 76 x 83in. (Robt. W. Skinner Inc.) $7,750 £4,353

Plains beaded and fringed hide cradleboard, Ute Reservation Period, 39in. high. (Robt. W. Skinner Inc.) $650 £365

A four-colour Chocktaw Indian plaited basket, 4½in. high, and a handled three-colour Cherokee basket, 11½in. high. (Robt. W. Skinner Inc.) $275 £166

Plains beaded hide boot moccasins, Southern Cheyenne/Arapaho, 1880's, 15in. high. (Robt. W. Skinner Inc.) $1,800 £1,011

Southwestern pre-historic pottery bowl, late 13th/ early 14th century, 16½in. diam. (Robt. W. Skinner Inc.) $3,300 £1,853

Plains beaded and quilled hide 'Possible' bag, Sioux, late 19th century, 20¾in. long. (Robt. W. Skinner Inc.) $1,500 £842

Late 19th century Plains carved red Catlinite pipehead, in the form of an eagle's claw clutching an ovoid-shaped bowl. (Robt. W. Skinner Inc.) $275 £154

Plains pony beaded and fringed hide dress, 19th century, formed of two skins, 51in. long. (Robt. W. Skinner Inc.) $7,200 £4,044

American Indian wood Kachina doll, Hopi of flattened form, probably 'Shalako Mana', 11in. high. (Robt. W. Skinner Inc.) $2,800 £1,696

Navajo pictorial weaving, woven on a burgundy ground in white, green, brown, black and pink, 43 x 57in. (Robt. W. Skinner Inc.) $900 £505

Eskimo/Northwest Coast polychrome wood mask, 19th century, cedar, 8½in. long. (Robt. W. Skinner Inc.) $2,200 £1,235

Southern Ojibwa engraved birchbark document scroll, Mide-Wiwim Society, 61in. long. (Robt. W. Skinner Inc.) $1,700 £955

Great Lakes loom beaded cloth bandolier bag, late 19th century, 36in. long. (Robt. W. Skinner Inc.) $850 £477

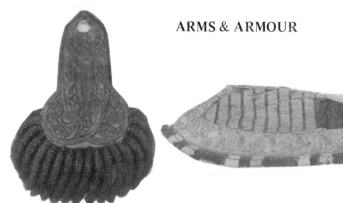

An officer's single epaulette of the 1st or the Royal Regt., gilt lace ornamental embroidered scarlet strap, 2½in., GC for age (gilt lace tarnished). (Wallis & Wallis) $650 £370

A Chinese horse armour with hemp backing, the body comprising two crupper and peytral panels of overlapping fish-scale plates. (Christie's) $401 £242

A composite Cuirassiers three-quarter armour, circa 1600, fingers lacking from gauntlets, pitted and cleaned overall. (Phillips) $4,536 £2,800

A Grenadier Guards Drummer's richly laced full dress tunic, a buff leather belt, full dress trousers, and a Guardsman's bearskin. (Christie's) $545 £300

A composite Continental armour mainly in early 17th century style, mounted on a fabric-covered wooden dummy, with realistically-carved, painted and bearded head set with glass eyes. (Christie's) $6,674 £3,800

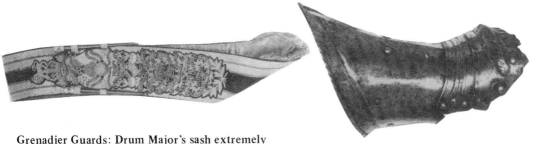

Grenadier Guards: Drum Major's sash extremely richly embroidered with a magnificent trophy of arms, thirty-four battle honours ending with France and Flanders 1914-18. (Christie's)
$1,278 £770

A left hand gauntlet circa 1580, deep roped knucklepiece, four lames, and cuff. (Wallis & Wallis)
$270 £155

A composite Continental armour in mid 16th century style, with roped borders and etched decoration, on a wooden stand. (Christie's)
$3,560 £2,000

A fine Black Watch broadsword by Wilkinson Sword Co. Ltd, London with 32½in. blade, an officer's Black Watch full dress doublet, a kilt and Black Watch sporran by Wm. Anderson & Sons Ltd. (Christie's) $1,550 £850

A decorative composite armour mainly in 16th century style, on a wooden display-stand with square base. (Christie's)
$1,602 £900

A post 1902 Lieutenant's full dress blue jacket of The Royal Horse Artillery, with scarlet collar, gilt cord and lace trim including 17 loops to chest. (Wallis & Wallis) $475 £260

A white Wolseley helmet with gilt chin-chain, a dark blue tunic with black velvet facings and with General's buttons, white leather gloves. (Christie's) $637 £350

A good Lieutenant's full dress scarlet tunic circa 1865 of the 18th (Royal Irish) Regt., with its crimson silk shoulder sash. (Wallis & Wallis) $455 £250

Pre-1914 Major's blue tunic of The Royal Regt. of Artillery. (James Norwich Auctions) $40 £25

A composite armour comprising: lacquered iron four-plate momonari kabuto with four lame shikiro and modern kuwagata, all contained in a wood box, some restoration. (Phillips) $2,464 £1,400

A yellow Skinner's kurta with plain shoulder chains, a fine pouchbelt and its Skinner's Horse title scroll. (Christie's) $4,500 £3,000

A good post 1902 Lt. Colonel's full dress scarlet doublet of The Gordon Highlanders, and a pair of tartan trews. (Wallis & Wallis) $365 £200

A pre-1914 officer's scarlet tunic of The Prince of Wales Leinster Regt. (James Norwich Auctions) $48 £30

A Prussian Rittmeister's dress tunic of the 14th Uhlan Regt., dark blue with maroon piping and cuffs. (Wallis & Wallis) $300 £172

An Edward VII blue mess jacket and waistcoat of The King's Own Norfolk Yeomanry, worn by Regt. Sgt. Major Hudgell. (James Norwich Auctions) $120 £75

A 19th century sugake-laced okegawa-do, unsigned, lacking armour-box. (Christie's) $4,928 £3,080

A fine Colonel's full dress scarlet tunic of The Royal Warwickshire Regt., with a crimson silk waistsash and tassels. (Wallis & Wallis) $400 £220

A silver cap badge of The Bedfordshire & Hertfordshire Regt., HM B'ham 1932. (Wallis & Wallis) $113 £69

An Imperial German World War I Zeppelin crew badge (Army). (Wallis & Wallis) $470 £285

A silver cap badge of The Duke of Cornwall's Light Infantry, HM B'ham 1899. (Wallis & Wallis) $74 £45

An officer's full-dress grenade badge of The Royal Dublin Fusiliers. (Wallis & Wallis) $231 £140

A cast brass badge of 602 (City of Glasgow) Bomber Squadron. (Wallis & Wallis) $96 £60

An other rank's white metal glengarry of The 7th Vol. Bn. The Argyll & Sutherland Highlanders. (Wallis & Wallis) $25 £16

An officer's gilt and silvered 1878 pattern helmet plate of The 88th (Connaught Rangers) Regt. (Wallis & Wallis) $222 £135

A pre-1855 officer's gilt and silver plated copper shoulder belt plate of The 1st Devon Militia. (Wallis & Wallis) $396 £240

A cast silvered pouch belt plate of The Canada Rifles. (Wallis & Wallis) $128 £80

BADGES

An other rank's white metal shako badge of The 74th (Highlanders). (Wallis & Wallis) $112 £70

A sterling silver cap badge of The 17th (Duke of Cambridge's) Lancers. (Wallis & Wallis) $140 £85

An Elizabeth II silver cap badge of The Green Jackets Brigade, HM B'ham 1958. (Wallis & Wallis) $49 £30

An Imperial German U-boat badge (as issued 1910), silvered finish. (Wallis & Wallis) $206 £125

Order of the Bath, Civil Division, Knight Commander's breast star, circa 1900, in silver with gold and enamel centre, in Garrard's case of issue. (Wallis & Wallis) $224 £140

A Victorian officer's gilt silvered and enamel fur cap grenade badge of The Royal Fusiliers. (Wallis & Wallis) $173 £105

Order of the Garter breast star in silver and enamels, 85mm. diam., mid Victorian period. (Wallis & Wallis) $3,200 £2,000

An officer's gilt and silvered shoulder belt plate of The Gordon Highlanders. (Wallis & Wallis) $165 £100

An officer's silvered Rifle Brigade pouch belt badge. (Wallis & Wallis) $107 £65

BADGES

An NCO's helmet plate of
The Ayrshire Yeomanry.
(Wallis & Wallis) $240 £150

An Imperial Turkish Empire
Air Force pilot's badge.
(Wallis & Wallis) $495 £300

A First Pattern Imperial
Austrian Naval pilot's
badge (1915). (Wallis &
Wallis) $165 £100

An officer's gilt and silver
grenade badge of The Royal
Welsh Fusiliers. (Wallis &
Wallis) $115 £70

An officer's gilt and silvered
plaid brooch of The High-
land Light Infantry. (Wallis
& Wallis) $627 £380

The Royal Guelphic Order,
Knight Commander's Civil
neck badge in gold, HM 1815,
and enamels. (Wallis & Wallis)
$1,520 £950

An officer's silver (not HM)
Maltese Cross shako plate
of The 6th Lancashire Rifle
Vols. (Wallis & Wallis)
$112 £68

A Victorian officer's silvered
and gilt shoulder belt plate
of The 3rd Bn., The Black
Watch (Royal Highlanders).
(Wallis & Wallis) $198 £120

A Victorian other rank's
white metal helmet plate
of The Volunteer Medical
Staff Corps. (Wallis & Wallis)
$99 £60

BADGES

A silver cap badge of The 7th/8th Bn. The West Yorkshire Regt., HM B'ham 1940. (Wallis & Wallis) $74 £45

A Victorian other rank's white metal Maltese Cross helmet plate of The Duke of Edinburgh's Own Vol. Rifles. (Wallis & Wallis) $160 £100

A pre-1881 other rank's glengarry of The 65th (Second Yorkshire North Riding) Regt. (Wallis & Wallis) $88 £55

An other rank's cap badge of The Jewish Bn. Royal Fusiliers. (Wallis & Wallis) $56 £35

A Georgian circular cast brass pouch badge of The 71st (Fraser's) Highlanders. (Wallis & Wallis) $528 £330

A pre-1881 officer's full-dress grenade badge of The 102nd (Royal Madras Fusiliers). (Wallis & Wallis) $231 £140

A Victorian officer's silvered helmet plate of The 1st Fifeshire Rifle Vol. Corps. (Wallis & Wallis) $176 £110

A pre-1855 officer's gilt and silvered shoulder belt plate of The 27th (Inniskilling) Regt. (Wallis & Wallis) $742 £450

A post-1902 officer's silvered helmet plate of The Cinque Ports Artillery Vols. (Wallis & Wallis) $148 £90

BADGES

A silver cap badge of The Reconnaissance Corps, HM B'ham 1944. (Wallis & Wallis) $181 £110

A silver cap badge of The Durham Light Infantry, HM B'ham 1930. (Wallis & Wallis) $115 £70

An officer's silver and enamel cap badge of The Coldstream Guards, HM B'ham 1970. (Wallis & Wallis) $56 £35

A post-1902 officer's full-dress grenade badge of The Royal Fusiliers (City of London Regt.). (Wallis & Wallis) $165 £100

A mantle(?) badge, featuring crowned device of St. Andrew with motto, in bullion weave with embroidery, velvet and sequins of Victorian period, 6 x 5in. (Wallis & Wallis) $80 £50

An Edward VIII other rank's white metal cap badge of The Royal Horse Artillery, by Firmin, London. (Wallis & Wallis) $104 £65

A 2nd pattern Victorian collar badge of The 21st Lancers. (Wallis & Wallis) $74 £45

An Imperial Austro-Hungarian pilot's badge. (Wallis & Wallis) $429 £260

A Victorian other rank's blackened glengarry of The Royal Irish Rifles. (Wallis & Wallis) $72 £45

BADGES

A Metropolitan Police helmet badge, GR VI. (James Norwich Auctions) $12 £8

A plastic cap badge of The Royal Artillery. (Wallis & Wallis) $164 £100

A Victorian officer's gilt and silvered helmet plate of The King's (Liverpool Regt.) (Wallis & Wallis) $156 £95

An officer's full-dress grenade badge of The Northumberland Fusiliers. (Wallis & Wallis) $181 £110

An officer's cast silver (not HM) glengarry badge of The Argyll & Sutherland Highlanders. (Wallis & Wallis) $128 £80

An Imperial Austrian pilot's badge, silvered eagle, with enamelled oak-leaf border. (Wallis & Wallis) $528 £320

A Victorian other rank's white metal helmet plate of The 4th Vol. Bn. The Scottish Rifles. (Wallis & Wallis) $144 £90

A 1st pattern Victorian collar badge of The 21st Lancers. (Wallis & Wallis) $148 £90

An officer's silver cap badge of The 5th Royal Inniskilling Dragoons Guards, HM B'ham 1948. (Wallis & Wallis) $80 £50

A Nazi Army officer's dagger, by Kolping, plated mounts, white grip, in
its plated sheath with hanging straps and belt lug. (Wallis & Wallis) $192 £120

A Prussian 1871 pattern brass hilted dress sword bayonet, saw-back blade
20in., by W.K.C., German silver crossguard, in its lacquered brass mounted
leather scabbard. (Wallis & Wallis) $140 £85

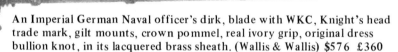

A Nazi Red Cross Man's dagger, blade retaining all original polish, plated
mounts, diced black grips, in its black painted steel sheath. (Wallis & Wallis)
$239 £145

An Imperial German Naval officer's dirk, blade with WKC, Knight's head
trade mark, gilt mounts, crown pommel, real ivory grip, original dress
bullion knot, in its lacquered brass sheath. (Wallis & Wallis) $576 £360

A Nazi model 1936 S.S. officer's dagger, by Boker, German silver
mounts, in its metal sheath with plated mounts and hanging
chains and belt clip. (Wallis & Wallis) $1,200 £750

A Nazi Naval officer's dirk, by W.K.C., blade retaining virtually all original polish,
wire bound white celluloid grip, in its gilt brass sheath. (Wallis & Wallis)
$239 £145

An Imperial German Naval Applicanten Naval dirk, blade 12½in., steel hilt with double
small folding shell guards, in its leather sheath. (Wallis & Wallis) $416 £260

A Nazi Naval officer's dirk, plain blade by Eickhorn, gilt mounts, wire bound white celluloid grip, in its gilt sheath with original bullion dress knot. (Wallis & Wallis)
$184 £115

A Nazi Hitler Youth bayonet, blade 8in., steel mounts, stylised eagle's head pommel, diced black grips, in its black painted metal scabbard. (Wallis & Wallis)
$128 £80

A Nazi Wehrmacht dress bayonet, plated blade 9¾in., by Everitz, plated mounts, stylised eagle's head pommel, real staghorn grips, in its black painted steel scabbard with leather frog. (Wallis & Wallis)
$112 £70

A Nazi Naval officer's dirk, by Eickhorn, plain double fullered blade, gilt mounts, white grip, in its gilt sheath with bullion dress knot. (Wallis & Wallis)
$240 £150

A 3rd Reich Naval officer's dirk, by Eickhorn, blade retaining all original polish, gilt mounts, wire bound white celluloid grip, bullion dress knot tied naval style, in its gilt sheath. (Wallis & Wallis)
$429 £260

A Nazi RAD officer's dagger, by Alcoso, plated mounts, white celluloid grip, in its plated sheath. (Wallis & Wallis)
$455 £276

A South African Air Force officer's dress dagger, plain, plated blade 9in., gilt brass crosspiece in form of eagle with wings spread, round fish-skin covered grip, gilt band mounts, in its leather covered sheath. (Wallis & Wallis)
$160 £100

DAGGERS

A Georgian Naval Officer's dirk circa 1790, straight double edged blade 15in., with single fullers, etched with crowned G. R., trophies of arms and other trophies. (Wallis & Wallis) $140 £80

An unusual all steel Indian katar, 15in., blade 9½in. with swollen armour piercing tip and raised ribs, hilt with broad flared sides deeply chiselled overall with flowers and foliage in relief. (Wallis & Wallis) $105 £60

A scarce 1907 Presentation bayonet, blade 17in., by Wilkinson, ordnance stamp at forte, etched: Presented to J. Clayton by The Wilkinson Sword Co. Ltd. on the completion of 2,000,000 Bayonets, 1915-1918'. (Wallis & Wallis) $140 £80

A rare 1st Pattern Field service fighting knife, tapering double edged blade 7in., by Wilkinson Sword, also etched at forte 'The Field Service Fighting Knife'. (Wallis & Wallis) $455 £260

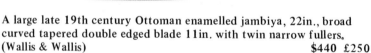

A large late 19th century Ottoman enamelled jambiya, 22in., broad curved tapered double edged blade 11in. with twin narrow fullers. (Wallis & Wallis) $440 £250

An unusual 19th century all steel Tibetan dagger, broad single edged blade 11in. with narrow fuller, steel hilt and large sheath mounts nicely chiselled overall with scrolling foliage. (Wallis & Wallis) $78 £45

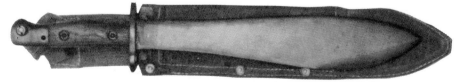

An Australian M.1944 Machete Paratroopers bayonet Bolo blade 11in., steel mounts, wood grip. (Wallis & Wallis) $130 £75

DAGGERS

An unusual 19th century Burmese/Thai dagger, straight single edged blade 11½in., stamped 'Manipurhaih', downturned brass crosspiece with chiselled lion's head terminals in full relief. (Wallis & Wallis)$300 £170

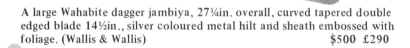

A scarce U.S.M.C. Stiletto fighting knife, double edged blade 6¾in., chequered solid alloy hilt with integral crosspiece, in a brown leather M6 sheath. (Wallis & Wallis) $315 £180

A large Wahabite dagger jambiya, 27¼in. overall, curved tapered double edged blade 14½in., silver coloured metal hilt and sheath embossed with foliage. (Wallis & Wallis) $500 £290

An attractive 19th century Indian bowie knife, blade 7in. with false edge, polished ivory grip, silver coloured metal mounts, recurved cross-piece chiselled with foliage. (Wallis & Wallis) $210 £120

A good quality Victorian Scottish dirk of The 78th (Ross-shire Buffs) Regt., straight single edged bifullered blade 12in. etched with crowned 'VR' cypher, '78 Highland' beneath elephant. (Wallis & Wallis)
$1,650 £950

A good Spanish Ripol type knife, 17½in., broad tapered single edged blade 11½in. chiselled brass sheath and hilt mounts. (Wallis & Wallis)
$140 £80

An unusual 19th century Turkish H.M. silver mounted trousse, 15½in., the three knives with curved fullered single edged blades 6¼in. to 4½in., hilts made from jade. (Wallis & Wallis) $630 £360

FLASKS

A good embossed copper powder flask (R. 355) 8in., graduated nozzle stamped G. & J. W. Hawksley. (Wallis & Wallis) $90 £55

A powder horn circa 1800, brass circular base plate engraved with the device of the Percy Tenantry, 13½in. long. (Wallis & Wallis) $135 £80

An embossed copper powder flask (R.535), 8in. embossed with panel of geometric and foliate ornament, patent brass top stamped James Dixon & Sons. (Wallis & Wallis) $87 £50

An 18th century Persian all steel powder flask, of swollen boat or swan form. (Wallis & Wallis) $107 £65

A good scarce Japanese cow horn powder flask, 5½in. very well made and polished, turned ivory spout and collar emanate from fluted horn tehenkanemono. (Wallis & Wallis) $160 £95

An engraved rifle horn with carved horntip powder measure, Midwest, dated 1843, in cartouche, 4½in. long. (Robt. W. Skinner Inc.) $1,200 £714

A good 18th/19th century Transylvanian stag horn powder flask, 6in. decorated overall with geometric devices. (Wallis & Wallis) $175 £100

A brass mounted Continental lanthorn powder flask, fixed baluster turned nozzle swivels on knuckle joint for cut off. (Wallis & Wallis) $150 £90

A 17th/18th century Persian Circassian walnut powder flask, 6in., sprung steel lever charger with shaped top. (Wallis & Wallis) $400 £240

An unusually large and scarce American embossed copper gun flask 'Indian Hunting Buffalo', 9½in. overall. (Wallis & Wallis) $175 £100

A scarce 18th century Persian silver mounted brass powder flask of swollen form, 5½in., engraved overall with flowers and foliage. (Wallis & Wallis) $265 £160

A good small copper pistol sized powder flask, 4¾in., common brass charger. (Wallis & Wallis) $87 £50

FUCHI-KASHIRA

An 18th century shakudo nanakoji fuchi-kashira decorated with serpents in takabori, gilt detail. (Christie's) $1,267 £792

A shibuichi migakiji fuchi-kashira, signed Hidekatsu, early 19th century. (Christie's) $880 £550

A 19th century shakudo nanakoji fuchi-kashira, inscribed Ishiguro Masa-yoshi. (Christie's) $968 £605

A 19th century fuchi-kashira, silver takazogan, inscribed Omori Eishu. (Christie's) $2,195 £1,372

A shakudo nanakoji fuchi-kashira, signed Kondo Mitsuyasu, circa 1800. (Christie's) $1,091 £682

An 18th century shakudo nanakoji gilt rimmed in fuchi-kashira, Soten style. (Christie's) $704 £440

A shibuichi fuchi-kashira, decorated with carp among gilt water-weeds, signed Tomohisa, Mito School, circa 1800. (Christie's) $844 £528

Early 19th century copper fuchi-kashira depicting Raiden among clouds on the kashira, unsigned. (Christie's) $440 £275

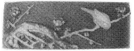

A shakudo nanakoji fuchi-kashira, iroe takazogan, reed warblers on branches of blossoming plum, signed Ganshoshi Nagatsune and kao. (Christie's) $739 £462

A 19th century shakudo migakiji fuchi-kashira decorated with Gentoku, signed Yasumasa. (Christie's) $563 £352

A shakudo migakiji fuchi-kashira decorated in taka-zogan with ants and their eggs, 19th century. (Christie's) $563 £352

A 19th century shakudo nanakoji fuchi-kashira, unsigned. depicting a cuckoo in flight. (Christie's) $563 £352

HELMETS

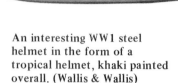

An officer's 1855 pattern shako bearing gilt plate of the 82nd Regiment with VR cypher on the gilt ball, upper lining missing. (Christie's) $728 £400

An interesting WW1 steel helmet in the form of a tropical helmet, khaki painted overall. (Wallis & Wallis) $100 £55

A good other ranks helmet of the 1st Dragoon Guards, brass skull and fittings, brass and white metal helmet plate, red horse hair plume. (Phillips) $810 £500

A Prussian M.1915 Ersatz (Pressed Felt) O.R's Pickelhaube of a Pioneer Battalion. (Wallis & Wallis) $245 £140

A good Spanish Officers shako, fawn cloth, leather peak and headband, simulated leather top. (Wallis & Wallis) $380 £210

A Hesse M. 1915 Infantryman's Pickelhaube, grey painted helmet plate and mounts leather lining and chinstrap. (Wallis & Wallis) $260 £150

Queen's Own Cameron Highlanders: officer's feather bonnet by W. Cater, Pall Mall. (Christie's) $584 £352

A well made modern copy of an English close helmet from a Greenwich armour, of good form and weight. (Wallis & Wallis) $500 £280

A Cabasset circa 1600, formed in one piece with 'pear stalk' finial, plain narrow brim. (Wallis & Wallis) $230 £130

HELMETS

A large round black hat with pale drab cotton cover bearing a large elaborate badge in wire embroidery of the Bersaglieri. (Christie's)
$127 £70

An English civil war period pikeman's 'pot', made in two pieces with sunken edges and steel rivetted borders. (Wallis & Wallis) $800 £460

An Italian black velvet fez by Unione Militare, Roma with an embroidered badge surmounted by Fasces. (Christie's) $218 £120

An officer's bearskin cap of the Royal Welsh Fusiliers with fine white metal mounted gilt grenade. (Christie's)
$475 £260

A Bavarian M.1915 Uhlan ORs Tschapska, grey painted helmet plate and mounts. (Wallis & Wallis) $315 £180

5th (Northumberland Fusiliers): officer's bearskin cap with regimental gilt grenade, inside is marked H.W. Archer, Esq., 5th Fusiliers. (Christie's) $639 £385

A very rare helmet of an experimental pattern for French Dragoon regiments circa 1900, bearing manufacturer's stamp: B. Franck et ses fils, Aubervilliers. (Christie's) $728 £400

An interesting composite close helmet made up for the Pisan Bridge Festival, the skull from a very rare Milanese armet circa 1440-1450. (Wallis & Wallis) $2,750 £1,500

A Rifles officer's Astrakhan busby, a tunic with scarlet facings and a composite pouch-belt with a whistle, chin-boss and badge. (Christie's) $435 £240

HELMETS

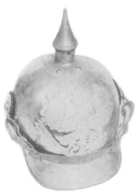

A Prussian Artillery officer's pickelhaube of The 10th Field Artillery Regt. (Wallis & Wallis) $496 £310

A scarce American Civil War Officers Dark Blue Kepi, black lace edge trim and side welts. (Wallis & Wallis) $475 £270

A Prussian Cuirassier trooper's helmet with grey metal helmet plate and spike. (Wallis & Wallis) $576 £360

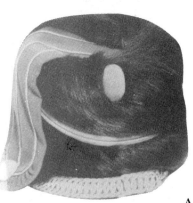

A Prussian Cuirassier officer's helmet with brown leather and silk inner lining. (Wallis & Wallis)
        $1,089 £660

An officer's fur busby of The 20th Hussars. (Wallis & Wallis)
        $544 £340

A Prussian Cuirassier officer's helmet, green leather lining to lobster tail and stepped peak. (Wallis & Wallis) $1,122 £680

A Victorian officer's blue cloth spiked helmet of The Royal Scots. (Wallis & Wallis)
        $478 £290

A closed cuirassier's Savoyard type burgonet with raised comb and pointed peak. (Christie's) $1,909 £1,155

A tall Cabasset circa 1600, formed in one piece with smooth finish and vestigial 'pear stalk' finial. (Wallis & Wallis) $350 £200

HELMETS

A Prussian Jager Zu Pferd trooper's helmet with grey metal finish to spike and mounts. (Wallis & Wallis) $600 £375

A Prussian Infantryman's ersatz (pressed felt) pickel-haube of The 87th Infantry Regt. (Wallis & Wallis) $432 £270

A distinctive beige/grey helmet of the Harrow Rifles with matching leather binding, label inside marked Chamberlayne. (Christie's) $690 £380

An Other Rank's brass 1871 pattern helmet of The 1st King's Dragoon Guards. (James Norwich Auctions) $520 £325

A Prussian NCO's lance cap of The 1st Guard Uhlan Regt. (Wallis & Wallis) $1,040 £650

Officer's helmet of The King's Own Norfolk Imperial Yeomanry, circa 1915. (James Norwich Auctions) $1,240 £775

Trooper's helmet of The King's Own Norfolk Imperial Yeomanry, circa 1910. (James Norwich Auctions) $577 £350

An early 17th century pike-man's pot helmet, formed in two pieces with engraved line decoration and brass rivets. (Wallis & Wallis) $455 £260

A French 1858 pattern Dragoon officer's helmet. (Wallis & Wallis) $2,145 £1,300

Early 19th century kabuto with a russet-iron sixty-two plate hoshi-bachi, rear plate signed Nagamichi. (Christie's) $2,816 £1,760

A post-1902 R.N. Flag officer's dark blue peaked cap. (Wallis & Wallis) $352 £220

A Nazi Naval officer's cocked hat with silk lining. (Wallis & Wallis) $192 £120

An officer's blue cloth peaked forage cap of The Somersetshire Light Infantry. (Wallis & Wallis) $304 £190

A Victorian officer's blue cloth spiked helmet of The Royal Engineers. (Wallis & Wallis) $400 £250

A Prussian other rank's lance cap as worn by The 1st and 2nd Uhlan Regt. (Wallis & Wallis) $800 £500

A Victorian officer's blue cloth spiked helmet of The Royal Scots. (Wallis & Wallis) $800 £500

A post-1902 officer's shako of The Highland Light Infantry. (Wallis & Wallis) $336 £210

A post-1902 officer's blue cloth spiked helmet of The Dorsetshire Regt. (Wallis & Wallis) $400 £250

HELMETS

An Imperial German Hussar officer's busby of The 2nd Leib Hussar Regt. (Queen Victoria of Prussia). (Wallis & Wallis) $2,887 £1,750

A 17th century kabuto with russet-iron hoshi-bachi, unsigned. (Christie's) $2,816 £1,760

A post-1902 officer's blue cloth ball-topped helmet of The Royal Army Medical Corps. (Wallis & Wallis) $315 £180

A Volunteer Artillery Officer's blue cloth ball topped helmet, silver plated mounts. (Wallis & Wallis) $265 £150

A Victorian officer's peaked forage cap of The Derbyshire Regt. (Wallis & Wallis) $304 £190

An Imperial Austrian Dragoon officer's helmet with silk and leather lining. (Wallis & Wallis) $1,732 £1,050

Helmet from the uniform of Col. Pilkington, 4th Vol. Bn. The King's Regt. (Wallis & Wallis) $1,320 £800

An officer's fur busby of The Royal Corps. of Signals, with leather lining. (Wallis & Wallis) $152 £95

An officer's blue cloth spiked helmet of The Royal Warwickshire Regt. (Wallis & Wallis) $496 £310

A Bavarian M.1915 Dragoon O.Rs Pickelhaube, grey painted helmet plate and mounts. (Wallis & Wallis) $210 £120

An Italian grey-green felt Alpini style hat bearing black embroidered badge of Alpine Artillery. (Christie's)
$110 £60

A Prussian Reservist Artillery Officer's M.1896 Pickelhaube, gilt finish to helmet plate. (Wallis & Wallis) $400 £225

A scarce American Civil War Union Cavalry O.R.'s Kepi known as the 'Bummers Cap'. (Wallis & Wallis) $175 £100

A Vic Officer's helmet of the Royal Horse Guards, plated brass skull, gilt peak binding. (Wallis & Wallis)
$2,200 £1,250

A good post 1902 Royal Artillery Officer's busby, scarlet bag, gilt grenade plume holder, white goatshair plume. (Wallis & Wallis) $225 £130

A good officers busby of the 15th (The King's) Hussars, scarlet bag with gilt braid trim and purl button. (Wallis & Wallis) $685 £390

A Wurttemberg Infantryman's Pickelhaube, grey painted finish to helmet plate, spike and mounts, leather lining and chinstrap. (Wallis & Wallis)
$210 £120

A good R.H.A. Officers Brown Fur Busby circa 1900, scarlet bag, 15in. white ostrich feather plume with white vulture feather base. (Wallis & Wallis) $370 £210

MEDALS

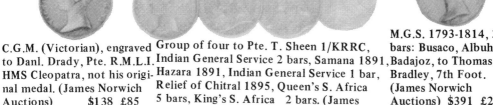

C.G.M. (Victorian), engraved to Danl. Drady, Pte. R.M.L.I. HMS Cleopatra, not his original medal. (James Norwich Auctions) $138 £85

Group of four to Pte. T. Sheen 1/KRRC, Indian General Service 2 bars, Samana 1891, Hazara 1891, Indian General Service 1 bar, Relief of Chitral 1895, Queen's S. Africa 5 bars, King's S. Africa 2 bars. (James Norwich Auctions) $320 £200

M.G.S. 1793-1814, 3 bars: Busaco, Albuhera, Badajoz, to Thomas Bradley, 7th Foot. (James Norwich Auctions) $391 £240

N.G.S. 1793, 1 bar Spartan 3rd May 1810, Henry Bourne. (Wallis & Wallis) $480 £300

Pair: 29th Ft. Sutlej (Feroz. in exergue), 1 bar Sobra'on Punjab, 2 bars Chilianwala, Goojerat, to Serjt. Timothy Dunne. (James Norwich Auctions) $330 £200

M.G.S. 1793, 1 bar Chateauguay (Sak Sotaontion, Warrior). (Wallis & Wallis) $1,560 £975

I.G.S. 1895, 3 bars: Relief of Chitral, Punjab Frontier, Tirah, to 3372 Pte. J. Henderson, 1st Bn. Gordon Highlanders. (James Norwich Auctions) $179 £110

Three: Canadian General Service, 1 bar Fenian Raid 1866, L.S. & G.C., Victorian issue, (935 Cr. Sergt. N. Lanc. R.), Vol. Force L.S., Edward VII, (1st Vol. Bn. L.N. Lancs. Regt.). (Wallis & Wallis) $288 £180

Afghanistan 1878-80 4 bars, Peiwar Kotal, Charasia, Kabul, Kandahar, to Driver W. Gibson 1/C. R.H.A. (James Norwich Auctions) $206 £125

ARMS & ARMOUR

A copper medal of Gotha und Altenberg for the campaign of 1814-15. (Wallis & Wallis) $156 £95

Deccan Medal 1778-1784, smaller issue in silver. (Wallis & Wallis) $352 £220

A hallmarked silver and gilt medal of The 1st Royal Edinburgh Vols., 2.3/10in. diam. (Wallis & Wallis) $371 £225

Mecklenburg: Order of the Griffin badge, in gilt and enamel, with neck ribbon section. (Wallis & Wallis) $132 £80

Order of the Bath, military companion's neck badge in silver gilt and enamel and with gold centres, in Garrard's case of issue, circa 1900. (Wallis & Wallis) $352 £220

Netherlands: Order of the House of Orange, pin-back breast badge in gilt and enamels. (Wallis & Wallis) $156 £95

Louisbourg Medal 1758, in silver, with a contemporary loop suspender, un-named as issued. (Wallis & Wallis) $1,480 £925

Prussia: Order of the Red Eagle, 4th class, in silver and enamel. (Wallis & Wallis) $148 £90

Seringapatam 1799, English striking, in silver with a contemporary loop suspender. (Wallis & Wallis) $336 £210

MEDALS

N.G.S. 1793, 1 bar Shannon Wh. Chesapeake, John Alexander. (Wallis & Wallis) $3,280 £2,050

Order of the Bath, military companion's neck badge, in silver gilt and enamel, circa 1950. (Wallis & Wallis) $336 £210

The Highland Society's medal 1804, in silver as given to The 42nd Highlanders (Black Watch) for the action at Alexandria 21st March 1801. (Wallis & Wallis) $296 £185

M.G.S. 1793, 2 bars Fort Detroit, Chrystler's Farm, J. Sterland, R. Arty. (Wallis & Wallis) $3,760 £2,350

Order of the Bath, military companion's neck badge, in gold and enamels, HM 1843. (Wallis & Wallis) $920 £575

Arctic Medal 1818-1855, un-named as issued. (Wallis & Wallis) $240 £150

Waterloo 1815, Charles Horsnail, 2nd Bn. 69th Foot, steel claw suspender. (Wallis & Wallis) $368 £230

Order of St. John, Knight of Grace, breast star in gold and enamelled, 2.1in. diam., with brooch-pin fastening. (Wallis & Wallis) $136 £85

Java Medal 1811, H.E.I.C.'s silver medal, 49mm. diam., with ring suspender. (Wallis & Wallis) $216 £135

Group of 3: Sutlej with Sobraon in exergue, no bar; Indian Mutiny, 1 bar Lucknow; Army LS & GC, to Pte. James Duntop, 1st Bn. 10th Foot. (James Norwich Auctions) $431 £265

Italy: Order of the Crown of Italy, 1st class neck badge in gilt and enamels. (Wallis & Wallis) $132 £80

Seven: D.C.M. Victorian issue (2nd Sept. 1898), Egypt undated, no bar Queen's Sudan, Q.S.A. 4 bars, K.S.A. both date bars, Khedive's Sudan 2 bars, Khedive's Star 1884-6. (Wallis & Wallis) $1,402 £850

Most Honourable Order of the Bath, military division, Knight Commanders set, comprising neck badge and breast star, in original Garrard's case of George V period. (Wallis & Wallis) $1,280 £800

Three: D.C.M. Edward VII issue, Q.S.A. 3 bars, K.S.A. both date bars, (Wallis & Wallis) $445 £270

Eleven: D.S.O. George V, M.C. George V, Mons trio with M.I.D., 1939-45 Star, Africa Star, Burma Star, Defence, War with M.I.D., Coronation (Mons Trio only named Lieut. & Major G. Le Q. Martel R.E.). (Wallis & Wallis) $1,216 £760

Three: Army of India, 1 bar Ava, (Ensign, 13th Foot), Sutlej for Ferozeshuhur, no bar (Capt. 62 Regt.), Indian Mutiny, 2 bars Relief of Lucknow, (Lieut. Col. C. W. Sibley, 64th Regt. (Wallis & Wallis) $1,200 £750

Pair: Sutleg for Moodkee with 3 bars, 31st Regt; Punjab 2 bars, Joseph Coles, 10th Foot. (Wallis & Wallis) $416 £260

The Orders and medals of Rear Admiral R. J. Prendergast, comprising Order of the Bath, Knight Commander (mil.) set of neck badge and breast star in silver gilt and enamels and neck badge in HM silver (1918), also group of five. (Wallis & Wallis) $1,440 £900

MEDALS

C.G.M. Victorian straight suspender, awarded in 1881, to William Bevis, Sick Berth Attendant, HMS Boadicea. (James Norwich Auctions) $7,498 £4,600

M.G.S. 1793, 1 bar Fort Detroit, J. Stagnell, Serjt. 41st Foot. (Wallis & Wallis) $1,520 £950

M.G.S. 1793-1814, 9 bars, to Hugh Hughes, 43rd Foot, top three bars loose. (James Norwich Auctions) $700 £430

A Victoria Cross miniature with blue ribbon, to Midshipman Duncan Gordon Boyes, Shimonoseki, Japan, Sept. 1864. (Lawrence Fine Art) $370 £198

Waterloo 1815, Charles Baxter 2nd Bn. 44th Regt. Foot, with steel claw and split ring. (Wallis & Wallis) $592 £370

Waterloo 1815, Serj. George Albert, 15th or King's Regt. Hussars. (Wallis & Wallis) $304 £190

N.G.S. 1793-1840, 2 clasps Acre 30 May 1799 and Egypt to Adam Sampson, served as Ordinary Seaman on HMS Tigre. (James Norwich Auctions) $1,467 £900

A German gilt medal, struck in 1914 to commemorate the entry of the German army into Paris. (Wallis & Wallis) $990 £600

77th Foot (2nd Middlesex), Regt. medal, silver, 35mm., engraved to George Thompson. (James Norwich Auctions) $692 £425

MEDALS

M.G.S. 1793-1814, 7 bars: Talavera, Fuentes d'Onor, Salamanca, Vittoria, Pyrenees, Nivelle, Orthes, to Peter Clifford, 24th Foot. (James Norwich Auctions) $537 £330

Boulton's Medal for Trafalgar, pewter, engraved C. Doran. (James Norwich Auctions) $244 £150

Crimea 1854, 3 clasps, Alma, Balaklava, Inkermann to Troop Serjt. Major R. Hooper, 13th Dragoons. (James Norwich Auctions) $896 £550

M.G.S. 1793, 1 bar Chrystler's Farm, Robt. Mardell, 49th Foot. (Wallis & Wallis) $1,520 £950

1st Foot (Royal Scots) Regt. medal, silver but not hall-marked, engraved to J. F. Miller/1st Foot. (James Norwich Auctions) $1,010 £620

N.G.S. 1793, 1 bar Boat Service 14th Dec. 1814, Henry Josephson, Gunner. (Wallis & Wallis) $880 £550

Punjab 1844, 1 bar Chilianwala, to Corpl. R. Horsley, 24th Foot. (James Norwich Auctions) $489 £300

C.G.M. Victorian straight suspender, awarded in 1874 to Dennis Driscoll, A.B., HMS Cleopatra. (James Norwich Auctions) $1,304 £800

Waterloo, Ensign George Drury, 33rd Regt. Foot, steel clip, straight bar suspender. (James Norwich Auctions) $570 £350

MEDALS

Waterloo, John Galley, 2nd Britt. 30th Reg. Foot, steel clip, thin 22mm. split ring suspender. (James Norwich Auctions) $293 £180

Indian Mutiny, 1 bar Lucknow, to Geo. Hawkings, 84th Regt. Another, 2 bars Defence of Lucknow, Lucknow, renamed 374 Pte. F. Paterson, 78th Highlanders. (James Norwich Auctions) $179 £110

M.G.S. 1793-1814, 3 bars: Busaco, Salamanca, Pyrenees, to Patrick Farrall, 11th Foot. (James Norwich Auctions) $391 £240

M.G.S. 1793-1814, 4 bars: Roleia, Vimiera, Talavera, Albuhera, to Samuel Bannister, 29th Foot. (James Norwich Auctions) $619 £380

Pair of Colour Sergt. John Burgess 97th Foot (later 2nd Batt. R. West Kents), Distinguished Conduct Medal, Crimea, 1 bar Sebastopol. (James Norwich Auctions)
$586 £360

I.G.S. 1895, 1 bar, Defence of Chitral 1895, to 1577 Naik Sham Sing, 14th Bengal Infantry. (James Norwich Auctions) $1,426 £875

M.G.S. 1793-1814, 7 bars: Talavera, Barrose, Vittoria, Pyrenees, Nivelle, Nive, Orthes, to R. Walsh, Serjt. 87th Foot. (James Norwich Auctions)
$912 £560

Pair of F. Frost, 9th Lancers: Punjab 2 bars; Indian Mutiny, 3 bars. (James Norwich Auctions)
$619 £380

M.G.S. 1793-1814, 4 bars: Albuhera, Ciudad Rodrigo, Salamanca, Toulouse, to E. Morgan, 23rd Foot. (James Norwich Auctions)
$423 £260

MEDALS

M.G.S. 1793-1814, 1 bar Egypt, to R. Baird, 42nd Foot. (James Norwich Auctions) $407 £250

Pair: Royal Household Faithful Service medal, Victorian issue, Jubilee 1887, in silver. (Wallis & Wallis) $416 £260

Waterloo, Serjt. John Gray, 1st Batt. 79th Regt. Foot, slightly damaged silver(?) clip, 17mm. split ring suspender. (James Norwich Auctions) $635 £390

Crimea 1854, 2 clasps, Balaklava, Inkermann, to George Adams, 1st Royal Dragoons. (James Norwich Auctions) $391 £240

Pair: 78th Highlanders, India General Service, 1 bar Persia. Indian Mutiny, 2 bars Defence of Lucknow, to F. Brownswood. (James Norwich Auctions) $330 £200

Waterloo 1815, Lieut. W. F. Fortescue, 1st Bn. 27th Regt. Foot. (Wallis & Wallis) $1,296 £810

A Nazi S.S. 12 Year service award, silver swastika with ribbon woven with silver thread, S.S. runes. (Wallis & Wallis) $280 £170

Pair: G.S.M. 1962, 1 bar N. Ireland, South Atlantic medal with rosette, together with an H.M.S. Ambuscade cap tally. (Wallis & Wallis) $272 £170

Baden: Order of the Zahringen lion, 5th class badge, in silver, glass and enamels. (Wallis & Wallis) $156 £95

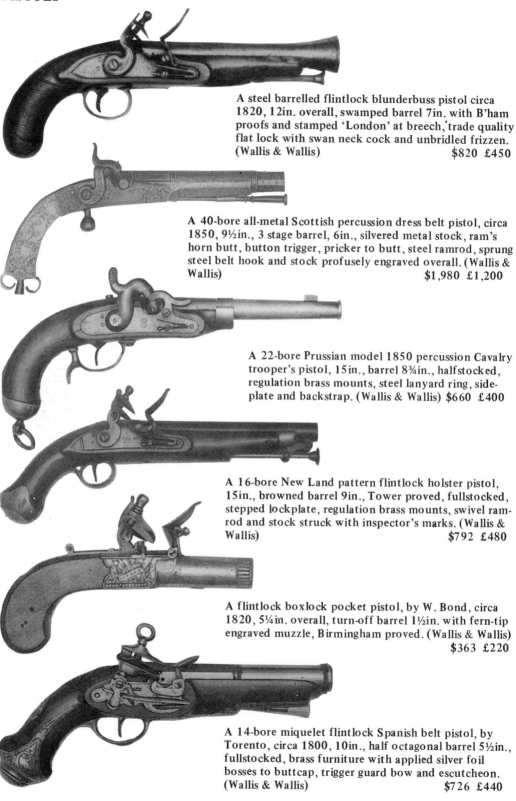

A steel barrelled flintlock blunderbuss pistol circa 1820, 12in. overall, swamped barrel 7in. with B'ham proofs and stamped 'London' at breech, trade quality flat lock with swan neck cock and unbridled frizzen. (Wallis & Wallis) $820 £450

A 40-bore all-metal Scottish percussion dress belt pistol, circa 1850, 9½in., 3 stage barrel, 6in., silvered metal stock, ram's horn butt, button trigger, pricker to butt, steel ramrod, sprung steel belt hook and stock profusely engraved overall. (Wallis & Wallis) $1,980 £1,200

A 22-bore Prussian model 1850 percussion Cavalry trooper's pistol, 15in., barrel 8¾in., halfstocked, regulation brass mounts, steel lanyard ring, side-plate and backstrap. (Wallis & Wallis) $660 £400

A 16-bore New Land pattern flintlock holster pistol, 15in., browned barrel 9in., Tower proved, fullstocked, stepped lockplate, regulation brass mounts, swivel ramrod and stock struck with inspector's marks. (Wallis & Wallis) $792 £480

A flintlock boxlock pocket pistol, by W. Bond, circa 1820, 5¼in. overall, turn-off barrel 1½in. with fern-tip engraved muzzle, Birmingham proved. (Wallis & Wallis) $363 £220

A 14-bore miquelet flintlock Spanish belt pistol, by Torento, circa 1800, 10in., half octagonal barrel 5½in., fullstocked, brass furniture with applied silver foil bosses to buttcap, trigger guard bow and escutcheon. (Wallis & Wallis) $726 £440

PISTOLS

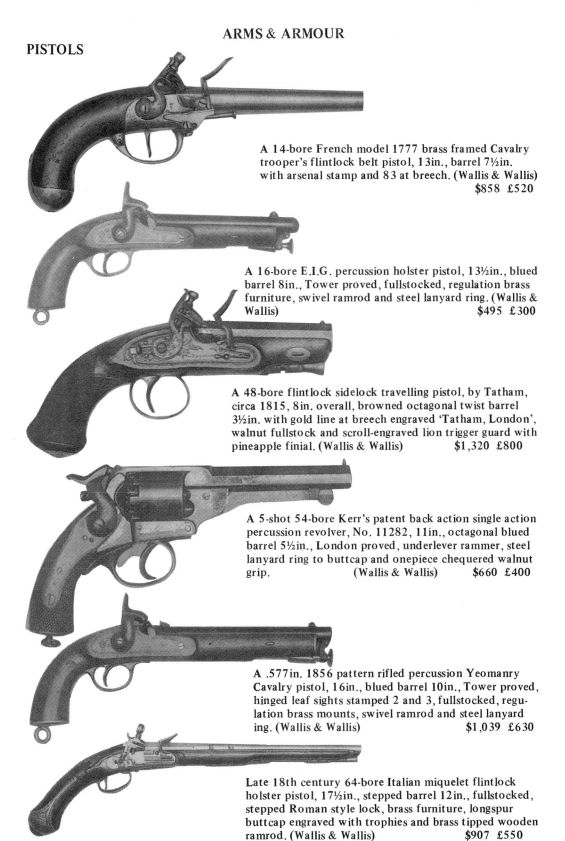

A 14-bore French model 1777 brass framed Cavalry trooper's flintlock belt pistol, 13in., barrel 7½in. with arsenal stamp and 83 at breech. (Wallis & Wallis)
$858 £520

A 16-bore E.I.G. percussion holster pistol, 13½in., blued barrel 8in., Tower proved, fullstocked, regulation brass furniture, swivel ramrod and steel lanyard ring. (Wallis & Wallis)
$495 £300

A 48-bore flintlock sidelock travelling pistol, by Tatham, circa 1815, 8in. overall, browned octagonal twist barrel 3½in. with gold line at breech engraved 'Tatham, London', walnut fullstock and scroll-engraved lion trigger guard with pineapple finial. (Wallis & Wallis)
$1,320 £800

A 5-shot 54-bore Kerr's patent back action single action percussion revolver, No. 11282, 11in., octagonal blued barrel 5½in., London proved, underlever rammer, steel lanyard ring to buttcap and onepiece chequered walnut grip.   (Wallis & Wallis)
$660 £400

A .577in. 1856 pattern rifled percussion Yeomanry Cavalry pistol, 16in., blued barrel 10in., Tower proved, hinged leaf sights stamped 2 and 3, fullstocked, regulation brass mounts, swivel ramrod and steel lanyard ing. (Wallis & Wallis)
$1,039 £630

Late 18th century 64-bore Italian miquelet flintlock holster pistol, 17½in., stepped barrel 12in., fullstocked, stepped Roman style lock, brass furniture, longspur buttcap engraved with trophies and brass tipped wooden ramrod. (Wallis & Wallis)
$907 £550

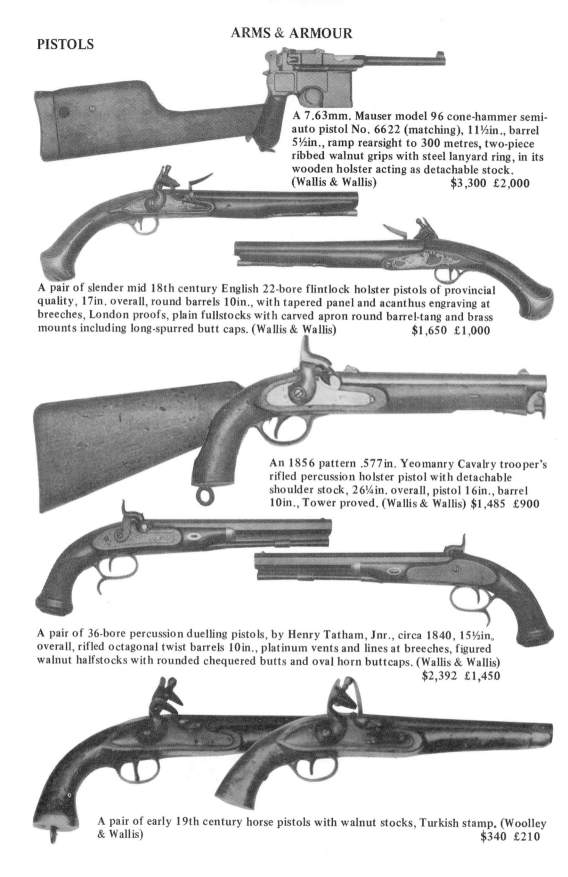

A 7.63mm. Mauser model 96 cone-hammer semi-auto pistol No. 6622 (matching), 11½in., barrel 5½in., ramp rearsight to 300 metres, two-piece ribbed walnut grips with steel lanyard ring, in its wooden holster acting as detachable stock. (Wallis & Wallis) $3,300 £2,000

A pair of slender mid 18th century English 22-bore flintlock holster pistols of provincial quality, 17in. overall, round barrels 10in., with tapered panel and acanthus engraving at breeches, London proofs, plain fullstocks with carved apron round barrel-tang and brass mounts including long-spurred butt caps. (Wallis & Wallis) $1,650 £1,000

An 1856 pattern .577in. Yeomanry Cavalry trooper's rifled percussion holster pistol with detachable shoulder stock, 26¼in. overall, pistol 16in., barrel 10in., Tower proved. (Wallis & Wallis) $1,485 £900

A pair of 36-bore percussion duelling pistols, by Henry Tatham, Jnr., circa 1840, 15½in. overall, rifled octagonal twist barrels 10in., platinum vents and lines at breeches, figured walnut halfstocks with rounded chequered butts and oval horn buttcaps. (Wallis & Wallis) $2,392 £1,450

A pair of early 19th century horse pistols with walnut stocks, Turkish stamp. (Woolley & Wallis) $340 £210

PISTOLS

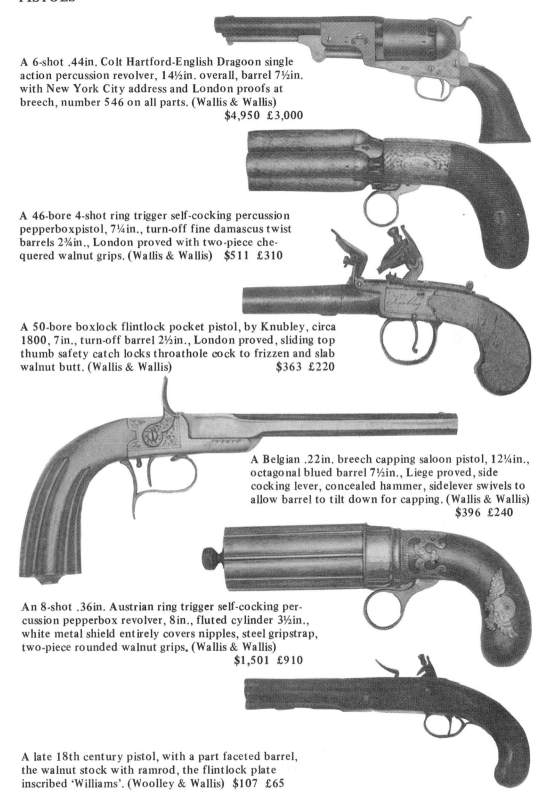

A 6-shot .44in. Colt Hartford-English Dragoon single action percussion revolver, 14½in. overall, barrel 7½in. with New York City address and London proofs at breech, number 546 on all parts. (Wallis & Wallis)
$4,950 £3,000

A 46-bore 4-shot ring trigger self-cocking percussion pepperbox pistol, 7¼in., turn-off fine damascus twist barrels 2¾in., London proved with two-piece chequered walnut grips. (Wallis & Wallis) $511 £310

A 50-bore boxlock flintlock pocket pistol, by Knubley, circa 1800, 7in., turn-off barrel 2½in., London proved, sliding top thumb safety catch locks throathole cock to frizzen and slab walnut butt. (Wallis & Wallis) $363 £220

A Belgian .22in. breech capping saloon pistol, 12¼in., octagonal blued barrel 7½in., Liege proved, side cocking lever, concealed hammer, sidelever swivels to allow barrel to tilt down for capping. (Wallis & Wallis)
$396 £240

An 8-shot .36in. Austrian ring trigger self-cocking percussion pepperbox revolver, 8in., fluted cylinder 3½in., white metal shield entirely covers nipples, steel gripstrap, two-piece rounded walnut grips. (Wallis & Wallis)
$1,501 £910

A late 18th century pistol, with a part faceted barrel, the walnut stock with ramrod, the flintlock plate inscribed 'Williams'. (Woolley & Wallis) $107 £65

PISTOLS

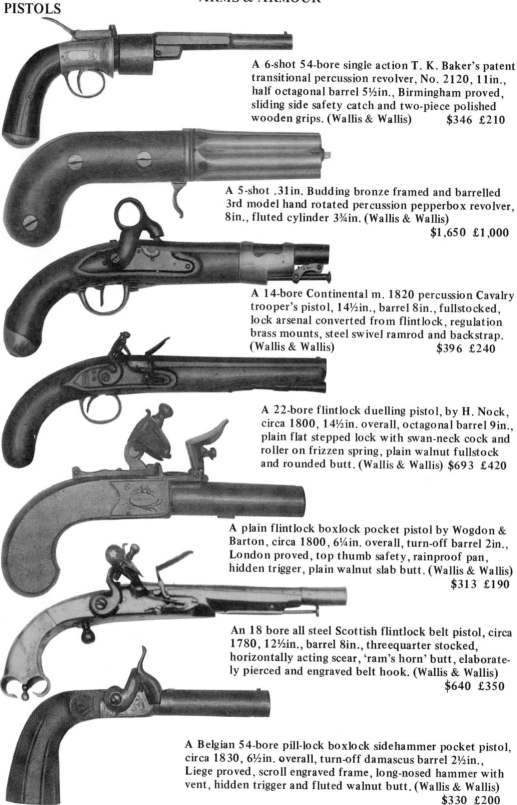

A 6-shot 54-bore single action T. K. Baker's patent transitional percussion revolver, No. 2120, 11in., half octagonal barrel 5½in., Birmingham proved, sliding side safety catch and two-piece polished wooden grips. (Wallis & Wallis) $346 £210

A 5-shot .31in. Budding bronze framed and barrelled 3rd model hand rotated percussion pepperbox revolver, 8in., fluted cylinder 3¾in. (Wallis & Wallis)
$1,650 £1,000

A 14-bore Continental m. 1820 percussion Cavalry trooper's pistol, 14½in., barrel 8in., fullstocked, lock arsenal converted from flintlock, regulation brass mounts, steel swivel ramrod and backstrap. (Wallis & Wallis) $396 £240

A 22-bore flintlock duelling pistol, by H. Nock, circa 1800, 14½in. overall, octagonal barrel 9in., plain flat stepped lock with swan-neck cock and roller on frizzen spring, plain walnut fullstock and rounded butt. (Wallis & Wallis) $693 £420

A plain flintlock boxlock pocket pistol by Wogdon & Barton, circa 1800, 6¼in. overall, turn-off barrel 2in., London proved, top thumb safety, rainproof pan, hidden trigger, plain walnut slab butt. (Wallis & Wallis)
$313 £190

An 18 bore all steel Scottish flintlock belt pistol, circa 1780, 12½in., barrel 8in., threequarter stocked, horizontally acting scear, 'ram's horn' butt, elaborately pierced and engraved belt hook. (Wallis & Wallis)
$640 £350

A Belgian 54-bore pill-lock boxlock sidehammer pocket pistol, circa 1830, 6½in. overall, turn-off damascus barrel 2½in., Liege proved, scroll engraved frame, long-nosed hammer with vent, hidden trigger and fluted walnut butt. (Wallis & Wallis)
$330 £200

PISTOLS

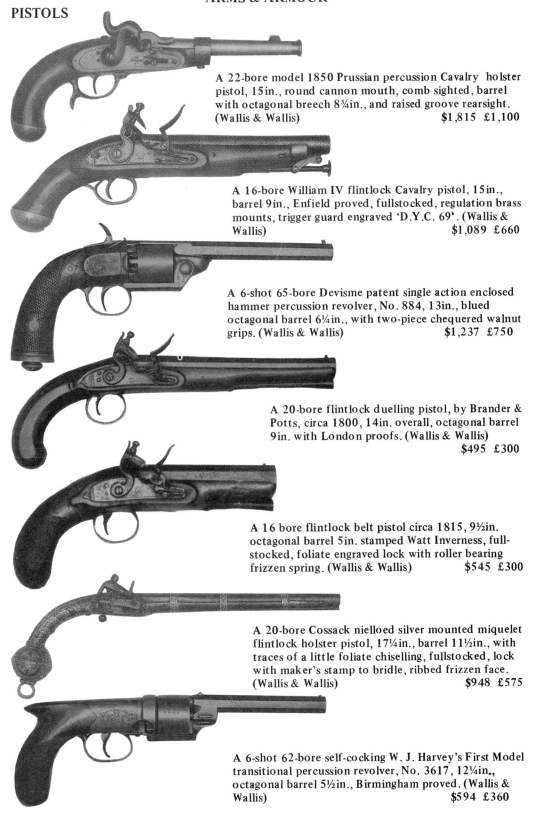

A 22-bore model 1850 Prussian percussion Cavalry holster pistol, 15in., round cannon mouth, comb sighted, barrel with octagonal breech 8¾in., and raised groove rearsight. (Wallis & Wallis) $1,815 £1,100

A 16-bore William IV flintlock Cavalry pistol, 15in., barrel 9in., Enfield proved, fullstocked, regulation brass mounts, trigger guard engraved 'D.Y.C. 69'. (Wallis & Wallis) $1,089 £660

A 6-shot 65-bore Devisme patent single action enclosed hammer percussion revolver, No. 884, 13in., blued octagonal barrel 6¼in., with two-piece chequered walnut grips. (Wallis & Wallis) $1,237 £750

A 20-bore flintlock duelling pistol, by Brander & Potts, circa 1800, 14in. overall, octagonal barrel 9in. with London proofs. (Wallis & Wallis)
$495 £300

A 16 bore flintlock belt pistol circa 1815, 9½in. octagonal barrel 5in. stamped Watt Inverness, fullstocked, foliate engraved lock with roller bearing frizzen spring. (Wallis & Wallis) $545 £300

A 20-bore Cossack nielloed silver mounted miquelet flintlock holster pistol, 17¼in., barrel 11½in., with traces of a little foliate chiselling, fullstocked, lock with maker's stamp to bridle, ribbed frizzen face. (Wallis & Wallis) $948 £575

A 6-shot 62-bore self-cocking W. J. Harvey's First Model transitional percussion revolver, No. 3617, 12¼in., octagonal barrel 5½in., Birmingham proved. (Wallis & Wallis) $594 £360

111

An unusual 19th century 16 bore all steel wheelock sporting gun in the Romantic Style, 43in., barrel 27in. with tubular rearsight chiselled as a dragon, openwork pierced steel butt of foliate design, stock engraved overall with foliage. (Wallis & Wallis) $875 £500

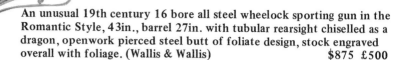

A 6.5mm. Steyr Model 1899 bolt-actionbox magazine sporting rifle, 47in. overall, barrel 26in., number 8493 on trigger guard, the barrel engraved 'Charles Lancaster, 151 New Bond St. London, W.' (Wallis & Wallis) $115 £65

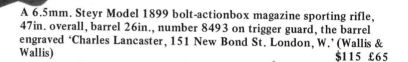

A .303in. B.S.A. Long Lee Enfield Military pattern bolt action rifle, 49½in. overall, barrel 30in., number G0725/1236, sliding and adjustable aperture rearsights, bayonet lug on fore end cap, sling swivels with leather sling. (Wallis & Wallis) $165 £95

A 6.5mm. Mannlicher Schoenauer M. 1903 bolt-action short sporting rifle, 38½in. overall, barrel 18in. number 2145, double set triggers single folding rearsight, the frame marked 'Oesterr. Waffenfabr. Ges. Steyr'. (Wallis & Wallis) $315 £180

A 24 bore Austrian rifled flintlock sporting carbine circa 1770, 34in., swamped octagonal barrel 19½in. with fixed sights, flattened lock, un-bridled frizzen, brass furniture, carved wooden trigger guard with brass inlay. (Wallis & Wallis) $875 £500

An attractive Indian flintlock rifle, circa 1830, 57in. damascus twist barrel with swollen muzzle, gold inlaid scrolls and foliage at breech and muzzle, fullstocked, English lock with Frenchstyle cock. (Wallis & Wallis) $840 £480

A matchlock gun with oak butt and stock, brass match-holder, spring, lock-plate, trigger and guard, the octagonal iron barrel signed Goshu Hino Yoshihisa saku, barrel length 77.8cm. (Christie's) $792 £495

An interesting Irish military style flintlock blunderbuss by Pattison of Dublin circa 1800, 34in., flared steel barrel 18in. stamped on octagonal breech 'Pattison Dublin', fullstocked, military style lock with throat-hole cock. (Wallis & Wallis) $700 £400

A 16-bore Austrian military flintlock carbine, 30in., barrel 14½in., two-third length stock, regulation steel mounts, finger scrolls to trigger guard, carved cheekpiece, steel ramrod and lanyard rings to extended side-plate. (Wallis & Wallis) $495 £300

A good .22in. LR Remington semi-auto take-down Model 24 rifle No. 101927, 45½in. overall including blued 7in. Parker Hale sound moder-ation, blued barrel 21in. with Remington address and Browning patent 1916, blued telescopic sight stamped with Winchester address. (Wallis & Wallis) $315 £180

A U.S. .30in. M1-A1 semi-automatic carbine with folding skeleton stock for airborne troops, 36in. overall, barrel 18in., number 370180, the action stamped 'InlandDiv', with sling swivels and webbing sling. (Wallis & Wallis) $455 £260

A French 11mm. Gras Model 1874 bolt action single shot military rifle 46¼in. overall, barrel 28in., number 18015, the frame stamped 'Manu-facture d'Armes St.Etienne Mle 1874'. (Wallis & Wallis) $160 £90

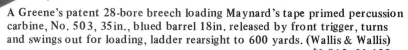

A Greene's patent 28-bore breech loading Maynard's tape primed percussion carbine, No. 503, 35 in., blued barrel 18 in. released by front trigger, turns and swings out for loading, ladder rearsight to 600 yards. (Wallis & Wallis)
$1,815 £1,100

A .450 in. Westley Richards 'monkey-tail' breech loading percussion sporting rifle, No. 5550.C, 42½ in., octagonal barrel 25 in., Birmingham proved, five-leaf rearsights to 500 yards, ladder rearsight to 1000 yards. (Wallis & Wallis)
$792 £480

A 40-bore Austrian percussion sporting rifle, by W. Leithner of Ischl, circa 1850, 38½ in., octagonal barrel 23½ in., fullstocked, swivel safety catch and foliate engraved steel furniture, carved cheekpiece, staghorn ramrod pipe, and brass tipped mahogany ramrod. (Wallis & Wallis) $1,773 £1,075

A 9-shot 36-bore P. W. Porter's patent vertically revolving turret percussion rifle, No. 630, 45 in., octagonal barrel 26 in., lever at side of frame allows action to hinge away for removing cylinder, underlever cocking lever cocks hammer and revolves cylinder. (Wallis & Wallis) $2,640 £1,600

A 30-bore Hall's patent American breech loading military flintlock Harper's Ferry rifled, dated 1837, 53 in., barrel 32¾ in., regulation steel mounts, 3 barrel bands, finger scroll to trigger guard, steel sling swivels and cleaning rod. (Wallis & Wallis) $1,980 £1,200

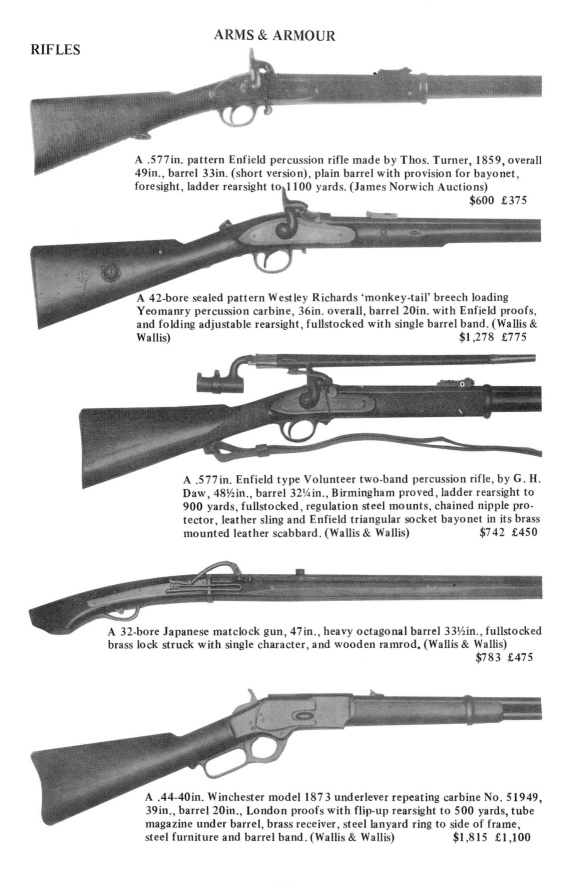

A .577in. pattern Enfield percussion rifle made by Thos. Turner, 1859, overall 49in., barrel 33in. (short version), plain barrel with provision for bayonet, foresight, ladder rearsight to 1100 yards. (James Norwich Auctions)

$600 £375

A 42-bore sealed pattern Westley Richards 'monkey-tail' breech loading Yeomanry percussion carbine, 36in. overall, barrel 20in. with Enfield proofs, and folding adjustable rearsight, fullstocked with single barrel band. (Wallis & Wallis)

$1,278 £775

A .577in. Enfield type Volunteer two-band percussion rifle, by G. H. Daw, 48½in., barrel 32¼in., Birmingham proved, ladder rearsight to 900 yards, fullstocked, regulation steel mounts, chained nipple protector, leather sling and Enfield triangular socket bayonet in its brass mounted leather scabbard. (Wallis & Wallis)

$742 £450

A 32-bore Japanese matclock gun, 47in., heavy octagonal barrel 33½in., fullstocked brass lock struck with single character, and wooden ramrod. (Wallis & Wallis)

$783 £475

A .44-40in. Winchester model 1873 underlever repeating carbine No. 51949, 39in., barrel 20in., London proofs with flip-up rearsight to 500 yards, tube magazine under barrel, brass receiver, steel lanyard ring to side of frame, steel furniture and barrel band. (Wallis & Wallis)

$1,815 £1,100

An 1871 pattern brass hilted Prussian dress sidearm, slightly curved blade, lined grip, in its brass mounted leather scabbard. (Wallis & Wallis)

$184 £115

A Prussian 1889 pattern Infantry officer's sword, straight double fullered plated blade, 32in., gilt hilt with pierced folding shell guard, wire bound fish-skin covered grip, in its black painted steel scabbard. (Wallis & Wallis) $80 £50

An Imperial German Prussian 1889 pattern high ranking officer's sword of The Garde Infantry Regt., straight double fullered blade 35in., chiselled gilt hilt, wire bound fish-skin covered grip mounted with enamelled guard star, in its plated scabbard. (Wallis & Wallis)

$2,062 £1,250

A Weimar Republic German Cavalry officer's Sabre, plated curved blade 33in., by R. Herder, plated plain stirrup guard and mounts, wire bound black grip, in its black painted steel scabbard. (Wallis & Wallis)

$168 £105

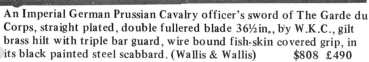

An Imperial German Prussian Cavalry officer's sword of The Garde du Corps, straight plated, double fullered blade 36½in., b'y W.K.C., gilt brass hilt with triple bar guard, wire bound fish-skin covered grip, in its black painted steel scabbard. (Wallis & Wallis) $808 £490

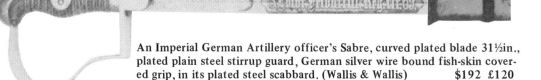

An Imperial German Artillery officer's Sabre, curved plated blade 31½in., plated plain steel stirrup guard, German silver wire bound fish-skin covered grip, in its plated steel scabbard. (Wallis & Wallis) $192 £120

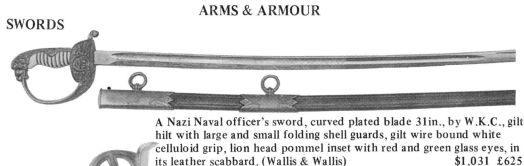

A Nazi Naval officer's sword, curved plated blade 31in., by W.K.C., gilt hilt with large and small folding shell guards, gilt wire bound white celluloid grip, lion head pommel inset with red and green glass eyes, in its leather scabbard. (Wallis & Wallis) $1,031 £625

A Prussian 1889 pattern Cavalry officer's sword, straight plated blade 32in., German silver hilt with folding guard, ribbed composition grip, in its black painted steel scabbard. (Wallis & Wallis) $56 £35

A Nazi artillery officer's Sabel, curved plated blade 37in., by Eickhorn, plated plain hilt with stirrup guard, wire bound, black grip, in its black painted steel scabbard. (Wallis & Wallis) $379 £230

An Imperial German Naval officer's sword, slightly curved, pipe backed plated blade, 29½in., etched with date 1861-1886, gilt brass hilt, folding sideguard, chiselled guard, lion's head pommel, wire bound ivorine grip, in its leather scabbard. (Wallis & Wallis) $304 £190

A dress sword of The King's Bodyguard for Scotland, The Royal Co. of Archers, slim blade 31in., by Johns & Co., gilt hilt, chiselled shell guard, chiselled knucklebow insert, fluted oval pommel, silver wire bound grip, in its patent leather scabbard. (Wallis & Wallis) $528 £320

An Imperial Prussian courtsword (Degen), slim blade 29½in., retaining all original polish, by WKC, gilt hilt with double shell guard, foliate chiselled urn pommel, wire bound grip, in its leather scabbard with gilt mounts. (Wallis & Wallis) $72 £45

ARMS & ARMOUR

An Imperial Wurttemberg Cavalry trooper's sword, plain curved blade 34in., by Lunceschloss, issue stamps for 1915, foliate pierced steel guard with state arms, steel mounts, wire bound fish-skin covered grip, in its steel scabbard. (Wallis & Wallis) $272 £170

A wakizashi with unusual scabbard diagonally banded in various styles of lacquer, signed Choshu ju Masasada, the blade, hirazukuri and almost musori, unsigned, 19th century, 36.5cm. long. (Christie's) $1,309 £770

An 1889 pattern Wurttemberg Cavalry trooper's sword, pipe back, clipped back blade, 32in., issue stamps for 1891, by Alex. Coppel, steel guard with marking of the 25th Dragoon Regt., ribbed composition grip, in its black painted steel scabbard. (Wallis & Wallis) $123 £75

A finely mounted aikuchi tanto, the kuroronuri saya decorated with kiri and kikumon in hiramakie and a gilt saya-kanamono en suite, mid 19th century, the blade 27.2cm. long, circa 1573. (Christie's) $6,688 £4,180

A Nazi Army officer's sword, plated curved blade 29in., by Eickhorn, gilt hilt with flattened stirrup knucklebow with oakleaf pattern, black, wire bound grip, in its black painted steel scabbard. (Wallis & Wallis) $192 £120

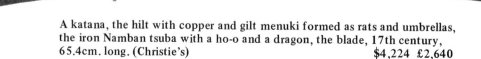

A katana, the hilt with copper and gilt menuki formed as rats and umbrellas, the iron Namban tsuba with a ho-o and a dragon, the blade, 17th century, 65.4cm. long. (Christie's) $4,224 £2,640

A Prussian 1889 pattern Cavalry officer's sword, plated blade, 33in., plated guard, ribbed composition grip, in its black painted metal scabbard. (Wallis & Wallis) $222 £135

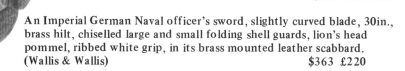

A wakizashi with natural wood scabbard, iron kojiri and fuchi-kashira, the cast iron tsuba depicting a woodcutter and a packhorse, the blade, signed Masatomi, 17th century, 39.1cm. long. (Christie's) $1,309 £770

An Imperial German Naval officer's sword, slightly curved blade, 30in., brass hilt, chiselled large and small folding shell guards, lion's head pommel, ribbed white grip, in its brass mounted leather scabbard. (Wallis & Wallis) $363 £220

An aikuchi tanto with fittings by Goto Ichijo, the blade signed Shinsoku, probably mid 15th century, 29.5cm. long. (Christie's) $7,744 £4,840

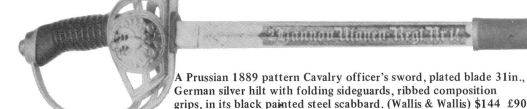

A Prussian 1889 pattern Cavalry officer's sword, plated blade 31in., German silver hilt with folding sideguards, ribbed composition grips, in its black painted steel scabbard. (Wallis & Wallis) $144 £90

A tanto blade signed Tairyusai Sokan horu dosaku, and dated Bunkyu ninen nigatsu no hi (February 1862), in brown leather covered scabbard with copper kojiri and fuchi-kashira depicting the Chinese heroes Kan U, Chohi and Gentoku, 33cm. long. (Christie's) $3,366 £1,980

ARMS & ARMOUR

A Victorian 1821 pattern Light Cavalry officer's sword, slightly curved blade 35in., by Henry Wilkinson, Pall Mall, officer's crest and initials, steel hilt, triple bar guard, silver wire bound fish-skin grip, in its steel scabbard. (Wallis & Wallis) $313 £190

A Saxony Cavalry officer's sword, curved blade 33in., by Ewald Cleff. Solingen, plain steel semi-basket guard, wire bound fish-skin covered grip, in its steel scabbard. (Wallis & Wallis) $128 £80

A Victorian 1854 Levee pattern Coldstream Guards officer's sword, blade 32in. of flattened diamond section, by Henry Wilkinson, Pall Mall, No. 22529, steel hilt, copper wire bound fish-skin covered grip, in its steel scabbard. (Wallis & Wallis) $462 £280

A Prussian 1889 pattern Cavalry trooper's sword, plain, pipe back, clipped back blade 33in., by Weyersberg Kirschbaum, steel guard with marking of The 2nd Guard Dragoon Regt., composition ribbed grip. (Wallis & Wallis) $48 £30

A George V Royal Naval officer's prize sword, blade 31in., by Henry Wilkinson, Pall Mall, No. 59467, retaining all original polish, gilt hilt, folding side-guard, lion's head pommel, bullion dress knot, gilt wire bound white fish-skin covered grip, in its leather scabbard. (Wallis & Wallis) $792 £480

An Imperial German Naval officer's sword, curved blade, 32in., gilt chiselled hilt, large and small folding sideguards, lion's head pommel, wire bound ivorine grip, in its leather scabbard with three gilt mounts. (Wallis & Wallis) $320 £200

SWORDS

A scarce 1887 pattern 19th Hussar officer's sword by Wilkinson, No. 42910 (made 1911), slightly curved fullered single edged blade, 35in., wire bound chequered patent solid grip, in its steel scabbard. (Wallis & Wallis) $313 £190

A late 19th century pattern Saxony Cavalry trooper's sword, pipe back, clipped back blade 30in., by Gebr. Weyersberg, steel guard with pierced state device, with issue marks of The 19th Hussar Regt., ribbed composition grip. (Wallis & Wallis) $96 £60

An Imperial German Naval officer's sword, curved blade 29½in., steel chiselled hilt, large and small folding sideguards, lion's head pommel, wire bound bone grip, in its leather scabbard. (Wallis & Wallis) $173 £105

A Prussian 1889 pattern Infantry officer's sword, straight double fullered blade, 32in., by Alex. Coppell, brass guard, wire bound leather covered grip, in its black painted steel scabbard. (Wallis & Wallis) $128 £80

A George V officer's sword of The Royal Horse Guards, blade 35in., retaining all original polish, original wash leather liner and bullion dress knot, silver wire bound fish-skin covered grip, in its plated scabbard. (Wallis & Wallis) $924 £560

An Imperial Bavarian Infantry officer's Sabre, plated curved blade 32in., gilt hilt with stirrup knucklebow, ribbed fish-skin covered grip, in its steel scabbard. (Wallis & Wallis) $112 £70

A 19th century sentoku tsuba formed as a serpent in marubori, signed Nagatsugu, 8.4cm. (Christie's) $3,344 £2,090

A 19th century iron tsuba with a crayfish in marubori, with gilt hirazogan seal of Munenori, 6.9cm. diam. (Christie's) $860 £506

Late 19th century otafuku-mokko sentoku hari-ishimeji tsuba decorated with two carp, signed Nagamasa. (Christie's) $8,800 £5,500

A shallow mokkogata tsuba decorated with Susano-o no Mikoto attacking the monster Yamata no orochi, Meiji period, 8.9cm. (Christie's) $1,672 £1,045

An iron higo tsuba formed as a blossoming plum tree, circa 1725, 7.8cm. diam. (Christie's) $561 £330

Mid 19th century hakkaku copper tsuba carved as a tree-trunk with an eagle, signed Ryuo (Ittosai). (Christie's) $7,040 £4,400

A large mokkogata iron tsuba, branches of bamboo in takabori, Kyo-shoami school, circa 1800, 8.7cm. (Christie's) $486 £286

Late 18th century iron tsuba, signed Bushu ju Masakata, 7.7cm. diam., and another, early Echizen school, 7cm. diam. (Christie's) $561 £330

Late 19th century hari-ishimeji tsuba decorated with Emma-O and a demonic attendant, inscribed Hamano Noriyuki, 9.6cm. (Christie's) $4,928 £3,080

TSUBAS

A hexagonal copper ishimeji tsuba decorated with a swallow-tail butterfly, signed Mitsumasa, Meiji period, 9.6cm. (Christie's)
$2,464 £1,540

Late 18th century ju-mokko-gata migakiji iron tsuba, Awa Shoami style. (Christie's)
$748 £440

A 19th century sentoku and copper tsuba formed as the eight-headed snake, signed Katsuchika, 8.8cm. (Christie's) $4,576 £2,860

An 18th century gilt rimmed shakudo mokkogata tsuba, unsigned, 7.6cm. (Christie's)
$1,122 £660

An iron tsuba with maple leaves and pine needles in ikizukashi, signed Suruga Takayoshi saku, circa 1850, 7.8cm. diam. (Christie's)
$935 £550

An 18th century mokkogata shakudo-nanakoji tsuba, Mino-Goto style, 7.1cm. (Christie's) $860 £506

An aorigata copper ishimeji tsuba decorated with Emma-o the King of Hell holding a shaku, 9.1cm. (Christie's)
$4,400 £2,750

A 19th century mokkogata iron tsuba, Edo Bushu school, 7.4cm. (Christie's)
$448 £264

A sentoku tsuba with canted corners decorated with a carp in copper takazogan, signed Tenkodo Hidekuni, 1825-91, 9.6cm. (Christie's)
$6,160 £3,850

An 18th century oval iron
tsuchimeji tsuba, Nara school,
7.7cm. (Christie's) $374 £220

Late 19th century copper
migakiji tsuba with wavy
rim, signed Sadakatsu, 9.2cm.
(Christie's) $2,992 £1,870

Late 18th/early 19th century
oval shakudo migakiji tsuba,
Shoki in shishiaibori with gilt
and silver detail, 7cm.
(Christie's) $1,672 £1,045

An iron tsuba, sections of a
saddle frame in yosukashi,
signed Choshu Hagi ju
Tomotsune saku, circa 1775,
7.5cm. diam. (Christie's)
                      $561 £300

Late 16th century Momo-
yama period tsuba decorated
with two men towing a boat,
8.6cm. (Christie's) $1,144 £715

A 19th century iron migakiji
tsuba decorated in takabori
and iroe takazogan with
Chinnan and Gama sennin,
7.6cm. diam. (Christie's)
                      $1,271 £748

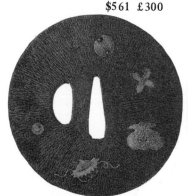

A 17th/18th century circular
iron tsuba decorated with the
takaramono in cloisonne enamels, unsigned, 8.5cm. diam.
(Christie's) $1,936 £1,210

A mokko-shaped Shakudo
tsuba chiselled with grass-
hoppers amidst numerous
flowers, gilt detail, 7.7cm.
(Phillips) $264 £150

An 18th century iron tsuba,
signed Choshu Hagi ju
Kawaji, 7.4cm. diam.
(Christie's) $374 £220

TSUBAS

An iron migakiji tsuba, signed Kageaki, with kao, and dated Bunsei junen (1827), 7.9cm. diam. (Christie's) $1,028 £605

Late 18th century oval iron tsuba, signed Chosu ju Masa-asada, 7.5cm. (Christie's) $561 £300

An oval iron migakiji tsuba decorated with branches of bamboo in kosukashi, circa 1875, 8.5cm. (Christie's) $2,057 £1,210

An 18th century iron soten tsuba depicting Kyoyu and Sofu in hikone-bori, 8.3cm. diam. (Christie's) $860 £506

An oval shakudo-nanakoji tsuba decorated in gilt, silver and copper takazogan with seven horses, 7.3cm. (Christie's) $1,320 £825

Mid 18th century circular iron tsuba formed as the madogiri or paulownia and window design in yosukashi and kebori, 8.5cm. (Christie's) $1,760 £1,100

A rounded-square shinchu and sahari tsuba decorated with Taira no Kiyomori seated on an engawa, signed Masanaga, Meiji period, 8.8cm. (Christie's) $1,936 £1,210

An oval shakudo-nanakoji tsuba decorated in silver and gilt takazogan with three rats and branches of mochi-bana, circa 1800, 6.6cm. (Christie's) $1,215 £715

A mokko-shaped Shakudo Nanako Tsuba decorated with flowers in gilt, the rim with gilt kiri-mon, 7.6cm. (Phillips) $563 £320

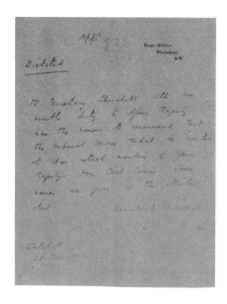

Benito Mussolini, document 1 page folio, Rome 15th Feb. 1940, promotion for an Air Force General, counter signed by King Victor Emmanuel. (Onslow's) $199 £120

Sir Winston Churchill, LS 1 page 4to, Home Office, Whitehall, 28th June 1911, to King George V. (Onslow's) $581 £350

Edith Cavell, ALS on postcard to her mother in Mundesley, Norfolk, 24th January 1913. (Onslow's) $249 £150

Edith Cavell (1865-1915), a worn German identity document, said to have been forged by Edith Cavell in order to assist a soldiers escape. (Onslow's) $166 £100

Anatoli V. Lunacharski (1875-1933), Lunacharski was a Bolshevist and served as Commissar for Education 1917-1929, signed, 6 x 4in. (Onslow's) $132 £80

Richard Strauss (1864-1949), Composer,
portrait photograph, inscribed and signed
Vienna, 5th February 1931, 10 x 8in.,
together with another of Strauss in 1917.
(Onslow's) $166 £100

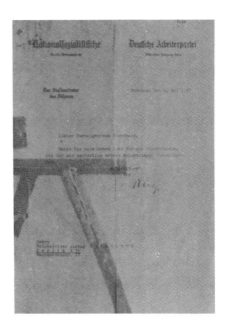

Rudolf Hess, Hitler's Deputy, TLS on
NSDAP letterheading 1 page 4to, Munich
8th May 1937, to A. Rosenberg. (Onslow's)
                                       $199 £120

Winston Churchill and Franklin D. Roosevelt,
'Short Snorter', an English £1 note, signed
by Winston Churchill, F. D. Roosevelt and
Stanley Matthews. (Onslow's) $830 £500

Heinrich Himmler (1900-1945), TLS 1 page
8vo, Berlin, 30th March 1938, to Nazi
Politician Alfred Rosenberg. (Onslow's)
                                       $282 £170

King George V and Queen Mary, studio
portrait photo, 14 x 18in., signed by both on
mount, dated 1911. (Onslow's) $166 £100

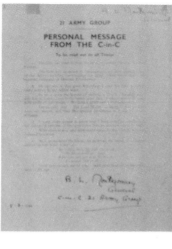

Archduke Franz Ferdinand (1863-1914), ALS 1 page 8vo with integral leaf, Cannes 23rd March 1896 to his accountant, Velicogna, in pencil. (Onslow's) $249 £150

D-Day, 6th June 1941, a printed Personal Message from the C-in-C of 21st Army Group General Sir Bernard L. Montgomery to be read out to all troops', 1 page 4to, dated 5th June 1941. (Onslow's) $166 £100

Samuel Pepys (1633-1703), manuscript letter, signed, 1 page legal folio, Navy Office 17th April 1671, also signed by two other officials. (Onslow's) $697 £420

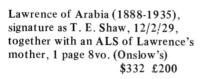

Lawrence of Arabia (1888-1935), signature as T. E. Shaw, 12/2/29, together with an ALS of Lawrence's mother, 1 page 8vo. (Onslow's) $332 £200

The Beatles, signatures of all four on album sheet, 5½ x 4in., an unsigned photo, greetings card signed by Brian Epstein and a signed pcm. on verso of Maharishi Yogi. (Onslow's) $315 £190

King Charles II, document signed as King, 1 page folio, 22nd June 1665, Whitehall, counter signed by Sir Wm. Morice, Secretary of State. (Onslow's) $348 £210

A clockwork fur covered rabbit automaton, emerging from a green cotton covered cabbage, 7½in. high, French, circa 1900. (Christie's) $544 £330

A varicoloured gold musical fob seal with commemorative portraits of Napoleon I and Josephine and an erotic automaton, Swiss, early 19th century, 42mm. high. (Christie's) $17,600 £10,757

Mid 19th century Swiss musical automaton of singing birds, 38in. high. (Christie's) $935 £571

A Leopold Lambert musical automaton doll, 'The Flower Seller', the Jumeau bisque head impressed 4, 19½in. high. (Lawrence Fine Art) $6,265 £3,500

A French musical clock diorama, signed Hy Marc, 37¾ x 26¾in. (Lawrence Fine Art) $2,774 £1,550

Mid 19th century automaton of a singing bird in a cage, the movement signed Bontems, Paris, 21½in. high. (Christie's) $1,760 £1,075

Mid 19th century Swiss gilt metal automaton with three singing birds, 21in. high. (Christie's) $3,300 £1,885

Early 20th century mother rocking baby automaton, German, the oak base contains the mechanism. (Robt. W. Skinner Inc.) $700 £424

A French automaton dancing couple by Theroude, on velvet lined circular base, 12in. high. (Lawrence Fine Art) $1,700 £950

An oak stick barometer, signed A. Ortelli, Birmingham, 38in. high. (Christie's)
$814 £440

An unusually small mahogany wheel barometer, signed Spelzini, London, 35in. high. (Christie's)
$1,548 £880

An early 19th century mahogany stick barometer, the plate signed J. Minolla, London, 38in. high. (Christie's)
$631   £385

A large Victorian oak wheel barometer, inscribed Fletcher and Sons, London, 46½in. high. (Christie's)
$569   £308

An early 19th century mahogany Sheraton shell wheel barometer, signed J. & P. Noseda, Walsall, 96cm. high. (Phillips) $470 £260

A stained oak stick barometer, inscribed Troughton and Simms, London, 39in. high. (Christie's)
$1,003 £528

A 19th century rosewood wheel barometer, signed F. Amadio & Son, London, 100cm. high, circa 1840. (Phillips)
$2,534 £1,400

A mahogany stick barometer, signed Josh. Croce, London, 39in. high. (Christie's)
$1,645 £935

BAROMETERS

A George III mahogany barometer, the dial signed Malacrida, London, 37½in. high. (Christie's)
$3,052 £1,650

A mahogany wheel barometer, inscribed Dring and Fage, London, 38½in. high. (Christie's) $447 £242

George II mahogany stick barometer with silvered face, signed F. Watkins, London, 40½in. high: $39,204 (Christie's) £24,200

A late 19th century mahogany wheel barometer, dial signed Leoni Taroni & Co., London, 36¼in. high. (Christie's) $865 £528

An oak wheel barometer, inscribed Gulliford, Dunster, 42in. high. (Christie's)
$407 £220

A good Georgian mahogany bow-front mercury barometer, inscribed J. Pastorelli, Liverpool, 37½in. high. (Christie's)
$3,750 £2,090

A Victorian mahogany wheel barometer with architectural pediment, inscribed A. Corti, Fecit, 38in. high. (Christie's)
$794 £418

A late 18th century mahogany stick barometer, signed Cary, London, 96cm. high. (Phillips) $1,086 £600

131

BAROMETERS

A mahogany wheel barometer with boxwood and ebony inlay, inscribed Rowe, Cambridge, 42in. high. (Christie's) $877 £462

A good mahogany bowfront mercury barometer, signed J. Blatt, Brighton. (Christie's) $610 £330

A George III satinwood barometer, the pewter dial signed C. Gaina, 43¼in. high. (Christie's) $1,972 £1,210

An early 19th century mahogany stick barometer, dial signed Manticha Fecit, 37in. high. (Christie's) $685 £418

An early 19th century mahogany stick barometer, signed Joseph Somalvico & Co., London, 98cm. high. (Phillips) $995 £550

A mahogany stick barometer with crested pediment, signed J.J. Wilson, 38in. (Christie's) $1,258 £715

A mahogany stick barometer, signed W. Field, Aylesbury, 39in. long. (Christie's) $1,548 £880

A mahogany wheel barometer, signed Vittory and Dannelli, Manchester. (Christie's) $1,452 £825

A 19th century mahogany ship's barometer, stamped J. Blair, Bristol, 36¼in. high. (Christie's)
$2,164 £1,320

Early 19th century mahogany stick barometer, signed Rizzi Fecit, 37in. long overall. (Prudential Fine Art) $660 £400

A large 19th century rosewood wheel clock barometer, signed J. Amadio, 128cm. high, circa 1835. (Phillips)
$3,620 £2,000

An 18th century George Adams Jnr. mahogany stick barometer, the scale signed G. Adams, London, 99cm. high. (Phillips) $1,810 £1,000

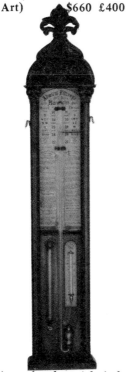

A 19th century mahogany ballooning barometer signed on the thermometer scale G & C Dixey, London, 36½in. high. (Christie's)
$1,353 £825

A good walnut Admiral Fitzroy's barometer (some damage), 48½in. high. (Christie's)
$813 £462

A mid-19th century rosewood stick barometer, signed J. Somalvico & Co., 97cm. high. (Phillips)
$579 £320

A very rare portable mercury barometer in ebonized carrying case, length of case 37in. (Christie's)
$1,149 £605

Book of Devotions, 146 leaves printed in
Latin on vellum, 18 full-page wood engravings, engraved pictorial borders. (Phillips)
$1,814 £950

Agricola (G.): Vom Bergwerck XII Bucher,
First German Edition. (Phillips)
$4,202 £2,200

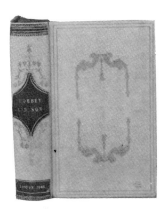

Dickens (C.): Dombey and
Son, 20 orig. parts bound in 1
vol., 40 engr. plates, by G.
Bellew of Dublin, 1848.
(Phillips) $687 £360

Surtees (R.S.): Jorrocks's
Jaunts and Jollities, second
edition, hand-col. front. title
and 13 plates by Henry Alken.
(Phillips) $1,050 £550

Rosel von Rosenhof (A.): Der
Monatlich-Herausgegeben
Insecten-Belustigung, 4 vol.s,
port. by J. M. Windler.
(Phillips) $3,960 £2,400

Combe (William): The English Dance of
Death, 2 vol.s, hand-col. front, and vig. title,
72 hand-col. plates by Rowlandson, 1 cover
detached. (Phillips) $1,337 £700

Dixon (W.S.): Loose Rein, 11 orig. parts, col.
plates, 1887. (Phillips) $787 £440

' The Last Ride', by Robert Browning, printed by Roycrofters , East Aurora, N.Y., 1900, copy no. 359. (Robt. W. Skinner Inc.) $450 £243

'Fringilla or Tales in Verse', by Richard D. Blackmore, published by Burrows & Co., Cleveland, 1895, illustrated by Will A. Bradley, no. 490 of 600 copies. (Robt. W. Skinner Inc.) $800 £432

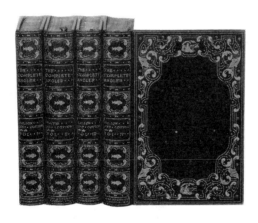

Walton (I.) and Cotton (C.): The Complete Angler, ed Sir H. Nicolas, extended to 4 vol.s with specially printed titles. (Phillips) $3,490 £1,950

Combe (W.): The Tour(s) of Doctor Syntax. (Phillips) $930 £520

Dickens (C.): The Mystery of Edwin Drood, 6 orig. parts, engr. port., title and 12 plates. (Phillips) $537 £300

Moliere (J. B. P.): Oeuvres, 6 vol.s, Nouvelle Edition, port., 33 plates by F. Boucher. (Phillips) $1,650 £1,000

A leather bound visitors book, 1909-1922, Used at Windsor Castle and St. James' Palace. (Prudential Fine Art) $478 £290

'Magic Lanterns: how made and how used with practical hints to unpractised lecturers', re-bound, London, E. G. Wood, 74 Cheapside, 1875. (Christie's) $110 £66

'Catalogue of Optical Lantern Slides', rebound in original wrappers, Bradford, Riley Brothers Ltd., n.d. ca 1911. (Christie's) $157 £93

George R. Sims — 'Ballads and poems' the complete works of Sims, with a portrait of the author, London, T. Vernon & Co. Ltd., n.d. (Christie's) $36 £22

A collection of ephemera relating to the cruise of Cunard's R.M.S. Lancastria from Liverpool to Gibraltar, North Africa and the Atlantic Isles, a quantity of menu cards and other literature. (Christie's) $83 £49

A Catalogue of Parts for Rolls-Royce, August 1914. (Onslow's) $305 £190

'The Story of a Passion", by Irving Bacheller, published by Roycrofters, 1901, hand-illuminated by Abby Blackmar, suede cover. (Robt. W. Skinner Inc.) $150 £81

Eleven lantern readings including 'Daisy's Influence', 'Labour and Victory' and 'A Famous Orator, An Evening with J. B. Gough' and others. (Christie's) $36 £22

Bassett-Lowke, New Illustrated Catalogue of Model Flying Machines, Aeroplanes, Balloons, Motor Fittings and Materials, May 1910. (Onslow's) $112 £70

BRONZE

A pair of Louis XVI ormolu mounted marble vases with fruiting finials and circular covers, 9in. high.
(Christie's) $1,653 £990

A pair of French figural bronze candelabra in the rococo style, 35cm. high.
(Phillips) $1,394 £850

A pair of Regency ormolu candlesticks, the bases with gardeners, the girl with a rake and the boy with a spade, 13in. high. (Christie's) $1,623 £990

Pair of Regency ormolu candlesticks of George II style, fitted for electricity, 9½in. high. (Christie's) $631 £385

A set of early 19th century bronze statuettes of the Four Seasons, with rectangular marble bases, 23cm. high. (Christie's) $1,194 £715

Late 19th century bronze vase, signed Seiya zo, 32cm. high. (Christie's) $654 £385

A Viennese cold painted bronze of a lion attacking an Arab mounted on a camel, incised beneath with the Bergman seal, 22cm. high. (Phillips) $1,467 £900

Pair of bronze oviform vases, signed Saito, Meiji period, 31.5cm. high. (Christie's) $3,872 £2,420

A 19th century bronze of Actaeon kneeling on a wounded stag, incised Holme. Cardwell Fect. Roma 1857, 83cm. high. (Christie's) $14,520 £8,800

An early 20th century Swiss bronze statuette of a nude man hurling a rock entitled 'Der Steinstosser', cast from a model by Hugo Siegwart, 37cm. high. (Christie's) $2,904 £1,760

'Penthesilia, Queen of the Amazons', a bronze figure cast from a model by A. Bouraine, 48.2cm. long. (Christie's) $1,443 £880

A 19th century French bronze statuette of Fanny Elssler, signed A. Barre fct. 1837, 43cm. high. (Christie's) $5,511 £3,300

A 19th century French bronze group of Hercules slaying the Cretan bull, after a model from the school of Giambologna, 56 x 61cm. (Christie's) $3,674 £2,200

Bronze bust of 'Dalila', by E. Villanis, circa 1890, seal of Societe des Bronzes de Paris. (Worsfolds) $1,440 £900

A 19th century French gilt bronze equestrian statuette of King Francois I, 42 x 41cm. (Christie's) $826 £495

'Apres la lecture', a bronze and ivory figure cast and carved from a model by D. Chiparus, 36.5cm. high. (Christie's) $10,824 £6,600

Three bronze groups, camel and rider, Arab horse and rider and mounted Indian, circa 1930, each 9in. high. (Prudential Fine Art) $2,268 £1,400

A 20th century French bronze group of a Scottish huntsman holding up a dead fox with a hound below, after P. J. Mene, 52cm. high. (Christie's) $1,102 £660

A late 19th/early 20th century Japanese bronze group of Death and a Maiden, with foundry stamp Dai Nippon Genryusai Seiya Zo. (Christie's) $1,837 £1,100

A 19th century French bronze group of the Voyage of the Nations, cast from a model by Edouard Drouot, 49cm. high. (Christie's) $2,722 £1,650

A late 19th century French 'Chryselephantine' bronze and ivory figure of 'La Liseuse', base signed A. Carrier-Belleuse, 62cm. high. (Christie's) $2,939 £1,760

A 19th century French bronze group of a putto riding a lion, 39.5cm. high. (Christie's) $1,102 £660

A bronze bust of a woman cast from a model by Dora Gordine, Paris, 1925, 36.8cm. high. (Christie's) $1,533 £935

A 19th century English bronze figure of a groom and a rearing horse, cast from a model by Joseph E. Boehm, 59cm. high. (Christie's) $7,260 £4,400

A 19th century French bronze statuette of the 'Tribunal', cast from a model by Paul Dubois, 50.5cm. high. (Christie's) $2,722 £1,650

A late 19th century French bronze model of a pointer called Aro, cast from a model by Alfred Barye, 18.5 x 25.5cm. (Christie's) $1,996 £1,210

A 19th century French gilt bronze statuette of Joan of Arc kneeling in prayer, signed Fremiet, 49cm. high. (Christie's) $2,939 £1,760

'Torch Dancer', a bronze and ivory figure cast and carved from a model by F. Preiss, 41.5cm. high. (Christie's) $6,314 £3,850

A late 19th/early 20th century bronze memorial relief, attributed to Sir Alfred Gilbert, 25cm. high. (Christie's) $551 £330

Bronze figure of Sagittarius, by E. M. Geyger, H. Gladenbeck u. Sohn, Berlin, 13in. high. (Worsfolds) $159 £95

A 19th century French bronze group of an Arab falconer, signed on the base P. J. Mene, 78 x 76cm. (Christie's) $14,520 £8,800

An early 20th century French patinated bronze bust of Omphale, cast from a model by E. Villanis, 53cm. high. (Christie's) $2,178 £1,320

A 19th century gilt bronze group of an 18th century scientist with pen and manuscript, seated beside a plate electrical machine, 13in. wide. (Christie's) $902 £550

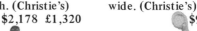

A fine bronze cast from a model by Le Faguays, of a female archer, 46cm. high. (Christie's) $1,353 £825

A 19th century English bronze of the Prince Consort, base incised Elkington on an ebonised wood stand, 54cm. high. (Christie's) $2,722 £1,650

'Russian Dancer', a bronze and ivory figure cast and carved after a model by F. Preiss, 32.4cm. high. (Christie's) $5,051 £3,080

Bronze figure of a woman, signed Oscar Glandebeck, circa 1900, 12in. high. (Lots Road Chelsea Auction Galleries) $304 £190

An Art Deco bronze and ivory figurine of a young bather reclining on a large rock. (Biddle & Webb) $7,498 £4,600

A bronze figure, 'Egyptian Priestess', 80cm. high. (Christie's) $1,443 £880

A 19th century French bronze statue of Cupid, after Denis-Antoine Chaudet, 60cm. high. (Christie's) $3,122 £1,870

An early 20th century Italian bronze bust of a maiden in folk costume, cast from a model by E. Rubino, 44cm. high. (Christie's) $762 £462

A 19th century French bronze figure of a nude woman, cast from a model by Aime Jules Dalou, 33cm. high. (Christie's) $10,890 £6,600

A bronze figure, cast from a model by H. Molins, as a female dancer, 58.5cm. high. (Christie's) $1,443 £880

A 19th century French bronze model of a stag, signed on the base Isidore Bonheur, 80 x 56cm. (Christie's) $11,022 £6,600

One of a pair of Charles X ormolu vases with pierced scrolling foliate handles, 14¼in. high. (Christie's) $2,755 £1,650

A 19th century French bronze group of Theseus combating the Minotaur, signed Barye, 44.5cm. high. (Christie's) $20,207 £12,100

A French bronze group of a mare and foal, base inscribed P. J. Mene and dated 1868, 46cm. high. (Christie's) $11,940 £7,150

An early 20th century Austrian bronze bust of Edward VII, cast from a model by J. Muhr, dated 1908, 40cm. high. (Christie's) $1,377 £825

A pair of mid 19th century gilt metal, bronze and white marble six-light candelabra, 26in. high. (Christie's) $3,630 £2,200

An early 19th century French bronze statuette of a Greek warrior on a giallo antico marble pedestal, 57.5cm. high. (Christie's) $2,087 £1,265

Pair of 19th century bronze figures of Mercury and Hebe, 2ft.9in. and 2ft.6in. high. (Lots Road Chelsea Auction Galleries) $800 £500

One of a pair of ormolu and white marble five-branch candelabra, 35in. high. (Christie's) $2,939 £1,760

A set of three French 19th century bronze and steel fire-irons, 33in. long, and smaller. (Christie's) $1,102 £660

'Girl with a riding crop', a bronze figure cast from a model by Bruno Zack, Made in Austria, 46cm. high. (Christie's) $3,968 £2,420

A bronze head of a negro girl, signed indistinctly A. Memiller(?), 43cm. high. (Christie's)

$3,674 £2,200

A late 19th century French bronze model of a grazing sheep, signed Rosa Bonheur, 14 x 21.5cm. (Christie's)

$1,194 £715

A 19th century French bronze head of a child, 'Bebe Endormi', cast from a model by Aime-Jules Dalou, 19cm. high. (Christie's)

$3,993 £2,420

A pair of Charles X ormolu and bronze three-light candelabra, 21in. high. (Christie's) $3,306 £1,980

'Con Brio', a bronze and ivory figure cast and carved from a model by F. Preiss, 29cm. high. (Christie's)

$9,020 £5,500

Pair of ormolu and bronze candlesticks formed as winged putti, 10¾in. high. (Christie's) $1,653 £990

One of a pair of Empire bronze and ormolu four-light candelabra, 30¼in. high.(Christie's)

$6,429 £3,850

A pair of ormolu and porcelain twin-branch wall-lights of Louis XV style, fitted for electricity, 14½in. high. (Christie's) $3,306 £1,980

One of a pair of late 19th century bronze vases formed in two sections, 68cm. high. (Christie's) $3,520 £2,200

An Oriental bronze architectural decoration with onion-shaped finial for a post top, 31in. high, 13in. diam. (Robt. W. Skinner Inc.) $700 £424

A mid 19th century French bronze group 'L'Accolade', base inscribed P. J. Mene, 34cm. high. (Christie's) $12,491 £7,480

A 19th century bronze group of Louis XIV on horseback, after a model by Girardon, 38cm. high, on ebonised and bronze mounted plinth. (Phillips) $20,375 £12,500

A 19th century English bronze figure of the young Prince of Wales standing on a bronze plinth inscribed T. Fowke Sc., London, 1864, 84cm. high. (Christie's) $15,427 £9,350

A 19th century French bronze group of a python attacking an Arab horseman, cast from a model by Antoine Louis Barye, circa 1835-40, 22 x 29cm. (Christie's) $23,595 £14,300

A 19th century bronze bust of a young boy, stamped Dalou, Cire Perdue A. A. Hebrard, 31cm. high. (Phillips) $2,934 £1,800

A 19th century bronze bust of a bearded 16th century scholar, his cloak cast with allegorical figures, 28cm. high. (Phillips) $1,304 £800

A 16th century gilt bronze plaque of the dead Christ supported by the Virgin and St. John, after Moderno, 7.5 x 5cm. (Phillips) $1,385 £850

One of a pair of Empire ormolu vases with overhanging lips, 6½in. high. (Christie's) $2,571 £1,540

A 19th century French bronze group of St. George and The Dragon, by E. Fremiet, 50cm. high. (Christie's) $4,719 £2,860

Late 19th century bronze models of elephants rearing in pain, signed Seiya and Saku, 29cm. and 22cm. long. (Christie's) $2,112 £1,320

A bronze figure cast from a model by Rudolf Kuchler, modelled as a male fencer, 37cm. high. (Phillips) $448 £280

A late 19th century French bronze group of a Scottish huntsman restraining two wolfhounds, cast from a model by P. J. Mene, 51cm. high. (Christie's) $3,674 £2,200

A 19th century animalier bronze group of two whippets playing with a ball, inscribed P. J. Mene, 16cm. high. (Phillips) $2,445 £1,500

'Au But', a bronze group of three male athletes, the base inscribed A. Boucher and foundry mark Siot Decauville, 28cm. high. (Phillips) $1,630 £1,000

An ancient Egyptian bronze mirror, 600 B.C., 8in. wide. (Robt. W. Skinner Inc.) $850 £515

A pair of late Louis XVI ormolu and white marble three-light candelabra, 18¼in. high. (Christie's) $2,939 £1,760

A 19th century French bronze group of Hebe and the Eagle of Jupiter, inspired by Rude, the base inscribed E. Drouot, 78cm. high. (Phillips) $4,564 £2,800

One of a pair of bronze
statues of Abyssinian cats,
32in. tall. (Chancellors
Hollingsworths) $972 £600

An early 20th century
German or French bronze
group of Saint George on
horseback, 55.5 x 36cm.
(Christie's) $918 £550

An early 20th century bronze
model of a seated blood-
hound bitch, base signed Paolo
Troubetskoy, 22.5cm. high.
(Christie's) $1,542 £935

A 19th century bronze group
of a whippet carrying a dead
hare in its mouth, inscribed
P. J. Mene, 7in. wide.
(Woolley & Wallis)
$1,166 £720

Art Deco bronze and ivory
figurine of a young woman
on a jetty holding a canoe
paddle. (Biddle & Webb)
$3,586 £2,200

One of a pair of ormolu and
bronze chenets of Louis XVI
style, 8¼in. high. (Christie's)
$642 £385

One of a pair of ormolu
mounted pink granite urns,
17½in. high. (Christie's)
$7,715 £4,620

'Bat Dancer', a bronze and
ivory figure cast and carved
from a model by F. Preiss,
23.5cm. high. (Christie's)
$5,412 £3,300

A George III ormolu mounted
blue-john pot-pourri vase, by
Matthew Boulton, 11in. high.
(Christie's) $2,851 £1,760

One of a pair of French 19th century bronze figures in Egyptian taste, on siena marble bases, 37cm. high. (Christie's) $907 £550

An early 20th century German bronze group of Europa and the Bull, cast from a model by A. Grath, 60 x 51cm. (Christie's) $3,306 £1,980

A 19th century bronze group of The Danseuses, after a model by Jean Baptiste Carpeaux, 53cm. high. (Christie's) $1,815 £1,100

A 19th century French bronze model of a lion crushing a serpent, after Barye, 40cm. high. (Christie's) $4,776 £2,860

A bronze and ivory figure cast and carved from a model by Kovats, 39cm. high. (Christie's) $12,628 £7,700

A 19th century bronze group of a retriever with a dead goose in its mouth, inscribed P. J. Mene, 7½in. wide. (Woolley & Wallis) $1,555 £960

A pair of Charles X bronze tazze with foliate rims and ribbed bases and handles, 10¼in. high. (Christie's) $2,939 £1,760

A mid 19th century French bronze figure of the 'Cheval Turc', signed Barye, 38.5 x 29.5cm. (Christie's) $82,665 £49,500

One of a pair of ormolu mounted crackle-glazed baluster vases, now converted to lamps, 13½in. high. (Christie's) $2,020 £1,210

A bronze mounted coconut shell in the form of a caricature of Louis Philippe, 18cm. high. (Phillips) $521 £320

One of a pair of George III ormolu cassolettes, 7¼in. high. (Christie's)
$1,782 £1,100

A Viennese cold painted bronze of a seated Indian brave, bearing the inscription C. Kauba and stamped Geschutzt 5806, 17cm. high. (Phillips) $1,271 £780

An early 20th century English bronze statuette of Peter Pan, after Sir George Frampton, 47.5cm. high. (Christie's) $4,900 £2,970

A pair of French 19th century bronze busts of a Nubian man and woman, also known as 'Venus Africaine', both signed Cordier, 83cm.and 79cm. high. (Christie's) $166,980 £101,200

An Art Deco bronze figure cast from a model by Lorenzl, modelled as a dancing girl, 43.9cm. high. (Phillips) $1,040 £650

'Valkyrie Rider', a parcel gilt bronze and ivory equestrian figure statue, signed L. Chalon, 54.5cm. high. (Christie's)
$8,118 £4,950

An Australian 'New Sculpture' bronze figure of Diana, by Sir Bertram Mackennal, 1905, 37cm. high. (Christie's)
$21,780 £13,200

A 19th century animalier bronze of a cock pheasant perched on a stump with weasel hiding beneath, the base inscribed J. Moigniez. (Phillips) $1,304 £800

A 19th century French bronze figure of La Baigneuse, cast from a model by Aime Jules Dalou, 41cm. high. (Christie's) $6,352 £3,850

A bronze figure of Herakles, Etruscan, 11.3cm. high. (Phillips) $852 £520

A 19th century bronze group of a mounted African Hunter, incised P. J. Mene, 46cm. high. (Phillips) $3,423 £2,100

A bronze and ivory figure cast and carved from a model by Marquetz and modelled as a girl with a long robe tied at the waist, 28.5cm. high. (Phillips) $608 £380

Pair of 19th century French bronze, copper and silver plated busts of 'La Juive d'Alger' and the 'Cheik Arabe de Caire', by Charles-Henri-Joseph Cordier, 86cm. high. (Christie's) $161,656 £96,800

A Roman bronze figure of Venus mounted on a wood base, 8.5cm. high, 1st-2nd century A.D. (Phillips) $902 £550

Mid 19th century bronze and ormolu inkwell, with shaped fitted top and pierced Gothic arcaded frieze, 6in. wide. (Christie's) $635 £385

A French bronze figure of a Neapolitan mandolin player, bearing the inscription Duret, 55cm. high. (Phillips) $1,222 £750

One of a pair of ormolu and tole peinte jardinieres of Louis XVI style with white porcelain flowerheads, 15½in. high. (Christie's) $10,103 £6,050

A Roman bronze bust of Athena, 8.5cm. high, 2nd century A.D. (Phillips) $309 £170

A pair of Roman bronze model feet, socketed, both 8cm. long, circa 2nd century A.D. (Phillips) $254 £140

Ming type miniature bronze horse. (G. A. Key) $97 £55

An Art Deco 'erotic' cold painted bronze figure case from a model by Nan Greb, 10¾in. high. (Christie's) $1,247 £770

Pair of Oriental bronze lions standing, approx. 18in. long. (G. A. Key) $708 £400

Bronze, 'Young Girl Looking Down at Frog', circa 1900, 18in. high. (J. M. Welch & Son) $688 £410

An 18th century bronze bell shaped mortar and pestle, 5in. high. (Christie's) $123 £77

A cold painted bronze figure of Cleopatra cast from a model by Nan Greb, 10in. across. (Christie's) $1,247 £770

A 19th century bronze two-handled koro with pierced lid and lion finial, 12½in. tall. (J. M. Welch & Son) $336 £200

A Roman bronze figure of the child, Harpokrates, 4.7cm. long, circa 2nd century A.D. (Phillips) $145 £80

A large bronze figure of a mountain lion. (Lawrences) $2,002 £1,100

A Romano British bronze fibula with linear decoration and onion-shaped terminals, 6.5cm. long, 3rd-4th century A.D. (Phillips) $58 £32

'Sword Dancer', a large cold painted bronze figure cast from a model by Nan Greb, 21¼in. high. (Christie's) $2,138 £1,320

A group of painted bronze miniature figures of animals, mainly characters from Beatrix Potter's books. (Christie's) $907 £550

An Egyptian bronze figure of Osiris, Late Dynastic Period, 15cm. high. (Phillips) $400 £220

Pair of bronze floriform candlesticks, attributed to Jarvie, Chicago, circa 1902, 14in. high. (Robt. W. Skinner Inc.) $3,100 £1,675

A bronze gun muzzle plate in the form of a King George V sovereign, 17.2cm. diam. (Christie's) $258 £154

Late 19th century bronze equestrian group of Louis XIV on horseback, the figure and saddle-cloth of gilt bronze, 10in. high. (Lalonde Fine Art) $280 £170

A George III brass bound
mahogany peat bucket,
16in. diam. (Christie's)
$2,904 £1,760

A George III brass bound
mahogany peat bucket with
later detachable tin liner,
15in. diam. (Christie's)
$902 £550

A George III brass bound
mahogany bucket of navette
shape with brass liner, 13½in.
wide. (Christie's) $631 £385

A George III brass bound
mahogany peat bucket with
carrying handles, 16in. diam.
(Christie's) $2,706 £1,650

A pair of painted leather fire
buckets, Newport, Rhode
Island, 1843, 12¼in. high.
(Christie's) $1,210 £731

A Regency brass bound
mahogany plate bucket
with carrying handle,
16½in. high. (Christie's)
$1,434 £880

A George III mahogany
brass bound plate pail with
brass carrying handles.
(Phillips) $1,804 £1,100

A Regency brass bound
mahogany bucket with
tin liner, 12in. wide.
(Christie's) $1,434 £880

A Georgian mahogany
caned plate bucket with
brass liner and loop handle,
14in. (Worsfolds)
$3,520 £2,200

A leather fire bucket, red painted rim, body painted black, legend reads 'No. 11 Daniel Waldo, 1756', Mass., 11in. high. (Robt. W. Skinner Inc.) $650 £365

A Georgian brass bound mahogany plate bucket with swing handle. (Geering & Colyer) $1,424 £800

A painted leather fire bucket, America, 1822, 12½in. high. (Robt. W. Skinner Inc.) $8,500 £5,059

A 19th century pair of painted and decorated leather fire buckets, New England, 12.3/8in. high. (Robt. W. Skinner Inc.) $1,600 £898

1st World War water carrier of kidney section, painted red and bearing crest, rope carrying handles, 21in. high. (Peter Wilson) $70 £40

Pair of 19th century painted leather fire buckets, New England, 13½in. high. (Robt. W. Skinner Inc.) $950 £533

A painted leather fire bucket, America, 11¾in. high. (Robt. W. Skinner Inc.) $850 £477

A George III brass bound mahogany bucket with lead lined body and foliate ring carrying handles, 8in. diam. (Christie's) $3,256 £1,760

A George III brass bound mahogany peat bucket with ribbed slatted sides and later tin liner, 14¾in. diam. (Christie's) $1,936 £1,100

A 17th century oak box, the moulded edge lid with iron hinges, 20.5in. long. (Woolley & Wallis) $198 £120

A French straw-work workbox worked in a three-coloured diapered pattern, pink, gold and green, 7½ x 5½ x 4in., circa 1750. (Christie's) $1,443 £825

An early 19th century veneered Anglo-Indian Colonial rectangular sarcophagus shape workbox, 14in. wide. (Woolley & Wallis) $2,970 £1,800

A 19th century mahogany domestic medicine chest by Fischer & Toller, 9½in. wide. (Christie's) $1,232 £770

A travelling dressing set with silver mounts, dated 1901, Birmingham, in an alligator skin case. (Lots Road Chelsea Auction Galleries) $680 £420

An Anglo-French silver and silver mounted dressing table set contained in a brass inlaid rosewood case, by C. Rawlings, 1821, and P. Blazuiere, Paris, 1819-38. (Christie's) $25,740 £14,300

Mid 19th century Victorian rosewood and mother-of-pearl inlaid sewing box with fitted interior. (G. A. Key) $462 £280

A George III mahogany cutlery urn with fitted interior, 25½in. high. (Christie's) $1,255 £770

A William and Mary trinket cabinet with star inlaid panels, fitted with ten drawers and enclosed by single door, 9½in. wide. (Prudential Fine Art) $1,444 £860

A rectangular box, containing two fitted boxes, the interiors nashiji, Meiji period, 8.7cm. long. (Christie's) $2,618 £1,540

A 19th century miniature stencilled sewing box, American, 10in. high, 14in. wide. (Christie's) $286 £161

An Indian fruitwood, ivory and micro-mosaic workbox with mirror-backed interior, 18in. wide. (Christie's) $1,996 £1,210

Regency mahogany tea caddy of sarcophagus form with brass lion ring handles. (G. A. Key) $264 £160

A mid 19th century wall salt box, inlaid with different woods, back inlaid with a sailing ship. (Woolley & Wallis) $429 £260

Early 19th century painted tin tea caddy, America, 5¼in. wide, 5in. high. (Robt. W. Skinner Inc.) $500 £280

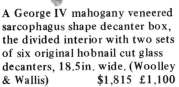

A George IV mahogany veneered sarcophagus shape decanter box, the divided interior with two sets of six original hobnail cut glass decanters, 18.5in. wide. (Woolley & Wallis) $1,815 £1,100

An 18th century suzuribako, the inside with suzuri and gourd-shaped shinchu tsuiteki, 21.3 x 18cm. (Christie's) $13,090 £7,700

Victorian bird's-eye walnut and rosewood crossbanded cigar casket with lift-up folding top, 11½in. wide. (Hobbs & Chambers) $445 £250

An oblong chased silver gilt singing bird box, circa 1900, 4½in. long. (Christie's) $1,540 £941

An oblong enamelled gilt singing bird box, circa 1900, 4in. long. (Christie's) $2,200 £1,344

A 19th century leather covered document box, the dome top with brass bail handle, 11½in. wide. (Christie's) $242 £146

A Spanish 17th century rose-wood and ivory inlaid table cabinet, 40cm. wide. (Phillips) $2,624 £1,600

A mahogany rotunda, the hinged fitted spherical box with three pairs of drawers with spreading pillars, 16in. wide. (Christie's) $3,048 £1,870

Late 16th century Momoyama period rectangular box with cover decorated in hiramakie, 19 x 12 x 11cm. (Christie's) $14,960 £9,350

Early 19th century tortoise-shell veneered tea chest with pagoda-shaped lid, 8in. wide. (Woolley & Wallis) $864 £540

An oak cigar box carved in the form of a kennel with a boxer, 10½in. wide. (Christie's) $871 £528

A George III burr-yew veneered tea chest, the interior with two lidded compartments, 7½in. wide. (Woolley & Wallis) $368 £230

A 19th century box of double clam shell shape, the interior nashiji, 13.4cm. long. (Christie's) $2,805 £1,650

Early Victorian Macassar ebony veneered sarcophagus-shaped workbox inlaid with mother-of-pearl, 12in. wide. (Woolley & Wallis) $486 £300

A William & Mary oyster walnut veneered lacemaker's box with brass escutcheon, 21in. long. (Woolley & Wallis) $1,360 £840

A 19th century cylindrical cosmetic box with an inner tray and three small containers, 9.3cm. diam., 8.8cm. high. (Christie's) $15,895 £9,350

A 19th century rounded rectangular suzuribako, 23 x 19.8cm. (Christie's) $3,366 £1,980

A Georgian fruitwood tea caddy in the form of an apple, 11cm. high. (Phillips) $820 £500

A Momoyama church-style chest with drop front, the interior with various-sized drawers, 89 x 65 x 52cm. (Christie's) $24,310 £14,300

Late 18th century document box (bunko), decorated in gold and silver hiramakie, takamakie and hirame on a nashiji ground, 40 x 30 x 15cm. (Christie's) $9,350 £5,500

A George III fiddle-back mahogany veneered tea chest with ivory escutcheon, 9¼in. wide. (Woolley & Wallis) $384 £240

Mid 18th century Batavian silver mounted burr-walnut casket, 13in. high. (Christie's) $1,194 £715

A grain-painted document box, probably New Hampshire, circa 1831, 24½in. wide. (Christie's) $440 £266

Late 16th century Momo-yama period small domed travelling casket, 21 x 12 x 10.5cm. (Christie's) $748 £440

Late 16th/early 17th century gourd-shaped roironuri suzuribako, 25.5cm. long. (Christie's) $11,220 £6,600

Mid 19th century gilt metal mounted tulipwood and kingwood coffre a bijoux in the style of B.V.R.B., 40in. high. (Christie's) $4,408 £2,640

Late 19th century mahogany slide cabinet of twenty-one drawers, containing slides by various makers, 12in. high. (Christie's) $1,172 £715

An Italian parcel gilt and painted casket on claw feet, 18in. wide. (Christie's) $1,745 £1,045

Late 16th century Momo-yama period Christian host box or pyx, 9cm. diam. (Christie's) $38,720 £24,200

A 19th century document box, the exterior covered with cherry-tree bark, 41.3 x 30.8 x 12.2cm. (Christie's) $14,080 £8,800

A 19th century silver rimmed suzuribako shaped as a koto, the interior fitted with a suzuri and an oval kikugata tsuiteki, 22.5cm. long. (Christie's) $11,220 £6,600

Victorian mother-of-pearl inlaid and painted papier mache two-division tea caddy, 7½in. wide. (Hobbs & Chambers) $136 £85

Early 19th century Indian ivory and micro-mosaic workbox with fitted interior. (Christie's) $1,270 £770

A grain-painted document box, 19th century, 11½in. wide, and another possibly Amish, 7¾in. wide. (Christie's) $770 £434

Eastern silver coloured metal Scribes box engraved with stylised script and geometric patterns. (Prudential Fine Art) $2,025 £1,250

A Victorian two bottle tantalus with silver plated mounts, 13¼in. long overall. (Christie's) $495 £290

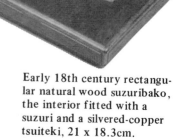

A 19th century leather covered document box, with brass bail handle and brass stud trim, 5¾in. high, 14in. wide. (Christie's) $275 £166

One of a pair of Chippendale mahogany urns, 24½in. high. (Woolley & Wallis) $8,000 £5,000

Early 18th century rectangular natural wood suzuribako, the interior fitted with a suzuri and a silvered-copper tsuiteki, 21 x 18.3cm. (Christie's) $2,057 £1,210

A painted and decorated 'Tree of Life' domed top box, American, circa 1840, 33in. long. (Robt. W. Skinner Inc.) $1,900 £1,130

A William and Mary walnut crossbanded marquetry lace box with hinged top, 50cm. wide. (Phillips) $1,755 £1,050

An Italian olivewood box with Tunbridgeware style crossbanding, approx. 9 x 6in. (G. A. Key) $67 £38

An early 19th century blond tortoiseshell tea chest, the hinged lid reveals two lidded compartments with silver plated knobs, 7in. long. (Woolley & Wallis) $429 £260

A Georgian Stilton box. (Hobbs Parker) $3,192 £1,900

A George III satinwood travelling necessaire box, the hinged lid enclosing a well-fitted interior, with leather label inscribed 'Manufactured by Bayley & Blew, 5 Cockspur Street, London', 15½in. wide. (Christie's) $2,645 £1,430

Mid 18th century George III inlaid mahogany tea caddy, English or American, 6½in. high, 9in. wide. (Christie's) $462 £260

Mid 19th century chip carved high domed painted poplar box, 13¾in. long. (Robt. W. Skinner Inc.) $325 £193

Victorian burr-walnut stationery box in the form of a miniature piano, 9¾in. wide. (Hobbs & Chambers) $332 £190

A William IV mahogany and rosewood writing slope, inlaid with cut brass, 44.5cm. long. (Osmond Tricks) $215 £115

A 19th century oval putty grained Shaker box, America, 5.7/8in. long. (Robt. W. Skinner Inc.) $3,300 £1,964

Bird's-eye maple Academy painted polychrome box, circa 1820, 12¼in. long. (Robt. W. Skinner Inc.) $3,600 £2,142

Mid 19th century coromandel veneered writing box inlaid with brass stringing, 16in. wide. (Peter Wilson) $334 £190

Mahogany collector's box decorated with brass stringing and vacant name plate, circa 1850, 7½in. wide. (Peter Wilson) $228 £130

A 19th century brass inlaid coromandel writing box, the interior with blue velvet lining, 14in. wide. (Hobbs & Chambers) $525 £300

A French tortoiseshell and enamel singing bird box, circa 1900, 4in. long. (Christie's) $2,200 £1,257

Late Georgian mahogany decanter box, oblong with lift-up top and compartmented interior, 1ft.9½in. wide. (Hobbs & Chambers) $1,602 £900

A painted box by Rufus Cole, N.Y., circa 1830, 13½in. long. (Robt. W. Skinner Inc.) $7,500 £4,464

Early 19th century inlaid sailor's art writing box, 20½in. long. (Robt. W. Skinner Inc.)
$1,800 £1,071

A painted and decorated Bentwood box, Germany, circa 1780, oval form with fitted lid, 18¾in. long. (Robt. W. Skinner Inc.)
$1,750 £1,041

A walnut writing box inlaid with broad Greek Key pattern borders, enclosing a blue leather-lined writing slope, 12in. wide. (Lalonde Fine Art)
$198 £120

A Regency tortoiseshell tea caddy. (Hetheringtons Nationwide) $704 £440

A painted maple lap desk, New York State, circa 1840, 19in. wide. (Christie's) $2,200 £1,330

An early 19th century French satinwood workbox, 12 x 35.5 x 26cm. (Phillips)
$2,492 £1,400

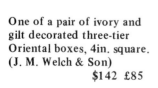

One of a pair of ivory and gilt decorated three-tier Oriental boxes, 4in. square. (J. M. Welch & Son)
$142 £85

A William and Mary oyster walnut veneered lace maker's box, the divided interior with pink satin padding and a frame, 23in. long. (Woolley & Wallis)
$1,122 £680

An Italian green stone inkstand, the cover set with seven lava cameos, 11.5cm. diam. (Lawrence Fine Art)
$699 £374

A two-compartment Tunbridge-ware tea caddy. (David Lay) $250 £140

A smoke grained dome-top box, American, circa 1830, 18¼in. long. (Robt. W. Skinner Inc.) $1,200 £714

A miniature putty grained blanket box, American, circa 1825, 14in. long. (Robt. W. Skinner Inc.) $1,800 £1,071

A Victorian Baccarat liqueur set, in an amboyna and marquetry case, signed, 13in. wide. (Hy. Duke & Son) $1,044 £580

A French gilt metal mounted velvet and leather small cartonnier with six drawers, the bases stamped L. Dromard F. cant Paris, 18, Rue St. Lazare, Ft. de Sieges, 12in. wide. (Christie's) $881 £495

A Regency tea caddy. (Hobbs Parker) $504 £300

A rosewood portable writing desk with countersunk brass handles, late Regency period, 14in. wide. (Lalonde Fine Art) $462 £280

A miniature Tunbridgeware cabinet with domed top and hinged door, 18cm. wide, 15cm. high. (David Lay) $360 £200

A George III laburnum tea caddy with a divided interior, on bracket feet, 10in. wide. (Christie's) $1,180 £638

A chrome Leica III camera No. 330547 with body cap, back plate engraved 'Leitz-Eigentum'. (Christie's) $865 £528

A Leica IIIa camera No. 252835 with 'R.P.' engraving on top plate. (Christie's) $99 £60

A grey Luftwaffen Leica IIIc camera No. 388254 engraved 'FI No. 38079' on top plate. (Christie's) $1,804 £1,100

A chrome Leica IIIc No. 379660 engraved 'Heer' on top plate. (Christie's) $2,525 £1,540

A Leica IIIc camera No. 476488 with a Leitz Summarit 5cm. f 1.5 No. 1500400 in Leitz box. (Christie's) $757 £462

A Leica IIIc camera No. 482153 with 'shark skin' vulcanite covering and a Leitz Summitar 5cm. f 2 No. 705438. (Christie's) $500 £308

A Leica I camera No. 176 with a Leitz Anastigmat f 3.5 50mm. and cap, a Leitz black enamelled rangefinder and double Leica film cassette holder. (Christie's) $17,138 £10,450

A replica UR-Leica camera top plate engraved and picked out in white 'Nachbildung der Ur-Leica'. (Christie's) $2,345 £1,430

A Leica I camera No. 8011 with a Leitz Elmar f 3.5 50mm. (Christie's) $902 £550

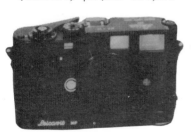  

A black Leica MP camera No. 72 with the Leicavit MP rapid winder. (Christie's) $9,922 £6,050

A model Ihagee Exakta camera No. 485606 with round magnifier in hood and an Ihagee Anast. Exaktar f 3.5 5.4cm. No. 771282. (Christie's) $1,082 £660

A Leica IIIa camera No. 197512 with a Leitz Summar 5cm. f 2 No. 409322 and a Leica-Motor No. 2388. (Christie's) $992 £605

A chrome Leica IIIb camera No. 351154 with a Leitz Elmar 5cm. f 3.5 No. 175134, camera baseplate engraved 'Robt. Ballantine, Glasgow'. (Christie's) $1,082 £660

A Leica I camera No. 17917 with a Leitz Elmar f 3.5 50mm. (Christie's) $1,082 £660

A grey Leica IIIc camera No. 372091 engraved on back plate 'Luftwaffen-Eigentum' with a Leitz Elmar 5cm. f 3.5 No. 547997. (Christie's) $2,525 £1,540

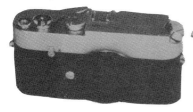

A Leica MDa camera No. 1379203 stamped on the top plate 'Y' (indicates Bundeswehr (German army) use). (Christie's) $1,443 £880

A Leica IIIc camera No. 364893 with a Leitz Summar 5cm. f 2 No. 218400. (Christie's) $577 £352

A Leica IIIb camera No. 280422 with body cap. (Christie's) $234 £143

A black dial Leica If camera No. 563478 back stamped in red 'A.P. 8886', with special mounting attachment on back. (Christie's) $1,353 £825

An E. Leitz Leica M2 camera No. 982920 with a Leitz Elmar 5cm. f 2.8 lens No. 1602272 in maker's leather e.r.c. and original box plus other accessories. (Christie's) $591 £352

A Leica I camera No. 740 with a Leitz Elmax f 3.5 50mm. and cap, a Leitz black enamelled rangefinder and double Leica film cassette. (Christie's) $4,510 £2,750

A Leica 24 x 36mm. Post camera No. 987591 engraved 'DPB' on top plate and with a Leitz Summaron f 2.8 35mm. No. 1931466 and cap. (Christie's) $2,164 £1,320

A black Leica M2 camera No. 956651 with push button rewind control. (Christie's) $1,172 £715

A Leica I camera No. 6460 with a Leitz Elmar f 3.5 50mm. (Christie's) $1,082 £660

A postcard Newman and Guardia Sibyl camera model No. 10 No. PC136 with a Zeiss Tessar f 4.5 15cm. No. 176722. (Christie's) $324 £198

An E. Leitz Leicaflex camera No. 1119417 with a Leitz Summicron-R f.2 50mm. lens, plus another two, in plastic case in maker's box. (Christie's) $1,016 £605

A Musashino Koki 6 x 9cm. Rittreck IIa s.l.r. camera No. 2747 with two Luminant lenses, one f3.5 10.5cm. and another f4.5 21cm. lens. (Christie's) $369 £220

A falling plate Svenska Express camera No. 2067 in black leather stamped in gilt on reverse 'Hasselblad Svenska Express'. (Christie's) $739 £440

An E. B. Koopman 28 x 28mm. 'The Presto' camera with four glass plates in situ and instruction book 'Presto Pocket Camera Primer'. (Christie's) $739 £440

An Eastman Kodak Co. 7 x 5in. No. 5 Folding Kodak camera (early satchel type) with lens set into an early sector shutter and an E.K. Co. roll film pack. (Christie's) $443 £264

An Ernemann-Werke 6½ x 9cm. Ermanox camera No. 1168134 with an Ernemann Ernostar f 1.8 12.5cm. No. 165405, film pack adapter and cloth dark slides. (Christie's) $1,443 £880

A 35mm. Globuscope 360° Panoramic camera No. 1094 with a Globuscope 25mm. f 3.5 - 22 lens with pouch case, film case and film resin all in maker's box. (Christie's) $1,623 £990

A 6 x 4½cm. Dallmeyer Speed camera No. D639 with a Dallmeyer Pentac f 2.9 3in. lens, film pack adapter and three d.d.s., all engraved and in maker's leather case. (Christie's) $240 £143

A Houghtons Ltd. 5 x 4in. tropical Sanderson camera, struts numbered '22425' with a Zeiss Tessar f 4.5 15cm. No. 600133 in a dial set Compur shutter. (Christie's) $757 £462

A Franke & Heidecke 4 x 4cm. grey Baby Rolleiflex camera with a Schneider Xenar f3.5 60mm. lens, in case. (Christie's) $203 £121

An Ilford/Kennedy Instruments 35mm. K.I. Monobrar camera in polished and cream enamelled metal with removable bellows, 35mm. film magazine and a Leica-fit lens panel. (Christie's) $811 £495

A black Leica M4-M camera No. 1206841 with an E. Leitz New York remote control winder No. 02787 and 'AA' battery pack. (Christie's) $6,133 £3,740

A Franke & Heidecke Rolleiflex Wide Angle camera No. W 2492220 with a Zeiss Distagon f.4 55mm. taking lens and a Heidosmat f.4 55mm. viewing lens. (Christie's) $1,663 £990

A half-plate brass and mahogany camera with a brass bound lens and focussing cloth, all in canvas bag. (Christie's) $277 £165

A C. P. Stirn No. 1 Concealed Vest camera No. 8364 with glass plate inside camera and two other circular glass plates. (Christie's) $887 £528

A Zeiss Ikon twin lens Contaflex camera No. Y84783 with a Zeiss Sonnar f 2 5cm. No. 1538892, and a rare Zeiss Sonnar f 2 8.5cm. No. 1799751. (Christie's) $1,804 £1,100

'The Rover Patent' detective camera by J. Lancaster & Son with a Lancaster Patent see saw shutter and internal brass plate holders. (Christie's) $406 £242

A Leica IIIg camera No. 891669 with a Leitz Super-Angulon f 4 21mm. No. 1645908. (Christie's) $1,443 £880

A chrome Leica IIIc camera No. 385817 engraved 'PATT 8665' on top plate. (Christie's) $1,353 £825

A Leica M1 camera No. 1091091 with lever rewind button. (Christie's) $1,533 £935

A double-stroke Leica Bundeseigentum M3 camera No. 910589 in olive green leather and metal. (Christie's) $1,804 £1,100

A dummy Leicaflex SL (un-numbered) camera with a dummy Summicron-R f 2 50mm. lens. (Christie's) $360 £220

A Leica Bundeseigentum M3 camera No. 927695 in olive green leather and metal. (Christie's) $2,525 £1,540

A Leica M3 camera No. 962596 with a Leitz Elmar 5cm. f 2.8 No. 1590342 and a Leica-Meter MC. (Christie's) $685 £418

A Leica Bundeseigentum M3 camera No. 910551 in olive green leather and metal back plate, the top plate with red painted eagle motif. (Christie's) $1,443 £880

A working cut away demonstration Leica M3 camera. (Christie's) $5,051 £3,080

A Leica III camera No. 290588 with a Leitz Elmar 5cm. f 3.5 in e.r.c. and a Sekonic Microlite meter No. 055071. (Christie's) $306 £187

A Leica Bundeseigentum M3 camera No. 910555 in olive green leather and metal. (Christie's) $1,623 £990

A Leica M2-R camera No. 1250189 with a Leitz Summicron f 2 50mm. No. 2279162. (Christie's) $2,345 £1,430

A double stroke Leica M3 camera No. 700396. (Christie's) $811 £495

A Leica I camera No. 3313 with a Leitz Elmar f 3.5 50mm. and a large dial rangefinder. (Christie's) $1,262 £770

A black Leica II camera No. 75570 with 'O' engraved on body lens flange and a Leitz Hektor 5cm. f 2.5. (Christie's) $631 £385

A Leica Ic camera No. 561235 with a Leitz Summicron 5cm. f 2 No. 1231582, a 5cm. f 2 No. 1231582, a 5cm. viewfinder and a chrome Leitz rangefinder. (Christie's) $811 £495

A Leica 24 x 36mm. Post camera No. 1273928 engraved 'DPB' on top plate and with a Leitz Summaron f 2.8 35mm. No. 2310896 and cap. (Christie's) $2,164 £1,320

A Leica Luftwaffen IIIb camera No. 3466697 with an extension winder and a Leitz Elmar 5cm. f 3.5 No. 5473888. (Christie's) $1,172 £715

A grey enamelled and bodied Leica IIIck camera No. 390080 with a white printed capital 'K' on the shutter blind, and a Leitz Summitar 5cm. f 2 No. 563508. (Christie's) $2,525 £1,540

A Leica R3 Safari camera No. 1483589 and A658 with carrying strap and a Leitz Safari Summicron -R f2 50mm. No. 2889714 in maker's box. (Christie's) $1,172 £715

A double-stroke Bundeseigentum M3 camera No. 920513 in olive green leather and metal. (Christie's) $1,804 £1,100

A Leica Bundeseigentum M1 camera No. 980455 in olive green metal and leather top plate engraved '5 + 13.5'. (Christie's) $1,623 £990

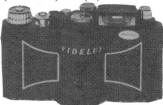

A Panon camera Shoko Co. Ltd. Widelux F7 camera No. 353785 with a Lux f 2.8 26mm. lens. No. 472230 in leather maker's e.r.c. (Christie's) $1,533 £935

A Leica Bundeseigentum M1 camera No. 9804888 in olive green leather and metal top plate engraved '5 + 13.5'. (Christie's) $2,706 £1,650

One of a pair of gilt metal and cut glass twelve-light chandeliers, fitted for electricity, 41in. high, 38in. diam. (Christie's) $5,511 £3,300

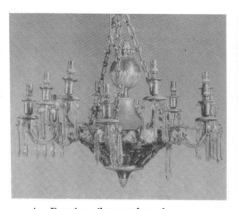

An Empire gilt metal twelve-branch hanging light, fitted for electricity, 18in. high, excluding chain suspension. (Christie's) $1,174 £660

An early Victorian brass eighteen-light chandelier in the Gothic style, 56in. high. (Christie's) $8,167 £4,950

A Regency bronze and ormolu colza oil chandelier, 38in. high, including chain suspension. (Christie's) $12,798 £7,150

Early 20th century hammered copper and bronze chandelier with seven Steuben shades, 20in. diam. (Robt. W. Skinner Inc.) $3,000 £1,785

Mid 19th century cut glass ten-light chandelier, fitted for electricity, 65in. high. (Christie's) $8,019 £4,950

A George III cut glass six-light chandelier with double inverted dish corona hung with pear shaped drops, 50in. high. (Christie's) $9,451 £5,280

An Art Deco glass and chromium plated metal chandelier of star form, circa 1930, 71cm. wide. (Christie's) $9,922 £6,050

A large cut glass twenty-light chandelier with scalloped corona issuing eight scrolls with arrow-head finials, 72in. high, 44in. diam. (Christie's) $47,256 £26,400

One of a set of four George III style five-light crystal wall lights, fitted for electricity, 23in. high, 21in. wide. (Christie's) $1,650 £942

A glass chandelier, the six branches complete with drops and glass chains. (G. A. Key) $743 £420

A Lalique plafonnier, hemispherical clear and opalescent glass, 31.5cm. diam. (Christie's) $1,804 £1,100

A George III style eight-light crystal chandelier, approx. 41in. high, 34in. diam. (Christie's) $962 £549

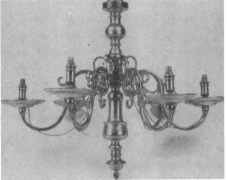

An 18th century Dutch brass six-light chandelier, fitted for electricity, 32in. high. (Christie's) $3,309 £1,870

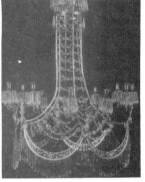

A 19th century Swedish brass and cut glass twelve-light chandelier, 37in. high, 27in. diam. (Christie's) $7,348 £4,400

A Regency bronze and ormolu eight-branch chandelier, each leaf cast double scroll arm supporting twin sconces, 100cm. diam., 123cm. drop. (Phillips) $12,250 £7,000

A Regency gilt bronze colza oil ceiling light, the foliate corona, with beaded and faceted drops hung with a cut glass dish, 99cm. drop, 59cm. diam. (Phillips) $14,000 £8,000

A 19th century French gilt bronze twelve-light chandelier, the extensively decorated baluster stem cast with triple cherub heads, circa 1880, 115cm. drop. (Phillips) $4,200 £2,400

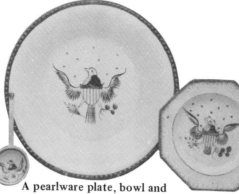

A 19th century creamware covered pitcher, entire surface in chequerboard pattern, brown glaze cut to cream, 6¼in. high. (Robt. W. Skinner Inc.) $125 £74

A pearlware plate, bowl and ladle with American Eagle decoration, early 19th century, plate 7¾in. diam., bowl 13½in. diam. and the ladle 2¾in. diam. (Christie's) $770 £434

Early 20th century Dedham pottery crackleware vase, decorated with blue iris, 7in. high. (Robt. W. Skinner Inc.) $550 £297

One of a pair of pearlware plates and a creamware plate, one 9¾in. diam., 1810-30. (Christie's) $286 £161

A Fulper pottery centrepiece on pedestal base, hammered olive-green on paler green glaze, circa 1915, 10½in. high. (Robt. W. Skinner Inc.) $1,600 £864

A Clifton Art pottery 'Indian Ware' vase, circa 1910, 10½in. high, 12in. diam. (Robt. W. Skinner Inc.) $300 £178

A two-colour Grueby pottery vase, Boston, Mass., circa 1905, 8¼in. high. (Robt. W. Skinner Inc.) $2,400 £1,297

One of two 19th century slip-decorated Redware dishes, American, 9¼in. and 11¾in. diam. (Christie's) $385 £217

Late 19th/early 20th century creamware mug, 4¾in. high, together with a jar and a castor. (Christie's) $528 £297

AMERICAN

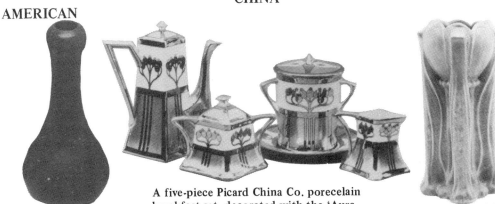

Late 19th century Chelsea
Keramic Art Works pottery
'oxblood' vase, 8in. high.
(Robt. W. Skinner Inc.)
$2,000 £1,190

A five-piece Picard China Co. porcelain
breakfast set, decorated with the 'Aura
Argenta Linear' design, artist signed by
Adolph Richter, circa 1910-30. (Robt. W.
Skinner Inc.) $550 £297

A Teco pottery moulded
lotus flower vase, Chicago,
circa 1905, designed by F.
Moreau, 11½in. high. (Robt.
W. Skinner Inc.)
$3,000 £1,621

A mid 19th century Moravian
slip-decorated Redware bowl,
probably Salem, N. Carolina
Jacob Christ type, 13½in. diam.
(Christie's) $264 £148

A Weller Sicard twisted pottery
vase, iridescent purples and
greens with snails in the design,
circa 1907, unsigned, 7½in.
high. (Robt. W. Skinner Inc.)
$600 £324

A 19th century slip-decorated
Redware dish, American, 10½in.
diam., and a bowl 7½in. diam.
(Christie's) $352 £198

A glazed ceramic grotesque
face jug, by H. B. Craig,
N. Carolina, ovoid with two
applied strap handles, 16½in.
high. (Christie's) $330 £186

A pair of late 19th century
painted chalkware doves,
American, 11½in. high.
(Christie's) $528 £297

A manganese decorated Redware
jar, by John W. Bell, 1880-95,
12½in. high. (Christie's)
$528 £297

Late 19th century painted chalkware horse, 10in. high. (Christie's) $286 £161

Saturday Evening Girls decorated planter, Boston, Mass., 1918, 9½in. long. (Robt. W. Skinner Inc.) $650 £351

A two-colour Grueby pottery vase, artist's initials A.L. for Annie Lingley, circa 1905, 8¼in. diam. (Robt. W. Skinner Inc.) $3,300 £1,783

A Grueby pottery vase, Boston, Mass., circa 1905, 13½in. high. (Robt. W. Skinner Inc.) $3,900 £2,108

A Zuni pottery jar, decorated in brown and red on a white ground, 27cm. high. (Phillips) $2,184 £1,200

A Rookwood pottery standard glaze portrait vase, decorated with portrait of a black African with a cap, 1897, 12in. high. (Robt. W. Skinner Inc.) $2,500 £1,351

A large Redware bowl or pot, probably Penn., 1870, 12in. diam. (Robt. W. Skinner Inc.) $1,100 £617

A 19th century painted chalkware cat, America, 10¾in. high. (Robt. W. Skinner Inc.) $850 £505

A Rookwood pottery jewelled porcelain vase, signed by Kataro Shirayamadani, Ohio, 1924, 7in. high. (Robt. W. Skinner Inc.) $1,400 £875

AMERICAN

A Clifton Art pottery 'Indian Ware' vase, circa 1910, 8in. high, 10in. diam. (Robt. W. Skinner Inc.) $325 £193

Saturday Evening Girls pottery decorated bowl, Mass., circa 1915, 11½in. diam. (Robt. W. Skinner Inc.) $600 £357

Grueby pottery butterscotch glazed vase, artist's initials W.P. for Wilamina Post, dated 3/12/06, 9in. diam. (Robt. W. Skinner Inc.) $6,500 £3,513

One of a pair of octagonal creamware plates and a similar soup plate, 1810-30, 8¾in. diam. (Christie's) $220 £124

Late 19th century Grueby Faience Co. bust of 'Laughing Boy', based on a statue by Donatello, 11in. high. (Robt. W. Skinner Inc.) $1,800 £972

One of a pair of pearlware plates, each octagonal painted with swags of lemons with brown leaves, 1810-20, 7¾in. diam. (Christie's) $198 £111

Early 20th century Dedham pottery crackleware vase, decorated with white iris on blue ground, signed, 7½in. diam. (Robt. W. Skinner Inc.) $2,200 £1,189

One of two 19th century slip-decorated Redware plates, American, 11¼in. and 12in. diam. (Christie's) $385 £217

A Newcomb pottery floral vase, New Orleans, circa 1928, initialled by Henrietta Bailey, 5¼in. high. (Robt. W. Skinner Inc.) $900 £486

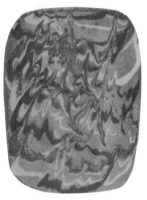

A Shawsheen pottery vase, probably Billerica, circa 1906, 6in. high. (Robt. W. Skinner Inc.) $200 £119

A Teco pottery double-handled vase, Illinois, circa 1910, 7in. high. (Robt. W. Skinner Inc.) $350 £208

One of two 20th century Van Briggle pottery vases, Colorado, one 2¾in. high, the other 5½in. high. (Robt. W. Skinner Inc.) $360 £225

A 19th century glaze and slip decorated redware platter, New England, 13½in. long. (Robt. W. Skinner Inc.) $2,600 £1,625

A Grueby pottery two-colour vase, elongated bottle neck on spherical cabbage form, circa 1905, 9¼in. high. (Robt. W. Skinner Inc.) $4,500 £2,812

A Teco Art pottery fluted vase, Illinois, circa 1905, 10½in. high. (Robt. W. Skinner Inc.) $1,200 £750

Saturday Evening Girls decorated pitcher, Mass., 1911, 9¾in. high. (Robt. W. Skinner Inc.) $950 £565

Early 20th century Grueby pottery vase, Mass., 4¾in. high. (Robt. W. Skinner Inc.) $450 £267

A Teco pottery four-handled vase, circa 1910, 7¼in. high. (Robt. W. Skinner Inc.) $650 £386

AMERICAN

Louwelsa Weller pottery Indian portrait vase, Ohio, circa 1915, 10¾in. high. (Robt. W. Skinner Inc.) $475 £296

Early 20th century Fulper pottery candle lantern, 10½in. high. (Robt. W. Skinner Inc.) $600 £357

A Grueby pottery vase, signed with logo, circa 1905, 11.7/8in. high. (Robt. W. Skinner Inc.) $2,600 £1,547

Late 19th century Chelsea Keramic Art Works covered jar, Mass., impressed CKAW, 5½in. high. (Robt. W. Skinner Inc.) $150 £90

A Merrimac pottery decorated vase, Mass., circa 1893, 4in. diam. (Robt. W. Skinner Inc.) $400 £238

Early 20th century pottery pitcher, New Hampshire, 8¼in. high. (Robt. W. Skinner Inc.) $150 £89

A Jervis Art pottery motto mug, 1906, 5¾in. high, 4in. diam. (Robt. W. Skinner Inc.) $200 £119

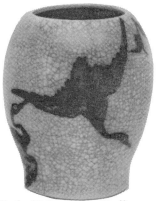
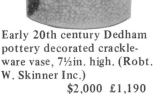

Early 20th century Dedham pottery decorated crackle-ware vase, 7½in. high. (Robt. W. Skinner Inc.) $2,000 £1,190

Early 20th century Grueby pottery two-colour vase, Mass., 10¼in. high. (Robt. W. Skinner Inc.) $3,000 £1,785

One of a pair of early 18th century Arita blue and white lobed dishes, Ming six-character marks, 15.5cm. wide. (Christie's)
$7,854 £4,620

One of two Arita oviform bottle vases decorated in kakiemon style, circa 1675, approx. 30cm. high. (Christie's) $12,320 £7,700

One of a pair of 17th century Arita standing puppies, 24cm. long. (Christie's)
$37,400 £22,000

Late 17th/early 18th century Arita blue and white oviform jar, 27cm. high. (Christie's)
$1,496 £935

A fine pair of Arita blue and white oviform jars and covers, Genroku period, 88cm. high, wood stands. (Christie's) $10,560 £6,600

One of a pair of late 17th/ early 18th century Arita Dutch decorated apothecary bottles, 26.5cm. high. (Christie's) $4,862 £2,860

Late 17th century Arita blue and white charger, 39cm. diam. (Christie's)
$2,112 £1,320

Late 17th century Arita blue and white oviform ewer with loop handle, 17cm. high. (Christie's) $2,464 £1,540

An 18th century Arita armorial foliate-rimmed shallow dish, 22cm. diam. (Christie's) $9,680 £6,050

ARITA

An 18th century Arita blue and white shallow dish decorated with the design of the 'Hall of One Hundred Boys', 20cm. diam. (Christie's) $3,179 £1,870

Late 17th century large Arita blue and white baluster vase and cover, 47cm. high. (Christie's) $8,800 £5,500

Early 18th century Arita foliate rim shallow dish, 20.5cm. diam. (Christie's) $1,776 £1,045

One of two Arita oviform bottle vases decorated in Kakiemon style, circa 1680, approx. 30cm. high. (Christie's) $7,480 £4,400

An Arita blue and white garniture comprising three oviform jars and covers and two trumpet-shaped beakers, Genroku period, jars and covers 37cm. high, the vases, 22.5cm. high. (Christie's) $9,350 £5,500

Late 17th century Arita blue and white ewer with loop handle, 24cm. high. (Christie's) $880 £550

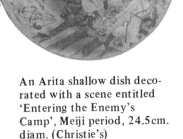

Late 17th century Arita blue and white charger. (Christie's) $2,805 £1,650

A 19th century Arita model of a tiger climbing on rocks among dwarf bamboo, 71cm. high. (Christie's) $5,610 £3,300

An Arita shallow dish decorated with a scene entitled 'Entering the Enemy's Camp', Meiji period, 24.5cm. diam. (Christie's) $1,496 £880

A KPM Berlin oval porcelain plaque painted with two cherubs, by Zapf, signed,10½in. across, impressed KPM. (Christie's) $1,322 £715

A Berlin Reliefzierrat rectangular indented tea caddy and cover, painted in colours with putti playing on clouds, circa 1700, 14.5cm. high. (Christie's) $4,114 £2,200

A Berlin rectangular plaque, painted at the Lamm decorating establishment by G. Meisel, after Boucher, 26.5 x 32.5cm., impressed KPM. (Phillips) $3,465 £2,100

A Berlin plaque painted after Murillo. with two peasant boys eating grapes and melon, circa 1875, 28 x 22.5cm. (Christie's) $3,085 £1,870

A Berlin two-handled campana vase painted in the neo-classical taste, 1803-1810, 45cm. high. (Christie's) $13,365 £8,250

A German porcelain rectangular plaque painted with a three-quarter length portrait of a young girl, 7½in. high. (Christie's) $855 £528

An 18th century Berlin figure of the Farnese Hercules, blue sceptre mark, 16cm. high. (Christie's) $78 £49

A Berlin rectangular plaque painted after Rubens, impressed sceptre, KPM and numeral marks, circa 1880, 33 x 20cm. (Christie's) $5,878 £3,520

A Berlin cylindrical coffee-cup and saucer with garlands of flowers between blue bands gilt with foliage, blue sceptre mark and gilt dot circa 1795. (Christie's) $1,260 £779

BERLIN

A KPM Berlin oval plaque painted by Zapf, signed, 10½in. across, impressed KPM and sceptre mark. (Christie's) $3,866 £2,090

A Berlin Celadon ground Tasse D'Amitie the saucer inscribed Le tems s'envole; votre amour est bien plus constant, circa 1805. (Christie's)$2,468 £1,320

A Berlin ecuelle and cover with Ozier moulded borders, blue sceptre mark, circa 1780, 19cm. wide. (Christie's) $1,682 £1,045

A Berlin plaque painted after Peter Paul Rubens, 39 x 31cm., KPM and sceptre mark. (Phillips) $8,684 £5,200

A pair of Berlin blue and white octagonal vases and covers, painted in the Oriental style with chinoiserie figures in landscapes (repairs to one neck), circa 1725, 44cm. high. (Christie's) $5,740 £3,280

A Berlin plaque painted after Raphael with a detail of the 'Madonna di San Sisto', late 19th century, 25.5 x 19cm. (Christie's) $1,542 £935

A Berlin oval plaque painted after A. Kauffmann with a Vestal Virgin, impressed KPM, sceptre, F and 5 marks, late 19th century, 27cm. high. (Christie's) $2,541 £1,540

A Berlin two-handled campana vase, on spreading foot and square base, circa 1825, 31cm. high. (Christie's) $10,760 £6,150

A K.P.M. oval portrait plaque of the young Christ, impressed marks, the plaque 10 x 8in. (Christie's) $393 £240

A Bow leaf moulded pickle-dish of ovate form, circa 1760, 11.5cm. wide. (Christie's) $1,828 £1,045

A Bow figure of a shepherd playing the bagpipes, circa 1757, 26.5cm. high. (Christie's) $1,732 £990

A Bow blue and white oval sauceboat, 1747-50, 22cm. wide. (Christie's) $1,089 £660

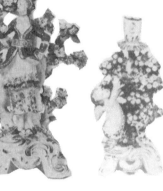

A pair of Bow figures of Eastern dancers, the lady wearing a purple coat over puce-fringed yellow skirt and flowered underskirt, the man with fur-lined yellow cloak, 24cm. (Phillips) $1,567 £950

A Bow figure candlestick, formed of a cupid kneeling on a rococo base (slight damage), anchor in red circa 1765. (Phillips) $1,076 £605

A pair of Bow candlestick figures of a stag and doe with mottled brown coats, circa 1765, 23.5cm. high. (Christie's) $4,356 £2,640

A Bow candlestick group of musicians, after Meissen models by Kaendler, circa 1760-65, 8¾in. high. (Christie's) $1,300 £750

A rare early Bow 'Muses' figure of Hope, the lady resting one arm on a puce column, her other on an anchor, 21.5cm. high. (Phillips) $1,472 £800

A Bow circular plate painted in famille rose with a Chinese lady, probably Lan Ts'ai Ho, 22.5cm. diam. (Phillips) $1,586 £950

BOW

A Bow leaf moulded sauce-boat, circa 1765, 16cm. long. (Christie's) $621 £352

A Bow porcelain figure of a nurse. (Hobbs Parker) $1,152 £720

A Bow leaf moulded sauce-boat with green stalk handle, circa 1765, 16cm. long. (Christie's) $3,272 £1,870

A pair of Bow candlestick figures of the New Dancers, circa 1765, 29cm. high. (Christie's) $1,996 £1,210

A rare Bow 'Muses' figure of Justice, the lady standing and wearing a black helmet and flowered white robe, 21cm. high. (Phillips) $1,067 £580

Two Bow figures symbolising the Elements, water depicted as Neptune, air as a nymph, 28.5cm. (Phillips) $1,656 £900

A Bow spirally moulded cane handle of tapering form, circa 1750, 5.5cm. high. (Christie's) $1,942 £1,110

A Bow flared pierced circular basket, painted in the Kakiemon palette with The Quail Pattern, circa 1756, 16.5cm. diam. (Christie's) $3,167 £1,810

A rare early Bow figure of Harlequin modelled in white, standing on a square base leaning against a tree trunk, 13.5cm. high. (Phillips) $1,656 £900

BRITISH

A pearlware Toby jug painted in Pratt colours, perhaps Yorkshire, circa 1800, 23.5cm. high. (Christie's) $907 £550

An English porcelain group of a recumbent cat with kittens, 4½in. wide, perhaps Derby, circa 1825. (Christie's) $887 £528

A pearlware figure of Napoleon as an Artillery Officer, circa 1840, 29cm. high. (Christie's) $1,089 £660

One of a pair of Yorkshire models of cows, one with a gardener, the other with a woman, 14.5cm. long. (Phillips) $4,676 £2,800

Early 20th century Arts & Crafts ceramic umbrella stand, stamped with logo, 'The Foley "Intarsio" England', 27½in. high. (Robt. W. Skinner Inc.) $700 £416

A Portobello cow creamer, with milkmaid on a stool, 16cm. wide. (Phillips) $734 £440

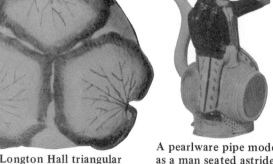

An H. & R. Daniel deep cream-ground vase, pattern no. 196, 197, circa 1830, and another similar. (Christie's) $235 £143

A Longton Hall triangular dish moulded with three cucumber leaves, circa 1755, 15cm. wide. (Christie's) $1,089 £660

A pearlware pipe modelled as a man seated astride a green barrel, perhaps Yorkshire, circa 1800, 15.5cm. high. (Christie's) $1,542 £935

BRITISH

A flask of Prince Albert, standing beside a pillar on which rests a crown, 28cm. high. (Phillips) $250 £150

A rectangular plaque, painted with Highland cattle and sheep, signed E. Townsend, 23.5 x 36cm. (Phillips) $1,753 £1,050

A creamware pipe modelled as a lady seated on a green barrel, perhaps Yorkshire, circa 1800, 17cm. high. (Christie's) $1,542 £935

A George Jones 'majolica' circular cheese dish and cover, circa 1880, 28cm. diam. (Christie's) $577 £330

A candle extinguisher in the form of a young lady's head, by James Hadley, 9cm. high, date code for 1892. (Phillips) $668 £400

A Holdcroft majolica jardiniere, square with canted corners, 21.1cm. high. (Christie's) $551 £330

A pearlware pipe modelled as a man, impressed with the name 'Jolly Pickman', circa 1800, 14.5cm. high. (Christie's) $1,542 £935

One of a pair of Caughley plates from the Donegal Service, painted at Chamberlain's factory, circa 1793, 21cm. diam. (Christie's) $1,724 £1,045

A pearlware puzzle jug, the serpent handle with three spouts, circa 1820, 29cm. high. (Christie's) $689 £418

A Longton Hall cabbage-leaf moulded teapot and cover, circa 1755, 11cm. high. (Christie's)
$19,965 £12,100

A large English delft bowl, painted in light blue with panels of parrots alternating with flower sprays, 34.5cm. diam. (Phillips) $1,528 £800

One of a pair of Caughley quatrefoil two-handled sauce tureens and covers, circa 1785, 15cm. wide. (Christie's) $2,178 £1,320

A creamware tall cylindrical mug, circa 1785, 12.5cm. high. (Christie's) $726 £440

An H. & R. Daniel blue-ground part tea service, comprising an 'Etruscan' shape teapot, cover and stand, a two-handled sugar bowl and cover, a milk jug, a slop-basin, eight teacups and saucers, pattern no. 3859, circa 1825. (Christie's) $726 £440

An 18th century blue and white pottery jug with loop handle, 7.75in. high. (Prudential Fine Art)
$214 £130

A Barr, Flight & Barr plate, decorated probably in London and in the manner of the Baxter workshop, 23.5cm. diam. (Phillips)
$501 £300

Hadley's porcelain vase and lid with cone finial, 4in. high. (G. A. Key) $280 £170

A London delft 'bleu persan' plate painted in white enamel with a seated Chinese figure, in Nevers style, 21.5cm. diam. (Phillips) $5,730 £3,000

BRITISH

A late Wemyss small model of a pig, 15.5cm. high, painted mark Wemyss, printed mark Made in England. (Phillips) $1,337 £700

Late 18th century creamware circular dish with petal-shaped rim, painted in Pratt-type colours, 14in. diam. (Lalonde Fine Art) $627 £380

A Foley 'Intarsio' 'Kruger' teapot and cover, designed by Frederick Rhead, modelled as the South African Statesman, 12.7cm. high. (Phillips) $563 £320

Carlton Ware lustre jug with gilt loop handle, the body painted and gilded with stylised floral and fan decoration, 5in. high. (Prudential Fine Art) $189 £115

A Ralph Wood figure of a harvester, circa 1775, 20cm. high. (Christie's) $3,085 £1,870

A Maw & Co. circular pottery charger painted in a ruby red lustre with winged mythical beast, 13½in. diam. (Christie's) $382 £209

A Maw & Co. pottery vase, the body painted in a ruby red lustre with large flowers and foliage all on a yellow ground, 13in. high. (Christie's) $644 £352

A Portobello cow creamer and cover, 13cm. wide. (Phillips) $601 £360

A Carlton Ware ginger jar and cover, the oviform body painted with clusters of stylised flowerheads, 10¾in. high. (Christie's) $801 £495

A Cistercian ware tyg, the conical cup with three loop handles, the black glaze stopping just above the foot, 6.8cm. high. (Phillips) $382 £200

A pair of pearlware figures of Mansion House dwarfs, their costumes in shades of yellow, brick-red, lime-green and brown, 16cm. and 16.5cm. high. (Phillips) $1,375 £720

A Longton Hall leaf dish, painted in the manner of the Trembley Rose painter, circa 1755, 22.5cm. wide. (Christie's) $653 £396

Belleek cream-ground shaped handled jug, black factory mark 'Robinson & Cleaver, Belfast', circa 1935. (Giles Haywood) $295 £180

Two George Jones majolica cheese dishes and covers, 25cm. and 24cm. high respectively, circa 1885. (Christie's) $1,815 £1,100

A Pratt ware Toby jug and cover, the man seated wearing ochre knee-breeches, blue coat and ochre, with caryatid handle, 26cm. high. (Phillips) $1,107 £580

A Leeds creamware tea canister of octagonal shape, 12.5cm. high, incised no. 25. (Phillips) $2,087 £1,250

A Swansea porcelain crested shaped rectangular dish with gilt twig handles, from the service made for T. Lloyd of Bronwydd, in 1819, 11in. long. (Dacre, Son & Hartley) $1,732 £1,050

A Sampson Hancock, Derby, group of Dr. Syntax chased up a tree by a bull, 17.5cm. high, red painted mark. (Phillips) $573 £300

A Pratt ware cow creamer, the animal with ochre sponging on a white body, the milkmaid wearing a blue bodice and spotted yellow skirt, 22cm. long. (Phillips) $802 £420

A Plymouth group of two putti emblematic of Spring, 14.5cm. high, impressed letters S & D (flower festoon R). (Phillips) $687 £360

A Victorian china two-handled footbath with 'bird' decoration. (J. M. Welch & Son) $623 £380

A Ralph Wood Vicar and Moses group, circa 1780, 24.5cm. high. (Christie's) $866 £495

Art Deco 'Shelley' teaset of five cups, six saucers, six side plates, cake plate and bowl, numbered R11792E. (J. M. Welch & Son) $134 £80

A 19th century pearlware transfer-printed coffee pot and cover, 10in. high. (Christie's) $528 £297

A Bretby pottery jardiniere, formed as a lion's head with glass eyes, 31cm. (Osmond Tricks) $710 £380

A 'scratch blue' saltglaze puzzle jug, the rim with three pinecone moulded spouts (two missing), 21.5cm. high. (Phillips) $5,348 £2,800

Early 19th century porcelain commemorative pottery jug with motto 'Success to Queen Caroline', 5.25in. high. (Prudential Fine Art) $247 £150

A late Wemyss model of a pig of small size, the body painted in green with scattered shamrock, 16cm. high. (Phillips) $1,566 £820

A pearlware cylindrical teapot and cover, applied with figures of Lord Rodney and Plenty, circa 1785, 13cm. high. (Christie's) $653 £396

A Longton Hall leaf dish, painted in the manner of the Trembley Rose painter, circa 1755, 27.5cm. wide. (Christie's) $1,452 £880

A Pilkington Lancastrian pottery vase by Richard Joyce, impressed Bee mark and date code for 1909, 11¾in. high. (Christie's) $1,006 £550

A pair of shell sweetmeat dishes, attributed to James Hadley, 22cm. wide, impressed and printed marks for 1882. (Phillips) $1,002 £600

'Guardian Vessel', a porcelain form by Ruth Barrett-Danes, 22.2cm. high. (Christie's) $1,262 £825

A Longton Hall strawberry leaf moulded plate, circa 1755, 23cm. diam. (Christie's) $3,448 £2,090

A Longton Hall white figure of a turkey of so-called 'Snowman' type, circa 1750, 18.5cm. high. (Christie's) $2,904 £1,760

An English slipware circular baking dish, 20.3cm. diam. (Phillips) $1,050 £550

A West Pans blue and white leaf moulded sauceboat with stalk handle, circa 1766, 20.5cm. wide. (Christie's) $508 £308

A pair of 19th century ironstone crescent-shaped serving dishes, 16in. long. (Prudential Fine Art) $218 £135

Shelley rectangular shaped cheese dish with matching handled cover 'Cloisello ware', 8in. long. (Giles Haywood) $106 £65

A creamware swelling jug painted in iron-red and black, circa 1770, 20.5cm. high. (Christie's) $1,270 £770

Pair of 'majolica' squirrel vases with branch handles, circa 1885, 31.5cm. high. (Christie's) $770 £440

A Caughley pounce pot, printed in underglaze blue with fruit and flower sprigs and insects, 8.5cm. high. (Phillips) $1,336 £800

An 18th century decorated baluster two-handled 'leech' jar with cover, approx. 14in. tall. (J. M. Welch & Son) $2,584 £1,700

A majolica glazed Stilton cheese dish and cover, probably by George Jones & Sons, late 19th century. (G. A. Key) $140 £85

'Bestiary Form', a porcelain jug form by Ruth Barrett-Danes, 28.5cm. high. (Christie's) $1,262 £825

A Cantonese circular bowl richly painted with panels of male and female figures within gilt cartouches, 16in. diam. (Anderson & Garland)
$1,274 £720

A 19th century oval covered Canton vegetable dish, China, 11in. long. (Robt. W. Skinner Inc.) $225 £140

Canton salad bowl, 19th century, shaped rim with notched corners, usual Canton scene. (Robt. W. Skinner Inc.) $650 £406

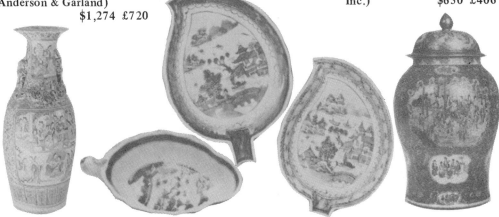

A Chinese Canton porcelain vase decorated in famille rose colours with panels of geishas on a floral ground, 2ft.½in. high. (Hobbs & Chambers) $313 £190

Three 19th century Canton dishes, two leaf-shaped relish dishes and an oval shallow sauceboat, 6¾in., 8in. and 7in. long. (Robt. W. Skinner Inc.) $325 £203

A 19th century Cantonese vase and cover decorated with Chinese household scenes. (Osmond Tricks)
$3,217 £1,950

Canton cider jug, mid 19th century, the domed cover with foo dog finial, height 8½in. (Robt. W. Skinner Inc.) $800 £432

Canton spittoon, 19th century, deep wide rim with Rain Cloud border, height 6¾in., rim diam. 7¾in. (Robt. W. Skinner Inc.) $600 £324

Shaped Canton shrimp dish, 19th century, typical Canton scene, diam. 10¼in. (Robt. W. Skinner Inc.) $275 £171

CARDEW

A stoneware casserole and cover by Michael Cardew, Wenford Bridge seals, circa 1970, 32cm. diam. (Christie's) $704 £440

An earthenware coffee pot and cover by Michael Cardew, impressed MC and Winchcombe Pottery seals, circa 1933, 17cm. high. (Christie's) $457 £286

A large stoneware teapot by Michael Cardew with strap handle and grip, Wenford Bridge seals, circa 1970, 23.4cm. high. (Christie's) $1,020 £638

An earthenware inscribed platter by Michael Cardew, decorated by Henry Bergen, Winchcombe Pottery seals, 42.7cm. diam. (Christie's) $1,760 £1,100

An unglazed stoneware teapot and cover by Michael Cardew, with bound cane handle, circa 1950, 17.8cm. high. (Christie's) $844 £528

A stoneware plate by Seth Cardew, impressed SC and Wenford Bridge seals, 35.6cm. diam. (Christie's) $228 £143

An earthenware cider flagon by Michael Cardew, circa 1970, 41cm. high. (Christie's) $704 £440

An Abuja large deep bowl on shallow foot, 34cm. wide. (Christie's) $246 £154

A large stoneware jar by Seth Cardew, the cylindrical body with four strap handles to the shoulder, 61.8cm. high. (Christie's) $492 £308

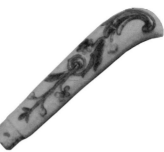

A Chelsea leaf dish with green vine-stock handle, red anchor mark, circa 1755, 21cm. wide. (Christie's) $3,850 £2,200

A Chelsea knife handle of facted octagonal shape, 11.5cm. long, red anchor period. (Phillips) $668 £350

An 18th century Chelsea 'Red Anchor' decorated bird of Paradise on a tree stump, 9in. high. (J. M. Welch & Son) $688 £420

A Chelsea cauliflower tureen and cover, red anchor mark to inside of base, circa 1755, 12cm. long. (Christie's) $4,235 £2,420

One of a pair of Chelsea-Derby groups of Renaldo, Armida, Cephalus and Procris, 20cm. high, incised numbers 75 and 76 with the initials J. W. (Phillips) $1,840 £1,000

A Chelsea-Derby Jardiniere of 'U' shape, Chelsea style with fabulous birds on rockwork and in the branches of leafy trees, 17cm. high. (Phillips) $1,485 £900

A Chelsea group of two children, naked except for a pink drapery, with large fish, 24cm. high. (Lawrence Fine Art) $1,458 £900

A Chelsea octagonal dish, painted in the Kakiemon palette with pheasants, circa 1750, 20.5cm. wide. (Christie's) $1,925 £1,100

A Chelsea white top of a Bonbon Nierre, modelled as Cupid and another, 5.5cm. high. (Lawrence Fine Art) $486 £300

CHELSEA

A red anchor Chelsea butter tub and cover, of circular straight sided shape, with two upright rectangular handles, set on three curved scroll feet, 13.5cm. diam., (one handle restored) circa 1752-6. (Phillips) $1,246 £700

A rare Chelsea model of a crouching leveret, 9cm. high. (Phillips) $9,936 £5,400

An 18th century Chelsea 'Red Anchor' half-circular flower holder, 12in. wide, 6½in. high. (J. M. Welch & Son) $885 £540

A Chelsea candlestick group, with leaf moulded candle nozzle and drip guard, 16.8cm. high, red anchor mark. (Phillips) $955 £500

A Chelsea group of two children, naked except for a white and gold drapery, seated on a rocky mound, 17.5cm. high. (Lawrence Fine Art) $1,539 £950

A Chelsea blue-ground square tapering vase, gold anchor mark, circa 1765, 32cm. high. (Christie's) $1,925 £1,100

A Chelsea-Derby figure of Diana, standing on a rocky, flower encrusted base, a stag at her feet (slight damage), circa 1770-5. (Phillips) $1,068 £600

A Chelsea cinquefoil scolopendrium dish, circa 1755, 20.5cm. diam. (Christie's) $3,850 £2,200

A rare Chelsea 'toy' figure of a gardener, pushing a roller over a grassy base strewn with applied flowers, 6.3cm. high. (Phillips) $1,196 £650

A Chinese famille verte armorial teapot, Yongzheng, circa 1724, (spout restored). (Woolley & Wallis) $928 £580

One of a pair of water-buffalo-head rhytons, 4½in. long. (Christie's) $3,262 £1,832

A fine blue and white bowl, painted in bright violet tones with a stylised lotus spray at the centre, 19.5cm. diam., fitted box. (Christie's) $3,495 £1,963

A large famille verte fish bowl with interior decoration, 45cm. high. (Dee & Atkinson) $480 £300

A blue and white pear-shaped vase, Yuhuchunping, painted with two mandarin ducks (minor rim chip), 26cm. high. (Christie's)$42,725 £24,002

A Chinese famille verte plate, Kangxi, circa 1725, 9¼in. diam. (Woolley & Wallis) $672 £420

Large mid 19th century Chinese Nanking ashet, 16½in. wide. (Peter Wilson) $721 £410

A rare Robin's egg blue Yixing wine ewer and cover, 18th century, 7¾in. high. (Christie's) $6,991 £3,927

A rare Chinese teapot and cover, decorated in London, the reverse inscribed '57 Miles to London', a milestone inscribed 'XIV Miles from London', 16cm., 1750-1760. (Phillips) $759 £460

CLARICE CLIFF

A Clarice Cliff Bizarre bowl, painted with crocus, 22.4cm. diam. (Osmond Tricks)
$196 £105

A Clarice Cliff wall pocket in the form of a pair of budgerigars, 23cm. high. (Osmond Tricks) $93 £50

A Clarice Cliff Bizarre 'Fantasque' octagonal bowl, painted with foxgloves and canterbury bells, 20.6cm. diam. (Osmond Tricks)
$93 £50

A Clarice Cliff Bizarre Latona vase of lotus shape with single handle, 30cm. high. (Osmond Tricks)
$1,140 £610

A Clarice Cliff Bizarre biscuit barrel with wicker handle, 16cm. (Osmond Tricks)
$252 £135

A Clarice Cliff 'Delicia' patterned jug. (Hobbs Parker) $574 £350

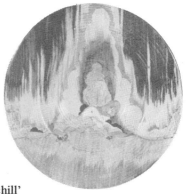

A large Clarice Cliff 'Fantasque' circular wall plate, 45.50cm. diam., printed marks and facsimile signature. (Phillips)
$1,568 £980

A large Clarice Cliff 'Churchill' Toby Jug, inscribed on base 'Going into Action, May God Defend the Right', 30.5cm. high, signed 'Clarice Cliff' No. 292'. (Phillips) $1,365 £750

A Wilkinson Bizarre pottery circular charger, by Clarice Cliff, 18¼in. diam. (Dacre, Son & Hartley)
$2,310 £1,400

COALPORT

One of two Coalport two-handled ecuelles and covers, painted in black with silhouette portraits of Queen Charlotte and George III, circa 1810, 16.5cm. wide. (Christie's) $4,356 £2,640

Part of a Coalport dessert service, the centre panels painted with floral bouquets on fawn ground, the compote 12¾in. wide, circa 1840. (Anderson & Garland) $1,699 £960

One of a pair of Coalport porcelain lozenge-shaped dessert dishes, painted in the manner of Thos. Baxter, circa 1810, 10¾in. by 8in. (Dacre, Son & Hartley) $1,732 £1,050

A late Coalport 'ramshead' vase and cover of shield shape, 18cm. high. (Phillips) $601 £360

A Coalport rectangular plaque with Cupid holding a dove, signed J. Rouse, 1856, 36.5 x 30.5cm. (Christie's) $1,996 £1,210

One of a pair of late Coalport vases with views of 'Dryburgh Abbey' and 'Hawthorndean', 29.5cm., green printed marks. (Phillips) $1,320 £800

A Coalport porcelain dessert plate from the service presented by Queen Victoria to the Emperor of Russia in 1845, 10in. wide. (Dacre, Son & Hartley) $2,557 £1,550

A Coalport vase of shield shape with scroll handles and square base, painted in the Baxter workshop, 32cm. (Phillips) $625 £340

A Coalport cabinet plate, signed by F.H. Chivers, with ripened fruit on an earthy ground, 10½in. across. (Christie's) $529 £286

COALPORT

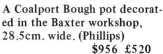

A 19th century Coalport porcelain peacock in gold and white on a rococo base, 6in. high. (G. A. Key) $222 £135

A pair of rare Coalport mantelpiece vases in neo-Classical style, painted almost certainly by Thomas Baxter, 29cm. high. (Phillips) $1,288 £700

A Coalport Bough pot decorated in the Baxter workshop, 28.5cm. wide. (Phillips) $956 £520

Large Coalport vase of baluster form, heavily applied with floral leaf decoration and griffin type handles, approx. 24in. high. (G. A. Key) $660 £400

A garniture of three early Coalport vases attributed to Charles Muss, 22cm. and 32cm. high, all signed underneath in gold CM. (Phillips) $1,072 £650

A Coalport vase of campana shape, with double scroll handles and leaf scroll moulded stem, on square base, 44cm. high. (Phillips) $3,056 £1,600

COPELAND

A Copeland 'orchid' vase, painted by T. Sadler, signed and dated 1904, 62.5cm. high. (Phillips) $1,910 £1,000

A Copeland part dessert service, the centres painted with named views, comprising twenty-four pieces, printed marks (some damage). (Christie's) $1,628 £880

A Copeland & Garrett rectangular shaped ceramic panel in oak frame, circa 1840, 32 x 8in. (Giles Haywood) $343 £180

A stoneware 'spade-form' vase by Hans Coper, circa 1970, 19.8cm. high. (Christie's)
$10,912 £6,820

An early small stoneware bowl by Hans Coper, with undulating rim, circa 1955, 14cm. diam. (Christie's)
$7,920 £4,950

A stoneware 'poppy head' shaped vase by Hans Coper, circa 1958, 13.8cm. high. (Christie's) $5,632 £3,520

A tall bulbous stoneware vase by Hans Coper, with narrow neck and flared rim, circa 1958, 33.4cm. high. (Christie's)
$7,920 £4,950

A bottle vase by Hans Coper, oviform body with short cylindrical neck, circa 1958, impressed HC seal, 65.2cm. high, (Christie's)
$23,760 £13,200

A stoneware 'spade-form' vase by Hans Coper, circa 1972, 23.4cm. high. (Christie's)
$16,720 £10,450

A tall 'hour-glass' vase by Hans Coper, impressed HC seal, 45.5cm. high. (Christie's)
$29,920 £18,700

A stoneware 'spade-form' vase by Hans Coper, 17.8cm. high. (Christie's)
$6,688 £4,180

A waisted cylindrical stoneware vase by Hans Coper, impressed HC seal, circa 1957, 18.6cm. high. (Christie's) $2,112 £1,320

An English delft polychrome posset pot, either London or Bristol, circa 1695, 24.5cm. wide. (Christie's)
$2,359 £1,430

One of two Bristol delft blue and white small rectangular flower-bricks painted with huts, circa 1760, 11.5cm. wide. (Christie's) $808 £462

A Bristol delft blue and white footed bowl, circa 1730, 26.5cm. diam. (Christie's) $2,178 £1,320

A London delft blue and white Royalist portrait plate, circa 1690, 22cm. diam. (Christie's)
$2,541 £1,540

A Delft mantel garniture, comprising two covered jars and a vase, vase 13in. high. (Christie's) $770 £434

A Lambeth delft blue and white octagonal pill slab, circa 1780, 26cm. high. (Christie's) $3,085 £1,870

A Bristol delft plate painted in a bright palette with a peacock, circa 1740, 21cm. diam. (Christie's)
$1,540 £880

A London delft vase painted in blue24cm. high. (Phillips)
$835 £500

A late 17th century Lambeth blue and white delftware dish, 14in. wide. (Dacre, Son & Hartley)		$656 £400

DERBY

A Derby Crown porcelain small lobed jardiniere, 19cm. wide, black printed mark. (Phillips) $768 £460

A pair of Derby figures of a sailor and his lass, Wm. Duesbury & Co., circa 1765, approx. 24cm. high. (Christie's) $1,996 £1,210

Bloor Derby porcelain sauce tureen and cover, Japan polychrome pattern with gilt work, circa 1820. (G. A. Key) $300 £170

A Derby figure of Justice represented by a blind lady in richly decorated Classical robes, 32cm. (Phillips) $1,104 £600

A Derby (Sampson Hancock) documentary rectangular plaque, signed and dated on the reverse Sampson Hancock May 31, 1865, 21.5 x 15.5cm. (Christie's) $726 £440

A Derby figure of a gallant seated on a tree stump, Wm. Duesbury & Co., circa 1760, 13cm. high. (Christie's) $1,179 £715

A Derby baluster jug, painted by Richard Dodson, 17cm. high, crown, crossed batons and D mark in red. (Phillips) $2,865 £1,500

Two Derby figures of John Wilkes and General Conway, Wm. Duesbury & Co., circa 1765. (Christie's) $2,178 £1,320

An attractive early Derby bell-shaped mug, painted with a bouquet of coloured flowers and scattered sprigs, the rim edged in brown, 11cm. (Phillips) $1,564 £850

DERBY

Derby handled cup and saucer, white ground with floral and gilded decoration, red mark to base, circa 1815. (Giles Haywood) $68 £42

A fine set of three 18th century Derby flower vases with named views. (Worsfolds) $4,704 £2,800

A Derby porcelain wine taster, circular with scalloped rim, leaf-shaped handle, circa 1770, 3.1/8in. long. (Christie's) $717 £419

A Derby figure of a flautist, Wm. Duesbury & Co., circa 1758, 15.5cm. high. (Christie's) $2,178 £1,320

A Derby set of the 'Four Quarters of the Globe', circa 1770, 22.5cm. high. (Phillips) $6,346 £3,800

An early Derby figure of a flautist, on a circular base with moulded puce scrolls, 14cm. (Phillips) $1,140 £620

An attractive small Derby model of a Pug, modelled and coloured with a gold studded collar around its neck, 6cm. high. (Phillips) $699 £380

A pair of Derby groups, both of a cow with calf in front of a flowering bocage background, 16cm. high. (Phillips) $840 £440

One of a pair of Derby plates, the centres painted with roses, thistles, bluebells, ferns and other flowers, 22.5cm. diam. (Phillips) $1,050 £550

'Smuts', Royal Doulton character jug, large, no number, designed by H. Fenton, introduced 1946, withdrawn circa 1948. (Louis Taylor) $676 £410

'The Wandering Minstrel' HN1224, designed by L. Harradine, introduced 1927, withdrawn 1938, 7in. high. (Louis Taylor) $1,402 £850

''Ard of 'Earing', large, D6588, designed by D. Biggs, introduced 1964, withdrawn 1967. (Louis Taylor)
$792 £480

Royal Doulton stoneware pottery jug, black leather ware, circa 1903, 8in. high. (G. A. Key) $108 £62

'North American Indian', a Royal Doulton character jug, 7in. high. (Anderson & Garland) $60 £34

'Coquette', no number, designed by Wm. White, introduced 1913, withdrawn 1938, 9.25in. high. (Louis Taylor) $1,567 £950

'Jarge', a Royal Doulton character jug, 6¾in. high. (Anderson & Garland)
$177 £100

A large Doulton Lambeth stoneware vase by Hannah Barlow and Frank Butler, 21in. high. (Christie's)
$1,425 £880

'The Mikado', a Royal Doulton character jug, small, D6507, designed by M. Henk, introduced 1959, withdrawn 1969. (Louis Taylor) $123 £75

DOULTON

'Brown-Haired Clown', a Royal Doulton character jug, large, D5610, designed by H. Fenton, introduced 1937, withdrawn 1942. (Louis Taylor)
$1,730 £1,050

Royal Doulton china model of a Siamese cat, 5½in. high, HN1655. (Prudential Fine Art) $33 £20

'Granny', Royal Doulton character jug, large, no number, designed by H. Fenton and M. Henk, introduced 1935. (Louis Taylor) $346 £210

Royal Doulton character jug, 'Old King Cole', with yellow crown and grey/white hair, 6in. high. (Prudential Fine Art) $5,445 £3,300

A Doulton Lambeth stoneware vase by Francis C. Pope, 16½in. high, impressed and incised artist monogram. (Christie's)
$644 £352

'Jockey', a Royal Doulton character jug, large, D6625, designed by D. Biggs, introduced 1971, withdrawn 1975. (Louis Taylor) $255 £155

Doulton Lambeth stoneware jug decorated with bacchanalian figures and verse, circa 1895, 7in. high. (G. A. Key)
$183 £105

'Boy with Turban', HN1210, designed by L. Harradine, introduced 1926, withdrawn 1938, 3.75in. high. (Louis Taylor) $495 £300

'Drake' (hatless), a Royal Doulton character jug, large, D6115, designed by H. Fenton, introduced 1940, withdrawn 1941. (Louis Taylor) $2,970 £1,800

DOULTON

Royal Doulton Dickens' ware part-toilet set, special back-stamp, 19th century. (Peter Wilson) $615 £280

A Lambeth stoneware figure, 'The Toiler', bearing initials LH, (Leslie Harradine), circa 1912, 9.25in. high. (Louis Taylor) $445 £270

A Sung flambe figure 'Boy on a Seahorse', signed Frederick Moore, 8.5in. high, probably a pilot. (Louis Taylor) $907 £550

A Royal Doulton flask, modelled by Leslie Harradine as Asquith, 18cm. high. (Phillips) $133 £80

Two Doulton Lambeth brown saltglazed stoneware figures, by George Tinworth, one play-ing a pipe, the other a tambour-ine, the tallest 4¾in. high. (Christie's) $1,181 £660

Royal Doulton figure, 'Harlequinade', HN585. (Warren & Wignall Ltd.) $640 £400

'Kathleen', HN1252, a Royal Doulton figure designed by L. Harradine, 7¾in. high. (Christie's) $433 £242

'Monty', D6202, a Royal Doulton character jug, 6in. high. (Anderson & Garland) $46 £26

'The Coming of Spring', HN1723, designed by L. Harradine, introduced 1935, withdrawn 1949, 12.5in. high. (Abridge Auctions) $875 £500

DOULTON

'One of the Forty', no number first version design, undecorated, hair crack in base, date 1924, 9.5in. high. (Louis Taylor) $330 £200

A flambe figure of a Seated Rabbit, 5.75in. high. (Louis Taylor) $132 £80

'Lady of the Georgian Period', HN41, designed by E. W. Light, introduced 1914, withdrawn 1938, 10.25in. high. (Louis Taylor) $1,072 £650

'Dog Begging with Lump of Sugar on nose', produced 1929, probably a prototype, 8in. high. (Louis Taylor) $759 £460

A pair of Royal Doulton stoneware vases by Hannah B. Barlow and Florrie Jones, 5½in. high. (Christie's) $354 £198

'Midinette', HN2090, a Royal Doulton figure designed by L. Harradine, 7¼in. high. (Christie's) $255 £143

'One of the Forty', no number, treacle glaze decoration, 6.5in. high. (Louis Taylor) $198 £120

Pair of Doulton Faience vases, dated 1885, 9½in. high. (Geering & Colyer) $356 £200

'Young Miss Nightingale', HN2010, a Royal Doulton figure designed by M. Davies, 9½in. high. (Christie's) $590 £330

'Gladys', HN1740, designed by L. Harradine, introduced 1935, withdrawn 1949, 5 in. high. (Louis Taylor)
$528   £320

'The Lady Jester', style two, HN1284, designed by L. Harradine, introduced 1928, withdrawn 1938, 4.25 in. high. (Louis Taylor) $1,089   £660

'Sweet and Twenty', HN1360, a Royal Doulton figure designed by L. Harradine, 5¾in. high. (Christie's) $315   £176

A Doulton, Burslem, ovoid vase, the panel painted by Fred Sutton, 17cm. high. (Phillips) $668   £400

A Royal Doulton group, 'The Flower Seller's Children', HN1342, 20cm. high. (Dee & Atkinson) $152   £95

A Royal Doulton Chang vase, 9in. high. (G. A. Key)
$513   £290

'White Haired Clown' Royal Doulton character jug, D6322 designed by H. Fenton, introduced 1951, withdrawn 1955.   (Abridge Auctions)
$840   £480

A Royal Doulton Limited Edition Tower of London jug. (Hobbs Parker)
$785   £450

'Dick Whittington', a Royal Doulton character jug, large, D6375, designed by G. Blower, introduced 1953, withdrawn 1960. (Louis Taylor) $239   £145

DOULTON

'Delight', HN1772, a Royal Doulton figure designed by L. Harradine, 7½in. high. (Christie's) $130 £75

Seated Bulldog with Union Jack, hat and cigar, 7.5in. high. (Louis Taylor)
$858 £520

A Royal Doulton figure, 'Rebecca', HN2805, 19cm. high. (Dee & Atkinson)
$136 £85

'Jarge', large, no number, designed by H. Fenton, introduced 1950, withdrawn 1960. (Louis Taylor)
$189 £115

'The Farmer's Boy', HN2520G, 9.25in. high. (Louis Taylor)
$759 £460

'Samuel Johnson', a Royal Doulton character jug, large no number, designed by H. Fenton, introduced 1950, withdrawn 1960. (Louis Taylor) $247 £150

A Doulton Lambeth style stoneware conservatory planter in the form of a weathered tree trunk. (Locke & England) $978 £600

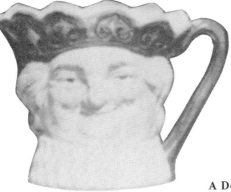

'Old King Cole', a Royal Doulton character jug, 5¼in. high. (Anderson & Garland)
$150 £85

A Doulton Lambeth stoneware jug, impressed factory mark and incised monograms for Florence Barlow and Mary Aitken, 8in. high. (Peter Wilson) $486 £300

209

CHINA

An earthenware two-handled
motto tankard by Michael
Cardew, impressed MC and
Winchcombe Pottery seals
(circa 1930), 10.1cm. high.
(Christie's) $356 £198

'Vertical Vessel', an earthenware vase by Gordon
Baldwin, dated '83, 50.7cm.
high. (Christie's) $528 £330

A small oval earthenware slip-
decorated dish by Charles
Tustin, impressed CT and
Winchcombe Pottery seals
(circa 1935), 20.4cm. diam.
(Christie's) $108 £60

A Poole pottery earthenware
oviform vase, painted by Anne
Hatchard, 28cm. high.
(Christie's) $425 £242

An earthenware cider flagon,
by Michael Cardew, Wenford
Bridge seals, circa 1970, 39cm.
high. (Christie's) $1,450 £825

A black earthenware hand-
built coiled amphora by
Fiona Salazar, 24.6cm. high.
(Christie's) $457 £286

A large earthenware jug by
Sidney Tustin, with strap
handle, impressed ST and
Winchcombe Pottery seals
(circa 1935), 16.5cm. high.
(Christie's) $99 £55

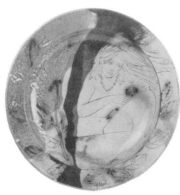

An earthenware charger by
Ljerka Njers, inscribed on the
reverse L. Njers 1983, 39.4cm.
wide. (Christie's) $554 £308

An early St. Ives slip decorated earthenware jug
with elaborate strap handle,
22.5cm. high. (Christie's)
                    $70 £44

EARTHENWARE

'Painting in the form of a
bowl', an earthenware bowl
by Gordon Baldwin, circa
1980, 38.4cm. diam.
(Christie's) $563 £352

'Painting in the form of a
bowl', an earthenware bowl
by Gordon Baldwin, dated
'82, 45.5cm. diam.
(Christie's) $739 £462

A grey earthenware bowl by
Birch, with shaped double
flanged rim, 26.5cm. wide.
(Christie's) $158 £99

An early St. Ives small
earthenware jug with strap
handle incised St. Ives
1927, 6.5cm. high.
(Christie's) $1,056 £660

A 16th century mediaeval
jug in buff coloured earthenware, probably Surrey,
18.5cm. high. (Phillips)
$764 £400

A Linthorpe earthenware
vase moulded on each side
with grotesque fish faces,
17.9cm. high. (Christie's)
$589 £385

A large earthenware dish by
Michael Cardew, impressed MC
and Winchcombe Pottery seals
(circa 1930), 36.6cm. wide.
(Christie's) $950 £528

A small earthenware jug by
Michael Cardew, impressed MC
and Winchcombe Pottery seals,
12.4cm. high. (Christie's)
$167 £93

'Vessel in the form of a Grey
Voice', an earthenware
sculpture in two parts by
Gordon Baldwin, dated '84,
base 38cm. square.
(Christie's) $633 £396

Early 20th century Gouda pottery covered urn, Holland, 16½in. high. (Robt. W. Skinner Inc.) $400 £238

Pair of 19th century Continental glazed and decorated stoneware figures, 'Policeman' and 'Woman', 12in. and 11in. tall. (J. M. Welch & Son) $151 £90

A mid 19th century Russian Toby jug from the Korniloff factory, 21.5cm. high. (Phillips) $1,085 £650

A model of a roistering Dutchman astride a Dutch gin cask, 37.5cm. high. (Christie's) $52,360 £30,800

A set of four Continental ceramic plaques, square, each depicting industrial and artisan subjects in the purist style, 10½in. sq., printed marks, each painted with Cocrah. (Christie's) $1,167 £638

Early 17th century Netherlands majolica syrup jar, painted in blue with scrolling foliage and plant pods, 23.5cm. high. (Phillips) $955 £500

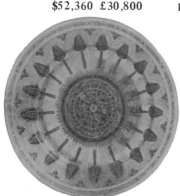

A Russian Imperial porcelain dinner plate, 23.5cm. diam., cypher mark of Nicholas I in blue. (Phillips) $668 £400

A Zurich figure of a shepherd, modelled by J. J. Meyer, 20cm. high, incised mark N I. (Phillips) $8,404 £4,400

A Cheese dish in the form of a bull's head. (Worsfolds) $184 £110

FAMILLE ROSE

A Chinese famille rose sauce-boat, Qianlong, circa 1760, 8¼in. across handle. (Woolley & Wallis) $640 £400

A pair of famille rose 18th century octagonal plates with the 'pseudo' 'tobacco pattern', 22in. diam. (Phillips) $356 £200

One of a pair of famille rose octagonal jardinieres, 10½in. wide. (Reeds Rains) $4,258 £2,550

An ormolu mounted famille rose baluster jar and cover with fruiting finial, the porcelain circa 1800, 21¾in. high. (Christie's) $2,388 £1,430

An 18th century Chinese famille rose plate, 43cm. diam. (David Lay) $450 £250

A famille rose Oviform vase with a scene of the eight Daoist Immortals below pine trees, 28cm. high. (Christie's) $10,098 £5,673

One of a pair of famille rose bowls, Yung Cheng marks and of the period, 7in. diam. (Phillips) $13,104 £7,200

A rare famille rose marbled-ground oviform vase, 15.5cm. high. (Christie's) $13,206 £7,419

A famille rose punch bowl, enamelled with panels of courtiers within key and floral pattern borders, 15½in. diam. (Greenslade & Co.) $1,780 £1,000

213

FRENCH

A 19th century Samson porcelain figure of Minerva, approx. 15in. high. (G. A. Key) $371 £210

Pair of French sweetmeat dishes formed as seated figures of a Girl and Boy, 5in. high. (G. A. Key) $495 £300

An 18th century French biscuit group modelled as a bearded god attended by two cupids, 40cm. high. (Christie's) $1,069 £660

One of a pair of Luneville shaped circular dishes painted in polychrome with chinoiserie figures with umbrellas, circa 1770, 33cm. diam. (Christie's) $5,667 £3,520

A pair of early 19th century Jacob Petit baluster vases on square bases with gilt mask handles, 71cm. high. (Wellington Salerooms) $6,720 £4,000

One of a pair of mid 18th century Strasbourg hexafoil plates, 24cm. diam. (Christie's) $796 £495

A Niderviller figure of 'La Jardiniere', on a circular base, 20.5cm. high. (Phillips) $458 £240

Pair of Samson porcelain figure ornaments, 'Presentation of Ribbons' and 'The Hairdresser', 7in. high. (G. A. Key) $672 £380

A 'Henri Deux style' candle-stick, by Charles Toft, 34cm. high. (Phillips) $1,336 £800

FRENCH

Late 18th/early 19th century
French biscuit group emble-
matic of America, 29cm. high.
(Christie's) $801 £495

A Rouen shaped circular plate
painted in a famille verte
palette, circa 1740, 25cm.
diam. (Christie's)
$1,948 £1,210

An 18th century French
biscuit figure emblematic
of Africa, 31.5cm. high.
(Christie's) $1,158 £715

Late 19th century Lachenal
Art pottery pitcher, French,
15¾in. high. (Robt. W.
Skinner Inc.) $400 £238

A Limoges teaset for six, the whole
covered in a mauve glaze, comprising teapot, hot water jug, sugar bowl
and cover, milk jug, six cups and
saucers, teapot 9¼in. high.
(Christie's) $483 £264

A Primavera pottery figure
depicting a female in broadly
flared pantaloons, 29cm.
high, stamped 'Primavera,
France', signed Levy. (Phillips)
$228 £130

One of a pair of Marseilles
(Veuve Perrin) shaped circular
plates painted en camaieu
vert with bouquets of flowers,
circa 1765, 25cm. diam.
(Christie's) $743 £462

An 18th century French
biscuit group emblematic
of Plenty, 34cm. high.
(Christie's) $801 £495

One of a pair of Moustiers
(Ferrat) shaped circular
plates painted with pairs
of parrots, circa 1770,
25cm. diam. (Christie's)
$619 £385

GERMAN

A Frankenthal figure of Pantolone from the Commedia dell'Arte, blue lion and monogram of Joseph Adam Hannong to base, circa 1760, 11.5cm. high. (Christie's) $6,058 £3,740

A Furstenberg globular teapot and cover, blue script F and figure 3 to base, circa 1765, 19cm. wide. (Christie's) $3,029 £1,870

A Brunswick Faience figure of a standing bagpiper, circa 1730, 18cm. high. (Christie's) $8,553 £5,280

Early 18th century Westerwald oviform tankard (Birnkrug) painted in blue and manganese on the grey body, 24cm. high. (Christie's) $534 £330

A Florsheim Faience inkstand, modelled as a chest of three serpentine-fronted drawers, 15cm. high. (Phillips) $2,254 £1,350

A German Faience tankard with pewter footrim mount, and cover with ball thumbpiece and engraved 'H. J. 1751', 25cm. high overall, the tankard circa 1730. (Christie's) $1,416 £880

A German plaque by Louis Renders, after David Neal, with Mary Queen of Scots' first encounter with Rizzio, signed, circa 1887, 29 x 21.5cm. (Christie's) $1,089 £660

Pair of Sitzendorf figurines, depicting flower girl and gardener boy, impress marks to base 'S' 'DEP' '15024', circa 1880. (Giles Haywood) $229 £140

A Hochst figure of harlequin wearing a multi-coloured suit and a conical hat, circa 1755, 16cm. high. (Christie's) $5,667 £3,520

216

GERMAN

An early Frankenthal figure of Pulchinella, impressed PH3 (for Paul Hannong) on base, circa 1755, 12cm. high. (Christie's) $8,910 £5,500

A Frankfurt Faience teapot and cover, painted in a bright blue with Chinese style figures, 13.5cm. high. (Phillips) $1,670 £1,000

A German Faience tankard painted in colours by a Nuremberg Hausmaler, with hinged pewter cover, the Faience 1740, 25.5cm. high. (Christie's) $16,929 £10,450

A Bottger gold Chinese milk jug and later domed cover gilt in the Seuter workshop, the porcelain circa 1725, 18cm. high. (Christie's) $1,211 £748

A Dresden Wolfsohn late 19th century china lobed dish, cover and stand. (Graves Son & Pilcher) $572 £320

A German Faience tankard (Walzenkrug), circa 1740, probably Erfurt, 24cm. high. (Christie's) $1,692 £1,045

Part of a Nymphenburg tea and coffee service painted in green and black with sprays of flowers and with iron-red borders, circa 1765. (Christie's) $2,302 £1,430

A Frankenthal group of four children, 23cm. wide, Carl Theodor mark in underglaze blue and dated 1783. (Phillips) $7,348 £4,400

A Dorotheenthal polychrome tankard, blue 'D' mark to base, circa 1735, with later cover, 25.5cm. high overall. (Christie's) $1,416 £880

Early 18th century German white Faience figure of a Callot dwarf modelled as a smoker, 46cm. high. (Christie's) $6,198 £3,850

Late 17th century Habaner Ware inscribed and dated beer jug, 30cm. high. (Christie's) $6,237 £3,850

A Hochst figure of a dancing girl modelled by Johann P. Melchior, blue crowned wheel mark, circa 1775, 13.5cm. high. (Christie's) $796 £495

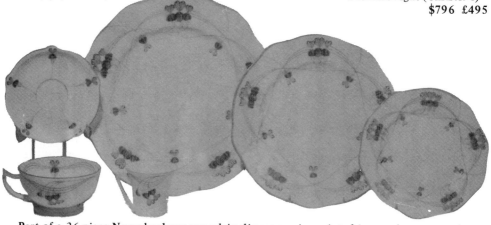

Part of a 36-piece Nymphenburg porcelain dinner service painted in purple, green and yellow enamels with stylised scrolling, flower-heads and stems. (Christie's) $992 £605

A Hochst group of Wandering Musicians, modelled by J. P. Melchior, underglaze blue wheel mark to base, circa 1770, 23cm. high. (Christie's) $7,128 £4,400

A German porcelain oval plaque painted with a portrait of a young girl, 14cm. high. (Christie's) $881 £528

A Frankenthal group of card players modelled by J. F. Luck, crowned CT mark and letter B for Adam Bergdoll to base, circa 1765, 17cm. high. (Christie's) $8,910 £5,500

GERMAN

A Hochst figure of a lady modelled by Johann P. Melchior as a sultan, circa 1770, 18cm. high. (Christie's) $1,239 £770

A pair of Nymphenburg plates, one of the five 'engravings' pinned to it with red and gilt nails, signed G. Sator inv. et Fecit, 24cm. diam. (Christie's) $2,851 £1,760

A Ludwigsburg figure of a lady with a muff modelled by Pierre F. Lejeune, circa 1760, 12.5cm. high. (Christie's) $1,328 £825

A pair of Hochst figures of musicians, blue wheel marks to bases, circa 1765, 16.5cm. high. (Christie's) $5,313 £3,300

A pair of Furstenberg white portrait busts modelled by J. C. Rombrich, probably of Schrader von Schiestedt and his wife, circa 1758/9, 15cm. high. (Christie's) $9,740 £6,050

A Frankenthal group of chess players modelled by J. F. Luck, blue crowned Carl Theodor mark, circa 1765, 17cm. high. (Christie's) $11,583 £7,150

A Bottger rectangular teapot and cover painted in Schwarzlot enriched in gilding by I. Preissler, circa 1720, 15cm. high. (Christie's) $60,214 £37,400

A Ludwigsburg group of dancers modelled by Franz Anton Pustelli, blue crowned crossed-C mark and incised UM 3 to base, circa 1760, 16cm. high. (Christie's) $19,602 £12,100

GERMAN

A German bisque porcelain figure group on oval base, 15in. high. (G. A. Key) $75 £45

Pair of Dresden Wolfsohn late 19th century china vases and covers, 12in. high. (Graves Son & Pilcher) $751 £420

A Sitzendorf porcelain classical figure group with polychrome decoration, 10in. high. (G. A. Key) $477 £270

Pair of German porcelain figures, decorated in blue and white, 13in. high. (G. A. Key) $379 £230

Late 19th century German porcelain table centrepiece, underglazed blue 'R' mark, 11½in. high. (Peter Wilson) $704 £400

Late 19th century pair of German porcelain figures, a dandy fruit gatherer with his female companion, 12in. tall. (G. A. Key) $354 £200

GOLDSCHEIDER

A Goldscheider ceramic wall plaque moulded as the head, neck and hand of a young woman, 7½in. high, printed marks. (Christie's) $194 £104

A Goldscheider alabaster figure carved by Dakon, of a clown, 30cm. high. (Christie's) $631 £385

A Goldscheider tin-glazed earthenware wall mask, Wien, Made in Austria, inscribed 8874, 36cm. high. (Christie's) $811 £495

GOSS

Parian bust of Southey. (Goss & Crested China Ltd.)
$260 £145

Glazed Florence Goss wall vase, with radiating hair and feathers, 120mm. high. (Goss & Crested China Ltd) $435 £250

Rye Cannon Ball without plinth. (Goss & Crested China Ltd.) $54 £30

Kirk Braddon Cross in brown washed parian. $140 £82 Unusually, the white parian example is more valuable. (Goss & Crested China Ltd) $325 £185

Parian bust of Lord Palmerston on socle base and fluted column, 335mm. high. (Goss & Crested China Ltd.) $270 £150

Shakespeare's House, half size. (Goss & Crested China Ltd.) $144 £80

The Trusty Servant of Winchester. (Goss & Crested China Ltd.) $2,430 £1,350

Large Carnarvon Ewer with Welsh Antiquities design of mistletoe and sickle, crossed daggers. (Goss & Crested China Ltd.) $72 £40

Coloured Parian bust of The Beautiful Duchess, who was Georgiana, Duchess of Devonshire. (Goss & Crested China Ltd.) $2,250 £1,250

IMARI

An Imari tall oviform jar decorated in coloured enamels and gilt on underglaze blue, Genroku period. (Christie's) $3,344 £2,090

An Imari charger decorated in iron-red enamel and gilt on underglaze blue, Genroku period, 55cm. diam. (Christie's) $2,057 £1,210

One of a pair of Imari double-gourd bottle vases, Genroku period, 33.5cm, high. (Christie's) $12,320 £7,700

One of a pair of pierced Imari plates, 8in. diam.. (R. K. Lucas & Son) $159 £95

An Imari model of a bijin decorated in iron-red, green, aubergine and black enamels and gilt, Genroku period, 37cm. high. (Christie's) $2,431 £1,430

A mid 19th century Japanese Imari goldfish bowl. (Miller & Co.) $787 £440

An Imari moulded kendi of typical form decorated in iron-red on underglaze blue, Genroku period, 27cm. high. (Christie's) $1,584 £990

An Imari jar decorated with a ho-o bird and a cockerel, Genroku period, wood cover, 39.5cm. high. (Christie's) $2,805 £1,650

An octagonal faceted Shoki-Imari bottle vase, circa 1660, 29cm. high. (Christie's) $4,288 £2,860

IMARI

An Imari globular bottle vase with tall neck decorated in coloured enamels and gilt with two cranes, circa 1700, 24.5 cm. high. (Christie's) $523 £308

An Imari bowl, Ming four-character mark, Genroku period, 25 cm. diam. (Christie's) $2,244 £1,320

An Imari jar and cover decorated in iron-red and black enamels and gilt on underglaze blue, Genroku period, 63 cm. high. (Christie's) $2,992 £1,870

An Imari barber's bowl, Genroku period, 28 cm. diam. (Christie's) $704 £440

An Imari model of an actor decorated in iron-red, green, aubergine and black enamels and gilt on underglaze blue, Genroku period, 39 cm. high. (Christie's) $3,553 £2,090

An Imari plate painted in under-glaze blue, iron-red, coloured enamels and gilt with 'La Dame au Parasol', circa 1740, 22.5 cm. diam. (Christie's) $2,992 £1,760

One of a pair of 19th century Chinese Imari style lidded vases of high shouldered ovoid form. (Peter Wilson) $915 £520

Late 17th century Ko-Imari jar decorated in iron-red, black, green and yellow ena-mels, 34 cm. high.(Christie's) $96,800 £60,500

One of a pair of late 19th century Imari moulded rectangular sake bottles, 27.5 cm. high. (Christie's) $1,122 £660

IMARI

Late 17th/early 18th century
Imari moulded condiment
ewer, 9 cm. high.
(Christie's)　　$633　£396

Pair of Imari ewers decorated in iron-red, green
enamels and gold on underglaze blue, Genroku period,
16.5 cm. high. (Christie's)
$3,168　£1,980

An Imari model of a leaping
carp on rockwork, Genroku
period, 32 cm. high.
(Christie's)　$2,992　£1,760

Late 17th century Ko-Imari
shaped square shallow dish,
14 cm. square. (Christie's)
$3,168　£1,980

Late 17th century Ko-Imari
model of a seated karashishi,
48.5 cm. high. (Christie's)
$56,100　£33,000

A large Imari fish bowl,
40 cm. high. (Dee &
Atkinson)　$496　£310

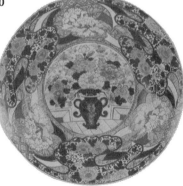

An Imari charger decorated
in iron-red and black enamels
and gilt on underglaze blue,
Genroku period, 54 cm. diam.
(Christie's)　$11,220　£6,600

An Imari octagonal jar,
Genroku period, 46 cm.
high. (Christie's)
$12,320　£7,700

An Imari charger, the roundel
containing a vase of cascading
chrysanthemum and peony
sprays on a veranda, Genroku
period, 55 cm. diam.
(Christie's)　$3,179　£1,870

IMARI

An Imari circular tureen and cover with applied loop finial, Genroku period, 23cm. diam. (Christie's) $2,992 £1,760

An Imari model of a bijin decorated in iron-red, green, black enamels and gilt on underglaze blue, 36cm. high. (Christie's) $3,553 £2,090

An Imari condiment set, ewer and cover decorated in iron-red and black enamels and gilt on underglaze blue, Genroku period, 9cm. high. (Christie's) $316 £198

Early 18th century Imari armorial dish decorated in iron-red and gilt on underglaze blue. (Christie's) $4,675 £2,750

A large Imari jar and a cover decorated in iron-red enamel and gilt on underglaze blue, Genroku period, the vase 61cm. high. (Christie's) $9,350 £5,500

An Imari charger decorated in iron-red and black enamels on underglaze blue, Genroku period, 60cm. diam. (Christie's) $2,244 £1,320

An Imari charger decorated in iron-red and gilt on underglaze blue, Genroku period, 53cm. diam. (Christie's) $6,545 £3,880

A pair of late 19th century Imari bijin, 48cm. high. (Christie's) $2,431 £1,430

An Imari shallow dish decorated in iron-red and gilt on underglaze blue, Genroku period, 25.5cm. diam. (Christie's) $841 £495

A Deruta blue and gold lustre charger, early 16th century, 41.5cm. diam. (Phillips) $7,258 £3,800

One of a pair of mid 16th century Venetian vasi a palli, 33cm. high. (Christie's) $21,252 £13,200

A Castelli armorial plate from the Grue workshop, 25cm. diam. (Phillips) $9,168 £4,800

A Faenza or Tuscan vase, circa 1500-20, 32.5cm. high. (Phillips) $1,753 £1,040

A Castelli rectangular plaque painted by Saverio Grue with Joseph sold by his brothers to the Midianites, circa 1770, 32.5 x 23.5cm. (Christie's) $10,626 £6,600

Early 17th century Central Italian circular plaque with a raised rim dated 1606, probably Deruta, 27cm. diam. (Christie's) $891 £550

Mid 16th century Castel Durante plate, 22cm. diam. (Phillips) $2,292 £1,200

An Urbino small albarello, workshop of Orazio Fontana, circa 1665-70, 15cm. high. (Phillips) $4,966 £2,600

A Venice vaso a palla with the portrait heads of two saints in cartouches, circa 1550, 28cm. high. (Christie's) $8,855 £5,500

ITALIAN

Early 16th century siena maiolica dish centre, probably from a tondino, the shield with the arms of the Penalva family of Portugal, 9.5cm. diam. (Phillips) $993 £520

A small pair of 19th century Italian albarello pots, the bases signed R.B., 4½in. high. (Christie's) $316 £198

An 18th century Savona polychrome tazza, painted in yellow, blue and green, mark in ochre, 35cm. high. (Phillips) $835 £500

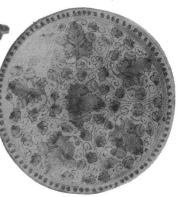

A Deruta gold lustre circular dish with the arms of Colonna in the central raised well, circa 1520, 29cm. diam. (Christie's) $7,128 £4,400

A pair of siena maiolica vases by Bartholomeo Terchi, one vase signed Bar: Terc(h)i: Romano: 1726, 56cm. high overall. (Phillips) $4,008 £2,400

Mid 17th century Montelupo circular dish painted with oak leaves, 32cm. diam. (Christie's) $566 £352

A Castelli small plate, painted with a putto in flight holding a book, 17cm. diam. (Phillips) $802 £420

An Urbino maiolica wet drug or syrup jar, workshop of Orazio Fontana, 1565-70, 34cm. high. (Phillips) $22,920 £12,000

Late 17th century Castelli plate painted in colours with a mounted hunting party, 23cm. diam. (Christie's) $4,633 £2,860

ITALIAN

A Naples creamware white group of the Madonna with the Infant Christ and St. John, inscribed Laudato Fecit 1794, 35cm. high. (Christie's) $7,128 £4,400

A 17th century Italian square tray, probably Deruta. (Christie's) $1,514 £935

One of a pair of 17th century Sicilian wet-drug jars with scroll handles, 25cm. high. (Christie's) $2,302 £1,430

An Urbino dish painted in the Patanazzi workshop with Abraham sacrificing Isaac, circa 1580, 35cm. diam. (Christie's) $8,910 £5,500

A Sicilian oviform vase painted with a portrait of a helmeted soldier, dated 1662, 37cm. high. (Christie's) $974 £605

A Castelli armorial circular dish, the centre painted with equestrian figures hawking, circa 1720, 40.5cm. diam. (Christie's) $8,500 £5,280

One of three 17th century Sicilian waisted albarelli, approx. 24cm. high. (Christie's) $891 £550

Two siena polychrome plates with scenes of the deer hunt and wolf hunt, circa 1740, 23.5cm. diam. (Christie's) $1,416 £880

A Sicilian waisted albarello painted with the head of a man in quatrefoil cartouche, 30cm. high, also another albarello and a wet-drug jar, all 18th/19th century. (Christie's) $2,125 £1,320

ITALIAN

A Deruta bottle for A. Graminis painted with the figure of Santa Barbara, circa 1530, 40cm. high. (Christie's) $8,910 £5,500

A Castelli rectangular plaque painted in the Grue workshop with the Flight into Egypt, circa 1720, 20 x 25.5cm. (Christie's) $2,479 £1,540

An 18th/19th century South Italian maiolica plaque painted with Christ, 38cm. high. (Christie's) $743 £462

A Deruta tondino painted in a palette of green, yellow, blue and orange, circa 1550, 21cm. diam. (Christie's) $1,960 £1,210

A 17th century baluster vase painted with yellow and green stylised flowers and foliage on a blue ground, 25cm. high. (Christie's) $1,069 £660

An Italian istoriato plate with the Judgement of Paris painted in colours, 1544, 27cm. diam. (Christie's) $17,820 £11,000

A Naples two-handled ecuelle, cover and stand painted with vignettes of five dated nocturnal eruptions of Vesuvius, circa 1794, stand 23.5cm. diam. (Christie's) $21,384 £13,200

A Pesaro istoriato tazza painted in colours by Sforza di Marcantonio with Anchises and Aeneas arriving at Pallanteum, circa 1550, 27cm. diam. (Christie's) $4,989 £3,080

A Castelli oval plaque painted by Saverio Grue with St. Francis, circa 1730, 38cm. high. (Christie's) $6,198 £3,850

ITALIAN

A 19th century Italian
alabaster bust of an allegory
of Sculpture, inscribed on
the reverse Vichi Firenze,
67cm. high. (Christie's)
$1,745 £1,045

An Urbino maiolica shallow
dish painted with Cain slaying
Abel, circa 1540, 25cm. diam.
(Christie's) $4,276 £2,640

Late 17th century S. Italian
Holy Water stoup, 33cm.
high. (Christie's)
$1,514 £935

A Castelli circular tondo
painted with the Dispute in
the Temple, circa 1725,
43cm. diam. (Christie's)
$1,062 £660

An Italian maiolica waisted
albarello painted with a
saint, circa 1600, 28cm.
high. (Christie's)
$1,593 £990

An early 18th century siena
circular dish painted with
two women with children,
31.5cm. diam. (Christie's)
$1,771 £1,100

A South Italian waisted
albarello painted with the
goddess Victory in a landscape, circa 1550, 28cm.
high. (Christie's)
$1,328 £825

A Castelli rectangular plaque
painted with the Meeting
between St. John and the
Infant Christ, circa 1690,
30 x 40cm. (Christie's)
$2,656 £1,650

One of three 17th century
Sicilian waisted albarelli
painted in yellow, green and
blue, approx. 23cm. high.
(Christie's) $1,514 £935

ITALIAN

Late 17th century S. Italian maiolica Holy Water stoup painted in colours, 31cm. high. (Christie's) $801 £495

An Urbino istoriato tazza painted in colours in the circle of Francesco Xanto Avelli with Marcus Curtius on horseback, circa 1545, 26.5cm. diam. (Christie's) $16,038 £9,900

A Savona blue and white fountain with loop-over handle, circa 1700, 59cm. high. (Christie's) $6,729 £4,180

An Urbino istoriato plate painted with the Temptation of Adam, circa 1560, 23cm. diam. (Christie's) $5,702 £3,520

A 17th century South Italian armorial waisted albarello, probably Sciacca, 29.5cm. high. (Christie's) $1,505 £935

An Urbino istoriato dish painted with the Death of Achilles, by Nicola Pellipario, circa 1535, 25.5cm. diam. (Christie's) $14,256 £8,800

One of two 17th century Sicilian drug jars with narrow necks, 23cm. high. (Christie's) $1,336 £825

Two Urbino armorial circular dishes, the centres with classical figure panels, circa 1580, 27.8cm. diam. (Christie's) $2,851 £1,760

A Castelli campana vase, probably painted by Liborio Grue, circa 1740, 41.5cm. high. (Christie's) $2,302 £1,430

One of a pair of Kakiemon
oviform jars and covers,
circa 1680, 29.5cm. high.
(Christie's)
$24,640 £15,400

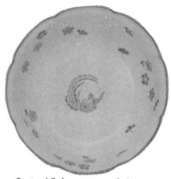

Late 18th century foliate
shaped Kakiemon bowl decorated in iron-red, blue, green,
yellow and black enamels,
18cm. diam. (Christie's)
$3,740 £2,200

Late 19th century Kinkozan
oviform vase and cover,
impressed seal mark, signed
Kinkozan zo, 15.5cm. high.
(Christie's) $2,431 £1,430

One of a pair of late 18th
century Kakiemon style
underglaze blue globular
bottle vases, 23.5cm. high.
(Christie's) $5,610 £3,300

Late 17th century model of
a Kakiemon seated tiger,
18.5cm. high. (Christie's)
$35,530 £20,900

A large octagonal oviform
jar and domed cover with
knop finial, Genroku period,
89cm. high. (Christie's)
$14,025 £8,250

A Kakiemon oviform vase
and cover, circa 1660, the
mounts 18th century, 19.5cm.
high. (Christie's)
$14,960 £8,800

Late 18th century Kakiemon
type underglaze blue koro
and cover, 14.3cm. diam.
(Christie's) $1,870 £1,100

One of a pair of Kaga ware
sake bottles (tokkuri),
21cm. high. (Christie's)
$3,179 £1,870

Late 19th century Kinkozan baluster vase, signed Dai Nihon Teikoku Kinkozan zo Kyoto Awata-yaki Shozan hitsu, 31cm. high. (Christie's) $5,610 £3,300

Late 17th/early 18th century Kakiemon type shallow dish, decorated in various coloured enamels and underglaze blue, 24.5cm. diam. (Christie's) $4,114 £2,420

Late 17th century Kakiemon underglaze blue oviform vase and cover, 36cm. high. (Christie's) $5,510 £3,300

Late 19th century Kinkozan oviform vase decorated in various coloured enamels and gilt on a dark green ground, 14cm. high. (Christie's) $2,244 £1,320

Pair of Kakiemon cockerels standing on rockwork bases, circa 1680, 28cm. high. (Christie's) $35,200 £22,000

A Kakiemon globular bottle vase, circa 1680, 28cm. high. (Christie's) $28,050 £16,500

Late 19th century Kinkozan oviform bottle vase decorated in coloured enamels and gilt, signed Kinkozan zo, 12.5cm. high. (Christie's) $2,805 £1,650

Late 19th century Yabu Meizan koro and cover with knop finial, signed, 9cm. diam. (Christie's) $1,870 £1,100

Late 19th century Kinkozan globular bottle vase, impressed seal mark, 26cm. high. (Christie's) $2,992 £1,760

CHINA

Late 17th century Kakiemon teabowl with later ormolu mounts, the bowl 6.75cm. diam., fitted box. (Christie's) $1,870 £1,100

An ormolu mounted Kakiemon porcelain vase of bombe shape, the porcelain late 18th century, 5in. wide. (Christie's) $1,653 £990

A decagonal Kakiemon foliate rim bowl, circa 1680, 18.5cm. wide. (Christie's) $4,114 £2,420

A 19th century Japanese Satsuma pottery coffee service of fifteen pieces, all decorated with panels of geishas and other figures on a gilt brocade ground. (Hobbs & Chambers) $330 £200

A Kakiemon shallow plate in iron-red, green, black, blue and yellow enamels on underglaze blue lines, circa 1680, 22cm. diam. (Christie's) $3,179 £1,870

A pair of late 19th century Japanese polychrome bottle vases, 25in. high. (Woolley & Wallis) $2,480 £1,550

One of a pair of late 17th/ early 18th century foliate rim Kakiemon type underglaze blue dishes, 20cm. diam. (Christie's) $528 £330

KANGXI

A Kangxi 'egg and spinach' bowl, a finely mottled glaze of green, yellow and brown splashes, 17.5cm. diam. (Christie's) $2,019 £1,134

A Kangxi Famille Verte deep bowl, painted in vivid enamels, 23cm. diam. (Christie's) $2,485 £1,396

A Kangxi yellow-glazed bowl, sides flaring into an everted rim, all under a lustrous yellow glaze, 19cm. diam. (Christie's) $2,330 £1,308

A Kangxi Famille Verte Foliate dish, painted in the Kakiemon style, 8¾in. diam. (Christie's) $1,398 £785

A Kangxi blue and white Yanyan vase with baluster body and flaring neck, 46cm. high. (Christie's) $2,175 £1,221

A Kangxi blue and white baluster jar, 10.8cm. high. (Christie's) $1,165 £654

A Kangxi rare documentary dated white-glazed stem cup, 10cm. high. (Christie's) $10,098 £5,673

An early Kangxi blue and white baluster vase, 20.5cm. high. (Christie's) $1,398 £785

A Kangxi Langyao dish, 7¾in. diam. (Christie's) $201 £112

A stoneware flask, by Bernard Leach, circa 1957, 33cm. high. (Christie's) $5,385 £3,520

A stoneware bowl by Bernard Leach, covered in a speckled olive-green glaze, circa 1970, 19.2cm. diam. (Christie's) $475 £297

A stoneware pear-shaped vase by Bernard Leach, covered in a blue-grey glaze over which brushed hakeme is incised with bell flowers, circa 1960, 26cm. high. (Christie's) $563 £352

A stoneware rectangular slab bottle by Bernard Leach, covered in a tenmoku glaze with shiny black and rich russet areas, circa 1962, 19.4cm. high. (Christie's) $457 £286

A stoneware oviform jar by John Leach, with everted rim decorated in wax-resist, 30.5cm. high. (Christie's) $352 £220

A Yingqing porcelain globular vase by Bernard Leach, covered in a bluish white glaze with blue black rim, circa 1965, 15cm. high. (Christie's) $492 £308

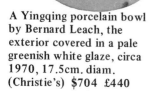

A Yingqing porcelain bowl by Bernard Leach, the exterior covered in a pale greenish white glaze, circa 1970, 17.5cm. diam. (Christie's) $704 £440

A tapering stoneware cylindrical vase by Bernard Leach, covered in an olive-green and pale green ash glaze with areas of russet brown, circa 1965, 30.4cm. high. (Christie's) $1,408 £880

A stoneware 'leaping deer' plate with everted rim decorated by Bernard Leach, circa 1965, 23.9cm. diam. (Christie's) $3,520 £2,200

LEACH

A porcelain bowl with compressed sides by Bernard Leach, circa 1960, 20.6cm. diam. (Christie's) $668 £418

A large stonewar jar by Bernard Leach, with lobed sides, circa 1965, 19.3cm. high. (Christie's) $1,232 £770

A stoneware bowl by Bernard Leach, on shallow foot, 25.2cm. diam. (Christie's) $880 £550

A stoneware flattened rectangular slab bottle by Bernard Leach, covered in an olive-green tea-dust glaze, 18.6cm. high. (Christie's) $668 £418

A large stoneware globular vase by Janet Leach, covered in a mottled olive-green ash glaze, circa 1980, 29.4cm. high. (Christie's) $281 £176

A tall stoneware jug by Bernard Leach, with incised strap handle, circa 1970, 27cm. high. (Christie's) $880 £550

A large stoneware 'fish' vase by Bernard Leach, circa 1970, 37.5cm. high. (Christie's) $9,680 £6,050

A pair of early slip decorated earthenware dishes attributed to Bernard Leach, circa 1935, 19.5cm. diam. (Christie's) $1,056 £660

A Yingqing porcelain slender oviform vase, by Bernard Leach, circa 1969, 36cm. high. (Christie's) $1,598 £1,045

LIVERPOOL

A Liverpool tin-glazed stone-ware small cylindrical mug, circa 1760, 6.5cm. high. (Christie's) $3,267 £1,980

A Liverpool blue and white moulded oval sauceboat, attributed to Wm. Ball's factory, circa 1758, 14.5cm. wide. (Christie's)
$3,993 £2,420

A Liverpool Delft blue and white bottle painted with chrysanthemum and other flowers, 9¾in. high, circa 1750. (Christie's)
$612 £350

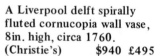

A Liverpool creamware jug, 21cm. high. (Phillips)
$1,252 £750

Two 19th century Liverpool transfer-printed pitchers, 10¾in. and 5½in. high respectively. (Christie's) $935 £565

A Liverpool delft spirally fluted cornucopia wall vase, 8in. high, circa 1760. (Christie's) $940 £495

A Liverpool creamware oviform jug, inscribed in black script W.B., 6¾in. high, circa 1800. (Christie's)$209 £110

An English delft blue and white dish, perhaps Liverpool, circa 1740, 30.5cm. diam. (Christie's) $2,722 £1,650

A 19th century Liverpool transfer-printed pitcher of baluster form with pulled spout and applied C-scroll handle. (Christie's)
$1,100 £665

LOWESTOFT

A Lowestoft bell-shaped mug, painted in colours, in the manner of the Tulip Painter, 14cm. high. (Phillips) $1,837 £1,100

An 18th century Lowestoft porcelain miniature sparrow-beak jug, 3½in. high. (Hy Duke & Son) $106 £60

A Lowestoft cylindrical mug, the scroll handle with thumb rest, 15cm. high. (Phillips) $3,173 £1,900

LUSTRE

A large Pilkingtons Lancastrian pottery vase, designed by Gordon Forsyth, painted in a golden lustre of foliage, 17in. high, circa 1919. (Christie's) $880 £500

Royal Lancastrian lustre pottery vase by W. S. Mycock, dated 1925, 9in. high. (Prudential Fine Art) $206 £125

Pilkington's Royal Lancastrian lustre two-handled baluster vase decorated by William S. Mycock, 8.25in. high. (Prudential Fine Art) $156 £95

MARTINWARE

A Martin Brothers stoneware vase, 23.5cm. high, signed 'Martin Bros. and dated '8-1903' and 'No. 6'. (Phillips) $296 £160

A Martin Brothers stoneware 'Gourd' vase, 17.5cm. high, signed 'Martin Bros., London & Southall', dated '2-1910. (Phillips) $222 £120

A Martin Bros. grotesque bird, covered in blue and olive-green glaze, 1915, 18.3cm. high. (Christie's) $2,692 £1,760

MASON'S

A Miles Mason rectangular
sugar bowl and cover, pattern no. 328 in gold, 17.5cm.
wide, an oval teapot stand
and a trio, circa 1815.
(Christie's) $127 £77

Mason's ironstone jug decorated with Imari pattern,
8in. high. (G. A. Key)
$136 £78

A Miles Mason sugar bowl and
cover painted with 'The Dragon
in Compartments' pattern, 16cm.
wide, with two others, 15cm. and
19cm. wide, 1810-15. (Christie's)
$707 £429

A Mason's ironstone part dinner service each piece decorated in the Imari colours, meat dish
48cm., circular underdish, 33cm., two vegetable dishes, 35cm., twelve dinner plates, 26cm.
diam., five soup plates, 26cm., two smaller dishes and two sauce tureen underdishes, 25
pieces. (Lacy Scott) $1,456 £880

A Miles Mason pale apricot-
ground D-shaped bough pot
and pierced dome cover,
circa 1805, 25cm. high.
(Christie's) $2,359 £1,430

A very rare garniture of Mason
vases, 19.5cm and 17cm. high.,
two vases impressed M. Mason.
(Phillips) $1,980 £1,200

Mason's pottery jug painted
and stamped mark, with
lizard handle and Imari pattern, 8in. high. (G. A. Key)
$192 £110

MEISSEN

A Meissen snuff box with hinged silver gilt mount, 7.5cm., the interior with KPM and crossed swords in blue, circa 1725. (Phillips)
$8,786 £4,600

A Meissen shaped plate, blue crossed swords mark and Pressnummer 16, circa 1755, 24cm. diam. (Christie's)
$13,370 £7,150

A Meissen large mythological centrepiece in three sections, 63cm. overall length, crossed swords mark. (Phillips)
$5,730 £3,000

One of a pair of Meissen vases with flared necks, 20.5cm. high, crossed swords marks (SR). (Phillips) $4,775 £2,500

An early Meissen teapot and cover, painted by J. G. Horoldt, 12.5cm. wide. (Phillips) $7,515 £4,500

A Meissen yellow ground quatrefoil coffee-pot and domed cover, blue crossed swords mark, gilder's mark M. to both pieces, circa 1742, 23cm. high. (Christie's)
$11,313 £6,050

A Meissen porcelain group of three Bacchantes, 8in. high. (Prudential Fine Art)
$825 £500

A Meissen tureen and cover, painted in the manner of C. F. Herold, 26cm. wide, crossed swords mark. (Phillips)
$5,921 £3,100

A 19th century Meissen porcelain group of the Reveller, 18th century style, 13½in. high. (Christie's) $935 £548

MEISSEN

A Meissen figure of Dr. Boloardo modelled by J. J. Kandler, circa 1742, 18.5cm. high. (Christie's) $8,553 £5,280

A Meissen KPM baluster teapot and domed cover, painted by P. E. Schindler, circa 1724, 15cm. wide. (Christie's) $12,474 £7,700

A Meissen figure of a tailor from the series of craftsmen modelled by J. J. Kandler, circa 1753, 23.5cm. high. (Christie's) $2,656 £1,650

A Meissen hunting group, blue crossed swords marks and incised X to base, circa 1755, 16cm. high. (Christie's) $1,603 £990

A Meissen deckelpokal, blue crossed swords mark to the base, and gilder's mark c to both pieces, circa 1725, 18cm. high. (Christie's) $13,282 £8,250

A Meissen group of a Mother and Children modelled by J. J. Kandler and P. Reinicke, circa 1740, 23.5cm. high. (Christie's) $2,673 £1,650

A Meissen tea caddy with domed shoulder, circa 1755, 10.5cm. high. (Christie's) $623 £385

A Meissen crinoline group of the gout sufferer modelled by J. J. Kandler, circa 1742, 19.5cm. wide. (Christie's) $9,740 £6,050

A Meissen cylindrical pomade pot and domed cover, painted in the manner of Gottfried Klinger, circa 1745, 15cm. high. (Christie's) $2,851 £1,760

MEISSEN

A Meissen figure of a Turkish woman playing the lute modelled by P. Reinicke, trace of blue crossed swords mark to base, circa 1755, 16.5cm. high. (Christie's) $980 £605

A Meissen KPM inverted baluster teapot and domed cover, painted in colours perhaps by Mehlhorn, circa 1724, 16cm. wide. (Christie's) $7,128 £4,400

A Meissen figure of a youth holding a rooster under his arm, circa 1755, 14.5cm. high. (Christie's) $531 £330

A large Meissen group of Count Bruhl's tailor on a goat, blue crossed swords and incised numeral marks, circa 1880, 43cm. high. (Christie's) $4,041 £2,420

A Meissen clock case and stand, blue crossed swords mark and Pressnummer 25 to the stand, circa 1745, the movement by LeRoy, 50cm. high overall. (Christie's) $7,969 £4,950

A pair of Meissen figures of a shepherd and shepherdess, faint blue crossed swords marks on bases, circa 1755, 14.5cm. high. (Christie's) $2,316 £1,430

A Meissen coffee pot and a cover, gilder's marks L. to cover and 65. , circa 1725, 19.5cm. high. (Christie's) $2,833 £1,760

A Meissen quatrefoil tureen, cover and stand, painted in colours with Watteaumalerei vignettes of amorous couples, circa 1750, the stand 28.5cm. wide. (Christie's)$8,553 £5,280

A Meissen kinderbuste, blue crossed swords and incised numeral marks, circa 1880, 25cm. high. (Christie's) $918 £550

MEISSEN

A Meissen green-ground quatrefroil teacup and saucer with ombrierte gilt cartouches of figures in landscapes, circa 1740. (Christie's) $1,151 £715

A Meissen two-handled quatrefoil tureen stand with shell and scroll handles, circa 1740, 41cm. wide. (Christie's) $5,346 £3,300

A Meissen baluster cream jug (small chip to spout), blue crossed swords mark to base, circa 1740, 9cm. high. (Christie's) $213 £132

A Meissen figure of a Turkish woman modelled by P. Reinicke, circa 1745, 17cm. high. (Christie's) $1,062 £660

A Meissen garniture of five vases and three covers, blue crossed swords marks and Pressnummern 21 to bases, circa 1738, the largest vase 46.5cm. high. (Christie's) $85,536 £52,800

A Meissen figure of Cupid as a soldier, blue crossed swords mark at back, circa 1755, 9.5cm. high. (Christie's) $354 £220

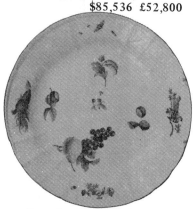

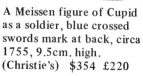

A Meissen baluster coffee pot and a cover, blue crossed swords mark and Dreher's mark +, circa 1728, 16.5cm. high. (Christie's) $1,682 £1,045

One of a pair of Meissen circular dishes, blue crossed swords marks, Pressnummern 20 and 21, circa 1745, 30.5cm. diam. (Christie's) $3,920 £2,420

A Meissen figure of a Gallant Dressing A Mops, modelled by J. F. Eberlein, circa 1745, 12cm. high. (Christie's) $2,138 £1,320

MEISSEN

A Meissen teacup and saucer, blue underglaze crossed swords marks and Pressnummern 64 and 66, circa 1750. (Christie's) $619 £385

An early Meissen sugar box and cover, the cover with half-length figures of Chinese, by J. G. Horoldt, 11cm. wide. (Phillips) $1,670 £1,000

A Meissen goldmalerei globular teapot and cover, 1725-30, 17cm. wide. (Christie's) $3,207 £1,980

A Meissen chinoiserie silver mounted tankard painted by J. E. Stadler, circa 1728, the Augsburg silver cover and thumbpiece by Hans J. Wild II, 18cm. high. (Christie's) $26,730 £16,500

An early Meissen beaker or chocolate cup with twisted stem handles. (Phillips) $1,002 £600

A Meissen small cylindrical tankard by Johann G. Horoldt, circa 1728, 10.5cm. high. (Christie's) $28,336 £17,600

A Meissen circular two-handled tureen and cover with Turk's head finial and Frauenkopf scroll handles, circa 1730, 32.5cm. high. (Christie's) $6,771 £4,180

A Meissen model of an elephant modelled by Kandler, 15cm. long. (Phillips) $1,336 £800

A Meissen figure of a musician in theatrical costume playing a lute, modelled by J. J. Kandler, circa 1745, 16.5cm. high. (Christie's) $8,910 £5,500

MEISSEN

A Meissen figure of the Marquis from the Cris de Paris series, circa 1756, 13cm. high. (Christie's) $3,385 £2,090

A Meissen shaped oval jagd tureen and cover with boar's head and shell finial, painted in the manner of C. F. Herold, circa 1740, 31.5cm. wide. (Christie's) $9,801 £6,050

A Meissen figure of a seamstress modelled by J. J. Kandler, circa 1753, 22.5cm. high. (Christie's) $2,656 £1,650

A Meissen two-handled ecuelle, cover and stand of round lobed form, circa 1745, the stand 18cm. diam. (Christie's) $2,656 £1,650

A Meissen monkey band of eighteen figures, from 11cm. to 18cm. high; two German monkey band figures, about 12.5cm. high; a Continental monkey figure of a drummer, 13.5cm. high and a faience music stand, 10cm. high, all late 19th century. (Christie's) $4,592 £2,750

A Meissen gold Chinese globular teapot and domed cover gilt at Augsburg by B. Seuter, circa 1725, 16.5cm. wide. (Christie's) $9,801 £6,050

A Meissen figure of Pulchinella from the Commedia dell'Arte modelled by J. J. Kandler, circa 1740, 14cm. high. (Christie's) $3,010 £1,870

A Meissen oviform rococo moulded teapot and cover painted in the manner of C. J. Albert, circa 1755, 15.5cm. wide. (Christie's) $908 £605

MEISSEN

A Meissen figure of the Courtesan from the Cries of London series, modelled by J. J. Kandler and P. J. Reinicke, circa 1754, 14cm. high. (Christie's) $2,851 £1,760

A pair of Meissen dancing children on rococo scroll bases, impressed numerals 24 to base, 12cm. high. (Christie's) $2,673 £1,650

A Meissen figure of harlequin with a jug modelled by J. J. Kandler, on an ormolu base in Louis XV style, circa 1737, 17.5cm. high. (Christie's) $3,896 £2,420

A pair of Meissen condiment groups modelled as a man and a woman, blue crossed swords and incised numeral marks, circa 1880, 20cm. high. (Christie's) $1,010 £605

Pair of Meissen Hausmalerei teacups and saucers painted by F. F. Meyer von Pressnitz, circa 1740. (Christie's) $4,958 £3,080

A Meissen three-footed cream pot and cover painted in colours with Watteaumalerei scenes of figures from the Commedia dell'Arte in park landscapes, circa 1745, 11cm. high. (Christie's) $1,782 £1,100

A Meissen figure of Cupid as a harlequin, circa 1765, 12cm. high. (Christie's) $1,416 £880

A Meissen baluster teapot and domed cover, blue crossed swords mark, gilder's mark 42, circa 1730, 15cm. wide. (Christie's) $16,929 £10,450

A Ming white-glazed Anhua-decorated bowl, 20.8cm. diam. (Christie's) $20,197 £11,346

A Ming Imperial yellow saucer-dish, a glaze of rich, warm yellow tones, 22.1cm. diam. (Christie's) $3,107 £1,745

A Ming blue and white stem bowl, painted in a vivid blue with two five-clawed dragons, 16.2cm. diam. (Christie's) $4,364 £2,451

A Ming Wucai saucer-dish, with a youthful Shoulao on a deer's back, 19cm. diam. (Christie's) $3,884 £2,182

A Ming blue and white vase, 4½in. high, wood stand. (Christie's) $7,379 £4,145

One of a pair of Ming dishes, in iron-red with three fish swimming, 8½in. diam. (Christie's) $8,545 £4,800

A Ming blue and white baluster jar, painted in violet-blue tones, 12.5cm. high. (Christie's) $4,364 £2,451

A fine Ming blue and white saucer-dish, 14.5cm. diam. (Christie's) $4,661 £2,618

An early 16th century large Ming blue and white baluster jar, Guan (minor restoration), 36.5cm. high. (Christie's) $7,768 £4,364

MINTON

A Minton pink-ground cabinet cup and saucer, circa 1825. (Christie's) $272 £165

A pair of Minton 'Dresden Scroll' vases and pierced covers in neo-rococo style, 29cm. high. (Phillips) $2,101 £1,100

A Minton Pilgrim vase, painted probably by A. Boullemier after W. S. Coleman, 20cm. high, date code possibly 1873. (Phillips) $434 £260

One of a pair of Minton porcelain dessert plates, one with swallow in flight, signed Leroy, the other with a bird perched on fuchsia branch, 9½in. diam. (Dacre, Son & Hartley) $2,062 £1,250

A massive Minton 'majolica' peacock after the model by P. Comolera, circa 1875, 153cm. high. (Christie's) $30,800 £17,600

A Minton porcelain dessert plate, the central pate-sur-pate panel signed L. Solon, circa 1880, 9¼in. wide. (Dacre, Son & Hartley) $495 £300

A Minton white and celadon glazed centrepiece modelled as three putti holding a basket, circa 1868, 26cm. high. (Christie's) $731 £418

A pair of Minton candlestick figures, both in richly decorated costumes and with flowered and striped designs, 22cm. high. (Phillips) $2,769 £1,450

A Minton 'majolica' garden seat modelled as a crouching monkey, circa 1870, 47cm. high. (Christie's) $12,512 £7,150

MINTON

A large Minton majolica umbrella stand modelled as a stork, impressed Minton 1916, 102cm. high. (Christie's) $4,592 £2,750

A Minton majolica jardiniere, the handles formed as satyrs impressed Minton and with date code for 1871, 26.5cm. high. (Christie's) $642 £385

A Minton majolica figure, 'Basket Carrier', with date code for 1868, 22.9cm. high. (Christie's) $514 £308

A Minton majolica bowl, impressed marks, numerals and date code for 1874, 31.5cm. diam. (Christie's) $1,452 £880

A Minton pale turquoise-ground 'Munster pot-pourri' vase and cover, circa 1830, 26cm. high. (Christie's) $544 £330

A Minton oval sugar bowl and cover, 13.5cm. wide, together with a trio and a saucer dish, circa 1805. (Christie's) $580 £352

A pair of Minton blue-ground 'Wellington' vases, the gilding perhaps by Thomas Till, circa 1830, 35cm. and 34.5cm. high. (Christie's) $3,630 £2,200

A Minton dark brown-ground pate-sur-pate plate, date code for 1873, 23.5cm. diam., together with another two plates. (Christie's) $471 £286

A Minton majolica barrel-shaped garden seat in the Oriental taste, date code for 1873, 50cm. high. (Christie's) $871 £528

MINTON

A Minton blue-ground centre-piece, circa 1835, 66cm. high. (Christie's) $5,445 £3,300

A Minton majolica cheese dish and cover with reclining bull finial, 29cm. high. (Christie's) $1,285 £770

A Minton majolica figure of a partially draped putto holding a lyre-shaped viol seated on a conch-shell, impressed Minton 1539 and with date code for 1870, 46.5cm. high. (Christie's) $3,674 £2,200

A Minton globular jug with loop handle, pattern no. 248, circa 1805, 16.5cm. wide. (Christie's) $308 £187

A Minton majolica vase, 'Monkey Match Pot', impressed Mintons 1692 and date code for 1873, 19cm. high. (Christie's) $551 £330

A Minton shaped rectangular basket of 'Clarence' shape, blue crossed swords mark, circa 1835, 18.5cm. wide. (Christie's) $580 £352

One of a pair of Minton yellow-ground cabinet plates, pattern no. G1276, 1874 and 1881, 24cm. diam. (Christie's) $726 £440

One of a pair of Minton majolica vases, twelve-sided oviform shape, date code for 1859 on one vase, 29cm. high. (Christie's) $918 £550

A pair of Minton majolica figures, 'Grape Gatherers', with date codes for 1866, 24.5cm. high. (Christie's) $734 £440

A Minton majolica-ware teapot and cover in the form of a Chinese actor holding a mask, 14cm. high, impressed Mintons, model no. 1838, date code for 1874. (Phillips) $660 £400

A Minton vase and cover by Louis Jahn, 50cm. high, impressed and printed marks. (Phillips) $1,670 £1,000

A Minton majolica-ware teapot and cover in the form of a monkey, 15.5cm. high, impressed Mintons, model no. 1844, date code for 1876. (Phillips) $1,023 £620

One of a pair of Minton majolica-ware figures of boys leaning on tall vine baskets, 23cm. high, model no. 421, date codes for 1868. (Phillips) £561 £340

A Minton aesthetic movement 'Cloisonne' vase, 18.5cm. high, impressed 'Minton'. (Phillips) $481 £260

A Mintons Kensington Gore pottery moon flask, 34.2cm. high. (Phillips) $555 £300

A Minton majolica-ware Neptune shell dish, 17cm. high, impressed Minton, shape no. 903 and date code for 1861. (Phillips) $462 £280

A Minton pate-sur-pate vase and cover by Marc Louis Solon, 35cm. high, date code for 1903. (Phillips) $3,340 £2,000

A fine Minton pate-sur-pate plate, signed Louis Solon, 24cm. high., printed Minton and A. B. Daniell & Sons retailer's mark. (Phillips) $1,380 £750

MOORCROFT

A bellied vase with waisted neck and foot rim, by Wm. Moorcroft, 6in. high. (Hetheringtons Nationwide) $140 £85

A twin-handled bowl, by Wm. Moorcroft, made for Liberty & Co., 23cm. wide. (David Lay) $306 £170

A ginger jar and cover, by Walter Moorcroft, factory mark and potter to the Queen, circa 1945, 11in. high. (Peter Wilson) $528 £300

PARIAN

Maisons bisque porcelain bust of Minerva, Charenton, France, late 19th century, marked base, 34½in. high. (Robt. W. Skinner Inc.) $2,500 £1,396

A Parian figural group of sleeping children 'Le Nid', circa 1875, signed 'Croisy', 15in. high. (Robt. W. Skinner Inc.) $750 £418

A Goss Parian bust of Queen Victoria, for Mortlock's of Oxford Street, 236mm. high. (Phillips) $400 £225

A Goss Parian wall vase with head of Georgiana Jewitt, white unglazed, chipped and marked. (Phillips) $116 £70

A large Parian group entitled 'Detected', signed R.J. Morris, 41cm. high. (Dee & Atkinson) $284 £160

A Sam Alcock & Co Parian seated portrait figure of Wellington with joined hands and crossed legs, 28cm. high. (Phillips) $498 £300

A Paris (Nast) green-ground cabinet cup and saucer, gilt marks, circa 1810. (Christie's) $220 £132

A pair of Paris (Jacob Petit) pink-ground vases of inverted baluster form, circa 1840, 18cm. high. (Christie's) $1,089 £660

A Paris veilleuse, the body painted with panels of buildings in extensive country landscapes, 9¾in. high. (Christie's) $437 £250

A pair of Paris royal-blue-ground two-handled vases, the oviform bodies painted after Teniers, circa 1820, 37cm. high. (Christie's) $3,630 £2,200

One of a pair of Paris (Jacob Petit) Mayblossom vases and covers, blue J.P. marks, circa 1830, 39.5cm. high. (Christie's) $1,653 £990

A pair of Paris gold-ground two-handled vases on square richly gilt bases, circa 1825, 42.5cm. high. (Christie's) $10,890 £6,600

A Paris (Schoelcher) royal-blue-ground cabinet cup and saucer, reserved and painted with a portrait of Helene, circa 1820. (Christie's) $404 £242

A massive Paris blue-ground 'Medici' vase, painted with Cupid, circa 1820, 54.5cm. high. (Christie's) $2,904 £1,760

A large Paris biscuit group entitled 'Le Nid' after the original sculpture by A. O. Croisy, circa 1880, 38.5cm. high. (Christie's) $2,388 £1,430

PARIS

A Paris (Jacob Petit) two-handled cup, cover and trembleuse-stand, blue JP marks, circa 1840, the stand 16.5cm. diam. (Christie's) $580 £352

Pair of early 19th century Paris (Dart Freres) white china elliptical dessert dishes, covers and fixed stands, 13in. diam. (Graves Son & Pilcher) $1,467 £820

A Paris (Jacob Petit) neo-renaissance oval two-handled pot-pourri vase and cover, circa 1840, 21.5cm. high. (Christie's) $235 £143

A Paris (Restoration) purple-ground tea service, each piece painted with a different scene after the fables of La Fontaine in a gilt panel, circa 1820. (Christie's) $4,455 £2,750

One of a pair of Paris ice-pails and covers with white and gilt caryatid handles, circa 1810, 39cm. high. (Christie's) $2,788 £1,760

A pair of Paris (Jacob Petit) vases modelled as figures of a boy and a girl, circa 1850, about 22cm. high. (Christie's) $508 £308

A Paris gilt bronze mounted vase, imitation incised interlaced L and blue marks, circa 1900, 44cm. high. (Christie's) $1,285 £770

One of a pair of stoneware bowls by Lucie Rie and Hans Coper, on shallow feet with compressed sides, circa 1958. (Christie's) $1,760 £1,100

A porcelain sgraffito bowl by Lucie Rie, circa 1958, 15.3cm. diam. (Christie's) $1,056 £660

A small stoneware sgraffito bowl by Lucie Rie, covered in a translucent finely crack-led mustard-yellow glaze, circa 1955, 6.1cm. high. (Christie's) $1,232 £770

A tall stoneware bottle vase, by Lucie Rie, circa 1967, 38.7cm. high. (Christie's) $6,688 £4,180

A sgraffito inlaid bowl and cover by Lucie Rie, the exterior with radiating inlaid purple lines, circa 1966, 18.2cm. diam. (Christie's) $3,872 £2,420

A stoneware bottle vase by Lucie Rie, with flared waves rim, flattened cylin-drical neck, circa 1975, 27.2cm. high. (Christie's) $2,112 £1,320

A small porcelain sgraffito bottle vase by Lucie Rie, 16.5cm. high. (Christie's) $668 £418

An early stoneware vase by Lucie Rie, covered in an olive-green glaze oxidising in places to a lustrous black, 27.1cm. high. (Christie's) $1,320 £825

A stoneware baluster vase by Lucie Rie, covered in a shiny deep-blue glaze with run matt-manganese rim, circa 1955, 31.7cm. high. (Christie's) $2,640 £1,650

RIE, LUCIE

A small stoneware sgraffito bowl by Lucie Rie, circa 1960, 12.2cm. diam. (Christie's) $616 £385

One of a pair of stoneware bowls by Lucie Rie and Hans Coper, each impressed with LR and HC seals, circa 1958, 8cm. high. (Christie's) $704 £440

A small stoneware sgraffito bowl by Lucie Rie, covered in a translucent finely crackled mustard-yellow glaze, circa 1950, 6cm. high. (Christie's) $1,144 £715

A porcelain bottle vase by Lucie Rie, with trumpet-shaped neck and rim, circa 1980, 26.7cm. high. (Christie's) $2,640 £1,650

A small stoneware bowl by Lucie Rie, covered in a mirror-black manganese glaze with white rim, circa 1953, 10cm. diam. (Christie's) $739 £462

A stoneware bottle vase by Lucie Rie, covered in a chalky-white glaze with puce and turquoise spiral, circa 1975, 24cm. high. (Christie's) $2,112 £1,320

A large stoneware milk jug with pulled handle by Lucie Rie, 15.8cm. high. (Christie's) $299 £187

A stoneware vase by Lucie Rie, covered in a pitted and mottled pale-pink, olive-green and brown glaze, circa 1966, 24cm. high. (Christie's) $5,280 £3,300

A stoneware bottle vase by Lucie Rie, covered in a finely pitted shiny white glaze thinning in places, circa 1968, 27.4cm. high. (Christie's) $5,984 £3,740

ROCKINGHAM

A Rockingham cottage pastille burner and stand, lavender colour with gilt details, 13cm. high. (Lawrence Fine Art) $435 £250

ROOKWOOD

A Rockingham porcelain octagonal plate, decorated in famille verte enamels, 35cm. diam. (H. Spencer & Sons) $435 £250

A Rockingham Cadogan teapot, of peach shape, 4½in. high, impressed Brameld. (Dreweatt Neate) $103 £55

Rookwood pottery Spanish water jug, Cincinnati, Ohio, 1882, cobalt blue glaze on strap handled, double spout round pitcher, 10in. high. (Robt. W. Skinner Inc.)
$125 £66

Rookwood Pottery Flower vase, Cincinnati, Ohio, 1886, spherical clay body, impressed 'RP/189/Y' and signed 'M.A.D.' by Matt Daly, 7½in. diam. (Robt. W. Skinner. Inc.) $200 £106

Rookwood pottery scenic vellum vase, signed and artist initialled by Sallie E. Coyne, 1913, 9in. high. (Robt. W. Skinner Inc.) $900 £486

Rookwood pottery silver overlay mug, Cincinnati, Ohio, 1891, marked 'Gorham Mfg. Co.' 6¼ in. high. (Robt. W. Skinner. Inc.)
$1,200 £638

A Rookwood pottery vase with sterling silver overlay, initialled C.C.L., for Clara C. Linderman, 1906, 7¼in. high. (Robt. W. Skinner Inc.)
$1,600 £952

Rookwood pottery flower pitcher, Cincinnati, Ohio, 1884, bulbous white clay body, signed 'AMB' by Anne Marie Bookprinter, 8¼in. high. (Robt. W. Skinner Inc.) $250 £132

ROOKWOOD

A Rookwood pottery decorated pitcher, artist's initials MLN for Maria Longworth Nichols, 1882, 6in. high. (Robt. W. Skinner Inc.)
$750 £446

Rookwood pottery dish, Cincinnati, Ohio, 1882, ginger clay body, signed by Nathaniel J. Hirschfield, diam 6½in. (Robt. W. Skinner Inc.)
$125 £66

A Rookwood pottery decorated creamer, Ohio, 1893, artist's initials O.G.R. for Olga Geneva Reed, 4¼in. high. (Robt. W. Skinner Inc.)
$175 £106

A Rookwood pottery scenic vellum vase, Ohio, initialled by artist Harriet E. Wilcox, 1918, 8in. high. (Robt. W. Skinner Inc.) $850 £505

A Rookwood pottery standard glaze pillow vase, 1889, artist's initials ARV for Albert R. Valentien, 14in. high. (Robt. W. Skinner Inc.)
$1,000 £595

A large Rookwood pottery standard glaze vase, Ohio, 1899, initialled AMV for Anna Marie Valentien, 19in. high. (Robt. W. Skinner Inc.)
$1,300 £812

A Rookwood pottery wax-resist floral vase, Ohio, 1929, artist initialled LNL for Elizabeth N. Lincoln, 17in. high. (Robt. W. Skinner Inc.)
$950 £593

A Rookwood pottery scenic vellum loving cup, initialled by Frederick Rothebusch, 1908, 7¼in. high. (Robt. W. Skinner Inc.) $1,000 £625

A Rookwood pottery vase, decorated by K. Shirayama-dani, Roman II for 1902, 38cm. high. (Christie's)
$2,345 £1,430

ROYAL DUX

Royal Dux 'Austria' Art Nouveau vase having fold-over leaf top, 14in. high. (Giles Haywood) $124 £65

Pair of Royal Dux figurines, flower girl carrying flower basket and boy with apron carrying basket, signed F. Otto, pink triangle to base. (Giles Haywood) $574 £350

Czechoslovakian Royal Dux figure of an Indian Boy playing a flute with a half nude female dancer, 9in. high. (G. A. Key) $284 £160

Royal Dux-style centrepiece designed as a young lady holding water lily, impress mark 8335, 12in. high. (Giles Haywood) $90 £55

A Royal Dux pottery toilette mirror, depicting an Art Nouveau maiden. (Phillips) $1,091 £620

A Royal Dux porcelain orna-ment formed as two Sirens near Conche Shell on a stemmed base, 18in. high. (G. A. Key) $447 £250

A Royal Dux group of two figures in classical dress on oval base with red triangle mark no. 1980, 16½in. high. (Prudential Fine Art) $439 £230

Pair of Royal Dux figurines, signed F. Otto, pink triangle to base, 17in. high. (Giles Haywood) $574 £350

A Royal Dux figure of a peasant boy leaning on a wooden pitcher, 59cm. high. (Abridge Auctions) $675 £385

SATSUMA

Late 19th century Kyo-
Satsuma oviform tea caddy,
signed Hakuzan, 12.5cm.
high. (Christie's)
$1,496 £880

Late 19th century Satsuma
model of a caparisoned
elephant decorated in
coloured enamels and gilt,
31cm. high. (Christie's)
$2,640 £1,650

Late 19th century Kyo-
Satsuma shallow dish, signed
Dai Nippon Setsuzan, 31.5cm.
diam. (Christie's)
$3,168 £1,980

A pair of Satsuma pottery
vases, decorated in a pink
and blue palette, 14in. high.
(G.A. Key) $264 £160

Late 19th century Satsuma
model of a lantern decorated
in various coloured enamels
and gilt, 50cm. high.
(Christie's) $3,344 £2,090

Pair of late 19th century Kyo-
Satsuma oviform vases, signed
Mitsu, 25cm. high. (Christie's)
$1,848 £1,155

A Satsuma oviform vase
decorated in various thickly
applied coloured enamels and
gilt, 152cm. high. (Christie's)
$9,350 £5,500

A 19th century Satsuma
pottery plaque decorated
with shaped panels of figures
dancing and feasting, 14in.
diam. (Hobbs & Chambers)
$1,248 £780

Late 19th century Satsuma
moulded oviform jar and
cover, depicting the story of
Bishamon and Kichigo-ten,
42cm. high. (Christie's)
$2,464 £1,540

SEVRES

Late 19th century Sevres pattern gilt bronze mounted two-handled centrepiece, 27.5cm. wide. (Christie's) $998 £605

A Sevres reeded cup and fluted saucer, date letter for 1768, and painter's mark of Thevenet Pere. (Christie's) $677 £418

A Sevres seau a demi-bouteille from the Duchesse du Barry service, date letters for 1771, and decorator's mark LB for Le Bel junior, 13cm. high. (Christie's) $8,553 £5,280

A Sevres plate, 23.5cm. diam., LL mark enclosing date letters EE for 1782, painter's marks for Capelle and probably Huny. (Phillips) $6,847 £4,100

Late 19th century Sevres pattern green-ground Napoleonic tapering oviform vase and cover, decorated by Desprez, 138cm. high. (Christie's) $8,712 £5,280

A Sevres plate, 24.3cm. diam., LL mark enclosing date letters EE for 1782, painter's mark probably for Huny. (Phillips) $3,674 £2,200

One of a pair of ormolu mounted and bleu celest Sevres style three-branch candelabra, 19th century, 24½in. high. (Christie's) $2,939 £1,760

A pair of late 19th century Sevres pattern blue-ground Napoleonic tapering oviform vases and covers, painted by J. Pascault, 152.5cm. high. (Christie's) $39,930 £24,200

Late 19th century Sevres pattern turquoise-ground gilt bronze mounted two-handled vase, fitted for electric light, the vase 31.5cm. high. (Christie's) $698 £418

SEVRES

A Sevres green-ground cup
and saucer, interlaced L
marks, date letters D for
1756 and R for 1770,
decorators' marks L B and
E. (Christie's) $891 £550

A Sevres circular tazza for
the Paris Exhibition of 1878,
36.5cm. high. (Christie's)
$1,724 £1,045

A Sevres green-ground large
cup and deep saucer, interlaced L marks and date
letter V for 1774 and
painter's mark B.g.
(Christie's) $392 £242

One of a pair of late 19th
century Sevres pattern
turquoise-ground gilt bronze
mounted jardinieres, 27cm.
high overall. (Christie's)
$2,204 £1,320

One of a pair of late Sevres
vases of 'Stephanus' shape,
designed by Carrier-Belleuse
in 1880, 55cm. high, mark
and date code for 1894.
(Phillips) $1,469 £880

A Sevres two-handled ecuelle,
cover and stand, blue interlaced L marks, date letter for
1775, and blue decorator's
mark for Thevenet, 25.5cm.
wide. (Christie's)
$1,603 £990

One of a pair of late 19th
century Sevres pattern gilt
bronze mounted ewers,
24.5cm. high. (Christie's)
$762 £462

A Sevres rose pompadour
lobed quatrefoil dish, blue
interlaced L marks enclosing
the date letter for 1762,
painter's mark of Micaud,
28cm. wide. (Christie's)
$2,494 £1,540

One of a pair of late 19th
century Sevres pattern green-
ground vases and covers,
42cm. high. (Christie's)
$2,359 £1,430

SEVRES

A Sevres blue-ground milk jug, incised os, interlaced L's enclosing the date letter for 1760, and the painter's mark of Aloncle, 10.5cm. high. (Christie's) $1,748 £935

A Sevres yellow ground ecuelle, cover and oval lobed stand, interlaced L's enclosing the date letter kk for 1788, the painter's mark cm for Commelin, 20cm. wide. (Christie's) $5,759 £3,080

A Sevres sucrier and cover interlaced L's enclosing date letter s for 1771 and mark possibly of Mereaud, 11.5cm. high. (Christie's) $2,262 £1,210

A Sevres baluster hot milk jug and cover, interlaced L's enclosing date letter u for 1773 and the painter's mark for Xhrouet, 15cm. high. (Christie's) $2,674 £1,430

A pair of Charles X Sevres plates, one painted with the Chateaux de Montargis, the other with the Grande Chartreuse a Grenoble, 22.3cm. diam., crowned entwined C's and dated 1824-25. (Phillips) $1,184 £620

A Sevres bleu lapis ground hot milk jug and cover, interlaced L's enclosing the letter D for 1756, two dots, and the mark of the painter Evans, 11cm. high. (Christie's) $4,731 £2,530

A Sevres blue-ground small cup and saucer with the date letter c for 1755. (Christie's) $2,057 £1,100

A Sevres tripod cream jug, interlaced L's enclosing date letter s for 1771 and the painter's mark b for Boulanger, 12.5cm. high. (Christie's) $2,674 £1,430

A Sevres bleu celeste ground cup and saucer, interlaced L's enclosing date letter M for 1765 and the painter's mark Cp for Chapuisaine. (Christie's) $1,748 £935

A Spode miniature taperstick with pattern no. 1166, 7.5cm. high., marked in red. (Phillips) $1,237 £750

Part of a Spodes new stone dinner service, impressed mark Spodes New Stone and pattern no. 3875 in red. (Lawrence Fine Art) $5,994 £3,700

An attractive pair of Spode candle extinguishers on a small rectangular tray with loop handle, 12.5cm., impressed workman's mark. (Phillips) $883 £480

A comprehensive Spode stone china dinner service, blue printed Spode stone china mark, and pattern no. in red. (Phillips) $2,392 £1,300

A Spode porcelain 'Beaded New Shape' jar and cover with gilt ball finial and loop handles, pattern No. 1166, 10½in. high. (Dacre, Son & Hartley) $7,410 £3,900

A pair of Spode porcelain cabinet cups, covers and stands marked in puce 'Spode 711' (circa 1805). (Dacre, Son & Hartley) $4,180 £2,200

A Spode footed vase with flared rim, decorated with 'Japan' pattern, 15.5cm. high. (David Lay) $322 £180

265

STAFFORDSHIRE

A Staffordshire pearlware sailor Toby jug, circa 1800, 29.5cm. high. (Christie's) $1,270 £770

A Staffordshire pearlware figure of a cow, circa 1800, 32.5cm. wide. (Christie's) $1,089 £660

A Staffordshire creamware Toby jug, circa 1800, 25.5cm. high. (Christie's) $635 £385

A Staffordshire saltglaze bear jug and cover, circa 1740, 24cm. high. (Christie's) $9,982 £6,050

A Staffordshire figure of a gentleman, circa 1810, 22.5cm. high. (Christie's) $544 £330

A Staffordshire figure of a doe of Ralph Wood type, circa 1770, 15.5cm. wide. (Christie's) $1,179 £715

A Staffordshire equestrian group of Obadiah Sherratt type, circa 1830, 22cm. high. (Christie's) $3,267 £1,980

A Staffordshire pearlware figure of a recumbent stag, circa 1800, 20.5cm. high. (Christie's) $635 £385

A Staffordshire creamware group of St. George and the Dragon of conventional Ralph Wood type, circa 1780, 28.5cm. high. (Christie's) $3,630 £2,200

STAFFORDSHIRE

A Staffordshire Toby jug of conventional type, circa 1780, 26cm. high. (Christie's) $907 £550

A Staffordshire creamware figure of a standing lion, circa 1810, 16cm. wide. (Christie's) $1,179 £715

A Staffordshire creamware Toby jug of Ralph Wood type, circa 1780, 25cm. high. (Christie's) $1,179 £715

A Staffordshire creamware spill-vase of Ralph Wood type, modelled as a gallant, circa 1780, 20cm. high. (Christie's) $635 £385

A pair of Staffordshire figures of a gardener and companion of Ralph Wood type, circa 1780, 19.5cm. high. (Christie's) $4,356 £2,640

A Staffordshire bust of Maria Foot of Obadiah Sherratt type, circa 1816, 29cm. high. (Christie's) $2,904 £1,760

A Staffordshire porcelain pastille-burner modelled as a two-storeyed pavilion, circa 1845, 16.5cm. high. (Christie's) $762 £462

A Staffordshire creamware recumbent stag, circa 1800, 15cm. wide. (Christie's) $762 £462

A Staffordshire spill vase musician group, circa 1830, 22.5cm. high. (Christie's) $2,541 £1,540

Large Staffordshire ornament of a recumbent lion, 12in. long. (G. A. Key) $85 £52

Pair of 19th century Staffordshire lions decorated in brown and cream with glass eyes and painted mouths, 12in. long. (G. A. Key) $280 £170

A Staffordshire saltglazed teapot and cover, modelled by Wm. Greatbatch for J. Wedgwood at Lane Delf, 11.5cm. high. (Phillips) $5,348 £2,800

A pair of South Staffordshire opaque tea caddies for Bohea and Green, circa 1760, about 13.5cm. high. (Christie's) $7,088 £3,960

One of a pair of Staffordshire pearlware dinner plates and two soup plates, early 19th century, one 10in. diam. (Christie's) $99 £55

A Staffordshire figure of Maritta Alboni as Cinderella seated in a shell-shaped carriage, circa 1850, 8¾in. high. (Christie's) $924 £550

A pair of Staffordshire models of the British lion, both holding beneath their paws the figure of Napoleon III, 24.2cm. high. (Phillips) $993 £520

A Staffordshire tipstaff moulded with Royal Garter, circa 1840, 11in. high. (Christie's) $332 £198

Pair of Victorian Staffordshire pottery flat-back deer spill vases, 12in. high. (Hobbs & Chambers) $347 £195

STAFFORDSHIRE

A Staffordshire model of a seated rabbit eating a lettuce leaf, 3½in. high, circa 1860. (Christie's) $314 £187

Early Staffordshire Walton type pottery model of a seated deer and a similar model of a standing deer, both 5¾in. high. (Hobbs & Chambers) $391 £220

Death of the Lion Queen, a Staffordshire pottery group of Ellen Bright, 36cm. high. (Phillips) $1,375 £720

A Staffordshire figure of the actor Menier in the part of Thelsitor from the play, 'Porga, circa 1850, 10¼in. high. (Christie's) $646 £385

Set of three early Staffordshire pottery figures on circular grassy mounds and square plinth bases, 6½in. high. (Hobbs & Chambers) $373 £210

A Staffordshire Phrenology bust by L. N. Fowler, late 19th century, 30cm. high. (Christie's) $1,058 £605

A Staffordshire Pratt type model of a deer, strongly coloured in ochre, 13.5cm. high. (Phillips) $668 £350

Pair of Staffordshire pottery spirit barrels with metal taps, 12in. high. (G. A. Key) $272 £165

A 19th century Staffordshire spill vase, 'Milk Sold Here', 13½in. tall. (J. M. Welch & Son) $699 £460

STAFFORDSHIRE

A Staffordshire glazed red-ware hexagonal teapot and cover, circa 1745, 14.5cm. high. (Christie's)
$816 £495

A Staffordshire white porcelain triple pastille burner, modelled as three Gothic pavilions, circa 1848. (Christie's) $816 £495

A Staffordshire saltglaze pecten-shell moulded baluster teapot and a cover, circa 1755, 13cm. high. (Christie's)
$1,996 £1,210

A Staffordshire erotic figure of a barmaid, circa 1820, 19cm. high. (Phillips)
$1,369 £820

A pair of Staffordshire pearlware figures of Mansion House dwarfs, after the Derby porcelain originals, 15cm. and 17cm. high. (Phillips) $2,254 £1,350

A Staffordshire saltglaze baluster milk jug and cover, circa 1755, 15.5cm. high. (Christie's) $3,630 £2,200

A pearlware 'Birds in Branches' group, probably Staffordshire, circa 1790, 19.5cm. high. (Christie's) $1,089 £660

An early creamware cow creamer and cover, 18cm. wide. (Phillips)
$2,254 £1,350

A Staffordshire pearlware figure of a cockerel, circa 1820, 25cm. high. (Christie's) $1,179 £715

STAFFORDSHIRE

A Staffordshire creamware oviform 'pebble-dash' teapot and cover of Whieldon type, circa 1760, 13cm. high. (Christie's) $18,150 £11,000

A 19th century Staffordshire cow creamer with willow pattern decoration in blue, 5¼in. high. (Robt. W. Skinner Inc.) $350 £218

A Staffordshire saltglaze globular teapot and cover, circa 1760, 6in. wide. (Christie's) $1,145 £682

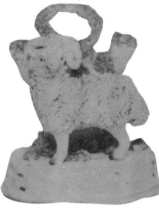

Early 19th century Staffordshire bust of John Wesley mounted on a marbleised pedestal base, 11½in. high. (Robt. W. Skinner Inc.) $175 £109

A Staffordshire spill-vase modelled as a ram, circa 1845, 4½in. high. (Christie's) $147 £88

A Staffordshire group of children, entitled 'Scuffle', 19cm. high. (Phillips) $412 £250

A Staffordshire seated dog, circa 1790, 3½in. high. (Christie's) $240 £143

A pair of early Staffordshire figures of Whieldon type, depicting a sailor and a soldier, 15cm. and 15.5cm. high. (Phillips) $7,682 £4,600

A Staffordshire figure of James Blomfield Rush, circa 1850, 10in. high. (Christie's) $1,626 £968

STONEWARE

A Westerwald stoneware inverted baluster kanne moulded all over with relief rosettes on a blue-ground, 32cm. high. (Christie's) $566 £352

A stoneware flask-shaped vase by Alan Wallwork, 32.1cm. high. (Christie's) $387 £242

A Bottger brown stoneware cylindrical tankard and hinged cover, circa 1715, 21.5cm. high. (Christie's) $31,878 £19,800

A stoneware cut-sided bottle vase by Shoji Hamada, with short neck and shallow foot, circa 1960, 29.1cm. high. (Christie's) $2,640 £1,650

A stoneware saltglazed press-moulded jar by Shoji Hamada, with paper label inscribed 56, 22cm. high. (Christie's) $2,816 £1,760

A stoneware oviform vase by Thomas Samuel Haile, covered in a grey-white glaze with dark olive-green splashes, 20.4cm. high. (Christie's) $158 £99

A tall St. Ives commemorative stoneware jug with strap handle, 29.1cm. high. (Christie's) $211 £132

A stoneware dish by Kitaoji Rosanjin, partly covered in a pale olive-green glaze, 19.1cm. diam. (Christie's) $1,408 £880

A stoneware teapot by Shoji Hamada, the cut-sided body with short spout and arched handle, 18.7cm. high. (Christie's) $1,496 £935

STONEWARE

Late 17th century Westerwald stoneware square flask, 22.5cm. high. (Christie's) $708 £440

A stoneware pinched and coiled bulbous vase by Betty Glandino, 28.4cm. high. (Christie's) $281 £176

A Pierre Fondu stoneware amphora vase, covered in an olive-brown and blue crystal-line glaze, 57.9cm. high. (Christie's) $1,082 £660

A tall flattened stoneware cylindrical vase by Joanna Constantinidis, 33.2cm. high. (Christie's) $264 £165

A stoneware dish by Ewen Henderson, with irregular rim, 35cm. wide. (Christie's) $528 £330

A stoneware asymmetrical sack-shaped vase by Ewen Henderson, 56cm. high. (Christie's) $1,760 £1,100

A St. Ives stoneware jug covered in a translucent inky-blue glaze, 19.2cm. high. (Christie's) $123 £77

A stoneware platter by Raymond Finch, decorated by Henry Bergen, Winch-combe Pottery seals, 39cm. diam. (Christie's) $1,056 £660

A stoneware jug by Janice Tchalenko, with pulled lip and strap handle, 24cm. high. (Christie's) $211 £132

A stoneware bowl by Kitaoji Rosanjin, covered in a finely crackled pale lavender translucent glaze with iron-brown rim, 25.2cm. diam. (Christie's) $5,984 £3,740

An unmarked stoneware butter crock with cover, American, circa 1850, 8¼in. diam. (Robt. W. Skinner Inc.) $450 £267

One of three early 18th century Westerwald salt-glazed stoneware rectangular inkwells, 14cm. wide. (Christie's) $566 £352

A decorated stoneware vase, attributed to Russell G. Crook, 1906-12, 9½in. high. (Robt. W. Skinner Inc.) $750 £446

A stoneware vase by John Ward, with oval undulating rim, 18.7cm. high. (Christie's) $158 £99

A narrow waved stoneware vase by Joanna Constantinidis, with sagged rim, 1984, 46.3cm. high. (Christie's) $616 £385

A large stoneware vase, by Seth Cardew, Wenford Bridge seals, circa 1984, 61cm. high. (Christie's) $302 £198

A saltglazed stoneware two-gallon batter jug, by Cowden & Wilcox, Penn., 1870-90, 11in. high. (Christie's) $1,870 £1,055

A stoneware elongated oviform vase by Shoji Hamada, 27.9cm. high. (Christie's) $1,760 £1,100

STONEWARE

A stoneware saltglazed deep bowl with flared rim by Shoji Hamada, 28.2cm. diam. (Christie's)
$2,112 £1,320

A three-gallon saltglaze stoneware crock, J. & E. Norton, Bennington, Vt., 10½in. high. (Robt. W. Skinner Inc.) $700 £393

A stoneware globular vase by Ruth Duckworth, covered in streaked and run green, brown and copper-red glazes, 23.9cm. high. (Christie's)
$528 £330

A stoneware vase, by John Ward, impressed JW seal, circa 1984, 22.4cm. high. (Christie's) $336 £220

A brown stoneware torso by Roger Perkins, 74.2cm. high. (Christie's) $281 £176

A stoneware oviform jar by Charles Vyse, 1928, 17cm. high. (Christie's) $252 £165

Two gallon Bennington stoneware jar, circa 1855, 13¾in. high. (Robt. W. Skinner Inc.)
$1,500 £842

'The Bull', a Poole pottery stoneware figure, designed by Harold and Phoebe Stabler, 33.5cm. high. (Christie's) $252 £165

An English saltglazed brown stoneware tobacco jar, modelled as a bear, probably early 19th century, 21cm. high. (Phillips) $4,202 £2,200

A saltglazed stoneware three-gallon jar, by Cowden & Wilcox, Penn., 1870-90, 12in. high. (Christie's) $418 £235

A stoneware jug by Thomas Samuel Haile, with strap handle, 19.9cm. high. (Christie's) $528 £330

'J. & E. Norton, Bennington, VT' two-gallon stoneware crock, 1850-59, 9¼in. high. (Robt. W. Skinner Inc.) $1,200 £714

A cobalt blue decorated and incised stoneware jug, New York, circa 1822, 13¾in. high. (Robt. W. Skinner Inc.) $21,000 £11,797

A stoneware bowl, by Eric James Mellon, dated 1982, 33.2cm. diam. (Christie's) $437 £286

One of two 19th century salt-glazed stoneware jugs, N. Carolina, 8½in. and 10½in. high. (Christie's) $770 £434

A saltglazed stoneware two-gallon jar, by G. A. Satterlee and M. Morey, 1861-85, and a two-gallon crock by P. Riedinger and A. Caire, 1857-78, 11½in. and 9½in. high. (Christie's) $385 £217

A large stoneware watercooler, double handled slightly ovoid form, America, 1866, 24¾in. high. (Robt. W. Skinner Inc.) $800 £476

A three-gallon saltglazed stoneware crock, J. & E. Norton, Bennington, Vt., 1850-59, 13½in. high. (Robt. W. Skinner Inc.) $1,500 £842

TERRACOTTA

A Cypriot terracotta chariot drawn by two horses, 7th-6th century B.C., 13cm. long. (Phillips) $656 £400

A terracotta figure of Eros, 4th-3rd century B.C., Boetia, 7.5cm. high. (Phillips) $426 £260

A Cypro-geometric bowl raised on three looped supports, circa 1700 B.C., 15cm. high. (Phillips) $1,230 £750

A 19th century French group of Bacchus and a Bacchante, cast from a model by Clodion, 33cm. high. (Christie's) $734 £440

A 19th century French terracotta bust of a little girl, attributed to Houdon, 39cm. high. (Christie's) $1,837 £1,100

A Cypriot terracotta equestrian figure, slight traces of red and black pigment, 7th-6th century B.C., 11.5cm. high. (Phillips) $311 £190

A Cypriot terracotta equestrian figure, 7th-6th century B.C., 15cm. high. (Phillips) $360 £220

A pair of 19th century French terracotta busts of 'L'Espiegle' and 'Le Printemps', signed J.-Bte-Carpeaux, 48cm. and 55cm. high. (Christie's) $5,143 £3,080

A terracotta figure of Eros, naked except for a drape across the shoulders, Boetia, 4th-3rd century B.C., 7cm. high. (Phillips) $328 £200

A Vienna (Dupaquier) covered 'pastetentopf' with loop handle, circa 1735, 15.5cm. wide. (Christie's)
$14,168 £8,800

A Vienna (Dupaquier) rect-angular casket and liner, circa 1728, in a contemporary fitted leather box, 16.5 x 12cm. (Christie's) $35,420 £22,000

A Vienna (Dupaquier) two-handled, double-lipped baroque moulded sauceboat painted in the Imari style, circa 1740, 24.5cm. wide. (Christie's)
$7,969 £4,950

Late 19th century 'Vienna' rectangular porcelain plaque, painted with three vestal virgins, 32 x 26cm. (Christie's) $1,285 £770

A Vienna (Dupaquier) cream-pot and cover painted by Johann P. Dannhoffer, circa 1725. (Christie's)
$5,313 £3,300

A 'Vienna' rectangular plaque painted by C. Meinelt after Murillo, signed and impressed blue enamelled beehive mark, circa 1880, 44 x 35cm. (Christie's) $16,533 £9,900

A pair of large Vienna-style ewer vases with gilt scrolled handles and ovoid bodies, 60cm. high. (Phillips) $4,008   £2,400

One of a set of six 'Vienna' porcelain plates, signed Wagner, 9½in. diam. (Capes Dunn) $3,043 £1,700

A Vienna Commedia dell'Arte group of Scaramouche and Pulchinella, circa 1750, 14.5cm. high. (Christie's)
$14,168 £8,800

WEDGWOOD

A rare Wedgwood 'Willow' lustre bowl, 23.5cm., Portland Vase mark, pattern Z5407. (Phillips) $495 £300

A Wedgwood majolica-ware three-piece strawberry set, 24.5cm., impressed Wedgwood, registration mark and GBX. (Phillips) $528 £320

A Wedgwood large octagonal Fairyland lustre bowl, 27.8cm. diam., Portland Vase mark and Z5125. (Phillips)
$1,567 £950

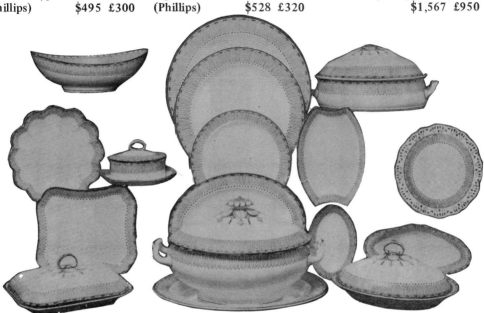

An extensive Wedgwood creamware dinner service, impressed Wedgwood marks 116 pieces. (Phillips) $10,725 £6,500

A Wedgwood majolica-ware 'Kate Greenaway' jardiniere, modelled as a lady's straw bonnet, 16.5cm., impressed Wedgwood and moulded registration mark. (Phillips)
$379 £230

A rare and important Wedgwood Sydney Cove medallion, titled below Etruria 1789, the reverse impressed, 5.7cm. overall diam. (Phillips)
$27,600 £15,000

A Wedgwood Fairyland lustre 'Malfrey Pot' and cover, 18cm. high, 26cm. diam., Portland Vase mark, Z5257, incised shape number 2308. (Phillips)
$907 £550

One of a pair of Wedgwood
dipped blue and white
jasper sphinx candlesticks,
circa 1810, 16.5cm. wide.
(Christie's) $4,235 £2,420

A Wedgwood pottery figure
of a bull designed by Arnold
Machin, 15½in. long.
(Christie's) $315 £176

A Wedgwood & Bentley
black basalt cylindrical inkwell, circa 1775, 7.5cm. diam.
(Christie's) $500 £286

A Wedgwood creamware oval
sauce tureen, cover and pierced
stand, painted in the manner of
James Bakewell, circa 1770,
the stand 26.5cm. wide.
(Christie's) $3,630 £2,200

A pair of mid 19th century
Wedgwood black basalt triton
candlesticks of conventional
type, 28cm. high. (Christie's)
$1,452 £880

A Wedgwood white biscuit
tripod vase and domed cover,
circa 1810, 25cm. high.
(Christie's) $1,925 £1,100

A Wedgwood Masonic
handled jug, white ground,
cobalt-blue neck and gilded
rim, circa 1935, 7in. high.
(Giles Haywood) $65 £40

A Wedgwood black basalt rectangular
plaque moulded with 'Death of a
Roman Warrior', circa 1800, 27 x
48.5cm. (Christie's) $3,085 £1,870

A Wedgwood 'Fairyland'
lustre vase and cover,
9¼in. high. (Christie's)
$1,969 £1,100

WEDGWOOD

Wedgwood Fairyland lustre footed bowl, 11in. diam. (Prudential Fine Art)
$1,567 £950

A creamware double rectangular tea caddy of Wedgwood/Whieldon type, circa 1760, 14.5cm. wide. (Christie's)
$2,722 £1,650

A Wedgwood black basalt encaustic-decorated pot-pourri vase, lid and pierced cover, circa 1820, 34cm. wide. (Christie's)
$1,815 £1,100

A Wedgwood & Bentley black basalt encaustic-decorated circular sugar bowl and cover, circa 1775, 11.5cm. diam. (Christie's) $2,904 £1,760

Two Wedgwood black basalt miniature busts of Homer and Aristophanes, circa 1785, 11cm. and 10cm. high. (Christie's) $2,502 £1,430

A Wedgwood solid pale-blue and white jasper cylindrical sugar bowl and cover, circa 1785, 10.5cm. diam. (Christie's) $673 £385

A Wedgwood & Bentley creamware large flower pot and stand, circa 1775, the stand 27cm. diam. (Christie's) $1,633 £990

Mid 19th century Wedgwood dipped lilac and white jasper centrepiece, 44.5cm. high. (Christie's) $3,657 £2,090

A Wedgwood Fairyland lustre black-ground small globular jar and cover, circa 1925, 8.5cm. high. (Christie's)
$2,359 £1,430

A rare and small Whieldon 'pear' teapot and cover, 8.5cm. high. (Phillips)
$11,408 £6,200

A Staffordshire creamware spirally moulded wall-pocket of Whieldon type, circa 1760, 21cm. high. (Christie's)
$871 £528

A creamware globular teapot and cover of Whieldon type with vine-stock spout, handle and finial, circa 1755, 11cm. high. (Christie's)
$871 £528

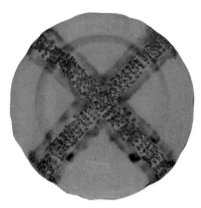

A creamware plate of Whieldon type, circa 1770, 24.5cm. diam. (Christie's) $1,633 £990

A Whieldon tortoiseshell coffee pot and cover, of baluster shape with domed cover, circa 1760. (Phillips)
$8,010 £4,500

A Staffordshire creamware pierced oval stand of Whieldon type, circa 1770, 24cm. wide. (Christie's)
$1,815 £1,100

A creamware globular teapot and cover of Whieldon type, circa 1760, 9.5cm. high. (Christie's) $1,597 £968

An Astbury/Whieldon glazed redware cylindrical mug with loop handle, 9.5cm. high. (Phillips)
$1,503 £900

A creamware miniature globular teapot and cover of Whieldon type, circa 1770, 8.5cm. high. (Christie's) $1,361 £825

WORCESTER

A large 'bow' vase, signed John Stinton, 30.5cm. high, shape no. 1428, date code for 1908. (Phillips)
$4,342 £2,600

Royal Worcester 'Sabrina' porcelain circular dished plate, signed R. Austin, 1929, 9.5in. diam. (Giles Haywood) $76 £40

A Grainger's Worcester pedestal ewer with a painted scene of swans, signed indistinctly, 10in. high. (Hetheringtons Nationwide)
$858 £520

An ovoid vase, the body well painted with two Highland cattle, signed H. Stinton, 21cm. high, shape no. 1762, date code for 1910. (Phillips)
$1,107 £580

Royal Worcester Hadley-style footed vase, designed as a jardiniere, 1906, 5in. high. (Giles Haywood)
$458 £240

A Royal Worcester porcelain jug (ice tusk), circa 1884, approx. 12in. tall. (G. A. Key)
$548 £310

Worcester porcelain jug, the blush ivory ground with hand-painted floral sprigs, circa 1902, 7in. high. (G. A. Key)
$346 £210

One of a pair of Grainger Worcester mugs with single spur handles, titled below painted panels, 'Drawing Cover' and 'The Death', 11.5cm. high. (Phillips)
$12,606 £6,600

A Dr. Wall Worcester quart mug with strap handle, circa 1770, 6.1/8in. high. (Robt. W. Skinner Inc.)
$275 £163

A Worcester yellow-ground honeycomb moulded oval dish, circa 1765, 30cm. wide. (Christie's) $23,100 £13,200

An 18th century Worcester blue and white teapot and cover decorated in underglaze blue with peonies. (Dee & Watkinson) $388 £240

A Chamberlains Worcester porcelain oval dish painted and gilded with 'Kylin' or 'Dragons in Compartments' pattern, 12½in. long, 9½in. wide. (Dacre, Son & Hartley) $1,122 £680

A Worcester sparrow-beak cream jug of pear shape, painted with the 'Arcade' pattern, 10cm. high, circa 1765-70. (Phillips) $734 £440

A Royal Worcester blue-ground three-piece garniture, decorated by Thomas Bott, the largest with TB monogram and 63, gilded by Josiah Davis, the largest 16in. high. (Christie's) $8,250 £4,714

A Royal Worcester two-handled, footed bulbous vase, by Harry Davis, model no. 1428, puce mark, 1932, 12in. high. (Giles Haywood) $10,027 £5,250

A Worcester blue-scale porcelain lobed circular plate, circa 1770, 19.5cm. diam. (Christie's) $1,361 £825

One of a pair of ovoid ewer-shaped vases, signed A. Shuck, 24cm. high, shape no. 1944, date codes for 1912. (Phillips) $2,387 £1,250

A Barr, Flight & Barr porcelain circular tureen and stand, the painted panel attributed to Thos. Baxter, 7in. high, 7½in. wide overall, circa 1810-15. (Dacre, Son & Hartley) $6,930 £4,200

WORCESTER

Worcester porcelain teapot, printed in a blue and white pattern of fence and tram-line design, circa 1770, 5½in. high. (G. A. Key) $619 £350

A Worcester shell-shaped pickle dish, circa 1755, 3.1/8in. wide. (Christie's) $831   £495

A Worcester creamboat of 'Chelsea Ewer' shape, circa 1765, 6.5cm. high. (Phillips) $1,035 £620

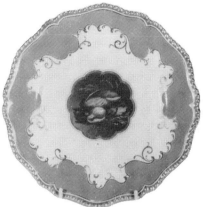

A Flight, Barr & Barr porcelain dessert plate with a central panel of painted shells, attributed to Smith, 8¼in. wide, circa 1813-19. (Dacre, Son & Hartley) $1,237 £750

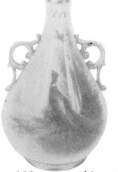

Royal Worcester china vase painted by Jas. Stinton, 5.75in. high, date code for 1909 and pattern no. 995. (Prudential Fine Art) $412 £250

A Grainger's Worcester porcelain tankard with boldy gilded borders, scrolling and handle, 5¼in. high, circa 1812-20. (Dacre, Son & Hartley) $1,980 £1,200

One of a pair of Worcester leaf dishes with green stalk handles, circa 1760, approx. 18cm. wide.(Christie's) $3,448 £2,090

A Royal Worcester footed pot-pourri, model no. 1286, black mark, signed R. Lewis, 10in. high. (Giles Haywood) $611 £320

A Worcester plate from The Duke of Gloucester Service, gold crescent mark, circa 1775, 22.5cm. diam. (Christie's) $23,595 £14,300

WORCESTER

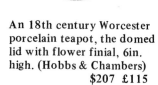

An early Worcester reeded coffee cup with a scroll handle, painted in Kakiemon style, circa 1753-55. (Phillips) $1,302 £780

One of a pair of Worcester Imari pattern leaf dishes, painted with The Kempthorne Pattern, circa 1770, 26.5cm. wide. (Christie's) $816 £495

An 18th century Worcester porcelain teapot, the domed lid with flower finial, 6in. high. (Hobbs & Chambers) $207 £115

A Worcester faceted part tea and coffee service painted with bouquets and scattered flowers and flower-sprays within gilt line rims, blue square seal marks, circa 1765, the teapot and sugar bowl painted by a different hand. (Christie's) $6,897 £4,180

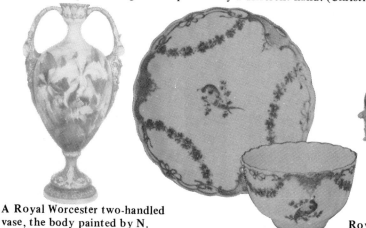

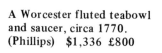

A Royal Worcester two-handled vase, the body painted by N. Roberts, signed, blue painted marks and date code for 1899, no. 2007, 49cm. high. (Christie's) $2,502 £1,430

A Worcester fluted teabowl and saucer, circa 1770. (Phillips) $1,336 £800

Royal Worcester two-handled footed bulbous vase, signed W. Hale, 1919, model no. 1428, 12in. high. (Giles Haywood) $5,921 £3,100

WORCESTER

An 18th century Worcester blue and white butter tub, cover and stand decorated in underglaze blue with roses and butterflies. (Dee & Atkinson) $388 £240

A Worcester faceted teapot, cover and stand, circa 1765, 14cm. high. (Christie's) $1,452 £880

A Worcester blue-scale bowl of Lady Mary Wortley Montagu pattern, painted in the atelier of James Giles, circa 1770, 16.5cm. diam. (Christie's) $998 £605

A Grainger, Lee & Co. Worcester tea service, painted in bright Imari style with panels of fences and foliage on blue and red grounds with zig-zag bands and flowerheads, pattern no. 575, some pieces with script marks. (Phillips) $1,503 £900

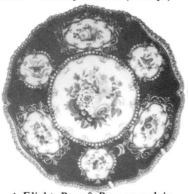

A Royal Worcester two-handled footed bulbous vase, by John Stinton, model no. 1428, puce mark, 1930, 12in. high. (Giles Haywood) $8,404 £4,400

A Flight, Barr & Barr porcelain dessert dish with paintings of flowers and butterflies, attributed to Henry Stinton, circa 1825, 10in. wide. (Dacre, Son & Hartley) $4,290 £2,600

A Worcester teapot and cover, circa 1758, 12.5cm. high. (Phillips) $2,171 £1,300

WORCESTER

One of a pair of Worcester blue-scale tapering hexagonal vases and covers, circa 1768, 28cm. and 29.5cm. high. (Christie's)
$23,595 £14,300

An 18th century Worcester porcelain dish decorated with a fable painting by Duvivier, 9½in. wide. (G. A. Key)
$858 £520

One of two Worcester porcelain mugs each with strap handle, open crescent mark to base, 3½in. high, circa 1760. (Lalonde Fine Art)
$396 £240

An early Worcester cream jug of pear shape with large sparrow-beak lip and scroll handle, 7cm. high, circa 1752-53. (Phillips)
$3,438 £1,800

One of a pair of Royal Worcester vases, date code for 1914, 10½in. high. (Reeds Rains) $599 £359

Royal Worcester flower bowl, shape no. 1713, green circle and crown mark, date code 1900, 9in. high. (Peter Wilson)
$680 £420

A Worcester 'blind earl' sweetmeat dish, painted in deep underglaze blue and with scattered insects, 15cm. long, crescent mark, circa 1765. (Phillips)
$3,915 £2,050

A Grainger's Worcester two-handled pedestal vase with landscaped decoration, signed J. Stinton, 11in. high. (Hetheringtons Nationwide)
$1,155 £700

Royal Worcester plate, signed James Stinton, puce mark, 1922, 10in. diam. (Giles Haywood) $248 £130

BRACKET CLOCKS

An 18th century mahogany bracket clock, the arched brass dial signed Sidney Smith, Sedgley, 48cm. high. (Phillips) $2,184 £1,300

A Regency 8-day striking twin fusee bracket clock in figured mahogany case, signed on dial Loof of Tunbridge Wells. (J. M. Welch & Son) $787 £480

A 19th century mahogany and brass mounted bracket clock, the bell topped case with carrying handle, 39cm. high. (Phillips) $1,596 £950

Mid 19th century George II ebony quarter-repeating bracket clock, signed Rich'd. Gregg, London, 13in. high. (Christie's) $5,280 £3,227

A Victorian walnut bracket clock, the case in Gothic style, 2ft.2in. high. (Phillips) $660 £400

Georgian style inlaid mahogany mantel or bracket clock with 8-day striking movement, the dial inscribed Finnigans Ltd., Manchester, 12½in. high. (Capes Dunn) $465 £260

A George III mahogany bracket timepiece, signed in the arch Perigal, Coventry Street, London, 26cm. high. (Phillips) $1,764 £1,050

A Victorian mahogany chiming bracket clock with chime/silent and selection of 8-bell or Westminster chime, 26in. high. (Christie's) $2,816 £1,760

A George III mahogany bracket clock, the circular enamel dial signed Biddell, London, 53cm. high. (Phillips) $2,352 £1,400

BRACKET CLOCKS

An early George III faded mahogany striking bracket clock, the dial signed Henry Sanderson, 18in. high. (Christie's) $5,808 £3,520

A 19th century bracket clock with 8-day movement, 29½in. high. (Dacre, Son & Hartley) $1,312 £800

A George III ebonised striking bracket clock for the Spanish market by Higgs y Diego Evans, 18¼in. high. (Christie's) $3,085 £1,870

A Regency Gothic mahogany bracket clock, the painted dial signed Manners & Sons, Stamford, 21½in. high. (Christie's) $1,542 £935

A Queen Anne ebonised bracket clock, the 6¼in. sq. dial signed James Tunn, London, 15in. high. (Christie's) $2,722 £1,650

Late 19th century mahogany 8-day domed bracket clock with silvered dial, 12in. high. (Giles Haywood) $393 £240

A Charles II ebonised striking bracket clock with 6¾in. sq. dial, backplate signed Nathaniel Hodges, 13¾in. high. (Christie's) $5,808 £3,520

A Charles II ebonised turntable bracket clock, by E. Bird, London, 19in. high. (Christie's) $11,797 £7,150

A William III ebonised striking bracket clock with gilt metal repousse basket top, dial signed Cha. Greeton, 14½in. high. (Christie's) $4,537 £2,750

BRACKET CLOCKS

An early Georgian ebonised bracket timepiece with gilt brass handle, the backplate signed Dan. Quare, London, 12¾in. high. (Christie's) $5,082 £3,080

An early George III dark japanned musical chiming bracket clock for the Turkish market, dial signed Edward Pistor, London, 23½in. high. (Christie's) $5,808 £3,520

A George III mahogany striking bracket clock, dial signed Devereux Bowly, London, 20in. high. (Christie's) $5,445 £3,300

A George II fruitwood striking miniature bracket clock with carrying handle, the backplate signed Wm. Hughes, 10in. high. (Christie's) $8,712 £5,280

A Charles II ebonised striking bracket clock, dial signed J. Windmills, London, 14¼in. high. (Christie's) $8,167 £4,950

A George II ebonised quarter striking bracket clock, the dial signed Jams. Snelling, London, 14¾in. high. (Christie's) $5,082 £3,080

A Queen Anne ebony striking and quarter repeating bracket clock, signed Sam. Aldworth, 14in. high. (Christie's) $8,167 £4,950

A George III mahogany striking bracket clock, signed Eardley Norton, London, 15¾in. high. (Christie's) $10,890 £6,600

A Queen Anne kingwood striking bracket clock, the dial signed Cha. Gretton, 14in. high. (Christie's) $29,040 £17,600

BRACKET CLOCKS

A George III satinwood bracket clock, the movement signed Tregent, Strand, London, 21in. high. (Christie's) $5,119 £2,860

A 19th century mahogany cased 8-day bracket clock, the silvered dial signed James Doig of Edinburgh, 16in. high. (J. M. Welch & Son) $273 £180

A Georgian green lacquered bracket clock, signed Stepn. Rimbault, London, 1ft.8in. high. (Phillips) $2,805 £1,700

An early 18th century ebonised bracket clock with brass dial, by Thomas Gardner, London, 18½in. high. (Graves Son & Pilcher) $2,058 £1,150

An 18th century C. European red lacquered quarter chiming bracket clock, the backplate signed Iohan Maurer in Prag, 57cm. high. (Phillips) $8,736 £5,200

A Victorian mahogany bracket clock, the movement by Streeter & Co., 18 New Bond Street, London, 15in. wide, 29in. high. (Anderson & Garland) $1,770 £1,000

A 19th century ebonised and brass mounted bracket clock, the silvered dial signed Payne, 163 New Bond St., London, 1ft.2½in. high. (Phillips) $1,650 £1,000

Mid 18th century George II ebonised quarter-chiming bracket clock, signed B. Gray, London, 15½in. high. (Christie's) $8,250 £5,042

A walnut chiming bracket clock, the three train fusee movement striking quarter hours on 8 bells or four gongs, 15in. high. (Christie's) $2,112 £1,320

BRACKET CLOCKS

A George IV mahogany lyre-form musical bracket clock, signed Frodsham, London, 37in. high. (Christie's) $6,600 £4,033

A William III quarter repeating ebony bracket clock, signed Claudius Du Chesne, Londini Fecit, 16½in. high. (Christie's) $19,694 £10,475

A Georgian mahogany quarter chiming bracket clock, the painted dial signed Geo. Wilkins, Soho, 2ft.2in. high. (Phillips) $2,392 £1,450

An 18th century ebony bracket clock, signed James Tregent, Leicester Square, London, 1ft.5½in. high. (Phillips) $4,125 £2,500

A late 17th century ebony 'double six hour' grande sonnerie bracket clock, the 6½in. square dial now inscribed Tompion Londini, 35.5cm. high. (Phillips) $15,120 £9,000

A Regency mahogany bracket clock, the arched brass dial signed Aynsth. & Jono. Thwaites, London, 1ft.6½in. high. (Phillips) $4,620 £2,800

A Queen Anne ebonised bracket clock, the dial signed Dan. Quare, London, 20in. high. (Christie's) $15,427 £9,350

A Victorian pollard oak Gothic Revival bracket clock, the dial signed Muller, Twickenham, 42in. high. (Reeds Rains) $1,169 £700

A Victorian director's bracket clock with 8-day fusee movement chiming on eight bells, 30in. high. (Hy. Duke & Son) $2,700 £1,500

CARRIAGE CLOCKS

A porcelain panelled carriage clock, the movement with the trademark of J. Dejardin, 7in. high. (Christie's) $4,180 £2,550

A gilt brass porcelain mounted striking carriage clock with porcelain dial, stamp of Achille Brocot, 6¼in. high. (Christie's) $3,085 £1,870

A lacquered brass carriage clock, signed on the dial in cyrillic, A. M. Geracimov, St. Petersburg, 8in. high. (Christie's) $1,320 £806

A lacquered brass petite sonnerie carriage clock, with the trademark of Francois-Arsene Margaine, 7in. high. (Christie's) $1,650 £1,008

A shagreen carriage clock of humpback form, dial signed Jump Paris 93 Mount Street (London), 7in. high. (Christie's) $1,542 £935

A 19th century French brass carriage clock, the lever movement striking on a gong with alarm and bearing the Drocourt trademark, 16.5cm. high. (Phillips) $873 £520

A gilt brass carriage clock with calendar and alarm, circa 1845, 7½in. high. (Christie's) $1,540 £941

A brass calendar carriage timepiece, enamel dial with chapter disc above gilt mask, 4¾in. high. (Christie's) $363 £220

A gilt brass and enamel striking carriage clock with uncut bimetallic balance to silvered lever platform, 5½in. high. (Christie's) $2,178 £1,320

CARRIAGE CLOCKS

A gilt brass porcelain mounted striking carriage clock, the dial and side panels painted in the Sevres style, 5½in. high. (Christie's)
$5,445   £3,300

A gilt brass grande-sonnerie calendar carriage clock with uncut compensated balance to the silvered lever platform, stamp of Drocourt, 6½in. high. (Christie's)
$6,352   £3,850

A gilt brass carriage clock with engraved side panels, signed Paul Buhre, St. Petersburg, the movement by F.-A. Margaine, 7in. high. (Christie's) $3,300   £2,016

A 19th century brass carriage clock with petit sonnerie and alarm movement, the enamel dial signed Dent, Paris, 4½in. high. (J. M. Welch & Son)
$927   £610

A miniature oval carriage timepiece with white enamel dial, 3in. high. (Christie's)
$704   £440

A grande sonnerie striking carriage clock, the white enamel dial signed A. Jackemann, Paris, 6in. high. (Christie's) $2,112   £1,320

A 19th century French gilt brass and porcelain mounted carriage clock, 18cm. high. (Phillips) $3,528   £2,100

A gilt brass carriage clock with gilt platform to lever escapement, 6¾in. high, including handle. (Christie's)
$880   £537

A gilt brass grande sonnerie carriage clock, 7½in. high, including handle. (Christie's)
$1,430   £874

CARRIAGE CLOCKS

A brass and glass panelled
carriage clock, dial inscribed
'Aird & Thomson, Glasgow',
5½in. high. (G. A. Key)
$595 £340

A 19th century French gilt
brass miniature carriage
timepiece, the lever movement with enamel dial,
3¾in. high, together with
a travelling case. (Phillips)
$1,452 £880

Large early English fusee
carriage clock with silvered
dial, by G. & W. Yonge,
London, 5½in. high. (G. A.
Key) $1,750 £1,000

A gilt brass quarter striking
carriage clock with uncut
compensated balance to
lever platform, 5in. high.
(Christie's) $998 £605

A 19th century French brass
carriage clock, 7in. high,
together with a leather travelling case. (Phillips)
$825 £500

An English petit sonnerie
carriage clock with white
enamel dial inscribed Lund
& Blockley, 6in. high.
(Graves Son & Pilcher)
$3,401 £1,900

A French gilt brass carriage
clock, the dial and side panels
decorated with scenes of
young couples, 7in. high.
(Phillips) $1,402 £850

A 19th century French gilt
brass and porcelain mounted
grande sonnerie carriage clock,
with trademark P.M., 18cm.
high. (Phillips) $7,728 £4,600

A 19th century French brass
carriage clock, the lever movement
striking on a gong, with push repeat
and with the Margaine trademark
on the backplate, 7¼in. high.
(Phillips) $858 £520

CARRIAGE CLOCKS

A French 19th century gilt brass carriage clock, the lever movement striking on a gong and bearing the Drocourt trademark, 7in. high. (Phillips) $1,402 £850

A gilt brass striking carriage clock, the backplate stamped J. Klaftenburger, 5¼in. high. (Christie's) $3,085 £1,870

A 19th century French miniature brass carriage time-piece, the lever movement bearing the Margaine trade-mark, 9.5cm. high. (Phillips) $672 £400

An ornate gilt repeating carriage clock, signed Bolviller a Paris, 6¼in. high. (Christie's) $1,322 £715

A quarter-repeating and cloisonne enamel carriage clock, 3in. high. (Christie's) $5,808 £3,300

A gilt brass bottom-wind striking carriage clock with split bimetallic balance to silvered levered platform, dial signed Le Roy et fils (etc.), 5½in. high. (Christie's) $871 £528

A 19th century French gilt brass grande sonnerie carriage clock, the lever movement striking on two gongs with push repeat, 20cm. high. (Phillips) $2,352 £1,400

A petite-sonnerie repeating and alarm carriage clock, with Arabic numerals and signed A H Rodanet, Paris, 6in. high. (Christie's) $1,424 £770

A 19th century French gilt brass carriage clock, the lever movement striking on a gong with push repeat, 19cm. high. (Phillips) $924 £550

297

CLOCK SETS

A French gilt marble and gilt metal garniture, with matching three-arm candelabra, 18in. high. (Christie's) $1,980 £1,100

A French veined marble garniture, 17in. high. (Christie's) $752 £418

A good ormolu and porcelain garniture, 18in. high. (Christie's) $2,772 £1,540

A French 19th century brass, enamel and porcelain mounted clock garniture, signed Lefranc, 1ft.3in. high, together with a pair of side urns. (Phillips) $2,722 £1,650

Late 19th century gilt metal clock set of Renaissance style, the clock 28in. high, the candelabra 39½in. high. (Christie's) $3,630 £2,200

An unusual 19th century enamelled and gilt brass 'Gothick' chamber clock and candlesticks, clock 22in. high. (Christie's) $5,500 £3,247

LANTERN CLOCKS

A brass lantern clock, the dial with brass chapter signed Wilmshurst, Odiham, 1ft.3in. high, together with an oak wall bracket. (Phillips) $1,732 £1,050

A French brass lantern clock, the circular chased dial with enamel numerals, 41cm. high. (Phillips) $1,008 £600

A brass lantern clock, 39.5cm. high (probably 17th century). (Phillips) $3,325 £1,900

A George II small brass lantern clock with silent escapement, chapter ring signed John Fletcher, 9in. high.(Christie's) $1,633 £990

A brass lantern clock, signed Chr. Gould, Londoni Fecit., late 17th century, 15in. high. (Christie's) $3,850 £2,273

A Georgian brass lantern clock, made for the Turkish market, signed Jno. Parks, London, 1ft.2½in. high. (Phillips) $990 £600

An early brass lantern clock, signed on the fret, Richard Beck, near Ye French Church, Londini, mid-17th century, 17½in. high. (Christie's) $5,060 £2,684

A Georgian brass miniature lantern clock made for the Turkish market, signed Robt. Ward, London, 5½in. high. (Phillips) $2,145 £1,300

A brass lantern clock with alarm, unsigned, 17th century, with restorations, 14½in. (Christie's) $2,860 £1,688

LONGCASE CLOCKS

Late 19th century mahogany 8-day rack striking longcase clock, by Seddon & Moss. (Peter Wilson) $5,984 £3,400

A William III walnut and marquetry longcase clock, the 12in. sq. dial signed John Marshall, 7ft.1in. high. (Christie's) $14,520 £8,800

Scottish 19th century mahogany longcase clock by D. Robinson, Airdrie, 7ft. tall. (Chancellors Hollingsworths) $1,472 £920

A George III mahogany musical longcase clock for the German market, the dial signed Jos. Herring, 8ft.11in. high overall.(Christie's) $14,520 £8,800

An 18th century walnut longcase clock, the 11in. square dial signed Jn°. Wise, London, 2.10m. high. (Phillips) $2,688 £1,600

Late 18th century oak and walnut crossbanded longcase clock, by Thos. Shaw, Lancaster, 88in. high. (Prudential Fine Art) $825 £500

Mid 17th century oak longcased 8-day clock, maker Wm. Webb, Wellington, 6ft.6in. high. (Giles Haywood) $1,312 £800

A reproduction longcase clock. (Miller & Co.) $2,937 £1,650

LONGCASE CLOCKS

A Georgian mahogany longcase clock, the dial with subsidiary seconds, 8ft. high. (Christie's) $5,082 £3,080

Westminster and Whittington mahogany longcase clock with brass and silver dial. (Ball & Percival) $3,444 £2,100

Early 19th century Federal painted tall-case clock, possibly Berks County, Penn., 96in. high. (Christie's) $2,530 £1,427

A Federal mahogany inlaid tall case clock, Mass., circa 1790, 91in. high. (Robt. W. Skinner Inc.) $7,000 £4,375

A George III mahogany regulator, the 10in. dial signed Holmes, London, 5ft.11½in. high. (Phillips) $9,075 £5,500

A large Regina oak longcase 15½in. disc musical box clock, with eighty-six discs, 252cm. high, circa 1900. (Phillips) $5,760 £3,600

A floral marquetry longcase clock, the dial signed Thos. Bradford, 6ft.6in. high. (Christie's) $12,100 £7,395

A Georgian mahogany longcase clock, signed Williams, Preston, 7ft. 6½in. high. (Phillips) $4,290 £2,600

A George III maho-
gany longcase clock,
the 13in. brass dial
signed Samuel Young,
Bonebury, 7ft.9in.
high. (Phillips)
$4,950 £3,000

A small oak 30-hour
striking longcase clock,
the 11in. brass dial by
Sam Hanley, circa
1750. (Peter Wilson)
$1,539 £950

A Georgian walnut
and inlaid longcase
clock, signed Jon.
Sales, Dublin, 8ft.
5½in. high.
(Phillips)
$3,696 £2,400

A George III maho-
gany longcase clock,
the dial signed Chas.
Cabrier, 7ft.11in.
high. (Christie's)
$7,260 £4,400

A carved oak longcase
clock, signed Edw.
Whitehead, Wetherby,
86in. high. (Christie's)
$1,056 £660

A 19th century maho-
gany regulator, by
Hepting, Stirling, 75in.
high. (Reeds Rains)
$1,068 £640

An Arts & Crafts oak
tallcase clock, by the
Colonial Mfg. Co.,
Zeeland, Michigan,
circa 1914, 84in.
high. (Robt. W.
Skinner Inc.)
$2,000 £1,081

An early 18th century
walnut and panel mar-
quetry longcase clock,
the 11in. square brass
dial signed Thos.
Stubbs, London,
2.10m. high.(Phillips)
$19,320 £11,500

LONGCASE CLOCKS

A Regency mahogany longcase clock, the 12in. silvered dial signed Grant, London, 7ft. high. (Phillips) $6,270 £3,800

An 18th century burr walnut longcase clock, the dial inscribed Robt. Maisley, London, 7ft. 6in. high. (Parsons, Welch & Cowell) $5,544 £3,300

A Georgian mahogany musical quarter chiming longcase clock, signed J. Cooke, Cambridge, 8ft.2½in. high. (Phillips) $4,620 £2,800

A longcase clock, by Tomlinson, London, with 8-day bell-striking movement, 76in. high. (Hy. Duke & Son) $2,430 £1,350

A Black Forest organ clock, the 24-key movement with thirty-six wood pipes, eight-air barrel and painted dial, 97in. high. (Christie's) $3,564 £2,200

An 18th century mahogany longcase clock, the 12in. brass dial signed Philip Lloyd, Bristol, 2.28m. high. (Phillips) $4,704 £2,800

An oak longcase clock, the dial signed Creighton B-Mena No. 120, 91in. high. (Christie's) $880 £550

An arabesque marquetry longcase clock, signed Rich. Colston, London, circa 1710, 7ft.4in. high. (Christie's) $11,550 £7,059

Late 18th century 30-hour oak long-cased clock, maker John Kent, Monmouth, circa 1790. (Giles Haywood) $369 £225

A Federal inlaid mahogany tall case clock, dial signed by David Wood, circa 1790, 90in. high. (Christie's) $33,000 £19,951

A late Stuart walnut and marquetry longcase clock with 11in. sq. dial, 7ft.0½in. high. (Christie's) $17,242 £10,450

A Federal cherry inlaid tall case clock, E. New Hampshire, circa 1800, 94in. high. (Robt. W. Skinner Inc.) $7,000 £4,166

A Federal mahogany inlaid tall case clock, by Samuel Foster, New Hampshire, 1798, 86in. high. (Robt. W. Skinner Inc.) $14,000 £8,333

A late 17th century walnut and panel marquetry longcase clock, the 10in. brass dial signed Bird, London, 6ft.8½in. high. (Phillips) $18,975 £11,500

An L. & J. G. Stickley tall case clock, signed with red handcraft decal, circa 1908, 81in. high. (Robt. W. Skinner Inc.) $15,000 £8,928

An 18th century oak longcase clock with brass and silvered dial, maker J. Barrow, London. (Dee & Atkinson) $1,620 £1,000

LONGCASE CLOCKS

A George I month-going walnut longcase clock, the chapter ring signed John May, 100in. high. (Christie's)
$9,982 £6,050

A late Stuart walnut and marquetry long-case clock, the 10¾in. sq. dial signed Fro-manteel, 7ft.11½in. high. (Christie's)
$23,595 £14,300

A George III maho-gany longcase clock, dial signed Joseph Nardin, London, 6ft. high. (Christie's)
$5,082 £3,080

A Pennsylvania Chip-pendale inlaid walnut tallcase clock, 88in. high. (Christie's)
$4,400 £2,483

A Chippendale walnut tall case clock, dial signed by Johnson, London, case probably Penn., 1770-90, 92in. high. (Christie's)
$2,420 £1,463

A mahogany longcase sidereal regulator with break circuit work, signed Wm. Bond & Sons, Boston, circa 1858, 64½in. high. (Christie's)
$28,600 £17,480

An 18th century walnut month going longcase clock, the dial signed Christop Gould Londini fecit, 6ft.10in. high. (Phillips)
$5,775 £3,500

A Georgian maho-gany quarter chiming longcase clock, the 12in. dial signed Wm. Haughton, London, 2.46m. high. (Phillips)
$6,720 £4,000

LONGCASE CLOCKS

Chippendale style mahogany eight-day longcase clock. (John Hogbin & Son)
$3,690 £2,250

A George II 8-day mahogany longcase clock, by Daniel Ray, Manningtree, 88in. high. (Lacy Scott)
$4,125 £2,500

Longcase clock with bombe marquetry case, enamel and brass dial. (Ball & Percival)
$4,756 £2,900

A painted pine tall case clock, by Silas Hoadley, Conn., circa 1825, 93½in. high. (Robt. W. Skinner Inc.)
$9,000 £5,357

An early 18th century walnut and panel marquetry longcase clock, signed J. Windmills, London, 7ft.2in. high. (Phillips)
$14,850 £9,000

A mahogany longcase clock, the brass dial inscribed Maple & Co. Ltd., London, 7ft. 11in. high. (Parsons, Welch & Cowell)
$1,142 £680

A mahogany granddaughter longcase clock with 7in. brass dial, 59½in. high. (Christie's)
$2,816 £1,760

A George III oak cased 8-day striking longcase clock, the dial signed J. Marr of Retford. (J. M. Welch & Son)
$1,018 £670

LONGCASE CLOCKS

Early 19th century
painted and carved
tallcase clock, Penn.,
98in. high. (Christie's)
$18,700 £10,553

Early 19th century
Lancashire maho-
gany longcase clock,
94½in. high. (Pru-
dential Fine Art)
$1,980 £1,200

A Federal maple tall
case clock, by Silas
Hoadley, circa 1820,
81in. high. (Robt. W.
Skinner Inc.)
$1,800 £1,125

A George II maho-
gany longcase clock,
the dial signed Christo.
Goddard, 8ft.5in. high.
(Christie's)
$4,719 £2,860

A Pennsylvania Chip-
pendale walnut tall-
case clock, the dial
signed C. Warner,
91in. high.
(Christie's)
$3,960 £2,234

An 18th century
Dutch oak longcase
clock, signed De
Wancker TotLoo,
98in. high.
(Christie's)
$1,362 £770

Art Nouveau mahogany tall
case clock, late 19th century,
by Gerr Suss, Hamburg,
96½in. high. (Robt. W.
Skinner. Inc.) $1,750 £930

A mid Georgian maho-
gany longcase clock,
inscribed Andrew
Reed, London.
(Locke & England)
$3,586 £2,200

Kneeling girl with clock, a bronze and ivory figure cast after a model by F. Preiss, 54.4cm. high. (Christie's) $14,071 £8,580

A Sevres pattern gilt bronze mantel clock, the movement by Gasnier a Paris, circa 1875, 41cm. wide. (Christie's) $1,361 £825

A Charles X ormolu mantel clock with circular dial signed 'Guyerde(?) aine Paris', 12in. wide. (Christie's) $1,102 £660

A George III giltwood mantel clock, the associated George I watch movement by William Webster, 13in. high. (Christie's) $1,623 £990

A George III ormolu mantel clock for the Oriental market, the dial signed W. Mahr, 19in. high. (Christie's) $7,260 £4,400

A Charles X ormolu and malachite mantel clock, the dial flanked by the brothers Horatii taking their oath, after J-L David, 21½in. wide. (Christie's) $6,980 £4,180

An Ato Art Deco table clock with a pair of bronze owls perched on top, 41.5cm. high. (Christie's) $811 £495

An early Victorian maple wood lancet mantel time-piece, the dial with inscription Thos. Cole, London, 10in. high. (Christie's) $2,178 £1,320

A Charles X ormolu and bronze mantel clock with silvered dial, 16in. high. (Christie's) $1,653 £990

308

MANTEL CLOCKS

Late 19th century Sevres pattern pink-ground porcelain gilt bronze mounted mantel clock, 34cm. high. (Christie's) $1,285 £770

A silvered bronze mantel clock, by Edgar Brandt, 30.6cm. high. (Christie's) $5,051 £3,080

A Louis Philippe ormolu mantel clock, the silvered dial signed A. C. Decauville A Paris, 24½in. high. (Christie's) $2,204 £1,320

An automaton clock in the form of a waterwheel in brickwork surround, 16in. high. (Christie's) $7,260 £4,400

A French brass four-glass clock with perpetual calendar, the calendar dial signed Achille Brocot, 13in. high. (Christie's) $4,900 £2,970

A Louis XVI ormolu and terracotta mantel clock, the dial signed Sotiau A Paris, with figures of Minerva and attendants, 18in. wide. (Christie's) $4,592 £2,750

A Charles X ormolu mantel clock with enamel dial surmounted by a bust of Aristotle flanked by a cherub, 19½in. high. (Christie's) $1,652 £990

A silvered bronze Art Deco table clock, signed R. Terras, 34.5cm. high. (Christie's) $1,623 £990

A Charles X bronze and ormolu mantel clock with circular dial surmounted by Cato amidst the ruins of Carthage, 17½in. wide. (Christie's) $2,020 £1,210

309

MANTEL CLOCKS

A Regency rosewood and brass inlaid mantel timepiece, the silvered dial signed Carpenter, London, 9½in. high. (Phillips) $3,135 £1,900

A 19th century French ormolu and bronze mantel clock, the gilt dial with enamel numerals, 1ft.10in. high. (Phillips) $1,320 £800

A 19th century French rosewood floral inlaid classical shaped 8-day mantel clock, 10in. high. (Giles Haywood) $278 £170

An ormolu mantel clock of Louis XVI style, the dial signed Antide-Janvier a Paris in oval vase-shaped case, 20in. high. (Christie's) $1,468 £825

'Inseparables', a Lalique square-shaped clock with blue and white painted dial, 11cm. high. (Christie's) $1,984 £1,210

An ormolu mantel clock of rococo style, 29in. high, 19½in. wide. (Christie's) $2,020 £1,210

A 19th century mahogany and brass inlaid mantel clock, the circular painted dial signed Condliff, Liverpool, 35cm.high. (Phillips) $1,176 £700

A Continental spelter mystery timepiece on a rectangular base, 32cm. high. (Phillips) $638 £380

An Austrian silver plated quarter chiming mantel clock, signed Carl Wolfe in Wien, 9½in. high. (Phillips) $693 £420

MANTEL CLOCKS

A 19th century French ormolu and porcelain mantel clock, 1ft.3in. high. (Phillips) $1,188 £720

An enamelled silver grande sonnerie world time table clock, signed Patek Philippe & Co., Geneve, 7½in. diam. (Christie's) $38,500 £23,531

A Paris (Jacob Petit) blue-ground clockcase and stand, the movement by Hrr. Marc a Paris, circa 1835, 34cm. high. (Christie's) $871 £528

A 19th century gilt bronze mantel timepiece, the silvered dial signed for Hunt & Roskell, London, 1ft.7¼in. high. (Phillips) $4,950 £3,000

An ormolu mantel clock with enamel dial and drum-shaped case, 12in. wide. (Christie's) $580 £352

An Empire ormolu and bronze mantel clock of lyre shape supported upon seated griffins, 10½in. high. (Christie's) $1,562 £935

A Regency mahogany and brass inlaid mantel time-piece, the circular enamel dial signed Scott, Horl^r to H.R.H. The Duke of Kent, 674, 26cm. high. (Phillips) $806 £480

An automaton clock in the form of a ship's bridge, 12½in. high. (Christie's) $3,465 £1,980

A Regency mahogany and brass inlaid mantel timepiece with circular enamel dial (damaged), 9½in. high. (Phillips) $429 £260

MANTEL CLOCKS

A George III ormolu mounted timepiece clock, by James Tregent, London, in the style of M. Boulton, 12½in. high. (Christie's) $11,797 £7,150

A 19th century French ormolu and porcelain mantel clock, the square dial signed Klaftenburger, London, together with a giltwood base, 46cm. high. (Phillips) $873 £520

An Austrian 19th century silver and enamel timepiece, with polychrome champleve dial, 18cm. high. (Phillips) $1,596 £950

A 19th century black slate mantel timepiece, signed Payne, 163 New Bond Street, 22cm. high. (Phillips) $429 £260

A Black Forest trumpeter clock in walnut case, 39in. high. (Christie's) $3,385 £2,090

A late 19th century walnut mantel clock, the dial signed Chas. Frodsham, Clockmaker to the Queen, No. 2057, 30cm. high. (Phillips) $1,260 £750

An Arts & Crafts mahogany mantel clock with bevelled glass, circa 1900, 12in. high. (Robt. W. Skinner Inc.) $500 £297

A Federal mahogany pillar and scroll clock, by E. Terry & Sons, Conn., circa 1820, 29in. high. (Robt. W. Skinner Inc.) $1,500 £937

Sterling silver 8-day travelling clock, Swiss movement 'Black Starr & Frost, New York', 4 x 2in. (Giles Haywood) $229 £140

MANTEL CLOCKS

A German gilt metal monstrance clock, the reverse with astrolabic dial, movement late 19th century, 18in. high. (Christie's)
$17,242 £10,450

A mid 19th century French ormolu and Sevres panel mantel clock, under glass dome, 18in. high. (G. A. Key) $840 £475

A Charles X vase-shaped mantel clock with enamel dial and swan-neck handles, 13in. high. (Christie's)
$1,377 £825

A 19th century French brass mantel clock, the enamel dial signed for Payne, Tunbridge Wells, 1ft.8in. high. (Phillips) $2,062 £1,250

A French champleve enamel four glass clock, the 8-day movement striking on bell, 13in. high. (Christie's)
$968 £605

A Victorian rosewood four-glass mantel clock, the back-plate signed French Royal Exchange, London, 9½in. high. (Christie's)
$2,722 £1,650

A 19th century French brass and porcelain mantel clock, 36cm. high. (Phillips)
$2,856 £1,700

A modern Swiss singing bird box in engine-turned lacquered brass case, surmounted by a French 8-day alarm clock, 6in. high, with travelling case. (Christie's) $2,138 £1,320

A Charles X ormolu mantel clock with circular dial and striking movement in a foliate drum case, 19in. high. (Christie's) $1,469 £880

MANTEL CLOCKS

A travelling clock in scroll and flower embossed silver case, by Charles James Fox, London, 1899, 3¼in. overall. (Dreweatt Neate) $710 £380

A Victorian lacquered brass mantel clock with French movement by F. Martie, 16in. high, 22in. wide. (Capes Dunn) $751 £420

A French ormolu and Sevres style panel clock, signed on the dial Lagarde A Paris, 49cm. high. (Wellington Salerooms) $4,368 £2,600

A large Victorian chiming mantel clock with brass and silver dial, 28in. high. (Ball & Percival) $1,584 £900

A French four-glass clock, the dial with enamelled swags above a mercury double chamber pendulum, the top and base of onyx, 27cm. high. (David Lay) $864 £480

A Swiss travelling clock, the enamel face inscribed 'Goldsmiths and Silversmiths Co. Ltd.', London import marks for 1913, 2½ x 1¼in. wide. (Dreweatt Neate) $1,122 £600

Late 18th century George III gilt and cut glass mounted floral painted quarter-chiming musical bracket clock for the Turkish market, signed Benj. Barber, London, 37½in. high. (Christie's) $52,800 £32,271

A French ormolu 8-day mantel clock with porcelain dial, circa 1870, 17in. high, on serpentine shaped base with glass dome. (Lacy Scott) $594 £360

Victorian 'ginger bread' framed shelf clock with an Ansonia Clock Co. striking movement. (G. A. Key) $112 £68

MANTEL CLOCKS

A Regency white marble and gilt bronze mantel timepiece, the gilt dial signed Viner, London, 8in. high. (Phillips) $742 £450

An Empire ormolu mounted clock, the dial within the wheel of Diana's chariot, 21¾in. wide. (Christie's) $2,349 £1,320

A 19th century French ormolu and porcelain mantel clock, the dial signed for F. Armstrong & Bros., Paris, 1ft.6½in. high. (Phillips) $858 £520

A Charles X ormolu and porcelain clock, the movement signed Le Roy, Paris 1102, 16in. high. (Christie's) $1,370 £770

An Arts & Crafts square oak mantel clock, by Seth Thomas Clock Co., 20th century, 12½in. high, 10½in. wide. (Robt. W. Skinner Inc.) $1,200 £648

Mid 19th century rosewood mantel clock with carrying case, signed James Murray, Royal Exchange London, 12in. high. (Christie's) $5,280 £3,227

A brass Eureka mantel timepiece, the enamel dial inscribed S. Fisher Ltd., 1ft.1in. high, under a damaged glass shade. (Phillips) $660 £400

A 19th century French ormolu and porcelain mantel clock, the enamel dial signed Vieyres & Repignon a Paris, 11in. high. (Phillips) $990 £600

A Charles X ormolu and bronze mantel clock with silvered dial, 15in. high. (Christie's) $2,153 £1,210

MANTEL CLOCKS

An ormolu mounted scarlet boulle bracket clock, dial signed V. Courtecuisse & Cie Lille, 45in. high. (Christie's) $3,122 £1,870

An Empire ormolu mantel clock, the movement signed James McCabe, London 2133, 12½in. high. (Christie's) $2,937 £1,650

Late 19th century enamelled silver gilt Renaissance style table clock, the case by H. Bohm, Vienna, 7½in. high. (Christie's) $1,320 £806

An oval four-glass lacquered brass 8-day striking mantel clock with enamel dial, 9½in. tall. (J. M. Welch & Son) $393 £240

A Louis Philippe ormolu, bronze and white marble mantel clock, with enamel circlet dial, 14in. high. (Christie's) $1,272 £715

An ormolu mounted scarlet boulle bracket clock, the glazed dial with Roman enamel numerals, 48in. high. (Christie's) $4,307 £2,420

A contre-partie polychrome boulle bracket clock, the enamel face signed Gille L'Aine a Paris, basically 18th century, 31in. high. (Christie's) $2,937 £1,650

A mantel clock in gilt metal case decorated with champ-leve enamelled panels of scarlet, green and blue flowers on a pale blue ground, 2½in. (Dreweatt Neate) $205 £110

A 19th century French ormolu mantel clock, the circular chased dial signed Hy. Marc a Paris, 41cm. high. (Phillips) $1,344 £800

MANTEL CLOCKS

A 19th century French ormolu and porcelain mantel clock, the decorated dial signed for Miller & Co., Bristol, 43cm. high. (Phillips) $873 £520

A 19th century French Empire style 8-day striking mantel clock, 17in. high. (J. M. Welch & Son) $561 £340

An alabaster and gilt pillar/vase clock with central milk-glass dial, 12in. tall, circa 1900. (J. M. Welch & Son) $228 £150

A gilt brass calendar strut clock attributed to Thos. Cole, London, the back-plate signed Hunt & Roskell, London, 5½in. high. (Christie's) $2,359 £1,430

A 19th century tortoiseshell and cut brass inlaid bracket clock, signed Lepeltier a Paris, 2ft.2½in. high. (Phillips) $1,567 £950

A 19th century rosewood cased four-glass mantel clock, dial signed French Royal Exchange, London, 9¼ x 6¼in. (J. M. Welch & Son) $3,444 £2,050

A 19th century French ormolu mantel clock, the case in the form of a lyre, 38cm. high, on an oval ebonised stand under a glass shade. (Phillips) $974 £580

An early 19th century time-piece inkstand, the movement with engine-turned gilt face by Edward Lock, 19cm. high, 18cm. wide. (David Lay) $594 £330

A Louis XV style red boulle bracket clock with two-train movement by Gay Vicarino & Co., Paris, 44cm. high. (Osmond Tricks) $785 £420

WALL CLOCKS

A French Louis XVI 3-month duration console clock, signed on a porcelain plaque Nicolas Texier a Philippeville, 23½in. high. (Christie's)
$7,524 £4,180

A George III brass wall clock, the dial signed Edwd. Pashier, London, 1ft.6½in. high. (Phillips) $2,310 £1,400

A French bracket wall clock, the white enamelled dial signed Causard Horloger Du Roy, Paris, the back plate stamped Vincenti, Paris. (Wellington Salerooms) $3,696 £2,200

A 19th century carved mahogany Vienna wall clock, 4ft.9in. high. (Giles Haywood)
$1,098 £575

A musical picture clock with figures on a river bank with the clock face in church tower, 29½ x 34½in. overall. (Christie's) $1,960 £1,210

A musical 19th century German carved wood wall clock, 6ft.11in. high. (Phillips) $11,220 £6,800

Early 19th century Federal mahogany giltwood and eglomise banjo clock, 33½in. long. (Christie's)
$1,760 £1,064

Early 19th century inlaid mahogany clock with brass bezel and convex 10in. dial. (Reeds Rains) $701 £420

Late 19th century softwood German wall clock, the white enamel dial with 8-day movement, 13in. high. (Peter Wilson) $680 £420

WALL CLOCKS

A 19th century mahogany wall timepiece, the brass dial signed Mattw. & Thos. Dutton, London, 2ft.2½in. high. (Phillips)
$4,125 £2,500

An 18th century striking Act of Parliament clock, signed Ino. Wilson, Peterborough, 56½in. high. (Christie's)
$1,881 £990

A 19th century 8-day rose-wood and oak cased wall clock with painted metal dial. (J. M. Welch & Son)
$155 £95

An ormolu and bronze clock with glazed enamel dial, indistinctly signed ... Armentieres, 32½in. high. (Christie's)
$2,204 £1,320

Mid 19th century wall clock in circular mahogany case, the enamel dial inscribed Ed. Russell, Foulsham. (G. A. Key)
$313 £190

A George III giltwood cartel clock with associated silvered dial signed Wm. Linderby, London, 34in. high. (Christie's) $4,989 £3,080

A Regency mahogany wall regulator, the movement of two week duration, 65in. high. (Christie's)
$5,020 £3,080

A Federal gilt and eglomise girandole clock, by Lemuel Curtis, Concord, Mass., circa 1816, 46in. high. (Christie's)
$13,200 £7,980

An early 19th century French brass octagonal cased portable or hanging clock, the movement signed Du Louier a Rouen. (Parsons, Welch & Cowell) $420 £250

A gold keyless openface free sprung fusee lever watch with winding indicator, signed Barraud & Lunds, London, 1893, 51mm. diam. (Christie's) $1,870 £1,142

A gold hunter-cased lever watch, signed Barraud & Lunds, London, 1882, 50mm. diam. (Christie's) $770 £470

A gold minute repeating keyless lever chronograph, signed Breguet No. 1310, 56mm. diam. (Phillips) $9,072 £5,400

A gold floral enamel dress watch, signed L. Gallopin & Co., Suc'rs to Henry Capt, Geneva, 44mm. diam. (Christie's) $1,980 £1,210

A gold openface chronograph, signed Vacheron & Constantin, Geneve, with an 18ct. gold fob, 51mm. diam. (Christie's) $1,980 £1,210

An enamelled gold pendant watch and chain, signed Ed. Koehn, Geneva, retailed by J. E. Caldwell & Co., Phila., 29mm. diam. (Christie's) $1,100 £672

A gold pair case verge watch, signed Wm. Robertson, London, 1793, together with an 18ct. gold chain, 52mm. diam. (Christie's) $1,320 £806

A platinum openface split-second chronograph, signed Patek Philippe & Co., 47mm. diam. (Christie's) $6,050 £3,697

An enamelled gold openface dress watch of Napoleonic interest, signed Movado, the 18ct. gold case with London import mark 1910, 47mm. diam. (Christie's) $3,080 £1,882

A finely enamelled gold open-face dress watch, signed Vacheron & Constantin, 47mm. diam. (Christie's) $3,300 £2,016

An 18ct. gold hunter-cased minute-repeating chrono-graph, signed Albert H. Potter & Co., Geneva, 52mm. diam. (Christie's) $10,450 £6,387

Early 19th century gold verge watch with retrograde second hand , probably Swiss, 55mm. diam. (Christie's) $2,090 £1,277

An 18ct. chased gold hunter-cased lever watch, signed Longines, with damascened nickel movement jewelled to the third wheel, 52mm. diam. (Christie's) $1,540 £940

A gold openface medical chronograph, signed Ulysse Nardin, Locle & Geneve, 55mm. diam. (Christie's) $2,200 £1,344

A gold openface lever watch, signed Jules Jurgensen, with-in a plain 18ct. gold case, 51mm. diam. (Christie's) $2,420 £1,479

An 18ct. gold minute repeat-ing keyless lever watch, the movement signed James Murray, London, 1882, 51mm. diam. (Phillips) $1,596 £950

A silver pair cased verge stop watch, the movement with pierced cock signed Wm. Graham, London, No. 11437, the cases marked London, 1797. (Phillips) $352 £210

A gold box hinge hunter-cased watch, by American Waltham Watch Co., within an engraved 14ct. gold box hinged case, 55mm. diam. (Christie's) $1,100 £672

A gold openface fusee lever watch, signed J. R. Arnold, Chas. Frodsham, London, 1853, 55mm. diam. (Christie's) $1,210 £739

An 18ct. gold openface dress watch, signed Patek Philippe & Co., with nickel 18-jewel movement and silvered dial, 45mm. diam. (Christie's) $825 £504

A large gold openface lever watch, signed Chronometro Gondolo, by Patek Philippe & Cie, 56mm. diam. (Christie's) $1,760 £1,075

A keyless gold openface minute-repeating watch with perpetual retrograde calendar, signed on the case Eugene Lecoultre, 54mm. diam. (Christie's) $9,900 £6,050

An engraved gold openface lever watch, signed Lucien Dubois, Locle, 48mm. diam. (Christie's) $1,210 £739

An 18ct. gold openface minute-repeating split-second chronograph with box and certificate, signed Jules Jurgensen, Copenhagen, 55mm. diam. (Christie's) $19,800 £12,101

An engraved gold hunter-cased pocket chronometer, signed on the cuvette Constantaras Freres, Constantinople, 55mm. diam. (Christie's) $1,320 £806

A Swiss silver Masonic keyless lever watch, the triangular case with mother-of-pearl dial, 60mm. high. (Phillips) $1,428 £850

An openface floral enamel silver gilt centre seconds watch for the Chinese Market, signed Bovet, Fleurier, 55mm. diam. (Christie's) $3,300 £2,016

WATCHES

Early 19th century silver openface clock watch, Swiss, the cuvette signed Breguet & Fils, the top plate signed Japy, 58mm. diam. (Christie's)
$1,650 £1,008

A gold openface lever watch, signed Paul Ditisheim, La Chaux-De-Fonds, 56mm. diam. (Christie's)
$2,420   £1,479

An 18th century gold and enamel pair cased watch, signed Geo. Phi. Strigel, London, 1770, 48mm. diam. (Phillips)
$3,192 £1,900

An 18ct. gold openface minute-repeating watch, signed Patek Philippe & Cie, 47mm. diam. (Christie's)
$7,150 £4,370

A verge watch, quarter-repeating on two visible bells, the gilt movement signed Georg Schmit, Neustadt, 56mm. diam. (Christie's)
$2,200 £1,344

An 18ct. gold openface quarter-repeating ruby cylinder watch, signed Ph. Fazy, dated 1816, probably Geneva, 52mm. diam. (Christie's) $935 £571

A gilt metal and tortoiseshell pair cased quarter repeating verge watch made for the Turkish market, signed Geo. Prior, London, 62mm. diam. (Phillips) $1,344 £800

A platinum dress watch with integral stand, retailed by Bucherer, Lucerne, 42mm. wide. (Christie's) $990 £605

An enamelled gold convertible cased cylinder watch, signed J. FS. Bautte & Co., Geneve, with gilt cylinder movement jewelled to the third wheel, 36mm. diam. (Christie's) $2,860 £1,748

A gold openface chronograph, Swiss, retailed by Tiffany & Co., New York, signed Tiffany, 53mm. diam. (Christie's) $990   £605

A Swiss gold minute repeating grande sonnerie keyless lever clock watch, the cuvette signed for Breguet No. 4722, 57mm. diam. (Phillips)
$38,640   £23,000

A Swiss gold openface watch, signed with Patent No. 98234, the 18ct. gold case, London, 1925, 51mm. diam. (Christie's) $935 £571

A small engraved gold pocket chronometer, signed Couvoisier & Comp'e, Chaux-De-Fonds, 46mm. diam. (Christie's)
$660 £403

An 18ct. gold openface chronograph, signed Patek Philippe & Co., Geneve, with nickel 23-jewel movement, 48mm. diam. (Christie's) $3,300 £2,016

A floral enamel silver gilt centre seconds watch for the Chinese Market, Swiss, mid 19th century, 57mm. diam. (Christie's)
$3,300   £2,016

A platinum openface dress watch, signed Patek Philippe & Co., Geneva, on movement and case, with original box and guarantee certificate, 44mm. diam. (Christie's) $2,640 £1,613

A platinum openface dress watch, signed Patek Philippe & Co., Geneva, with nickel 18-jewel lever movement, 44mm. diam. (Christie's)
$1,870 £1,142

A 14ct. rose gold openface dress watch and chain, signed Vacheron & Constantin, Geneve, with 17-jewel nickel lever movement, 42mm. diam. (Christie's) $1,540 £941

An 18ct. gold openface minute-repeating split-second chronograph, Swiss, retailed by Tiffany & Co., 54mm. diam. (Christie's)
$6,600 £4,033

Mid 19th century gold openface pivoted detent chronometer for the American market, Swiss, the dial signed William F. Ladd, 46mm. diam. (Christie's) $550 £336

A gold openface free sprung fusee lever watch with winding indicator, signed Aldred & Son, Yarmouth, the 18ct. gold case, London, 1891, 53mm. diam. (Christie's)
$1,320 £806

A Continental silver pair cased verge watch, signed Blanc Pere & Fils, Geneve, the silver champleve dial signed P. B., London, 50mm. diam. (Phillips) $806 £480

A gold openface Masonic watch, with nickel 19-jewel movement, signed Dudley Watch Co., Lancaster, Pa., 45mm. diam. (Christie's)
$1,650 £1,008

An enamelled gilt metal verge watch, signed Gregson A Paris, with white enamel dial, 53mm. diam. (Christie's)
$935 £571

A gold openface split second chronograph, signed C. H. Meylan, Brassus, 48mm. diam. (Christie's) $825 £504

A platinum openface dress watch, signed Patek Philippe & Cie, Geneve, on movement and case, 44mm. diam. (Christie's) $1,760 £1,075

An 18ct. gold openface dress watch, signed Patek Philippe & Co., Geneve, with nickel 18-jewel cal. 17-170 lever movement, 44mm. diam. (Christie's) $2,420 £1,479

WRISTWATCHES

A stainless steel and gold self-winding wristwatch with centre seconds, signed Rolex Oyster Perpetual. (Christie's) $1,320 £806

A 14ct. gold curvex wristwatch, signed Gruen, with curved cushion shaped 17-jewel movement, (Christie's) $1,100 £672

A 14ct. gold self-winding wristwatch with centre seconds, signed Rolex Oyster Perpetual, with a 14ct. gold bracelet. (Christie's) $2,090 £1,277

An 18ct. gold wristwatch, signed Patek Philippe & Co., retailed by Cartier. (Christie's) $3,850 £2,353

A lady's stainless steel wristwatch with calendar, signed Patek Philippe & Co., Geneva, Nautilus model. (Christie's) $1,210 £739

A gold self-winding wristwatch with centre seconds, signed Omega Seamaster, the leather strap with 14ct. gold buckle. (Christie's) $330 £201

An early waterproof wristwatch, signed Rolex, within a silver case hinged to outer protective silver case. (Christie's) $1,650 £1,008

A 14ct. gold curvex wristwatch, signed Gruen Watch Co., with curved nickel 17-jewel movement. (Christie's) $2,200 £1,344

A thin 18ct. gold wristwatch, signed Vacheron & Constantin, with nickel 17-jewel movement, the leather strap with 18ct. gold buckle. (Christie's) $1,430 £874

WRISTWATCHES

A stainless steel self-winding wristwatch with centre seconds, signed Rolex Oyster Perpetual, with steel bracelet. (Christie's) $462 £282

An 18ct. gold self-winding wristwatch with perpetual calendar, signed Patek Philippe & Co. (Christie's) $13,750 £8,404

A stainless steel self-winding wristwatch with centre seconds, signed Rolex Oyster Perpetual. (Christie's) $825   £504

An 18ct. white gold minute repeating wristwatch, signed Vacheron & Constantin, Geneva. (Christie's) $60,500 £36,977

A gold wristwatch, signed Movado, with nickel 17 jewel movement, within a circular 14ct. gold case with unusual lugs. (Christie's) $935   £571

A gold self-winding wrist-watch with centre seconds, signed Rolex Oyster Perpetual, the leather strap with 14ct. gold buckle. (Christie's) $1,980   £1,210

A gold self-winding wrist-watch, signed Patek Philippe & Co., within a signed 18ct. gold waterproof case. (Christie's) $2,640 £1,613

An 18ct. gold wristwatch, retailed by Cartier, the move-ment signed Jaeger Lecoultre, with oblong duoplan nickel movement. (Christie's) $6,050 £3,697

An 18ct. gold wristwatch, signed Vacheron & Constantin, with nickel 17-jewel P 453/3B movement, signed on move-ment and case. (Christie's) $2,200 £1,344

WRISTWATCHES

An 18ct. thin white gold wristwatch, signed Patek Philippe & Co., the nickel 18-jewel movement with Geneva Observatory seal. (Christie's) $1,980 £1,210

An 18ct. white gold timezone wristwatch, signed Patek Philippe & Co., Geneva, with nickel 18-jewel cal. 27-HS 400 movement. (Christie's) $9,350 £5,714

A platinum wristwatch, signed Audemars Piguet, on the movement and case, inscribed and dated 1926 in the interior. (Christie's) $6,600 £4,033

An 18ct. gold self-winding wristwatch with centre seconds, signed Rolex Oyster Perpetual, with gold bracelet. (Christie's) $1,430 £874

An 18ct. rose gold world time wristwatch, signed Patek Philippe & Co., Geneva, with nickel movement jewelled through the centre. (Christie's) $35,200 £21,514

A stainless steel and gold self-winding wristwatch with centre seconds, signed Rolex Oyster Perpetual. (Christie's) $528 £322

A stainless steel wristwatch, signed Patek Philippe & Co., with shaped oblong 18-jewel nickel lever movement. (Christie's) $1,430 £874

A stainless steel wrist chronograph, signed Longines, within a waterproof stainless steel case. (Christie's) $660 £409

A gold wristwatch, signed International Watch Co., Schaffhausen, with leather strap with 14ct. gold buckle and a spare crystal. (Christie's) $1,650 £1,008

WRISTWATCHES

An 18ct. gold bracelet watch, signed Vacheron & Constantin, on movement, case and bracelet. (Christie's) $2,420 £1,479

A stainless steel self-winding wristwatch with centre seconds, signed Rolex Oyster Perpetual, Submariner. (Christie's) $770 £470

An enamelled gold wristwatch, retailed by Cartier, the movement signed European Watch & Clock Co. (Christie's) $9,900 £6,050

A stainless steel self-winding wristwatch with centre seconds, signed Rolex Oyster Perpetual, Explorer, with Oyster crown and steel bracelet. (Christie's) $462 £282

A stainless steel chronograph, signed Longines, with lever movement. (Christie's) $220 £134

An 18ct. gold self-winding wristwatch, signed Rolex Oyster Perpetual Day Date, with 18ct. gold bracelet. (Christie's) $3,300 £2,016

A steel duoplan wristwatch, signed Jaeger, with oblong nickel lever movement, the white dial signed Cartier. (Christie's) $1,980 £1,210

A stainless steel and gold self-winding wristwatch with centre seconds, signed Rolex Oyster Perpetual, with 14ct. gold and stainless steel bracelet. (Christie's) $1,980 £1,210

A wristwatch, signed Rolex Prince, the 9ct. gold case bearing Glasgow import mark for 1930. (Christie's) $3,850 £2,353

WRISTWATCHES

An 18ct. white gold and hardstone skeletonised wristwatch, signed Chopard, Geneve, with original leather strap and 18ct. white gold buckle. (Christie's) $7,150 £4,370

A platinum wristwatch, signed Patek Philippe & Co., Geneva, signed on movement and case. (Christie's) $7,150 £4,370

A stainless steel wristwatch, signed Patek Philippe & Co., Geneve, with nickel 18-jewel movement. (Christie's) $1,320 £806

A large silver and stainless steel aviator's hour angle watch, to the designs of Charles A. Lindbergh, by Longines. (Christie's) $7,700 £4,706

A lady's 18ct. gold self-winding wristwatch, signed Rolex Perpetual Super Precision, signed on movement and case. (Christie's) $1,320 £806

A gold self-winding wristwatch with calendar, signed Universal, Geneva, within an 18ct. gold case. (Christie's) $605 £369

A gold and stainless steel self-winding wristwatch with centre seconds, signed Rolex Oyster Perpetual, with original guarantee certificate. (Christie's) $1,430 £874

A gold and stainless steel wristwatch with calendar, signed Patek Philippe & Co., Geneva, Nautilus model with reeded black dial. (Christie's) $3,850 £2,353

An 18ct. gold wristwatch with centre seconds, signed Audemars Piguet, with nickel 20-jewel movement with gold train. (Christie's) $2,420 £1,479

WRISTWATCHES

An 18ct. gold skeletonised wristwatch, signed Vacheron & Constantin, with signed 18ct. gold buckle to leather strap. (Christie's)
$4,950 £3,025

An 18ct. gold shaped oblong wristwatch, signed Patek Philippe, signed on movement and case. (Christie's)
$4,950 £3,025

A platinum wristwatch, signed Patek Philippe & Co., with nickel 18-jewel movement, signed on movement and case. (Christie's) $4,950 £3,025

A steel wrist chronograph, signed Breguet, and another signed Henry K. Tournheim-Tourneau, without calendar. (Christie's) $1,760 £1,075

An 18ct. gold wristwatch, signed Patek Philippe & Co., Geneva, with circular nickel movement jewelled to the centre. (Christie's)
$3,080   £1,882

A gold wristwatch with calendar, signed Movado, within a reeded 14ct. gold case, and a self-winding 14ct. gold wristwatch, signed Bulova. (Christie's)
$990   £605

An 18ct. gold wristwatch, signed Patek Philippe & Co., with nickel 18-jewel lever movement. (Christie's)
$1,650 £1,008

A stainless steel and gold self-winding centre seconds wrist-watch with calendar, signed Rolex Oyster Perpetual. (Christie's) $777 £470

An 18ct. thin gold wrist-watch, signed Patek Philippe, with nickel 18-jewel cal. 10-200 movement. (Christie's)
$1,320 £806

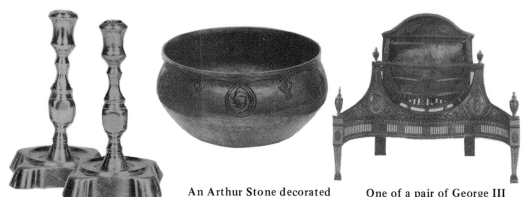

A pair of 19th century brass candlesticks, each with urn-turned drip-pan, 6¾in. high. (Christie's) $308 £186

An Arthur Stone decorated copper bowl, Mass., circa 1910, stamped with Stone logo, 5¼in. diam. (Robt. W. Skinner Inc.) $5,040 £3,000

One of a pair of George III brass and blacked steel basket grates, 40½in. wide, 34in. high. (Christie's) $17,930 £11,000

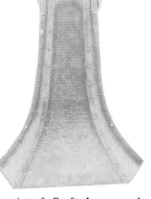

A late 19th century ship's brass plaque, enamelled with H.M.S. Centurion Comm[n] 1895-98, 14in. diam. (Christie's) $258 £154

An Arts & Crafts hammered copper fireplace hood, circa 1910, 43in. high, 12½in. wide at top, 36in. wide at bottom. (Robt. W. Skinner Inc.) $900 £486

A Victorian copper oval jelly mould, orb and sceptre mark, 5.5in. high. (Woolley & Wallis) $140 £85

Early 20th century hammered copper lamp base with mother-of-pearl mountings, 13in. high. (Robt. W. Skinner Inc.) $400 £250

Early 20th century brass bottle bar with 'optic' taps, overall length 37in. (Christie's) $715 £419

A brass electric bridge searchlight with polished mirror reflector, 9in. diam., and two brass deck lamps and reflectors. (Christie's) $924 £550

A late Victorian brass coal box with domed lid and pierced finial, 17in. wide. (Christie's) $551 £330

A brass pen tray in the form of a roaring hippopotamus with hinged back, 12½in. wide. (Christie's) $5,808 £3,520

A circular copper jelly mould with a swirl top, 5.5in. (Woolley & Wallis) $148 £90

A copper and brass diver's helmet, date 8.29.41, with clamp screws, valves, plate glass windows and guards, 20in. high. (Christie's) $2,032 £1,210

A copper and brass masthead lamp with spirit lamp and moulded glass lens, 23½in. high, and another lamp labelled Toplight. (Christie's) $332 £198

An enamelled hammered copper humidor, by R. Cauman, Boston, circa 1925, 6½in. high. (Robt. W. Skinner Inc.) $425 £252

A pair of brass candlesticks, one with a caryatid shaft, the other with Atlantes shaft, 11in. high. (Christie's) $587 £352

Four 19th century brass chambersticks, 9½in. and 4½in. high. (Robt. W. Skinner Inc.) $350 £212

Pair of Federal brass andirons, probably Boston, circa 1810, 18in. high. (Robt. W. Skinner Inc.) $700 £437

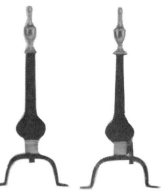

A fine pair of 20th century brass candlesticks, 8½in. high. (Robt. W. Skinner Inc.) $375 £202

A hammered copper wine pitcher, no. 80, by the Stickley Bros., circa 1905, 15in. high. (Robt. W. Skinner Inc.) $150 £81

Pair of knife blade andirons, America, circa 1780, 25½in. high. (Robt. W. Skinner Inc.) $800 £476

A hammered brass umbrella stand, possibly Belgium circa 1900-20, 24in. high. (Robt. W. Skinner Inc.) $650 £351

Pair of relief decorated copper plaques, signed by Raymond Averill Porter, 1912 and 1913, 10½ x 9½in. (Robt. W. Skinner Inc.) $600 £324

One of a pair of brass candlesticks, each with cylindrical candlecup 7½in. high. (Christie's) $175 £105

A bronze mounted copper diver's helmet, overall height 20in, maker's plate of 'Siebe Gorman & Co. Ltd., Submarine Engineers, London'. (Wallis & Wallis) $1,200 £750

Pair of Georgian brass door stops, the moulded bases with weighted iron insets, 13¾in. high. (Woolley & Wallis) $736 £460

An Onondaga Metal Shop hammered copper and repousse wall plaque, circa 1905, 20in. diam. (Robt. W. Skinner Inc.) $5,500 £2,972

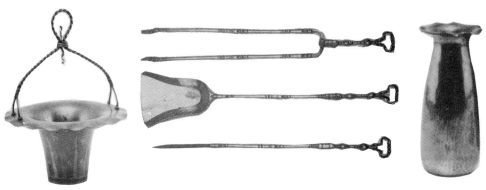

A Roycroft copper and brass wash handled basket, East Aurora, N.Y., circa 1920, 9in. diam. (Robt. W. Skinner Inc.) $100 £54

A set of three George III brass fire-irons with shaped ring handles and baluster shafts, 24in. long. (Christie's) $1,960 £1,210

A Karl Kipp copper vase, model no. 218, East Aurora, N.Y., circa 1919, 6½in. high. (Robt. W. Skinner Inc.) $275 £148

A triangular hammered copper umbrella stand, with single panel of stylised poppies, circa 1900, 23in. high. (Robt. W. Skinner Inc.) $425 £229

Set of brass postage scales and full set of weights. (McKenna's) $473 £260

A hammered copper chamber-stick, by Gustav Stickley, circa 1913, 9¼in. high. (Robt. W. Skinner Inc.) $700 £378

A pair of brass dome-base candle-sticks, each with ring-turned cylindrical candlecup, 9in. high. (Christie's) $715 £403

A hammered copper jar with enamelled cover, Boston or Worcester, Mass., circa 1915, 4½in. diam. (Robt. W. Skinner Inc.) $400 £216

A pair of Federal brass andirons and matching fire tools, New York, 1800-25, andirons 20in. high. (Christie's) $1,980 £1,117

A Dutch silver corkscrew by J. J. Koen of Amsterdam, 3¼in. high. (Christie's) $305 £175

A Dutch silver and mother-of-pearl corkscrew, apparently unmarked, circa 1780, 3¼in. high. (Christie's) $825 £483

A Dutch silver and mother-of-pearl corkscrew, circa 1800, maker's mark apparently **DP** with vase of flowers between, 3¼in. high. (Christie's) $1,100 £644

A 19th century Dutch silver corkscrew, the platform handle with the cast figures of a man in 18th century dress and two rearing horses, 4in. high. (Christie's) $880 £515

A Dutch silver corkscrew, by Josephius Servatius Anderlee, Amsterdam, 1785, 3½in. high. (Christie's) $770 £451

A Dutch silver corkscrew, struck with date letter for 1908, 4in. high. (Christie's) $935 £548

Early 19th century King's screw double action corkscrew, with turned bone handle and helical worm, nickel side handle. (Christie's) $462 £270

A George III silver corkscrew, by Thos. Willmore, 1798, 3¾in. high, the second of silver and mother-of-pearl, late 18th century, 3¾in. high. (Christie's) $1,320 £773

Hull's 'Royal Club' side lever corkscrew, with helical worm. (Christie's) $880 £515

Early 19th century Thomason-type double action corkscrew with open frame, turned bone handle and helical worm. (Christie's) $528 £309

Early 19th century Thomason-type double action corkscrew, with horn handle. (Christie's) $550 £322

Early 19th century Thomason-type double action corkscrew, with turned bone handle and helical worm. (Christie's) $825 £483

A Dutch silver and mother-of-pearl corkscrew, struck with indistinct maker's mark, circa 1780, 3.1/8in. high. (Christie's) $880 £515

A Dutch silver corkscrew, by Johannes Van Geelen, Gouda, 1799, the handle cast in the form of a lion passant on a scroll base, 3¾in. high. (Christie's) $1,320 £773

A Dutch silver corkscrew, by L. Olfers, Groningen, the handle cast as a galloping horse on a scroll base, 3¾in. high. (Christie's) $935 £548

A George II silver combination corkscrew and nutmeg grater, apparently unmarked, circa 1750, 3½in. long. (Christie's) $1,540 £902

Late 19th century silver 'lady's legs' folding corkscrew, probably American, marked Sterling, height closed 2in. high. (Christie's) $418 £245

A 19th century Dutch silver corkscrew, the curled platform handle with the cast figure of a cow, 3½in. high. (Christie's) $605 £354

A Dutch silver corkscrew, circa 1760, unmarked, 3½in. high. (Christie's) $520 £306

Early 19th century Thomason-type double action corkscrew, with turned bone handle. (Christie's) $1,760 £1,031

A Dutch silver corkscrew, struck with date letter for 1895, 4in. high. (Christie's) $880 £515

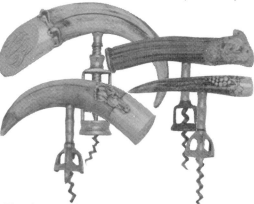

Two horn and two tusk-handled corkscrews, comprising a frame corkscrew; another with Williamson's type bell cap; an antler-handled example with grape-vine chased silver mount and another antler-handled example carved with a bulldog's face silver cap. (Christie's) $1,760 £1,031

A varied grouping, comprising a gold miniature golding bow corkscrew; a gold mounted amber-handled perfume corkscrew; a gold combination keyholder and corkscrew; two repousse silver mounted pocketknife/corkscrews and a silver handled T-bar corkscrew. (Christie's) $2,200 £1,289

An English gold roundlet corkscrew, by J. C. Vickery, London, 1912, 9ct., 3½in. long closed, gross weight 1oz. 5dwt. (Christie's) $495 £290

A cast iron bar corkscrew, black painted with gold decoration, origin unknown. (Christie's) $1,100 £644

A German 'folding lady' corkscrew, circa 1900, height closed 2.5/8in. (Christie's) $605 £354

Late 18th century silver corkscrew by Cocks & Bettridge of Birmingham, 3in. high. (Christie's) $255 £145

Early 19th century variant of Thomason's double action corkscrew with elliptical brass turning handle and helical worm. (Christie's) $1,540 £902

A Dutch silver and mother-of-pearl corkscrew, apparently unmarked, circa 1775, 3in. high. (Christie's) $770 £451

Nine, 19th/20th century, silver mounted corkscrews. (Christie's) $1,430 £838

Three German 'lady's legs' folding corkscrews, the celluloid legs clothed in variously striped and coloured stockings and high lace-up boots, average height 2¾in. (Christie's) $605 £354

'Amor', a German figural folding corkscrew, formed as a Bakelite soldier and his lady, circa 1900, height closed 2¾in. (Christie's) $572 £335

A rotary eclipse bar corkscrew, in brass, with steel helical worm and wood side handle. (Christie's) $770 £451

Late 19th century American silver mounted and mother-of-pearl corkscrew, stamped Sterling, 4¼in. wide. (Christie's) $528 £309

A late 18th century open robe of chine silk with linen lined bodice, the matching petticoat altered and accompanying stomacher. (Phillips)
$6,048   £3,600

An early 19th century Turkish coat woven with rows of florets in red, green and yellow silks on an ivory ground and trimmed with blue braid, lined. (Phillips)
$75 £45

An early 17th century purse of red silk with gold thread embroidery and having applied seed pearls, garnets and sequins, lined. (Phillips)
$1,344 £800

A late 18th century gentleman's waistcoat, the ivory silk fronts embroidered in pastel silk threads with sprays of spring flowers. (Phillips) $159 £95

A pair of mid 19th century North American Eastern Woodlands Indian gloves of light brown leather, lined, probably Cree. (Phillips)
$235 £140

The Court dress of King Otto of the Hellenes, circa 1835. (Christie's) $14,437 £8,250

A pair of mid 19th century ivory silk stockings, initialled 'AB' numbered 36, the instep decorated with an inset of Brussels needlepoint lace. (Phillips) $854 £480

A 19th century Chinese robe of midnight-blue silk embroidered in coloured silks. (Phillips) $486 £300

A mid 18th century open robe of calimanco, the bodice part lined in linen and with front lacing. (Phillips) $504 £300

A gown of red cotton printed overall with multi-coloured cones, scrolls and floral motifs, circa 1870's. (Phillips) $504 £300

An early 19th century Chinese robe of K'o-ssu woven mainly in green, blue and white silks and gold thread, lined. (Phillips) $1,980 £1,100

A late 19th century bridal veil of tamboured net designed with flower sprays and sprigs, 2 x 2m. (Phillips) $320 £180

An Indonesian shawl of cotton Ikat woven mainly in madder and indigo, 2.32 x 1.28m., Sumba. (Phillips) $259 £160

A pair of late 19th century American Woodlands Indian gauntlets of brown leather, probably Cree. (Phillips) $672 £400

A 19th century Chinese vest of midnight blue silk, embroidered in pekin knot and satin stitch, lined. (Phillips) $828 £460

A deshabille of pale pink crepe de chine trimmed and inset with lace, circa 1900. (Christie's) $385 £220

Two early 20th century Chinese summer gauze robes, one with dragon and cloud motif, the other with goldfish and seaweed motif. (Robt. W. Skinner Inc.) $525 £318

An evening dress of ivory silk with yellow and black stripes, by Vincent Lachartroulle, 8 Rue Auber, Paris, circa 1900. (Christie's) $1,155 £660

Early 20th century German bisque bathing belle with painted facial feature and auburn wig held in a net cap, 3in. high. (Lawrence Fine Art) $469 £264

A composition shoulder headed doll, by Joel Ellis of the Cooperative Doll Co., 11in. high. (Christie's) $326 £198

Early 20th century German bisque bathing belle, lying propped on her elbows and one leg raised, in original pink net costume. (Lawrence Fine Art) $509 £286

A terracotta headed creche figure modelled as a Turk with moustache and pigtail, painted wooden hands and feet, 19in. high. (Christie's) $610 £330

A pair of advertising dolls modelled as the 'Bisto Kids', designed by Will Owen, 11in. high, circa 1948. (Christie's) $386 £209

A composition character headed doll modelled as Lord Kitchener, in original clothes with Sam Browne hat and puttees, 19in. high. (Christie's) $305 £164

A German bisque head doll, marked 283/297, Max Handwerck, 24¾in. high. (Geering & Colyer) $468 £260

A bisque headed doll's house doll modelled as a man with cloth body and bisque hands, 6in. high. (Christie's) $235 £143

A German bisque head doll, marked Heubach-Koppelsdorf, 250-4, 25¾in. high. (Geering & Colyer) $468 £260

Early 20th century German bisque bathing belle, resting on one hand, the other raised shielding her eyes, 3½in. high. (Lawrence Fine Art) $587 £330

A composition mask faced googlie eyed doll, with smiling watermelon mouth, wearing spotted dress, 10½in. high. (Christie's) $610 £330

A composition headed Motschmann type baby doll with dark inset eyes, painted curls and floating hands and feet, 8in. high, circa 1850. (Christie's) $689 £418

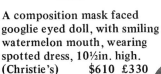

A 'Chad Valley' boxed set of Snow White and the Seven Dwarfs in Original clothes, Snow White with painted pressed felt face, jointed velvet body, the blue velvet bodice with pale blue and pink slashed sleeves and short cape, 17in. high, the Dwarfs 9½in. high. (Christie's) $5,291 £2,860

A composition mask faced googlie eyed doll, with smiling watermelon mouth, wearing pinafore and bonnet, 9in. high. (Christie's) $345 £187

A French bisque headed doll with cork pate, the leather shoes impressed with a number 11, a bee and a Paris Depose, 25in. high. (Ambrose) $2,430 £1,350

A Hebe bisque headed doll, marks indistinct, with open mouth and upper teeth, sleeping blue eyes and long fair plaited hair, 24in. high. (Lawrence Fine Art) $332 £187

A painted head doll with blue eyes, the felt body in original, clothes, 16in. high, marked Lenci, circa 1930. (Christie's) $202 £121

A painted cloth character doll with blue shaded eyes, ginger wool wig and jointed legs, 18in. high, with Deans Rag Book Co. Ltd. circa 1926. (Christie's) $330 £198

A bisque headed character child doll, marked 231 DRMR 248 FANY A2/0M, 14in. high. (Christie's) $3,993 £2,420

An 18th century group of Italian creche figures, six average height 9in., four average height 11½in., and two at 14½in. (Robt. W. Skinner Inc.) $3,700 £2,242

A papier mache mask faced doll with turquoise blue eyes, the cloth and wood body in original Central European costume, 15½ in. high, circa 1860. (Christie's) $330 £198

Two all bisque doll's house dolls with fixed blue eyes, blonde wigs and moulded socks and shoes in original national costume, 4in. high. (Christie's) $183 £110

A bisque headed child doll with fixed brown eyes and blonde wig, 10in. high, marked 1079 DEP S&H. (Christie's) $312 £187

A bisque headed clockwork Bebe Premier Pas with kid upper legs and blonde wig, 17½in. high, by Jules Nicholas Steiner, circa 1890. (Christie's) $1,837 £1,100

A painted wooden child doll the jointed wooden body (one foot missing) 17in. high, probably by Schilling. (Christie's) $330 £198

A bisque headed child doll with closed mouth, fixed blue eyes, blonde wig and composition body, 7in. high, marked 16. (Christie's) $183 £110

A pair of all bisque doll's house dolls with blue painted eyes, 5in. high, marked 1503 and 1603 on the legs, by Kestner, circa 1910. (Christie's) $238 £143

A pair of all bisque doll's house dolls modelled as roguish girls, jointed at neck, shoulder and hip, 3½in. high. (Christie's) $762 £462

One of two bisque headed doll's house dolls with blue sleeping eyes, one with brown wig, 5½in. high, one marked Halbig K*R 13. (Christie's) $477 £286

An all bisque doll's house doll, marked 253 12 on the head and body, 5¼in. high, and an all bisque standing character boy, 3¼in. high. (Christie's) $163 £99

A bisque figure of a seated fat baby, marked 95 and the Heubach square mark, stamped in green 68, 5in. high, together with two child dolls. (Christie's) $170 £99

345

Heubach Koppelsdorf bisque headed doll, 20½in. high. (Hobbs & Chambers) $385 £220

Bisque headed German doll marked 'Mignon', 22in. high. (Warren & Wignall Ltd.) $440 £275

A Simon & Halbig bisque headed Jutta character doll, impressed 'Jutta 1914 12', circa 1920, 21in. high. (Hobbs & Chambers) $704 £440

A bisque headed bebe with fixed blue yeux fibres and pierced ears, 15in. high, impressed 6 body stamped Jumeau Medaille d'or Paris. (Christie's) $1,928 £1,155

A bisque figure of a seated naked woman with moulded black bobbed hair, 3in. high. (Christie's) $163 £99

A bisque headed character doll with closed mouth, blue painted eyes, blonde wig and jointed composition body, 18in. high, marked K*R 114.46. (Christie's) $4,041 £2,420

Pedigree Coronation doll in original clothes, 14in. high. (Giles Haywood) $36 £22

Set of six late 19th century all bisque dolls, German, mounted in candy box, inscribed on cover 'found in the nursery of a ruined old chateau — Verdun, France — 1917', 4in. high. (Robt. W. Skinner Inc.) $650 £393

A bisque headed doll's house doll modelled as a man with full beard and hair, 6½in. high. (Christie's) $344 £209

Charlotte Norris, a wax-over-composition headed doll with smiling mouth, the stuffed body with pink kid arms, 23in. high, 1840-45. (Christie's) $514 £308

A bisque group of two googly-eyed figures in original hats, by William Goebel, 3½in. high. (Christie's) $508 £308

A bisque headed doll jointed at neck, shoulder, thigh and knee, 7in. high, marked 199 2/0, also a doll's house doll, 5in. high. (Christie's) $275 £165

A cloth character doll, the head in five sections, 16in. high, by Kathe Kruse, and The Katy Kruse dolly book, published 1927. (Christie's) $1,745 £1,045

A pair of poured wax portrait dolls, modelled as Edward VII and Queen Alexandra, 21in. high, by Pierotti. (Christie's) $1,837 £1,100

A bisque headed doll, impressed SFBJ 236 Paris 12, with composition toddler body, circa 1910, 24in. high. (Hobbs & Chambers) $960 £600

A bisque headed doll's house doll modelled as a man, 6½in. high. (Christie's) $326 £198

A bisque figure of a chubby baby, impressed No. 9902, 4½in. high, and a bisque figure of a baby playing with his toes, 5½in. long, impressed Gebruder Heubach. (Christie's) $635 £385

A bisque headed doll's house doll modelled as a man with a black-painted moustache and hair, 7in. high. (Christie's) $217 £132

A 19th century enamel box, in South Staffordshire style, 7¼in. long. (Christie's) $1,100 £628

Mid 19th century Austro-Hungarian jewelled and enamelled silver gilt and metal theatrical axe and shield, Vienna, the axe 38½in. long, the shield 20in. diam. (Christie's) $44,000 £25,142

An 18th century German enamel box with French reeded silver mounts, 8cm. wide. (Phillips) $1,586 £950

A 19th century Limoges polychrome enamel plaque, in the 16th century style, after Pierre Reymong, 7.1/8 x 5.1/8in. (Christie's) $990 £565

A South German double-ended enamel snuff box of waisted form, circa 1740, 2.5/8in. high. (Christie's) $3,920 £2,420

A German rectangular enamel snuff box painted in colours with battle scenes from the Seven Years' War, circa 1760, 3in. wide. (Christie's) $5,445 £3,300

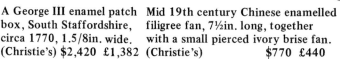

A George III enamel patch box, South Staffordshire, circa 1770, 1.5/8in. wide. (Christie's) $2,420 £1,382

Mid 19th century Chinese enamelled filigree fan, 7½in. long, together with a small pierced ivory brise fan. (Christie's) $770 £440

An Austrian enamelled Art Nouveau cigarette case, in the style of Alphonse Mucha, circa 1900. (Phillips) $1,137 £650

A South Staffordshire George III enamel bonbonniere, circa 1770, 3in. long. (Christie's) $4,180 £2,388

A George III enamel bottle ticket, Birmingham or South Staffordshire, circa 1770, 3in. long. (Christie's) $264 £154

An Arts & Crafts period enamelled plaque depicting a galley, 14in. wide. (Christie's) $295 £176

A 19th century French enamel plaque of Eve, signed L. Penet, in ebonised frame, 39 x 27cm. (Christie's) $2,388 £1,430

A 19th century cloisonne vase decorated with birds and flowers, 21in. high, damaged. (Lots Road Chelsea Auction Galleries) $2,560 £1,600

An Austrian enamelled cigarette case, the cover depicting a Caucasian warrior. (Phillips) $1,050 £600

A South Staffordshire oval enamel patch box, transfer-printed and painted on the cover with Bristol Hot Wells, circa 1800, 1¾in. long. (Christie's) $544 £330

Mid 19th century Limoges polychrome enamel triptych, in the Nazarene Style, 22.1/8in. high, 19.3/8in. wide when open. (Christie's) $1,980 £1,131

An enamel wine funnel, South Staffordshire, circa 1770, 4¼in. long. (Christie's) $1,980 £1,160

A late 18th century fan, the leaf an etching in brown of heraldic devices, with ivory sticks, 25cm. long. (Phillips) $518 £320

A French fan with carved, pierced, painted and gilt ivory sticks decorated with mother-of-pearl, circa 1760, 28cm. long. (Phillips) $2,430 £1,500

A Chinese fan of carved and pierced ivory, circa 1760, 25.5cm. long. (Phillips) $680 £420

A fan with plain ivory sticks and 18ct. gold loop at pivot, the leaf of Brussels bobbin and needlepoint applique, circa 1890, 27cm. long. (Phillips) $680 £420

A Chinese telescopic fan with black and gilt lacquer sticks, circa 1840, 26cm. long extended, in original box. (Phillips) $615 £380

A Chinese silver gilt filigree fan with mainly blue and green enamel decoration, circa 1830, 19.5cm. long. (Phillips) $907 £560

A late 19th century fan with ivory sticks, the leaf of Brussels point de gaze, 35cm. long, in original box inscribed J. Duvelleroy, London. (Phillips) $684 £380

A French fan, the ivory sticks decorated with chinoiserie, circa 1760, 28cm. long. (Phillips) $648 £400

A French fan with gilded ivory sticks and
ivory silk leaf painted with lovers at an altar,
circa 1770, 28cm. long. (Phillips) $405 £250

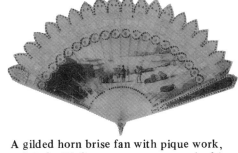

A gilded horn brise fan with pique work,
painted with figures on a quay overlooking
a bay, circa 1810, 16cm long. (Phillips)
$324 £200

A fan with carved, pierced, silvered and gilt
mother-of-pearl sticks and the chicken-skin
leaf painted and gilded, circa 1760, 30cm.
long, probably German. (Phillips) $777 £480

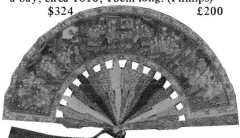

A Chinese fan with carved and pierced
shaped sticks of tortoiseshell, mother-of-
pearl, stained and unstained ivory and metal
filigree with enamel decoration, circa 1840,
28cm. long, in box. (Phillips) $777 £480

A Chinese cabriolet fan with black, pink,
silver and gilt lacquer sticks, circa 1830,
28.5cm. long, in original box with label
printed in Spanish. (Phillips) $1,053 £650

A fan with carved, pierced, silvered and gilt
mother-of-pearl sticks and an 18th century
pastiche, signed Donzel, circa 1870, in a
shaped, glazed case. (Phillips) $2,268 £1,400

A 19th century painted fan, the guards inlaid
with green enamel, porcelain plaques, semi-
precious stones and pearls, probably French,
11¼in. long. (Christie's) $880 £502

A French fan, the carved, pierced and painted
ivory sticks decorated with red and green
florets, circa 1760, 26cm. long, and a shaped
case. (Phillips) $1,053 £650

BEDS

A Gustav Stickley spindle-sided baby's crib, no. 919, circa 1907, 56½in. long. (Robt. W. Skinner Inc.) $1,400 £833

Early 18th century Spanish or Venetian parcel gilt and polychrome hanging cradle of navette form, 49½in. wide. (Christie's) $3,674 £2,200

Mission oak double bed with exposed tenons, circa 1907, 58½in. wide. (Robt. W. Skinner Inc.) $2,500 £1,351

An Empire grain painted tall post bed, possibly Mahantango Valley, Penn., circa 1825, 51in. wide. (Robt. W. Skinner Inc.) $2,800 £1,666

A German figured walnut single bedstead on turned tapering legs and bun feet, 74in. long, 34in. wide. (Christie's) $1,070 £605

A four-poster bedstead decorated with leafage, six drawing curtains, 97in. high. (Lawrence Fine Art) $2,286 £1,210

A mahogany four-poster bedstead, labelled Heal & Son, Makers of Bedsteads and Bedding, London W, 74in. wide, 92in. high. (Christie's) $5,808 £3,520

Late 18th/early 19th century pine deception bedstead, Penn., in the form of a slant-front desk with four sham graduated long drawers, the back enclosing a hinged bedstead, 48in. high, 93in. long. (Christie's) $880 £496

A Federal carved mahogany four-post tester bedstead, probably Mass., 1800-20, 66in. wide. (Christie's) $12,100 £7,315

BEDS

A mahogany four-post bed with blind-fret carved canopy, hung with aquamarine watered silk, 54½in. wide, 97in. high. (Christie's)
$6,582 £3,520

An L. & J. G. Stickley slatted double-bed, signed with red (Handcraft) decal, 58in. wide. (Robt. W. Skinner Inc.)
$10,000 £5,952

A French Louis XV style walnut and carved bedstead, 48in. wide. (J. M. Welch & Son) $243 £160

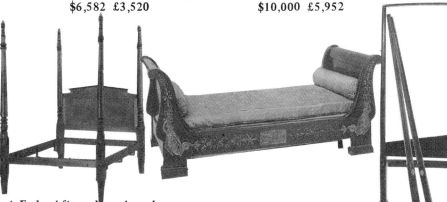

A Federal figured maple and ebonised high-post bedstead, Mass., 1810-20, 59in. wide. (Christie's) $1,430 £864

An Empire mahogany and ormolu mounted Lit en Bateau with cushion and bolsters. (Phillips) $5,460 £3,000

A Chippendale mahogany tall post bed, Goddard-Townsend School, Rhode Island, circa 1770, 54in. wide, 86in. high. (Robt. W. Skinner Inc.) $7,000 £4,166

A 19th century Italian blue-painted and parcel gilt four-post double bedstead, 71in. wide, 103in. high. (Christie's)
$1,996 £1,210

A Federal carved and inlaid walnut field bedstead, New England, 1800-20, 57in. wide. (Christie's)
$7,150 £4,322

One of a pair of mahogany Mission oak beds, possibly Roycroft, circa 1912, 42in. wide. (Robt. W. Skinner Inc.)
$650 £406

BOOKCASES

A Gustav Stickley double-door bookcase, no. 719, circa 1912, 60in. wide. (Robt. W. Skinner Inc.) $3,600 £2,142

A Gustav Stickley V-top bookrack, signed with red decal in a box, 1902-04, 31in. wide, 31in. high. (Robt. W. Skinner Inc.) $1,400 £833

A Sidney Barnsley walnut bookcase on two stepped trestle ends, 106.8cm. wide. (Christie's) $11,781 £7,700

A mahogany breakfront library bookcase with four astragal glazed doors enclosing adjustable shelves, 8ft.2in. wide. (Parsons, Welch & Cowell) $5,376 £3,200

Victorian, American walnut bookcase, the top section with two glazed doors, 3ft. 9in. wide. (G. A. Key) $885 £500

An L. & J. G. Stickley two-door bookcase, no. 654, circa 1910, 50in. wide. (Robt. W. Skinner Inc.) $3,000 £1,875

A two-door bookcase, with mitred mullions, by Gustav Stickley, circa 1902-03, 35½in. wide. (Robt. W. Skinner Inc.)$6,000 £3,243

A George III mahogany break-front bookcase with two pairs of geometrically glazed cup-board doors, 116in. wide. (Christie's) $34,485 £20,900

A mahogany bookcase on plinth base, partly late 18th century, 60½in. wide. (Christie's) $12,705 £7,700

BOOKCASES

A Regency mahogany dwarf bookcase on ormolu paw feet, 46in. wide. (Christie's) $14,767 £8,250

George III mahogany breakfront bookcase having double-opening glazed doors, 7ft. wide. (Giles Haywood) $7,258 £3,800

One of a pair of Regency brass inlaid mahogany dwarf bookcases, the sides with lion-mask and ring handles, 33½in. wide. (Christie's) $53,163 £29,700

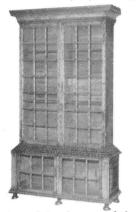

An oak book-press of the Pepys model, on bun feet, 57in. wide, 96½in. high. (Christie's) $7,009 £3,960

A Regency mahogany breakfront bookcase with partly replaced moulded cornice, 122in. wide. (Christie's) $16,736 £9,350

One of a pair of Regency mahogany bookcases with ebony stringing and later scrolled broken pediments, 52¼in. wide. (Christie's) $21,780 £13,200

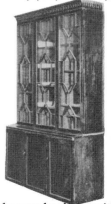

A mahogany bookcase with three glazed cupboard doors and three panelled cupboard doors with plinth base, 83in. wide. (Christie's) $3,406 £2,090

A Regency brass inlaid and mounted mahogany breakfront open bookcase with Gothic pierced galleried top, 94in. wide. (Christie's) $98,450 £55,000

A mahogany bookcase with moulded arcaded cornice above three glazed cupboard doors, 54½in. wide. (Christie's) $3,610 £1,980

BOOKCASES

A Regency mahogany bookcase, double glazed doors with brass strip and trellis fronts. (Locke & England) $1,304 £800

A Georgian carved mahogany breakfront library bookcase with four glazed astragal doors, 2.50m. wide. (Phillips) $31,160 £19,000

A French inspired walnut bookcase, upper section with three velvet-lined shelves, 49in. wide. (Locke & England) $4,401 £2,700

A Gustav Stickley two-door bookcase, no. 718, signed with large red decal, circa 1904-05, 54in. wide. (Robt. W. Skinner Inc.) $3,600 £2,250

An Arts & Crafts oak bookcase, the cupboard doors with copper hinges, 101.3cm. wide. (Christie's) $613 £374

A Regency rosewood dwarf bookcase with later rectangular verde antico marble top, 49in. wide. (Christie's) $1,353 £825

L. & J. G. Stickley single door bookcase with keyed tenons, no. 641, circa 1906, 36in. wide. (Robt. W. Skinner Inc.) $2,400 £1,500

A Regency mahogany bookcase in the Gothic style, 132¾in. wide. (Christie's) $20,619 £12,650

An ormolu mounted tulipwood bibliotheque in the Transitional style, 30in. wide. (Christie's) $3,306 £1,980

BOOKCASES

A mid Victorian walnut bookcase with three glazed and three panelled doors, 89in. wide. (Christie's) $7,260 £4,400

An early George III mahogany breakfront bookcase with scrolling pediment, 85½in. wide. (Christie's) $124,740 £77,000

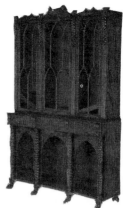

A George IV mahogany bookcase with undulating cornice flanking a broken scrolled pediment, 66in. wide. (Christie's) $14,520 £8,800

A Gustav Stickley two-door bookcase with keyed tenons, no. 716, 42½in. high. (Robt. W. Skinner Inc.) $2,500 £1,562

A 19th century Continental breakfront heavily carved bookcase, 10ft. wide. (Giles Haywood) $4,202 £2,200

A late Victorian walnut library bookcase, by Maple & Co., 183cm. wide. (Osmond Tricks) $1,650 £1,000

A George III mahogany bookcase with a pair of geometrically glazed cupboard doors, 52in. wide. (Christie's) $12,342 £7,480

A George III mahogany breakfront bookcase with two pairs of geometrically glazed doors, 82in. wide. (Christie's) $16,137 £9,900

One of a pair of Regency simulated rosewood and parcel gilt bookcases, 71½in. wide, 111in. high.(Christie's) $133,650 £82,500

BOOKCASES

 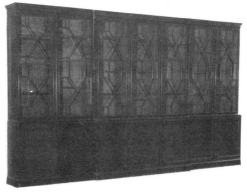 

A Victorian mahogany glazed bookcase, 3ft.9in. wide. (Giles Haywood) $2,387 £1,250

A mahogany breakfront bookcase, 182in. wide, 101in. high. (Christie's) $10,463 £6,380

A Regency mahogany bookcase with waved top and sides, 36in. wide. (Christie's) $1,793 £1,100

George IV mahogany breakfront library bookcase with four panel glazed, folding doors enclosing adjustable shelves, 113in. wide. (Prudential Fine Art) $6,930 £4,200

A grain painted wall shelf with scalloped sides, New England, circa 1840, 25½in. wide. (Robt. W. Skinner Inc.) $1,600 £952

An early 19th century mahogany breakfront library bookcase, 8ft.8in. wide. (Phillips) $9,828 £5,400

 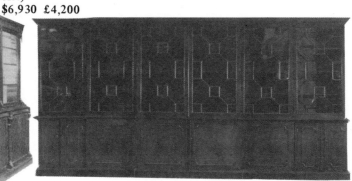 

An early 19th century figured mahogany bookcase, 158 x 208cm. high. (Wellington Salerooms) $7,728 £4,600

A George III mahogany double breakfront library bookcase, 220in. wide. (Christie's) $17,930 £11,000

Late 19th century satin walnut bookcase cupboard with two-door glazed and leaded upper section, 41in. wide.. (J. M. Welch & Son) $537 £320

BUREAU BOOKCASES

A George III mahogany bureau bookcase, with four graduated drawers. (Phillips)
$3,280 £2,000

A Chippendale walnut desk and bookcase with four graduated long drawers, on ogee bracket feet, 85in. high. (Christie's) $5,500 £3,072

A Georgian oak bureau bookcase, with two panel doors, bureau with fitted interior and four drawers, 81in. high. (Lawrence Fine Art)
$3,118 £1,650

A Chippendale mahogany desk and bookcase with four graduated long drawers, on ball-and-claw feet, 94in. high. (Christie's) $3,850 £2,150

A mahogany bureau bookcase, with fitted interior above four long drawers, 83in. high. (Lawrence Fine Art)
$3,950 £2,090

A small Chippendale mahogany desk bookcase, Mass., circa 1780, 34in. wide. (Robt. W. Skinner Inc.)
$14,000 £8,333

A George III satinwood secretaire cabinet of Sheraton style, the solid cylinder enclosing a fitted interior, 34½in. wide. (Christie's) $19,057 £11,550

A George III mahogany and inlaid bureau bookcase with single astragal glazed door, 33in. wide. (Dacre, Son & Hartley)
$3,772, £2,300

A walnut veneered bureau bookcase, the drawers oaklined. 31in. wide. (Woolley & Wallis) $3,240 £2,000

BUREAU BOOKCASES

A William and Mary period walnut bureau bookcase, on bun feet, 3ft.6in. wide. (Jacobs & Hunt)
$51,330 £29,000

A walnut bureau cabinet with a pair of bevelled glazed cupboard doors enclosing a partly fitted interior with two candle slides, 39¼in. wide. (Christie's)
$6,864   £4,160

A mid Georgian red walnut bureau cabinet, the cupboard doors enclosing a partly fitted interior with candle slides, 41in. wide. (Christie's)
$16,335   £9,900

A tiger marked walnut veneered bureau cabinet, basically 18th century, 3ft.7½in. wide. (Woolley & Wallis) $6,480 £4,000

A Chippendale mahogany desk and bookcase, possibly Charleston, S. Carolina, 1760-90, 53in. wide, 109in. high. (Christie's)$242,000 £146,313

A Queen Anne walnut bureau cabinet with two arched later glazed cupboard doors enclosing shelves, 31in. wide. (Christie's) $47,256 £26,400

A George III mahogany slope front bureau beneath a later but matching bookcase, 99cm. wide. (David Lay)
$2,340 £1,300

A William and Mary walnut bureau cabinet, the sloping flap enclosing a fitted interior, 42in. wide. (Christie's)
$16,236 £9,900

A William and Mary stained burr-elm bureau cabinet with moulded double-domed cornice, on later turned oak feet, 43½in. wide. (Christie's)
$49,225 £27,500

BUREAU BOOKCASES

Late 18th century mahogany bureau bookcase with fitted interior, 84in. high, (some restoration). (Brown & Merry) $5,278 £2,900

A George I walnut bureau cabinet with arched broken pediment, 40in. wide. (Christie's) $35,442 £19,800

A late Victorian mahogany and inlaid bureau bookcase. (Hobbs Parker)
          $1,628 £1,100

A Georgian mahogany, satinwood crossbanded and inlaid bureau bookcase, 4ft. wide. (Phillips) $5,642 £3,100

A George III mahogany bureau/cabinet in two parts, circa 1775, 7ft.6in. high, 4ft.4in. wide. (Ambrose)
          $6,120 £3,400

A walnut bureau bookcase with moulded cornice above a pair of glazed cupboard doors, 35¾in. wide. (Christie's)
$14,602   £8,250

A George I walnut bureau cabinet on bracket feet, 41½in. wide, 82in. high. (Christie's)
          $24,948 £15,400

A George I walnut bureau bookcase with two candle slides, 3ft.4in. wide. (Prudential Fine Art)
          $9,020 £5,500

A late 18th/early 19th century Dutch walnut and floral marquetry bureau cabinet in three parts, 1.39m. wide. (Phillips)
          $17,220 £10,500

BUREAUX

A Chippendale mahogany slant top desk, the fall-front reveals a fitted interior, Mass., circa 1780, 40in. wide. (Robt. W. Skinner Inc.)
$5,500 £3,273

A Georgian mahogany bureau. (Hobbs Parker)
$1,120 £700

An oak bureau, the hinged writing fall disclosing a fitted interior, on bracket feet, 3ft. wide. (Prudential Fine Art)
$1,377 £820

An 18th century George II mahogany fall-front bureau. (Warren & Wignall Ltd.)
$1,000 £625

A George III mahogany bureau, the sloping lid enclosing a fitted interior, 37in. wide. (Christie's)
$3,247 £1,980

An early Georgian walnut bureau, banded with elm, the sloping flap enclosing a fitted interior and well, 36½in. wide. (Christie's)
$9,735 £5,500

An early Georgian walnut bureau, the sloping flap enclosing a fitted interior including a well, 39½in. wide. (Christie's) $9,345 £5,280

A Chippendale mahogany block-front slant top desk with fitted interior, Salem, Mass., 1760-90, 43½in. wide. (Christie's) $22,000 £13,301

A Georgian mahogany bureau. (Hobbs Parker)
$2,000 £1,250

BUREAUX

An 18th century oak bureau.
(Hobbs Parker) $1,088 £680

Georgian mahogany fall-
front bureau with fitted
interior. (Ball & Percival)
$4,756 £2,900

An Edwardian mahogany
fall-front bureau with rosewood crossbandings, 2ft.6in.
wide. (G. A. Key) $460 £260

An 18th century Colonial
padoukwood bureau, 3ft.
1½in. wide. (Phillips)
$6,916 £3,800

A George III fruitwood bureau,
the flap top opening to reveal
serpentine interior, 96cm.
wide. (Lacy Scott)
$4,732 £2,600

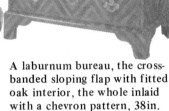
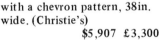

A laburnum bureau, the crossbanded sloping flap with fitted
oak interior, the whole inlaid
with a chevron pattern, 38in.
wide. (Christie's)
$5,907 £3,300

A figured mahogany bureau
on bracket feet with fitted
interior. (Broader & Spencer)
$2,268 £1,400

A Chippendale tiger maple
slant lid desk, the fall-front
reveals a stepped interior,
New England, circa 1780,
36in. wide. (Robt. W. Skinner
Inc.) $4,500 £2,678

A Chippendale mahogany
slant lid serpentine desk, Mass.,
circa 1780, 41½in. wide.
(Robt. W. Skinner Inc.)
$7,500 £4,213

BUREAUX

An early 18th century walnut, crossbanded and featherstrung bureau, the sloping fall enclosing a fitted interior, 87cm. wide. (Phillips) $4,100 £2,500

A Chippendale maple slant top desk, the fall-front opening to reveal a fitted interior, circa 1790, 36in. wide. (Robt. W. Skinner Inc.) $1,600 £1,000

A Chippendale birch reverse-serpentine front desk, Mass., 1765-85, 42½in. wide. (Christie's) $10,450 £6,318

George I walnut feather crossbanded fall-front bureau with fitted interior, circa 1720, 30in. wide. (Giles Haywood) $8,200 £5,000

A Chippendale mahogany slant-front desk with fitted interior, N.Y., 1760-90, 44¼in. wide. (Christie's) $4,400 £2,660

A Chippendale walnut slant-front desk with fitted interior, Penn., 1760-80, 41in. wide. (Christie's) $3,300 £1,995

A Federal inlaid mahogany cylinder-top desk with fitted interior, Baltimore, 1790-1810, 41in. wide. (Christie's) $14,300 £8,645

A Chippendale carved figured maple slant front desk, Rhode Island, 1760-80, 38in. wide. (Christie's) $12,650 £7,648

A Queen Anne walnut bureau, the crossbanded sloping flap enclosing a fitted interior, 36½in. wide. (Christie's) $18,040 £11,000

BUREAUX

A George III mahogany bureau with sloping lid enclosing an interior of serpentine drawers and pigeonholes, 42¾in. wide. (Christie's) $3,608 £2,200

A George III mahogany bureau, the sloping flap enclosing a fitted interior, 41in. wide. (Christie's) $2,164 £1,320

A George I walnut bureau with crossbanded sloping flap enclosing a fitted interior, 34in. wide. (Christie's) $15,334 £9,350

A George I walnut bureau inlaid with chequered lines, the slant lid enclosing a fitted interior, 41½in. wide. (Christie's) $20,493 £12,650

Early 19th century walnut and herringbone banded bureau on bun feet, 40in. wide. (Prudential Fine Art) $6,156 £3,800

An oyster-veneered laburnum bureau, the sloping lid enclosing a fitted interior with a well and central door, 31¾in. wide. (Christie's) $7,484 £4,620

A George II burr-yewwood bureau, the sloping fall enclosing an oak fitted and graduated interior, 88cm. wide. (Phillips) $9,020 £5,500

A Queen Anne maple desk on frame, the fall-front opens to interior of four drawers and valanced compartments, 24in. wide, circa 1760. (Robt. W. Skinner Inc.) $2,700 £1,687

A Georgian mahogany bureau with four tapered drawers and octagonal brass handles, 36in. wide. (Jacobs & Hunt) $2,080 £1,300

BUREAUX

A George III mahogany cylinder bureau, the roll flap reveals a fitted interior with a pull-out blue baize ratcheted writing top, 3ft.4in. wide. (Woolley & Wallis)
$11,550 £7,000

An early Georgian burr-yew and burr-walnut bureau, the sloping flap enclosing a fitted interior, 39in. wide. (Christie's) $5,082 £3,080

An Edwardian mahogany and marquetry inlaid cylinder front bureau with fitted interior, 32in. wide. (J. M. Welch & Son) $672 £400

Late 19th century ormolu mounted marquetry and trellis parquetry bureau a cylindre with musical trophy, 44in. wide. (Reeds Rains) $5,010 £3,000

A mid 19th century Danish oak bureau cabinet. (Miller & Co.) $2,640 £1,475

A George I burr-walnut bureau with hinged flap enclosing a fitted interior, 41¾in. wide. (Christie's) $6,855 £4,180

An inlaid pollard oak writing bureau with fitted interior, on bracket feet, 3ft. wide. (Ball & Percival) $4,136 £2,350

A Chippendale walnut desk, the hinged lid with moulded bookrest opening to a fitted interior, probably Virginia, 1760-80, 36in. wide. (Christie's) $6,050 £3,657

A mid Georgian walnut bureau inlaid with boxwood lines, the sloping flap enclosing a fitted interior, 34¼in. wide. (Christie's) $6,897 £4,180

CABINETS

One of a pair of 19th century Continental serpentine-fronted walnut inlaid and crossbanded side cabinets, 26in. wide. (Giles Haywood) $3,533 £1,850

One of a pair of mid 19th century satinwood, seaweed marquetry and ebonised credenzas, 172cm. wide. (Wellington Salerooms) $13,440 £8,000

Late 19th century lacquer cabinet formed in four sections, 216 x 135 x 44cm. (Christie's) $70,400 £44,000

A Regency ebonised, parcel gilt and Chinese lacquer dwarf cabinet with bowed breakfront black and yellow marble top, 68½in. wide. (Christie's) $48,114 £29,700

An Edwardian mahogany and marquetry inlaid side cabinet with carved and glazed door, 23in. wide. (J. M. Welch & Son) $364 £240

A mid 19th century burr-walnut, kingwood crossbanded and satinwood inlaid side cabinet with bow-fronted central section, 69in. wide. (Dacre, Son & Hartley) $5,445 £3,300

An Arts & Crafts oak cabinet with repousse hammered copper panels, circa 1900, 31¾in. wide. (Robt. W. Skinner Inc.) $1,000 £540

Mid 19th century burr-walnut marquetry inlaid and crossbanaded credenza with ormolu mounts, 75in. wide. (J. M. Welch & Son) $2,542 £1,550

A 19th century Oriental side cabinet with mother-of-pearl inlaid panels. (McKenna's) $1,092 £600

CABINETS

A giltmetal mounted ebony and scarlet boulle side cabinet with later black-painted top, 50in. wide. (Christie's) $2,178 £1,320

Late 17th century style oak and fruitwood panelled two-door cupboard, 48in. wide. (J. M. Welch & Son)
$912 £600

A 19th century French style ebony veneered side cabinet with cast gilt brass mounts, 4ft. wide. (Woolley & Wallis) $992 £620

Burr-walnut, rosewood and marquetry gilt metal mounted breakfront side cabinet, 45¾in. wide. (Prudential Fine Art) $3,840 £2,400

One of a pair of late 19th century ormolu mounted ebonised side cabinets, 28½in. wide. (Christie's)
$4,537 £2,750

A Regency parcel gilt and rosewood side cabinet with eared white marble top with concave sides, 38½in. wide. (Christie's)
$19,602 £12,100

Edwardian inlaid mahogany music cabinet with four drawers and open shelf. (Lots Road Chelsea Auction Galleries) $495 £300

A late 17th/early 18th century japanned and decorated cabinet on carved and silvered stand, 1.18m. wide, 1.65m. high. (Phillips) $9,840 £6,000

One of a pair of Japanese lacquer cabinets on stands, decorated in gilt on red and black, 19in. wide. (Parsons, Welch & Cowell)
$1,377 £820

CABINETS

Late 16th century Spanish walnut and red-painted cabinet with two frieze drawers, 48in. wide. (Christie's) $34,903 £20,900

A Regency rosewood and parcel gilt dwarf cabinet with eared rectangular white marble top, 51in. wide. (Christie's) $14,256 £8,800

One of two Regency brass inlaid and parcel gilt rosewood side cabinets with verde antico marble tops, one 37in. wide, the other 45in. wide. (Christie's) $19,602 £12,100

A Regency ormolu mounted rosewood and ebonised side cabinet, 29in. wide. (Christie's) $37,411 £20,900

A Chinese Export black lacquer cabinet-on-stand, mid 19th century, 41in. wide. (Christie's) $7,172 £4,400

A 19th century French design mahogany breakfront side cabinet on bun turned feet, 3ft.10in. wide. (Woolley & Wallis) $3,300 £2,000

A William IV parcel gilt painted and oak cabinet-on-stand, painted with the arms of the Duke of Westminster, 43in. wide. (Christie's) $15,262 £8,250

A mid Victorian ormolu mounted ebony breakfront side cabinet, 85½in. wide. (Christie's) $7,623 £4,620

A Flemish ivory inlaid ebony and tortoiseshell cabinet-on-stand, the cabinet 17th century, 40in. wide. (Christie's) $4,776 £2,860

A Flemish walnut, tortoiseshell and ebonised cabinet-on-stand, 30¼in. wide. (Christie's) $2,571 £1,540

A Regency rosewood side cabinet, the doors with panels of pleated red silk, 43in. wide. (Christie's) $3,427 £2,090

Late 17th century Flemish ebony cabinet-on-stand with hinged top, the interior painted in the style of Keirincx, 30¾in. wide. (Christie's) $8,266 £4,950

A figured walnut veneered cabinet-on-chest, the drawers with brass swan-neck handles, 3ft.2in. wide. (Woolley & Wallis) $4,860 £3,000

A Regency rosewood and parcel gilt side cabinet in the Southill manner, 59½in. wide. (Christie's) $44,550 £27,500

A mid Victorian walnut marquetry side cabinet with shaped, foliate edged back-plate, 29½in. wide. (Christie's) $1,837 £1,100

A 19th century satinwood cabinet in the French style, crossbanded with kingwood, 2ft.9in. wide. (Warners Wm. H. Brown) $4,800 £3,000

A 19th century serpentined boulle dwarf corner cabinet, brass inlaid into red tortoise-shell, 2ft.6in. wide. (Lots Road Chelsea Auction Galleries) $1,252 £750

A mid Victorian tulipwood, ebony and marquetry side cabinet with later eared serpentine top, 44½in. wide. (Christie's) $3,490 £2,090

CABINETS

A George III mahogany cabinet-on-stand, the panelled doors enclosing seven various-sized drawers, 32in. wide. (Christie's) $5,379 £3,300

A Regency rosewood and parcel gilt side cabinet, 42¾in. wide. (Christie's) $26,730 £16,500

A 19th century Spanish marquetry cabinet-on-stand, the interior with twenty-two various sized panelled doors, 49.1/8in. wide. (Christie's) $6,980 £4,180

One of a pair of mid Victorian figured walnut and marquetry side cabinets, 31½in. wide. (Christie's) $3,267 £1,980

A Regency mahogany and ebony strung D-shaped side cabinet with a reeded edge, 1.45m. (Phillips) $7,872 £4,800

A side cabinet, the chromium plated metal frame supporting two walnut shelves, 125cm. wide. (Christie's) $360 £220

One of a pair of Regency pollard oak side cabinets, attributed to G. Bullock, 53½in. wide. (Christie's) $392,040 £242,000

One of a pair of George IV mahogany side cabinets, the doors filled with ormolu trellis and pleated faded pale green silk, 22in. wide. (Christie's) $6,813 £4,180

A Regency mahogany breakfront side cabinet with moulded top and three panelled doors, 63in. wide. (Christie's) $1,793 £1,100

CANTERBURYS

A Regency mahogany canterbury with carrying handle and one division with spindle uprights, 18in. wide. (Christie's)
$4,123 £2,530

A Victorian carved mahogany canterbury. (Hobbs Parker) $841 £550

A mahogany canterbury with concave rectangular top and three pierced divisions, 18½in. wide. (Christie's) $2,032 £1,155

A 19th century mahogany canterbury on turned legs with brass castors, 1ft.9in. wide. (Hobbs & Chambers) $957 £580

A 19th century canterbury with spiral turned uprights and shaped lower drawer, 22in. wide. (Lots Road Chelsea Auction Galleries) $512 £320

A Victorian mahogany trolley with canterbury beneath, approx. 2ft. x 1ft.6in. (G. A. Key) $177 £100

A rosewood canterbury with X-shaped divisions centred by roundels, 20in. wide. (Christie's) $2,868 £1,760

An early Victorian mahogany canterbury on tapering legs. (David Lay) $805 £450

A Regency mahogany canterbury with three divisions on spindle supports, 18¾in. wide. (Christie's) $1,984 £1,210

CANTERBURYS

Mid 19th century figured walnut music canterbury with ebony inlay and one short drawer, 25in. wide. (Lalonde Fine Art)
$528 £320

Mid 19th century rosewood canterbury on china castors. (Brown & Merry)
$1,092 £600

A Victorian carved mahogany canterbury. (Hobbs Parker) $604 £360

An early Victorian rosewood veneered canterbury on turned legs. (David Lay)
$1,074 £600

A 19th century walnut canterbury on barley-twist supports, 26in. wide. (Locke & England)
$1,222 £750

An early Victorian walnut canterbury of three divisions, 23½in. wide. (Locke & England) $978 £600

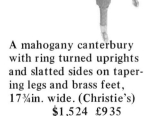

A mahogany canterbury with ring turned uprights and slatted sides on tapering legs and brass feet, 17¾in. wide. (Christie's)
$1,524 £935

A Regency mahogany canterbury with four pierced divisions and a frieze drawer, 19in. wide. (Christie's)
$2,868 £1,760

A Regency mahogany canterbury with slatted divided top, the base with a drawer, 20½in. wide. (Christie's) $4,477 £2,420

DINING CHAIRS

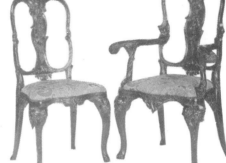

One of a set of eight George IV simulated rosewood dining chairs with cane filled seats. (Christie's)
$8,068 £4,950

Two of a set of five rosewood mahogany and marquetry inlaid occasional chairs, circa 1900. (J. M. Welch & Son)
$1,271 £775

One of a set of six mid Victorian rosewood shaped back standard chairs with drop-in seats. (Hetheringtons Nationwide)
$1,840 £1,150

One of a set of six carved mahogany Chippendale style single dining chairs with serpentine front rails and cabriole legs. (J. M. Welch & Son) $1,107 £675

Two of a set of twelve mid 18th century Portuguese walnut dining chairs, including a pair of open armchairs. (Christie's)
$14,685 £8,250

One of a set of nine Regency mahogany rosewood and brass inlaid dining chairs. (Phillips)
$12,740 £7,000

A rush-seated oak sidechair, by Joseph P. McHugh & Co., N.Y., circa 1900, 36in. high. (Robt. W. Skinner Inc.)
$300 £187

One of a set of twelve Regency mahogany dining chairs in the manner of Gillows. (Christie's)
$33,858 £20,900

Two of a set of six Federal painted fancy chairs, N.Y., 1800-15, 33¾in. high. (Christie's) $3,850 £2,327

DINING CHAIRS

One of a pair of mid
Victorian oak hall chairs,
the arched back carved
with a crest and the date
1873. (Christie's)
$1,270 £770

Two of a matching set of eight
Hepplewhite style dining chairs
with tapestry upholstered seats.
(J. M. Welch & Son)
$3,772 £2,300

One of a set of six stencilled
green-painted side chairs,
probably New York, circa
1820, 33¼in. high.
(Christie's) $2,860 £1,729

One of a set of six Queen
Anne cedar side chairs,
Bermuda, 1730-40, 41in.
high. (Christie's)
$28,600 £17,291

One of a set of eight George
III mahogany dining chairs,
including a pair of open armchairs. (Christie's)
$38,665 £20,900

Mid 18th century Chinese
carved padoukwood side
chair. (Phillips)
$10,920 £6,000

A Chippendale cherrywood
side chair with a square slip
seat, Mass,, 1780-1800,
38in. high. (Christie's)
$715 £432

Two of a set of eight William IV
mahogany dining chairs, the
Trafalgar seats covered in floral
needlework tapestry. (Capes
Dunn) $3,043 £1,700

A Queen Anne maple side
chair with rush seat, 41in.
high. (Christie's)
$495 £299

DINING CHAIRS

One of a set of eight balloon-back rosewood framed single dining chairs with upholstered seats, circa 1820. (J. M. Welch & Son) $4,455 £2,700

One of a pair of painted and decorated sidechairs, New England, circa 1820, 34in. high. (Robt. W. Skinner Inc.) $1,900 £1,130

One of a set of eight rosewood framed balloon-backed single chairs, circa 1850. (J. M. Welch & Son) $2,624 £1,600

One of a matched set of six late 18th/early 19th century single elm and beech ladder-back dining chairs. (Lacy Scott) $2,970 £1,800

One of a set of four Victorian mahogany balloon-back dining chairs with red velvet stuff-over serpentine fronted seats. (Hobbs & Chambers) $462 £260

One of a set of six late 19th century Chippendale design mahogany dining chairs with drop-in seats. (Lacy Scott) $4,950 £3,000

One of a set of six Chippendale carved mahogany side chairs, Phila., 1775-85, 38.5/8in. high. (Christie's) $34,100 £20,616

Child's Shaker ladder-back sidechair, New York, circa 1870, 26¼in. high. (Robt. W. Skinner Inc.) $550 £343

A Queen Anne walnut side chair on cabriole legs, Newport, 1730-60, 42½in. high. (Christie's) $3,300 £1,995

DINING CHAIRS

One of a pair of late Federal fancy chairs, probably by Hugh and John Finlay, Baltimore, circa 1815, 29in. high. (Christie's) $15,400 £9,310

Shaker maple tilter ladderback sidechair with rush seat, circa 1875, 39½in. high. (Robt. W. Skinner Inc.) $600 £375

One of a set of eight oak high-backed single dining chairs with panel seats. (J. M. Welch & Son) $721 £440

Regency mahogany hall chair with scroll and shell carved shaped back. (Prudential Fine Art) $445 £270

A painted maple and ash fanback Windsor sidechair, New England, circa 1780, 35in. high. (Robt. W. Skinner Inc.) $600 £375

One of a set of four William IV mahogany dining chairs with drop-in seats on fluted and turned front supports. (Prudential Fine Art) $1,089 £660

One of a pair of Classical Revival tiger maple sidechairs, America, circa 1830, 31½in. high. (Robt. W. Skinner Inc.) $2,400 £1,428

A fine George I dining chair, walnut veneered on elm, with drop-in seat. (Lacy Scott) $3,300 £2,000

A leather upholstered dining chair, no. 355, by Gustav Stickley, circa 1910, 33¼in. high. (Robt. W. Skinner Inc.) $950 £513

DINING CHAIRS

One of a pair of Chippendale period carved mahogany dining chairs with slip-in seats. (Phillips) $1,230 £750

One of a set of twelve Regency simulated rosewood and parcel gilt dining chairs comprising six armchairs and six side chairs. (Christie's) $28,512 £17,600

One of a set of six George III mahogany dining chairs with bowed padded seats. (Christie's) $7,530 £4,620

One of a set of eighteen Regency oak and parcel gilt dining chairs, attributed to George Bullock, 19in. wide, 34¾in. high. (Christie's) $142,560 £88,000

Two of a set of twenty mahogany dining chairs of George III style, including two armchairs and five side chairs of late 18th century date, one labelled Coutts & Findlater Ltd., Sunderland. (Christie's) $13,530 £8,250

One of a set of ten mahogany dining chairs of George III style including a pair of open armchairs. (Christie's) $10,463 £6,380

One of a set of four Regency blue-painted and parcel gilt side chairs with cane-filled backs and seats with squabs. (Christie's) $2,359 £1,430

Two of a set of six Sheraton design mahogany dining chairs including one carver. (Worsfolds) $3,198 £1,950

One of a set of six Louis Philippe walnut dining chairs, each with cartouche-shaped back and bowed cane-filled seat. (Christie's) $1,194 £715

DINING CHAIRS

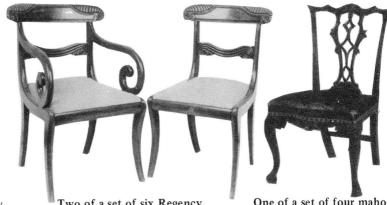

A George III mahogany
dining chair with padded
seat on moulded square
legs. (Christie's)
$681 £418

Two of a set of six Regency
mahogany dining chairs with
drop-in seats, on sabre supports.
(Prudential Fine Art)
$4,428 £2,700

One of a set of four mahogany dining chairs, each
with a serpentine toprail.
(Christie's)
$18,150 £11,000

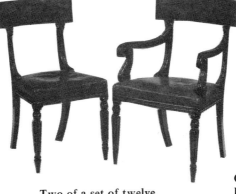

One of a set of six Louis
Philippe carved giltwood
and gesso salon chairs in
the manner of Fournier.
(Phillips) $8,200 £5,000

Two of a set of twelve
Regency mahogany dining
chairs in the style of Gillows.
(Christie's) $30,294 £18,700

One of a set of eight George
III mahogany dining chairs,
including one armchair, on
square tapering legs.
(Christie's) $6,096 £3,740

One of a set of seven Regency
mahogany dining chairs including an open armchair, with
drop-in seats. (Christie's)
$3,066 £1,870

Two of a set of twelve George III
carved mahogany dining chairs,
including a pair of elbow chairs,
in the Hepplewhite taste.
(Phillips) $24,600 £15,000

One of a set of seven mahogany dining chairs including
one armchair of Regency
style, early 19th century.
(Christie's) $2,755 £1,650

DINING CHAIRS

One of a set of five George III mahogany dining chairs, with two open armchairs. (Christie's) $3,066 £1,870

One of a set of six Regency mahogany dining chairs with cane-filled seats and button squab cushions. (Christie's) $2,541 £1,540

One of a set of six George IV ebonised and brass inlaid dining chairs with cane seats. (Christie's) $1,815 £1,100

A Country Queen Anne Transitional maple sidechair, attributed to the Gaines family, circa 1740, 41¾in. high. (Robt. W. Skinner Inc.) $2,900 £1,726

One of a set of six William IV mahogany dining chairs, including an open armchair, with moulded bowed top-rails. (Christie's) $3,630 £2,200

One of a set of twelve Regency cream-painted and parcel gilt dining chairs, including two armchairs. (Christie's) $15,147 £9,350

One of a set of eight George III mahogany dining chairs, including an armchair and a side chair ensuite, of later date. (Christie's) $7,260 £4,400

One of a set of four Regency black and gilt-painted dining chairs with cane seats. (Christie's) $1,226 £748

One of a pair of George III white-painted side chairs, the seats covered in pale blue silk. (Christie's) $1,361 £825

DINING CHAIRS

One of a set of four George III mahogany dining chairs inlaid with rosewood, the padded seats upholstered in pale yellow repp.
(Christie's) $3,085 £1,870

One of a set of four Regency mahogany dining chairs, including two armchairs, the padded seats covered in green leather. (Christie's)
$2,178 £1,320

Regency child's correction chair. (Worsfolds)
$656 £400

One of a set of six Regency parcel gilt and ebonised dining chairs, four inscribed in ink 'Pink Room'.
(Christie's) $1,443 £880

One of a pair of birch laminated side chairs by Gerald Summers. (Christie's)
$6,113 £3,740

One of a matched set of six Wigan ladder-back chairs in ash and elm, circa 1780.
(Prudential Fine Art)
$1,793 £1,100

One of a pair of mid Georgian walnut dining chairs, the drop-in seats covered in buttoned yellow shot silk.
(Christie's) $13,899 £8,580

One of a set of eight Regency dining chairs, the padded drop-in seats upholstered in yellow velvet. (Christie's)
$3,247 £1,980

One of a pair of George II cream-painted hall chairs, with the painted arms of the Duke of Northumberland. (Christie's)
$8,553 £5,280

DINING CHAIRS

One of a set of eight mahogany dining chairs including a pair of open armchairs with pierced ladder-backs. (Christie's) $8,167 £4,950

Two of a set of five Gustav Stickley dining chairs with rush seats, circa 1907, 37in. high. (Robt. W. Skinner Inc.) $1,700 £1,062

One of a set of four 18th century mahogany dining chairs. (Warren & Wignall Ltd.) $1,200 £750

One of a set of four George III mahogany dining chairs including an open armchair. (Christie's) $8,712 £5,280

Two of a set of twelve mahogany dining chairs, including a pair of open armchairs, the calico covered seats on turned fluted tapering legs. (Christie's) $10,527 £6,380

One of a set of four George IV mahogany dining chairs with bowed tablet toprails and drop-in seats. (Christie's) $1,255 £770

One of a set of ten George III mahogany dining chairs with tablet toprails and moulded X-shaped splats. (Christie's) $8,553 £5,280

Two of a set of seven late Georgian mahogany framed dining chairs, including two carvers. (Prudential Fine Art) $1,467 £900

One of a set of ten Regency green-painted and parcel gilt dining chairs. (Christie's) $24,948 £15,400

DINING CHAIRS

One of a set of eight mid Georgian mahogany hall chairs with cartouche-shaped solid backs. (Christie's) $10,692 £6,600

Two of a set of six 20th century Adirondack splint seat chairs, one armchair and five sidechairs, 38in. high. (Robt. W. Skinner Inc.) $475 £296

One of a pair of George III mahogany side chairs with oval padded backs and bowed seats. (Christie's) $811 £495

One of a set of ten Regency ebonised dining chairs with solid tablet toprails carved with rosettes. (Christie's) $7,260 £4,400

One of a set of four George III mahogany dining chairs and a similar open armchair. (Christie's) $3,968 £2,420

One of a set of six George III mahogany dining chairs with pierced shield-shape backs, bowed padded seats and square tapering legs. (Christie's) $4,356 £2,640

One of a set of four Regency brass inlaid simulated rosewood dining chairs with drop-in and cane-filled seats. (Christie's) $1,804 £1,100

Two of a set of eight mahogany inlaid chairs, Edwardian. (Warren & Wignall Ltd.) $3,040 £1,900

One of a set of four Regency brass mounted simulated rosewood dining chairs on sabre legs. (Christie's) $1,443 £880

FURNITURE

One of a set of four mid 19th century giltwood fauteuils of Louis XVI style. (Christie's)
$2,178 £1,320

One of a pair of Regency mahogany wing armchairs, upholstered in hide. (Christie's) $7,260 £4,400

A mid Victorian ebonised oak open armchair by J. Kendell & Co., the back and seat with squabs. (Christie's) $816 £495

A George III mahogany wing armchair upholstered in pale blue repp. (Christie's)
$3,406 £2,090

A late Regency mahogany hall porter's chair with arched hooded back and seat covered in brown leather, 61½in. high. (Christie's)
$4,303 £2,640

A George III white and green-painted bergere with padded back, sides and seat covered in pale green cloth. (Christie's) $980 £605

A mahogany armchair of George III style, the padded serpentine back, arms and seat upholstered in floral repp. (Christie's)
$541 £330

Late 19th century wing easy chair with reclining action. (Lots Road Chelsea Auction Galleries)
$810 £500

A walnut fauteuil, the car-touche-shaped back and bowed seat upholstered in gros and petit-point needle-work. (Christie's)
$1,775 £1,045

EASY CHAIRS

One of a pair of George III parcel gilt and cream painted open armchairs with bowed seats. (Christie's)
$5,379 £3,300

A Louis XVI stained beechwood fauteuil with oval padded back and bowed seat covered in foliate repp. (Christie's) $1,194 £714

One of a pair of Hepplewhite carved mahogany elbow chairs in the French taste with serpentine stuffover seats. (Phillips) $9,512 £5,800

A Regency mahogany bergere chair with caned back and seat. (Woolley & Wallis)
$1,101 £680

An early Victorian oak open armchair attributed to A. W. N. Pugin, the back and seat upholstered in contemporary foliate cut velvet. (Christie's)
$8,910 £5,500

An early George III mahogany open armchair with padded back and seat upholstered in pink and brown cut velvet. (Christie's) $24,948 £15,400

A George III giltwood open armchair arributed to Thos. Chippendale. (Christie's)
$3,029 £1,870

A George III mahogany library armchair, the padded back and seat covered in red leather. (Christie's)
$8,606 £5,280

One of a pair of giltwood fauteuils of Louis XVI style. (Christie's)
$1,542 £935

EASY CHAIRS

A Chippendale mahogany easy chair, Penn., 1780-1800, 47¾in. high. (Christie's) $8,800 £5,320

A Victorian walnut framed sewing chair on cabriole legs. (G. A. Key) $619 £350

A Chippendale upholstered wing chair, New England, circa 1810, 45¾in. high. (Robt. W. Skinner Inc.) $1,800 £1,125

A Federal inlaid mahogany lolling chair with serpentine front, possibly Portsmouth, New Hampshire, 1800-10, 43in. high. (Christie's) $11,000 £6,650

Part of a late 19th century suite of furniture of Louis XV style, comprising a canape and four fauteuils, labelled E. G. Gaze Meubles Anciens Dorures, Rue Charles V. No. 8 Paris, the canape 86in. wide. (Christie's) $14,520 £8,800

A Federal mahogany lolling chair, Mass., circa 1815, 44in. high. (Robt. W. Skinner Inc.) $5,500 £3,273

One of a pair of George II mahogany side chairs upholstered in gros and petitpoint needlework, the needlework early 18th century. (Christie's) $44,550 £27,500

One of a pair of upholstered easy armchairs by Howard & Sons. (Christie's) $3,306 £1,980

A Regency mahogany chair with concave back, on square tapered splay feet. (King & Chasemore) $2,700 £1,500

EASY CHAIRS

One of a pair of early Victorian rosewood open armchairs with cartouche-shaped buttoned padded backs and serpentine seats. (Christie's) $11,654 £7,150

A Victorian carved walnut nuring chair, upholstered in velvet. (King & Chasemore) $468 £260

A Country Federal child's mahogany wing chair, New England, circa 1770, 30¼in. high. (Robt. W. Skinner Inc.) $5,500 £3,273

Mid 18th century walnut wing armchair with high arched back, outscrolled arms and squab cushion. (Christie's) $5,062 £2,860

One of a pair of walnut bergeres upholstered in green velvet, on moulded cabriole legs and scrolled toes. (Christie's) $1,633 £990

A Queen Anne walnut easy chair on cabriole legs with pointed slipper feet, N.Y., 1735-55. (Christie's) $22,000 £13,301

One of a set of three mahogany open armchairs of Louis XV style, upholstered in strawberry damask. (Christie's) $9,020 £5,500

Victorian button-back armchair upholstered in champagne velvet dralon.) (County Group) $283 £175

A gentleman's 19th century wing armchair upholstered in floral tapestry, on cabriole supports with claw and ball feet. (Greenslade & Co.) $516 £290

One of a pair of giltwood
fauteuils of Louis XVI
style, upholstered in floral
tapestry. (Christie's)
$1,996 £1,210

A wing armchair with shaped
back on stretcher base. (Lots
Road Chelsea Auction Galleries) $388 £240

One of a set of six Louis XVI
carved beechwood fauteuils
en cabriolet with stuffover
bowed seats. (Phillips)
$15,580   £9,500

A George III cream painted
and parcel gilt open arm-
chair with oval padded back
and serpentine seat.
(Christie's) $2,330 £1,430

An early George III walnut
wing armchair with padded
back, bowed seat with a
squab cushion. (Christie's)
$12,474 £7,700

One of a set of eight George
III giltwood open armchairs
with heart-shaped backs and
serpentine seats. (Christie's)
$44,550 £27,500

One of a pair of George III
mahogany library armchairs,
the padded backs, arms and
seats covered in close-nailed
beige velvet. (Christie's)
$9,801 £6,050

Victorian spoon-back and
buttoned chair in walnut
frame, upholstered in green
and gold cut-patterned
velvet. (County Group)
$442 £265

A Louis XVI carved giltwood
bergere with arched upholstered panel back and padded
scroll arm supports with stuffover serpentine seat. (Phillips)
$951 £580

EASY CHAIRS

Mid 18th century giltwood fauteuil with padded cartouche-shaped back and serpentine feet. (Christie's) $918 £550

One of a pair of mahogany open armchairs of George III design, covered in light cream damask. (Christie's) $5,808 £3,520

A Louis XV giltwood fauteuil, the cartouche-shaped padded back and bowed seat covered in embroidered silk. (Christie's) $1,561 £935

A Louis XV walnut fauteuil with cartouche-shaped back and bowed seat. (Christie's) $2,204 £1,320

A mahogany framed tub-shaped low seat chair with stuffed overseat. (County Group) $83 £50

A Louis XVI giltwood fauteuil with padded oval back and circular seat covered in green damask. (Christie's) $2,020 £1,210

A Regency mahogany bergere with rectangular padded back, arm-rests and seat, the sides filled with split cane. (Christie's) $4,719 £2,860

One of a matched pair of Louis XV fauteuils with cartouche-shaped padded backs and seats upholstered in salmon repp. (Christie's) $2,388 £1,430

A Regency mahogany library armchair, the cane filled back and seat with red leather squab cushions. (Christie's) $3,406 £2,090

389

ELBOW CHAIRS

One of a set of ten George III painted open armchairs, the padded and caned seats with pink and ivory striped silk squab cushions. (Christie's) $17,820 £11,000

One of a pair of Regency mahogany open armchairs with blue brocade covered drop-in seats, (Christie's) $4,123 £2,530

A Regency mahogany reading chair with horseshoe-shaped toprail and vertical bar splats. (Christie's) $3,207 £1,980

One of a set of eight Regency mahogany dining chairs, including two elbow chairs, with stuffover seats. (Phillips) $7,872 £4,800

Early 20th century wicker arm rocker, 31in. wide. (Robt. W. Skinner Inc.) $200 £119

One of a pair of 19th century hardwood elbow chairs with marble inset panel splats and cane seats, (Phillips) $3,116 £1,900

One of a set of twelve Spanish walnut open armchairs, seven upholstered in distressed gilt leather, five in cream cotton. (Christie's) $8,450 £5,060

A Gustav Stickley spindle-sided cube chair, no. 391, circa 1907, 26in. wide. (Robt. W. Skinner Inc.) $16,000 £9,523

One of a pair of Charles X gilt metal mounted mahogany side chairs with padded drop-in seats. (Christie's) $2,204 £1,320

ELBOW CHAIRS

A Regency mahogany
library armchair with cane-
filled back and seat with
yellow repp squab cushion.
(Christie's) $1,533 £935

A George II mahogany
elbow chair on cabriole
legs with trifid pad feet.
(Phillips) $1,804 £1,100

One of a pair of Regency
blue-painted and parcel
gilt armchairs with padded
arm rests and seats, both
stamped T. Gray.
(Christie's)$19,057 £11,550

A Chippendale carved
mahogany elbow chair
with slip-in gros point
needlework seat and arm
supports. (Phillips)
$1,804 £1,100

A Gustav Stickley bent arm
spindle Morris chair, circa
1907, with spring cushion
seat. (Robt. W. Skinner Inc.)
$1,300 £7,738

A Regency cream and parcel
gilt open armchair with cane-
filled seat and sabre legs.
(Christie's) $902 £550

One of a set of five Regency
green-painted and parcel
gilt open armchairs, the
caned seats with yellow silk
squab cushions. (Christie's)
$23,166 £14,300

A Gustav Stickley bird's-eye
maple wide slat cube chair,
circa 1903-04, no. 328.
(Robt. W. Skinner Inc.)
$3,000 £1,785

A mahogany open armchair
of George II style, with
padded drop-in seat.
(Christie's) $3,448 £2,090

ELBOW CHAIRS

A Victorian woven canework rocking armchair. (Osmond Tricks) $198 £120

A wicker patio chair designed by Terence Conran. (Christie's) $134 £88

A Plail Bros. barrel-back armchair, Wayland, N.Y., circa 1910, 33in. high. (Robt. W. Skinner Inc.) $900 £562

A George III carved mahogany elbow chair in the Hepplewhite taste with serpentine stuffover seat. (Phillips) $2,460 £1,500

One of a pair of Venetian silver and brown-painted grotto chairs, each with a mussel shell-shaped back, dolphin arms and clam shell-shaped seat on carved base with pearls. (Christie's)
$5,482 £3,080

A Regency mahogany library bergere with cane back, sides and seat with cushions. (Phillips)
$2,132 £1,300

A Queen Anne mahogany armchair, Mass., circa 1750, 42in. high. (Robt. W. Skinner Inc.) $60,000 £35,714

An adjustable back armchair, attributed to J. Young & Co., circa 1910, 31½in. wide. (Robt. W. Skinner Inc.)
$800 £476

A Chippendale maple corner chair, the square slip seat above a deep double-ogee-shaped skirt, 1760-80. (Christie's) $3,850 £2,327

ELBOW CHAIRS

George IV mahogany elbow chair with carved back rail and centre splat. (J. M. Welch & Son) $524 £320

A leather upholstered dining armchair, by Gustav Stickley, circa 1910, no. 355A, 36¼in. high. (Robt. W. Skinner Inc.) $1,800 £972

One of a set of eight well matched early 19th century Macclesfield dining chairs with rush seats. (Brown & Merry) $5,005 £2,750

An oak and oak veneered armchair with scenic inlay, circa 1910, unsigned, 37in. high. (Robt. W. Skinner Inc.) $1,400 £756

A mahogany Hepplewhite style chair with tapered legs and splayed feet. (Hetheringtons Nationwide) $480 £300

George III oak corner chair with cabriole front leg and pad foot. (Brown & Merry) $1,055 £580

A George II white-painted and parcel gilt open elbow chair in the manner of Thos. Chippendale. (Christie's) $1,452 £880

Plail Bros. barrel-back rocker, with spring cushion seat, N.Y., circa 1910, 31½in. high. (Robt. W. Skinner Inc.) $325 £203

One of a set of ten hand-carved mahogany chairs, the seats with brown leather style covers. (Lots Road Chelsea Auction Galleries) $1,452 £880

ELBOW CHAIRS

One of a pair of Empire mahogany fauteuils with scrolled padded backs and bowed seats upholstered in green silk. (Christie's) $3,306 £1,980

An L. & J. G. Stickley adjustable back flat armchair, no. 412, circa 1909, 35in. wide. (Robt. W. Skinner Inc.)
$2,700 £1,607

One of a set of eight George III mahogany dining chairs, including a pair of open armchairs. (Christie's)
$7,216 £4,400

One of a set of eight early Victorian rosewood open armchairs of George II style. (Christie's)
$15,240 £9,350

A Gustav Stickley slat-sided cube chair, no. 331, circa 1910, 25¼in. wide. (Robt. W. Skinner Inc.)
$5,250 £3,125

One of a pair of oak framed ecclesiastical chairs. (Lots Road Chelsea Auction Galleries) $501 £300

A Regency ebonised bergere with deep curved toprail and upholstered back and seat covered in pale green leather. (Christie's) $13,365 £8,250

A Gustav Stickley oak 'Eastwood' chair with original rope support for seat, circa 1902. (Robt. W. Skinner Inc.) $28,000 £16,666

One of a set of twelve parcel gilt and black-painted open armchairs of Regency style with cane-filled backs and seats, redecorated. (Christie's) $25,256 £15,400

ELBOW CHAIRS

A George III mahogany
open armchair, the padded
drop-in seat covered in
needlework. (Christie's)
$1,172   £715

A late Louis XVI beechwood
fauteuil bureau with circular
caned seat, stamped I. B.
Lelarge. (Christie's)
$4,592 £2,750

One of a pair of Spanish
walnut armchairs with
close-nailed rectangular
leather backs and seats.
(Christie's) $2,020 £1,210

One of a pair of George III
mahogany open armchairs
with oval padded backs
and bowed seats upholstered
in green repp. (Christie's)
$11,583   £7,150

One of a set of ten Regency
carved mahogany dining
chairs on sabre legs, including
two armchairs. (Phillips)
$5,904 £3,600

One of a pair of Regency
mahogany armchairs, the
arms with turned supports
and padded seats. (Christie's)
$4,690 £2,860

Late 18th century blue-
painted and parcel gilt
fauteuil, possibly Scandinavian. (Christie's)
$4,776 £2,860

William IV mahogany
framed library armchair,
with leatherette cushions.
(Lots Road Chelsea Auction
Galleries) $567 £350

A Regency mahogany arm-
chair with cane-filled back
and seat with red leather
squab cushion. (Christie's)
$1,262 £770

ELBOW CHAIRS

A Gustav Stickley child's arm rocker, no. 345, signed with small red decal and paper label, circa 1904-06. (Robt. W. Skinner Inc.) $500 £297

Mid 19th century pine desk chair, the tablet set with a photograph of Abraham Lincoln, 31in. high. (Christie's) $1,650 £997

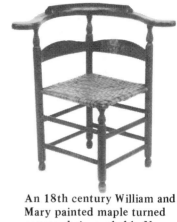

An 18th century William and Mary painted maple turned corner chair, probably New England, 32in. high. (Robt. W. Skinner Inc.) $2,700 £1,607

An early 19th century elm-wood and ash miniature Windsor chair. (J. M. Welch & Son) $393 £240

Early 19th century green-painted rocking settee, New England, 31in. wide. (Christie's) $1,980 £1,197

An oak framed chair with carved narrow back and shaped arms. (Lots Road Chelsea Auction Galleries) $583 £360

A Federal cherrywood lolling chair, Mass., 1785-1800, 42½in. high. (Christie's) $6,050 £3,657

A Gustav Stickley bow arm-chair, no. 335, circa 1905, signed with small red decal, 37½in. high. (Robt. W. Skinner Inc.) $5,500 £3,437

One of a set of four classical Revival painted armchairs, circa 1820, 32in. high. (Robt. W. Skinner Inc.) $2,600 £1,625

ELBOW CHAIRS

An early 18th century child's painted maple ladder-back armchair with rush seat, New England, 30½in. high. (Robt. W. Skinner Inc.) $550 £327

An 18th century Continental fruitwood open elbow chair. (Hobbs & Chambers)
$612 £350

A William and Mary American walnut elbow chair with caned back panel and seat with squab cushion. (Woolley & Wallis)
$1,188 £720

A walnut framed Queen Anne style carver chair with drop-in seat. (McKenna's)
$819 £450

Early 20th century spindle-back lift seat hall bench, style no. 542, unsigned, 46in. wide. (Robt. W. Skinner Inc.)
$425 £265

A 19th century hardwood Windsor stickback elbow chair with pierced splat. (Hobbs & Chambers)
$409 £230

One of a pair of Regency simu-lated bamboo bergeres in the Brighton Pavilion taste, with blue linen covered squab cushions. (Christie's) $22,385 £12,100

A walnut open armchair, the arched back carved with two angels and trophies with blue and gilt leather panel. (Christie's) $973 £550

A Gustav Stickley adjustable back drop armchair, no. 369, circa 1907, signed with red decal, 38in. high. (Robt. W. Skinner Inc.) $4,500 £2,812

ELBOW CHAIRS

An ash and maple bow-back knuckle arm Windsor chair, probably Conn., circa 1780, 33½in. high. (Robt. W. Skinner Inc.)$6,000 £3,571

A bent arm spindle Morris chair, no. 369, by Gustav Stickley, with adjustable back, 24in. high. (Robt. W. Skinner Inc.) $14,000 £7,567

A stencil decorated rocking chair, probably Mass., circa 1820, 44in. high. (Robt. W. Skinner Inc.) $1,000 £595

One of a pair of 19th century oak Jacobean elbow chairs profusely carved with mythical beasts. (Lots Road Chelsea Auction Galleries) $873 £520

A tall spindle-back armchair, no. 386, by Gustav Stickley, 49½in. high. (Robt. W. Skinner Inc.)
$12,000 £6,486

A Chippendale mahogany corner chair, Newport, Rhode Island, 1750-70, 32½in. high. (Christie's) $27,500 £16,626

A George III mahogany Windsor armchair with comb-back and yoke-shaped arms. (Christie's)
$10,692 £6,600

A child's spindle back arm rocker, unsigned, circa 1915, 24¼in. high. (Robt. W. Skinner Inc.) $375 £202

An American 19th century tin sack-back Windsor arm-chair, 36in. high. (Christie's)
$286 £161

ELBOW CHAIRS

One of six matching elm Windsor open arm elbow chairs. (Geering & Colyer) $5,518 £3,100

An Edwardian child's adjustable high chair. (McKenna's) $273 £150

A Victorian slat-back stretcher armchair. (James Norwich Auctions) $113 £65

A yewwood and inlaid elbow chair with wheel-shaped back and two front tapered legs. (Hetheringtons Nationwide) $800 £500

Mid 19th century birch armchair with rush seat. (Peter Wilson) $437 £270

Early 19th century ash and elm comb-back Windsor armchair. (Prudential Fine Art) $336 £210

Edwardian elbow chair, the padded seat and back panel upholstered in tapestry. (County Group) $158 £95

One of a set of seven turned maple folding deck chairs, upholstered with gold, green and blue striped cotton velvet. (Christie's) $3,520 £2,011

One of a pair of 19th century rosewood chairs, on shaped legs. (John Hogbin & Son) $3,772 £2,300

CHESTS OF DRAWERS

An early Georgian walnut and elm chest with two short and three graduated long drawers on later bun feet, 36½in. wide. (Christie's) $1,262 £770

A George II mahogany chest with rectangular top and brushing slide, 28½in. wide. (Christie's) $8,068 £4,950

An early Georgian burr-yew chest with two short and four graduated long drawers, 43in. wide. (Christie's) $8,167 £4,950

A Gustav Stickley chest-of-drawers, no. 901, with wooden pulls, circa 1907, 37in. wide. (Robt. W. Skinner Inc.) $1,300 £773

A George III mahogany chest with moulded rectangular top, on bracket feet, 38in. wide. (Christie's) $1,996 £1,210

A Chippendale curly maple chest-of-drawers, probably New Hampshire, 1775-1810, 39in. wide. (Christie's) $6,600 £3,990

A Charles II oak chest-of-drawers with oyster walnut veneered front, 3ft.3in. wide. (Woolley & Wallis) $2,268 £1,400

A George I walnut chest with crossbanded and quartered chamfered top, 35in. wide. (Christie's) $5,737 £3,520

A Regency mahogany bow-fronted chest, the top cross-banded with satinwood, 36in. wide. (Christie's) $4,329 £2,640

CHESTS OF DRAWERS

A George III Cuban mahogany chest, the drawers oak lined, 32in. wide. (Woolley & Wallis) $1,536 £960

A Country Federal maple painted four-drawer chest, possibly Maine, circa 1800, 38¾in. wide. (Robt. W. Skinner Inc.) $3,700 £2,312

A George III mahogany chest with crossbanded moulded serpentine top, 39in. wide. (Christie's) $10,463 £6,380

A Chippendale poplar blanket chest, New England, circa 1780, 37¾in. wide. (Robt. W. Skinner Inc.) $950 £593

An early 18th century walnut veneered crossbanded and featherstrung chest, fitted with a slide, 81cm. (Phillips) $5,904 £3,600

A Chippendale curly maple five-drawer chest, New England, circa 1780, 37¼in. wide. (Robt. W. Skinner Inc.) $1,000 £625

A George III mahogany chest with serpentine top and leather-lined dressing slide, 37in. wide. (Christie's) $9,922 £6,050

A Gustav Stickley nine-drawer tall chest, no. 913, circa 1907, 36in. wide, 50in. high. (Robt. W. Skinner Inc.) $4,000 £2,500

A Federal mahogany and mahogany veneer bowfront bureau, possibly Penn., circa 1815, 41½in. wide. (Robt. W. Skinner Inc.) $850 £531

CHESTS-OF-DRAWERS

George II mahogany chest with brushing slide above two short and three graduated long drawers, 36½in. wide. (Reeds Rains) $2,087 £1,250

A Chippendale mahogany chest-of-drawers, Penn., circa 1780, 38in. wide. (Robt. W. Skinner Inc.) $3,500 £2,083

A mahogany bowfront chest-of-drawers with ivory inset escutcheons. (Broader & Spencer) $1,263 £780

A Country Chippendale tiger maple blanket chest, New England, circa 1760, 37¾in. wide. (Robt. W. Skinner Inc.) $9,500 £5,654

A Queen Anne painted maple tall chest on a tall bracket base, New England, circa 1750, 36in. wide. (Robt. W. Skinner Inc.) $6,500 £3,869

A Chippendale tiger maple tall chest on bracket feet, replaced brasses, New England, circa 1790, 38½in. wide. (Robt. W. Skinner Inc.) $5,500 £3,273

A grain painted pine five-drawer chest, New England, circa 1780, 37¾in. wide. (Robt. W. Skinner Inc.) $6,000 £3,571

A Chippendale cherry and pine four-drawer bureau on ogee bracket feet, Conn., circa 1780, 39½in. wide. (Robt. W. Skinner Inc.) $4,250 £2,529

A Queen Anne painted pine two-drawer blanket box, the lift-lid above three false drawers and two working drawers, probably Mass., circa 1750, 38¾in. wide. (Robt. W. Skinner Inc.) $2,400 £1,428

CHESTS-OF-DRAWERS

A George III mahogany bow-front chest with four long graduated drawers, on French bracket feet, 3ft.1in. wide. (Lalonde Fine Art) $858 £520

Early 19th century mahogany chest-of-drawers, having oval burr walnut inset with rosewood crossbanding, 3ft.5in. wide. (Lawrences) $1,428 £850

Early 19th century oak square fronted chest of four long graduated drawers, 32in. wide. (J. M. Welch & Son) $470 £280

A George III mahogany chest of two short over three long graduated drawers on shaped bracket feet, 36in. wide. (Hy. Duke & Son) $1,116 £620

A George II mahogany chest crossbanded with rosewood, 37in. wide. (Christie's) $8,606 £5,280

A 19th century mahogany square-front chest of three graduated drawers, 21in. wide. (J. M. Welch & Son) $520 £310

An early 18th century mahogany chest of four long graduated drawers. (Hobbs Parker) $2,608 £1,620

A Chippendale maple tall chest-of-drawers with original pulls, circa 1780, 36in. wide. (Robt. W. Skinner Inc.) $6,500 £3,869

A small Georgian mahogany chest of four long drawers. (Hobbs Parker) $1,897 £1,150

A Federal inlaid mahogany bowfront chest-of-drawers on French feet, Mass., 1790-1810, 40¾in. wide. (Christie's) $4,180 £2,527

A Regency mahogany bowfronted chest with four graduated drawers, 42in. wide. (Christie's)
$3,944 £2,420

A Chippendale carved mahogany reverse-serpentine chest-of-drawers, Mass., 1760-80, 39½in. wide. (Christie's)
$19,800 £11,971

A Chippendale carved maple five-drawer chest, attributed to the Dunlap family, New Hampshire, circa 1780, 40½in. wide. (Christie's)
$22,000 £13,301

A George III mahogany dressing chest, containing three long drawers, 97cm. wide. (Phillips)
$2,460 £1,500

A nine-drawer tall chest with cast bronze faceted pulls, by Gustav Stickley, circa 1904-06, 36in. wide. (Robt. W. Skinner Inc.) $7,000 £3,783

A George I walnut bachelor's chest with two short and three graduated long drawers on bracket feet, 30in. wide. (Christie's) $30,294 £18,700

An 18th century mahogany chest with four long graduated drawers, 74cm. wide. (David Lay) $1,288 £720

A Chippendale cherrywood block-front chest-of-drawers, Boston, Mass., 1760-80, 34in. wide. (Christie's)
$49,500 £29,927

CHESTS OF DRAWERS

A Chippendale mahogany serpentine bureau, New England, circa 1780, 38¼in. wide. (Robt. W. Skinner Inc.) $5,000 $3,125

A George II mahogany bachelor's chest with hinged top and on bracket feet, 32in. wide. (Christie's) $3,247 £1,980

Georgian inlaid mahogany Lancashire chest. (Ball & Percival) $3,116 £1,900

A Queen Anne walnut chest, the drawers oak-lined with brass drop handles, 103cm. wide. (Dee & Atkinson) $770 £480

A mahogany chest-of-drawers with brass lion's head handles, on platform base, 43in. wide. (County Group) $292 £175

A George I walnut bachelor's chest, the crossbanded top lined with velvet enclosing a well, 33in. wide. (Christie's) $13,365 £8,250

A Chippendale mahogany reverse-serpentine chest-of-drawers, Mass., 1760-80, 43in. wide. (Christie's) $19,800 £11,971

Georgian mahogany bachelor's chest of four graduated drawers with brushing slide above, approx. 2ft.6in. wide. (G. A. Key) $2,722 £1,650

A Victorian teak military secretaire chest with baize lined fall-front, 3ft.6in. wide. (Prudential Fine Art) $1,815 £1,100

FURNITURE

An early 18th century walnut chest on chest, three short and three long boxwood strung drawers with three graduated drawers, 102cm. (Phillips) $5,576 £3,400

A George I walnut tallboy, fitted with three short and six long drawers, original brass handles, on bracket feet, 74in. high. (Dreweatt Neate) $12,852 £6,800

A George I burr-walnut secretaire tallboy crossbanded and inlaid with chevron bands, 42¼in. wide. (Christie's) $29,535 £16,500

A mahogany veneered tall-boy chest on bracket feet, 3ft.7in. wide. (Woolley & Wallis) $2,430 £1,500

The John Mills family Chippendale cherrywood chest-on-chest, by Major Dunlap, New Hampshire, circa 1780, 41½in. wide. (Christie's) $66,000 £39,903

A Queen Anne maple chest-on-chest, in two sections, New Hampshire, 1740-70, 41in. wide. (Christie's) $14,300 £8,645

A George III mahogany tall-boy with two short and six graduated long drawers, 40in. wide. (Christie's) $7,876 £4,400

A mahogany bowfront chest-on-chest on splay feet, 3ft.6in. wide. (Lots Road Chelsea Auction Galleries) $2,720 £1,700

An early 18th century walnut chest on chest, three short and seven long drawers, on bracket feet, 194 x 106cm. (Phillips) $4,900 £2,800

CHESTS-ON-CHESTS

George I figured walnut tallboy, in two sections, 3ft.6in. wide. (Prudential Fine Art) $6,560 £4,000

A George II walnut chest-on-chest, molded cornice and three short drawers, over six long drawers, 69¾in. high. (Robt. W. Skinner Inc.) $6,750 £3,770

A George I walnut tallboy on bracket feet, 42in. wide, 69in. high. (Christie's) $11,048 £6,820

A Chippendale maple chest-on-chest, Mass., circa 1780, 38in. wide. (Robt. W. Skinner Inc.) $8,750 £5,468

A George I walnut tallboy chest, with three short and six long drawers, on shaped bracket feet, 5ft.9in. x 3ft.8in. (Phillips) $10,850 £6,200

A George I walnut tallboy with moulded cavetto cornice, 43in. wide. (Christie's) $12,705 £7,700

An early George III carved mahogany tallboy chest on bracket feet, 1.14m. wide. (Phillips) $5,248 £3,200

Early 18th century walnut chest on bracket feet, 28in. wide. (Chancellors Hollingsworths) $2,755 £1,650

A George III mahogany chest-on-chest with two short and six long drawers. (Chancellors Hollingsworths) $2,004 £1,200

CHESTS-ON-STANDS

Black lacquer bowfront chest with chinoiserie decoration, 2ft. wide. (Warners Wm. H. Brown) $960 £600

Spanish Colonial painted chest-on-stand, Mexican/New Mexican, 38in. wide. (Robt. W. Skinner Inc.) $1,800 £1,011

A walnut chest-on-stand with brass escutcheons and handles, 98cm. wide. (Dee & Atkinson) $2,025 £1,250

A William and Mary walnut chest on later stand, crossbanded and herringbone inlaid with walnut and rosewood, 102cm. wide. (Lacy Scott) $2,275 £1,250

An Ernest Gimson walnut bureau cabinet on stand, circa 1906, 99.5cm. wide. (Christie's) $16,830 £11,000

William and Mary design walnut veneered chest-on-stand, the drawers with brass drop handles. (Worsfolds) $1,280 £800

An early 19th century Chinese Export dark green and gilt lacquer coffer-on-stand, 31½in. wide. (Christie's) $2,330 £1,430

A Queen Anne carved maple high chest-of-drawers, in two sections, New England, 1750-60, 39in. wide. (Christie's) $20,900 £12,636

An early George III mahogany chest-on-stand, the sides with carrying handles, 30¾in. wide. (Christie's) $9,075 £5,500

CHESTS-ON-STANDS

A Queen Anne cherry high-boy on four cabriole legs, Conn., circa 1770, 37¼in. wide. (Robt. W. Skinner Inc.) $11,500 £6,845

A Queen Anne walnut chest-on-stand, the drawers fitted with pierced brass handles, 40in. wide. (Chancellors Hollingsworths)
$2,754 £1,700

Mid 19th century North Italian ebony and ivory inlaid cabinet-on-stand, 58¼in. wide. (Christie's) $27,412 £15,400

A Queen Anne curly maple bonnet top highboy, New England, circa 1770, 36¾in. wide. (Robt. W. Skinner Inc.) $3,500 £2,187

A walnut chest-on-stand with moulded quartered top, basically early 18th century, 40in. wide. (Christie's)
$2,345 £1,430

A walnut and mulberry inlaid chest-on-stand, circa 1770. (McKenna's) $13,650 £7,500

Late 17th century oak chest-on-stand with four long graduated drawers with brass furniture, 3ft.2in. wide. (Hobbs & Chambers)
$1,750 £1,000

An early Georgian figured and pollard oak chest-on-stand, 43in. wide. (Christie's)
$7,398 £4,180

A William and Mary oyster-veneered walnut marquetry cabinet-on-stand, 51in. wide. (Christie's) $19,602 £12,100

CHIFFONIERS

Victorian mahogany chiffonier with serpentine front, 41in. wide. (County Group)
$183 £110

A Regency mahogany chiffonier inlaid with ebonised lines, 26¾in. wide. (Christie's)
$5,231 £3,190

A Regency brown-painted chiffonier, decorated with yellow lines, 34¼in. wide. (Christie's) $2,689 £1,650

Early Victorian figured mahogany chiffonier with raised and carved back, 36in. wide. (J. M. Welch & Son)
$590 £360

A Regency mahogany chiffonier the top surface crossbanded with rosewood, 33in. wide. (Lacy Scott) $1,732 £1,050

A late Regency rosewood chiffonier, the recessed panelled doors filled with gilt trellis and backed with green watered silk, 40in. wide. (Christie's)
$2,178 £1,320

A Regency mahogany dwarf chiffonier on short square section tapering legs, 67cm. wide, 150cm. high. (David Lay) $3,150 £1,750

One of a pair of Regency rosewood chiffoniers with brass galleries and mirrored doors, 47in. wide. (Worsfolds)
$6,552 £3,900

A Victorian mahogany and ebony banded chiffonier with galleried and mirrored upper section, 48in. wide. (J. M. Welch & Son) $759 £460

COMMODES & POT CUPBOARDS

One of a pair of painted bedside tables with concave-fronted rectangular tops, 22¼in. wide. (Christie's) $7,128 £4,400

A Louis XVI mahogany and brass mounted oval pot cupboard with marble top and dummy drawer door, 1ft6½in. high. (Phillips) $2,625 £1,500

A mahogany bowfronted bedside cupboard with three-quarter galleried top, stamped Gillows, Lancaster, 15¾in. wide. (Christie's)
$1,548 £880

One of a pair of late 18th/early 19th century Italian walnut bedside commodes, 16¼in. wide. (Christie's)
$5,482 £3,080

A set of Regency mahogany bedside steps with three red leather-lined treads, the top hinged, the middle sliding, previously fitted with a commode, 20½in. wide. (Christie's)
$1,645 £880

One of a pair of French mid 19th century mahogany bedside cabinets, 20¾in. wide. (Christie's) $2,937 £1,650

George III inlaid feathered mahogany commode fitted with two dummy drawers and cupboard under, 23in. wide. (Lalonde Fine Art)
$363 £220

A Georgian mahogany tray-top commode cupboard, 31in. high, 22in. square. (J. M. Welch & Son)
$330 £200

Early 19th century Shaker pine commode with hinged slant lid opening to reveal a shelf interior, 18in. wide. (Robt. W. Skinner Inc.)
$4,500 £2,678

COMMODE CHESTS

A South Italian walnut and marquetry commode with four graduated long drawers, 73in. wide. (Christie's) $5,143 £3,080

A George III painted commode, the top with concave sides, 47¾in. wide. (Christie's) $23,166 £14,300

Early 18th century German gilt metal mounted kingwood commode, 46in. wide. (Christie's) $6,429 £3,850

A George III ormolu mounted black and gold lacquer commode with serpentine top, 36in. wide. (Christie's) $33,473 £18,700

A gilt metal mounted marquetry commode, the waved crossbanded quartered top inlaid with a songbird amid a cornucopia of flowers, 31½in. wide. (Christie's) $1,745 £1,045

Hepplewhite style commode in flame figured mahogany framed in burr-walnut with boxwood and ebony stringing, 3ft. wide. (Capes Dunn) $1,074 £600

A French provincial oak commode with serpentine top and three long drawers, 51½in. wide. (Christie's) $5,143 £3,080

A serpentine fronted three-drawer walnut commode of early Georgian design, 3ft.6in. wide. (Lots Road Chelsea Auction Galleries) $15,200 £9,500

A George III mahogany commode with chamfered serpentine top, the top drawer fitted with a leather-lined slide, 38in. wide. (Christie's) $11,420 £6,380

COMMODE CHESTS

A Regency kingwood commode, the brass bound bowfronted top crossbanded with strapwork, 46½in. wide. (Christie's) $7,348 £4,400

A George III satinwood commode banded with mahogany, the four doors with rosewood banded oval centres, 54in. wide. (Christie's) $24,948 £15,400

Mid 18th century Dutch kingwood and tulipwood commode, 53in. wide. (Christie's) $4,592 £2,750

Late 18th century North Italian walnut and parquetry commode, 50½in. wide. (Christie's) $6,265 £3,520

Mid 18th century fruitwood commode with mottled later marble slab, probably German, 32½in. wide. (Christie's) $1,928 £1,155

One of a pair of early George III mahogany serpentine commodes, in the style of Thos. Chippendale, 51¼in. wide. (Christie's) $196,020 £121,000

Mid 18th century Swedish ormolu mounted kingwood bombe commode by C. G. Wilkom, 42½in. wide. (Christie's) $7,715 £4,620

Late 18th century Italian neoclassic inlaid walnut commode, 53in. wide. (Christie's) $7,150 £4,085

A mahogany commode with eared serpentine rectangular top and two short and three long graduated drawers, 51in. wide. (Christie's) $29,535 £16,500

FURNITURE

CORNER CUPBOARDS

A Federal poplar corner cupboard, with glazed door opening to three shelves, 1800-20, 41½in. wide. (Christie's) $1,870 £1,130

One of a pair of directoire fruitwood corner cabinets with mottled black marble tops, 30½in. wide. (Christie's) $2,755 £1,650

A mahogany corner cupboard with glazed door enclosing two shelves. (Worsfolds) $1,920 £1,200

George III mahogany bow-fronted corner wall cupboard, 27½in. wide. (Prudential Fine Art) $1,458 £900

A Federal pine and poplar corner cupboard, in two sections, 1800-20, 53in. wide. (Christie's) $4,400 £2,660

Georgian bowfronted oak and crossbanded two-door hanging corner cupboard, 37in. high, 28in. wide. (J. M. Welch & Son) $590 £360

Early 20th century Sheraton design standing corner cabinet, 3ft.6in. wide. (Lalonde Fine Art) $1,320 £800

A Chippendale red-painted corner cupboard, on ogee bracket feet, 88in. high. (Christie's) $3,300 £1,843

A painted and decorated Mahantongo Valley corner cupboard, Penn., circa 1825, 50in. wide. (Robt. W. Skinner Inc.) $15,000 £8,426

414

CORNER CUPBOARDS

A satinwood standing corner cupboard, the panelled doors painted in the classical style of Kauffman, 80cm. wide, 196cm. high. (David Lay) $1,440 £800

An 18th century black lacquered two-door hanging corner cupboard, 21in. wide. (G. A. Key) $511 £310

A painted pine Federal corner cupboard, America or England, circa 1800, 49in. wide. (Robt. W. Skinner Inc.) $3,000 £1,785

Late Georgian mahogany bowfronted corner cabinet inlaid with boxwood lines, 2ft.6in. wide. (Lots Road Chelsea Auction Galleries) $972 £600

A mahogany bowfronted corner display cabinet, 22in. wide. (Giles Haywood) $561 £340

A 19th century pine hanging corner cupboard, the door with rat-tailed hinges, 49in. high, 40in. wide. (Christie's) $2,090 £1,179

A Federal cherry corner cupboard, possibly Penn., circa 1820, 50in. wide. (Robt. W. Skinner Inc.) $2,200 £1,375

One of a pair of 18th century South German walnut corner cabinets with bowed panel doors, 42in. wide. (Christie's) $4,283 £2,420

A Federal pine corner cupboard, New England, mid-19th century, with molded cornice, 90in. high. (Christie's) $3,520 £1,966

A George II mahogany cabinet with a pair of arched doors,
50in. wide. (Christie's)
$235,386 £145,300

A poplar hanging cupboard,
Ephrata, Penn., 1743-60,
18½in. wide, 24½in. high.
(Christie's) $990 £558

Early 17th century German
oak cupboard fitted with
four panelled doors, 51¼in.
wide. (Christie's)
$5,511 £3,300

A Federal blue-painted cupboard with two glazed doors,
possibly N. Jersey, 1775-1810,
50in. wide. (Christie's)
$7,150 £4,322

An 18th century Chippendale
pine step-back cupboard in
two sections, Penn., 73½in.
wide. (Christie's)
$13,200 £7,449

A painted pine stepback
cupboard, Virginia, circa
1840, 38in. wide. (Robt. W.
Skinner Inc.) $2,000 £1,250

A Country poplar cupboard,
red-brown grain painted to
simulate mahogany, Penn.,
circa 1825, 55in. wide. (Robt.
W. Skinner Inc.)
$6,000 £3,571

A 17th century oak spice
cupboard fitted with twenty-
three drawers. (Lawrence
Butler & Co.) $4,100 £2,500

A Country Federal pine step-
back cupboard, circa 1800,
50in. wide. (Robt. W. Skinner
Inc.) $800 £500

CUPBOARDS

A painted and grained pine
Empire cupboard, New
England, circa 1830, 18¼in.
deep. (Robt. W. Skinner Inc.)
$900 £505

Mid/late 18th century Chippen-
dale poplar hanging cupboard,
Penn., 36½in. high, 27in. wide.
(Christie's) $1,045 £589

An 18th century carved pine
buffet, Canada, 58in. wide.
(Robt. W. Skinner Inc.)
$1,000 £625

Federal pine cupboard, possibly
Penn., circa 1820, 42½in. wide.
(Robt. W. Skinner Inc.)
$2,400 £1,348

A 17th century Flemish
carved oak side cupboard,
4ft.4in. wide. (Phillips)
$3,822 £2,100

A Shaker painted pine and
poplar cupboard, possibly
N.Y., circa 1830, 28in. wide,
86¾in. high. (Robt. W.
Skinner Inc.) $3,500 £2,083

Early 19th century sponge-
decorated step-back cupboard
in two sections, Penn., 56in.
wide. (Christie's)
$12,650 £7,138

Chinese objets d'art display
cabinet, circa 1890-1900.
(Locke & England)
$7,172 £4,400

A Country Federal cupboard,
Penn., circa 1820, 48in. wide,
86½in. high. (Robt. W.
Skinner Inc.) $1,200 £750

George IV mahogany davenport, the sliding top section with three-quarter pierced brass gallery, 20in. wide. (Christie's) $2,990 £1,870

Victorian burr-walnut harlequin davenport with sliding desk top internally lined with satinwood, 24in. wide. (Giles Haywood) $1,435 £875

A George IV rosewood davenport with sliding top and lined writing surface, 22in. (Christie's) $2,153 £1,210

A Regency mahogany davenport, writing slope enclosing two short drawers and pen drawer, and with pull out writing slide and four drawers, 50cm. wide. (Phillips) $4,592 £2,800

A Wheeler & Wilson type S. Davis & Co. walnut 'Davenport' treadle sewing machine, serial no. 21535, 96cm. high, 63cm. wide, circa 1870. (Phillips) $2,080 £1,300

A mid Victorian amboyna and ebony davenport, the cupboard doors enclosing a fitted interior, 22in. wide. (Christie's) $1,452 £880

A Victorian rosewood davenport, with fitted side cupboard enclosing four trays and pull-out hinged drawer, 26in. wide. (Lalonde Fine Art) $1,188 £720

Mid Victorian figured walnut davenport with serpentine front and raised stationery box with hinged lid, 21in. wide. (Lalonde Fine Art) $1,650 £1,000

A Victorian burr walnut davenport, inlaid with marquetry and geometric boxwood lines, 23¼in. (Christie's) $4,525 £2,420

DAVENPORTS

A late Victorian rosewood davenport, inlaid with ivory marquetry and geometric lines. (Christie's) $1,821 £990

An early Victorian calamander davenport with pierced scrolling three-quarter gallery and leather-lined sloping top, 21in. wide. (Christie's) $2,178 £1,320

A Victorian walnut davenport. (Hobbs Parker) $1,191 £740

A mid Victorian ebony and amboyna davenport with sloping lid and tambour, 23½in. wide. (Christie's) $1,561 £935

A Regency mahogany and ebony banded davenport, the fall-front writing section with brass galleried rail, 16½in. wide. (J. M. Welch & Son) $9,900 £6,000

A Regency burr-yew davenport with pierced gothic brass gallery and leather-lined sloping top, 20¼in. wide. (Christie's) $3,066 £1,870

A George IV mahogany davenport by Gillows of Lancaster, with gilt metal three-quarter gallery and red leather-lined sloping flap, 20¼in. wide. (Christie's) $8,140 £4,400

A William IV burr-yew davenport with three-quarter spindle gallery and green leather-lined sloping flap, 20½in. wide. (Christie's) $11,228 £6,380

An early Victorian walnut davenport with three-quarter gallery, sloping flap enclosing a fitted interior, stamped Johnstone & Jeanes, London 11544, 23¼in. wide. (Christie's) $3,308 £1,760

DISPLAY CABINETS

A Dutch mahogany and marquetry display cabinet on square tapering legs and bun feet, 41in. wide. (Christie's) $4,776 £2,860

A mid Victorian ormolu mounted and walnut side cabinet, 62in. wide. (Christie's) $2,571 £1,540

An 18th/19th century Dutch oak display cabinet with bombe base, 7ft. wide. (Prudential Fine Art) $4,785 £2,900

A Limbert single door china cabinet, no. 1347, Grand Rapids, Michigan, circa 1907, 34¼in. wide. (Robt. W. Skinner Inc.) $1,900 £1,027

A Dutch marquetry display cabinet with moulded arched cornice, a glazed door and sides enclosing scalloped shelves, 34¾in. wide. (Christie's) $1,762 £990

A satinwood display cabinet with crossbanded, herringbone and line inlay in various woods, 3ft.4in. wide. (Warners Wm. H. Brown) $3,120 £1,950

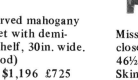

One of a pair of mid 19th century brass mounted and kingwood side cabinets, 42½in. wide. (Christie's) $2,904 £1,760

Edwardian carved mahogany display cabinet with demi-lune display shelf, 30in. wide. (Giles Haywood) $1,196 £725

Mission oak two-door china closet, no. 2017, circa 1910, 46½in. wide. (Robt. W. Skinner Inc.) $350 £218

DISPLAY CABINETS

Sheraton Revival mahogany glazed china cabinet, 3ft. wide. (G. A. Key)
$726 £440

A brass mounted ebonised vitrine cabinet with simulated green marble top, 48in. wide. (Christie's)
$816 £495

An Edwardian mahogany china cabinet on tapering rectangular legs with spade feet, 3ft. wide. (G. A. Key)
$654 £370

One of a pair of black and gold lacquer display cabinets of drum-shape, 30in. wide, 63½in. high. (Christie's) $2,886 £1,760

An early Victorian display cabinet on cabriole legs with eagle's claw and ball feet, 64in. wide. (Christie's)
$5,737 £3,520

One of a pair of William IV rosewood display cabinets, 25½in. wide. (Christie's)
$12,342 £7,480

A William IV faded rosewood glazed display cabinet with mirrored and shelved super-structure, 30in. wide. (J. M. Welch & Son) $2,805 £1,700

A mahogany display cabinet in the Arts & Crafts style, 53in. wide. (Prudential Fine Art) $777 £480

American Dutch-style bombe-fronted walnut and oak glazed display cabinet, 6ft. wide, 7ft. 6in. high. (Giles Haywood)
$1,640 £1,000

DRESSERS

A mid Georgian oak dresser, the waved frieze with three drawers on square tapering legs, 78½in. wide. (Christie's) $3,427 £2,090

An 18th century oak and crossbanded mahogany Lancashire dresser base. (Warren & Wignall Ltd.) $2,560 £1,600

A George III oak and fruit-wood dresser on ogee bracket feet, 64½in. wide, 77in. high. (Christie's) $21,384 £13,200

An 18th century oak dresser with two shelves, the base with four drawers, on turned supports, 63in. wide, 76in. high. (Lacy Scott) $3,960 £2,400

An early 18th century brown oak dresser with wavy frieze. (John Hogbin & Son) $5,330 £3,250

A painted pine step-back cupboard, the top section with two open shelves, possibly Canada, circa 1800, 59¾in. wide. (Robt. W. Skinner Inc.) $4,750 £2,827

An 18th century oak dresser with three brass handled drawers, 185cm. wide. (Dee & Atkinson) $3,645 £2,250

An oak enclosed dresser base fitted with two drawers and two panelled cupboards, 56in. wide. (J. M. Welch & Son) $577 £380

A George III oak dresser fitted with three drawers and shaped apron, 73in. wide. (J. M. Welch & Son) $3,444 £2,100

DRESSERS

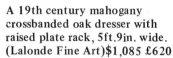

A 19th century mahogany crossbanded oak dresser with raised plate rack, 5ft.9in. wide. (Lalonde Fine Art)$1,085 £620

A 17th century oak dresser base on turned legs, 68in. wide. (Parsons, Welch & Cowell) $4,200 £2,500

A Georgian oak and elm dresser with plate rack, 4ft.2in. wide. (Lots Road Chelsea Auction Galleries) $2,821 £1,550

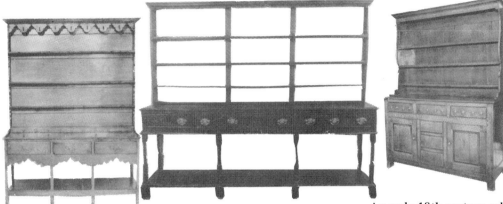

An 18th century oak dresser, 150cm. wide, 200cm. high. (David Lay) $4,654 £2,600

Late 18th century George III oak dresser, 8ft. wide, 6ft.6in. high. (Ambrose) $2,970 £1,650

An early 18th century oak dresser, the delft rack with moulded top and shelves, 65in. wide. (Dacre, Son & Hartley) $11,550 £7,000

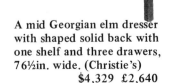

An 18th century and later oak dresser on bracket feet, 57½in. wide. (Christie's) $5,097 £2,880

A mid Georgian elm dresser with shaped solid back with one shelf and three drawers, 76½in. wide. (Christie's) $4,329 £2,640

A late George III fruitwood dresser and shelves, 54in. wide. (Hy. Duke & Son) $3,780 £2,100

DUMB WAITERS

A mid Georgian mahogany dumb-waiter with three graduating tiers, 43½in. high. (Christie's)
$3,448 £2,090

A Regency mahogany two-tier dumb-waiter on arched tapering tripartite base, 38in. high. (Christie's) $2,151 £1,320

Three-tier mahogany circular dumb-waiter, designed in the Georgian Chippendale mould. (G. A. Key) $825 £500

One of a pair of Georgian mahogany dumb waiters, each with three graduated tiers, 19 x 23½in. in diam. (Prudential Fine Art) $7,955 £4,300

A Sheraton period two tier mahogany dumb waiter, the two tiers with hinged flaps, 37in. high. (Prudential Fine Art) $1,387 £750

A mid 19th century mahogany circular three tier dumb waiter, with three moulded swept feet. (Peter Wilson) $1,852 £980

An early George III mahogany three-tier dumb waiter, the graduated trays revolving on turned waisted spiral cut stems, 24in. diam. (Woolley & Wallis) $2,475 £1,500

A George III style mahogany dumb-waiter with triple rimmed circular moulded tiers, 46in. high. (Christie's) $968 £605

A George III mahogany three-tier folding dumb waiter with sabre legs and brass castors, 177 x 71cm. (Phillips) $1,680 £880

424

KNEEHOLE DESKS

A Regency mahogany partner's desk with rounded rectangular leather-lined top, 67in. wide. (Christie's) $4,356 £2,640

An early John Makepeace, Andaman padouk and leather-covered desk, by M. Doughty, D. Pearson and A. Freeman, 199cm. wide, and a chair. (Christie's) $3,247 £1,980

A mahogany kneehole desk with leather-lined top and nine drawers, 53in. wide. (Christie's) $1,804 £1,100

A William III walnut and featherstrung kneehole bureau on later bun feet. (Phillips) $13,940 £8,500

A George I walnut, cross-banded and featherstrung kneehole desk, on bracket feet, 76cm. wide. (Phillips) $6,560 £4,000

A mid Georgian walnut kneehole desk on bracket feet, 34in. wide. (Christie's) $2,722 £1,650

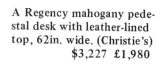

George I walnut feather crossbanded kneehole desk, circa 1720, 32in. wide. (Giles Haywood) $8,610 £5,250

A Victorian figured walnut kneehole writing desk with brass gallery, 4ft.6in. wide. (Prudential Fine Art) $3,444 £2,100

A Regency mahogany pedestal desk with leather-lined top, 62in. wide. (Christie's) $3,227 £1,980

KNEEHOLE DESKS

A small Regency mahogany partner's desk with leather-lined top, 54in. wide. (Christie's)
$3,267 £1,980

A desk, the top suspended on tubular steel U-shaped supports, with cantilever chair, desk 164.4cm. wide. (Christie's)
$1,262 £770

A William IV walnut pedestal desk with serpentine leather-lined top and two frieze drawers, 63½in. wide. (Christie's)
$12,117 £7,480

A Regency rosewood partner's desk with knob handles and original William IV locks. (James Norwich Auctions)$17,136 £10,200

A French Art Deco beechwood writing desk on trestle ends, 105.4cm. wide. (Christie's)
$992 £605

A Cotswold School oak kneehole desk and armchair, desk 152cm. wide. (Christie's)
$631 £385

An early Gustav Stickley flat-top, kneehole desk, circa 1902-03, 54in. wide. (Robt. W. Skinner Inc.)
$1,400 £833

A mahogany veneered writing desk, designed by Frank L. Wright, produced by Heritage-Henredon Furniture Co., circa 1955, 52in. wide. (Robt. W. Skinner Inc.)$1,100 £594

KNEEHOLE DESKS

An early Victorian oak and burr-walnut partner's desk of Gothic style, 84in. wide. (Christie's) $7,260 £4,400

A mid Victorian bird's-eye maple ebonised partner's desk, 75in. wide. (Christie's) $11,726 £7,150

A partner's mahogany desk with inset leather writing surface, circa 1900, 84 x 60in. (J. M. Welch & Son) $5,376 £3,200

A shaped front oak pedestal desk with tooled leather top and nine drawers below, circa 1900, 48in. wide. (J. M. Welch & Son) $852 £520

Satin walnut pedestal desk with nine drawers, circa 1900, 36in. wide. (J. M. Welch & Son) $742 £450

An oak 'Shannon' roll-top pedestal desk with fitted interior and ten drawers below, 53½in. wide, circa 1900. (J. M. Welch & Son) $951 £580

A partner's mahogany desk on plinth base with carrying handles, 61½in. wide. (Christie's) $6,897 £4,180

A Chippendale-design mahogany pedestal desk with scale-carved border and blind-fret decoration to drawer fronts, 4ft. wide. (Prudential Fine Art) $4,200 £2,500

A George III mahogany pedestal desk with leather-lined top, fitted with three frieze drawers, 44in. wide. (Christie's) $16,038 £9,900

A George II ormolu mounted mahogany and parcel gilt kneehole desk attributed to John Boson, 55¾in. wide. (Christie's) $240,570 £148,500

A Louis XIV boulle and rose-wood bureau mazarin, the top inlaid in pewter with scrolling foliage and strapwork, 45in. wide. (Christie's) $11,940 £7,150

An early Georgian walnut kneehole coffer with leather-lined top, 35in. wide. (Christie's) $4,633 £2,860

A Regency mahogany cylinder desk with stencilled label 'A. Ardley & Son Office Fitters, 11 Great St, 27 Wormwood Street', 46in. wide. (Christie's) $4,329 £2,640

A George II red walnut kneehole desk with narrow folding leather-lined top, 37in. wide. (Christie's) $4,811 £2,970

A George I walnut kneehole desk with crossbanded top, 49½in. wide. (Christie's) $42,768 £26,400

An early Victorian burr-yew kneehole desk, 48in. wide. (Christie's) $3,448 £2,090

An 18th century Italian walnut kneehole desk with moulded rectangular quartered top, 42½in. wide. (Christie's) $11,940 £7,150

LOWBOYS

An early Georgian oak low boy with mahogany crossbandings, with one frieze drawer above two short drawers, 33in. high. (Lawrence Fine Art)
$2,910 £1,540

A walnut side table with three drawers on cabriole legs and pad-feet, 30½in. wide. (Christie's) $2,402 £1,320

A George II walnut lowboy fitted with three drawers with original handles, on cabriole legs, 35¾in x 20¼in. (Dreweatt Neate)
$10,584 £5,600

A Dutch oak lowboy, fitted with two short and one long drawer, on cabriole legs, 28½in., part 18th century. (Christie's) $1,265 £715

An 18th century rectangular mahogany lowboy, the three cockbeaded drawers with brass bail handles, 32in. wide. (Parsons, Welch & Cowell)
$5,880 £3,500

A mid Georgian mahogany side table on cabriole legs and pad feet, 29¼in. wide. (Christie's) $1,460 £825

A walnut lowboy with two short and one long drawer on cabriole legs and pad feet, 28½in. wide. (Christie's) $3,066 £1,860

An 18th century oak lowboy with drawers, shaped frieze, cabriole legs and pad feet, 2ft6in. wide. (Phillips)
$1,215 £650

A George I walnut lowboy, the quartered top crossbanded in ash, with three drawers, brass handles, shaped apron on cabriole legs, 29in x 18in. (Dreweatt Neate)
$7,182 £3,800

A scarlet and gold lacquer six-leaf screen decorated in black and gilt, each leaf 21¾in. wide, 97in. high. (Christie's) $26,730 £16,500

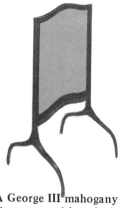

A George III mahogany fire-screen with arched glazed sliding panel, 19¼in. wide. (Christie's) $466 £286

An inlaid oak three-panelled screen, designed by Harvey Ellis for Gustav Stickley, circa 1903-04, 66¾in. high, each panel 20in. wide. (Robt. W. Skinner Inc.) $18,000 £10,714

A four-leaf screen covered in Brussels verdure tapestry, the tapestry 17th century, each leaf 84½ x 25½in. (Christie's) $11,022 £6,600

Regency carved giltwood ornate three-fold fire-screen, upper section with ten mirrored glass panels, 3ft.6in. wide. (Giles Haywood) $902 £550

A mid 18th century firescreen panel worked in tent stitch with mainly red and blue wools and ivory silk, 61 x 45cm. (Phillips) $1,344 £800

A Regency painted three-leaf screen, decorated with panels of chinoiserie landscapes with courtly figures, each panel 63½ x 24½in. (Christie's) $13,365 £8,250

An early Victorian rosewood fire-screen with glazed panel, 29in. wide. (Christie's) $573 £352

An early 19th century Chinese coromandel lacquer six-leaf screen, each leaf 80½ x 17½in. (Christie's) $3,267 £1,980

SCREENS

An early Gustav Stickley leather fire-screen, 1902, 35in. high, 31in. wide. (Robt. W. Skinner Inc.) $2,000 £1,190

An early George III walnut polescreen, the adjustable panel with gros and petit-point needlework, 51in. high. (Christie's) $3,741 £2,090

Early 19th century Chinese five-leaf black and gold lacquer screen, each leaf 83½ x 21½in. (Christie's) $8,068 £4,950

A painted leather three-leaf screen, decorated overall with an English rustic scene, 36 x 48in. (Christie's) $726 £440

Parcel gilt and gesso pole screen on tripod base with silk embroidered panel, 53in. high. (Worsfolds) $574 £350

A late Victorian scrapwork four-leaf screen with coloured figures and scenes, each leaf 66½ x 22¼in. (Christie's) $1,452 £880

A Dutch leather four-leaf screen painted with exotic birds, shrubs and vases of flowers and fruit on a gilt ground, the leather 18th century, each leaf 20 x 74¾in. (Christie's) $2,722 £1,650

A Regency mahogany fire-screen with sliding panel and pilaster uprights, 25in. high. (Christie's) $448 £275

A late Victorian ebonised, parcel gilt and scrapwork three-leaf screen, each leaf 70 x 23¾in. (Christie's) $2,541 £1,540

FURNITURE

A 19th century two-leaf screen depicting a scene with Europeans watching dancers and musicians on stage, each panel approx. 60 x 83cm. (Christie's) $3,553 £2,090

A mid Georgian mahogany polescreen with needlework panel, 54½in. high. (Christie's) $896 £550

An 18th century Chinese scarlet and gilt lacquer eight-leaf screen, each leaf 85½ x 21¾in. (Christie's) $18,826 £11,550

A wood and copper phone screen, circa 1910, 12in. high, 13in. wide. (Robt. W. Skinner Inc.) $125 £67

A mid-Victorian rosewood cheval firescreen, the panel with a petit-point vase of flowers and fruit, on scrolled legs carved with foliage, 25¾in. wide, 46½in. high. (Christie's) $827 £440

A wrought-iron and pierced copper fire-screen, circa 1900, 34½in. wide. (Robt. W. Skinner Inc.) $300 £162

A 19th century Chinese lacquer and hardstone eight-leaf screen, each panel 91 x 21¾in. (Christie's) $17,451 £10,450

A mahogany polescreen with petit-point floral panel on a dark brown ground, on claw feet, 23in. wide. (Christie's) $617 £330

A 19th century six-leaf screen depicting pine groves in Kano style, each panel approx. 152 x 61cm. (Christie's) $3,553 £2,090

432

SECRETAIRES

George III Provincial oak and crossbanded mahogany secretaire cabinet on bracket feet, 3ft.6in. wide. (Hobbs & Chambers) $2,187 £1,250

A Federal mahogany veneered inlaid secretary/desk, Mass., circa 1800, 38in. wide. (Robt. W. Skinner Inc.) $2,750 £1,636

A George II period red walnut secretaire tallboy chest on ogee bracket feet, 3ft.8½in. wide. (Geering & Colyer)
    $3,150 £1,750

A French style mahogany marquetry inlaid escritoire having brass gallery over fall-front enclosing fitted interior, 2ft.7in. wide. (Lawrences) $3,731 £2,050

Early 19th century faded mahogany veneered secretaire with fitted interior, 31in. wide. (Woolley & Wallis)
    $1,360 £840

A Queen Anne figured walnut secretaire on later bun feet, 43¼in. wide, 66¾in. high. (Christie's) $26,730 £16,500

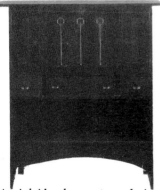

An inlaid oak secretary, designed by Harvey Ellis for Gustav Stickley, circa 1903-04, 42in. wide. (Robt. W. Skinner Inc.)
    $93,000 £55,357

Late 17th century period Export lacquer escritorio or writing cabinet, 89 x 49 x 65cm. high, the George I stand 18th century, 76.5cm. high. (Christie's)
    $12,320 £7,700

A Queen Anne walnut cabinet-on-chest, the glazed doors enclosing a fitted interior with eleven various-sized drawers, 44in. wide. (Christie's)
    $17,820 £11,000

433

SECRETAIRE BOOKCASES

A 19th century inlaid mahogany secretaire bookcase with glazed upper section, 3ft.4in. wide. (Hobbs & Chambers) $4,025 £2,300

A George III satinwood cabinet with gothic arched cornice, 48¼in. wide. (Christie's) $6,275 £3,850

A George III mahogany secretaire cabinet with moulded cornice, 43½in. wide. (Christie's) $5,297 £3,520

A Georgian mahogany secretaire bookcase. (Hobbs Parker) $1,600 £1,000

Late 19th century French ormolu mounted kingwood and rosewood vitrine with secretaire-a-abattant, 33in. wide. (Graves Son & Pilcher) $10,203 £5,700

A Queen Anne walnut and featherstrung double dome secretaire cabinet on chest, 1.05m. wide. (Phillips) $15,580 £9,500

A George III mahogany secretaire cabinet with a pair of Gothic glazed cupboard doors, 43in. wide. (Christie's) $8,712 £5,280

A Regency rosewood, tulipwood crossbanded and strung secretaire dwarf bookcase, 78cm. wide. (Phillips) $6,560 £4,000

A Regency mahogany cabinet with a pair of geometrically glazed doors enclosing shelves, 40in. wide. (Christie's) $3,944 £2,420

SECRETAIRE BOOKCASES

A George III mahogany secretaire cabinet, 49in. wide, 101in. high. (Christie's)
$13,447 £8,250

A William IV mahogany secretaire bookcase, the upper section fitted with adjustable shelves, 4ft.1in. wide. (Prudential Fine Art)
$1,968 £1,200

A Regency mahogany secretaire cabinet on partly replaced bracket feet, 46½in. wide. (Christie's) $2,151 £1,320

A George I cream lacquer secretaire cabinet with bow-shaped moulded cornice, 43¾in. wide, 86½in. high. (Christie's)
$427,680 £264,000

Mid 19th century classical mahogany veneered desk and bookcase, mid-Atlantic States, 88in. high. (Christie's)
$1,045 £589

An early 18th century walnut and featherstrung double dome secretaire cabinet on chest, 1.09m. wide. (Phillips)
$19,680 £12,000

A George III mahogany secretaire cabinet, the base with a leather-lined secretaire drawer, 43in. wide. (Christie's) $9,861 £6,050

An early 19th century mahogany secretaire bookcase, the two doors with satinwood strung astragals, 51in. wide. (Parsons, Welch & Cowell)
$2,772 £1,650

A late 18th century mahogany secretaire bookcase on swept bracket feet, 118cm. wide. (Wellington Salerooms)
$6,048 £3,600

435

SETTEES & COUCHES

One of a pair of early Victorian rosewood sofas, the moulded shaped backs and bowed seats with buttoned upholstery, 96in. wide. (Christie's) $15,240 £9,350

A Regency ivory and green-painted beechwood daybed upholstered in crimson damask on fluted sabre legs, 87in. wide. (Christie's) $3,811 £2,310

Mid 19th century walnut frame three-seater settee covered in button down embossed velvet fabric. (Locke & England) $815 £500

A George III cream-painted and parcel gilt sofa, the padded back, arms and seat with spirally-turned spreading arm supports, 77in. wide. (Christie's) $2,178 £1,320

An early Gustav Stickley settle with arched slats, 1901-03, 60in. wide. (Robt. W. Skinner Inc.) $27,000   £16,071

A Regency oak and parcel gilt sofa, attributed to George Bullock, 61½in. wide. (Christie's) $106,920 £66,000

A Regency parcel gilt and ebonised sofa, the padded back, arms and bowed seat with squab cushions, 72in. wide. (Christie's) $1,415 £858

A Regency cream-painted sofa with rectangular button back, sides and squab covered in brown silk, 76in. wide. (Christie's) $2,706 £1,650

SETTEES & COUCHES

An early Victorian oak daybed in the Gothic style, the padded seat covered in green leather, 77in. wide. (Christie's) $3,993 $2,420

A Louis XV parcel gilt and grey-painted canape, with waved upholstered back and seat, 77in. wide. (Christie's) $4,408 £2,640

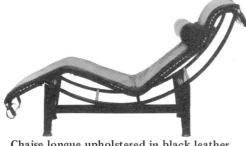

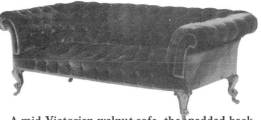

Chaise longue upholstered in black leather, designed by Le Corbusier, 1926. (Lots Road Chelsea Auction Galleries) $496 £310

A mid Victorian walnut sofa, the padded back, outscrolled arms, back and seat upholstered in buttoned slate-blue velvet, on cabriole legs, 80in. wide. (Christie's) $1,815 £1,100

An Empire bird's eye maple sofa with panelled back, padded arms and seat covered in white calico, 76in. wide. (Christie's) $3,426 £1,925

A walnut sofa of William and Mary style with padded back, outscrolled arms and seat upholstered with fragments of 17th century tapestry, 82in. wide. (Christie's) $9,801 £6,050

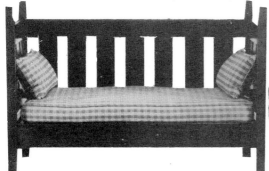

A Gustav Stickley slat-back settle, no. 206, circa 1904-06, 60in. wide. (Robt. W. Skinner Inc.) $15,000 £8,928

A mid Victorian walnut sofa, the buttoned back upholstered in celadon green velvet with deep fringe, 78in. wide. (Christie's) $2,204 £1,320

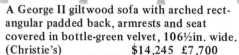

A George II giltwood sofa with arched rectangular padded back, armrests and seat covered in bottle-green velvet, 106½in. wide. (Christie's) $14,245 £7,700

A painted and stencil decorated settee, Penn., circa 1830, with J. Swint Chairmaker stamped on base, 76¼in. long. (Robt. W. Skinner Inc.) $2,000   £1,190

Early 18th century Dutch green painted hall bench, 72in. wide. (Christie's) $8,811 £4,950

A mahogany sofa with slightly arched back and serpentine seat upholstered in russet velvet, 76in. wide. (Christie's) $902 £550

An Art Nouveau mahogany and marquetry settle on three arched trestle supports, circa 1890, 185cm. wide. (Christie's)
                              $1,514 £990

A Gustav Stickley tall spindleback settee, no. 286, signed with decal, circa 1906, 48in. wide. (Robt. W. Skinner Inc.) $36,000 £21,428

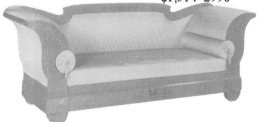

One of a pair of Biedermeier maplewood sofas with double scrolling padded backs, arms and seats, 101in. wide. (Christie's) $16,643 £9,350

A painted and decorated settee, the rolled crest rail above three slats and twelve spindles, Penn., circa 1825, 76in. long. (Robt. W. Skinner Inc.) $2,750 £1,636

SETTEES & COUCHES

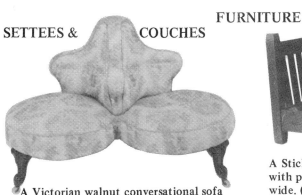

A Victorian walnut conversational sofa
upholstered in figured damask, on scrolling
feet, 50in. wide. $1,262 £770
(Christie's)

A Stickley Bros. slat-back settle, signed
with paper label, Quaint, circa 1910, 72in.
wide. (Robt. W. Skinner Inc.) $4,500 £2,432

A Victorian carved mahogany shaped settee
with button back, 80in. wide. (J. M. Welch
& Son) $1,246 £820

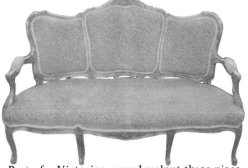

Part of a Victorian carved walnut three-piece
suite. (Hobbs Parker) $1,310 £780

An oak bench, the padded back and squab
cushion covered in tapestry, on turned legs
and moulded stretchers, 57½in. wide.
(Christie's) $1,070 £605

A 19th century pine settle with
backrest, the seat with three drawers under,
74in. wide. (Greenslade & Co.) $729 £410

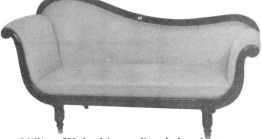

William IV double scroll-ended mahogany
framed shaped settee with rising back rail
and four small turned legs, 75in. long. (J.
M. Welch & Son) $571 £340

A Victorian walnut sofa, the seat and padded
arms upholstered in moquette, raised on
scrolling legs, 74in. wide, complete with easy
chair. (Anderson & Garland) $2,478 £1,400

439

A mid Victorian carved rosewood settee with serpentine front and cabriole legs, 78in. wide. (Dacre, Son & Hartley) $1,558 £950

A George III white painted and parcel gilt sofa with rounded arched back, sides, seat and squab covered in green repp on turned tapering fluted legs, 98½in. wide. (Christie's) $2,330 £1,430

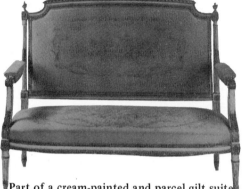

Part of a cream-painted and parcel gilt suite of Louis XVI style, comprising a pair of chaises, a pair of fauteuils and a canape, the canape 56in. wide. (Christie's) $2,722 £1,650

A George III carved mahogany twin chairback settee in the Chinese and Gothic Chippendale taste. (Phillips) $13,940 £8,500

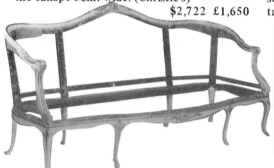

A George III parcel gilt and cream painted sofa, the waved back and serpentine seat lacking upholstery, 84in. wide. (Christie's) $4,123 £2,530

A Gustav Stickley bird's-eye maple wide slat settee, no. 214, circa 1903-04, 50¼in. wide. (Robt. W. Skinner Inc.) $4,000 £2,380

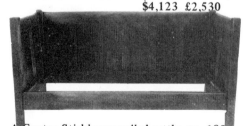

A Gustav Stickley panelled settle, no. 189, signed with large red decal with signature in a box, 1901-03, 84in. long. (Robt. W. Skinner Inc.) $6,250 £3,720

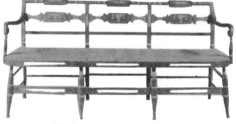

A stencilled green-painted triple chair-back settee, probably New York, circa 1820, 74¼in. long. (Christie's) $2,860 £1,729

SETTEES & COUCHES

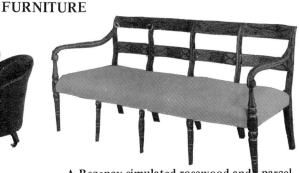

A mid Victorian walnut sofa with arched deep buttoned back, curved sides and serpentine seat covered in bottle green velvet, 79½in. wide. (Christie's) $2,178 £1,320

A Regency simulated rosewood and parcel gilt quadruple chairback settee, the seat covered in white calico, 71in. wide. (Christie's) $2,178 £1,320

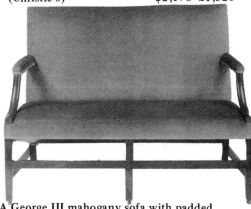

A walnut three-seater settee in the George II style, having triple carved vase splat and shaped arms, 62in. long. (Chancellors Hollingsworths) $640 £440

A George III mahogany sofa with padded rectangular back and seat with square legs and plain stretchers, 49in. wide. $2,541 £1,540 (Christie's)

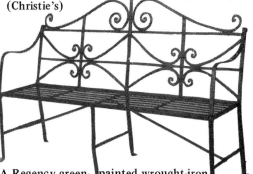

A Biedermeier walnut sofa with arched padded back, scrolling arms and seat covered in striped silk with two bolsters, 62½in. wide. (Christie's) $4,592 £2,750

A Regency green-painted wrought-iron garden seat with scrolling pierced back and pierced seat, 66in. wide. (Christie's) $3,630 £2,200

A 'lip' sofa, after a design by Salvador Dali, upholstered in red nylon stretch fabric. (Christie's) $1,894 £1,155

A classical mahogany sofa upholstered in red woven horsehair bordered with brass nails, attributed to Duncan Phyfe, N.Y., circa 1816, 94in. wide. (Christie's) $18,700 £11,306

A Federal inlaid mahogany sideboard, the serpentine top edged with line inlay, 72¾in. wide. Mass., 1790-1815. (Christie's)
$16,500 £9,975

A George III mahogany veneered bowfronted sideboard, crossbanded in rosewood and inlaid stringing, 5ft. wide. (Woolley & Wallis)
$6,642 £4,100

A Limbert sideboard with arched mirrored backboard with corbel detail, Michigan, circa 1910, 47¾in. wide. (Robt. W. Skinner Inc.)
$1,200 £648

A George III mahogany sideboard with D-shaped top crossbanded with satinwood, 47½in. wide. (Graves Son & Pilcher)
$8,592 £4,800

A George III mahogany sideboard with bowed breakfront top and a frieze drawer, 71in. wide. (Christie's)
$7,530 £4,620

A mid Victorian pollard oak sideboard with arched mirror backplate, 102in. wide. (Christie's)
$2,755 £1,650

SIDEBOARDS

An eight-legged sideboard, model no. 961, plate rail with V-board panelled back, by Gustav Stickley, circa 1902-04, 70in. wide. (Robt. W. Skinner Inc.) $3,750 £2,027

A Federal inlaid mahogany sideboard with serpentine front, Baltimore, 1790-1810, 72in. wide. (Christie's) $41,800 £25,272

A Gustav Stickley oak sideboard with open plate rack, circa 1905-06, 49in. wide. (Robt. W. Skinner Inc.) $1,300 £773

A Limbert mirrored sideboard, no. 1453 3/4, circa 1910, 48in. wide. (Robt. W. Skinner Inc.) $475 £296

A 19th century brass bound military unit, 6ft.10in. wide. (Geering & Colyer)
                                    $1,890 £1,050

A George III mahogany and inlaid sideboard of concave outline with crossbanded top containing a short central and two deep drawers in the arched apron, 185cm. wide. (Phillips) $4,756 £2,900

A George III mahogany sideboard with waved serpentine top, possibly Scottish, 83½in. wide. (Christie's) $18,150 £11,000

A Sheraton breakfront mahogany inlaid and crossbanded sideboard, 183cm. wide. (Dee & Atkinson) $2,880 £1,800

A George III mahogany sideboard, the breakfront bowed top crossbanded with satinwood, 71¾in. wide. (Christie's) $5,412 £3,300

A Stickley Bros. sideboard, Grand Rapids, Michigan, 1912, 60in. wide. (Robt. W. Skinner Inc.) $425 £265

George III mahogany bowfronted kneehole sideboard fitted with centre drawer flanked by cellarette, small cupboard and one larger cupboard with four sliding trays. (Prudential Fine Art) $6,232 £3,800

Regency mahogany bowfronted sideboard with ebony and satinwood stringing, 72in. wide. (Worsfolds) $1,428 £850

Early 19th century sideboard on turned legs with central drawer, cellarette drawer and cupboard, 5ft. wide. (Lots Road Chelsea Auction Galleries) $1,263 £780

A George III mahogany bowfronted sideboard crossbanded in satinwood, 77in. wide. (Christie's) $5,808 £3,520

SIDEBOARDS

A George III Scottish mahogany sideboard, the eared rectangular superstructure formerly with a gallery and with bowed tambour doors, 71¾in. wide. (Christie's) $3,968 £2,420

A Federal inlaid mahogany sideboard with bowed serpentine top, Mass., 1790-1810, 72¾in. wide. (Christie's) $6,600 £3,990

A George III mahogany sideboard with bow-fronted top and frieze drawer above an arched recess, 69½in. wide. (Christie's) $11,583 £7,150

A George III mahogany sideboard with triple-bowed top, 90¼in. wide. (Christie's) $4,719 £2,860

Early Gustav Stickley sideboard, no. 967, with long copper strap hardware and square copper pulls, 60in. wide. (Robt. W. Skinner Inc.) $9,500 £5,650

Antique inlaid mahogany sideboard. (John Hogbin & Son) $2,050 £1,250

A Regency mahogany veneered breakfront sideboard, banded in satinwood with stringing, 6ft. wide. (Woolley & Wallis) $2,880 £1,800

A George III mahogany sideboard with D-shaped top with a frieze drawer and arched recess, 71in. wide. (Christie's) $6,494 £3,960

A three-tiered muffin stand, by Charles Rohlfs, Buffalo, N.Y., 1907, 34in. high. (Robt. W. Skinner Inc.) $1,300 £702

An 18th century Japanese sword stand, for court tachi, 26in. high. (Robt. W. Skinner Inc.) $700 £424

A mahogany three-tier etagere with rectangular top and square supports, 18½in. wide. (Christie's) $1,258 £715

An Art Nouveau oak hall stand with circular mirror, stylish hooks and embossed copper panels, 36in. wide. (Lots Road Chelsea Auction Galleries) $567 £350

Regency dark mahogany small fly press with two small drawers to the front, on squat circular feet. (G. A. Key) $875 £500

An Italian walnut pedestal with shaped rectangular top on a bombe support, 50¼in. high. (Christie's) $2,020 £1,210

A Regency brass and rosewood etagere with four rectangular trays, 16½in. wide, 39½in. high. (Christie's) $13,783 £7,700

A cane-sided plant stand, probably Limbert, circa 1910, 23in. high, the top 16in. sq. (Robt. W. Skinner Inc.) $475 £282

A magazine stand with cutouts, Michigan, 1910, 20in. wide. (Robt. W. Skinner Inc.) $700 £416

STANDS

An Edwardian mahogany and inlaid pedestal jardiniere with liner. (J. M. Welch & Son)
$380 £250

A set of George III mahogany library steps with moulded handrail and leather-lined treads, 104in. high. (Christie's) $6,891 £3,850

A rosewood grained one-drawer poplar stand, American, circa 1830, top 21 x 16in. (Robt. W. Skinner Inc.)
$6,250 £3,720

An L. & J. G. Stickley slat-sided magazine rack, no. 46, circa 1910, signed with decal, 42in. high. (Robt. W. Skinner Inc.) $2,100 £1,312

A Regency mahogany teapoy with folding top enclosing a divided interior, 26¾in. wide. (Christie's)
$9,768 £5,280

Early 20th century Mission oak magazine stand with cut out arched sides, 49in. high. (Robt. W. Skinner Inc.)
$500 £312

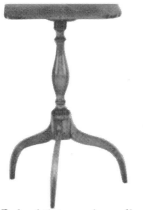

A Federal tiger maple candlestand, New England, circa 1810, top 17 x 17½in. (Robt. W. Skinner Inc.)
$1,300 £812

A Gustav Stickley slat-sided folio stand, no. 551, 1902-03, 40½in. high, 29½in. wide. (Robt. W. Skinner Inc.)
$3,000 £1,785

A drink stand, by L. & J. G. Stickley, no. 587, circa 1912, 16in. sq. (Robt. W. Skinner Inc.) $650 £351

447

STANDS

A Regency mahogany three-tier etagere with circular shelves and ring-turned supports, 14in. diam. (Christie's) $1,548 £880

An 18th century spinning wheel with turned wood spindles. (J. M. Welch & Son) $262 £160

A Country Federal birch candlestand, possibly New Hampshire, circa 1810, 27¼in. high. (Robt. W. Skinner Inc.) $325 £203

A Regency mahogany torchere, fitted for electricity, 54in. high. (Christie's) $13,365 £8,250

A Regency ebony and oak open display stand, attributed to George Bullock, 80in. wide, 82½in. high. (Christie's) $187,110 £115,500

An early Victorian oak reading stand with rectangular easel-supported top, 19in. wide. (Christie's) $2,359 £1,430

An L. & J. G. Stickley magazine rack, no. 45, circa 1912, 44½in. high. (Robt. W. Skinner Inc.) $1,300 £812

A fine pair of George III giltwood torcheres, 49in. high. (Christie's) $40,986 £25,300

A painted Country candlestand, circa 1810, 26¼in. high, 17in. diam. (Robt. W. Skinner Inc.) $1,800 £1,071

STANDS

A Regency mahogany double music stand with candleholders, 108cm. high. (Osmond Tricks)
$5,115 £3,100

Country Federal tiger maple one-drawer stand, New England, circa 1810, top 19¾ x 20in. (Robt. W. Skinner Inc.)
$7,200 £4,285

Late Regency rosewood brass inlaid teapoy with sarcophagus shaped top, 17in. wide. (Lalonde Fine Art)
$2,310 £1,400

A carved wood hallstand depicting bear and cubs. (Ball & Percival)
$5,808 £3,300

A marquetry panelled oak smoking rack, possibly Stickley Bros., Michigan, circa 1910, style no. 264-100, 22in. high, 24in. wide. (Robt. W. Skinner Inc.)
$130 £81

A black and gold-painted umbrella stand with scrolling foliate sides, 32in. wide. (Christie's) $902 £550

A Chippendale walnut dish-top stand, Phila., 1770-90, 20¾in. diam. (Christie's)
$8,250 £4,987

A matched pair of Italian giltwood torcheres with circular platforms, 49½in. high. (Christie's)
$1,653 £990

An ebonised hardwood Oriental jardiniere stand with inset rouge marble top. (Peter Wilson)
$550 £340

STOOLS

A Gustav Stickley upholstered footstool with tacked leather surface, no. 300, circa 1905, 20½in. wide. (Robt. W. Skinner Inc.) $1,600 £952

A Gustav Stickley mahogany footstool, no. 302, signed with red decal, 1905-05, 4½in. high. (Robt. W. Skinner Inc.) $900 £562

A Queen Anne walnut stool with a slip-in gros point needlework seat, on cabriole legs. (Phillips) $2,975 £1,700

A George III mahogany stool, the seat covered in close-nailed green cloth with crewelwork flowers, on cabriole legs, 23½in. wide, 17in. high. (Christie's) $8,140 £4,400

An oak stool of William and Mary style with machined tapestry circular seat and turned scrolled legs, 19in. wide. (Christie's) $1,050 £600

Victorian rosewood stool on cabriole legs with scroll feet and brass castors, 18in. square. (Peter Wilson) $372 £230

A George III mahogany stool with drop-in seat covered in blue and red floral needlework, 19in. wide. (Christie's) $3,544 £1,980

A leather upholstered footstool, no. 300, by Gustav Stickley, 20in. wide, circa 1905. (Robt. W. Skinner Inc.) $950 £513

A 19th century Continental carved giltwood rectangular stool covered in floral material. (Peter Wilson) $915 £520

STOOLS

A George I walnut stool with close-nailed rectangular padded seat, on claw-and-ball feet, 19½in. wide. (Christie's) $3,291 £1,760

A Gustav Stickley footstool with notched feet, style no. 726, circa 1902-04, 12¼in. wide. (Robt. W. Skinner Inc.) $700 £378

A Victorian walnut dressing stool, the upholstered seat with shell carved serpentine apron. (David Lay) $540 £300

A walnut stool with concave waisted padded drop-in seat on cabriole legs, 26½in. wide. (Christie's) $2,336 £1,320

A William and Mary walnut stool with square padded top covered in floral needlework, 15½in. square. (Christie's) $2,468 £1,320

An unusual mahogany stool, the rectangular gros and petit point needlework drop-in seat, on cabriole legs and paw-feet, 19in. wide. (Christie's) $1,028 £550

A 19th century mahogany dressing stool in George I style, with upholstered serpentine seat on four cabriole legs. (David Lay) $432 £240

An early Victorian oak stool in the Gothic style, with padded seat covered in close-nailed green leather, 51in. wide. (Christie's) $8,712 £5,280

Late 17th century oak joint stool. (Brown & Merry) $1,274 £700

One of a pair of early 19th
century late Federal mahogany
footstools, 12¾in. long.
(Christie's) $7,700 £4,655

An early Victorian oak hall
stool the octagonal arms with
scrolled ends and solid seat,
25in. wide. (Christie's)
$1,452 £825

A Regency oak footstool,
attributed to George
Bullock, with padded seat
covered in white-striped
blue silk, 13½in. square.
(Christie's)
$22,275 £13,750

One of a pair of North Italian
giltwood rococo stools, the
serpentine seats upholstered
with maroon velvet with silver
thread borders, 23in. wide.
(Christie's) $28,473 £17,050

One of a pair of giltwood
fender stools of William
and Mary style, 72in. wide.
(Christie's) $6,133 £3,740

A Regency rosewood piano
stool with adjustable padded
seat, 14in. wide. (Christie's)
$1,742 £990

A George I walnut stool, the
top upholstered in gros and
petit-point floral needlework,
on square cabriole legs, 26in.
wide. (Christie's)
$15,752 £8,800

A George II mahogany stool,
the padded seat covered in
yellow velvet, 24in. wide.
(Christie's) $3,993 £2,420

A tabouret with cut corners,
by L. & J. G. Stickley, no.
560, circa 1912, 16in. wide.
(Robt. W. Skinner Inc.)
$750 £405

STOOLS

A Regency oak window-seat, attributed to George Bullock, the solid seat with squab cushion, 38in. wide. (Christie's)
$67,716 £41,800

A Regency mahogany gout stool with buttoned brown leather upholstery, 26¼in. wide. (Christie's)
$1,936 £1,100

A Gustav Stickley piano bench, no. 217, plank sides with D-shaped handles, circa 1907, 36in. long. (Robt. W. Skinner Inc.)
$800 £476

A walnut stool, the padded seat covered in floral needle-work on turned baluster legs, with scrolled feet, 17¾in. wide. (Christie's) $3,385 £2,090

A Regency pollard oak, oak and holly commode stool, by George Bullock, 22in. wide. (Christie's)
$2,904 £1,760

One of a pair of Regency oak and ebonised stools attributed to George Bullock, 24½in. wide. (Christie's)
$37,411 £20,900

Mid 19th century rosewood stool, the padded seat covered in floral needlepoint, 17¼in. wide. (Christie's)
$902 £550

Early 20th century octagonal oak garden seat, unsigned, 16in. diam. (Robt. W. Skinner Inc.)
$425 £265

One of a pair of giltwood stools of Louis XVI style with padded seats, 21in. wide. (Christie's)
$1,469 £880

SUITES

Part of a suite of George II ebonised and parcel gilt seat furniture with velvet upholstered rectangular padded backs and seats on foliate cabriole legs and claw feet, comprising six side chairs, an armchair and two sofas, the sofas 69in. long. (Christie's) $77,330 £41,800

Early 20th century Plail & Co., barrel-back settee and matching armchairs, 46¼in. long. (Robt. W. Skinner Inc.) $4,800 £2,857

Part of a suite of George III mahogany seat furniture comprising eight side chairs, each with arched rectangular back and serpentine seat covered in pink striped material with plain moulded frames, the sofa 77in. long. (Christie's) $18,315 £9,900

Part of a suite of Regency parcel gilt and simulated rosewood seat furniture comprising a set of six open armchairs, four with red velvet covered squab cushions, two chairs and the settee with blue velvet covered squabs, the settee 76¾in. long. (Christie's)

$22,385 £12,100

A suite of George III mahogany seat furniture, now parcel gilt and cream painted, comprising five open armchairs and a sofa, the sofa 60½in. wide. (Christie's)

$88,605 £49,500

An Edwardian mahogany and boxwood strung five-piece salon suite. (Phillips) $2,002 £1,100

CARD & TEA TABLES

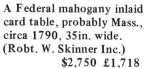

A George III satinwood card table on square tapering legs and spade feet, 35½in. wide. (Christie's) $3,993 £2,420

A Federal inlaid mahogany card table with D-shaped top, Mass., 1790-1810, 34in. wide. (Christie's) $4,400 £2,660

A Federal mahogany inlaid card table, probably Mass., circa 1790, 35in. wide. (Robt. W. Skinner Inc.) $2,750 £1,718

A George III mahogany tea table, the serpentine twin-flap top with carved border on chamfered moulded square legs, 36in. wide. (Christie's) $2,541 £1,540

A George II mahogany demi-lune tea table with single gate action. (Locke & England) $1,059 £650

A mid Georgian mahogany card table, the eared rectangular twin-flap top with guinea wells, 29½in. wide. (Christie's) $2,722 £1,650

An early George III mahogany card table, the top with candle sconces, 35in. wide. (Christie's) $18,040 £11,000

A Federal inlaid mahogany card table on five square tapering legs, New England, 1800-20, 32.7/8in. wide. (Christie's) $715 £432

A mid Victorian gilt metal mounted mahogany and amboyna card table with leather-lined eared shape rectangular top, 35in. wide. (Christie's) $4,408 £2,640

CARD & TEA TABLES

A Regency mahogany tea table with crossbanded D-shaped top, 39in. wide. (Christie's) $1,443 £880

A Queen Anne figured maple octagonal tilt-top tea table, Conn., 1730-40, 33in. wide, 26in. high. (Christie's) $19,800 £11,971

One of a matched pair of George III mahogany card tables, one with chamfered folding baize-lined top, the other a tea table, one 39½in. wide, the other 19in. wide. (Christie's) $8,910 £5,500

A mid Georgian mahogany card table with hinged top enclosing a baize-lined interior, possibly American, 35¾in. wide. (Christie's) $3,630 £2,200

A Chinese Export black and gilt lacquer tea table with triple-flap top, early 19th century, 30in. wide. (Christie's) $3,085 £1,870

One of a pair of George III figured mahogany card tables, the D-shaped tops crossbanded and lined with baize, each 36in. wide. (Christie's) $17,138 £10,450

A George III mahogany card table with baize-lined serpentine top, 35½in. wide. (Christie's) $2,345 £1,430

A George III mahogany inlaid and crossbanded D-shaped card table with fold-over top, 36in. wide. (Dacre, Son & Hartley) $1,394 £850

A William and Mary walnut card table with crossbanded folding suede-lined top, 33½in. wide, 30¼in. high. (Christie's) $13,365 £8,250

CARD & TEA TABLES

A Regency rosewood card table inlaid with boxwood dots in a burr-yew band, 33¾in. wide. (Christie's) $2,330 £1,430

A George III satinwood and marquetry card table, the baize-lined D-shaped top crossbanded with rosewood, 42¼in. wide. (Christie's) $8,910 £5,500

Late Georgian mahogany fold-over tea table, 30in. square, open. (J. M. Welch & Son) $1,180 £720

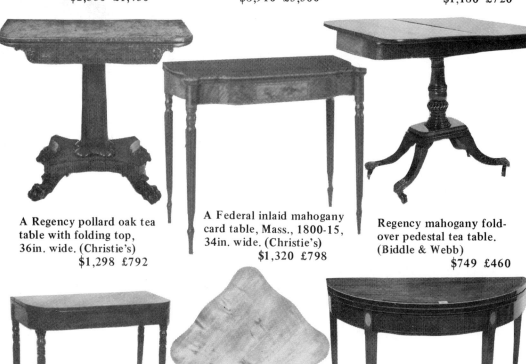

A Regency pollard oak tea table with folding top, 36in. wide. (Christie's) $1,298 £792

A Federal inlaid mahogany card table, Mass., 1800-15, 34in. wide. (Christie's) $1,320 £798

Regency mahogany fold-over pedestal tea table. (Biddle & Webb) $749 £460

An early 19th century D-end mahogany fold-over card table on turned and tapered legs, 36in. square. (J. M. Welch & Son) $328 £200

A Country Chippendale maple tea table, New England, circa 1780, 33½in. wide. (Robt. W. Skinner Inc.) $850 £477

An 18th century demi-lune mahogany card table, 36in. wide. (Warren & Wignall Ltd.) $1,088 £680

CARD & TEA TABLES

A Federal carved mahogany card table, attributed to Henry Connelly, circa 1810, 36in. wide. (Christie's) $2,640 £1,596

A William IV mahogany fold-over card table on scrolled feet, 36in. wide. (J. M. Welch & Son) $590 £360

An early Victorian figured mahogany fold-over card table on slender turned legs, 36in. square. (J. M. Welch & Son) $623 £410

A Federal inlaid mahogany card table on four tapering legs, Baltimore, 1790-1810, 36¼in. diam. (Christie's) $3,850 £2,327

A Chippendale birch tea table, the serpentine tip top on a vase and ring turned post and tripod cabriole leg base, circa 1780, 37in. wide. (Robt. W. Skinner Inc.) $800 £500

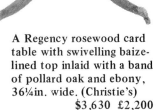

A Regency rosewood card table with swivelling baize-lined top inlaid with a band of pollard oak and ebony, 36¼in. wide. (Christie's) $3,630 £2,200

A Regency kingwood card table with baize-lined crossbanded rectangular top, 36in. wide. (Christie's) $1,815 £1,100

A mid Georgian mahogany card table, the eared top with counter wells and a frieze drawer, 24½in. wide. (Christie's) $9,323 £5,720

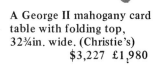

A George II mahogany card table with folding top, 32¾in. wide. (Christie's) $3,227 £1,980

CARD & TEA TABLES

An Art Deco mahogany fold-over card table in the Chinese Chippendale style, 38in. sq. (J. M. Welch & Son)
$369 £220

Regency mahogany fold-over card table with baize top. (Brown & Merry)
$1,092 £600

An Hepplewhite mahogany and marquetry half-round card table in the French taste, 96cm. wide. (Phillips) $9,512 £5,800

A mid Georgian mahogany tea and card table with eared triple-flap top, 32½in. wide. (Christie's)
$9,020 £5,500

One of a pair of late Regency rosewood folding card tables with baize lined interior, 3ft. wide. (Hobbs & Chambers)
$3,382 £1,900

A George III mahogany folding card table, D-shaped with rosewood crossbanded top and baize lined interior, 3ft. wide. (Hobbs & Chambers)
$528 £320

Regency rosewood fold-over tea table. (Brown & Merry)
$1,547 £850

A Federal mahogany inlaid card table, shaped top with elliptic front, Boston, circa 1810, 36in. wide. (Robt. W. Skinner Inc.) $1,000 £625

A Chippendale mahogany tea table, America, circa 1780, 31in. diam. (Robt. W. Skinner Inc.)
$1,200 £714

CARD & TEA TABLES

Victorian mahogany circular tilt-top tea table on a canon and wrythen turned column, 3ft. diam. (G. A. Key)
$437 £250

One of a pair of 19th century French walnut and parcel gilt card tables, 89cm. wide. (Wellington Salerooms)
$8,736 £5,200

A Chippendale carved walnut dish-top birdcage tea table, probably Lancaster, Penn., 1760-90, 32¾in. diam. (Christie's) $2,640 £1,489

A Federal mahogany inlaid card table, probably Mass., circa 1790, 36in. wide. $1,600 (Robt. W. Skinner Inc.) £952

An early Victorian rosewood fold-flap card table inset with circular baize having central multi-panelled bulb support on scroll feet. (Hetheringtons Nationwide) $896 £560

A Federal mahogany inlaid card table, the shaped top with half-serpentine ends, Mass., circa 1790, 35½in. wide. (Robt. W. Skinner Inc.) $6,500 £3,869

A George II style mahogany card table, the fold-over top fitted with candlestands and money wells, 2ft.8in. wide. (Greenslade & Co.)
$3,204 £1,800

An 18th century mahogany fold-over card table, lined blue baize, on cabriole legs with ball and claw feet. (Jacobs & Hunt)
$3,894 £2,200

A George III mahogany fold-top tea table with boxwood stringing. (David Lay)
$984 £550

CENTRE TABLES

An Italian giltwood and pietra dura centre table, ink label beneath stretcher 'Monsieur R. O. Milne Florence 18.4.99', 26¾in. wide. (Christie's)
$6,171 £3,740

A Regency rosewood centre table by Gillows, with tip-up top on spreading hexagonal stem and concave sided triangular base, 54½in. diam. (Christie's)
$23,166 £14,300

A tortoiseshell, walnut and parcel gilt centre table, the crossbanded top bordered with ivory, 33in. wide. (Christie's)
$11,583 £7,150

Early 19th century Italian scagliola circular table top on a mahogany tripartite pedestal, 34½in. diam. (Christie's)
$11,583 £7,150

A George IV pollard oak centre table with circular top, 47½in. diam. (Christie's)
$3,993 £2,420

A Napoleon III ormolu mounted Sevres pattern porcelain and mahogany centre table, 33in. diam. (Christie's) $11,940 £7,150

A Morris & Co. walnut centre table, 69cm. diam. (Christie's) $811 £495

A Salvatore Meli ceramic and glass centre table, 120.5cm. wide. (Christie's)
$11,726 £7,150

A mid Victorian oak and parcel gilt centre table 30½in. diam. (Christie's)
$6,534 £3,960

CENTRE TABLES

An early 18th century oak centre table on tapering cabriole legs and pad feet, the gallery initialled 'W', 29½in. wide. (Christie's) $1,353 £825

An early Victorian rosewood centre table with well figured circular tip-up top, 48in. diam. (Christie's) $5,020 £3,080

One of two ormolu mounted kingwood and parquetry centre tables of Louis XVI style, 37in. wide and 39¼in. wide. (Christie's) $6,429 £3,850

A walnut centre table with circular top and scrolling supports, 25½in. diam. (Christie's) $2,204 £1,320

A mid Victorian rosewood centre table on spirally-turned twin column end-standards, 45¾in. wide. (Christie's) $1,633 £990

An early Victorian pollard oak centre table with an Italian circular specimen marble top, 22¼in. diam. (Christie's) $1,713 £1,045

A Dutch mahogany and ebony oval centre table on square tapering legs headed by rosettes, on ball feet, 36in. wide. (Christie's) $1,837 £1,100

A mahogany centre table with circular specimen marble top, 19½in. diam. (Christie's) $1,815 £1,100

An early Victorian ebonised and parcel gilt centre table with Italian scagliola top, 36¼in. diam. (Christie's) $14,256 £8,800

CENTRE TABLES

A gilt and cream-painted centre table with brass bound rectangular scagliola top, 51½in. wide. (Christie's) $8,553 £5,280

A Regency pollard oak centre table, attributed to George Bullock, with octagonal tip-up top, 53½in. diam. (Christie's) $35,442 £19,800

One of a pair of George IV mahogany centre tables with slightly later rounded rectangular tops, 67in. wide. (Christie's) $26,730 £16,500

An early Victorian figured walnut centre table with tip-up top, 57½in. wide. (Christie's) $1,996 £1,210

A mid Victorian ormolu mounted marquetry centre table with shaped oval top, 58in. wide. (Christie's) $4,356 £2,640

An early Victorian mahogany circular snap-top table, 100cm. diam. (David Lay) $984 £550

A Victorian walnut centre table, the rectangular top with burr-walnut banding, 75 x 117cm. (David Lay) $805 £450

A Regency rosewood and parcel gilt centre table with moulded circular tip-up top, 53½in. diam. (Christie's) $29,040 £17,600

A George IV rosewood veneered centre table with D-ends, 65 x 134cm. (David Lay) $1,350 £750

CENTRE TABLES

A Victorian figured walnut centre table with double serpentine shaped top, circa 1880, 47 in. long. (Peter Wilson) $1,654   £940

Mid 19th century drawingroom centre table in veneered figured walnut with oval tilt-top, 5ft. long. (Lalonde Fine Art) $792   £480

A giltwood and specimen marble centre table on entwined dolphin supports, 47½ in. wide. (Christie's) $21,659   £12,100

A mid Victorian ebony and marquetry centre table with sixteen-sided tip-up top, 46½ in. wide. (Christie's) $5,143   £3,080

A mid Victorian wrought-brass centre table, the black slate top inlaid with gothic brass strapwork enamelled in green, red and blue, 30in. wide. (Christie's) $6,352   £3,850

An early Victorian amboyna and marquetry centre table in the style of E. H. Baldock, 54in. diam. (Christie's) $9,075   £5,500

Victorian oval top walnut centre table on carved and turned stretcher supports, circa 1880. (Brown & Merry) $1,274   £700

A Regency brass inlaid rose-wood centre table, the two frieze drawers with lion-mask handles, 41in. wide. (Christie's) $11,814   £6,600

An early Victorian oak and walnut centre table in the manner of A. W. N. Pugin, 59½ in. wide. (Christie's) $1,837   £1,100

CONSOLE TABLES

Mid 18th century rococo turquoise-painted and parcel gilt console table, possibly Genoese, 43in. wide. (Christie's) $12,859 £7,700

One of a pair of oyster-veneered walnut and cream-painted console tables with crossbanded serpentine tops, 69½in. wide. (Christie's) $4,041 £2,420

Early 19th century white-painted and gilded pier table with eared rectangular black marble top, 41in. wide, 33in. high. (Christie's)$37,422 £23,100

A Regency parcel gilt and ebonised console table with mottled rounded rectangular black marble top, 39in. wide. (Christie's) $4,636 £2,810

One of a pair of carved mahogany rococo console tables of bracket design, 98cm. wide. (Phillips) $18,040 £11,000

A Federal mahogany inlaid console table, Baltimore, circa 1800, 37½in. wide. (Robt. W. Skinner Inc.) $8,500 £5,059

One of a pair of William IV mahogany and bronze corner console tables with mottled green scagliola tops, 28in. wide. (Christie's) $3,586 £2,200

One of a 19th century pair of black and gilt japanned and parcel gilt console tables of early Georgian style, 57in. wide. (Christie's) $4,537 £2,750

One of a pair of early 19th century mahogany pier tables each with black marble top, 19in. wide. (Christie's)$16,038 £9,900

CONSOLE TABLES

An Empire mahogany console table with grey marble top and frieze drawer, 28½in. wide. (Christie's) $1,469 £880

A Regency parcel gilt and rosewood console table with white marble top, 47¾in. wide. (Christie's) $2,689 £1,650

One of a pair of Empire mahogany marble-top pier tables, probably Boston, circa 1830, 49in. wide. (Christie's) $4,400 £2,660

A Louis XV oak console table with shaped veined grey marble top, 35in. wide. (Christie's) $4,041 £2,420

A Louis XVI console table with a 'D' shaped marble top, 3ft.4¾in. wide. (Phillips) $7,700 £4,400

A pine console table with rectangular white marble top, now painted to simulate verde antico, 32in. wide. (Christie's) $8,712 £4,950

A Regency mahogany console table with moulded black mottled green marble top, with mirror glazed back, 35½in. wide. (Christie's) $6,314 £3,850

Mid 18th century German giltwood console table with grey marble eared serpentine top, 37in. wide. (Christie's) $20,207 £12,100

One of a pair of Empire mahogany veneer marble-top pier tables, attributed to the shop of Duncan Phyfe, N.Y., 1834-40, 41½in. wide. (Christie's) $24,200 £14,631

DINING TABLES

A Regency mahogany and satinwood breakfast table with tip-up top, 59in. wide. (Christie's) $16,137 £9,900

A Queen Anne maple dining table with oval drop-leaf top, Rhode Island, circa 1760, 50in. wide open. (Robt. W. Skinner Inc.) $7,500 £4,464

A Queen Anne mahogany drop-leaf dining table, New England, 1750-70, 50in. deep with leaves open. (Christie's) $8,800 £5,320

A George III mahogany library table with leather-lined circular top and four frieze drawers and four false drawers, 47in. diam. (Christie's) $13,365 £8,250

A Federal painted maple dining table with rounded drop leaves, New England, circa 1800, 42in. wide. (Robt. W. Skinner Inc.) $4,000 £2,380

One of a pair of George IV rosewood breakfast tables with circular tip-up tops, 47½in. diam. (Christie's) $14,256 £8,800

A Regency mahogany breakfast table with rounded rectangular tip-up top, 53¼in. wide. (Christie's) $3,630 £2,200

A rosewood dining table of circular form, carved collar decoration to column. (McKenna's) $1,456 £800

Early 19th century faded mahogany tip-top pedestal dining table, 56 x 46in. (J. M. Welch & Son) $541 £330

DINING TABLES

A George IV mahogany breakfast table with cross-banded circular top, 54in. wide. (Christie's)
$6,855 £4,180

A George II period mahogany oval top drop-leaf dining table, 5ft.4in. by 6ft. opened. (Geering & Colyer)
$8,280 £4,600

A Regency rosewood breakfast table with circular tip-up top, 53¾in. diam. (Christie's) $6,237 £3,850

A George IV oval mahogany snap top breakfast table on a ring turned bulbous column and quadruple scrolled supports, 4ft.6in. x 4ft. (Prudential Fine Art)
$1,650 £1,000

A Regency rosewood circular breakfast table on platform base with three brass lion paw feet, 120cm. diam. (Osmond Tricks) $1,870 £1,000

Round pedestal base dining table, Hastings Co., Michigan, circa 1915, signed with decal on pedestal top, 54in. diam. (Robt. W. Skinner Inc.)
$1,200 £750

A Regency mahogany breakfast table with tip-up top, 56in. wide. (Christie's)
$2,525 £1,540

A dining table, the five legs joined by flared stretchers, by Gustav Stickley, circa 1905-07, 54in. diam. (Robt. W. Skinner Inc.)
$6,800 £3,675

A Victorian burr-walnut and marquetry inlaid oval pedestal 'loo' table, 50 x 40in. (J. M. Welch & Son)
$592 £390

DRESSING TABLES

A Chippendale tiger maple dressing table on cabriole legs, probably Penn., circa 1780, 33¾in. wide. (Robt. W. Skinner Inc.)$20,000 £11,904

An Arts & Crafts dressing table by George Walton, 134.2cm. wide. (Christie's) $992 £605

A Georgian mahogany bow-fronted dressing table with drawer on squared supports, 3ft. wide. (Greenslade & Co.) $765 £430

An early George III mahogany dressing table, the well fitted interior with sliding easel mirror, 24½in. wide. (Christie's) $16,929 £10,450

A 19th century inlaid mahogany kneehole dressing table with lift-up top enclosing a fitted interior, 4ft.1in. wide. (Hobbs & Chambers) $1,072 £650

A Country Federal dressing table, painted blue with applied gold decoration, New England, circa 1820, 30¾in. wide. (Robt. W. Skinner Inc.) $1,900 £1,130

A Federal painted dressing table, New England, circa 1820, 35in. wide. (Robt. W. Skinner Inc.) $1,800 £1,071

A George III satinwood, tulipwood crossbanded and marquetry serpentine dressing table in the French taste, 69cm. wide. (Phillips) $5,740 £3,500

A George III satinwood and marquetry dressing table in the manner of John Cobb, 27½in. wide. (Christie's) $27,730 £16,500

DRESSING TABLES

A George III mahogany and satinwood dressing table, adjustable mirror, and false drawer, 49½in. open. (Dreweatt Neate)
$2,835 £1,500

Late George III figured mahogany kneehole dressing table with end fold-over flaps concealing lidded and other compartments, 3ft.3in. wide. (Lalonde Fine Art)
$1,402 £850

Part of an Edwardian mahogany three-piece bedroom suite, the dressing table with swing mirror, label Warings, London. (Peter Wilson)
$2,728 £1,550

A George II oak dressing table, circa 1740, raised on cabriole legs ending in trifid feet, 29½ in. high. (Robt. W. Skinner. Inc.)
$1,100 £614

A Scandinavian mahogany and parcel-gilt dressing-table with bronzed dolphin supports and two convex drawers flanked by two small drawers, early 19th century, 54½in. high. (Christie's) $5,291 £2,860

Part of an Art Deco Macassar ebony bedroom suite, the dressing table 47in. across. (Christie's) $3,207 £1,980

A George III satinwood and ebony inlaid dressing table, circa 1785, top enclosing mirror and compartments, 34in. high. (Robt. W. Skinner. Inc.)
$2,750 £1,536

A George IV mahogany dressing table by Gillows of Lancaster, 50¾in. wide. (Christie's) $3,944 £2,420

A George III satinwood and rosewood banded table , after a design by Thomas Sheraton, 30in. wide. (Christie's)
$6,771 £4,180

Mid 18th century Chippendale drop-leaf table, 3ft.4in. x 5ft.3in. (Woolley & Wallis) $2,560 £1,600

A Classical Revival mahogany table, possibly New York, circa 1830, 50in. wide, open. (Robt. W. Skinner Inc.) $1,300 £773

A drop-leaf table, by Gustav Stickley, no. 638, circa 1912, 42in. long, 40in. wide, open. (Robt. W. Skinner Inc.) $2,800 £1,513

A late Regency mahogany pedestal two-flap table with four hipped splay supports and brass claw feet and castors. (Greenslade & Co.) $712 £400

A mid Georgian mahogany drop-leaf table with twin-flap top, on cabriole legs, 48in. wide. (Christie's) $3,993 £2,420

A Queen Anne mahogany drop-leaf table, Newport, 1740-60, 47.7/8in. wide. (Christie's) $4,950 £2,992

A Queen Anne maple and birch drop-leaf table, New England, circa 1760, 39¼in. wide. (Robt. W. Skinner Inc.) $1,000 £625

An oak drop-leaf table, no. 638, by Gustav Stickley, circa 1906, 42in. long extended. (Robt. W. Skinner Inc.) $2,100 £1,135

A Chippendale cherrywood drop-leaf table, with wavy stretchers, Conn., 1760-80 (Christie's) $1,980 £1,197

GATELEG TABLES

A William and Mary walnut gateleg table, probably New England, circa 1740, 56in. wide. (Robt. W. Skinner Inc.) $3,700 £2,202

A small 18th century oval oak gateleg table, 3ft.7in. long. (Greenslade & Co.) $302 £170

George II mahogany drop-leaf gateleg table with rectangular top, 55in. long open. (Abridge Auctions)$1,000 £625

Early 18th century oak, oval top, gateleg table with solid shaped ends, 52in. wide extended. (Abridge Auctions) $1,750 £1,000

A Gateleg table with oval twin-flap top and moulded channelled trestle ends, basically 17th century, 46in. wide. (Christie's) $2,141 £1,210

An oak gateleg table with oval twin-flap top on ring-turned legs and moulded stretchers, basically 17th century, 36½in. wide. (Christie's) $1,460 £825

A figured walnut inlaid Sutherland table with four turned columns and turned gatelegs with porcelain castors, 35in. wide. (Peter Wilson) $915 £520

A William and Mary maple gateleg table with oval drop-leaf top, New England, circa 1740, 41in. long, 51in. wide. (Robt. W. Skinner Inc.) $2,500 £1,488

Victorian figured walnut oval Sutherland table on turned end pedestals, 42 x 35in. (J. M. Welch & Son) $453 £270

LARGE TABLES

A Jacobean draw-leaf table, having planked and clamped top, supported on trestle ends, the draw-leaf top extending to 16ft. (Locke & England) $3,260 £2,000

A Regency mahogany extending dining table with rounded rectangular end-sections and concertina action, 53 x 88½in. including two extra leaves. (Christie's) $12,210 £6,600

A George III mahogany two-pillar dining table, the rounded oblong top with thumb mould edge, 5ft.6in. x 3ft.11in. (Hobbs & Chambers) $2,681 £1,625

A Regency mahogany patent extending dining table with D-shaped folding top, including three extra leaves, 2.83 x 1.30m. extended. (Phillips) $9,020 £5,500

A mid Georgian walnut supper table with twin-flap top, club legs and pad feet, 54in. wide, open. (Christie's) $3,608 £2,200

A mahogany twin-pedestal D-end dining table, including two extra leaves, 1.37 x 3.01m. extended. (Phillips) $13,940 £8,500

Late 19th century Regency style mahogany D-end dining table having inlaid ebony and sycamore stringing, 6ft.6in. long. (Giles Haywood) $792 £480

A dining table, centre section 4ft. x 4ft., and two D-end tables, 4ft. x 2ft. making one table 8ft. x 4ft. (J. M. Welch & Son) $1,312 £800

LARGE TABLES

A 1930's Art Deco mahogany octagonal topped dining table supported on eight carved legs with mask decoration and honeycombed stretcher, 78in. x 55in. (J. M. Welch & Son) $1,260 £750

Early 19th century Shaker tiger maple and cherry trestle base dining table, Canterbury, New England, 71¼in. wide. (Robt. W. Skinner Inc.) $86,000 £51,190

A Georgian style two-pedestal oval dining table with centre leaf, 86 x 36in., circa 1900. (J. M. Welch & Son) $1,246 £820

A late George III D-end mahogany dining table with gateleg centre section on fourteen square channelled tapering legs, stamped R. Bradley, Warrington, 43 x 102in. (Christie's) $6,776 £3,850

One of a pair of mahogany serving tables with moulded shaped tops and recessed concave stepped fluted and beaded friezes, 66in. wide. (Christie's) $8,606 £5,280

A mid Victorian mahogany D-end dining table. (Miller & Co.) $2,774 £1,550

A Country maple and pine painted harvest table, New England, circa 1800, 72in. long. (Robt. W. Skinner Inc.) $2,800 £1,666

A mahogany D-ended dining table (converted to accommodate two centre leaves), circa 1800, 89 x 48in. (J. M. Welch & Son) $1,489 £980

OCCASIONAL TABLES

A Regency mahogany Pembroke table with twin-flap rounded rectangular top, 38½in. wide. (Christie's) $1,972 £1,210

An Italian porphyry and serpentine marble low table with moulded square top, 47¼in. wide. (Christie's) $15,614 £9,350

A Georgian mahogany supper table with inlaid D-shaped top, 37in. wide. (Prudential Fine Art) $1,874 £1,150

A Gustav Stickley table with twelve Grueby tiles, 1902-03, 23¾in. wide. (Robt. W. Skinner Inc.) $49,000 £26,486

An 18th century circular mahogany pedestal wine table with 'dished' top, 20in. diam. (J. M. Welch & Son) $311 £190

An 18th century Country Queen Anne painted oak and maple tea table, 33½in. long. (Robt. W. Skinner Inc.) $6,600 £3,928

A Gustav Stickley round oak tabouret, no. 604, signed with small red decal, 1905-06, 26in. high, 20in. diam. (Robt. W. Skinner Inc.) $1,800 £1,125

An Edwardian mahogany marquetry inlaid two-tier tea table, having removable tray top. (Lawrences) $1,243 £740

A painted Windsor table, the top with breadboard sides, possibly New Hampshire, circa 1800, top 23¾ x 17¾in. (Robt. W. Skinner Inc.) $750 £468

OCCASIONAL TABLES

A Regency mahogany flap-top supper table with inlaid ebony stringing, 3ft. wide. (Woolley & Wallis)
$1,166 £720

A 19th century Chinese hardwood low table, 82 x 34cm. (David Lay) $666 £370

A Roycroft oak piano bench, N.Y., circa 1910, signed with logo, 36in. long. (Robt. W. Skinner Inc.) $2,400 £1,428

A George III mahogany tripod table the crossbanded rectangular top with canted angles, 19in. long. (Greenslade & Co.)
$818 £460

A mahogany drop-leaf table with knuckle supports, single drawer and four moulded swept legs with brass paw castors, circa 1850, 38 x 42in. open. (Peter Wilson)
$1,126 £640

A Regency satinwood and ebony inlaid vitrine on four tapering legs joined by X-framed stretcher, 23in. sq. (Hetheringtons Nationwide)
$1,600 £1,000

A nest of three shaped mahogany tables with rosewood crossbanding and turned frames. (David Lay) $411 £230

A late Regency design mahogany Pembroke table, 3ft.6in. fully extended. (Lalonde Fine Art) $693 £420

A George III mahogany pie-crust tripod snap-top occasional table with circular top, 1ft.9in. diam. (Hobbs & Chambers) $1,485 £900

OCCASIONAL TABLES

A walnut tilt-top cellar table, 29½in. diam., 26in. high, together with a pair of turned wood stools. (Christie's) $418 £245

An L. & J. G. Stickley occasional table, no. 543, circa 1912, 29¼in. diam. (Robt. W. Skinner Inc.) $300 £187

A Regency rosewood tripod table with rounded square top edged with boxwood, 17in. square. (Christie's) $3,085 £1,870

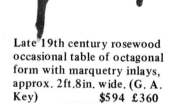

Mission oak 'knock-down' table, unsigned, circa 1910, 30in. diam. (Robt. W. Skinner Inc.) $225 £140

A set of Regency rosewood quartetto tables, the largest 56cm. wide. (Phillips) $3,608 £2,200

Late 19th century rosewood occasional table of octagonal form with marquetry inlays, approx. 2ft.8in. wide. (G. A. Key) $594 £360

One of two gilt metal, ebony and marquetry tables ambulantes, 21in. wide. (Christie's) $1,089 £660

A Heal's oak book table, the hexagonal top on six gadrooned legs, 80.5cm. wide. (Christie's) $673 £440

A mahogany veneer drum table, the single drawer fitted with compartments, Baltimore, 1810-20, 20in. diam. (Christie's) $11,000 £6,650

OCCASIONAL TABLES

A brass inlaid rosewood tripod table with circular top, on brass claw and ball feet, 18½in. diam. (Christie's) $811 £495

An Oriental rosewood circular two-tier table on ball and claw feet, 24in. diam. (Chancellors Hollingsworths) $496 £310

A mahogany tripod table, the circular top with a pierced balustrade, 14½in. diam. (Christie's) $902 £550

A Gustav Stickley square table with cut corners, no. 612, circa 1905-06, signed with small red decal, 29¾in. sq. (Robt. W. Skinner Inc.) $950 £593

A nest of four 19th century Chinese scarlet and gold lacquer quartetto-tables, 22in. wide to 13in. wide. (Christie's) $4,989 £3,080

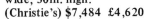

A George III mahogany architect's table with rect-angular easel top, 39½in. wide, 30in. high. (Christie's) $7,484 £4,620

A Regency brass inlaid mahogany tripod table, 18½in. wide. (Christie's) $902 £550

Mid 19th century Italian scagliola circular table top painted with two fishermen with their catch, 33¼in. diam. (Christie's) $6,429 £3,850

A mid Georgian mahogany tripod table, the top with pierced gallery, 25in. wide. (Christie's) $5,412 £3,300

OCCASIONAL TABLES

A George III scarlet
japanned tripod table with
chinoiserie tip-up top,
30in. diam. (Christie's)
$1,394 £850

A kingwood and marquetry
petit table of Louis XV
style, the top inlaid with a
hunting scene, 17in. wide.
(Christie's) $1,179 £715

A mahogany tripod table
with serpentine tip-up top
and spirally ribbed ring-
turned pedestal on arched
tripod base, 21½in. diam.
(Christie's) $8,019 £4,950

A mahogany tripod table
with circular tip-up pie-
crust top, 32in. diam.
(Christie's) $1,793 £1,100

An early Victorian low table
with out-curved foliate border and gadrooned frieze,
29½in. wide. (Christie's)
$6,454 £3,960

A Sheraton period mahogany
crossbanded and strung drum
top table, 60cm. diam.
(Phillips) $9,512 £5,800

A mahogany tripod table
with circular tip-up top,
27¾in. diam. (Christie's)
$2,345 £1,430

An ormolu mounted maho-
gany and parquetry gueridon
in the manner of Weisweiler,
18in. diam. (Christie's)
$2,204 £1,320

One of a pair of Regency
brass inlaid rosewood
tripod tables, 18in. wide,
28in. high. (Christie's)
$19,723 £12,100

OCCASIONAL TABLES

An early George III mahogany occasional or wine table with a circular snap-top, 52cm. diam. (Phillips) $1,640 £1,000

George III mahogany pedestal reading table with adjustable slope, 24in. wide. (Prudential Fine Art) $2,460 £1,500

An early Victorian oak occasional table in the style of A. W. N. Pugin, with octagonal parquetry top, 20¼in. wide. (Christie's) $1,452 £880

A gilt metal mounted mahogany gueridon in the style of Weisweiler, stamped Wright and Mansfield, 27¼in. diam. (Christie's) $6,980 £4,180

A mahogany silver table with serpentine top on moulded cabriole legs, 33in. wide. (Christie's) $18,711 £11,550

A Regency mahogany cheese table with divided bowed rectangular top, 22in. wide. (Christie's) $1,804 £1,100

A Regency rosewood and mahogany small table in the manner of G. Bullock, 22in. wide. (Christie's) $4,356 £2,640

One of a pair of silver mounted and malachite gueridons in the style of Weisweiler, possibly Russian, 15¾in. diam. (Christie's) $44,088 £26,400

A gilt metal mounted burr-walnut jardiniere on cabriole legs, 22½in. wide. (Christie's) $907 £550

A Gustav Stickley hexagonal leather-top table, no. 624, circa 1910-12, 48in. diam. (Robt. W. Skinner Inc.) $7,000 £4,166

A Georgian mahogany pie-crust tip-top pedestal table, 24in. diam. (J. M. Welch & Son) $790 £520

William and Mary cherry and pine hutch table, Hudson River Valley, circa 1750, 44in. diam. (Robt. W. Skinner Inc.) $6,400 £3,809

A painted birch and pine one-drawer stand, possibly Maine, circa 1810, top 24¼ x 19in. (Robt. W. Skinner Inc.) $4,000 £2,380

A Regency mahogany drum table with leather-lined circular top and four frieze drawers, 37in. diam. (Christie's) $8,659 £5,280

An Edwardian mahogany nest of three oval tables on sabre legs. (David Lay) $519 £290

An occasional table, no. 609, by Gustav Stickley, circa 1904-05, unsigned, 36in. diam. (Robt. W. Skinner Inc.) $900 £486

A Regency mahogany tripod table with circular tip-up top, 16½in. wide. (Christie's) $1,713 £1,045

A Country Queen Anne maple tavern table, the oval overhanging top on shaped skirt and block-turned tapering legs, circa 1740, 33in. wide. (Robt. W. Skinner Inc.) $8,500 £5,089

OCCASIONAL TABLES

An 18th century maple tavern table with breadboard ends, New England, the top 40 x 24½in. (Robt. W. Skinner Inc.) $2,700 £1,687

A George III mahogany breakfast table on baluster turned shaft and ribbed splayed legs, 43in. wide. (Christie's) $1,435 £880

A Limbert oval occasional table, style no. 146, circa 1907, 36in. long. (Robt. W. Skinner Inc.) $2,200 £1,309

A Gustav Stickley round leather-top table, no. 645, circa 1907, 36in. diam. (Robt. W. Skinner Inc.) $2,100 £1,250

Set of four mahogany quartetto tables. (Worsfolds) $1,344 £820

An occasional table with cut corners, possibly early Gustav Stickley, circa 1902-04, 29in. high. (Robt. W. Skinner Inc.) $1,100 £594

A painted 'Windsor' tavern table, possibly Rhode Island, circa 1780, 28in. wide. (Robt. W. Skinner Inc.) $6.000 £3,571

A George III mahogany tripod table, the later octagonal top with pierced border, 10½in. wide. (Christie's) $2,868 £1,760

A Limbert oval table with cut-out sides, Grand Rapids, Michigan, circa 1907, no. 146, 45in. long. (Robt. W. Skinner Inc.) $1,200 £648

PEMBROKE TABLES

A George III satinwood Pembroke table with twin-flap top, 37½in. wide, open. (Christie's) $9,845 £5,500

A George III satinwood and burr-yew Pembroke table with twin-flap top, 46in. wide. (Christie's) $11,583 £7,150

A mahogany Pembroke table with twin-flap top and one frieze drawer on cabriole legs, 34¼in. wide, open. (Christie's) $1,262 £770

A George III mahogany, tulipwood crossbanded and boxwood strung oval Pembroke table, 79cm. x 1m. (Phillips)$3,608 £2,200

An Hepplewhite period carved mahogany and tulipwood crossbanded Pembroke table with hinged top, 91.5 x 46cm. extended. (Phillips) $22,140 £13,500

Early 19th century mahogany Pembroke table on four slender turned legs, 36in. square. (J. M. Welch & Son) $250 £165

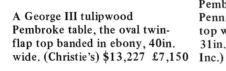

A George III tulipwood Pembroke table, the oval twin-flap top banded in ebony, 40in. wide. (Christie's) $13,227 £7,150

A Chippendale mahogany Pembroke table, possibly Penn., circa 1780, the shaped top with serpentine leaves, 31in. wide. (Robt. W. Skinner Inc.) $1,300 £812

A George III mahogany Pembroke table in the French taste with twin-flap serpentine top, 38½in. wide. (Christie's) $9,438 £5,720

PEMBROKE TABLES

A Regency mahogany
Pembroke table in the manner
of Gillows, on ribbed tapering
legs, 42in. wide. (Christie's)
$1,344 £825

A Federal mahogany inlaid
Pembroke table with D-shaped
leaves, probably New York,
circa 1800, 39¾in. wide open.
(Robt. W. Skinner Inc.)
$3,500 £2,083

Late George III mahogany
Sheraton design ovoid top
Pembroke table, 33in. wide.
(Locke & England)
$1,059 £650

A George III mahogany
inlaid and oval Pembroke
table with hinged top,
86 x 108cm. extended.
(Phillips) $1,804 £1,100

An early George III mahogany
Pembroke table with rectangu-
lar twin-flap top, 33¼in. wide.
(Christie's) $1,633 £990

A George III mahogany
Pembroke table with twin-
flap top and frieze drawer,
42in. wide, open. (Christie's)
$1,161 £660

A Georgian mahogany
Pembroke table on square
tapering fluted supports and
castors, 2ft.4in. wide.
(Greensalde & Co.)
$534 £300

A George III satinwood
Pembroke table with a
frieze drawer, 39¼in. wide.
(Christie's) $5,379 £3,300

A well figured mahogany
Pembroke table banded in
satinwood, above square
tapering legs to brass castors,
31in. long. (Woolley & Wallis)
$1,980 £1,200

SIDE TABLES

A George I gilt gesso side table with rectangular verde antico marble top, 35½in. wide. (Christie's)
$8,019 £4,950

A mid Georgian mahogany side table with single-flap top, 34in. wide. (Christie's)
$998 £605

One of a pair of George III satinwood and marquetry side tables with D-shaped tops crossbanded in rosewood, 54½in. wide. (Christie's)
$33,858 £20,900

A George II mahogany side table with frieze drawer, on club legs and pad feet, 27¼in. wide. (Christie's)
$2,525 £1,540

Regency painted pine side table fitted with a frieze drawer, 30in. wide. (Prudential Fine Art)
$1,840 £1,150

One of a pair of George III mahogany side tables, each with serpentine top and plain frieze, 28in. wide. (Christie's)
$19,602 £12,100

A George I walnut side table, the quartered top crossbanded with burr-walnut, 30¾in. wide. (Christie's) $14,256 £8,800

A George III mahogany side table with serpentine top and one frieze drawer, 28in. wide. (Christie's)
$7,260 £4,400

Mid 18th century Venetian pine side table with moulded serpentine top, 35in. wide. (Christie's) $1,745 £1,045

SIDE TABLES

A George III sycamore, marquetry and gilt gesso elliptical side table, 1.23m. wide. (Phillips) $11,480 £7,000

A George III mahogany side table in the manner of Thos. Chippendale, 46½in. wide. (Christie's) $21,384 £13,200

A George III satinwood, marquetry and giltwood elliptical side table in the manner of Wm. Moore of Dublin, 1.23m. wide. (Phillips) $9,512 £5,800

A rosewood side table with rectangular specimen marble top with three-quarter brass gallery, 45½in. wide. (Christie's) $7,623 £4,620

A Regency mahogany and fruitwood side table, 27in. wide. (Christie's) $2,722 £1,650

One of a pair of Italian giltwood side tables, each with a serpentine eared green marble top, 59½in. wide. (Christie's) $18,370 £11,000

An early Georgian walnut side table with later veneered rectangular top, 32in. wide. (Christie's) $5,412 £3,300

An Italian grey-painted side table with moulded rectangular mottled yellow and pink marble slab, 39½in. wide. (Christie's) $4,408 £2,640

An early Georgian oak side table on scrolling lappeted cabriole legs and hoof feet, 34in. wide. (Christie's) $6,133 £3,740

FURNITURE

An English mahogany veneered serpentine front serving table, 4ft.9in. wide, together with a pair of matching pedestals, 3ft. 9in. high, circa 1780. (Woolley & Wallis) $5,120 £3,200

A mahogany side table, the rounded rectangular top with inset mottled green marble and one frieze drawer, 11¾in. wide. (Christie's)$1,082 £660

One of a pair of George III mahogany side tables, each with a serpentine top, 64½in. wide. (Christie's) $35,640 £22,000

A mahogany serving table with rectangular top and bowfronted centre, 84in. wide. (Christie's) $3,247 £1,980

One of a pair of Regency mahogany side tables, comprising a card table and a tea table, 36in. wide. (Christie's) $10,399 £6,380

A George III mahogany satinwood and yew side table, the crossbanded D-shaped top inlaid with a batswing motif, 70in. wide. (Christie's) $5,412 £3,300

A mahogany veneered side table, designed by Frank L. Wright, circa 1955, 21½in. wide, red decal on back. (Robt. W. Skinner Inc.) $800 £432

A 19th century Irish carved mahogany hall or side table, the apron carved in relief with a mask, 1.80m. wide. (Phillips) $6,232 £3,800

One of a pair of French style ormolu mounted small tables, by Donald Ross of Denmark Hill, circa 1870, tops 16 x 13½in. (Graves Son & Pilcher) $6,802 £3,800

SIDE TABLES

A library table with one drawer, by L. & J. G. Stickley, signed with Handcraft label, 42in. wide. (Robt. W. Skinner Inc.) $950 £513

A George III mahogany serving table with crossbanded serpentine top on moulded tapering legs, 57in. wide. (Christie's) $5,445 £3,300

A George III giltwood side table with associated specimen marble top, 49¼in. wide. (Christie's) $19,690 £11,000

One of a pair of black and gold japanned side tables of Regency style with D-shaped tops, 61in. wide. (Christie's) $6,897 £4,180

A Regency mahogany bedside table with rounded rectangular twin-flap top, 29½in. wide. (Christie's) $1,082 £660

A George III mahogany serving table with moulded rectangular top and blind-fret frieze on chamfered square legs, 71½in. wide. (Christie's) $6,237 £3,850

A Regency style walnut and marquetry side table with single frieze drawer. (Hetheringtons Nationwide) $1,600 £1,000

An early Victorian giltwood and composition side table with shaped serpentine moulded green marble top, 81in. wide. (Christie's) $6,352 £3,850

A Country Federal grain painted maple tray table, possibly New Hampshire, circa 1820, top 17 x 16½in. (Robt. W. Skinner Inc.) $3,250 £1,934

SOFA TABLES

A Regency rosewood sofa table with twin-flap top crossbanded with yew-wood and zebrawood, 59¾in. wide, open. (Christie's)
$12,474 £7,700

Regency rosewood brass inlaid sofa table with plate glass top, 34in. wide. (Prudential Fine Art) $1,539 £950

A Regency rosewood and satinwood sofa table with rounded rectangular twin-flap top, 60½in. wide, open. (Christie's) $5,051 £3,080

A William IV rosewood sofa table fitted with two short frieze and two dummy drawers. (Lots Road Chelsea Auction Galleries)
$1,662 £950

A Regency rosewood and boxwood strung sofa table with hinged top, 1.50m. x 53cm. extended. (Phillips) $7,380 £4,500

Late Regency rosewood veneered sofa table with twin-flap top with inlaid brass marquetry and stringing, 3ft.1in. wide. (Woolley & Wallis)
$3,240 £2,000

A Regency mahogany sofa table, the twin-flap top crossbanded in rosewood, 62½in. wide. (Christie's)
$5,808 £3,520

A Regency mahogany sofa table, the twin-flap top crossbanded with rosewood, 57¾in. wide. (Christie's)
$3,066 £1,870

A Regency rosewood sofa table, the twin-flap top with canted corners and two frieze drawers, 58.5/8in. wide. (Christie's)
$3,048 £1,870

SOFA TABLES

A Regency brass inlaid rosewood sofa table, 60¼in. wide, open. (Christie's) $60,588 £37,400

Late Regency figured mahogany sofa table with rosewood crossbanding and line inlay, 4ft.11in. fully extended. (Lalonde Fine Art) $825 £500

A Regency mahogany sofa table with twin-flap top and two frieze drawers, 61in. wide, open. (Christie's) $3,484 £1,980

A good Regency rosewood and maple banded sofa table, the rounded rectangular top over two frieze drawers, 128cm. (Phillips) $6,888 £4,200

A regency rosewood and satinwood inlaid sofa table, with two drawers, 142cm x 63cm. (Phillips) $13,125 £7,500

A George III mahogany sofa table with twin-flap top and two frieze drawers, 52in. wide, open. (Christie's) $4,690 £2,860

A 19th century Dutch marquetry sofa table, 23½ x 52in. extended. (J. M. Welch & Son) $1,444 £860

A mahogany sofa table with drop leaves, 23in. long extending to 46in. (County Group) $651 £390

A 19th century walnut crossbanded sofa table with two drawers on stretcher frame and brass capped feet and castors. (Jacobs & Hunt) $4,956 £2,800

An early 19th century figured mahogany pedestal work box with fold-over top, drawer and work-basket, 20 x 14½in. (J. M. Welch & Son) $656 £400

A painted satinwood work table with pleated silk basket, 22in. wide. (Christie's) $1,984 £1,210

A 19th century walnut work table with shaped hinged top, on four fluted baluster supports. (David Lay) $450 £250

A Regency octagonal oak workbox crossbanded and inlaid with geometric mahogany and satinwood lozenges, 15½in. wide, 31in. high. (Christie's) $1,179 £715

Early 19th century mahogany work table with two drop-flaps, end drawer and dummy drawer, 2ft.4in. wide. (Lots Road Chelsea Auction Galleries) $560 £350

A satinwood workbox-on-stand with hinged top enclosing a blue silk padded interior above a sliding well, labelled John Bagshaw & Sons, Liverpool, 11¾in. wide. (Christie's) $689 £418

A Country Federal inlaid cherry work table, New England, circa 1800, top 20 x 19¼in. (Robt. W. Skinner Inc.) $3,500 £2,083

A Victorian burr walnut inlaid work table with rising top, drawer and slide (writing slope missing), 24in. wide. (King & Chasemore) $1,044 £580

A George III oak work table with twin-flap top crossbanded with rosewood, 29in. wide. (Christie's) $2,689 £1,650

WORKBOXES & GAMES TABLES

Federal mahogany and mahogany veneer and satinwood work table, circa 1820, 18¼in. wide. (Robt. W. Skinner Inc.) $2,600 £1,547

An early 19th century Chinese lacquer work table with hinged top and fitted interior, 25in. wide. (Robt. W. Skinner Inc.) $2,300 £1,369

A Chinese Export lacquer games table with eared triple-flap top, 32½in. wide. (Christie's) $2,886 £1,760

Mid 19th century giltwood and composition games table with square pietra dura top inlaid with chess squares, 21in. wide. (Christie's) $2,178 £1,320

A Country Federal maple and pine painted and grained two-drawer work table, possibly Mass., circa 1820, top 19 x 17½in. (Robt. W. Skinner Inc.) $14,000 £8,333

A mid Victorian parcel gilt, painted and sycamore work table with hinged top, 19½in. wide. (Christie's) $1,633 £990

A work table with original 'vinegar painted' ochre decoration, New England, circa 1830, 21in. wide. (Robt. W. Skinner Inc.) $2,000 £1,190

A Regency faded mahogany and rosewood work-table, the rounded rectangular top with two frieze drawers, 20in. wide. (Christie's) $3,608 £2,200

A cherry and tiger maple work table, the bottom drawer fitted with bag frame, St. Louis, circa 1830, 26in. wide. (Robt. W. Skinner Inc.) $1,400 £875

WRITING TABLES & DESKS

A Regency mahogany bonheur du jour, the superstructure with three-quarter solid gallery and six small drawers, 19in. wide. (Christie's) $2,904 £1,760

A Regency mahogany Carlton House desk with balustraded three-quarter brass gallery, 61½in. wide. (Christie's)
$213,840 £132,000

A Regency rosewood cylinder bureau crossbanded and inlaid with boxwood lines, 25¾in. wide. (Christie's)
$8,910 £5,500

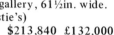

A Louis Philippe burr-walnut and tulipwood table a ecrire with brass bound top, 31½in. wide. (Christie's)
$3,674 £2,200

Shop-O'-The-Crafters slant front desk, Ohio, circa 1906, style no. 279, signed with paper label, 42in. wide. (Robt. W. Skinner Inc.) $450 £281

A parcel gilt walnut and marquetry bureau mazarin with folding rectangular top, 41½in. wide. (Christie's)
$9,185 £5,500

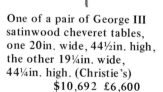

A gilt metal mounted mahogany bureau a cylindre on fluted turned tapering legs, 30in. wide. (Christie's)
$4,041 £2,420

An ormolu mounted kingwood bureau plat of Regency style with leather-lined top, 69in. wide. (Christie's)
$10,890 £6,600

One of a pair of George III satinwood cheveret tables, one 20in. wide, 44½in. high, the other 19¼in. wide, 44¼in. high. (Christie's)
$10,692 £6,600

WRITING TABLES & DESKS

An L. & J. G. Stickley flat top writing desk, circa 1905, 40in. wide. (Robt. W. Skinner Inc.) $550 £327

A Regency mahogany library table, the frieze with two drawers, 46½in. wide. (Christie's) $2,868 £1,760

A lady's Edwardian inlaid rosewood desk, the back fitted with two mirror panels. (Chancellors Hollingsworths) $810 £500

A Gustav Stickley flat-top writing desk, style no. 720, signed with red decal, circa 1907, 38¼in. wide. (Robt. W. Skinner Inc.) $1,100 £687

An ormolu mounted kingwood and marquetry double-sided bureau of Louis XV style, 51in. wide. (Christie's) $12,705 £7,700

A mid 19th century American Wooton Desk Co. burr-walnut panelled office desk. (Locke & England) $8,476 £5,200

An L. & J. G. Stickley drop-front writing desk, no. 613, writing surface with fitted interior, circa 1910, 32in. wide. (Robt. W. Skinner Inc.) $650 £406

Partner's Victorian mahogany table with leather-lined writing surface, 4ft. 6in. x 3ft.6in. (Lots Road Chelsea Auction Galleries) $1,148 £700

An Italian bureau base inlaid with Renaissance style decoration and ivory panels. (Lots Road Chelsea Auction Galleries) $1,023 £620

WRITING TABLES & DESKS

A brass-mounted mahogany writing-table with rectangular leather-lined top and frieze drawer on turned tapering legs, 31in. wide. (Christie's) $2,645 £1,430

Victorian mahogany library table with shaped end supports and turned centre stretcher, 48 x 26in. (J. M. Welch & Son) $852 £520

Lady's Regency rosewood writing/work table with five small drawers with workbox slide under. (Worsfolds) $1,848 £1,100

A Transitional style tulipwood and ormolu mounted desk, inlaid with boxwood and ebony lines, of bowed form, 36in. (Christie's) $1,468 £825

A 20th century mahogany Carlton House desk with leather inset writing slide, 41in. wide. (Peter Wilson) $1,036 £640

A Kingwood and tulipwood bureau-de-dame of bombe shape, sloping flap enclosing a fitted interior, 30½in. wide. (Christie's) $4,070 £2,200

A school master's grain painted pine desk with slant lift lid, New England, 1830, 3ft. wide. (Robt. W. Skinner Inc.) $750 £468

An inlaid oak drop-front desk, designed by Harvey Ellis for Gustav Stickley, 1903-04, style no. 706, 30in. wide. (Robt. W. Skinner Inc.) $20,000 £11,904

An Edwardian mahogany Carlton House writing table on square tapering legs, 45in. wide. (Parsons, Welch & Cowell) $3,528 £2,100

WRITING TABLES & DESKS

Mid 19th century mahogany library writing table, 58in. long. (Peter Wilson)
$1,337 £760

A 19th century French walnut and parcel gilt library table, 135cm. wide. (Wellington Salerooms) $7,056 £4,200

An Edwardian mahogany inlaid kidney-shaped pedestal writing desk, 4ft. wide. (King & Chasemore) $2,700 £1,500

A Gustav Stickley desk, no. 721, circa 1912, 29in. high. (Robt. W. Skinner Inc.)
$425 £252

A rosewood bonheur-du-jour, the rectangular top with leather-lined panel and pierced three-quarter gallery, with three drawers, 46in. high. (Christie's) $4,884 £2,640

A 19th century inlaid walnut amboyna and ebonised writing desk with hinged stationery compartment, 26½in. wide. (Reeds Rains) $1,235 £740

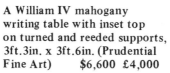

An Edwardian mahogany writing table, interior fitted with a rising stationery rack and drawers, 26in. high. (Christie's) $3,866 £2,035

A William IV mahogany writing table with inset top on turned and reeded supports, 3ft.3in. x 3ft.6in. (Prudential Fine Art) $6,600 £4,000

A Sheraton Revival rosewood and marquetry small cylinder desk, 28in. wide. (Dreweatt Neate) $2,232 £1,200

WRITING TABLES & DESKS

A George III mahogany writing table, now with Regency leather-lined top, 60in. wide. (Christie's) $74,844 £46,200

A black and gold lacquer Carlton House desk decorated with chinoiserie panels of flowers, landscapes and figures, 59½in. wide. (Christie's) $4,510 £2,750

A Regency mahogany writing table with rectangular leather-lined top, 45in. wide. (Christie's) $5,737 £3,520

A Victorian walnut bonheur du jour decorated with ormolu handles and mounts. (Lots Road Chelsea Auction Galleries) $2,754 £1,700

An ormolu mounted king-wood and tulipwood bonheur-du-jour, 28in. wide. (Christie's) $5,082 £3,080

A late Victorian ormolu mounted ebonised bonheur-du-jour mounted with Sevres style plaques, 43in. wide. (Christie's) $1,452 £880

A brass mounted mahogany writing desk with a tambour roll-top, 26½in. wide. (Christie's) $2,204 £1,320

A George III mahogany writing table with leather-lined top and arched secretaire drawer, 50½in. wide. (Christie's) $8,068 £4,950

A satinwood veneered bonheur du jour, Maple & Co. trade label, 28.5in. wide. (Woolley & Wallis) $1,620 £1,000

WRITING TABLES & DESKS

An ormolu mounted mahogany and marquetry bureau plat in the manner of B.V.R.B., stamped G. Durand, 45½in. wide. (Christie's) $4,592 £2,750

An early George III mahogany architect's table with rectangular easel-supported top, 39¼in. wide. (Christie's) $9,801 £6,050

A Regency mahogany writing table in the manner of Gillows, with eared leather-lined top and three frieze drawers, 48in. wide. (Christie's) $40,986 £25,300

A Carlo Bugatti ebonised and rosewood lady's writing desk with pewter and ivory inlay, 75.5cm. wide. (Christie's) $6,314 £3,850

A Dutch ebonised and lacquer writing table, the top with inset panel of courtly figures boating in a water landscape, 34½in. wide. (Christie's) $4,225 £2,530

A German oak green stained writing desk in the style of C. A. Voysey, 110.5cm. wide. (Christie's) $5,772 £3,520

A Regency rosewood bonheur du jour, the open superstructure with shelves and two cupboards, 34½in. wide. (Christie's) $5,445 £3,300

A Louis XVI ormolu mounted bureau a cylindre with three-quarter galleried white marble top and three drawers above a panelled cylinder, 49¾in. wide. (Christie's) $11,022 £6,600

A late Victorian satinwood bonheur-du-jour on square tapering legs, 33¾in. wide. (Christie's) $3,993 £2,420

499

Late 16th century Momoyama period coffer with domed hinged lid, 79 x 44 x 53.8cm. (Christie's) $6,688 £4,180

Late 18th/early 19th century painted pine blanket chest, Penn., 50in. wide. (Christie's) $3,300 £1,995

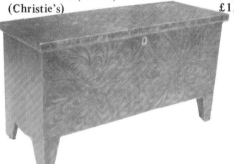

A painted and grained pine blanket box, New England, circa 1810. (Robt. W. Skinner. Inc.) $1,300 £773

A 17th century oak coffer with a rectangular cover over a lunette frieze and a triple panelled front, on stile supports, 44in. wide. (Hy. Duke & Son) $810 £450

An oak and poplar chest with drawer, probably Conn., 1690-1710, 48½in. wide. (Christie's) $20,900 £12,636

A 17th century gilt metal kingwood coffre fort with oyster-veneered top and fallflap, possibly Flemish, 15½in. wide. (Christie's) $1,557 £880

A painted pine blanket chest, New England, circa 1800, 43in. wide. (Robt. W. Skinner Inc.) $1,700 £1,011

Late 18th century Mediterranean ivory inlaid olivewood coffer, 67in. wide. (Christie's) $3,306 £1,980

TRUNKS & COFFERS

A vinegar painted blanket box, probably New England, circa 1830, 39in. wide. (Robt. W. Skinner Inc.) $1,100 £654

A carved and grain painted blanket chest, America, circa 1820, 44in. wide. (Robt. W. Skinner Inc.) $4,000 £2,380

A grain painted blanket box, the moulded lift-top on dovetailed base and cut-out bracket feet, Conn., circa 1850, 40½in. wide. (Robt. W. Skinner Inc.) $650 £386

A painted and decorated pine blanket chest, Schoharie County, N.Y., circa 1810, 40¾in. wide. (Robt. W. Skinner Inc.) $8,500 £5,059

A 19th century yellow grain-painted miniature blanket chest on French feet, 14in. high, 22in. wide, 12¾in. deep. (Christie's) $1,760 £993

A mid-Victorian walnut Ottoman, rectangular top and bracket feet, 33in. wide. (Christie's) $1,964 £1,045

Mid 17th century Flemish oak coffer, the interior fitted with a well, the coffered front inlaid with ivory and ebony, 52½in. wide. (Christie's) $1,561 £935

Early 19th century North African ivory and hardwood inlaid walnut chest, 40½in. wide. (Christie's) $2,020 £1,210

TRUNKS & COFFERS

A painted and decorated rectangular box, fabric lined, America, circa 1830, 30 in. long. (Robt. W. Skinner Inc.) $2,750 £1,636

Late 17th century Italian walnut cassone, heavily carved to front and sides, 85 in. long. (Brown & Merry) $3,185 £1,750

Late 18th/early 19th century Chippendale tiger maple two drawer blanket chest, New England, 38¾in. wide. (Christie's)
$2,640   £1,596

A Federal painted poplar blanket chest, probably Penn., 1800-30, 50 in. wide. (Christie's) $6,600 £3,990

An experimental Gustav Stickley cedar-lined chest, circa 1901-02, 27¾in. wide. (Robt. W. Skinner. Inc.) $9,000 £5,357

A red-painted two drawer blanket chest, labelled by F. W. Spooner Vermont, 1836, 42 in. wide. (Christie's)
$660 £399

A putty painted pine blanket chest, New England, circa 1820, 38½in. wide. (Robt. W. Skinner. Inc.) $8,500 £5,059

An oak coffer, panelled rising lid, with panelled and carved front, 56 in. wide. (Locke & England) $1,059 £650

TRUNKS & COFFERS

Early 19th century grain painted blanket box, New England, 38¼in. wide. (Robt. W. Skinner Inc.) $750 £446

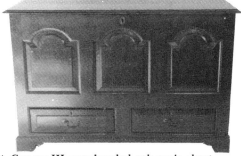

A George III crossbanded oak mule chest with plain top, panelled sides, arched panelled front and two drawers, on bracket feet, 4ft.1in. wide. (Hobbs & Chambers) $825 £500

An eagle-painted pine blanket chest, possibly Hanover area, York County, Penn., circa 1808, 52in. wide. (Christie's) $8,800 £4,966

A painted blanket chest, Pennsylvania, dated 1760, 21in. high, 51½in. wide, 24½in. deep. (Christie's) $385 £217

An oak coffer with panelled rising top, front and sides, inlaid with lozenge and star motifs, 3ft.9in. wide. (Geering & Colyer) $961 £540

A 19th century painted pine and poplar dower chest, Penn., 48in. wide. (Robt. W. Skinner Inc.) $6,000 £3,571

Early 17th century Italian oak bridal chest with walnut facings and coloured marble inlays. (Worsfolds) $2,624 £1,600

Early 19th century grain painted pine six board chest with hinged lid, probably New England, 47¾in. wide. (Robt. W. Skinner Inc.) $1,800 £1,071

503

WARDROBES & ARMOIRES

Mid 18th century Tyrolean cream and black-painted armoire on later bun feet, 55in. wide, 73½in. high. (Christie's) $4,592 £2,750

Late 18th century Dutch brass mounted mahogany armoire, 74in. wide. (Christie's) $16,533 £9,900

A George IV mahogany wardrobe on bun feet, 85½in. high, 55in. wide. (Christie's) $2,151 £1,320

An Arts & Crafts breakfront oak wardrobe by George Walton, 230.2cm. wide. (Christie's) $6,855 £4,180

An early 19th century gentleman's mahogany wardrobe, the gilded Nelson mask handles celebrating The Battle of Trafalgar 1805, 122cm. wide. (Wellington Salerooms)
$2,016 £1,200

An English Arts & Crafts walnut combination wardrobe with ebony crossbanding, 66in. wide. (Reeds Rains) $567 £340

An Arts & Crafts walnut wardrobe by Cope & Collinson, 188cm. wide. (David Lay) $1,890 £1,050

A George III gentleman's mahogany linen press, 49 x 85in. high. (Lacy Scott) $2,062 £1,250

A maple and walnut kas, in two sections, N.Y., or N. Jersey, 1750-1800, 72in. wide. (Christie's)
$4,400 £2,660

WARDROBES & ARMOIRES

A Louis XV oak armoire with foliate overhanging cornice, minor restoration, 64in. wide. (Christie's) $3,916 £2,200

Late 18th century Dutch walnut kas on turned onion feet, 67in. wide. (Christie's) $1,533 £935

A 19th century mahogany and marquetry linen press on splay bracket feet, 42in. wide. (Parsons, Welch & Cowell) $3,360 £2,000

A Gustav Stickley two-door wardrobe, no. 920, 1904-06, 33in. wide. (Robt. W. Skinner Inc.) $3,100 £1,845

An 18th century William and Mary walnut schrank, Penn., 74¼in. wide. (Christie's) $7,700 £4,345

A George III mahogany clothes press, the base with two short and one long drawer, 53in. wide. (Christie's) $3,406 £2,090

A Regency satinwood clothes press, the base with two short and two graduated long drawers, 50½in. wide. (Christie's) $16,736 £9,350

An early George III mahogany clothes press on panelled bracket feet, 49½in. wide, 79in. high. (Christie's) $6,494 £3,960

A French 18th century Provincial chestnut armoire with a pair of arched triple fielded panel doors, 59½in. wide. (Christie's) $7,398 £4,180

A 19th century enclosed washstand with lift-top revealing a rising mirror. (Lots Road Chelsea Auction Galleries) $968 £550

George III mahogany corner wash-stand with fitted shelf, additional shelf beneath having central drawer, 3ft3in. high. (Phillips) $520 £280

A late 18th century mahogany washstand with side carrying handles, 45cm. wide. (Wellington Salerooms) $1,344 £800

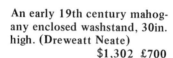

A mid Georgian mahogany washstand on turned supports, 31in. high. (Christie's) $973 £550

An early 19th century mahogany enclosed washstand, 30in. high. (Dreweatt Neate) $1,302 £700

A 19th century painted pine washstand, painted old pink over other colours, America, 15½in. wide. (Robt. W. Skinner Inc.) $800 £449

A painted and decorated washstand, New England, circa 1830, 15¼in. wide. (Robt. W. Skinner Inc.) $300 £168

An Empire rosewood washstand, the moulded rectangular top with three recesses, 42in. wide. (Christie's) $1,958 £1,100

Classical Revival mahogany washstand, probably Boston, circa 1815, 18¼in. diam. (Robt. W. Skinner Inc.) $3,600 £2,250

WHATNOTS

A Regency mahogany three-tier whatnot, 16in. wide. (Christie's) $1,623 £990

A Victorian mahogany three-tier carved and turned buffet. (J. M. Welch & Son)
$516 £340

A Regency mahogany whatnot with four rectangular shelves, 20in. wide. (Christie's)
$1,839 £1,045

A Regency rosewood and brass etagere with four rectangular tiers, the top with pierced gallery, 39¼in. high. (Christie's)
$14,245 £7,700

A Victorian walnut and marquetry four-tier corner whatnot on turned supports. (J. M. Welch & Son) $511 £310

A Regency mahogany whatnot with two tiers, ring-turned supports and two drawers, 24in. wide. (Christie's) $2,525 £1,540

A Regency mahogany whatnot with four rectangular tiers, 19in. wide. (Christie's) $2,525 £1,540

A grain painted pine and poplar etagere, New England, circa 1820, 35½in. wide. (Robt. W. Skinner Inc.)
$450 £267

A Regency mahogany whatnot with three shelves, 16in. wide. (Christie's)
$1,262 £770

WINE COOLERS

Late 18th century George III mahogany cellaret, the sides with brass carrying handles, 17¾in. wide. (Christie's) $4,950 £2,901

An Irish George III mahogany wine waiter of rectangular shape with divided and undulating galleried top, 26in. wide. (Christie's) $13,783 £7,700

Late 18th century George III brass bound mahogany cellaret, the hinged top enclosing a lead-lined fitted interior, 18½in. wide. (Christie's) $4,400 £2,579

A George III mahogany and brass bound octagonal cellaret with hinged top, 46cm. wide. (Phillips) $3,936 £2,400

A Regency mahogany sarcophagus cellaret with revolving panelled doors enclosing a fitted interior for six bottles, 33in. wide. (Christie's) $5,020 £3,080

A mahogany cellaret, the waved body with detachable tin-liner, 15in. wide. (Christie's) $1,262 £770

A satinwood cellaret crossbanded with tulipwood and inlaid with burr-walnut ovals, 20in. wide. (Christie's) $3,048 £1,870

A George IV mahogany wine cooler of sarcophagus shape with stepped hinged top enclosing a lead-lined interior, 28in. wide. (Christie's) $1,645 £935

A Georgian mahogany wine cooler with brass carrying handles. (McKenna's) $1,729 £950

WINE COOLERS

A Regency mahogany wine cooler of sarcophagus shape with lead-lined interior, 31¾in. wide. (Christie's)
$10,399 £6,380

A George III mahogany brass bound hexagonal cellaret, 15in. wide, 27½in. high. (Graves Son & Pilcher)
$2,058 £1,150

An early 19th century mahogany cellaret with lead lining and set on four bun feet, 79 x 47cm. (Wellington Salerooms)
$2,184 £1,300

A George III mahogany cellaret with octagonal hinged top enclosing a later divided interior, 19in. wide. (Christie's)
$2,904 £1,650

A George IV mahogany cellaret with lead-lined interior, 34in. wide. (Christie's) $2,345 £1,430

A George III brass bound mahogany cellaret with a lead-lined interior, 19in. wide. (Christie's)
$3,968 £2,420

A George III brass bound mahogany wine cooler, the tapering oval body with scrolling handles, 28½in. wide. (Christie's)
$5,033 £2,860

A George IV mahogany sarcophagus cellaret with hinged lid, lead-lined interior and Bramah lock, 33in. wide. (Christie's)
$1,533 £935

A George III mahogany wine cooler, the oval lid enclosing a detachable tin liner, 26in. wide. (Christie's)
$8,269 £4,620

GLASS

BEAKERS

Mid 19th century Bohemian engraved cylindrical beaker with scenes and quotes from The Lord's Prayer, 5½in. high. (Christie's) $550 £314

Late 18th/early 19th century engraved Masonic toasting glass, 4¾in. high. (Christie's) $1,760 £993

A Venetian Zwischengoldglas beaker with panelled sides and a scene of The Last Supper, after da Vinci, 3¾in. high. (Christie's) $1,320 £754

BOTTLES

Early 18th century sealed wine bottle of olive-green tint and onion shape, 18cm. high. (Christie's) $787 £440

A sealed wine bottle of upright form and olive-green tint, the body with a seal inscribed M Stripp/Lyskerd, circa 1745, 23.5cm. high. (Christie's) $275 £154

A 19th century brownish green carboy with gilt scrolled label for Acet Distill, 11½in. high. (Christie's) $360 £220

An early sealed wine bottle in dark green glass, bearing a seal 'Thos. Abbott 1728', 19.5cm. high. (Phillips) $1,375 £720

A Nuremburg engraved serving bottle, the neck with foliate and scrolling floral foliage bands, circa 1700, 25cm. high. (Christie's) $1,535 £858

A sealed wine bottle of upright form and olive-green tint, dated 1747, 21.5cm. high. (Christie's) $511 £286

BOWLS

A cut glass punch bowl with Van Dyke edge above a band of diamonds, 16½in. diam. (Christie's) $1,100 £628

A Victorian vaseline glass bowl with an off-white exterior and pink interior, approx. 9in. wide. (G. A. Key) $61 £35

Galle Cameo glass bowl, wide raised rim on shallow round bowl, 'Galle' signature, diam. 6in. (Robt. W. Skinner Inc.) $550 £307

An Irish cut turnover fruit bowl, circa 1800, 36cm. wide. (Christie's) $2,520 £1,400

Late 19th century Bohemian rose bowl on stand, 16½in. high. (Peter Wilson) $1,231 £760

A Venetian deep bowl, on a radially ribbed spreading foot, second half of the 15th century. (Christie's) $1,980 £1,100

Early 19th century Cork Glass Co. engraved finger bowl, 13cm. diam. (Christie's) $1,082 £605

One of two Daum Cameo glass rosebowls, crimped ruffled rim decorated with cameo-cut sprays of violets, signed 'Daum/Nancy', diam. 7in. (Robt. W. Skinner Inc.) $800 £446

A Schwarzlot decorated armorial deep bowl in the manner of Preissler, Bohemia or Saxony, circa 1736, 25cm. diam. (Christie's) $5,513 £3,080

Art glass bowl, attributed to Victor Durand, diam. 4¾in. (Robt. W. Skinner Inc.) $100 £55

A Lalique opalescent bowl, the blue opalescent glass moulded with a frieze of budgerigars, 24cm. diam. (Christie's) $2,886 £1,760

One of a pair of 'Lynn' finger bowls and one stand, the bowl 12cm. diam., the stand 15.5cm. diam., circa 1775. (Christie's) $393 £220

Late 19th century Venetian pedestal bowl in blotched pink and opaque white and clear aventurine glass, 10½in. high. (Lalonde Fine Art) $297 £180

Two of ten George III glass wine rinsers, circa 1810, 5in. diam. (Christie's) $660 £386

An Irish cut oval turnover fruit bowl, circa 1800, 28cm. wide. (Christie's) $720 £400

Daum Cameo glass bowl/ planter, flared wide rim on squat round body, signed 'Daum/Nancy/France', diam. 10½in. (Robt. W. Skinner Inc.) $1,600 £893

Steuben centrepiece bowl with adjusting holder, diam. 12in. (Robt. W. Skinner Inc.) $475 £265

'Lys', a Lalique opalescent bowl moulded with four lily flowers, 24cm. diam. (Christie's) $902 £550

CANDLESTICKS

A pedestal stemmed candlestick with detachable waxpan, circa 1750, 25cm. high. (Christie's) $720 £400

A pair of Charles X gilt metal and cut glass candlesticks and a dressing table mirror en suite, the candlesticks 6¾in. high, the mirror 13¼in. high. (Christie's) $2,153 £1,210

One of a pair of harlequin cut glass twin branch wall lights, 30in. high. (Christie's) $2,151 £1,320

A pedestal stemmed candlestick and a detachable waxpan, 18th century, 25cm. high. (Christie's) $864 £480

A fine pair of gilt metal and Bohemian glass candlesticks, mid 19th century, 15in. high. (Christie's) $7,832 £4,400

A pedestal stemmed candlestick, the cylindrical nozzle with everted rim, mid 18th century, 19.5cm. high. (Christie's) $360 £200

One of a pair of Venetian glass table lustres, 38.5cm. high. (Phillips) $1,050 £550

An opaque twist taperstick, the slender nozzle with everted rim, circa 1765, 18.5in. high. (Christie's) $3,938 £2,200

One of a pair of Regency ormolu and cut glass twin-light candelabra with flaming finials, 16in. high. (Christie's) $3,029 £1,870

DECANTERS

Two George III glass decanters, classic-shaped with panel-cut shoulders and bases, circa 1800, 9.7/8in. high and 8½in. high. (Christie's) $605 £354

A George III glass decanter, Indian club-shaped with wide neck, circa 1790, overall height 29cm. (Christie's) $935 £548

A Victorian decanter stand with three oval glass decanters, one in green, one in ruby and one in clear glass, by Elkington & Co., 12in. high. (Christie's) $915 £572

A Venini 'Vetro pesante inciso' decanter and stopper designed by Paolo Venini, circa 1957, 18.5cm. high. (Christie's) $1,232 £770

An Archimede Seguso 'Compisizione Piume' carafe, circa 1960, 29cm. high. (Christie's) $7,920 £4,950

A Venini 'Vetro pesante inciso' decanter and stopper, 27.5cm. high. (Christie's) $1,046 £638

A Venini 'Vetro pesante inciso' carafe, dark brown cased in clear glass, circa 1957, 25.5cm. high. (Christie's) $1,232 £770

A pair of Georgian mallet-shaped decanters facet cut with bull's eye stoppers, 27cm. high, and another matching, 28.5cm. high. (Osmond Tricks) $445 £270

A 'Lynn' decanter of club shape with horizontally ribbed sides and kick-in base, circa 1775, 23.5cm. high. (Christie's) $945 £528

DISHES

Tiffany glass Floriform dish, gold iridescent bowl form with scalloped and crimped irregular rim, marked 'L.C.T', diam. 4½in. (Robt. W. Skinner Inc.) $175 £97

A 17th century Venetian diamond engraved tazza, 20cm. diam. (Christie's) $3,544 £1,980

North Country machine-pressed milk glass oval butter dish cover on wood plinth, 2.5in. (Giles Haywood) $19 £10

A 'Non-Such' blue glass dish, by Isaac Jacobs, circa 1805, 18.5cm. diam. (Christie's) $3,544 £1,980

An opaque twist sweetmeat glass, the double ogee bowl with everted dentil rim, circa 1765, 9.5cm. high. (Christie's) $511 £286

Mid 19th century cobalt blue blown glass cuspidor, American, 5in. high, 9in. diam. (Robt. W. Skinner Inc.) $250 £156

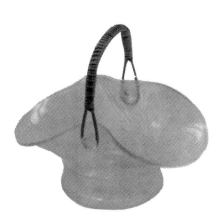

A North Country pressed crystal shaped dish designed as a basket with cane handle, circa 1900, 4in. high. (Giles Haywood) $22 £12

One of a pair of Charles X ormolu and cut glass sweetmeat dishes with ring finials, the dishes supported by mermaids and tritons, 20in. high. (Christie's) $8,223 £4,620

A Schneider cameo glass dish of circular shape, 39cm. diam., signed 'Charder' for Charles Schneider. (Phillips) $528 £300

An Art Deco glass decanter set, the decanter 20.5cm. high and six octagonal glasses, 6.5cm. high. (Phillips)

$774 £440

Early 19th century glass liqueur set, in a mahogany fitted chest, probably French, chest 11in. long. (Christie's)

$935 £548

A WMF Art Deco moulded glass liqueur set on a stand with moulded handle. (Woolley & Wallis)

$247 £150

Two Lalique clear glass decanters and stoppers, the spherical bodies moulded with fine vertical ribbing and twenty glasses en suite. (Christie's) $801 £495

Four liqueur drinking glasses, on tall flaring stems with various sized bowls, possibly Austrian, each 6½in. high. (Christie's) $1,279 £715

An Art Deco decanter and glasses, the decanter 22.5cm. high and six liqueur glasses 5cm. high (one glass chipped). (Phillips)

$264 £150

GOBLETS

Mid 18th century Newcastle engraved composite stemmed goblet on a folded conical foot, 16.5cm. high. (Christie's) $511 £286

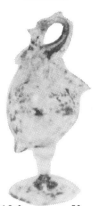

Late 19th century Venetian goblet vase in nacreous marbled pink and amber, and clear aventurine glass, 12½in. high. (Lalonde Fine Art) $280 £170

An engraved Bohemian goblet and cover, 38.5cm. high. (Phillips) $1,680 £880

A baluster goblet with a round funnel bowl, the solid lower part with a tear, circa 1710, 16.5cm. high. (Christie's) $945 £528

One of three large Vedar glass goblets, the bowls enamel painted with continuous frieze of naked females and peacocks, 7½in. high, signed XVII. (Christie's) $1,248 £682

Mid 18th century engraved composite stemmed goblet with bell bowl, 21.5cm. high. (Christie's) $2,559 £1,430

A colour twist goblet with an ogee bowl, circa 1765, 19.5cm. high. (Christie's) $3,544 £1,980

A James Powell flower form goblet, milky vaseline glass, the flower form bowl with frilly rim, 30cm. high. (Christie's) $1,178 £770

Mid 18th century Newcastle light baluster engraved goblet, the bell bowl with a border of laub-und-Bandelwerk, 17cm. high. (Christie's) $590 £330

517

GOBLETS

A heavy baluster goblet, the ovoid bowl drawn from a stem terminating in an angular knop, circa 1710, 17.5cm. high. (Christie's) $2,165 £1,210

A 19th century crystal glass, the hollow bulbous knopped stem containing a Swingewood opal cat and three amethyst mice, circa 1890, 5in. high. (Giles Haywood) $343 £180

An ale glass, the slender funnel bowl with crisp wrythen moulded lower part, circa 1730, 15cm. high. (Christie's) $630 £352

An Almeric Walter pate-de-verre goblet, designed by Henri Berge, 6¼in. high. (Anderson & Garland) $1,595 £900

A James Powell goblet, milky vaseline glass, 21cm. high. (Christie's) $420 £275

An Absolon rummer of emerald-green tint, the ovoid bowl decorated in gilt with a sailing ship heightened in black, circa 1800, 12cm. high. (Christie's) $905 £506

A baluster goblet with bell bowl, the stem with two true baluster sections, circa 1710, 17.5cm. high. (Christie's) $472 £264

Late 17th century Netherlands green tinted roemer, the stem applied with raspberry prunts, 15cm. high. (Christie's) $1,279 £715

An engraved pedestal stemmed goblet with round funnel bowl, circa 1750, 17.5cm. high. (Christie's) $905 £506

GOBLETS

A pedestal stemmed goblet with straight-sided funnel bowl, circa 1750, 16cm. high. (Christie's) $630 £352

An emerald green incised twist goblet with cup-shaped bowl, circa 1765, 14cm. high. (Christie's)
$2,362 £1,320

A facet stemmed engraved goblet with funnel bowl, circa 1785, 19.5cm. high. (Christie's) $511 £286

One of three large Vedar goblets, the bowls enamel painted with continuous frieze of dancing putti, 7½in. high, signed Vedar XIII, XX, VIII. (Christie's)
$1,245 £682

A German Royal armorial goblet and a cover, the glass possibly Thuringia, the engraving Potsdam, 1720-25, 32cm. high overall. (Christie's) $3,150 £1,760

One of a pair of Venetian ruby glass goblets with panels of The Road to Calvary, 9in. high. (Christie's) $605 £345

A baluster goblet with straight-sided funnel bowl, circa 1715, 16.5cm. high. (Christie's)
$393 £220

A gilt decorated emerald green goblet with cup-shaped bowl, circa 1765, 14cm. high. (Christie's) $1,673 £935

A mammoth baluster goblet, the funnel bowl with a solid lower part, circa 1710, 30.5cm. high. (Christie's)
$3,544 £1,980

GLASS

A baluster goblet with round funnel bowl on a small knop, on a conical folded foot, 20cm. high. (Phillips) $668 £400

Late 19th century Venetian goblet in pale pink and clear aventurine glass, 15½in. high. (Lalonde Fine Art) $396 £240

A baluster goblet, the round funnel bowl with a tear to the solid lower part, circa 1715, 15.5cm. high. (Christie's) $393 £220

A baluster goblet, the bell bowl supported on an annulated knop above a true baluster stem and short plain section, circa 1715, 21cm. high. (Christie's) $748 £418

A Bohemian engraved amber flash goblet, the flared fluted bowl on a fluted knopped stem, circa 1840, 26cm. high. (Christie's) $984 £550

A baluster toastmaster's glass, the funnel bowl set on an inverted baluster stem enclosing a tear, circa 1710, 12cm. high. (Christie's) $630 £352

A 'single flint' goblet, the straight-sided funnel bowl with a solid lower part, circa 1700, 18cm. high. (Christie's) $984 £550

A 19th century crystal glass, the hollow bulbous knopped stem containing a black Swingewood cockerel and hen, circa 1890, 5in. high. (Giles Haywood) $229 £120

A plain stemmed goblet, the bucket bowl inscribed Success to Sir Francis Knollys, circa 1760, 19.5cm. high. (Christie's) $590 £330

JUGS

An ovoid glass claret jug with a star design, the plain mount with bracket handle, 7¾in. high. (Christie's) $144 £88

An Elton squat globular jug with elongated spout, 16.5cm. high. (Osmond Tricks)
$187 £100

A Hukin & Heath EPNS mounted large cut glass claret jug, 12in. high. (Hetheringtons Nationwide)
$304 £190

D. Christian cameo glass pitcher, shaped upright pouring lip and applied handle on slender cylindrical form, signature 'D. Christian/Meisenthal/Loth', height 10¼in. (Robt. W. Skinner Inc.)
$1,400 £782

An early serving bottle, the compressed globular body with a kick-in base, circa 1700, 14.5cm. high. (Christie's) $1,530 £850

A hand cut crystal tall pitcher with notched handle, circa 1890. (Du Mouchelles)
$300 £171

A Continental silver mounted ewer, the silver cap with embossed fruit decoration, on a lead crystal base, 10in. high. (Hetheringtons Nationwide)
$152 £95

An Elton jug with bifurcated spout and handle above, 18cm. high. (Osmond Tricks)
$504 £270

A 19th century Arts & Crafts period claret jug, by Heath & Middleton, Birmingham, 1893. (Peter Wilson) $422 £240

A clear and frosted glass oval tray with DT monogram mark, for Dorothy Thorpe, 25¼ x 17¾in. (Christie's) $495 £282

Early 18th century posset jar and cover, 21.5cm. high. (Christie's) $2,756 £1,540

Lalique opaque blue stained glass circular inkwell moulded with four mermaids, 6¼in. diam. (Reeds Rains)
$868 £520

A Bohemian pewter and porcelain mounted ruby overlay tankard and cover, engraved in the manner of Pfhol, circa 1860, 25cm. high. (Christie's) $708 £396

A pair of 19th century glass specie jars enamelled in white on the inside and enamelled colours with the Royal Arms, 18.1/8in. high. (Christie's) $844 £528

A cranberry triple trumpet-shaped three-branch blown glass epergne on circular crimped base. (Hetheringtons Nationwide) $448 £280

A St. Louis patterned concentric millefiori wafer-stand, 3.3/8in. high. (Christie's) $715 £408

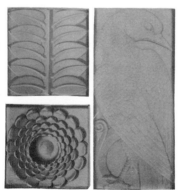

Three of eight Lalique satin glass panels, three rectangular and five of square shape, one panel signed R. Lalique. (Christie's) $1,804 £1,100

An English cameo glass biscuit barrel with plated mount, swing handle and cover, 17cm. diam. (Phillips) $1,337 £700

MISCELLANEOUS

A Victorian glass epergne, opaline and green tinted decoration, 23in. high. (Peter Wilson) $457 £260

A Lalique glass inkwell. (Hobbs Parker) $1,890 £1,125

A flask of flattened oviform shape, the sides with a band of trailed loop ornament above 'nipt diamond waies', circa 1695, 13.5cm. high.(Christie's) $945 £528

A Lalique clear and frosted glass presse-papier, the plaque intaglio moulded with the figure of St. Christopher carrying the infant Christ, 4½in. high. (Christie's) $712 £440

A pair of Nancy pate de verre bookends fashioned as dolphins, signed X Momillon, 6½in. high. (Lots Road Chelsea Auction Galleries) $4,550 £2,500

An Art Deco glass cocktail shaker with silver mounts, Birmingham, 1936, 8in. high. (Dreweatt Neate) $748 £400

A Millville steel die sailing boat mantel ornament, attributed to Michael Kane, 5½in. high. (Christie's) $1,210 £691

A pair of early 19th century urn-shaped honey jars with domed covers and cut knop finials, 12in. high, overall. (Anderson & Garland) $566 £320

Two of six 19th century cut glass stirrup cups, four 6¼in. high, the other two 7in. high. (Christie's) $550 £322

A Baccarat flat bouquet weight, 3in. diam. (Christie's) $13,200 £7,542

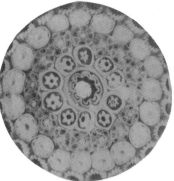

A Bacchus concentric mille-fiori paperweight, the dark green central cane encircled by five rows of canes in red, white and blue, 8.5cm. diam. (Phillips) $751 £450

A Baccarat close concentric millefiori mushroom weight on a star-cut base, 3.1/8in. diam. (Christie's) $1,870 £1,068

A Baccarat faceted blue-flash patterned millefiori weight, 3.1/8in. diam. (Christie's) $3,080 £1,760

A Millville rose pedestal weight, the flower with numerous bright yellow petals, 3¾in. high. (Christie's) $1,320 £754

A Baccarat faceted pink-ground sulphide weight, the crystallo-ceramie portrait of St. Joseph, named below, 2.5/8in. diam. (Christie's) $440 £251

A St. Louis faceted blue-berry weight, 2½in. diam. (Christie's) $2,090 £1,194

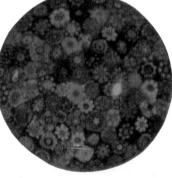

A Clichy close millefiori small paperweight, the canes includ-ing a pink and a white rose, 5.2cm. diam. (Phillips) $1,085 £650

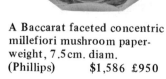

A Baccarat faceted concentric millefiori mushroom paper-weight, 7.5cm. diam. (Phillips) $1,586 £950

PAPERWEIGHTS

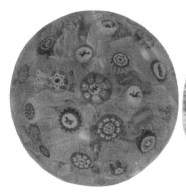

A Baccarat millefiori paper-weight, one cane dated B. 1847, 7.5cm. diam. (Phillips) $1,135 £680

A Clichy pink-ground patterned concentric millefiori weight, 3.1/8in. diam. (Christie's) $2,420 £1,382

A Mount Washington magnum pink rose weight, 4in. diam. (Christie's) $4,400 £2,514

A French (unknown factory) strawberry weight, 3.1/8in. diam. (Christie's) $3,850 £2,200

An Almaric Walter pate-de-verre paperweight designed by H. Berge, 8cm. high. (Christie's) $15,334 £9,350

A St. Louis double clematis paperweight, the two rows of pink striated petals with yellow match-head stamen, on a green leafy stalk, 6.4cm. diam. (Phillips) $764 £400

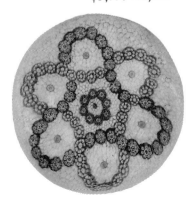

A Baccarat patterned millefiori white carpet-ground weight, 3in. diam. (Christie's) $6,050 £3,457

A St. Louis blue dahlia weight on a star-cut base, 2¾in. diam. (Christie's) $1,650 £942

A Clichy triple-colour swirl paperweight, 7.4cm. diam. (Phillips) $1,536 £920

A Clichy 'barber's pole' chequer paperweight, the spaced canes with a central pink rose, 6.8cm. diam. (Phillips) $1,623 £850

A New England blown pear weight, 3¼in. diam. (Christie's) $1,320 £754

A Baccarat garlanded sulphide weight, the crystallo-ceramie portrait of Sir Walter Raleigh in profile, 2¾in. diam. (Christie's) $990 £565

A Mount Washington magnum pink dahlia weight, 4¼in. diam. (Christie's) $28,600 £16,342

A St. Lous faceted upright bouquet weight on a star-cut base, 3.1/8in. diam. (Christie's) $2,530 £1,445

A Baccarat pink clematis-bud weight on a star-cut base, 3¼in. diam. (Christie's) $1,980 £1,131

A Baccarat snake weight, 3in. diam. (Christie's)
                   $9,350 £5,342

A Millville rose pedestal weight, the flower with numerous dark red petals, 3½in. high. (Christie's) $880 £502

A St. Louis concentric mille-fiori mushroom weight, on a star-cut base, 3.7/8in. diam. (Christie's) $1,650 £942

PAPERWEIGHTS

A Clichy blue-ground concentric millefiori weight, 2.5/8in. diam. (Christie's) $550 £314

A New England small blown pear weight, 2¾in. diam. (Christie's) $715 £408

A Baccarat pale-blue double-overlay mushroom weight on a star-cut base, 3in. diam. (Christie's) $1,650 £942

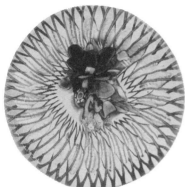

A St. Louis upright bouquet weight, 3in. diam. (Christie's) $2,640 £1,508

A Baccarat pink-ground sulphide weight, the sulphide portrait of Washington, named on the shoulder, 2¾in. diam. (Christie's) $1,320 £754

A Clichy swirl weight, the alternate pale-pink and white staves radiating from a central large coblat-blue and white cane, 3.1/8in. diam. (Christie's) $1,540 £880

A St. Louis fruit paperweight, set with two pears, an apple and four cherries lying on a bed of leaves, 7.8cm. diam. (Phillips) $734 £440

A New England blown apple weight, the fruit of bright pink tint, 2½in. diam. (Christie's) $1,210 £691

A St. Louis orange dahlia weight on a star-cut base, 2.11/16in. diam. (Christie's) $19,800 £11,314

A St. Louis purple dahlia weight on a star-cut base, 2¾in. diam. (Christie's) $2,860 £1,634

A Clichy faceted pink double-overlay concentric millefiori mushroom weight on a strawberry-cut base, 3.1/8in. diam. (Christie's) $5,500 £3,142

A Clichy close concentric millefiori weight, 2.1/8in. diam. (Christie's) $3,520 £2,011

A Sandwich blue poinsettia weight, the pale-blue flower with twelve petals, 2½in. diam. (Christie's) $550 £314

An Almaric Walter pate-de-verre paperweight, the blue glass moulded as a bird, 12cm. high. (Christie's) $902 £550

A Baccarat garlanded butterfly weight, on a star-cut base, 3.1/8in. diam. (Christie's) $2,420 £1,382

A St. Louis concentric millefiori paperweight, one cane dated SL 1848, 6.8cm. diam. (Phillips) $2,254 £1,350

A Gillinder flower weight, 2.7/8in. diam. (Christie's) $935 £534

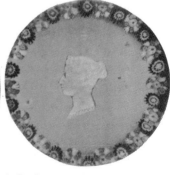

A St. Louis amber flash garlanded sulphide weight, the portrait of the young Victoria in profile, 2½in. diam. (Christie's) $1,430 £817

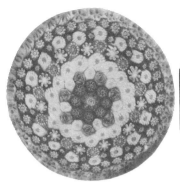

A Clichy close concentric millefiori weight, 2.7/8in. diam. (Christie's) $3,520 £2,011

A Baccarat faceted green-ground sulphide huntsman weight, 3.3/8in. diam. (Christie's) $1,760 £1,005

A St. Louis faceted upright bouquet weight, 2¾in. diam. (Christie's) $2,420 £1,382

A Baccarat blue pompom and bud weight, 3.1/8in. diam. (Christie's) $13,200 £7,542

A sulphide paperweight, the lobed globular surmount inset with a crystallo-ceramie bust of Voltaire, 12.5cm. diam., possibly reduced. (Phillips) $501 £300

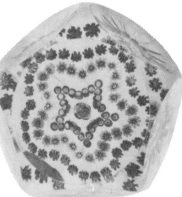

A Clichy faceted patterned millefiori weight, 3in. diam. (Christie's) $1,320 £754

A Baccarat faceted sulphide huntsman paperweight, 8.5cm. diam. (Phillips) $918 £550

A St. Louis crown weight, 2¾in. diam. (Christie's) $2,090 £1,194

A St. Louis concentric millefiori mushroom paperweight, the base star cut, 7.5cm. diam. (Phillips) $1,169 £700

SCENT BOTTLES

Daum Cameo and enamelled glass perfume bottle with conforming stopper, signature 'Daum/Nancy', height 4½in. (Robt. W. Skinner Inc.)
$1,400 £782

A cameo citrine-ground silver mounted scent bottle, the silver with maker's mark JNM, London, 1884, 14.5cm. long. (Christie's) $472 £264

One of a pair of blue tapering scent bottles and stoppers, gilt in the atelier of James Giles, circa 1760, in a contemporary Birmingham gilt metal filigree case, circa 1760, the case 5cm. high. (Christie's) $1,673 £935

An opaque scent bottle of pear shape, one side inscribed I*E:CAY, Newcastle-upon-Tyne, circa 1785, 8.5cm. long. (Christie's) $196 £110

A facet cut green scent bottle, stopper and gold screw cover, gilt in the atelier of James Giles, circa 1765, 6cm. long. (Christie's) $1,673 £935

A crystal perfume bottle/ink well with matching stopper, 3.5in. high. (Giles Haywood) $28 £15

A cameo scent-bottle and stopper of tapering form with waisted neck, circa 1880, 14.5cm. high. (Christie's) $900 £500

A Webb cameo glass scent phial with Tiffany white metal hinged cap, 6½in. high. (Christie's) $748 £418

An opaque white scent bottle of tear-drop form, gilt in the atelier of James Giles, circa 1770, 8cm. long. (Christie's) $826 £462

SCENT BOTTLES

A cameo silver gilt mounted scent bottle and screw cover, maker's mark for Sampson Mordan, London, 1884, 15cm. long. (Christie's)
$354 £198

An English cameo scent bottle, in the form of a swan's head, marked Birmingham 1888, 16cm. (Phillips)
$1,732 £1,050

Coralene decorated perfume bottle with matching beaded stopper, height 6¾in. (Robt. W. Skinner Inc.) $250 £139

An opaque scent bottle of flattened pear shape, one side inscribed A*B 1780, Newcastle-upon-Tyne, 7.5cm. long. (Christie's)
$630 £352

An Apsley Pellatt cut-glass sulphide scent bottle and stopper, 5.3/8in. high. (Christie's) $1,100 £628

A gilt decorated blue scent bottle and stopper, decoration in the atelier of James Giles, circa 1765, 18cm high. (Christie's)
$1,620 £900

Continental amber glass, shaped perfume bottle with matching stopper, 6in. high. (Giles Haywood) $28 £15

A Lalique scent bottle and stopper, the clear glass impressed and moulded with stylised marguerites, 13.2cm. high. (Christie's)
$324 £198

A bottle-shaped cut crystal perfume bottle and matching stopper, with silver spoon and silver rim, hallmarked Sheffield, 1912, 4in. high. (Giles Haywood)
$61 £32

STAINED GLASS

A 16th century Flemish stained glass panel of the parable of Dives and Lazarus, 23.5 x 17.5cm. (Christie's) $1,194 £715

A set of four late 18th or early 19th century English painted glass panels of female allegories of Justice, Faith, Hope and Charity, probably by Thos. Jarvis, after Sir J. Reynolds, each panel 72 x 40cm. (Christie's) $3,490 £2,090

One of a pair of 18th century English oval stained glass armorial panels, 46 x 34.5cm. (Christie's) $734 £440

A large 19th century English stained glass panel showing a lady in Renaissance costume at the prie-dieu, 100 x 55cm. (Christie's) $826 £495

An Art Deco leaded stained glass panel by Jacques Gruber, 70.2cm. wide, 50.3cm. high. (Christie's) $5,772 £3,520

A large rectangular glass panel by John Hutton, sand blasted and wheel engraved with Perseus before the Three Graces, 206.5 x 97cm. (Christie's) $2,706 £1,650

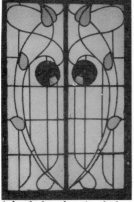

A leaded and stained glass panel by George Walton, after a design by Charles Rennie Mackintosh, 133.6cm. high, 91.4cm. wide. (Christie's) $1,082 £660

A 17th century French rectangular stained glass panel centred with an oval of the martyrdom of St. Stephen, 46.5 x 59cm. (Christie's) $918 £550

A large 19th century English stained glass panel of Mary Queen of Scots, 151 x 80cm. (Christie's) $1,837 £1,100

TUMBLERS

A Charpentier engraved cylindrical tumbler with a recumbent sheep, a dog, hat and crook, circa 1820, 9cm. high. (Christie's) $756 £420

One of a pair of 'Lynn' flared tumblers with horizontally ribbed sides, circa 1775, 11.5cm. high. (Christie's) $315 £176

A Bohemian 'Zwischengoldglas' fluted tumbler, initialled 'IHS', circa 1730, 8cm. high. (Christie's) $1,530 £850

Possibly late 18th century Central European enamelled 'Jagd' tumbler, 16.5cm. high. (Christie's) $6,694 £3,740

A lower Austrian 'Zwischengold' tumbler by Johann Mildner, the cylindrical body set with a double-walled medallion, circa 1788, 8.5cm. high. (Christie's) $1,530 £850

An Austrian 'Zwischengold' Armorial tumbler by Johann Mildner, set with a double walled medallion, circa 1794, 12cm. high. (Christie's) $5,760 £3,200

A Baccarat double medal cylindrical tumbler with cut foot and sunray base, 10.5cm. high. (Christie's) $1,378 £770

A gilt decorated blue tumbler from the atelier of James Giles, circa 1765, 10.5cm. high. (Christie's) $1,338 £748

A Charpentier dated cylindrical tumbler engraved with Cupid standing beside an urn, circa 1823, 9cm. high. (Christie's) $905 £500

An Elton twin-handled vase, the rim crimped to form two spouts, 15.5cm. high. (Osmond Tricks) $327 £175

A Venetian green glass bud vase, designed as a dolphin on circular foot, circa 1920, 7in. high. (Giles Haywood) $38 £20

'Le Figurines Et Masques', a Lalique clear and frosted glass vase, 9¾in. high. (Christie's) $1,811 £990

One of a pair of late 18th century ormolu and blue cut glass vases, Swedish or Russian, 9½in. high. (Christie's) $5,482 £3,080

An Almeric Walter pate-de-verre two-handled mortar pattern vase, designed by Henri Berge, 5in. high. (Anderson & Garland) $1,858 £1,050

A blue-flashed and acid-etched cylindrical vase of the Art Deco period. (G. A. Key) $177 £100

A cameo vase overlaid in white on a matt cranberry-red ground, by Thomas Webb & Sons, circa 1885, 23cm. high. (Christie's) $787 £440

Lalique pale brown opaque glass, 'Six Figurines et Masques' vase, 9½in. high. (Prudential Fine Art) $2,310 £1,400

A Galle cameo glass vase, the oviform body with flaring neck, 5¼in. high. (Christie's) $392 £242

VASES

A James Powell vase, milky vaseline glass, the body narrowing at the shoulder to a frilled rim, 30cm. high. (Christie's) $589 £385

An Elton globular vase with three short flared necks, incised with a pink floral spray, 13cm. high. (Osmond Tricks) $149 £80

A St. Louis crown shot vase, the everted rim with pink and white twisted ribbon border, 3¾in. high. (Christie's) $1,760 £1,005

An Elton single-handled vase of waisted baluster form, overall gold lustre crackle glaze, 22cm. high. (Osmond Tricks) $467 £250

'Gui', a Lalique opalescent glass vase, the body moulded with mistletoe, traces of blue staining, 7in. high. (Christie's) $845 £462

An Elton globular vase with tall neck and flared rim, over-all crackled gold lustre glaze, 19cm. high. (Osmond Tricks) $430 £230

A Galle cameo glass vase, the flattened spherical body with slender stem overlaid in red and etched with berried foliage, 7in. high. (Christie's) $748 £462

An Elton baluster vase, the neck with six loop handles, 19cm. high. (Osmond Tricks) $317 £170

One of a pair of opaline vases brightly painted with coloured flower bouquets, 49.5cm. high. (Phillips) $2,674 £1,400

A Gabriel Argy-Rousseau pate-de-verre vase, 12cm. high. (Christie's)
$3,427 £2,090

'Béliers', a Lalique vase with two handles moulded as rams, 19cm. high. (Christie's) $902 £550

'Languedoc', a Lalique vase, the body deeply moulded with bands of stylised leaves, 22.6cm. high. (Christie's) $2,164 £1,320

A Stourbridge cameo glass vase, the mid-blue ground overlaid in white and carved all-over with trailing wall-flowers, 12cm. high. (Phillips) $1,169 £700

A James Powell vase, milky vaseline glass, the flattened bulbous base pinched into four arms supporting a floppy quatrefoil rim, 16.5cm. high. (Christie's) $673 £440

A Gabriel Argy-Rousseau pate-de-verre vase, the body moulded with tall stemmed plants with hanging red pods, 6in. high. (Christie's) $3,207 £1,980

A miniature Daum enamelled and acid etched vase enamelled with Sweet Violets, 4.3cm. high. (Christie's) $793 £484

Mid 19th century decalcomania slender oviform vase and a ball cover, the vase 40.5cm. high. (Christie's)
$1,575 £880

A Seguso 'valva' vase designed by Flavio Poli, grey cased in amethyst coloured glass, circa 1958, 15cm. high. (Christie's)
$4,400 £2,750

A Daum double-overlay carved vase of flattened globular shape, 11.5cm. high. (Christie's) $1,172 £715

A Venini vase designed by Ludovico de Santillana, the grey glass with irregular applied white drips, circa 1962, 20.5cm. high. (Christie's) $352 £220

'Caudebec', a Lalique vase with two semi-circular handles, 14.5cm. high. (Christie's) $902 £550

An Orrefors cylindrical flared vase designed by Simon Gate, wheel engraved with naked maidens on classical columns, 17.5cm. high. (Christie's) $865 £528

A pair of Lithyalin vases, in sealing wax red glass, with trumpet necks and circular feet, 23cm. high. (Phillips) $1,085 £650

A Venini 'vaso a Canne', flaring cylindrical shape with waved rim, circa 1950, 22cm. high. (Christie's) $3,168 £1,980

A Gabriel Argy-Rousseau pate-de-verre vase, the body moulded with black spiders spinning their webs amongst leaves, 4¾in. high. (Christie's) $5,702 £3,520

A Louis XVI ormolu mounted blue glass vase and cover, 11in. high. (Christie's) $459 £275

A Daum enamelled and acid etched vase of rounded cube form, 11.5cm. high. (Christie's) $2,345 £1,430

VASES

A large Galle carved and acid etched double-overlay 'vase aux ombelles', with cameo signature Galle, 63.5cm. high. (Christie's) $5,412 £3,300

A Daum Art Deco acid etched vase, bell-shaped, 28cm. high. (Christie's) $992 £605

A Venini cylindrical vase, composed of three equal cylinders of purple, amber and smoke-grey glass, 24cm. high. (Christie's) $1,353 £825

'Martins Pecheurs', a black Lalique vase, with impressed signature R. Lalique, 23.5cm. high. (Christie's) $8,659 £5,280

A Lalique vase, the milky opaque glass moulded with intertwined brambles, 23cm. high. (Christie's) $793 £484

A Daum acid textured two-handled vase, engraved signature Daum Nancy with the Cross of Lorraine, France, 25.5cm. high. (Christie's) $1,443 £880

A Venini 'vetro a Granulari' vase, designed by Carlo Scarpa, circa 1951, 20cm. high. (Christie's) $12,320 £7,700

'Albert', a Lalique vase, the topaz glass with two handles moulded as eagles' heads, 17.3cm. high. (Christie's) $1,713 £1,045

'Bacchantes', a Lalique opalescent glass vase moulded in relief with naked female dancing figures, 24.5cm. high. (Christie's) $13,530 £8,250

VASES

A Daum vase, circular base and waisted cylindrical shape with flared rim, 35.1cm. high. (Christie's) $1,172 £715

A Venini vase designed by Fulvio Bianconi, concave lozenge shape internally decorated with a 'tartan' pattern, 27.5cm. high. (Christie's) $98,560 £61,600

A Daum enamelled and acid etched vase, enamelled Daum Nancy with Cross of Lorraine, 21.6cm. high. (Christie's) $1,262 £770

A Daum Art Deco acid etched vase, oviform with tall neck, 29cm. high. (Christie's) $1,533 £935

'Coqs et Plumes', a Lalique flaring cylindrical vase, 15.5cm. high. (Christie's) $865 £528

A Lalique vase, the satin finished glass moulded with marguerites, highlighted with amber staining, 20.5cm. high. (Christie's) $902 £550

A Daum Art Deco acid etched vase, the smoky-blue glass deeply etched with oval and circular panels, 33.5cm. high. (Christie's) $2,345 £1,430

'Oran', a large Lalique opalescent glass vase moulded in relief with flowerheads and foliage, 26cm. high. (Christie's) $7,216 £4,400

A Galle cameo baluster vase, the amber and milky white glass overlaid in purple, carved with fuschia, 16cm. high. (Christie's) $902 £550

VASES

A large Barovier & Toso patchwork vase, the white and mauve glass forming a chequer-pattern overall, 44.5cm. high. (Christie's) $3,608 £2,200

'Rampillon', an opalescent Lalique vase, 12.6cm. high. (Christie's) $613 £374

A tall Daum carved and acid etched mould-blown vase, baluster shape, engraved with the Cross of Lorraine, 44cm. high. (Christie's) $4,329 £2,640

A Gabriel Argy-Rousseau pate-de-verre vase of swollen cylindrical shape, 9.5cm. high. (Christie's) $2,525 £1,540

An Archimede Seguso vase, tomato-red cased with clear glass and with gold foil inclusions, circa 1960, 37cm. high. (Christie's) $1,760 £1,100

A Loetz oviform vase, the body with four dimples, 25.4cm. high. (Christie's) $1,353 £825

A Venini vase designed by Fulvio Bianconi, 1949, 21cm. high. (Christie's) $7,040 £4,400

A 19th century Viennese rock crystal and enamel vase in the form of a fish, the cover surmounted by an enamelled figure of Neptune, 31cm. high. (Phillips) $14,670 £9,000

An ormolu mounted cut glass vase of slightly tapering form with waved top and ram mask handles, 14in. high. (Christie's) $551 £330

VASES

A Galle carved acid etched triple overlay landscape vase, 50.5cm. high. (Christie's) $10,824 £6,600

'Danaides', a Lalique vase moulded with six nude maidens pouring water from urns, 18.3cm. high. (Christie's) $2,525 £1,540

A carved double-overlay cameo vase, bearing an incised Galle chinoiserie signature, 25cm. high. (Christie's) $3,608 £2,200

A Lalique clear glass stained vase moulded with grass-hoppers on blades of grass with blue and lime-green staining, 27.4cm. high. (Christie's) $4,690 £2,860

A Venini vase designed by Fulvio Bianconi, circa 1950, 32cm. high. (Christie's)
$11,440 £7,150

A Venini vase designed by Thomas Stearns, asymmetric bubble shape, circa 1962, 25cm. high. (Christie's) $7,392 £4,620

A Galle carved and acid etched double-overlay landscape vase, 29cm. high. (Christie's) $8,659 £5,280

'Violettes', a Lalique vase, the satin finished opalescent glass partially blue stained and moulded with eight overlapping leaves, 15.7cm. high. (Christie's) $1,443 £880

A vase attributed to Ferro Lazzarini and the design to Flavio Poli, circa 1960, 32cm. high. (Christie's)
$1,584 £990

WINE GLASSES

A 'Newcastle' baluster wine glass on a wide conical foot, 19.2cm. high. (Phillips) $701 £420

Late 18th/early 19th century green pedestal stemmed wine flute, 15.5cm. high. (Christie's) $1,986 £1,100

A baluster wine glass, the bell bowl with a tear to the lower part, circa 1720, 15.5cm. high. (Christie's) $590 £330

An engraved composite stemmed wine glass of drawn trumpet shape, circa 1750, 17.5cm. high. (Christie's) $826 £462

A baluster dram glass with short round funnel bowl on a bladed knop containing a tear, 10.7cm. high. (Phillips) $217 £130

A quadruple knopped opaque twist wine glass, the bell bowl supported on a double series opaque twist stem with four knops, circa 1770, 17cm. high. (Christie's) $551 £308

A George III wine glass, the plain stem with single series opaque twist, with saucer-top bowl, circa 1760, 6½in. high. (Christie's) $242 £141

A coloured wine glass of blue/green tint, the double ogee bowl supported on a plain stem and foot, circa 1765, 15cm. high. (Christie's) $1,378 £770

A baluster cordial glass, the trumpet bowl with solid base containing a tear, 16.5cm. high. (Phillips) $567 £340

542

WINE GLASSES

A George III wine glass with facet cut stem and tapering bowl, circa 1775, 6.1/8in. high. (Christie's) $220 £128

A baluster wine glass, the funnel bowl with solid base on conical folded foot, 16.5cm. high. (Phillips) $400 £240

Mid 18th century pale-green tinted wine glass for the European market, 16cm. high. (Christie's) $315 £176

An opaque twist champagne glass, the double ogee bowl with everted rim, circa 1765, 18cm. high. (Christie's) $1,476 £825

A George III wine glass, the plain stem with double series opaque twist, part-fluted tapering bowl, circa 1760, 5.3/8in. high. (Christie's) $264 £154

A baluster toastmaster's glass on a conical firing foot, 13.5cm. high. (Phillips) $217 £130

A Beilby opaque twist wine glass, the funnel bowl enamelled in white with floral swags pendant from the rim, circa 1770, 15.5cm. high. (Christie's) $1,870 £1,045

Late 18th/early 19th century coloured wine glass of dark blue/green tint with bucket shaped bowl, 15cm. high. (Christie's) $295 £165

A 'Lynn' opaque twist wine glass on a conical foot, circa 1770, 14.5cm. high. (Christie's) $826 £462

A large oblong gold snuff-box, the plaque early 18th century, the box 19th century, 3½in. long. (Christie's)
$24,288 £13,200

A Swiss oval gold snuff-box, the medallion painted with a warrior courting his lady, Geneva, circa 1800, maker's initials AI crowned, 2¾in. long. (Christie's)
$11,132 £6,050

A French oblong gold snuff-box, the cover with initials RH in monogram, by Veuve Blerzy, Paris, 1809-19, 3¼in. long. (Christie's)
$5,667 £3,080

A Swiss bombe oblong gold snuff box, probably by Joli & Chenevard, Geneva, circa 1830, 2¾in. long. (Christie's) $5,544 £3,080

A French gold mounted onyx and enamel scent bottle of amphora form, circa 1870, 3¼in. high. (Christie's) $2,673 £1,650

An Austrian narrow oval gold and enamel snuff box, circa 1780, 2¾in. long. (Christie's) $7,128 £4,400

An Irish octagonal gold Freedom Box, maker's initials IK incuse probably for James Kennedy, Dublin, 1798, 22ct. in case, 3.5/8in. long. (Christie's)
$16,830 £9,350

An important Louis XV rectangular gold snuff-box with diagonal bands of flowers, by Jean-Baptiste Bertin, Paris, 1749-50, 3in. long. (Christie's)
$36,432 £19,800

A fine Swiss gold and enamel card case, one side painted with a gallant taking leave of his loved one, circa 1830, 3¾in. long. (Christie's)
$5,667 £3,080

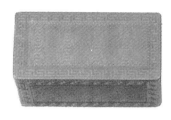

A German gold snuff box, the cover signed Gaab, Augsburg, circa 1755. (Christie's) $7,920 £4,400

A Louis XV narrow rectangular gold snuff box, by Germain Chaye, Paris, 1765, with the poincons of J. J. Prevost, in case, 3in. long. (Christie's) $5,940 £3,300

A French oblong gold snuff box, by Jean-Baptiste Fossin, with Paris gold standard mark and excise mark for 1819-38, 3.1/8in. long. (Christie's) $8,910 £4,950

A Swiss gold and enamel snuff box of lobed oval form, the hinged cover painted en grisaille with a musical trophy, circa 1820, 3½in. long. (Christie's) $8,019 £4,950

A gold etui case, the body chased with flowers and bearing the Royal cypher. (Wellington Salerooms) $8,064 £4,800

A Swiss oval gold and enamel snuff box, the hinged cover painted en grisaille with an allegorical trophy of the sciences, circa 1820, 2.7/8in. long. (Christie's) $8,019 £4,950

A Swiss oblong gold snuff box champleve enamelled in black, probably by G. L. Malacreda, Geneva, circa 1830, 2¾in. long. (Christie's) $4,752 £2,640

An Irish circular gold Freedom Box, maker's initials IK incuse probably for James Kennedy, Dublin, 1798, 22ct. in case, 2¾in. diam. (Christie's) $7,524 £4,180

A French oblong gold snuff box, the cover painted on enamel with a portrait of George Annesley, 3in. long. (Christie's) $8,910 £5,500

A gun tackle double block with 1¼ and 1.1/8in. lignum vitae sheaves, 10in. long. (Christie's) $469 £264

A 28-second sand glass, the case with turned oak ends, four pine struts and beech packing, 4½in. high. (Christie's) $6,853 £3,850

A turned and carved elm wood bowl with two hand-holds, 11¾in. diam. (cracked). (Christie's) $1,860 £1,045

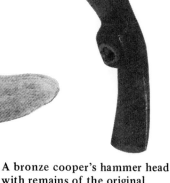

A plain pewter shoe buckle, 2½in. wide. (Christie's) $48 £27

A wooden shoe last, 9in. long. (Christie's) $234 £132

A bronze cooper's hammer head with remains of the original handle, 7½in. across. (Christie's) $587 £330

A 24-pounder gun ramrod head, stamped '24' and 'H'; 5½in. diam. (Christie's) $685 £385

A leather firebucket with stitched sides and bottom and simple rope handle, originally repaired circa 1758, the rope replaced with a piece salvaged from the wreck 'Invincible', 9½in. high. (Christie's) $391 £220

An elm heart block, stamped 'XIIII', 14in. long. (Christie's) $293 £165

An elm bull ring with rope lanyard, 8in. diam. x 4½in. bore. (Christie's) $215 £121

A green glass Madeira wine bottle with concave bottom and lipped neck, 9¼in. high. (Christie's) $783 £440

One of two cast iron grenades with wooden fuses. (Christie's) $587 £330

A shaped wooden scrubbing brush with some bristles remaining, 4.7/8in. long. (Christie's) $58 £33

Parts of a seaman's incomplete leather boot, 10½in. long. (Christie's) $106 £60

One button 23mm. diam., bearing Arabic number 14 within circle with dot. (Christie's) $145 £82

One of two wicker baskets, one with both handles. (Christie's) $117 £66

One of two cast iron grenades both with wooden fuses, one marked 'X' and one with canvas fuse cover. (Christie's) $1,566 £880

An elm clew block, without pin or sheave, stamped 'XVI', 16in. long. (Christie's) $881 £495

A wooden gun tackle single block with 1¼in. sheave, stamped 'X', 10in. long. (Christie's) $744 £418

An ornate pewter shoe buckle, 2½in. wide, (centre missing). (Christie's) $97   £55

A stave built oak bucket with rope handle, 10in. high x 14in. diam. (Christie's)
                $626 £352

A gun cartridge piercing spike with turned beech wood handle, 4in. long, (spike broken). (Christie's) $509 £286

A leather shoe of welt construction, the uppers partially cut away, 9in. long. (Christie's)
             $1,076 £605

A stoneware jug complete with handle and lipped neck, 9½in. high. (Christie's) $1,468 £825

An elm heart block, 12in. diam. (Christie's) $293 £165

A pigment barrel with original bindings, 9¾in. long. (Christie's) $352 £198

An apron of lead with four mounting holes, 5½in. sq. (Christie's) $156 £88

A single pulley block with 2¼in. lignum vitae sheave, stamped 'XVIII', 18in. long. (Christie's) $430 £242

Part of a set of parrel tackle comprising two bars of ash or elm, 12in. long, and two trucks, 2¾in. long, and another similar. (Christie's) $391 £220

A sailor's square wooden dinner plate, with fiddle, 11¾ x 11¾in. (Christie's) $1,664 £935

A spirit barrel of approx. 2 gals. capacity, built of fourteen oak staves originally bound with four iron hoops, 17½in. high. (Christie's) $430 £242

A stave built oak save-all or bucket, with wicker binding and pegged oak bottom, and remains of original rope handle, 10¼in. high x 14½in. diam. (Christie's) $352 £198

A 14-second sand glass, the case with turned oak ends, four pine struts and beech packing, 5½in. high. (Christie's) $5,482 £3,080

An elm clew block with 2in. lignum vitae sheave, stamped 'XVI', 16½in. long. (Christie's) $587 £330

A leather firebucket with stitched sides and bottom, complete with handle, 10in. high, (restored). (Christie's) $1,272 £715

A 32-pounder gun ramrod head stamped '32' and 'I', 6in. diam. (Christie's) $509 £286

Late 19th century four-case roironuri inro, 8.5cm. high, with an attached ojime with fish, squid and seaweed in Hiramakie. (Christie's) $3,520 £2,200

A 19th century three-case Kinji inro, signed Tatsuke Takamasu. (Christie's) $4,114 £2,420

A 19th century four-case inro, signed Nikkosai, 8.5cm. long. (Christie's) $3,366 £1,980

Late 19th century lozenge-shaped inro, signed on a mother-of-pearl tablet Yasuyuki, 9cm. long. (Christie's) $5,610 £3,300

A 19th century five-case roironuri inro, 10cm. high, with an attached agate ojime. (Christie's) $5,632 £3,520

Early 19th century five-case fundame inro, signed Kaji-kawa saku with red tsuba seal, 9.2cm. high, and an ivory ojime of a monkey. (Christie's) $1,230 £770

A 19th century three-case inro, signed Tojo saku, with an attached coral ojime, 7cm. long. (Christie's) $13,090 £7,700

Early 19th century three-case circular inro, signed Kanshosai, with a silvered-metal ojime, 8.3cm. diam. (Christie's) $3,179 £1,870

A 19th century five-case inro, signed Jokasai, with an attached soft metal ojime, 9.4cm. long. (Christie's) $7,106 £4,180

A 19th century sleeve inro
with attached soft-metal
ojime and a wood and ivory
netsuke, the inro 10.2cm.
long, the netsuke 4.2cm. high.
(Christie's) $6,545 £3,850

An 18th century four-case
inro, signed Gyokumin, with
an attached agate ojime and
a kagamibuta with ivory bowl
and shibuichi disc, inro 7.7cm.
high, netsuke 4.5cm. diam.
(Christie's) $1,230 £770

A 19th century four-case
inro, signed Shokasai, with
an attached gold stone ojime,
8.7cm. long. (Christie's)
            $2,431 £1,430

Late 18th/early 19th
century four-case nashiji
inro, unsigned. (Christie's)
      $4,114 £2,420

A 19th century four-case
inro, signed Kajikawa saku,
8.3cm. long. (Christie's)
            $1,683 £990

A 19th century four-case
inro decorated in gold takamakie and inlaid with coral,
amber, metal and other
materials, 7.2cm. long.
(Christie's) $2,431 £1,430

A 19th century four-case
inro, signed Shokasai,
8.5cm. high. (Christie's)
        $1,936 £1,210

A 19th century three-case
inro, unsigned, with an
attached coral ojime, 7cm.
long. (Christie's)
            $2,805 £1,650

Early 19th century three-case
silver lined iron inro, signed
Toshinaga, the iron ojime with
a silver frog, 5.7cm. long.
(Christie's) $2,431 £1,430

An 18th century brass way-wiser dial, signed Made by Tho. Wright Infrumt maker to ye Prince of Wales, 6¼in. diam. (Christie's)
$865 £528

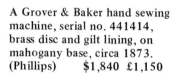

A Grover & Baker hand sewing machine, serial no. 441414, brass disc and gilt lining, on mahogany base, circa 1873. (Phillips) $1,840 £1,150

A small cricular brass sextant, signed Thos. Harris & Son, London. (Greenslade & Co.)
$267 £150

A late 19th century oxodized brass surveying aneroid barometer, by Pidduck & Sons, Hanley, 6in. diam. (Christie's)
$211 £132

A 19th century brass compound binocular microscope signed Ross, London, No. 4119, in mahogany case, 20¾in. high. (Christie's) $968 £605

A brass stamp box by W. Avery & Son, 2½in. high. (Christie's) $396 £242

A brass cased dip-circle by F. E. Becker & Co., on adjustable stand, 10¾in. high. (Christie's) $528 £330

A polished teak and brass ship's wheel of eight spokes, inscribed William Cory & Son Ltd., overall diam. 54in. (Christie's) $776 £462

A Country painted globe, New England, circa 1810, 15in. diam., 37in. high. (Robt. W. Skinner Inc.)
$5,500 £3,273

A late 18th century demonstration apparatus, signed Fraser, Instrument Maker to his Majesty, London, 12¼in. wide. (Christie's) $528 £330

A Melloni's thermopile by Griffin & Tatlock Ltd., with telescopic stand and the associated tangent galvanometer, 9in. high. (Christie's) $158 £99

A wood and brass magic lantern with brass bound lens and chimney with a slide holder and a small quantity of slides in wood box. (Christie's) $277 £165

An 18th century silver and silver gilt equinoctial automatic dial, unsigned, but of the Johan Willebrand type. (Christie's) $3,520 £2,200

An Italian brass ship's pedestal telegraph with enamelled dial, lever and pointer, two lamps and chain drive, 42in. high. (Christie's) $1,108 £660

An early 19th century universal equinoctial ring dial, unsigned, 6in. diam. (Christie's) $1,496 £935

A Betts's portable terrestrial globe arranged so as to fold like an umbrella, 15in. diam. (Christie's) $563 £352

A Kriegsmarine micrometer sextant, signed C. Plath, Hamburg, No. 21536, with certificate dated 21.XI.42, 6½in. index arm radius, in wooden box, 12½in. wide. (Christie's) $295 £176

A mid 19th century brass propeller pitchometer signed Edwin Craven, Maker, Hull, 16.3/8in. long, with brass carrying handle. (Christie's) $462 £275

A two-day marine chronometer in two-tier glazed mahogany box, the 4½in. silvered dial with Arabic numerals, signed Thomas Mercer, No. 28271, in travelling box. (Christie's) $776 £462

A set of early Victorian mahogany jockey scales with ivory plaque De Grave & Co., Makers, London, 39in. wide. (Christie's) $4,329 £2,640

A 19th century single cupping set by J. Laundy, with lacquered brass syringe and shaped glass cup, the case 5in. wide. (Christie's) $422 £264

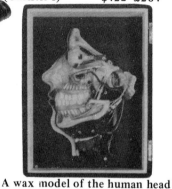

A 17th century brass sector, unsigned, 18in. long. (Christie's) $1,936 £1,210

A 19th century lacquered brass 2in. refracting telescope, signed Watson & Son, London, in mahogany case, 32¼in. long. (Christie's) $865 £528

A wax model of the human head showing the nerves, arteries, veins and muscles, in an ebonised and glazed case, 9¾in. high, by Lehrmittelwerke, Berlin. (Christie's) $302 £198

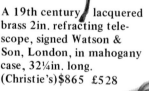

A 19th century lacquered brass drum pattern French cross, trade label for J. & W. E. Archbutt, in mahogany case, 6¾in. wide. (Christie's) $211 £132

A pair of early Victorian terrestrial and celestial globes, by Malby & Son, London, dated 1850. (Lacy Scott) $2,227 £1,350

A 19th century bone saw and three dental elevators. (Christie's) $153 £93

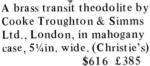

A brass transit theodolite by Cooke Troughton & Simms Ltd., London, in mahogany case, 5¼in. wide. (Christie's) $616 £385

A collapsible A. H. Baird patent stereoscope with a quantity of stereocards in wood box. (Christie's) $396 £242

A mid 18th century brass theodolite, by Benjamin Cole, the telescope 15¾in. long. (Christie's) $2,464 £1,540

A 17th century fruitwood nocturnal, unsigned, main plate 4.1/8in. diam., index arm length 7.3/8in. (Christie's) $2,956 £1,760

The 'Improved Phantasmagoria Lantern, by Carpenter & Westley, with patent argand solar lamp with a quantity of lantern slides. (Christie's) $369 £220

An early 19th century lacquered brass azimuth sighting instrument, signed Narrien, London, 9½in. wide. (Christie's) $2,164 £1,320

A 19th century gilt Sheffield two-draw monocular, signed Watkins & Hill, 2.1/8in. diam. (Christie's) $246 £154

A 19th century mahogany inclined plane, with arc engraved 0°-40°, 27¾in. wide. (Christie's) $126 £77

A sextant by Lilley & Son, London, in wooden case. (Greenslade & Co.) $551 £310

One of a pair of William IV terrestrial and celestial globes by W. Harris, dated 1836, 40in. high, 22in. diam. (Christie's) $26,730 £16,500

A late 18th century 'Ladder Scale', the 1oz. and 2oz. beams stamped De Grave & Co. London, 16.1/8in. wide. (Christie's) $811 £495

A French terrestrial globe signed J. Forest, on ebonised base, 23in. high. (Christie's) $734 £440

Early 19th century lacquered brass universal equinoctial ring dial, signed Dollond, London, in original fishskin covered case, 9½in. diam. (Christie's) $5,772 £3,520

A mid 19th century lac-quered brass theodolite by Troughton & Simms, 11½in. wide. (Christie's)
$1,262 £770

A late 19th century desk calendar compendium, 3¼in. diam. (Christie's)
$270 £165

A 19th century brass double-rack action twin cylinder vacuum pump, unsigned, 14in. high. (Christie's)
$992 £605

A brass vacuum pump of small size, unsigned, with tall jar and a lacquered brass vacuum chamber with cap and glass insulated ball and hook, 6in. high. (Christie's) $234 £143

A Wimshurst pattern plate machine by Philip Harris Ltd., Birmingham, 21.5/8in. wide, and a pair of brass and ebonite discharge forks. (Christie's) $811 £495

Late 19th century sectional model of the eye, the plaster body decorated in colours and with glass lenses, 6¾in. high. (Christie's) $541 £330

A lacquered brass 3in. refracting telescope signed Watson & Son, London, 45¼in. long. (Christie's) $757 £462

A mid Victorian terrestrial globe by Thos. Malby & Son, 19in. high. (Christie's) $2,345 £1,430

A 17th century silver perpetual calendar, unsigned, with suspension loop, 1in. diam. (Christie's) $902 £550

A lacquered and oxidised brass compound monocular microscope, by W. Watson & Sons Ltd., London, and other items in a mahogany case, 13in. high. (Christie's) $505 £308

One of a pair of mid 18th century terrestrial and celestial table globes with Latin inscription, 17in. wide, 19in. high. (Christie's) $13,365 £8,250

A Pascal's apparatus, unsigned, 14in. wide, with three different shaped glass vessels mounted in brass collars to fit the limb. (Christie's) $811 £495

Late 18th century lacquered brass compound monocular microscope, unsigned, 8¾in. long. (Christie's) $3,247 £1,980

A 19th century cupping set by Weiss, London, with two glass cups in plush lined fitted case, 5½in. long. (Christie's) $432 £264

A two-day marine chronometer, the 4in. dial signed Kelvin Bottomley & Baird Ltd., Glasgow, and numbered 9550, in a brass bound mahogany box. (Phillips) $1,567 £950

A late 19th century oxidised and lacquered brass simple theodolite, signed on the plate R. W. Street & Co., in mahogany case, 15¾in. wide. (Christie's) $577 £352

A late 18th century pocket dental scaling kit, with mirror in a shagreen case, 2¼in. wide. (Christie's) $286 £176

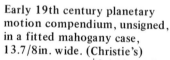

A demonstration refracto- meter, unsigned, with a set of twelve lenses. (Christie's) $360 £220

Early 19th century planetary motion compendium, unsigned, in a fitted mahogany case, 13.7/8in. wide. (Christie's) $2,164 £1,320

A George II glass celestial globe by Thomas Heath, 15in. diam., engraved by John Cowley. (Christie's) $66,748 £40,700

A sheet brass letter balance signed Parnell, London and inscribed Hall's Patent, 5¼in. wide. (Christie's) $234 £143

A black enamelled and lac- quered brass Grand Theo- dolite by T. Cooke & Sons, 16in. high. (Christie's) $2,345 £1,430

A 19th century Norrenberg's polariscope, unsigned, with mirrors and calibrated scales. (Christie's) $631 £385

A 19th century German diptych dial signed J. Kleininger on the compass rose, 3.1/8in. long. (Christie's) $342 £209

A deflection magnetometer on mahogany base with adjustable feet, 13in. high. (Christie's) $938 £572

A lacquered brass aneroid barometer signed J. Gold-schmid, Zurich, 3in. diam. (Christie's)
     $541 £330

A 'Geryk' vacuum pump, 23in. high, a Callendar's apparatus by Griffin & George Ltd. on a stand and a compression/expansion demonstration apparatus. (Christie's) $216 £132

An early 19th century lacquered brass and mahogany vacuum pump, 18¾in. long, with an extensive collection of accessories. (Christie's)
     $8,298 £5,060

A late Victorian terrestrial table globe with turned walnut shaft, 17½in. high. (Christie's) $396 £242

A 19th century lacquered brass compound monocular microscope, the base signed Ross, London, No. 3354, with a few accessories, 13¾in. high. (Christie's) $902 £550

A 19th century brass theodolite, signed by Troughton & Simms, 9½in. high. (Christie's) $811 £495

A 19th century amputation saw by Weiss, with anti-clog teeth and ebony handle, 15½in. long. (Christie's)
     $144 £88

An iron trivet, posnet and toaster. (Christie's)
$121 £68

A 17th century Spanish iron strongbox with hinged top, the sides with carrying handles, 20½in. wide. (Christie's)
$1,460 £825

Late 19th/early 20th century painted and gilded tin and wrought-iron wall mounted trade sign, American or English, 42½in. high, 39in. wide. (Christie's)
$4,180 £2,358

A pair of ebonised torcheres with iron nozzles and circular drip-pans, 58½in. high. (Christie's) $3,674 £2,200

A Regency black-painted and cast iron basket grate in the manner of George Bullock, 31in. wide. (Christie's)
$4,719 £2,860

A pair of wrought-iron torcheres with circular foliate platforms, 55in. high. (Christie's)
$2,388 £1,430

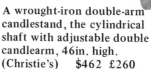

A pair of 17th century iron stirrups finely inlaid in silver hirazogan with a chrysanthemum and water design (kikusui), each signed Kashu ju Morisada saku. (Christie's)
$1,589 £935

A wrought-iron double-arm candlestand, the cylindrical shaft with adjustable double candlearm, 46in. high. (Christie's) $462 £260

A pair of mid 19th century American painted cast iron dressing glasses, 21in. high. (Christie's) $770 £465

An 18th century wrought iron bound salt bucket with swing handle, 7¼in. diam. (Christie's) $203 £121

A rare Eley percussion cap measure, 4¾in., cast 'W & C Eley London', with solid steel nipples graded in sizes 4-24 with military cap at top. (Wallis & Wallis) $297 £180

A polished steel grate of George III style, the pierced frieze filled with key-pattern, 32½in. wide, 35in. high. (Christie's) $2,468 £1,320

One of six pairs of wrought and cast iron andirons. (Christie's) $550 £310

An impressive iron 17th century 'Armada' chest, 37 x 19 x 20in. (Wallis & Wallis) $3,052 £1,850

19th century white painted iron stickstand modelled as a boy holding a serpent, 2ft.10in. high. (Lots Road Chelsea Auction Galleries) $400 £250

A white metal and polished steel basket grate of serpentine form, 21in. wide, 21in. high. (Christie's) $3,702 £1,980

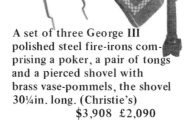

A set of three George III polished steel fire-irons comprising a poker, a pair of tongs and a pierced shovel with brass vase-pommels, the shovel 30¼in. long. (Christie's) $3,908 £2,090

A George III polished steel basket grate, 33in. wide. (Christie's) $3,247 £1,980

A 19th century German miniature ivory tankard with silvered metal mounts, 10.5cm. high. (Christie's) $3,674 £2,200

Late 18th century ivory Kitsune mask, 3.5cm. high. (Christie's) $345 £187

A 19th century carved ivory bust of a bishop in the Gothic style, on silver metal base with lion supports at each corner, 16cm. high. (Phillips) $896 £550

Late 19th century ivory carving of a farmer holding a birdcage, 33cm. high. (Christie's) $2,640 £1,650

An 18th century ivory work-box of octagonal form, 22.5cm. wide. (Phillips) $684 £420

Late 19th century ivory carving of a hunter, signed Kozan saku, 22cm. high. (Christie's) $792 £495

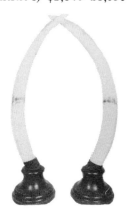

A pair of curved ivory elephant tusks on ebonised bases, 6ft. high, overall. (Prudential Fine Art) $2,788 £1,700

Late 19th century boxwood, rootwood and ivory group of doves attending their young, signed Mitsuhiro, 49cm. high. (Christie's) $18,700 £11,000

An ivory carving of a sennin, eyes inset in dark horn, stylised seal mark, 20.5cm. high. (Christie's) $935 £550

A 19th century ivory okimono of a farmer with a fox and a hare, dressed as humans, 6cm. high. (Christie's) $748 £440

A 19th century ivory mask of a Buaku, signed Ryuraku, 3.8cm. high, (age cracks). (Christie's) $566 £306

A 19th century German carved ivory lidded tankard with caryatid handle, 13¾in. high. (Capes Dunn) $8,055 £4,500

Late 19th century ivory carving of a scholar, signed Akira, 26cm. high. (Christie's) $704 £440

A pair of Chinese 19th century ivory handscreens with ivory handles hung with ornaments and silk tassels, 13½in. long, contained in a fitted brocade case. (Christie's) $1,870 £1,068

Late 19th century ivory carving of a kannon, signed Masayuki, 33cm. high, wood stand. (Christie's)
$4,114 £2,420

A 19th century Dieppe ivory tazza, by E. Blard, 17.5cm. high. (Christie's) $2,204 £1,320

A 19th century Japanese ivory group on wood stand, signed, 8¾in. high. (Capes Dunn) $841 £470

A 19th century Japanese ivory tusk vase, 12in. high, with a lobed wooden base and wood stand, 23in. high overall. (Capes Dunn)
$501 £280

Late 19th century Uncle Sam animated ivory cane, when button on hat is pressed his jaw drops, America, 35in. long. (Robt. W. Skinner Inc.) $1,400 £833

A Napoleonic prisoner-of-war period bone-ivory games box, raised on four cabriole legs, 8½in. wide. (Christie's) $1,386 £825

Late 19th century ivory carving of a fisherman, signed Shizuhisa, 29cm. high. (Christie's) $968 £605

A carved ivory figure of a young woman, signed Gogyoku saku, Meiji period, 32.2cm. high. (Christie's) $1,589 £935

Late 19th century stained ivory group of four children playing beside a drum, 21cm. high. (Christie's) $2,618 £1,540

Mid 14th century Flemish or German carved ivory relief, 6½ x 3.5/8in. (Christie's) $14,300 £8,171

Late 19th century carved ivory okimono group of a fisherman and a boy assistant, signed Ogawa Munekata, 13cm. high. (Christie's) $1,496 £880

Pair of 19th century carved ivory figures of a swain and his lass, 14cm. high. (Phillips) $1,793 £1,100

A 19th century Dieppe ivory tazza, its stem carved with a classical female figure, 18cm. high. (Christie's) $2,020 £1,210

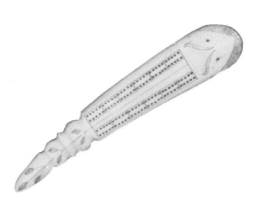

A 19th century carved ivory figure of a cherub playing a flute, 33cm. overall. (Phillips) $1,630 £1,000

A 19th century walrus tusk modelled in the form of a cribbage board, 11¼in. long. (Christie's) $517 £308

Late 19th century carving of a kannon standing beside a seated attendant holding a koro, signed Ryushin, 32cm. high. (Christie's) $2,992   £1,760

A 19th century German ivory flagon carved in relief with scenes of Scipio, 53cm. high. (Phillips) $14,670 £9,000

Late 19th century ivory and wood group of a scholar with children, 16cm. high. (Christie's) $2,992 £1,760

Late 19th century carved sectional ivory okimono of a man and a small boy, signed Munehisa, 15.5cm. high. (Christie's) $1,589 £935

Late 19th century carved sectional ivory okimono of a street vendor, signed Munehisa, 15.8cm. high. (Christie's) $654 £385

Late 19th century ivory vase and cover inlaid in shibayama style, signed Gyokiukendo san, 20cm. high. (Christie's) $5,610 £3,300

Late 19th century ivory carving of an itinerant basket seller, signed Hododa, 35.3cm. high. (Christie's) $4,114 £2,420

A 20th century sterling silver and opal pin, 1¾in. diam. (Robt. W. Skinner Inc.) $325 £175

Four 19th century onyx cameos, probably Italian, one signed L. Rosi, oval 1-1½in. high. (Christie's) $1,210 £691

A Victorian mourning brooch centred by a woven hair panel within a half pearl surround, and with a foliate scroll gold border. (Lawrence Fine Art) $473 £253

An oval carved shell cameo with a profile of a classical maiden in 9ct. gold openwork brooch mount. (Prudential Fine Art) $189 £115

A Victorian gold mounted shell cameo necklace, the thirteen carved shell cameos depicting Lorenzo de Medici, probably Italian, circa 1850. (Christie's) $2,750 £1,571

An antique pink topaz and cannetille gold necklace and earrings, in a fitted case from Hunt & Roskell, late Storr & Mortimer. (Lawrence Fine Art) $6,788 £3,630

An Arts & Crafts oval white metal brooch designed by Arthur Gaskin, 4.5cm. long. (Christie's) $1,082 £660

An 18ct. gold, diamond and baroque pearl floral spray brooch. (Hobbs & Chambers) $2,640 £1,650

A diamond pendant brooch with detachable brooch pin and pendant ring. (Lawrence Fine Art) $7,405 £3,960

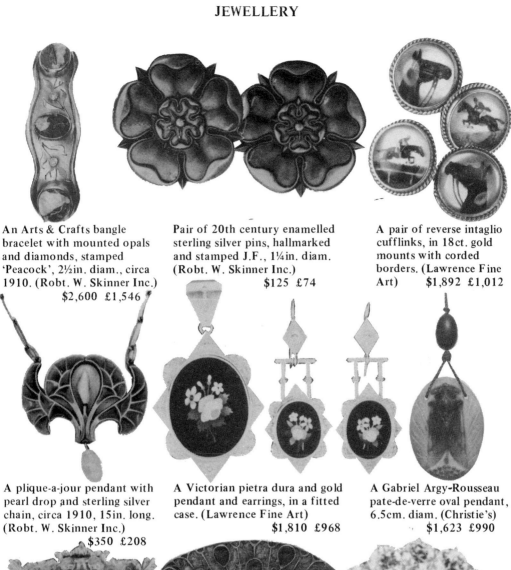

An Arts & Crafts bangle bracelet with mounted opals and diamonds, stamped 'Peacock', 2½in. diam., circa 1910. (Robt. W. Skinner Inc.) $2,600 £1,546

Pair of 20th century enamelled sterling silver pins, hallmarked and stamped J.F., 1¼in. diam. (Robt. W. Skinner Inc.) $125 £74

A pair of reverse intaglio cufflinks, in 18ct. gold mounts with corded borders. (Lawrence Fine Art) $1,892 £1,012

A plique-a-jour pendant with pearl drop and sterling silver chain, circa 1910, 15in. long. (Robt. W. Skinner Inc.) $350 £208

A Victorian pietra dura and gold pendant and earrings, in a fitted case. (Lawrence Fine Art) $1,810 £968

A Gabriel Argy-Rousseau pate-de-verre oval pendant, 6.5cm. diam. (Christie's) $1,623 £990

A Swiss enamel brooch, the rectangular panel painted in colours with Madonna and Child with the infant St. John after Raphael. (Lawrence Fine Art) $740 £396

A Guild of Handicrafts Ltd. silver and enamel brooch designed by C. R. Ashbee, London hallmarks for 1907, 7.8cm. long. (Christie's) $16,236 £9,900

A diamond roundel brooch with fourteen brilliant cut diamonds in an open circle. (Lawrence Fine Art) $1,604 £858

A plique-a-jour pin with fresh-water pearls, probably French, circa 1910, marked 800, 1½in. long. (Robt. W. Skinner Inc.) $200 £119

9ct. gold and plique-a-jour Art Nouveau wing brooch in Egyptian style, 4¼in. wide, maker's mark HL conjoined. (Capes Dunn) $547 £306

A Russian diamond, sapphire, ruby and plique-a-jour enamel moth brooch, St. Petersburg maker's mark JV. (Lawrence Fine Art) $16,661 £8,910

An early George III moss agate and garnet ring on a gold shank with memorial inscription and dated 1765. (Lawrence Fine Art) $514 £275

A 19th century sapphire and diamond frog brooch, set in silver and gold. (Dreweatt Neate) $6,358 £3,400

An emerald and diamond cluster ring, in a basket mount on a plain gold shank. (Lawrence Fine Art) $1,357 £726

An oval diamond set gold mounted shell cameo brooch, 1¾in. high. (Christie's) $2,860 £1,634

Zuni silver and turquoise bracelet, openwork silver cuff, 3¼in. diam. (Robt. W. Skinner Inc.) $650 £365

A 19th century oval gold mounted onyx cameo pendant brooch, the frame set with pearls and with black enamel ropework, 2½in. high. (Christie's) $1,650 £942

An old cut diamond and pearl three stone ring, centre stone approx. 1.65ct. (Dreweatt Neate) $3,459 £1,850

A Murrle Bennett gold wirework oval brooch, with opal matrix and four seed pearls, stamped MB monogram and 15ct. on the pin, circa 1900. (Christie's) $336 £220

A diamond bracelet composed of 17 graduated stones in a half-hoop gold setting. (Morphets) $2,537 £1,450

A diamond solitaire ring, the stone weighing 4.23ct, claw set on an 18ct gold shank. (Lawrence Fine Art)
$7,816 £4,180

An opal and diamond bangle with nine oval cabochon opals divided by pairs of old cut diamonds on a hinged 15ct. gold band. (Lawrence Fine Art)
$1,604 £858

A diamond set bound scroll double dress clip set in white gold, combining to form a brooch with white metal conversion. (Dreweatt Neate)
$2,150 £1,150

A 15ct. gold and enamelled ceremonial coat-of-arms pendant, made by Spencer of London. (Dreweatt Neate)
$299 £160

Victorian gold, diamond and turquoise ring. (Hobbs & Chambers) $464 £290

A 19th century large sapphire cluster ring set in silver and gold with leaf pierced scrolling shoulders. (Dreweatt Neate) $1,271 £680

A 19th century oval gold mounted shell cameo brooch, probably Italian, 2½in. high. (Christie's) $1,650 £942

Zuni silver and turquoise bracelet, large single stone carved in the form of a leaf, 3in. diam. (Robt. W. Skinner Inc.) $375 £210

A gold mounted pink coral carved brooch, the openwork scrolling foliage frame set with four small diamonds, 2¼in. high. (Christie's) $1,760 £1,005

An 18ct. gold bracelet set with eight sapphires alternating with seven diamonds. (Worsfolds)
$504 £300

A double trapezoid shaped amethyst brooch bordered by small rose cut diamonds, calibre jet and seed pearls. (Dreweatt Neate) $897 £480

A diamond and half pearl ring, all claw set on a gold shank. (Lawrence Fine Art) $678 £363

One of a pair of oak and leaded glass wall lanterns, circa 1910, 23in. long. (Robt. W. Skinner Inc.) $1,100 £594

A hammered copper and mica table lamp, circa 1910, 14¾in. high. (Robt. W. Skinner Inc.) $1,400 £833

A conch shell and hammered copper table lamp, designed by E. E. Burton, California, circa 1910, 24in. high. (Robt. W. Skinner Inc.)
$3,400 £2,023

A Bradley & Hubbard table lamp with gold iridescent shade, Mass., circa 1910, 15in. high. (Robt. W. Skinner Inc.) $700 £416

Pair of 19th century gilt metal cherub lamps with hexagonal shades, 14in. high. (Lots Road Chelsea Auction Galleries). $384 £240

A Tiffany Studio lamp with green-blue Favrile glass moulded as a scarab, N.Y., circa 1902, 8½in. high. (Robt. W. Skinner Inc.)
$3,000 £1,875

A Le Verre Francais acid etched table lamp with three-pronged wrought-iron mount, 42.2cm. high. (Christie's)
$2,886 £1,760

A Handel adjustable desk lamp, with green glass shade, circa 1920, 12¾in. high. (Robt. W. Skinner Inc.)
$750 £446

A Satsuma pottery gilt bronze mounted oil lamp base, 12in. high. (Reeds Rains) $668 £400

An Art Deco frosted glass lamp painted in colours with banding and linear decoration, 31cm. high. (Phillips) $563 £320

A hammered copper table lamp with mica shade, Old Mission Kopperkraft, San Francisco, circa 1910, 13¾in. high, 15in. diam. (Robt. W. Skinner Inc.) $2,700 £1,687

A Degue Art Deco glass lamp, 35cm. high. (Phillips) $352 £200

A Daum enamelled and acid etched landscape table lamp with wrought-iron mounts, 48.5cm. high. (Christie's) $5,231 £3,190

A pair of Regency bronzed and ormolu lamps, fitted for electricity, 30¾in. high, 13in. diam. (Christie's) $28,512 £17,600

A Tiffany Studios enamelled copper electric lamp base, circa 1900, 15in. high. (Robt. W. Skinner Inc.) $3,700 £2,202

Muller Freres cameo glass illuminated column table lamp and mushroom shaped shade, 23in. high. (Prudential Fine Art) $825 £500

A copper and leaded glass piano lamp, cone-shaped slag glass shade, incised mark 'KK', 13¾in. high. (Robt. W. Skinner Inc.) $400 £216

A copper and amber glass lantern, style no. 324, by Gustav Stickley, circa 1906, 15in. high, globe 5¼in. diam. (Robt. W. Skinner Inc.) $7,500 £4,054

A 19th century French
marble bust of Psyche,
by Albert Carrier-Belleuse,
60cm. high. (Christie's)
$4,592 £2,750

An early 20th century
Italian white marble statue
of a female nude, by Alfredo
Pina, 81cm. high. (Christie's)
$15,427 £9,350

A 19th century marble bust
of 'Jeunefille', probably
Flora, by Albert Carrier-
Belleuse, 62cm. high.
(Christie's) $6,429 £3,850

A marble bust of Prince
Albert, in Classical drapes,
signed on the reverse W.
Theed, 1857, 35cm. high
overall. (Phillips)
$2,526 £1,550

A 19th century Italian marble
figure of a Bacchante, in the
style of Bartolini, 85cm. long.
(Christie's) $8,266 £4,950

A 19th century marble
head of Aphrodite, after
the Antique, 49cm. high.
(Christie's) $3,448 £2,090

A 19th century Italian neo-
classical bust of a classical
lady, in the manner of
Canova, 47cm. high.
(Christie's) $5,445 £3,300

A pair of early 19th century
Venetian coloured marble busts
of a Blackamoor boy and girl,
55cm. high. (Christie's)
$8,266 £4,950

A 19th century marble
figure of the Apollino, on
oval grey marble base,
62cm. high. (Phillips)
$847 £520

A 19th century Italian marble figure of Apollo Belvedere, 127cm. high. (Christie's)
$10,890 £6,600

A marble stele, possibly Roman period from Sicily, 21cm. high. (Phillips)
$492 £300

A 19th century marble figure of a girl, by Joseph Gott, 31cm. high. (Christie's) $1,452 £880

A 19th century marble group of Apollo and Daphne, incised P. Barranti, Firenze, 117cm. high. (Phillips)
$1,141 £700

A 19th century American marble group of two children asleep on a mattress, by Wm. Rinehart, 37 x 90 x 48cm. (Christie's) $68,970 £41,800

A 19th century English marble figure of Venus and Cupid, by Joseph Gott, 124cm. high, on a marble pedestal 110cm. high. (Christie's)
$30,855 £18,700

A 19th century English marble bust of a gentleman wearing a toga, by Theed, 71cm. high. (Christie's)
$918 £550

One of a pair of 19th century mottled pink marble urns, 30in. high. (Christie's)
$6,429 £3,850

A 19th century Italian marble neo-classical bust of a vestal, after Canova, 50cm. high. (Christie's)
$7,260 £4,400

An early 19th century Irish marble bust of Angelica Catalani, by Thos. Kirk, 1824, 79cm. high. (Christie's) $8,167 £4,950

An Italian sienna marble miniature sarcophagus, the lid with scrolling ends, 8in. wide. (Christie's) $1,996 £1,210

White marble bust of a young woman in 19th century dress and Neapolitan bonnet, on socle, 31in. high. (Lots Road Chelsea Auction Galleries) $1,670 £1,000

A 19th century French marble figure of a nymph, by Jean Baptiste Carpeaux, 95cm. high. (Christie's) $7,482 £4,180

A pair of 19th century polychrome marble busts of a blackamoor and his wife, 62cm. and 60cm. high. (Christie's) $8,860 £4,950

A 19th century English marble figure of Ino teaching Bacchus to dance, by Joseph Gott, 145cm. high, on a veined marble pedestal 110cm. high. (Christie's) $344,850 £209,000

A mid 19th century Swedish marble statue of a nymph stepping forward to bathe, by J. Lundberg, after J. N. Bisstrom, 153cm. high. (Christie's) $13,777 £8,250

A Roman marble relief of Eros, 20 x 30cm., 2nd-3rd century A.D. (Phillips) $728 £400

A 19th century English marble figure of Susannah, by Joseph Gott, 120cm. high, supported on an original pedestal 110cm. high. (Christie's) $87,120 £52,800

A 19th century English
marble bust of General George
Guy Carlton L'Estrange, by
Wm. Theed, 1853, 70cm. high.
(Christie's) $1,815 £1,100

A 19th century Italian marble
figure of a child pulling a thorn
from a spaniel's foot, by G. M.
Benzoni, 1846, 80cm. high,
standing on marble column,
110cm. high. (Christie's)
$15,752 £8,800

A 19th century English
marble bust of King Arthur,
by Charles Francis Fuller,
68cm. high. (Christie's)
$2,559   £1,430

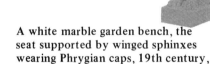

A 19th century Italian
marble figure of Venus
De'Medici, 102cm. high.
(Christie's) $3,306 £1,980

A white marble garden bench, the
seat supported by winged sphinxes
wearing Phrygian caps, 19th century,
70in. wide. (Christie's)
$14,256 £8,800

A 19th century white marble
figure of a barefoot peasant
girl on a grey marble plinth,
22in. high. (Lots Road Chelsea
Auction Galleries) $340 £210

A neo-classical marble bust
of Napoleon, 59cm. high.
(Phillips) $1,956 £1,200

A pair of 19th century Florentine marble
figures of Love Found and Love Abandoned, by Pasquale Romanelli, 1876 and
1877, 160cm. and 155cm. high, the
plinths 60cm high. (Christie's)
$78,760 £44,000

A 20th century English
marble bust of Pharaoh's
Daughter, by John Adams-
Acton, 1904, 69cm. high.
(Christie's) $7,876 £4,400

A burr-yew wood miniature chest inlaid with lines, on bracket feet, 11in. wide. (Christie's) $4,633 £2,860

A 19th century miniature wallpapered bandbox, American, 4½in. high. (Robt. W. Skinner Inc.) $325 £196

A 19th century miniature, Empire mahogany veneer chest-of-drawers, New England, 15in. wide. (Robt. W. Skinner Inc.) $600 £375

A 19th century painted miniature ladder-back arm-chair, American. (Robt. W. Skinner Inc.) $225 £136

A William and Mary walnut oyster veneer and cross-banded chest of small size. (Phillips) $3,280 £2,000

A 19th century miniature tilt-top tea table, 13in. high. (Robt. W. Skinner Inc.) $275 £166

A Victorian mahogany and marquetry banded miniature chest of five drawers, 14in. wide. (J. M. Welch & Son) $330 £200

A mid Georgian walnut minia-ture chest, the base with one long drawer on bracket feet, 13½in. wide. (Christie's) $2,141 £1,210

A 19th century miniature, Empire mahogany and pain-ted chest-of-drawers, American, 19½in. wide. (Robt. W. Skinner Inc.) $800 £484

A Regency giltwood convex mirror with eagle cresting and moulded berried apron, 40 x 23¾in. (Christie's)
$4,356 £2,640

Late 17th century beadwork mirror with four ladies surrounded by exotic animals, flowers and insects, 30 x 26in., English. (Christie's)
$3,272 £1,870

A table top mirror on shoe foot base, by Gustav Stickley, circa 1910, 21¼in. high. (Robt. W. Skinner Inc.)
$800 £432

Shop-O'-The Crafters mahogany wall mirror, Ohio, 1910, 27½in. high, 30½in. wide. (Robt. W. Skinner Inc.)
$750 £468

A mirror clock with polychrome stencilled eglomise tablet framing the painted iron dial, circa 1825, 31in. long. (Robt. W. Skinner Inc.)
$1,500 £892

A William and Mary looking glass, walnut burl veneer, 1690-1700, 28½in. high. (Robt. W. Skinner Inc.)
$2,000 £1,190

Early 19th century kingwood and tulipwood cheval mirror with rectangular plate, 66 x 25½in. (Christie's)
$5,878 £3,520

A painted and carved Federal courting mirror, painted in old red and black with yellow ochre, circa 1820, 12in. high. (Robt. W. Skinner Inc.)
$4,750 £2,827

A scarlet japanned toilet mirror, the serpentine base with five drawers, 16in. wide. (Christie's)
$627 £385

A George III giltwood pier glass by Thos. Chippendale Snr. or Jnr., 127½ x 64¼in. (Christie's)
$40,986 £25,300

A Regency giltwood over-mantel with verre eglomise panel painted with a rustic scene, 55in. wide.
(Christie's) $2,541 £1,540

A George III giltwood mirror with shaped rectangular plate, 40 x 21½in. (Christie's)
$4,690 £2,860

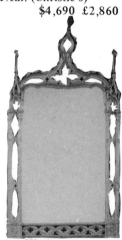

A WMF electroplated pewter mirror, stamped marks B 2/0 GK H, 40cm. high.
(Christie's) $757 £462

A William and Mary walnut and rolled paper mirror, 31½ x 28½in. (Christie's)
$17,820 £11,000

A George III giltwood mirror with later shaped rectangular plate and pierced gothic sur-round, 64 x 34½in.
(Christie's) $10,335 £6,380

A Regency carved giltwood convex mirror, bearing a label T. Rushworth & Son, 1.77m. x 1.06m. (Phillips)
$5,248 £3,200

A walnut and gilt metal mirror with convex moulded surround, 41 x 27½in.
(Christie's) $1,745 £1,045

A giltwood mirror of rococo style. 45 x 31in.
(Christie's) $1,452 £880

A giltwood mirror with shaped rectangular plate in a rockwork frame, 37¾ x 20¼in. (Christie's)
$1,443 £880

A Gustav Stickley hall mirror, style no. 66, circa 1905-06, 28in. high, 36in. wide. (Robt. W. Skinner Inc.) $1,200 £714

One of a pair of Queen Anne gilt gesso girandoles, 37 x 22¼in. (Christie's)
$53,460 £33,000

Late 18th century Louis XV parcel gilt and cream-painted mirror, 57 x 39½in. (Christie's) $4,592 £2,750

Late 17th/early 18th century Flemish ebony, tortoiseshell and ivory mirror, 27½ x 24½in. (Christie's) $3,306 £1,980

A George III giltwood mirror with later rectangular plate and mirrored slips with beaded frame, 55 x 25in. (Christie's) $3,765 £2,310

A WMF polished pewter mirror, the frame cast with a partly draped maiden, stamped marks, 28.9cm. high. (Christie's)
$1,443 £880

A George III giltwood over-mantel, 88 x 71in. (Christie's)
$46,332 £28,600

An early Georgian walnut toilet mirror with shaped plate, on later bun feet, 16½in. wide. (Christie's)
$1,353 £825

A giltwood mirror, the moulded frame with pierced foliate and C-scroll cresting and apron, 42½ x 22in. (Christie's) $896 £550

A George I giltwood mirror, the bevelled oval plate bordered with egg-and-dart ornament, 38 x 25½in. (Christie's) $21,384 £13,200

A giltwood pier glass with divided shaped plate, 105½ x 59in. (Christie's)
$4,408 £2,640

A mid Georgian walnut and parcel gilt mirror with later rectangular plate and eared foliate surround, 50 x 27in. (Christie's) $9,861 £6,050

A Queen Anne marginal wall mirror with arched bevelled plate and divided frame giltwood surround, 92 x 64cm. (Phillips) $10,660 £6,500

A mid Georgian walnut and parcel gilt mirror with bevelled rectangular plate, 53½ x 26in. (Christie's)
$6,352 £3,850

A Chippendale period carved giltwood wall mirror, 1.1m. x 53cm. (Phillips)
$10,660 £6,500

A George I walnut toilet mirror, the base with three short drawers and a concave long drawer, 17in. wide. (Christie's)
$2,151 £1,320

Late 18th century brass mounted, mahogany and parcel gilt cheval mirror, probably German, 77½ x 46½in. (Christie's)
$5,143 £3,080

One of a pair of George III giltwood mirrors by Thos. Chippendale Snr. or Jnr., 77½ x 46½in. (Christie's) $392,040 £242,000

A giltwood mirror, the rockwork cresting supporting a stylised pagoda with a Chinese man, 55 x 38in. (Christie's) $1,623 £990

One of a pair of George II giltwood mirrors, 56 x 35½in. (Christie's) $53,460 £33,000

An early George III mahogany and parcel gilt fret carved wall mirror, 1.30m. x 67cm. (Phillips) $9,020 £5,500

A WMF Secessionist electroplated mirror, 34cm. high. (Christie's) $1,353 £825

A walnut and parcel gilt mirror of George I style, 60 x 34in. (Christie's) $1,623 £990

An early Georgian walnut mirror with shaped rectangular divided bevelled plate, 31½ x 15¼in. (Christie's) $1,118 £682

A George III giltwood mirror with later oval plate and fluted surround, 44½ x 32in. (Christie's) $2,494 £1,540

A Queen Anne black and gold japanned toilet mirror, the base with three short and two serpentine long drawers, 17¾in. wide. (Christie's) $1,075 £660

Late 18th century, possibly German, giltwood mirror, 49 x 29in. (Christie's) $6,980 £4,180

A 19th century Federal giltwood girandole mirror, 54½in. high, 40in. wide. (Christie's) $7,700 £4,655

A Regency giltwood convex mirror, the circular plate with ebonised surround, 43 x 26in. (Christie's) $1,613 £990

A Regency giltwood mirror with rectangular plate, the frieze with verre eglomise panel, 38½ x 22½in. (Christie's) $1,270 £770

A Regency giltwood convex mirror with ebonised fluted slip, 25½in. diam. (Christie's) $907 £550

A George II giltwood mirror, previously with candle branches, 50¾ x 30¾in. (Christie's) $11,583 £7,150

One of a pair of George III giltwood mirrors with oval plates, 48 x 30in. (Christie's) $51,678 £31,900

A Regency colonial calamanderwood toilet mirror, 28in. wide. (Christie's) $1,905 £1,155

A George III giltwood mirror with later pear-shaped divided plate, 61 x 32½in. (Christie's) $12,474 £7,700

A Regency giltwood convex mirror with candle branches, 35 x 25in. (Christie's) $1,542 £935

A giltwood mirror with rectangular bevelled plate, 53 x 43in. (Christie's) $1,724 £1,045

One of a pair of giltwood mirrors with oval plates, 62 x 31½in. (Christie's) $3,227 £1,980

A silver gilt dressing table mirror, in the Charles II style, the reverse engraved Mappin & Webb, 24in. high. (Christie's) $7,128 £4,400

A George I giltwood mirror with rectangular plate and channelled frame, 40¼ x 29in. (Christie's) $1,633 £990

A giltwood Italian mirror with rectangular plate, 92 x 47in. (Christie's) $4,041 £2,420

A Chippendale period carved giltwood cartouche-shaped mirror, 1.7m. x 60cm. (Phillips) $8,200 £5,000

An Austrian shaped rectangusilver dressing table mirror, maker's mark M & K, Vienna, 1846, 26½in. high, weight of frame 40oz. (Christie's) $8,910 £5,500

One of a pair of early George III giltwood mirrors, 90 x 44in. (Christie's) $60,588 £37,400

One of a pair of gilt metal twin-light wall-lights, 13½in. high. (Christie's) $1,194 £715

A Russian papier mache box realistically painted with a scene of two fishermen on a riverbank, signed and dated. 19 x 17.5cm. (Phillips) $423 £260

A 19th century leather, metal-work and agate tobacco pouch, kagamibuta netsuke and ojime, the netsuke signed Naohiro, 15cm. wide and 5.4cm. diam. (Christie's) $3,532 £2,090

'The Tap Dancer', a life-size metal figure of a young negro, 185cm. high. (Christie's) $3,608 £2,200

John Speede 'The Countie Pallatine of Lancaster', hand-coloured engraved map with English text on the reverse, circa 1676, 15 x 20in. (Capes Dunn) $268 £150

Mid 19th century North Italian parcel gilt and painted sedan chair, 30½in. wide, 69in. high. (Christie's) $14,696 £8,800

The Glasgow Herald £650 Golf Tournament at Gleneagles Open to the World's Players May 1920, poster 40 x 30in. (Onslow's) $93 £60

A Victorian child's sledge, painted red on shaped metal runners. (Lots Road Chelsea Auction Galleries) $486 £300

A Victorian glass dome containing a collection of foreign stuffed birds. (G. A. Key) $115 £65

Pacific Northwest Coast Attu circular basket with cover, 4in. high. (Christie's)
$1,980 £1,131

An American 19th century papercut picture, depicting two eagles with flags, 5¾ x 7½in. (Christie's)
$1,100 £620

A 19th century pouch 8 x 7.5cm, with a boxwood seated baku netsuke, signed Gyokumin, 4.6cm. long. (Christie's)
$5,205 £3,080

A black and white poster, advertising 'Kathleen Mavourneen', Theatre Stamford, 1871. (James Norwich Auctions)
$21 £14

Christopher Saxton and Philip Lea 'The County Palatine of Lancaster', engraved and hand-coloured map and Lancaster town map with castle, circa 1693, 15½ x 18½in. (Capes Dunn)
$268 £150

A lead winged cherub with dolphin fountain, 26in. high. (Lots Road Chelsea Auction Galleries)
$992 £620

A 19th century Palekh School icon, depicting St. Roman in a wooded landscape, by Ovchinnikov, 17.5 x 11cm. (Phillips)
$2,934 £1,800

A baby carriage with maker's name plate attached, A. Mitchell, Margate, height to hood 31in. (Worsfolds)
$537 £320

Poster for George Humphrey's bookstore, by M. Louise Stowell, 1896, 11 x 15½in. (Robt. W. Skinner Inc.)
$300 £187

Victorian gilded metal watch stand designed as a mother-of-pearl bird-bath. (Giles Haywood) $98 £60

Papier mache and lacquered vesta box with striker to the base, late 19th century period, Continental. (G. A. Key) $262 £150

A Hepple & Co. malachite fish pattern jug, 7in. high. (Anderson & Garland) $106 £60

An Empire gilt metal frame, with moulded acanthus leaf and Vitruvian scroll border and pierced olive leaf cresting, 12 x 8¼in. (Christie's) $2,153 £1,210

A fine pair of gilt metal and malachite candlesticks with vase-shaped nozzles, 6¾in. high. (Christie's) $2,755 £1,650

A Norwich General firemark, Policy No. 7522, 1799-1802, made of lead. (James Norwich Auctions) $248 £160

A late 19th century French plaster bust of 'L'Espiegle', signed on the shoulder J. B. Carpeaux, 51cm. high. (Christie's) $2,571 £1,540

A micro-mosaic panel of the Colosseum, signed G. Rinaldi, 59 x 77cm. (Phillips) $34,230 £21,000

An Egyptian mummified hawk, 22cm. long, Late Dynastic Period. (Phillips) $473 £260

An alabaster peep egg with three scenes of the Crystal Palace, 4½in. high. (Christie's) $175 £104

Stone fountain base, 3ft. 6in. diam. (Lots Road Chelsea Auction Galleries) $448 £280

A 19th century stag-antler pipe-case and tobacco box, signed Seiryu, 20.2cm. and 9.5cm. (Christie's) $8,365 £4,950

Late 17th/early 18th century gentleman's green velvet undress hat embroidered in silver and gold thread, 8½in. (Hy. Duke & Son) $1,440 £800

A rock crystal relief plaque depicting the life of Christ, in the Gothic style, 5¼ x 3½in., mounted in a leather case. (Christie's) $1,430 £817

A Russian icon: The Mother of God Vladimirskaya, Moscow 1861, maker's mark cyrillic I.A., 31 x 27cm. (Lawrence Fine Art) $1,337 £715

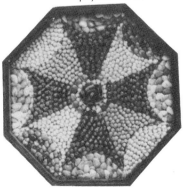

A late 19th century French original plaster half length portrait of Mme. La Baronne Cecile Demarcay, signed J. B. Carpeaux, 80cm. high. (Christie's) $29,392 £17,600

One of three 19th century shell pictures in octagonal wooden frames, 11in. wide. (Lots Road Chelsea Auction Galleries) $480 £300

One of a pair of gilt metal sconces of 17th century design, 15in. high. (Christie's) $642 £385

587

A 19th century tin and alloy inkwell depicting 'Mr Punch', 3in. wide. (Giles Haywood) $82 £50

A 19th century sailor's woolwork ship picture in original mahogany veneered frame, 39.5 x 61cm. (David Lay) $1,404 £780

Late 19th century red lacquered mask of a Karasu Tengu, signed Somin, 5cm. high. (Christie's) $2,442 £1,320

A large Maori nephrite adze head of rounded rectangular form, 17cm. long. (Phillips) $582 £320

Isaac Taylor III, a family conversation group, silhouette painted on glass, 12.5/8in. high. (Christie's) $1,425 £880

A Maori bone comb, 12.7cm. high. (Phillips) $254 £140

A Solomon Islands shell ornament, Kap Kap, the tridacna clam shell base with turtle shell disc attached, 11.7cm. diam. (Phillips) $691 £380

A pale celadon jade carving of a Maiden Immortal standing beside a deer, 8½in. high, carved giltwood stand. (Christie's) $4,620 £2,640

A model of a horse-drawn gypsy caravan, the interior furnished in traditional manner, 20½in. long, excluding shafts. (Lawrence Fine Art) $372 £209

One of a pair of 19th century lacquered coasters, 5½in. diam. (Hobbs & Chambers) $525 £300

A 19th century sedan chair, the interior with buttoned and studded leather, complete with carrying bars. (Jacobs & Hunt) $3,894 £2,200

A Davidson jade green square shaped Tutankhamen bowl, circa 1923, 6in. sq. (Anderson & Garland) $77 £44

Late 19th century American Toleware painted and stencilled chocolate pot, 8½in. high. (Christie's) $1,100 £620

Augustin Edouart, a full-length group silhouette of the Lambe family, Hogarth frame, 12in. high. (Christie's) $1,514 £935

Mid 19th century Chinese Export lacquer tea caddy of quatre-foil shape, 10in. wide. (Christie's) $682 £416

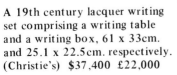

A 19th century lacquer writing set comprising a writing table and a writing box, 61 x 33cm. and 25.1 x 22.5cm. respectively. (Christie's) $37,400 £22,000

An apple green and mottled white jade carving of Guanyin, 18in. high, fixed pierced stand. (Christie's) $66,000 £37,714

A needlework pocketbook worked in Queens stitch with silk yarns, Penn., circa 1818, 4 x 6in. (Robt. W. Skinner Inc.) $450 £267

A builder's mirror back half model of the single screw cargo ship 'Persistence', 15 x 49¼in. overall. (Christie's) $5,544 £3,300

A fully planked un-rigged boxwood model of H.M.S. Circe, circa 1875, built by T. Wake, Stockwood, 5 x 17in. (Christie's) $1,201 £715

A 19th century model of a Gloucester fishing schooner, 'Columbia', fully rigged with wooden sails, 20.3/8in. long. (Robt. W. Skinner Inc.) $900 £545 £!

A live steam spirit-fired wooden model of the paddle tug 'Alert' of Yarmouth, 21 x 39in. (Christie's) $2,679 £1,595

A fully planked and rigged model of a 72-gun man-o'-war, built by P. Rumsey, Bosham, 26 x 37in. (Christie's) $2,772 £1,650

An exhibition standard 1:384 scale model of H.M.S. Rattlesnake, circa 1781, built by J. Evans, Whyteleaf. (Christie's) $2,956 £1,760

An exhibition standard 'One Metre' class steam boat 'Papua', BH 19, built by A. Broad, Bromley, 8 x 40in. (Christie's) $554 £330

A well detailed wood and metal static display model of the Leander class frigate H.M.S. Aurora, Pennant No. F10, stand 14 x 16in. (Christie's) $1,016 £605

A wood waterline model of the R.M.S. Edinburgh Castle built by Bassett-Lowke, the ship 30in. long, in glazed case. (Onslow's) $612 £400

A fully planked and rigged bone and wood model of a topsail schooner built by P. Rumsey, Bosham, 10 x 14in. (Christie's) $702 £418

A 1:48 scale fibreglass, wood and metal, electric-powered model of the coastal cargo ship S.S. Talacre of Liverpool, built by R. H. Phillips, 13 x 33in. (Christie's) $739 £440

A 1/24 scale fully planked electric powered model of the Herring Drifter 'Supernal', built by G. Wrigley, 1979/80 from drawings by R. Neville, 24 x 24in. (Christie's) $2,402 £1,430

A contemporary model of Sir Henry Segrave's record breaking power boat Miss England, length of vessel 12in., in glazed case. (Onslow's) $520 £340

A model of the single screw tug 'Devonmoor', built by J. Gregory, Plymouth, 18 x 34in. (Christie's) $1,663 £990

A finely carved and detailed contemporary early 19th century boxwood model of the 28-gun man-o'-war H.M.S. Nelson, 13½ x 10½in. (Christie's) $15,708 £9,350

A contemporary mid 19th century model of the Paddle Steamer 'Atlanta', 18½ x 41in. (Christie's) $8,316 £4,950

Marklin, gauge 1, clockwork 4-4-0 locomotive and tender No. 1031. (Phillips) $684 £420

Marklin for Gamages, gauge 1, clockwork 0-4-0 G.N.R. locomotive and tender No. 294. (Phillips) $521 £320

Hornby pre-war gauge 0 No. 0 vans, including two milk, ventilated refrigerator, perishable, meat; two No. 2 high capacity wagons and a Bing LNWR open wagon. (Christie's) $392 £242

Marklin gauge 1 (e-rail) electric model of a Continental 4-4-0 'Compound' locomotive and six-wheeled tender No. 65/13041. (Christie's) $356 £220

A Stevens's model dockyard, 3¼in. gauge live-steam spirit fired brass model of an early 2-2-0 locomotive, in original box, circa 1900. (Christie's) $338 £209

A Hornby pre-war gauge 0 No. 2 tank Passenger train set, in original box. (Christie's) $748 £462

Hornby No. 00 train, early 1920's clockwork tin printed MR locomotive and tender No. 483, with key. (Phillips) $138 £85

Bing, gauge 1, clockwork 0-4-0 locomotive and tender No. 48, (unnamed). (Phillips) $456 £280

A Bing for Bassett-Lowke gauge O clockwork model of the LMS 4-4-0 'Compound' locomotive and tender No. 1053 'George the Fifth', (James Norwich Auctions) $176 £110

A Bassett-Lowke gauge 0, 3-rail, electric model of the GWR 2-6-0 'Mogul' locomotive and tender No. 4331, in original paintwork. (Christie's) $1,089 £660

A gauge 0 clockwork model of the LNER 4-4-0 No. 2 special locomotive and tender No. 201, 'The Bramham Moor', by Hornby. (Christie's) $1,069 £660

A 4in. gauge LMS model tank engine, heavy goods type, steam driven, on oak stand. (Woolley & Wallis) $1,944 £1,200

A Hornby pre-war gauge 0 clockwork No. 2 tank goods set, in original box, and an M1 locomotive. (Christie's) $498 £308

A 7¼in. gauge model of the Great Eastern Railway 0-4-0 locomotive No. 710, steel boiler with 7in. barrel and superheater, cylinders 2.1/8in. x 3¾in., driving wheels 8in. diam. (Onslow's) $3,519 £2,300

A Bing gauge 0 clockwork model of the LNER 4-6-0 locomotive and tender No. 4472, 'Flying Fox', in original paintwork. (Christie's) $534 £330

An early gauge 1 (3-rail) electric (4v) model of the LNWR 4-4-0 'Compound' locomotive and tender No. 2663, 'George The Fifth', by Marklin, circa 1912. (Christie's) $801 £495

An early 20th century single cylinder horizontal mill engine, complete with mahogany lagged brass bound cylinder, 2½ x 3in. (Onslow's) $397 £260

A 4½in. scale model of a Burrell single cylinder, two-speed, three-shaft general purpose traction engine, built by Lion Engineering Co., 1971, length of engine 68in. (Onslow's) $6,120 £4,000

An exhibition standard 1½in. scale model of the Allchin single cylinder two-speed four-shaft General Purpose Traction Engine (Royal Chester'. (Onslow's) $2,295 £1,500

A model of an early 20th century twin cylinder horizontal mill engine, complete with mahogany lagged copper bound cylinders, 2½ x 5in. (Onslow's) $734 £480

A Stuart Major Beam engine, cylinder, 2¼ x 4in., on wood stand in glazed case. (Onslow's) $780 £510

An early 20th century wood model of the 1860 horse-drawn goods wagon owned by Carter Paterson & Co, London and Suburban Express Carriers, 17in. long. (Onslow's) $489 £320

Large monoplane model, made by Charles R. Witteman, Staten Island, New York, circa 1912, 62in. long, wingspan 78in. (Robt. W. Skinner Inc.) $2,000 £1,123

An exhibition standard 2in. scale model of the Clayton Undertype Articulated wagon, built by E. W. D. Sheppard. (Onslow's) $2,295 £1,500

'Tammany Bank', a cast iron mechanical bank, the seated gentleman with articulated right arm, 5¾in. high, by J. and E. Stevens Co., circa 1875. (Christie's)$175 £100

'Artillery', a cast-iron money-box, with a moulded cannon, and a World War I tank, by Starkies, circa 1915, 10in. long. (Christie's) $254 £154

A cast iron money bank of a golly, 15.5cm. high. (Phillips) $165 £100

'Bull Dog Bank', a cast-iron mechanical moneybox, by J. & E. Stevens, circa 1880, 7¾in. high. (Christie's) $326 £198

'Trick Dog', a mechanical cast-iron moneybox, by J. & E. Stevens, circa 1888, 8¾ x 3in. (Christie's) $544 £330

Late 19th century American cast iron mechanical bank, 'Stump Speaker', 9½in. high. (James Norwich Auctions) $168 £95

'Stollwerck Bros. Post Savings-Bank', modelled as a chocolate dispenser, circa 1911, 6½in. high. (Christie's) $285 £176

'United States and Spain', a mechanical cast-iron money-box, by J. & E. Stevens, circa 1898, 8½ x 2½in. (Christie's) $1,996 £1,210

'Transvaal Moneybox', a mechanical cast-iron money-box of Paul Kruger. (Christie's) $235 £143

Grenouille, a Lalique glass frog, script R. Lalique France marks (chips to leg and base), 2½in. high. (Onslow's) $1,094 £680

An enamel, double sided, sign for Castrol Wakefield Motor Oil, 13 x 20in. (Onslow's) $136 £85

'Coq Nain', a coloured car mascot, the topaz and satin finished glass moulded as a cockerel, 20.2cm. high. (Christie's) $4,510 £2,750

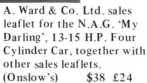

A nickel plated mascot of a girl bather standing in a seashell, 7in. high. (Onslow's) $209 £130

A. Ward & Co. Ltd. sales leaflet for the N.A.G. 'My Darling', 13-15 H.P. Four Cylinder Car, together with other sales leaflets. (Onslow's) $38 £24

Five publicity booklets by W. Heath Robinson, Connolly Land, Cattle Culture, Nothing Takes The Place of Leather and others; and two others similar by A. Leete and H. M. Bateman. (Onslow's) $193 £120

Brooklands Automobile Racing Club, an aluminium and enamel Junior Car Club badge, 3½in. high. (Onslow's) $177 £110

Pratts, two gallon petrol can, repainted. (Onslow's) $57 £36

A Smith's four position light switch and ammeter combined, with bezel action, suitable for Bentley, 3½in. diam. (Onslow's) $80 £50

A Lalique clear and frosted glass car mascot of 'Victoire — Spirit of the Wind', 10in. long. (Prudential Fine Art) $9,454 £5,800

Napier Motors British Made Throughout, enamel, double sided, 16 x 25in. (Onslow's) $322 £200

'Tete de Belier', a Lalique car mascot, moulded as a ram's head, 9.5cm. high. (Christie's)$27,060 £16,500

A Doxa timepiece with second hand, nickel plated case, 6 o'clock side winder, 2½in. diam. (Onslow's) $193 £120

A nickel plated Michelin type pressure gauge, contained in original printed tinplate box, with instructions. (Onslow's) $225 £140

L'Allumage Moderne Magneto Lavalette Eisemann, hand-coloured lithograph after E. Montaut, 17¾ x 35¼in. (Onslow's) $386 £240

An early 20th century cold painted metal car mascot of a dragonfly golfer seated on a composition golf ball, 6in. high. (Woolley & Wallis) $693 £420

Redline, two gallon petrol can, original black and gold paint. (Onslow's) $48 £30

Tete de coq, a Lalique glass cockerel's head (chip to comb), 7in. high, on glass base. (Onslow's) $563 £350

Official programme to
the 7th Monte Carlo Rally,
1928. (Onslow's) $80 £50

A chromium plated trophy,
modelled as a Bugatti radiator
grill and badge, mounted on
wood stand, 9in. high.
(Onslow's) $837 £520

The late Hon. C. S. Rolls,
monochrome postcard.
(Onslow's) $32 £20

A chromium plated and
enamelled Aero-Club Brooklands badge, stamped 418,
3½in. high. (Onslow's)
             $853 £530

Perche, a Lalique glass mascot,
script Lalique France marks,
4in. high. (Onslow's)
             $402 £250

A chromium plated speed
nymph, 5½in. high, mounted
on a radiator cap. (Onslow's)
             $112 £70

A Souvenir of Brooklands,
published by Temple Press,
1938; The Brooklands Year-
book, 1939; and Brooklands
Speed & Distance Tables,
revised edn. 1931. (Onslow's)
             $161 £100

'Archer', a Lalique car
mascot, in clear and grey
stained glass, with chrome
metal radiator mounts,
11.8cm. high. (Christie's)
             $721 £440

D. N. Ingles, Be Up-To-Date
— Shellubricate, printed tin,
with table of grades of oils
listing cars and aeroplane
engines, 25 x 17in. (Onslow's)
             $161 £100

Official programme to the 20th Annual 500 Mile Sweepstakes, Indianapolis, May 30th 1934. (Onslow's) $152 £95

Join The R.A.C., printed tin-plate hanging leaflet box, 11in. high, with some membership leaflets. (Onslow's) $120 £75

A circular enamel sign for Mercedes Benz, convex, 16in. diam. (Onslow's) $338 £210

A chromium plated and enamelled B.A.R.C. Brooklands badge, stamped 803, 3½in. high. (Onslow's) $660 £410

'Spirit of the Wind', a red-ashay car mascot on chromium plated metal mount, 11.5cm. high. (Christie's) $1,353 £825

A brass electric Klaxon horn, suitable for Rolls-Royce, 9in. high. (Onslow's) $128 £80

W. D. & H. O. Wills Ltd, Raymond Mays on the E.R.A. at Brooklands, cardboard advertising display for Will's Star Cigarettes, 27 x 19in. (Onslow's) $627 £390

'Vitesse', a Lalique car mascot moulded as a naked female, 18.5cm. high. (Christie's) $9,020 £5,500

Le Sport & Le Tourisme Automobile, June 1925, French text, mounted plates. (Onslow's) $128 £80

Circuit des Ardennes Belges 1906, hand-coloured lithograph, after E. Montaut, 17¾ x 35¼in. (Onslow's) $386 £240

Le Panhard et Lavassor Gagnant du Championnat de la Mer en 1908, hand-coloured lithograph, after E. Montaut, 17¾ x 35¼in. (Onslow's) $354 £220

German Grand Prix 1937, Caracciola in the Mercedes receiving pit instructions from team manager Neubauer, by Carlo Demand, signed, charcoal heightened with white, 17 x 36in. (Onslow's) $3,381 £2,100

Rover, One of Britain's Fine Cars, oval bevelled glass mirror with inscription in gold, 14 x 24in. (Onslow's) $322 £200

Belsize Motor Vehicles Of Every Description, printed tin, 23 x 30in. (Onslow's)
                                    $322 £200

A sales brochure for the Bentley 3 Litre, No. 7, issued Oct. 1924, prices in text. (Onslow's)
                                    $418 £260

An enamel, double sided, advertising sign, Humber, 12 x 28in. (Onslow's) $136 £85

Motor 'B.P.' Spirit, enamel, double sided, 15 x 24in. (Onslow's) $104 £65

Le Dirigeable Republique Motor Panhard et Lavassor, hand-coloured lithograph, after E. Montaut, 17¾ x 35¼in. (Onslow's)
$386 £240

A sales brochure for Sheffield Simplex Motor Cars, 1914 Season, plates some colour, loosely inserted letter from the Co. (Onslow's)
$209 £130

Vauxhall, oval bevelled glass hanging display, 12 x 18in. (Onslow's)
$338 £210

Renault 1911, hand-coloured lithograph, after Gamy, 14½ x 25½in. (Onslow's)
$354 £220

An enamel, double sided, sign Fill Up Here With National Benzole Mixture, 12 x 18in. (Onslow's)
$104 £65

Monaco Grand Prix 1937, by Michael Wright, signed, watercolour and gouache, 30 x 27in. (Onslow's)
$1,610 £1,000

Coupe des Voitures Legeres 1911, hand-coloured lithograph, after Gamy, 17¾ x 35¼in. (Onslow's)
$434 £270

An enamel advertising sign for Guaranteed Shell Lubricating Oil, Single, Double, Triple, three enamels. (Onslow's)
$152 £95

5eme Grand Prix Automobile Monaco 23 Avril 1933, by G. Ham, colour lithograph, 47 x 31½in. (Onslow's)
$3,220 £2,000

A nickel plated Heath's bulb horn, with nickel plated flexible extension and mounting bracket. (Onslow's)
$201 £125

The artist, Frederick Gordon Crosby, in his MG 16/80, signed and dated 1929, water-colour heightened with white, 24 x 19in. (Onslow's)
$2,254 £1,400

A catalogue for Beatonson Wind Shields 1913, plates, prices in text, together with other sales literature. (Onslow's) $38 £24

A bronze figure of a weight lifter, with winged feet holding a weight inscribed 30cwt., 6in. high, probably from a commerical vehicle. (Onslow's)
$322 £200

Monaco Grand Prix 1928, Bugatti and Mercedes at the station hairpin, by James Dugdale, watercolour heightened with white, 17 x 20½in. (Onslow's) $177 £110

A pair of copper and brass fire engine sidelights, with oil burners, bevelled glass, carrying handles and mounting brackets, 12in. high. (Onslow's)
$177 £110

Official programme to the 1906 Tourist Trophy, advertisements, partly complete score sheet. (Onslow's)
$289 £180

A pair of carriage lamps, with silvered interiors, the candle burners inscribed H. & A. Holmes, Litchfield, Sheffield, Derby and London, 22in. long. (Onslows's) $161 £100

A Bugatti poster, after Gerold, 38 x 53in. (Onslow's) $322 £200

B.P. Super, glass petrol pump globe, 18in. square. (Onslow's) $72 £45

Official programme to the Royal Irish Automobile Club, Irish International, Grand Prix, Phoenix Park, Dublin, July 12th-13th 1929. (Onslow's) $96 £60

Avus 1937, Auto Unions, by Phil May, signed, watercolour, 8½ x 10½in. (Onslow's) $104 £65

Coq Nain, a Lalique glass small cockerel, script Lalique France marks, 8¼in. high. (Onslow's) $483 £300

XVIII Mille Miglia 1951, silk handkerchief, framed and glazed, 31in. square. (Onslow's) $338 £210

A pair of brass Lucas King of the Road No. 416 oil sidelights, with bevelled glass and mounting brackets, 11½in. high. (Onslow's) $209 £130

Thornton & Co. Ltd. Latest Styles and Patterns for Motorcycle Water-proofs, Oiled Silks and Cottons, Season 1913-14, folding wallet containing material samples and illustrations of clothing. (Onslow's) $25 £16

A pair of silver trophies with moulded foliate decoration, inscribed Essex Motor Club Brooklands, August 13th 1921, H. Merton 2nd Prize, 4in. high. (Onslow's) $322 £200

603

A Sublime Harmony musical box playing six operatic airs, trade label of C. Scotcher & Son, Birmingham, 21in. wide, the cylinder 13in. (Christie's) $3,207 £1,980

A gramophone with 'The Gramophone Co., Maiden Lane, London, W.C.' label, a 7in. diam. turntable and four single sided E. Berliner's 7in. diam. records, circa 1900-10. (Hobbs & Chambers)$1,600 £1,000

A key-wind part-overture musical box, No. 20420, playing 'Zampa' overture in two parts and ten other airs, 19in. wide, the cylinder 11½ x 3in. diam. (Christie's)$2,851 £1,760

A Harmonia 16¼in. disc musical box with single comb movement and walnut veneered case, 23in. wide, with ten discs. (Christie's) $1,782 £1,100

A 'Margot' forty-four-note piano orchestrion by H. Peters & Co., Leipsig, in oak case, 97in. high, with two barrels 24 x 10½in. diam. and weight. (Christie's) $6,771 £4,180

A 9½in. Symphonium disc musical box with 'Sublime Harmony' combs, with one disc. (Christie's) $1,069 £660

An Edison Amerola 1A phonograph, No. SM 950 in mahogany case with two-minute and four-minute traversing mandrel mechanism, 49in. high. (Christie's) $1,782 £1,100

An Amourette organette in the form of a chalet, with seventeen discs, 14in. wide, the discs 9in. (Christie's) $801 £495

A Symphonion musical mantel clock in walnut case, the hinged top concealing a 5¾in. periphery-drive double comb Symphonion movement, 18½in. high, with one disc. (Christie's) $855 £528

A forty-four key dumb organist pinned for six listed hymn tunes, in mahogany case with crank, 31in. wide. (Christie's) $1,158 £715

An Edison Bell 'Commercial' electric phonograph, No. 21164, the motor in oak base with accessories drawer. (Christie's) $1,336 £825

A mandolin musical box, No. 15838, playing six airs, 33in. wide overall, the cylinder 19½in. (Christie's) $4,633 £2,860

An Edison Diamond Disc phonograph, Chippendale Laboratory Model (C19) No. SM 106640, 51½in. high, with nineteen discs. (Christie's) $748 £462

A Melodia fourteen-note organette by American Mercantile Co., on gilt stencilled walnut case with label of Bradford & Teale, London, with two rolls. (Christie's) $498 £308

An oak Berliner 7in. record cabinet with folding lid, spaces for 32 records, containing seven American issue Berliners by Cal. Stewart and others. (Christie's) $712 £440

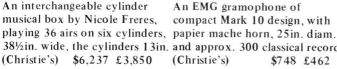

An interchangeable cylinder musical box by Nicole Freres, playing 36 airs on six cylinders, 38½in. wide, the cylinders 13in. (Christie's) $6,237 £3,850

An EMG gramophone of compact Mark 10 design, with papier mache horn, 25in. diam. and approx. 300 classical records. (Christie's) $748 £462

A bells and drum in view cylinder music box, by B. A. Bremond, circa 1875, box 21in. long. (Christie's) $2,530 £1,546

An Edison Fireside phonograph, Model A No. 25426, the K reproducer, crane and 36 two-minute and four-minute wax cylinders in cartons. (Christie's) $748 £462

A Polyphon 15.5/8in. periphery-drive disc musical box with winding handle and twelve discs. (Phillips) $1,440 £900

A musical box by J. Thibouville Lamy & Co., No. 69701, playing twelve airs, 23in. wide, the cylinder 13in., 1890-1900. (Christie's) $1,514 £935

A 24.5/8in. upright Polyphon with coin mechanism and drawer, in glazed walnut case, 46in. high, with twenty-seven discs. (Christie's) $8,019 £4,950

An early Edison electric phonograph mechanism, in oak case with glass cover, with rear part of a Bettini carrier arm (lacks Edison carrier arm, Bettini reproducer and horn). (Christie's) $1,960 £1,210

A 15.5/8in. Regina table disc musical box with double comb long bedplate movement in oak case and twelve zinc discs. (Christie's) $2,138 £1,320

An Apollo horn gramophone with double-spring motor in oak case with part wood tone-arm and laminated oak horn, circa 1912. (Christie's) $1,158 £715

A Celestina twenty-note organette in gilt stencilled walnut case, with fourteen rolls and nineteen new rolls. (Christie's) $1,336 £825

A musical box playing 12 airs, tune sheet and inlaid lid, 26in. wide, the cylinder 14in. (Christie's) $4,633 £2,860

An HMV Intermediate Monarch gramophone with mahogany case and horn, 1911 (soundbox replaced). (Christie's) $1,158 £715

A 19th century chased brass cased rectangular musical box with a hinged cover revealing a singing bird, 4.25in. long. (Woolley & Wallis) $495 £300

A musical box by Ducommun Girod, playing eight operatic and other airs, in bevelled corner case, 23¾in. wide, the cylinder 13in. (Christie's) $1,692 £1,045

An eighteen-key chamber barrel organ by Longhurst(?), London, with three barrels, drum, triangle and four musical stops, in mahogany case with simulated pipes to the Gothic front, 71in. high. (Christie's) $1,514 £935

'Golden Marenghi', 46 key Fairground organ, circa 1905, 7ft. x 7ft. (Onslow's) $28,764 £18,800

An HMV Model 203 cabinet gramophone, 5A soundbox and re-entrant tone chamber, the mahogany case with gilt internal fittings. (Christie's) $3,564 £2,200

A 15.5/8in. table polyphone with twin combs and 17 discs. (Christie's) $2,316 £1,430

A coin-operated table-top Buffet Tirelire musical box, the 17cm. cylinder with zither attachment, in walnut case, 47.5 x 42cm. (Osmond Tricks) $1,720 £920

A 19.5/8in. upright Polyphon with coin mechanism and drawer, in glazed walnut case, 38in. high. (Christie's) $6,237 £3,850

A Gramophone & Typewriter Ltd. Style No. 6 gramophone in panelled oak case and Concert soundbox, travelling arm and brass horn, circa 1901. (Christie's) $1,603 £990

Early HMV wind-up table gramophone with original gilt pleated circular diaphram. (Lawrence Butler & Co.) $820 £500

A Gramophone & Typewriter Ltd. New Style No. 3 gramophone with 7in. turntable, now with Columbia soundbox and brass horn. (Christie's) $1,452 £880

A 15¾in. Polyphon disc musical box playing on single comb, in walnut case, 19¼in. wide, complete with winding handle and forty-one discs. (Hobbs & Chambers) $1,408 £880

An early Kammer & Reinhardt 5in. Berliner Gramophone, with three Berliner records. (Phillips) $2,080 £1,300

A Britannia 'smoker's cabinet' upright 9in. disc musical box in walnut case, 26½in. high, with fourteen discs. (Christie's) $2,494 £1,540

A Zither Marmonique Piccolo musical box by Paillard, Vaucher Fils, playing eight airs, 22in. wide, the cylinder 13in. (Christie's) $2,316 £1,430

An Edison Home phonograph, early Model A, with automatic reproducer, and modern brass witch's hat horn. (Christie's) $427 £264

A Sublime Harmony Tremelo musical box with tune sheet and bird's-eye maple case, 24½in. wide. (Christie's) $1,782 £1,100

A viola by Wm. H. Luff, London, dated 1971, 16½in. long. (Phillips) $6,048 £3,600

A violoncello by Henry Jay, in London, circa 1760, 28.7/8in. long, with a lightweight case by Paxman. (Phillips) $8,064 £4,800

A viola by G. Lucci, Roma, 1978, 16½in. long, with a bow in a modern shaped case. (Phillips) $2,856 £1,700

A violin by N. Vuillaume, Paris, circa 1840, 14.1/8in. long, in case. (Phillips) $7,360 £4,600

A violoncello by Ch. J. B. Collin-Mezin, length of back 30in. (Phillips) $7,160 £4,000

A violin by Claude Pierray, in Paris, circa 1720, 14.5/16in. long, with a water-proof case by W. E. Hill & Sons. (Phillips) $4,200 £2,500

A violin by G. A. Chanot, dated 1906, 14.3/16in. long, in case. (Phillips) $2,520 £1,500

A violin by G. Pyne, London, 1921, 14in. long, with a silver mounted bow by J. Hel, in case. (Phillips) $1,680 £1,050

A violin by Salomon of Reims, 1746, length of back 14. 13/16in., in an oblong, velvet-lined and fitted case. (Phillips)
$2,970 £1,800

A Florentine violin, circa 1770, bearing the label Lorenzo and Tommaso Carcassi, anno 1773, length of back 14in. (Phillips)
$9,075 £5,500

An English violin, bearing the label of G. Pyne, Maker London, 1888, 14.1/8in. long, with bow. (Phillips)
$2,880 £1,800

A viola, by B. Banks of Salisbury, circa 1770, length of back 15.3/8in., in a shaped and lined velvet case. (Phillips)
$9,308 £5,200

A violin by J. A. Chanot, 1899, length of back 14.1/8in., with a silver mounted bow, in case. (Phillips)
$5,728 £3,200

A violin by Wm. E. Hill & Sons, London, 1904, length of back 14in., in a mahogany case. (Phillips)
$8,055 £4,500

A violoncello by Wm. Forster, London, circa 1784, 29in. long, in wood case. (Phillips)
$6,720 £4,000

A violin by Carolus F. Landulphus, 1766, length of back 13. 15/16in., with a silver mounted bow, in an oak case. (Phillips)
$57,280 £32,000

A Neapolitan violon-
cello, circa 1750,
attributed to G.
Gagliano, 29.7/16in.
long, with a silver
mounted bow and
cover. (Phillips)
$58,800 £35,000

A viola by F.
Gagliano in Naples,
14½in. long, upper
bouts 7.1/8in. long,
lower bouts 9in.
(Phillips)
$17,600 £11,000

A violoncello, circa
1750, of the Tyro-
lesse School, label-
led Carlo Tunon,
1732, 29.3/16in.
long, in wood case.
(Phillips)
$7,056 £4,200

A violin by J. N.
Leclerc, circa 1770,
14in. long, with
two bows, in case.
(Phillips)
$2,520 £1,500

A violin by Alfred
Vincent, dated
1922, 13.14/16in.
long, in a shaped
case, by E. Withers.
(Phillips)
$3,024 £1,800

A violin by Dom
Nicolo Amati of
Bologna, 1714,
14.1/16in. long,
in case. (Phillips)
$15,120 £9,000

A viola, circa 1830,
of the Kennedy
School, 15.5/16in.
long, with two bows,
in an oblong case.
(Phillips)
$2,436 £1,450

A violin attributed
to R. Cuthbert,
1676, 13.7/8in.
long, in case.
(Phillips)
$1,310 £780

A viola, circa 1780, length of back 15¾in., in an oblong fitted case. (Phillips) $11,550 £7,000

A violin by Richard Duke in London, circa 1770, length of back 14in. (Phillips) $6,930 £4,200

A viola by Giuseppe Lucci, length of back 16½in., in a case lined in green velvet by Gewa. (Phillips) $3,795 £2,300

A violin by Antonio Capela, 1972, length of back 14in., in shaped case. (Phillips) $198 £120

A violin by William Glenister, 1904, length of back 14. 1/16in., with a bow. (Phillips) $1,567 £950

A violin by Vincenzo Sannino, 1910, length of back 14.1/16in, with a shaped case and cover. (Phillips) $10,725 £6,500

A violin by Joannes Gagliano of Naples, circa 1790, length of back 14in., in case. (Phillips) $9,308 £5,200

A violin by Lorenzo Arcangioli of Florence, circa 1840, length of back 13.7/8in. (Phillips) $6,930 £4,200

A violin by Ferd. August Homolka, length of back 13. 15/16in., with two bows, in marquetry case. (Phillips)
$5,012 £2,800

A French viola, circa 1900, labelled Joannes Baptista Guadagnini, length of back 15.7/8in., in fitted case. (Phillips)
$3,300 £2,000

A violin by J. Werro, bearing the maker's label Fecit a Berne 1922, length of back 14.1/8in. (Phillips)
$3,960 £2,400

A violin by Joseph Hill, 1756, length of back 14in. (Phillips)
$5,940 £3,600

A violin by Charles J. B. Collin-Mezin, length of back 14. 1/8in., with two bows in case. (Phillips)
$2,805 £1,700

A violin by F. W. Chanot, London, A.D. 1890, length of back 14in., with two bows, in water-proof case. (Phillips)
$4,833 £2,700

A violoncello by H. Derazey in Mirecourt, circa 1860, length of back 29in., with a silver mounted French bow. (Phillips)
$6,444 £3,600

A violin by H. L. Hill, London, circa 1825, length of back 14in., with a bow in leather case. (Phillips)
$7,160 £4,000

Early 19th century brass mounted mahogany sedan clock, 7in. diam. (Christie's) $306 £187

A silver medallion by B. Andrieu, circa 1800, 2in. diam. (Christie's) $288 £176

A bronze bust of Napoleon on spreading plinth, signed 'Noel R', 12¼in. high. (Christie's) $1,082 £660

A 19th century ivory rotunda with stepped roof and fluted columns framing a statuette of Napoleon, 7in. high, 5½in. diam. (Christie's) $7,576 £4,620

Napoleon I: Letter signed 'Napoleon', to the Archduke Charles, Compiegne, 24 March 1810, one page, sm. 4to, mounted beside a colour printed engraving of Napoleon's head. (Christie's) $3,427 £2,090

A 19th century brass carriage clock with enamel dial and statuette of Napoleon, 8in. high. (Christie's) $721 £440

After Vauthier: Notables de a France revolutionaire, by E. Bovinet, engravings, 400 x 273mm. (Christie's) $1,082 £660

A Continental biscuit porcelain equestrian group of Napoleon crossing the Alps after the painting by David, mid 19th century, 8in. wide, 10½in. high. (Christie's) $2,164 £1,320

Napoleon I: Document signed 'Napol', one page, large folio, printed heading the crest, Moscow, 12 October 1812. (Christie's) $1,353 £825

An Empire ormolu mounted mahogany fauteuil de bureau with revolving circular seat covered in ochre leather, 21½in. diam. (Christie's) $99,220 £60,500

Early 19th century circular tortoiseshell box, the cover painted with Napoleon on horseback, 3in. diam. (Christie's) $541 £330

A trooper's helmet of the French Cuirassiers (Second Empire) with chin-chain, mane and tuft, 18in. high. (Christie's) $1,804 £1,100

A 19th century bronze bust of Napoleon as First Consul, 36cm. high. (Christie's) $635 £385

Napoleon I: Document signed 'Nap', granting a pardon to Jean-Marie Merle, who had been sentened to 5 years hard labour in 1805 for desertion, one page, oblong folio, 395 x 505mm.. (Christie's) $1,984 £1,210

An ivory statuette of Frederick the Great on eight-sided base carved with relief portraits of ladies, 7¼in. high. (Christie's) $4,690 £2,860

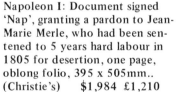

Napoleon I: Endorsement signed 'N', 26 May, 1813, one page, folio, printed heading of Ministere de la Guerre, Bureau de la Gendarmerie. (Christie's) $631 £385

One of two early 19th century French shallow circular boxes, possibly Grenoble, 3½in. diam. (Christie's) $270 £165

Early 19th century marquetry coach panel inlaid in shaded woods with Napoleon on horseback, 27¾ x 19½in. (Christie's) $1,262 £770

A 19th century French bronze bust of Napoleon, inscribed on the reverse J. Berthoz, 24cm. high. (Christie's) $689 £418

An Empire scarlet morocco leather despatch box with brass hasp backplate, clips and angles, 27in. wide. (Christie's) $7,216 £4,400

A Continental biscuit porcelain bust inscribed 'Napoleon I', 16½in. high. (Christie's) $2,886 £1,760

After Jean Baptiste Isabey: Napoleon a Malmaison, by C. L. Lingee and J. Godefroy, mixed method engraving, 637 x 433mm. (Christie's) $505 £308

A bronze equestrian statue of Napoleon issuing instructions from a galloping horse, on a breccia marble base, 10in. wide, 11½in. high. (Christie's) $631 £385

An Empire ormolu toilet mirror, with inscription '. . . taken by a Sergeant of the 11th Lt. Dragoons from Napoleon's Carriage dressing case . . .', 12 x 8in. (Christie's) $1,102 £660

A 19th century bronze bust of Napoleon, signed 'Linedon' on verde antico marble plinth, 18½in. high. (Christie's) $1,713 £1,045

A 19th century ormolu and porphyry encrier, the pentray centred by a bust of the Emperor with initial N below, 14½in. wide. (Christie's) $2,886 £1,760

A 19th century French bronze figure of Napoleon, the base inscribed Vela. F. 1867, and on the reverse F. Barbedienne, 28cm. high. (Christie's) $1,361 £825

A 19th century French bronze bust of Napoleon The First, after Ambrogio Colombo, 32cm. high. (Christie's) $998 £605

A 19th century bronze, ormolu and verde antico paperweight mounted with a trophy of Napoleon's hat, sword and scroll, 6in. wide. (Christie's) $1,984 £1,210

A bronze bust of Napoleon, signed 'Noel Ruffier', 11½in. high. (Christie's) $1,443 £880

After Robert Lefevre: Joseph Napoleon, Roi de Naples et de Sicile, by L. C. Rouolle, coloured mixed method engraving, 436 x 324mm. (Christie's) $396 £242

A 19th century French bronze statue of Napoleon on Horseback, on rouge marble base, 61cm. high. (Christie's) $2,755 £1,650

Pellerin & Co., Publishers: Genie; Musique de la Garde Republicane; Fanfare de Dragons; Hussards; Chasseurs; and Musique de Hussards, coloured engravings, 373 x 265mm. (Christie's) $144 £88

After Cornillet: Napoleon au Palais des Tuileries; and Napoleon assis, after F. Flameng, 304 x 210mm. (Christie's) $505 £308

A 19th century bronze group of Napoleon and a French soldier, 6½in. wide, 7in. high. (Christie's) $631 £385

A 19th century bronze bust of Napoleon signed 'Noel R', on spreading verde antico marble plinth, 6½in. high. (Christie's) $216 £132

A pair of late 19th century Sevres pattern porcelain circular plaques painted with scenes from Napoleon's Campaigns, the plaques 17½in. diam. (Christie's)
$18,040 £11,000

A silver circular medallion after B. Andrieu, one side with a scene of Prometheus chained to the rock with an eagle pecking at his liver, date 1816 below, 3in. diam. (Christie's)
$216 £132

A gilt metal painted plaster roundel with relief portrait of Napoleon, 3½in. diam., and a bronzed lead relief medallion of Napoleon crossing the Alps, signed Andrieu, F. (Christie's) $324 £198

Two miniatures, one of Napoleon, signed T. Perdult(?), and another of Josephine signed S. Laupua (?), 6¾in. high. (Christie's) $1,623 £990

Apres vous Sire! (Campagne de 1813); and On n'passe pas..., by N. T. Charlet and P. L. Debucourt, mixed method aquatints, 420 x 479mm. and smaller. (Christie's)
$469 £286

After Jean Baptiste Isabey and Charles Percier: L'Empereur, en petit Costume; and L'Imperatrice, en petite Costume, by Ribault, coloured engravings, 443 x 240mm. and smaller. (Christie's) $324 £198

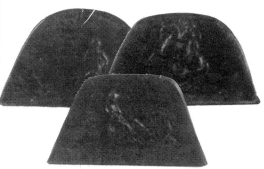

Three early 19th century horn snuff boxes shaped as tricorn hats, 3.1/8in. long. (Christie's) $1,172 £715

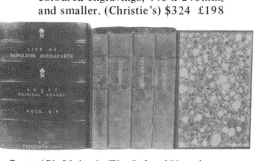

Scott (Sir Walter): The Life of Napoleon Buonaparte, First Edn., 9 vols., with an autograph letter signed (with initials) from Scott to J. Ballantyne, 8vo. Edinburgh, 1827. (Christie's) £811 £495

A bronzed equestrian statue of Napoleon crossing the Alps, 4½in. wide, and a gilt metal relief of Napoleon crossing the Alps, 6in. wide. (Christie's) $811 £495

A rectangular metal mounted frame with oval miniatures of Napoleon and Josephine, signed Derval, 7½in. long, and another oval gilt metal frame with an image of Napoleon, 2¼in. high. (Christie's) $1,082 £660

One of a pair of oak egg cups with silver plaques inscribed NB 1798, framing an obelisk, 3in. high, and two copper measures, 2in. diam. (Christie's) $1,353 £825

A 20th century ivory netsuke, Boyasha Sonjiro, signed Nasatoshi, 5 cm. high. (Christie's) $6,692 £3,960

An ivory netsuke of a grazing deer, unsigned, circa 1800, 6.2cm. high. (Christie's) $4,833 £2,860

An 18th century ivory netsuke of Shoki and Oni, unsigned, 7.7cm. high. (Christie's) $2,974 £1,760

A 19th century cloudy amber netsuke of Fukurokuju, 6.3cm. high. (Christie's) $1,301 £770

Early 18th century wood netsuke of a bitch and puppies, signed Matsuda Sukenaga, 6.8cm. long. (Christie's) $1,673 £990

A boxwood netsuke of Daruma, signed Sansho (1871-1936), 4.3cm. high. (Christie's) $7,807 £4,620

A 19th century boxwood netsuke of a large snake holding a rat in its jaws, signed Masanori, 5cm. wide. (Christie's) $2,992 £1,870

Late 18th century wood netsuke of Roshi seated on a mule (seal netsuke), 7cm. high. (Christie's) $1,766 £1,045

An ivory seal netsuke carved as a well-known foreigner who came to Nagasaki, signed Mitsumasa, circa 1880, 4.8cm. high. (Christie's) $792 £495

A 19th century Hirado ware netsuke of Gama Sennin, impressed signature Masakazu, 8.1cm. high. (Christie's) $1,022 £605

An 18th century ivory netsuke of a grazing horse, unsigned, 7cm. high. (Christie's) $3,346 £1,980

A 20th century ivory netsuke of Ryujin, signed Masatoshi, 9.2cm. high. (Christie's) $6,506 £3,850

A 19th century metal netsuke of a Kendo mask, signed Nagayasu saku, 3.8cm. high. (Christie's) $3,718 £2,200

Early 19th century wood netsuke of an ostler trying to shoe a horse, 4.8cm. long. (Christie's) $2,416 £1,430

A 20th century stag-antler netsuke of an owl, signed Masatoshi, 4.5cm. high. (Christie's) $5,948 £3,520

A wood netsuke of a dog with one foot on a clam shell, Kyoto School, circa 1780, 3.4cm. high. (Christie's) $1,936 £1,210

Late 18th century ivory netsuke of Moso and bamboo shoot, signed Awataguchi, 8.4cm. high. (Christie's) $5,205 £3,080

A 19th century wood netsuke of three human skulls, signed Yoshiharu, 5.3cm. wide. (Christie's) $2,602 £1,540

Late 19th century Imari ware netsuke of the monkey showman, 5.5cm. high. (Christie's) $1,115 £660

A 19th century zelkova wood Karashishi mask, 5.2cm. long. (Christie's) $780 £462

An ivory netsuke of Rakan, signed Kuya, 4.5cm. high, with tomobako. (Christie's) $5,019 £2,970

A 19th century ivory netsuke of a cherry tree and morning mist (ryusa manju), signed with a kao, 4.3cm. diam. (Christie's) $1,394 £825

A wood netsuke of the demon's arm, signed Kyusai, 7.2cm. long. (Christie's) $3,346 £1,980

A 19th century ivory netsuke of a nine-tailed fox, signed Baihosai, with seal Naomitsu, 7.4cm. diam. (Christie's) $2,788 £1,650

An ivory netsuke of a seated kirin, signed Yoshimasa, circa 1800, 10.5cm. high. (Christie's) $44,616 £26,400

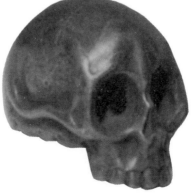

A 19th century metal netsuke of a human skull, signed Yoshihide, 3.5cm. long. (Christie's) $2,044 £1,210

A 19th century ivory netsuke of Songoku the magical monkey, signed Mitsuhiro, 5.2cm. high. (Christie's) $13,013 £7,700

A wood netsuke of Yamabushi, signed Soko (1879-1942), 5.3cm. high, with tomobako. (Christie's) $22,308 £13,200

Early 19th century wood netsuke Ko-omote mask, 5.9cm. high. (Christie's) $1,022 £605

A 19th/20th century coloured and inlaid ivory netsuke of a courtier, signed Yasuaki, with seal Kodama, 4.6cm. high. (Christie's) $4,461 £2,640

Mid 19th century ivory netsuke of a tsuba, signed Hojitsu, 4.4cm. high. (Christie's) $3,532 £2,090

An 18th century ivory netsuke of an Amagatsu doll, signed Masanao (of Kyoto), 5.5cm. high. (Christie's) $48,334 £28,600

A 19th century ivory, shishiai-bori and kebori netsuke of Asahina Saburo and Sogo No Goro, signed Kosai Moritoshi and kao, 6.1cm. diam. (Christie's) $2,230 £1,320

Early 19th century lacquered wood netsuke of Tososei, unsigned, 6.3cm. high. (Christie's) $1,580 £935

An ivory netsuke carved as a tsuitate depicting Tekkai Sennin exhaling his spiritual essence, circa 1840, 5cm. high. (Christie's) $880 £550

A 19th century ivory netsuke of a rat on a corn cob, 9.4cm. long. (Christie's) $2,230 £1,320

An 18th century ivory
netsuke of a dog and awabi
shell, signed Tomotada,
3.5 cm. high. (Christie's)
$12,083 £7,150

A wood netsuke of a recumbent camel, signed Sosui,
4.3cm. long. (Christie's)
$13,942 £8,250

A 19th century wood netsuke
of Hideyoshi playing horse,
4cm. high. (Christie's)
$2,602 £1,540

A 19th century wood netsuke
of Jurojin and stag, signed
Masakatsu, 4.3cm. wide.
(Christie's) $17,660 £10,450

An ivory netsuke of Omori
Hikoshichi and the witch,
signed Shoko, 5.2cm. high,
with tomobako. (Christie's)
$13,013 £7,700

A 19th century boxwood
netsuke of a seated figure
of a monster-man, 4.8cm.
high. (Christie's)
$3,718 £2,200

A 19th century boxwood
netsuke of a Bugaku mask,
signed Shugetsu saku,
3.9cm. high. (Christie's)
$1,487 £880

A 19th century wood net-
suke of a dragon in thunder
clouds, signed Homi,
3.9cm. diam. (Christie's)
$1,208 £715

A 19th century ivory netsuke
of an Otafuku mask, signed
with a kao, 4cm. high.
(Christie's) $2,044 £1,210

A 19th century ivory netsuke of Karashishi and young with a tama, signed Eijusai Masayoshi, 4cm. wide. (Christie's) $13,942 £8,250

A 19th century ivory netsuke of Yuramosuke, signed Anrakusai, 3.4cm. high. (Christie's) $2,974 £1,760

An 18th century wood netsuke of two goats, signed Tametaka, 3.5cm. high. (Christie's) $13,013 £7,700

Late 19th century ivory, stained and inlaid netsuke of a Temple servant, signed Yasumasa, 4.9cm. high. (Christie's) $3,532 £2,090

Early 19th century wood netsuke of a demon mask, signed Gyokuzan, 6.3cm. high. (Christie's) $892 £528

Early 19th century wood netsuke of a mushroom cluster, traces of signature, 4.7cm. high. (Christie's) $1,301 £770

An ivory netsuke of a Daruma doll, signed Mitsuhiro and kao (1810-75), 4cm. high. (Christie's) $4,089 £2,420

A 19th century wood netsuke of rats on an otafuku mask, signed Tadahisa, 4cm. long. (Christie's) $2,602 £1,540

A 19th century ivory netsuke, Takaramono, 4.5cm. diam. (Christie's) $2,044 £1,210

An 18th century ivory netsuke of a fox and cub, unsigned, 5.8cm. wide. (Christie's) $2,416 £1,430

A 19th century ivory, shishiai-bori netsuke, Setsubun, signed Moritoshi and kao, 5.3cm. diam. (Christie's) $1,301 £770

A 19th century ivory netsuke of a bat, signed Mitsutoshi koku, Kyo no junin, 3.9cm. high. (Christie's) $8,923 £5,280

A 17th/18th century stag-antler netsuke of a monster head, 4cm. high. (Christie's) $1,673 £990

Mid 19th century ivory netsuke of dancing Shojo, signed Otoman, 4.1cm. high. (Christie's) $5,202 £3,080

A wood netsuke of an oni pounding something in a mortar, 3.2cm. high, and another of Daruma, both mid 19th century. (Christie's) $1,320 £825

An ivory netsuke of a gourd and ladybird, signed Ohara Mitsuhiro and kao (1810-75), 3.9cm. high. (Christie's) $4,089 £2,420

An ivory, stained and painted netsuke of a fly on an octopus tentacle, signed Mitsuhiro and kao, 5.6cm. long. (Christie's) $13,013 £7,700

An ivory netsuke of a skeleton playing a biwa (manju netsuke), signed Hakuo, circa 1830, 3.9cm. diam. (Christie's) $4,461 £2,640

A 19th century wood netsuke of a primitive fish, unsigned, 8cm. long. (Christie's)
$706 £418

A 19th century ivory, shishiai-bori and kebori netsuke, despatching a wolf, signed Harushige and kao, 5.6cm. diam. (Christie's)
$1,508 £935

An ivory netsuke of a tiger and monkey, signed Kaigyokusai, with seal Masatsugu, 3.9cm. long. (Christie's)
$24,167 £14,300

An 18th century ivory seal netsuke formed as a kara-shishi, 4.2cm. high, 19th century netsuke. (Christie's)
$563 £352

Late 17th century ivory netsuke of Hotei, unsigned, 5.3cm. high. (Christie's)
$1,022 £605

A wood netsuke of the Rakan Nakasaina Sonja, signed Shoko, 5.2cm. high, with tomobako. (Christie's) $20,449 £12,100

A 19th century ivory and metal netsuke of Rochishin uprooting a willow tree, 4.8cm. diam. (Christie's)
$929 £550

Early 19th century wood netsuke of Yamabushi sounding conch shell horn, 6.4cm. long. (Christie's)
$2,230 £1,320

A 20th century ebony netsuke of a bat and young, signed Masatoshi, 4cm. wide. (Christie's) $8,923 £5,280

1928 Bank of Australasia £1. (Phillips)
$356 £220

Canada: 1897 Dominion $1. (Phillips)
$518 £320

Zanzibar: 1916 20 rupees. (Phillips)
$1,620 £1,000

Southern Rhodesia: 1951 10/-. (Phillips)
$251 £155

1857 Mosenthal Brothers £5 issued at Cape
Town. (Phillips) $469 £290

Gibraltar: 1914 (6 August) £1. (Phillips)
$550 £340

£1 1915 overprinted for use in the Dardanelles.
(Phillips) $1,944 £1,200

Barbados: 1938 Royal Bank of Canada $5.
(Phillips) $170 £105

Mauritius: 1919 1 rupee. (Phillips) $275 £170

Jersey: Jersey Mercantile Union Bank £1 uni-face colour trial in blue by Charles Skipper & East. (Phillips) $777 £480

Hong Kong: 1929 Hong Kong & Shanghai Banking Corporation $10 specimen. (Phillips) $243 £150

1916 Mercantile Bank of India $10. (Phillips) $324 £200

Malaya: 1942 $100. (Phillips) $267 £165

Zanzibar: 1928 (1st February) Government 10 rupees. (Phillips) $2,025 £1,250

Ireland: Northern Bank £100, 1919. (Phillips) $194 £120

Australia: c. 1900 Bank of New South Wales £100 unissued. (Phillips) $745 £460

A rectangular pewter-rimmed kobako, unsigned, circa 1800, 9.3 x 8.3cm. (Christie's) $1,320 £825

One of a pair of Art Nouveau pewter vases, attributed to WMF, with glass liners, stamped A K & Cie, 36cm. high. (Christie's) $1,713 £1,045

German pewter three-handled soup tureen with boar mount, by Kayserzinn, 15in. high. (Worsfolds) $420 £250

A Victorian pewter egg cruet with four spoons. (G. A. Key) $126 £70

A Glasgow style pewter and enamel cigar box, with an enamel plaque of a maiden holding an apron of fruit, 8¾in. wide. (Christie's) $288 £180

A Swedish art pewter inkwell by Svenskt Tenn, Stockholm, 12.5cm. high. (David Lay) $68 £38

Liberty & Co. Tudric pewter two-handled motto cup, London, circa 1910, 7.7/8in. high. (Robt. W. Skinner Inc.) $225 £121

A glass jar with pewter cover and mounting, after a design by Peter Behrens, 6¼in. high. (Robt. W. Skinner Inc.) $450 £267

An 18th century large baluster pewter pitcher (hallmarked with two sets of cross keys). (J. M. Welch & Son) $486 £320

A 19th century American Dixon & Son pewter teapot, with wooden handle. (Du Mouchelles) $150 £81

A Liberty Tudric pewter biscuit box, the lid with twin handle over square section base, 11cm. high. (Phillips) $171 £90

A 19th century pewter salt dip, on claw feet with hinged lids. (Du Mouchelles) $150 £81

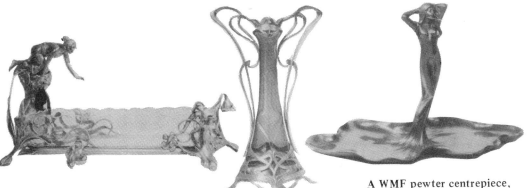

A WMF pewter centrepiece with rectangular clear glass tank, stamped marks, 55.5cm. wide, 31.4cm. high. (Christie's) $1,353 £825

One of a pair of WMF pewter and glass vases, stamped marks, 48cm. high. (Christie's) $902 £550

A WMF pewter centrepiece, cast as a young girl with flowing robe forming an irregular-shaped tray, 22.5cm. high. (Christie's) $721 £440

A pewter bell-based candlestick, with flaring drip-pan above a cylindrical candlecup, 9in. high. (Christie's) $66 £39

A pewter-rimmed kobako decorated with chrysanthemums by the East Fence, box 17th century, 7.9cm. long. (Christie's) $1,144 £715

A Chinese octagonal pewter wine pot, glass panels depicting domestic scenes. (Du Mouchelles) $350 £195

'Journal of my trip to Ceylon, Australia and Tasmania, W. G. Hardy, 1894', disbound album containing approx. 120 albumen prints, majority 6½ x 9½in., small 4to. (Christie's) $577 £352

'The Expression of the Emotions in Man and Animals', by Charles Darwin with seven heliotype plates, 8vo., London: John Murray, 1872. (Christie's) $104 £55

Three Midgets, whole plate tin-type, gilt highlights, gilt edged oval paper matt, 1850s/60s; and another. (Christie's) $90 £55

F.E. Currey, Iris and chrysanthemum, two platinum prints, 7½ x 5½in. and 8 x 6in., unmounted (1880s or early 90s). (Christie's) $376 £198

A pair of portrait photographs of George VI and Queen Elizabeth, by Dorothy Wilding, in original fitted cases, 26cm. x 35cm. (Phillips) $5,440 £3,400

The Far East, Australasia, South America, South Africa and Europe, two albums, containing 360 albumen prints, 240 cartes-des-visites, oblong 4to. and half morocco, 1860s and 1870s. (Christie's) $1,804 £1,100

Bill Brandt, Parlourmaid and under-parlourmaid ready to serve dinner, gelatin silver print, 35¼ x 30in., with photographer's ink stamp and initials 'B.B.' on reverse, 1930s. (Christie's) $1,985 £1,045

Francis Frith (1822-1898), Egypt and Sinai, ten albumen prints, each 6 x 8in., six signed, 1857. (Christie's) $459 £242

Bill Brandt (1906-1984), Antonio Tapies' left eye, gelatin silver print, 28 x 24in., with photographer's ink stamp and initials 'B.B.' on reverse, 1964. (Christie's) $731 £385

Silvy, Caldesi, Notman, Robinson and others, a collection of cartes-des-visite and cabinet cards, 29 albums, majority full morocco,1850s/1890s. (Christie's)
$1,443 £880

6th Inniskilling Dragoons, an album of 24 photographs, majority salt prints and oval 5¼ x 4¼in., cont. half red morocco, 4to. (Christie's)
$324 £198

One of a collection of ambrotypes and daguerreotypes, quarter-plate portrait of a butcher hand-tinted in pink to emphasise the raw meat and his cheeks. (Christie's)
$902 £550

Angus McBean, 'Toumanova 'surrealized' as La Sylphide', gelatin silver print, 19¼ x 14¾in., signature and date 'London '38' in pencil on card. (Christie's) $271 £143

Jane Brown, Edith Sitwell, gelatin silver print, 15 x 11in., mounted on card, 1959. (Christie's) $167 £88

J. Dupont, Foot artist at work, albumen print, 9¾ x 7¾in., signature 'J. Dupont Phot. Anvers' (1870s). (Christie's)
$585 £308

Japanese costume portraits and topography, album of forty-six albumen prints and a three-print panorama, oblong 4to, dated 1896. (Christie's) $469 £286

Yousuf Karsh, Ernest Hemingway, gelatin silver print, 12 x 10in., titled and credited, 1957. (Christie's)$271 £143

James Linton, calotype, 7½ x 5½in., unmounted, letter 'A' stamped in ink on reverse, 1844-45. (Christie's)
$940 £495

A spinet by Longman Lukey & Co., London, circa 1771. Overall length 75in. (Phillips) $1,023 £550

An Operaphone cabinet gramophone in the form of a grand piano, in mahogany case with Thorens soundbox, internal horn enclosed by the 'keyboard fall', 34in. long. (Christie's) $891 £550

An overstrung boudoir grand pianoforte, seven and a quarter octaves, by John Broadwood & Sons, in a satinwood case. (Christie's) $2,178 £1,320

A Steinway upright oak piano, circa 1903, Serial 107781, decorated by Edwin Willard Deming. (Christie's) $28,600 £16,342

A classical rosewood and mahogany pianoforte, labelled by A. Babcock, Boston, circa 1820, 67in. wide. (Christie's) $2,860 £1,733

An Aeolian Grand 58-note player organ with 19 musical stops and walnut case, 64in. wide, 1898. (Christie's) $1,782 £1,100

Late 18th century wing-shaped spinet, the hardwood case stained dark walnut, overall length 73in. (Phillips) $5,370 £3,000

A 48-note street barrel piano in veneered case, playing 10 airs, on painted hand-cart. (Christie's) $1,960 £1,210

A fine single manual Harpsichord, by Jacob & Abraham Kirkman, in a cross banded mahogany case, 87 x 37¼in. on modern trestle stand. (Christie's) $23,628 £13,200

An Eavestaff overstrung under-dampered 'mini-piano' with green drag point slab shaped deco case, also matching stool. (Peter Wilson) $1,134 £700

An important Steinway parlour concert grand piano, circa 1904, 91in. long, together with a duet stool, 44in. long. (Christie's)
          $66,000 £37,714

A forty-seven note coin-slot barrel piano with ten-air barrel in varnished birch case and engraved glass panel, 40in. wide. (Christie's)
          $855 £528

Gernard Lens, a gentleman facing right in beige coat, signed with gold monogram, gilt metal mounts, rectangular wood frame, oval 2.7/8in. high. (Christie's) $1,069 £660

James Peale, a lady in white shawl and bonnet, signed with initials and dated 1800, oval 3in. high. (Christie's) $1,960 £1,210

Thomas Flatman, a self-portrait, on vellum, signed and dated 1678, gold frame, oval 2½in. high. (Christie's) $10,335 £6,380

George Engleheart, a miniature of Capt. John Cummings in the uniform of The 8th Dragoons, signed and dated 1806, oval 3½in. high. (Christie's) $6,237 £3,850

George Engleheart, a lady in decollete white dress with frilled border, gold frame, oval 2.7/8in. high. (Christie's) $5,346 £3,300

John Cox Dillman Engleheart, a gentleman in dark blue coat with gold buttons, signed on the reverse and dated 1814, oval 2.5/8in. high. (Christie's) $980 £605

Philip Jean, a gentleman in blue coat with gold buttons, gold frame with plaited hair reverse, oval 2¾in. high. (Christie's) $1,336 £825

Attributed to Pierre Chasselat, a lady seated on a bench in a landscape, set in the lid of a tortoiseshell box with gold rims, 2.5/8in. diam. (Christie's) $3,920 £2,420

John Cox Dillman Engleheart, a gentleman in black coat and waistcoat, gold frame, oval 2.7/8in. high. (Christie's) $534 £330

Andrew Plimer, an officer in scarlet uniform with blue facings and silver lace, gold frame, oval 3in. (Christie's) $3,207 £1,980

John Smart, a miniature of Miss Elizabeth Cottingham of County Clare, signed and dated 1777, gold frame, oval 2in. high. (Christie's) $10,335 £6,380

James Green, a gentleman possibly the Rt. Hon. Edward Ellice, gold frame, oval 3.1/8in. high. (Christie's) $981 £606

Philip Jean, a gentleman in blue coat with gold buttons, gold frame, oval 2.5/8in. high. (Christie's) $715 £440

David Des Granges, a miniature of a lady in black dress with lace border and white lace collar, on vellum, oval 2.3/8in. high. (Christie's) $8,019 £4,950

Studio of Richard Gibson, a gentleman believed to be Sir John Germaine, on vellum, oval 3.1/8in. high. (Christie's) $1,782 £1,100

George Place, a miniature of an officer of the Weymouth Vol. Artillery, gilt metal frame, oval 4¾in. high. (Christie's) $5,346 £3,300

John Smart, Jane Palmer in ermine-bordered pale blue surcoat, signed with initials and dated 1777, gold frame, oval 1¾in. high. (Christie's) $7,128 £4,400

John Comerford, Capt. James Hughes in the blue uniform of The 18th Dragoons (Hussars), signed and dated 1807, oval 3in. high. (Christie's) $2,138 £1,320

After Pierre Adolph Hall, a gentleman in white-lined blue coat with gold borders, gilt metal frame with split pearl border, 2¾in. diam. (Christie's) $1,158 £715

English School, circa 1800, a gentleman in black coat with large lace ruff, set in the lid of a tortoiseshell box, 1¾in. diam. (Christie's) $712 £440

In the manner of Charles Henard, a lady seated in a green chair mixing poison, 2½in. diam. (Christie's) $2,316 £1,430

Richard Gibson, a gentleman facing right in armour and white linen collar, on vellum, gilt metal frame with reeded border, oval 2¼in. high. (Christie's) $2,494 £1,540

Captain and Mrs. Wm. Croome, by G. Engleheart, both signed and dated 1811 and 1812, later gold frames, ovals, 3¼in. high. (Christie's) $8,316 £4,620

Thomas Flatman, a nobleman called John Maitland, 2nd Earl and Duke of Lauderdale, on vellum, signed with initial, oval 2.1/8in. high. (Christie's) $7,128 £4,400

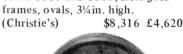

Mme. Aimee Zoe Lizinka de Mirbel (nee Rue), a miniature, possibly of Queen Adelaide, signed and dated 1830, rectangular 4.1/8in. high. (Christie's) $5,346 £3,300

Continental School, a nobleman in gold bordered crimson coat, oil on copper, oval 3in. high. (Christie's) $356 £220

Ozias Humphrey, after Sir Godfrey Kneller, Lionel, 1st Duke of Dorset, gold frame, 6½in. high. (Christie's) $1,247 £770

Jacques Charlier, after
Francois Boucher, two
nymphs and two putti,
ormolu frame with beaded
border, 2¾in: diam.
(Christie's) $4,633 £2,860

Jean Baptiste Isabey, a
miniature of a gentleman in
brown coat, signed, gilt metal
frame, 2¾in. diam. (Christie's)
$8,553 £5,280

Andrew Plimer, a miniature of
an officer in scarlet uniform,
gold frame, oval 2¼in. high.
(Christie's) $4,455 £2,750

Christian Frederick Zincke, a
portrait of a lady, enamel,
gilt metal frame, oval 1¾in.
high. (Christie's) $1,564 £986

John Taylor, a pair of plum-
bagos of William and Cyril
Jackson, oval 5in. high.
(Christie's) $1,960 £1,210

D.M., a miniature of a gentleman in blue coat with large
buttons, on vellum, signed in
gold with monogram and
dated 1665, oval 2.3/8in. high.
(Christie's) $2,494 £1,540

John Smart, a miniature of
Peter Johnston, signed
with initials and dated 1803,
gold frame, oval 3½in. high.
(Christie's) $10,692 £6,600

Aldani, a miniature of a
gentleman seated on a stone
wall, signed, gilt metal frame,
rectangular 3.1/8in. high.
(Christie's) $1,782 £1,100

William Grimaldi, a portrait
of a child seated beside a
tree with a blue finch on his
hand, signed, gold frame, oval
2¾in. high. (Christie's)
$6,237 £3,850

Yoshijuro Urishibawa: Paeonies and Fresias, one of four woodcuts printed in colours, circa 1910, 303 x 201mm. and smaller. (Christie's)
$2,032 £1,210

Albrecht Durer: St. Jerome in his Study, engraving, watermark Three Balls (?), 245 x 189mm. (Christie's)
$5,913 £3,520

Henry Moore: Reclining Figures and Reclining Mother and Child, lithograph printed in colours, 1971 and 1974, 299 x 239mm. (Christie's) $1,386 £825

Pierre-Auguste Renoir: La Danse a la Campagne, Deuxieme Planche, soft-ground etching, circa 1890, on wove paper, 220 x 135mm. (Christie's)
$8,553 £5,280

Henry Moore: Girl Seated At Desk VII, lithograph printed in colours, 1974, on J. Green wove paper, 242 x 175mm. (Christie's) $1,570 £935

Dame Elisabeth Frink: Geoffrey Chaucer, etching illustrating Chaucer's Canterbury Tales, Leslie Waddington Prints Ltd., London, 1972, 588 x 694mm. (Christie's) $702 £418

David Hockney: Black Tulips, lithograph, 1980, signed, dated and numbered 80/100, published by Waddington, 112 x 76cm. (Phillips) $5,670 £3,500

Laura Knight: At The Fair, aquatint, signed in pencil, mount-stained, taped to front mount, 26 x 21cm. (Phillips) $486 £300

Andy Warhol: Hand-coloured Flower, lithograph, signed with initials, 102 x 68cm. (Phillips) $1,944 £1,200

Henry Moore: Three reclining
Figures on Pedestals, lithograph
printed in colours, 1966, on
Arches, signed and dated in
pencil, 312 x 263mm.
(Christie's) $2,656 £1,540

Jacques Villon: L'Italienne,
after A. Modigliani, aquatint
printed in colours, circa
1927, on wove paper, signed,
497 x 309mm. (Christie's)
        $6,771 £4,180

David Hockney: Rue de Seine,
etching, 1971, on J. Green
mould-made wove paper,
numbered 92/150, 537 x
435mm. (Christie's)
        $8,019 £4,950

Three, Les Maitres de l'Affiche, Volumes I-V, Imprimerie Chaix, Paris 1896-1900, sheet
403 x 315mm. (Christie's) $21,384 £13,200

Marc Chagall: Cirque avec
Clowne-jaune, lithograph
printed in colours, 1967, on
Arches, numbered 83/150,
675 x 496mm. (Christie's)
        $7,484 £4,620

David Hockney: Potted
Daffodils, lithograph, 1980,
signed, dated and numbered
81/95 in pencil, 112 x 76cm.
(Phillips) $5,670 £3,500

Shuho Yamakawa, oban tate-e,
okubi-e of a young woman,
signed, entitled Yukimoyoi,
dated 1927, 38.5 x 26.5cm.
(Christie's) $1,108 £693

Jacques Villon: Le Paysan, after V. van Gogh, aquatint printed in colours, 1927, on wove paper, signed, 400 x 317mm. (Christie's) $1,692 £1,045

Kathe Kollwitz: Zwei Schwatzende Frauen mit zwei Kindern, lithograph, 1930, on wove paper, 296 x 262mm. (Christie's) $5,346 £3,300

Alexei Gan: Twenty Years of Works by Vladimir Mayakovsky. lithograph printed in colours, 1930, on wove paper, 614 x 438mm. (Christie's) $891 £550

Marc Chagall: Ile Saint-Louis (M. 225), lithograph printed in colours, 1959, on Arches, 517 x 668mm. (Christie's) $17,820 £11,000

Norman Wilkinson: A Land Locked Salmon, etching, signed in pencil, 21.5 x 30cm. (Phillips) $178 £110

Alphonse Maria Mucha: Reverie, lithograph printed in colours, 1896, on wove paper, 639 x 477mm. (Christie's) $3,920 £2,420

El Lissitsky: Pro Dva Kvadrata (Of Two Squares), Skythen Verlag, Berlin, 1922, album of lithographs printed in colours, 1920, 280 x 225mm. (Christie's) $8,910 £5,500

Otto Dix: Kupplerin, lithograph printed in red, yellow and blue, 1923, numbered 5/65, 482 x 367mm. (Christie's) $35,640 £22,000

Erich Heckel: Hockende, woodcut, 1913, on soft wove paper, watermark Saskia, first state of two, 417 x 306mm. (Christie's) $11,583 £7,150

George Braque, Composition (Nature morte I) (V. 8), etching, 1911, on Arches, 350 x 215mm. (Christie's) $21,222 £13,100

Jacques Villon: Nu, after P. A. Renoir, aquatint printed in colours, 1923, on Arches, signed in pencil, numbered 193/200, 602 x 450mm. (Christie's) $3,920 £2,420

Marc Chagall: L'Odyssee, two volumes, printed on Arches, containing 43 colour lithographs and 39 lithographs printed in grey in the text, the next text being a translation of Homer. (Phillips) $38,880 £24,000

Marc Chagall: Hymen, from Daphne et Chloe (M. 349), lithograph printed in colours, 1961, on Arches, numbered 52/60, 422 x 643mm. (Christie's) $40,986 £25,300

Paul Delvaux: La Reine de Saba, screenprint in colours, 1982, on Arches, 596 x 431mm. (Christie's)
$1,336 £825

Erich Heckel: Mannerbildnis, woodcut printed in black, olive-green, brown and blue, 1919, second state of three, 463 x 327mm. (Christie's)
$92,664 £57,200

Marc Chagall: Femme de l'Artiste, lithograph printed in colours, 1971, on Arches, 649 x 503mm. (Christie's)
$33,858 £20,900

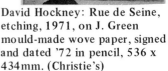

Utamaro, a triptych, signed, published by Yamaguchiya Tobei, each sheet approx. 36 x 24cm. (Christie's) $7,392 £4,620

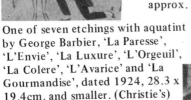

One of seven etchings with aquatint by George Barbier, 'La Paresse', 'L'Envie', 'La Luxure', 'L'Orgeuil', 'La Colere', 'L'Avarice' and 'La Gourmandise', dated 1924, 28.3 x 19.4cm. and smaller. (Christie's) $432 £264

David Hockney: Rue de Seine, etching, 1971, on J. Green mould-made wove paper, signed and dated '72 in pencil, 536 x 434mm. (Christie's) $8,870 £5,280

Jean Morin: Tete de Mort, after P. Champaigne, engraving, watermark proprietary, 315 x 324mm. (Christie's) $2,217 £1,320

Jacques Villon: Portrait de jeune Femme, drypoint, 1913, on BFK Rives, watermark Eug Delatre, numbered 7, from the edition of approx. 30, 651 x 498mm. (Christie's) $53,460 £33,000

Mikhail Larionov, N. Goncharova, V. Tatlin and I. Rogovin: Alexei Kruchenykh and Velimir Khlebnikov, Mirskontsa (Worldbackwards), paper collage and lithographs, 1912, 189 x 154mm. (Christie's) $14,256 £8,800

Christopher Richard Wynne Nevinson: After a German Retreat, Labour Battalion making a Road through a captured Village, lithograph printed in dark brown, 1918, 235 x 308mm. (Christie's) $2,032 £1,210

Rolf Nesch: Negerrevue, etching with drypoint and aquatint printed in black, orange-red and deep mustard yellow, 1930, on thick fibrous Japan, 353 x 555mm. (Christie's) $32,076 £19,800

Edward Wadsworth: Mine-sweepers in Ports, woodcut, on thin Japan, signed and dated 'Liverpool 1918', 50 x 135mm. (Christie's) $6,468 £3,850

Louis Icart: Mimi, drypoint with aquatint printed in colours, 1927, on wove paper published by Les Graveurs Modernes, Paris, 534 x 356mm. (Christie's) $1,016 £605

Conrad Felixmuller: Ich zeichnend (Selbstbildnis mit Akt), woodcut, 1924, on wove paper, 545 x 335mm. (Christie's) $2,494 £1,540

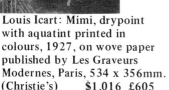

A Walt Disney celluloid depicting 'Turtle and Chipmunk', from 'Snow White and the Seven Dwarfs' 1934, 5 x 5¼in. (Robt. W. Skinner Inc.) $950 £575

Henri de Toulouse Lautrec: Eldorado: Aristide Bruant, lithograph printed in colours, 1892, on two sheets of thin tan wove paper, 930 x 1,354mm. (Christie's) $32,076 £19,800

Henri de Toulouse-Lautrec: Le Jockey, lithograph, 1899, on Chine, second (final) state, from the edition of 100, 504 x 359mm. (Christie's) $18,711 £11,550

Utamaro, hashira-e, the famous lovers Koharu and Jihei, signed, published by Murataya, 64.1 x 13.6cm. (Christie's) $2,112 £1,320

James Abbott McNeill Whistler: Thames Police, etching with drypoint, on laid paper, third (final) state, 149 x 224mm. (Christie's) $1,293 £770

Paul Cesar Helleu: Madame Wolffe, drypoint, printed in colours, signed in pencil, 54 x 33.6cm. (Phillips) $3,888 £2,400

Tsuguji Foujita: Le Songe, lithograph, circa 1964, on wove paper, signed in pencil, 510 x 660mm. (Christie's) $1,386 £825

Roy Lichtenstein: Crake!, offset lithograph printed in colours, 1964, on wove paper, signed and dated in pencil, 474 x 687mm. (Christie's) $5,544 £3,300

Georges Roualt: Christ en Croix, aquatint printed in colours, 1936, on Montval, 657 x 495mm. (Christie's) $53,460 £33,000

Ernst Ludwig Kirchner: Halbakt, lithograph, 1909, on smooth wove paper, 256 x 149mm. (Christie's) $39,204 £24,200

Henri Matisse: Marie-Jose en Robe jaune, aquatint printed in five colours, 1950, on Arches, numbered 50/100, 538 x 418mm. (Christie's) $71,280 £44,000

Louis Icart: Parfum des Fleurs (Le Divan), etching with drypoint and aquatint printed in colours, 1937, 447 x 643mm. (Christie's) $1,848 £1,100

Pablo Picasso: Personnages masques et Femme Oiseau, etching with aquatint, 1934, on Montval, watermark Vollard, from the edition of 250, 249 x 348mm. (Christie's) $5,346 £3,300

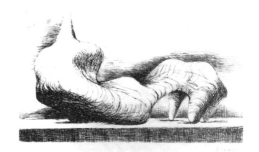

Richard Hamilton: I'm dreaming of a Black Christmas, silkscreen and collotype printed in colours, 1971, on wove paper, signed in pencil, numbered 40/150, published by Petersburg Press, London, with margins, 517 x 760mm. (Christie's) $1,755 £1,045

Henry Moore: Reclining Figure Point, etching with aquatint, 1976, on wove paper, watermark Bisonte, second (final) state, signed in pencil, numbered 41/100, 170 x 245mm. (Christie's) $2,032 £1,210

Jacob Kramer: Vorticist Figure, lithograph, circa 1920, on laid paper, 417 x 252mm. (Christie's) $2,402 £1,430

Marc Chagall: Now the King loved Science and Geometry, Plate X from Four Tales from the Arabian Nights, lithograph printed in colours, 1948, 380 x 286mm. (Christie's) $27,621 £17,050

Theodore Alexandre Steinlen: Motocycles Comiot, lithograph printed in colours, 1899, on two joined sheets of thin tan wove paper, 1,885 x 1,280mm. (Christie's) $13,365 £8,250

Pablo Picasso: Minotaure caressant une Femme, etching, 1933, on Montval, watermark Vollard, from the edition of 250, 299 x 370mm. (Christie's) $13,810 £8,525

Jacques Villon: Les Joueurs de Cartes, after P. Cezanne, aquatint printed in colours, 1929, on Arches, signed, 487 x 601mm. (Christie's) $2,851 £1,760

Kunisada/Kunichika/Chikanobu and others, an album containing 54 oban tate-e, 35.2 x 24.8cm. (Christie's) $1,760 £1,100

Harunobu, Chuban yoko-e, a young couple dallying, signed, 20.7 x 28cm. (Christie's) $2,376 £1,485

Henri Matisse: Odalisque a la Culotte de Satin rouge, lithograph, 1925, on Chine volant, 191 x 272mm. (Christie's) $62,370 £38,500

Pablo Picasso: Cheval mourant, etching, 1931, on wove paper, from the edition of 103, 222 x 311mm. (Christie's) $5,346 £3,300

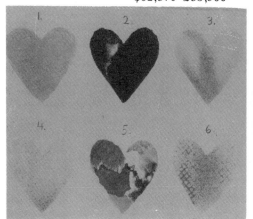

Jim Dine: Dutch Hearts, Petersburg Press, London, 1970, lithographs printed in colours with collage, on hand-made Hodgkinson wove paper, 416 x 506mm. (Christie's) $13,365 £8,250

Otto Mueller: Zwei auf den Safa sitzende Madchen, lithograph with handcolouring, 216 x 269mm. (Christie's) $24,948 £15,400

Appliqued quilt, America, late 19th century, red cotton patches arranged in a 'Princess Feather' pattern, 96 x 98in. (Robt. W. Skinner Inc.) $1,100 £607

Mid 19th century pieced and appliqued quilt, the calico patches arranged in 'conventional rose' pattern, 80 x 84in. (Robt. W. Skinner Inc.) $425 £265

Mid 19th century crib quilt, the red, yellow and green calico patches arranged in the 'Star of Bethlehem' pattern, 28in. square. (Robt. W. Skinner Inc.) $400 £250

Mid 19th century patchwork crib quilt, worked in mosaic pattern with various calicos, American, 42 x 44in. (Robt. W. Skinner Inc.) $1,800 £1,071

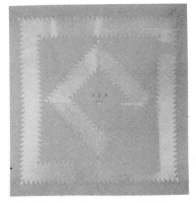

An appliqued album quilt, cross stitch name in corner 'Miss Lydia Emeline Keller, 1867', American, 84 x 86in. (Robt. W. Skinner Inc.) $2,100 £1,250

An Amish pieced cotton quilt, Lancaster County, Penn., circa 1900, with later embroidery JEB, 1920, 83½ x 85in. (Christie's) $352 £198

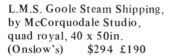

L.M.S. Goole Steam Shipping, by McCorquodale Studio, quad royal, 40 x 50in. (Onslow's) $294 £190

G.N.R., handlamp, marked Algarkirk and Yarmouth Vauxhall, 12in. high, and another, internals missing. (Onslow's) $184 £110

L.M.S. Southend-on-Sea, by Charles Pears, quad royal, 40 x 50in. (Onslow's) $124 £80

A tinplate salver, produced for the Stockton & Darlington Railway Centenary, depicting Locomotion and head of Stephenson, 12in. diam. (Onslow's) $13 £8

A silver gilt circular director's pass, inscribed South Devon, Cornwall & West Cornwall railways No. 4. (Onslow's)

$436 £260

London & Birmingham Railway Centenary Medal, 1838-1938, in presentation case. (Onslow's) $23 £14

North British Railway, copper lamp with bull's-eye lens , mounted with brass plate inscribed Hawick Up Home, internals missing, 24in. high. (Onslow's) $252 £150

Liverpool & Manchester Railway, three engravings, two hand-coloured, and Tallis's Railway Map of Great Britain. (Onslow's) $75 £45

A silver circular director's pass, inscribed Cornwall Railway Lord Robartes. (Onslow's) $588 £350

Railways Wanted Board, with movable Slide In and Outs, 22in. high, and L.M.S. wood fire buckets notice. (Onslow's) $11 £7

Poster by H. G. Gawthorn, L.N.E.R. Capacity — Mobility Dog Tooth Loading Dock, Ardwick, Manchester, quad royal. (Onslow's) $302 £180

L.B.S.C.R., handlamp, later burner. (Onslow's) $100 £60

A gold medallion of the Metropolitan Railway, The Queen's Jubilee 1887. (Onslow's) $1,176 £700

Stratford-upon-Avon & Midland Junction Railway, Beware of Trains cast iron sign, 14½ x 21½in. (Onslow's) $126 £75

A silver and enamelled medallion of The Great Eastern Railway, dated 1922. (Onslow's) $36 £22

A silver shield-shaped free pass, inscribed Lambourn Valley Railway. (Onslow's) $470 £280

To London By Sleeper From Edinburgh (Waverley) to King's Cross, by Alexeieff, published by L.N.E.R., quad royal, 40 x 50in. (Onslow's) $4,960 £3,200

L. & Y.Ry. Victoria Station, Manchester, porcelain door plate with two door knobs. (Onslow's) $201 £120

'Mons Meg', Edinburgh, Travel
By L.N.E.R. East Coast Route,
by Frank Newbould, quad
royal, 40 x 50in. (Onslow's)
$682 £440

S.E.R., square front handlamp, stripped. (Onslow's)
$50 £30

L.N.E.R. Redcar, by Frank
Newbould, quad royal, 40
x 50in. (Onslow's)
$232 £150

L.N.E.R. The Norfolk Coast,
by Picking, quad royal, 40 x
50in. (Onslow's) $620 £400

Caledonian Railway, enamel
double sided trespass sign,
dated 1st August 1893, 17 x
22in. (Onslow's) $100 £60

L.M.S. Lowestoft Through
Express Services From The
North and Midlands, by F.
Newbould, quad royal, 40 x
50in. (Onslow's) $387 £250

L.N.E.R. North Berwick, by
Frank Newbould, quad royal,
40 x 50in. (Onslow's)
$728 £470

G.W.R., handlamp, the glass
and burner inscribed G.W.R.
(Onslow's) $142 £85

Brighton Works 1902, cast
brass builder's plate, 6½in.
long. (Onslow's) $520 £310

S.R. 'The 'Golden Arrow' Service and 'The Motorist' Service Leaving Dover, 1932, by K. Shoesmith, quad royal, 40 x 50in. (Onslow's) $387 £250

M.R., handlamp, later burner, 12½in. high. (Onslow's) $42 £25

L.M.S. Spend A Day At Port Sunlight . . ., 1932, by A. Lambart, quad royal, 40 x 50in. (Onslow's) $465 £300

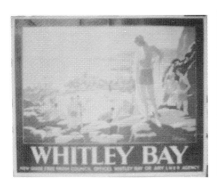

L.N.E.R. Whitley Bay, by Littlejohns, quad royal, 40 x 50in. (Onslow's) $434 £280

L.M.S. Luggage in Advance, double royal, 40 x 25in. (Onslow's) $403 £260

L.M.S. The Irish Mails, by Bryan De Grineau, quad royal, 40 x 50in. (Onslow's) $279 £180

L. & N.W. Railway No. 650 Claughton Class Lord Rathmore dropping down from Grayrigg at Okenholme 1922, by Gerald Broom, signed, on board, 23½ x 35½in. (Onslow's) $420 £250

North Eastern Railway, guard's wood whistle. (Onslow's) $20 £12

G.W.R. King Class James I, by Vic Welch, signed, gouache on board, 12½ x 19½in. (Onslow's) $117 £70

M.R. Blackwell to Barnt Green, second class 1874. (Onslow's) $117 £70

Newington Road to Dalston Junction, second class 1867. (Onslow's) $487 £290

St. Austell to Bodmin Road, Express Train, second class, reverse overprinted C.R. Express. (Onslow's) $218 £130

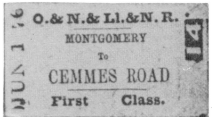

O. & N. & L.1. & N.R. Montgomery to Cemmes Road, first class 1876. (Onslow's) $218 £130

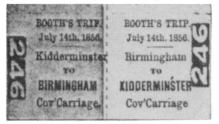

Booth's Trip, July 14th, 1856, Kidderminster to Birmingham Cov' Carriage. (Onslow's) $58 £35

Cornwall Railway Penryn to Par by ordinary train, second class 1879. (Onslow's) $100 £60

New Cross to Blackfriars, second class 1866, overprinted with the letter B. (Onslow's) $168 £100

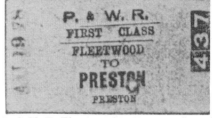

P. & W. R. Fleetwood to Preston, first class 1878. (Onslow's) $117 £70

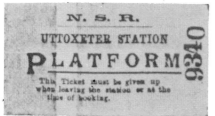

N.S.R. Platform Uttoxeter Station and three others. (Onslow's) $252 £150

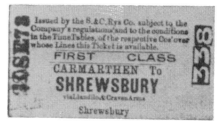

S. & C.R. Carmarthen to Shrewsbury, first class 1878. (Onslow's) $100 £60

Bryan Ferry, 'Don't Stop the Dance' promotional poster, Limited Edition 52/100, signed, 97 x 66cm.
(Phillips) $701   £420

A black peaked 'Boy' cap, decorated by Boy George, together with a publicity photograph of Boy George. (Phillips) $3,674 £2,200

Elvis Presley, signed colour photo of Elvis, 10 x 8in. (Onslow's) $182 £110

A black, turquoise, green and purple fluorescent body suit worn by Kim Wilde on her video for 'The Second Time'. (Phillips) $300 £180

The Who, John Entwhistle's Guild 'Brown' solid brass guitar, Serial No. 102232, with case. (Phillips)
$2,171 £1,300

Ivor Novello Award Certificate of Honour, 1974/75, presented to Mike Batt, The Wombles. (Phillips)
$250 £150

A presentation silver disc for 'Blondes Have More Fun', 1978, presented to Rod Stewart by B.P.I. for U.K. sales of £150,000. (Phillips)
$1,169 £700

Paul McCartney Live Aid, 1985, a 20 x 16in. silver print, Limited Edition 2/3, signed, signed on the front by David Bailey. (Phillips)
$2,505 £1,500

Status Quo, a presentation silver disc 'Blue for You', 1976, presented to Phonogram Ltd. for U.K. sales of more than £100,000. (Phillips) $567 £340

Phil Collins Live Aid, 1985, a 20 x 16in. silver print, Limited Edition 8/8, signed by David Bailey on the reverse. (Phillips)$1,252 £750

Elvis Presley: 'I'm left, You're right, She's Gone/Baby lets Play House', 45 rpm record on the Sun label, (Sun 217), circa May 1955. (Phillips) $411 £220

A good signed publicity photograph of The Beatles, 21.5 x 15cm. (Phillips) $673 £360

A superb pair of Michael Jackson's purple lace-up dancing shoes, heavily studded with purple glass stones. (Phillips) $7,480 £4,000

The Who, Pete Townshend's Fender Telecaster three-colour sunburst guitar AO25167 Japanese. (Phillips)$2,338 £1,400

Hot Chocolate, Errol Brown's Yamaha six-string guitar FG 140, with etched titles of the band's hit songs on the front. (Phillips) $2,004 £1,200

An extremely rare drawing by Michael Jackson in blue ball point pen entitled 'Your Girlfriend' and signed, 18 x 11.5cm. (Phillips) $1,870 £1,000

A poster, John's Children, pro-duced by Track Records, to promote a new single 'Des-demona', released in 1967, 51cm. sq. (Phillips) $66 £40

An excellent handwritten letter from Jimi Hendrix to a member of the Universal Autograph Collector's Club, written in red biro, circa 1967. (Phillips) $2,992 £1,600

A black and white photograph of Elvis Presley, signed on the front, 10 x 18in. (Phillips) $374 £200

Led Zeppelin: John Bonham's Ludwig drum set, together with a charity ball invitation, signed on the back by John Bonham, circa July 1978. (Phillips) $5,610 £3,000

The Rolling Stones: Keith Richard. An original black and white photograph, mounted, framed and glazed, 43 x 37cm. (Phillips) $121 £65

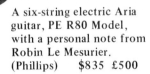

M.T.V. 'Man on the Moon' video music award, awarded to Jack Sonni, rhythm guitarist for Dire Straits, for Best Video of the Year, 'Money for Nothing', 31cm. high. (Phillips) $634 £380

A six-string electric Aria guitar, PE R80 Model, with a personal note from Robin Le Mesurier. (Phillips) $835 £500

A pair of Michael Jackson's white lace-up dance shoes, each signed twice in blue ink. (Phillips) $7,106 £3,800

Bee Gees, a presentation gold disc for the single 'Night Fever', presented to Polydor Ltd. to recognise the sale in the U.K. of more than 500,000 copies. (Phillips) $634 £380

Elvis Presley's full length Eastern style green and gold bedrobe. (Phillips) $2,992 £1,600

John Lennon and Yoko Ono, a promotional poster 'Hair Peace' for 'Wedding Album', released in 1969, 79cm. sq. (Phillips) $267 £160

Late 19th century Anatolian Yastik, possibly Mudjur, 2ft. 10in. x 1ft.10in. (Robt. W. Skinner Inc.) $375 £223

Late 19th/early 20th century Kazak rug, the brick-red field with four deep and pale blue abrashed medallions, 8ft. x 4ft.7in. (Robt. W. Skinner Inc.) $1,800 £1,072

Late 19th century Serapi carpet, 8ft.7in. x 11ft.8in. (Robt. W. Skinner Inc.) $6,000 £3,571

Late 19th/early 20th century cloudband Kazak rug, 8ft.8in. x 4ft.1in. (Robt. W. Skinner Inc.) $1,900 £1,067

A Heriz carpet, the ivory field set with stepped medallion, 135 x 175in. (Giles Haywood) $1,910 £1,000

A Shirvan rug with short kilim strip at each end, (slight overall wear), 10ft.2in. x 4ft.6in. (Christie's) $1,752 £990

An Agra rug, the magenta field woven with a palmette trellis in pink, blue, green and cream, 7ft.7in. x 5ft.1in. (Lawrence Fine Art) $1,566 £880

A Kelim, the tomato red field woven with a stylised blue tree bearing lozenge flowers, 12ft. x 5ft.10in. (Lawrence Fine Art) $391 £220

A 19th century needlework carpet with coloured geometric foliage on a black ground, 14ft.7in. x 9ft. (Christie's) $25,454 £14,300

Late 19th/early 20th century Heriz carpet, 7ft.10in. x 11ft. (Robt. W. Skinner Inc.) $2,400 £1,428

A Soumac small carpet, the tomato red field with four elongated lozenge medallions and half medallions in green, cream and magenta, 9ft.3in. x 6ft.3in. (Lawrence Fine Art) $1,135 £638

Marion Dorn, an abstract small carpet woven in khaki and pale blue green, 8ft. x 4ft. 2in. (Lawrence Fine Art) $783 £440

Late 19th century Kazak rug, Southwest Caucasus, 7ft.11in. x 4ft.5in. (Robt. W. Skinner Inc.) $750 £421

A hooked rug, the beige field centering a brown spotted dog, dated 1892, America, 27in. wide, 53in. long. (Robt. W. Skinner Inc.) $275 £154

A Kazak runner, the indigo field with five sunburst medallions, 44 x 118in. (Hy. Duke & Son) $1,980 £1,100

A Hamadan small carpet, the camel field with rows of beige boteh and centred by a blue lozenge pole medallion, 10ft. 1in. x 5ft.7in. (Lawrence Fine Art) $626 £352

A Kazak Karatchoph rug, the tomato red field woven with a cream octagon within diced spandrels, dated 1862, 4ft.5in. x 4ft.9in. (Lawrence Fine Art) $12,139 £6,820

A Tabriz rug, the honey field woven with a flower filled vase within mille fleur spandrels, 6ft.6in. x 4ft.7in. (Lawrence Fine Art) $1,958 £1,100

A Shirvan Prayer rug, the saffron mihrab with a trellis design with palmettes and ivory arch, 1.35m. x 93cm. (Phillips) $1,820 £1,110

A large Soumac carpet with burgundy field, 11ft.10in. x 9ft. (Christie's)
  $53,793 £33,002

One of a pair of Kashan column and vase design Persian carpets, 80 x 52in., circa 1930. (Giles Haywood)
  $574 £350

A Malayir rug, the ivory field with palmettes and floral sprays, with a short kilim strip at one end, 6ft. 3in. x 3ft.4in. (Christie's)
  $2,868 £1,760

A Shiraz carpet, the indigo field scattered with a variety of birds and floral motifs, 10ft.3in. x 7ft.6in. (Christie's) $3,048 £1,870

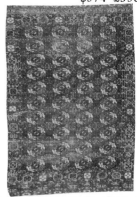

A Tekke carpet, the shaded sang-de-boeuf field with four columns of linked Tekke guls divided by minor cruciform motifs, 8ft.1in. x 5ft.9in. (Christie's) $1,234 £748

Caucasian three medallion Persian carpet, 93 x 52in., circa 1930. (Giles Haywood)
  $459 £280

A Malayir rug, the indigo field with a variety of stylised floral motifs, 11ft. 3in. x 4ft.5in. (Christie's)
  $3,048 £1,870

An antique East Anatolian part cotton and metal thread Prayer Kilim, 7ft. 2in. x 4ft.7in. (Christie's)
  $1,633 £990

A Hereke rug, the ivory field with eau-de-nil tracery vine around a turquoise flower-head lozenge, 5ft.11in. x 4ft. (Christie's) $2,178 £1,320

An antique Kuba rug, 5ft.8in. x 3ft.3in. (Christie's)
$2,087 £1,265

A Kazak rug, the brick field with three hooked medallions, 6ft.9in. x 4ft.8in. (Woolley & Wallis)
$960 £600

A Shirvan Prayer rug, the indigo field with rows of alternately facing serrated boteh, 5ft. x 3ft.5in. (Christie's) $1,361 £825

One of a pair of Kashan rugs of prayer influence, 2.10 x 1.38m. and 2.11 x 1.37m. (Phillips)
$4,264 £2,600

A Kuba rug with ivory field and a short braided strip at each end, 5ft.4in. x 2ft.11in. (Christie's) $1,724 £1,045

A Konagkend rug, the indigo field with stylised ivory floral lattice in a broad indigo stylised kufic border, 5ft.1in. x 4ft.1in. (Christie's)
$1,016 £616

A Malayir rug, the indigo field with herati pattern and small stylised birds, 10ft. x 5ft.2in. (Christie's) $1,524 £935

A Kirman rug with a short kilim strip at each end, one end with an inscription 'Moaven al-Tajar, 6ft.4in. x 4ft.4in. (Christie's)
$4,123 £2,530

A Fereghan rug, 6ft.4in. x 4ft.7in. (Christie's) $2,510 £1,540

Early 20th century Yomud Asmalyk, the pale ivory field with a repeating rust, coral, red and turquoise trellis, 2ft.2in. x 3ft.10in. (Robt. W. Skinner Inc.) $325 £203

Late 19th century kuba rug, East Caucasus, 3ft. 9in. x 3ft.2in. (Robt. W. Skinner Inc.) $550 £343

A Qashqai Kilim, the brick-red field with diagonal rows of multi-coloured radiating hooked lozenges, 9ft.10in. x 5ft.2in. (Christie's) $1,179 £715

A hand-knotted rug attributed to Henry van de Velde, 146.5cm. long, 95.9cm. wide. (Christie's) $1,533 £935

A Shirvan rug with a broad kilim strip at each end, dated AH1321 (1905AD), 10ft.7in. x 5ft.5in. (Christie's) $1,972 £1,210

A Bergama rug, the rust field with a stepped ivory and cruciform central panel and stellar cochineal medallions, 1.85 x 1.44m. (Phillips) $984 £600

A Perepedil rug, the indigo field with traditional 'wurma' motifs, stylised peacocks and all over angular designs, 1.56 x 1.06m. (Phillips) $2,624 £1,600

A Herez carpet, the terra-cotta field with green palmette pendant indigo medallion with all over angular designs, 3.76 x 2.78m. (Phillips) $8,200 £5,000

Late 19th century Soumak bagface in shades of blue, turquoise and camel, 1ft.7in. x 1ft.8in. (Robt. W. Skinner Inc.) $300 £187

A Karabagh Kilim, the black field with three large bouquets surrounded by sprays with perching birds and stylised human figures, 12ft.1in. x 5ft.2in. (Christie's) $1,542 £935

A Mahal carpet, the ivory field with an all over design with palmettes, lanceolate leaves and panels, 4.38 x 3.42m. (Phillips) $4,920 £3,000

A Melas rug, the indigo field with three large brick lobed and hooked medallions, 6ft.5in. x 3ft.9in. (Woolley & Wallis) $544 £340

A 19th century rectangular hooked rug, American, 2ft. 7in. x 5ft.2in. (Robt. W. Skinner Inc.) $1,100 £687

Late 19th century Bordjalou kazak, 6ft.2in. x 3ft.7in. (Robt. W. Skinner Inc.) $400 £250

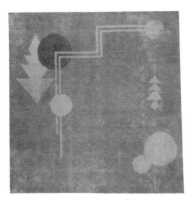

Early 20th century Heriz carpet, N.W. Persia, 11ft. 7in. x 7ft.9in. (Robt. W. Skinner Inc.) $3,700 £2,312

A hand-woven Art Deco carpet, the powder-pink field with circle and triangle motif, in beige, emerald green and eau de nile, 273 x 296cm. (Christie's) $1,804 £1,100

Early 20th century Heriz carpet, N.W. Persia, 11ft. 7in. x 8ft.1in. (Robt. W. Skinner Inc.) $2,700 £1,687

A Kashan pictorial Natanz rug, silk pile, circa 1920, 4ft.6in. x 6ft.6in. (Peter Wilson) $1,539 £950

A Kashan rug with central medallion on a deep pink field within a deep blue floral border, 6ft. x 4ft. (Lots Road Chelsea Auction Galleries) $1,377 £820

One of a pair of Kirman rugs, the ivory field with centre medallion and three line border, 6ft.2in. x 3ft.11in. (Worsfolds) $672 £400

An Agra rug, the cream field woven with palmettes and floral sprays, 7ft.8in. x 4ft. 11in. (Lawrence Fine Art) $8,811 £4,950

A Louis Philippe Aubusson rug woven with floral sprays on a chocolate ground, 6ft.1in. x 6ft.6in. (Christie's) $4,699 £2,640

Late 19th century Bidjar rug, Northwest Persia, 5ft.2in. x 8ft.6in. (Robt. W. Skinner Inc.) $1,900 £1,067

A Kazak runner, the madder field with four pale green medallions, 49in. wide, 142in. long. (Hy. Duke & Son) $468 £260

Late 19th/early 20th century Bidjar carpet, Northwest Persia, with red Herati filled field, 9ft. x 12ft. (Robt. W. Skinner Inc.) $7,500 £4,213

Early 20th century Heriz carpet, Northwest Persia, 10ft.4in. x 8ft. (Robt. W. Skinner Inc.) $3,100 £1,741

Late 19th/early 20th century East Caucasian rug, 5ft.5in. x 4ft.3in. (Robt. W. Skinner Inc.) $1,700 £955

Mid 19th century Aubusson carpet woven with a central floral spray on a celadon ground, 6ft.8½in. x 6ft.4½in. (Christie's) $5,874 £3,300

A Karabagh Kilim, the black ground with two bouquets in a floral spray frame, 13ft.8in. x 6ft.2in. (Christie's) $3,894 £2,200

Late 19th century Sewan Kazak, Southwest Caucasus, 5ft.5in. x 6ft.11in. (Robt. W. Skinner Inc.) $1,600 £898

A 19th century needlework carpet, in mainly autumnal shades of a beige ground, 6ft.4½in. x 6ft.7in. (Christie's) $17,622 £9,900

A wool pile carpet, signed on reverse 'Orendi', circa 1900-20, 7ft.7in. by 10ft.6in. (Robt. W. Skinner Inc.) $4,500 £2,432

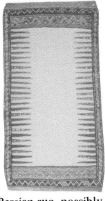

A Persian rug, possibly Shiraz, the camel flat weave field with brown finger indents, 5ft.6in. x 3ft.1in. (Lawrence Fine Art) $744 £418

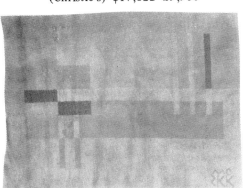

Edward McKnight Kauffer, an abstract rug woven in shades of brown, yellow and blue, 5ft.3in. x 3ft.10in. (Lawrence Fine Art) $783 £440

A Caucasian Kilim, the shaded blue field with diagonal rows of stepped lozenges, 9ft.8in. x 5ft.1in. (Christie's) $428 £242

665

A needlework sampler, 'Sina Halls Sampler Wrought at Wallingford, August 10, 1811', worked in a variety of stitches on moss-green linsey-woolsey ground, 15¾ x 17½in. (Robt. W. Skinner Inc.) $14,000 £8,333

A sampler 'Wrought by Harriot Wethrell May Aged 10 years, Plymouth Massachusetts, June 10th 1830', 16¼ x 16½in. (Robt. W. Skinner Inc.) $1,900 £1,130

A mid 19th century Armenian needlework sampler by Souepile Kedeasian, the linen ground embroidered in red and pink threads, 45 x 58cm. (Phillips) $160 £90

A needlework sampler by Eliz. Matilda Whitcombe aged 11, 1846, embroidered in coloured silks on a wool ground, 43 x 32cm. (Phillips) $569 £320

Needlework sampler, 'Rhoda Roger's Sampler wrought in the 11 years of her age 1804', Mass. (Robt. W. Skinner Inc.) $6,000 £3,370

A mid 19th century needlework sampler by Sarah Redfern, 1.04 x 0.77m., framed and glazed. (Phillips) $890 £500

Needlework picture, entitled 'The Beggar's Petition', by Sarah Hadley, 1841, 24 x 24in. (Robt. W. Skinner Inc.) $2,800 £1,573

An 18th century sampler, by Kezi Ladell, July 11, 1799, 37 x 21cm. (David Lay) $358 £200

A needlework family register, 'Wrought by Hannah Winchell, 1822', 22½ x 23½in. (Robt. W. Skinner Inc.) $2,600 £1,547

A needlework picture, signed Anne Oram and dated 1824, worked in polychrome threads on natural ground, 10 x 12in. (Christie's) $440 £248

An early 18th century needlework sampler, the linen ground embroidered in coloured silks, 46 x 21cm. (Phillips)
$1,513 £850

A needlework sampler made by 'Anna Braddock . . . A work wrought in the 14th year of her age, 1826', 22½ x 26in. (Robt. W. Skinner Inc.) $38,000 £22,619

Late 18th century framed needlework sampler, by Charlotte Richardson 13 years, Dec. 1786, American, 17 x 20in. (Robt. W. Skinner Inc.) $1,500 £937

A needlework sampler 'Susannah Styles finished this work in the 10 years of her age 1800', worked in silk yarns on wool ground, 13in. square. (Robt. W. Skinner Inc.)
$1,000 £595

Sampler with alphabet verse and figures of plants and birds, dated 1824, 17 x 13in. (Lots Road Chelsea Auction Galleries)
$501 £300

A needlework sampler by Mary Ann Cash, 1801, the linen ground worked in coloured silks, 37 x 30cm. (Phillips) $356 £200

A 17th century needlwork sampler by Anna Stone, the linen ground worked in pink, green and blue silk threads, 41 x 19cm. (Phillips)
$1,176 £700

Needlework sampler, 'Betsey Stevens, her sampler wrought in 10th year of her age AD 1796', silk yarns on linen, 15 x 16in. (Robt. W. Skinner Inc.) $3,000 £1,685

Folkestone Pier and Lift Co. 1888 £10 shares, vignette of Queen Victoria, Red seal. (Phillips) $51 £32

The Mediterranean Electric Telegraph, 1854, Bearer certificate for 1 x £10 share. (Phillips) $58 £36

Waveney Steam Drift Fishing Co. Ltd. 1909-18. Ord. £1 shares. (Phillips) $72 £45

The London & Brighton Railway Co. 1847, fixed interest bearer certificate No. 4 for £50 at 5%. (Phillips) $939 £580

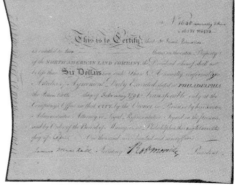

Pullman's Palace Car Company 1898, $100 shares. Vignette of St. Pancras Station and The Pullman Car Works, Detroit. (Phillips)
                    $98 £60

The North American Land Company, 1795, two shares. Handsigned by Robt. Morris, a signatory of the Declaration of Independence. (Phillips) $518 £320

A pair of glace black kid slippers, embroidered with bouquets of flowers, trimmed with pale blue silk, circa 1840. (Christie's) $924 £528

A pair of shoes of mustard coloured ribbed silk with 3in. heels, English, circa 1770, inscribed Miss Alsorne. (Christie's) $2,117 £1,210

A pair of glace black kid slippers embroidered with flowers in coloured silks on the front and heel, lined and trimmed with pink silk, circa 1840. (Christie's) $962 £550

A pair of ladies' high heeled shoes of crimson damask, trimmed with gold lace with 2in. heels, 9in. long, early 18th century. (Christie's) $1,455 £770

A pair of ladies' high heeled shoes of ivory silk, circa 1730. (Christie's) $3,118 £1,650

A pair of early 18th century lady's shoes of duck-egg-blue silk worked with gold thread embroidery and sequin decoration. (Phillips) $2,670 £1,500

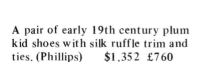

A pair of early 19th century plum kid shoes with silk ruffle trim and ties. (Phillips) $1,352 £760

A pair of mid 19th century boots of brown and white leather, lined with pink kid, and a pair of white kid boots. (Christie's) $1,540 £880

A pair of lady's shoes of dark blue morocco, with low wedge heels, circa 1790. (Christie's) $1,663 £880

SILVER

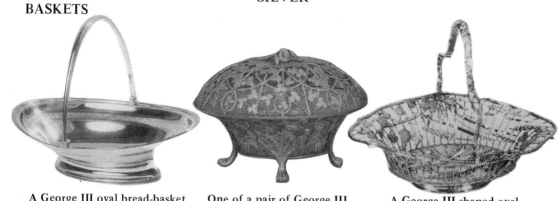

A George III oval bread-basket on spreading foot, by Henry Nutting or Hannah Northcote, 1801, 14in. long, 26ozs. (Christie's) $2,024 £1,100

One of a pair of George III silver gilt oval dessert baskets and covers, by Wm. Pitts, 1803, with frosted glass liners, 12½in. long, 95oz. (Christie's) $15,147 £9,350

A George III shaped oval bread basket, on moulded oval foot, by John Vere and William Lutwyche, 1766, 14in. long, 32ozs. (Christie's)$5,348 £2,860

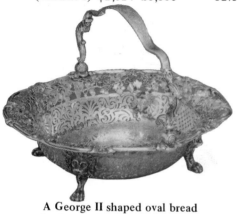

A George II shaped oval bread basket on four lion's mask and claw feet, the handle engraved with a crest, by Peter Archambo, 1741, 14½in. long, 63ozs. (Christie's) $11,313 £6,050

A Wiener Werkstatte electro-plated basket, designed by Josef Hoffmann, 26cm. high. (Christie's) $1,623 £990

A George II shaped oval bread basket, by Benjamin Godfrey, 1741, 11¾in. long, 51oz. (Christie's) $12,474 £7,700

A George III beaded and pierced oval swing-handle cake basket, London 1777, 13in. 21.75oz. (Christie's) $1,275 £682

A pierced and engraved fruit basket, by Robert Hennell, London, 1788, 14in. long. (Brown & Merry) $3,005 £1,650

A George III oval cake basket, by Michael Plummer, 1793, 36.9cm., 24.6oz. (Lawrence Fine Art) $1,851 £990

A George III oval bread basket, by William Plummer, 1782, 15in. long, 42oz. (Christie's) $9,266 £5,720

A George III oval cake basket, the spreading foot and rim pierced with slats, by Robert Hennell, 1787, 14¼in. long, 25ozs. (Christie's) $2,944 £1,600

George III oblong cake basket with reeded swing handle, Dublin, 1806. (Reeds Rains) $734 £440

A George III oval cake basket on moulded foot, by Paul Storr, 1799, 14¾in. long, 34oz. (Christie's) $6,930 £3,850

A cake basket with pierced foliate handle, by Udall & Ballou, circa 1900-10, 11in. high overall, 14¾in. long, 49oz. (Christie's) $2,860 £1,729

A Victorian oval cake basket, pierced fret sides in George III style, by Henry Hyde, London, 1859. (Woolley & Wallis) $1,353 £820

A George III shaped oval bread basket, by William Kidney, 1745, 15in. long, 83oz. (Christie's) $13,860 £7,700

A George III sugar basket with concave corners, reeded borders and swing handle, by John Robins, London, 1796, 6¾in., 8.1/3oz. (Dreweatt Neate) $935 £500

A George III shaped oval bread basket, on rim foot, with openwork sides, by John Vere and William Lutwyche, 1765, 13¼in. long, 29ozs. (Christie's) $3,291 £1,760

SILVER

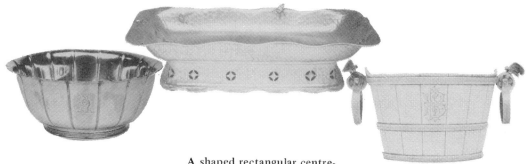

A George II circular fluted bowl, by Benjamin Godfrey, 1739, 6¾in. diam., 12oz. 7dwt. (Christie's) $4,719 £2,860

A shaped rectangular centre-piece bowl, by Tiffany & Co., 1878-91, 4½in. high, 18.3/8in. wide, 8½in. deep, 67oz.10dwt. (Christie's) $15,400 £9,310

A nut bowl, in the form of a barrel-stave bucket, by Gorham Manuf. Co., 1869, 2¼in. high, 4¾in. wide, 3oz. (Christie's) $418 £252

A George I Irish plain circular Monteith bowl, by David King, Dublin, 1715, 10¾in. high, 63oz. (Christie's) $39,930 £24,200

A George I plain circular sugar bowl and pear-shaped cream jug, by George G. Jones, 1726, 15oz.15dwt. (Christie's) $12,830 £7,920

Large plated punch bowl by Viners with embossed decoration. (G. A. Key) $78 £45

A yachting trophy punch bowl, by Gorham Manuf. Co., 1884, the interior gilt, 9¼in. high, 18¼in. wide, 117oz. (Christie's) $41,800 £25,272

A Monteith bowl, by Samuel Kirk & Son, Baltimore, 1880-90, 5½in. high, 9½in. diam., 25oz. (Christie's) $1,430 £864

A George II Irish small circular punch bowl, by Robert Calderwood, Dublin, 1732, 7.5/8in. diam., 23oz. (Christie's) $12,705 £7,700

BOWLS

An Edwardian hammered sugar bowl, in Art Nouveau style, by A. E. Jones, Birmingham, 1908, 4¼in. diam., 4.5oz. (Hobbs & Chambers) $165 £100

An Italian white metal punch bowl, by Gannazzi, stamped 800 (circa 1940), 46.9cm. diam., 1.464kg. (Christie's) $2,886 £1,760

A sterling silver bowl, by Arthur Stone, 1910-37, 5.3/8in. diam., 7 troy oz. (Robt. W. Skinner Inc.) $1,300 £702

A Georg Jensen footed bowl, stamped marks GJ 925.S 4, 7.6cm. high, 129.2gr. (Christie's) $613 £374

A George I sugar bowl and cover, possibly by James Goodwin, London, 1719, 4in. diam. (Woolley & Wallis) $3,712 £2,250

A Georg Jensen bowl and cover, stamped with C. F. Heise assay mark 100B and with London import marks for 1925, 11.9cm. high, 242gr. (Christie's) $1,172 £715

A large two-handled circular bowl, by Elkington & Co., Birmingham, 1908, 13½in. diam., 100oz. (Christie's) $2,673 £1,650

A silver gilt bowl, by Gorham Manuf. Co., Providence, 1884, 3¾in. high, 6oz. (Christie's) $1,210 £731

A bowl, circular with flaring rim, by Josiah Austin, Boston, circa 1750-70, 3in. high, 5¾in. diam., 6oz. (Christie's) $14,300 £8,645

A Victorian casket of square bombe form, by S. S. Drew and E. Drew of J. Drew & Sons, 1890, 20.5cm. (Lawrence Fine Art) $1,028 £550

Early 20th century German silver singing bird box, 4in. long. (Christie's) $2,640 £1,508

A silver cigar box, cedar lined, double container, central cutter and tools with spirit light, London, 1899. (Brown & Merry) $1,055 £580

A George III silver gilt circular box and cover, by Joseph Ash, 1810, 4½in. diam., 10oz.16dwt. (Christie's) $3,385 £2,090

A small silver spice box in the form of a skull, the hinged back revealing six compartments, ¾in. wide. (Christie's) $544 £330

One of a pair of George III silver gilt oval toilet boxes, by D. Smith and R. Sharp, 1783, 7.5/8in. long, 55oz. (Christie's) $20,872 £12,650

A Victorian fisherman's creel vesta case, the interior with Essex crystal depicting two trout, by Thos. Johnson, 1882, 5.5cm. long. (Phillips) $3,062 £1,750

An Arts & Crafts hammered silver box, by Chas. Horner, Birmingham hallmarks for 1902, 15.3cm. long, 5oz. 12dwt. (Christie's) $721 £440

A French silver gilt casket of bombe triangular form on four scroll feet, by Lhote, the miniatures by Paillet, 7½in. wide. (Christie's) $3,993 £2,420

BOXES

A silver gilt box, the lid inset with an enamel plaque, Birmingham hallmarks for 1922 and maker's monogram SB, 9cm. long, 2oz.17dwt. gross wt. (Christie's)

$252 £165

A box, the lid pierced and embossed with figures, a carriage and horses, bells, scrolls and flowers, by Wm. Comyns, London, 1903, 5¾in. long. (Dreweatt Neate)

$336 £180

A 19th century Swiss shaped oblong silver gilt and enamel singing bird box, the movement by Chas. Bruguier, 3½in. long. (Christie's) $5,082 £3,080

A Dutch silver gilt shaped square tobacco box and cover, by Pieter Meeter, Leewarden, 1770, 5in. sq., 20oz. (Christie's)

$7,128 £4,400

A French circular blonde tortoiseshell box, the cover with a grisaille miniature of Napoleon, Marie-Louise and the King of Rome, circa 1815, 2¾in. diam. (Christie's)

$907 £550

An Arts & Crafts rectangular silver box, by W. Hutton & Sons Ltd., London hallmarks for 1901, 11.1cm. long, 11oz. 4dwt. gross weight. (Christie's) $396 £242

A sterling silver box with pierced enamel hinged cover, Worcester, Mass., 1925, 3¾in. wide. (Robt. W. Skinner Inc.)

$475 £256

A German silver and enamel singing bird box, struck with English import hallmarks for 1926, 4in. long. (Christie's)

$3,300 £1,885

A green stained box, by George Anton Scheidt, with pierced and chased white metal mount of scrolling tendrils, 6.3cm. long. (Christie's) $396 £242

CANDELABRA

One of two plated candelabra with two lights on swept reeded arms, not matching. (G. A. Key) $141 £80

One of a pair of five-light candelabra, by Tiffany & Co., New York, 1885-91, 18¾in. high, 133oz.10dwt. (Christie's) $18,700 £11,306

Hallmarked silver three-light candelabrum, Birmingham Assay. (G. A. Key) $175 £100

One of a pair of George II two-light candelabra, by Wm. Cripps, 1750, the branches unmarked, the branch sockets and drip-pans probably later replacements. (Christie's) $18,150 £11,000

A pair of George I style three light candelabra, each on hexagonal base with scroll branches, by Richard Comyns, 1964, 71ozs, 11¼in. high. (Christie's) $2,879 £1,540

One of a pair of George III cast candelabra, by Wm. Eaton, London, 1816, 380oz., 51cm. high. (Wellington Salerooms) $4,032 £2,400

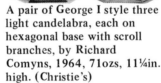

One of a pair of ormolu twin-light candelabra of Louis XVI style, 13in. high. (Christie's) $2,204 £1,320

A pair of George III three-light candelabra and two matching candlesticks, by John Scofield, 1792 and 1795, 19½in. high, weight of branches 96oz. (Christie's) $71,280 £44,000

One of a pair of large five-light candelabra with four detachable scroll branches, 30¼in. high. (Christie's) $3,630 £2,200

CANDELABRA

One of a pair of Georg Jensen five-branch candelabra, designed by Harald Nielsen, 40cm. high. (Christie's) $25,256 £15,400

A pair of Old Sheffield plate three-light candelabra, each on circular base and with fluted tapering column, by Matthew Boulton and Co., circa 1815, 21in. high. (Christie's)
$1,840   £1,000

A massive Victorian ten-light candelabrum, by John Mortimer and John S. Hunt, circa 1843, 38in. high. (Christie's)
$82,280 £44,000

A Victorian five-light candelabrum, by Robert Garrard, 1841, 30½in. high, 254oz. (Christie's) $7,260 £4,400

A pair of three light candelabra, each on oval fluted base, with two reeded branches and central light, Birmingham, 1950, 18½in. high. (Christie's)
$3,291 £1,760

One of a pair of George III three-light candelabra, by Richard Cooke, 1800 and 1804, 16¾in. high, 128oz. (Christie's) $16,929 £10,450

One of a pair of late 19th century German cast rococo style seven-light candelabra, by J. D. Schleissner & Sons, Hanau, 54cm. high, 234.5oz. (Phillips) $6,125 £3,500

Pair of Sheffield plated three-light candelabra, 55cm. high. (Lawrence Fine Art)
$2,159 £1,155

One of two Victorian ten-light candelabra, by Barnard Bros, 1846 and C. F. Hancock, 1895, 32¼in. high, 458oz. (Christie's) $21,384 £13,200

677

Two of four George IV table candlesticks, by J. & T. Settle, Sheffield, 1824, 11¾in. high. (Christie's) $4,455 £2,750

Pair of silver candlesticks, decorated in the Adam style, by John Round & Sons Ltd., Sheffield, 1902, 6½in. tall. (G. A. Key) $676 £410

Two of four George II table candlesticks, by John Cafe, 1747, 9¾in. high, 84oz. (Christie's) $8,910 £5,500

A pair of George III Irish table candlesticks, by A. Boxwell, Dublin, 1781, 10½in. high, 45oz. (Christie's) $3,742 £2,310

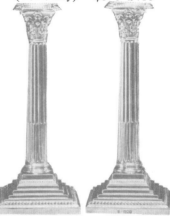

Pair of late Victorian candlesticks, formed as Corinthian columns, by Charles Stuart Harris, London, 1898, 29cm. high, weighted. (Osmond Tricks) $1,496 £800

A pair of Queen Anne tapering baluster candlesticks, by Wm. Turell, 1713, 19.5cm. high, 30oz. (with later nozzles). (Phillips) $25,375 £14,500

A pair of George III table candlesticks on square bases with detachable nozzles, by Jonathan Alleine, 1777, 10½in. high, 56oz. (Christie's) $6,897 £4,180

A pair of Louis XV Provincial candlesticks, 8.5in. high, Lille, circa 1765. (Woolley & Wallis) $4,125 £2,500

A pair of Victorian, Adam style Corinthian column table candlesticks, by H. Wilkinson of Sheffield, London, 1871, 13in. high. (Hy. Duke & Son) $1,692 £940

CANDLESTICKS

Two of a set of four George II cast candlesticks, by James Gould, 1738, two nozzles by J. Baddeley, 1821, 7¾in. high, 72oz. (Christie's)
$15,427   £9,350

Two of four George II table candlesticks, by Samuel Courtauld, 1757, 10¾in. high, 86oz. (Christie's)
$11,583 £7,150

A pair of James Dixon & Sons silver candlesticks, Sheffield hallmarks for 1904, 22cm. high. (Christie's) $1,262 £825

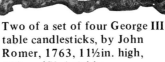

A pair of George III silver reeded and fluted column candlesticks, maker's mark I.P. & Co., John Parsons & Co., Sheffield, 1783, 11¼in. high. (Geering & Colyer)
$1,557   £875

Two of a set of four George III table candlesticks, by John Romer, 1763, 11½in. high, 139oz. (Christie's)
$22,687 £13,750

A pair of George IV table candlesticks, by S. C. Younge & Co., Sheffield, 1821, 11¾in. high. (Christie's) $2,851 £1,760

Two of a set of four George III Corinthian column candlesticks, by Emick Romer, 1762, 11½in. high. (Christie's) $9,801 £6,050

A pair of Old Sheffield plate candlesticks, designed to commemorate famous and contemporary British Admirals and their naval victories over the French during the late 18th century, 21cm. high. (Phillips)
$1,715 £980

Two of a set of four George II table candlesticks, by Wm. Cafe, 1757, 9¾in. high, 57oz. (Christie's) $25,839 £15,950

CASTERS

One of a pair of Dutch silver gilt octagonal pear-shaped casters, by Albert de Thomese, The Hague, 1733, 7¾in. high, 22oz. (Christie's) $4,989 £3,080

A pair of William IV vase-shaped casters, by Robert Hennell, London, 1834, 5¾in. high, 10.75oz. (Christie's) $712 £440

A Queen Anne sugar caster, by Simon Pantin I, 1709, 19cm. high, 10oz. (Phillips) $2,362 £1,350

One of a pair of George IV casters, by William, Charles and Henry Eley, 1824, 11.8cm. high. (Lawrence Fine Art) $925 £495

A set of three Charles II casters, the smaller casters, 1682, 6in. high, the larger 1683, 7in. high, 22oz. (Christie's) $71,280 £44,000

An amber, coral and malachite sugar caster, designed by Anton Rosen, stamped marks GJ 826 GJ, 19.9cm. high. (Christie's) $3,608 £2,200

An Edwardian plain baluster sugar caster, by Elkington & Co., Birmingham, 1909, 8in. high, 12oz. (Christie's) $249 £154

A set of three George I plain octagonal casters, by Edward Vincent, 1716, 5.7/8in. and 7½in. high, 27oz. (Christie's) $11,253 £6,820

An early 18th century style lighthouse sugar caster on a skirted foot, London, 1932, 7in. high, 9oz. (Christie's) $213 £132

CENTREPIECES

A WMF electroplated centrepiece with cut glass liner of
oval section modelled in full
relief with young lovers,
21in. across. (Christie's)
$1,017 £638

A sterling silver Martele oval
centrepiece, by Gorham Mfg.
Co., dated 1881 to 1906, 38
troy oz., 12¾in. long. (Robt.
W. Skinner Inc.)
$2,750 £1,636

A WMF plated centrepiece of
twin-handled boat-shape with
clear glass liner, 46cm. long.
(Phillips) $672 £420

A George III epergene with
four scroll branches each with
detachable dish, by Thomas
Pitts, 1766, 98oz. (Christie's)
$13,612 £8,250

A French centrepiece, by
Christofle, Paris, 24¾in. high,
8,947gr. (Christie's)
$13,860 £7,700

A Victorian plated centrepiece, the
simulated coral mount supported by
three dolphins, 11in. high, together
with a matching pair of single dolphin
centrepiece bases, 8in. high.
(Christie's) $541   £330

A baroque style centrepiece,
Sheffield, 1903, approx.
20in. high, approx. 158oz.
(Peter Wilson) $5,104 £2,900

A centrepiece bowl, by Gorham
Manuf. Co., 1880, 3.1/8in. high,
7½in. diam., 11oz.10dwt.
(Christie's) $605 £365

An Austro-Hungarian brightly
coloured silver gilt centrepiece
finely modelled as a crowned
ostrich, by Hermann Bohm,
Vienna, circa 1880, 15in. high.
(Christie's) $35,640 £19,800

CHAMBERSTICKS

SILVER

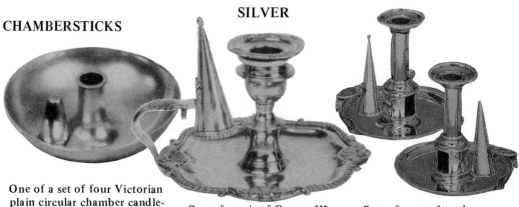

One of a set of four Victorian plain circular chamber candlesticks, by Robt. Garrard, 1878, 7in. diam., 63oz. (Christie's) $6,930 £3,850

One of a pair of George III shaped circular chamber candlesticks, by B. & J. Smith, 1808, the nozzles 1809, 6in. diam., 28oz. (Christie's) $3,762 £2,090

Part of a set of twelve George III circular chamber candlesticks, by M. Boulton, Birmingham 1803, 125oz. (Christie's) $30,294 £18,700

CHOCOLATE POTS

A George II plain cylindrical chocolate pot, on moulded spreading foot, by Isaac Cookson, Newcastle, 1731, 9¾in. high, 29ozs. (Christie's) $6,592 £3,520

A sterling silver Martele chocolate pot, by Gorham Mfg. Co., circa 1900, 11½in. high, 23 troy oz. (Robt. W. Skinner Inc.) $3,500 £2,083

A George II plain tapering cylindrical chocolate pot, on moulded circular foot, 1738, 9¼in. high, 24ozs. (Christie's) $3,496 £1,870

A George I Irish plain tapering cylindrical chocolate pot, by Thos. Williamson, Dublin, 1715, 11¼in. high, gross 32oz. (Christie's) $8,167 £4,950

A Louis XV plain pear-shaped chocolate pot, by Jean Gouel, Paris, 1734, 9.5/8in. high, weight without handle 840gr. (Christie's) $5,808 £3,520

A Queen Anne plain tapering cylindrical chocolate pot, by Robt. Timbrell and J. Bell I, 1709, 10¼in. high, gross 27oz. (Christie's) $6,336 £3,520

CIGARETTE CASES

A late Victorian cigarette case enamelled on cover with a coaching scene, by J. Wilmot, Birmingham, 1896. (Phillips) $509 £280

A good 19th century Russian niello cigarette case, cover depicting a despatch carrier being driven by a peasant in a horse-drawn carriage, Gustav Klingert, Moscow, 1888, 8.5cm. long. (Phillips) $618 £340

A Russian cigarette case with separate hinged vesta compartment, probably by Dmitri Nikolaiev, Moscow, circa 1890. (Phillips) $402 £230

CLARET JUGS

A William IV pear-shaped claret jug, by James Franklin, 1835, 11½in. high, 31oz. (Christie's) $1,692 £1,045

A pair of Victorian silver gilt mounted glass claret jugs, by W. & G. Sissons, Sheffield, 1872, 11in. high. (Christie's) $3,385 £2,090

A William IV large vase-shaped claret jug, 1837, maker's mark IW overstriking another, perhaps that of Chas. Fox, 17in. high, 65oz. (Christie's) $5,808 £3,520

One of a pair of French silver mounted glass claret jugs, circa 1880, 10¼in. high. (Christie's) $4,174 £2,530

One of a pair of Victorian silver mounted glass claret jugs, by Henry Wilkinson & Co., Sheffield, 1862, 9in. high. (Christie's) $3,920 £2,420

An early Victorian vase-shaped claret jug, by Henry Wilkinson & Co., Sheffield, 1838, 12¾in. high, 23oz. (Christie's) $1,692 £1,045

A pair of George III silver wine coasters, by Rebecca Emes and Edward Barnard, London, 1815, 6.1/8in. diam. (Christie's)
$2,420 £1,418

One of a pair of George III coasters, by Thos. Nash I, London, 1767, 12cm. diam. (Osmond Tricks)
$3,300 £2,000

A Victorian silver articulated two-division wine wagon, maker's mark R. & S., Robert & Slater, Sheffield 1859. (Geering Colyer)
$3,115 £1,750

One of a pair of George III decanter stands, by Rebecca Emes and E. Barnard, London, 1802. (Woolley & Wallis)
$2,310 £1,400

Two George III silver wine coasters, the first by S. Herbert & Co., London, 1765, the second Dublin, circa 1765, 5½in. diam. (Christie's)
$2,750 £1,612

A pair of George IV circular wine coasters, by S. C. Younge & Co., Sheffield, 1821, 14.8cm. diam. (Lawrence Fine Art)
$3,268 £1,748

One of a pair of George IV wine coasters, by Rebecca Emes and Edward Barnard, London, 1825, 7in. diam. (Christie's) $2,860 £1,676

One of four George IV wine coasters, by Smith, Tate, Hoult & Tate, Sheffield, 1823. (Christie's) $5,940 £3,300

One of a pair of George III wine coasters, by Wm. Burwash, London, 1814, 6½in. diam. (Christie's)
$2,420 £1,418

Pair of George III circular wine coasters, by William Plummer, 1782. (Christie's)
$4,356 £2,420

One of a pair of decanter stands on turned wood bases, by Elkington & Co. (Woolley & Wallis)
$577 £350

Pair of George III coasters with wrigglework band decoration, by Robt. Hennell, London, 1792. (Reeds Rains) $1,503 £900

COFFEE POTS

A George III oval coffee pot, stand and lamp, on three reeded scroll feet, by Benjamin and James Smith, 1811, 10¼in. high, 37ozs. (Christie's) $1,851 £990

A Georgian style coffee pot, the domed hinged cover with ivory oval mushroom knop, Sheffield, 1891, 24½oz. (Lalonde Fine Art)
$627 £380

A George II Provincial coffee pot with scroll embellished spout and acorn finial, by Wm. Partis, Newcastle, 1743, 24cm. high, 32.5oz. (Phillips)
$2,887 £1,650

A George I plain tapering cylindrical coffee pot, by Wm. Spackman, 1718, 9¼in. high, gross 21oz. (Christie's) $4,989 £3,080

A George II plain tapering cylindrical coffee pot, by Peze Pilleau, 1732, 8¾in. high, gross 28oz. (Christie's)
$4,989 £3,080

A George I Irish plain tapering cylindrical coffee pot, by J. Hamilton, Dublin, 1715, 9½in. high, gross 29oz. (Christie's)
$7,920 £4,400

A George III plain pear-shaped coffee pot, by Francis Crump, 1765, 10½in. high, gross 29oz. (Christie's)
$3,207 £1,980

A William IV pear-shaped coffee pot, by Paul Storr, 1836, finial by J. S. Hunt, 8¾in. high, 32oz. (Christie's) $3,630 £2,200

A George I plain tapering cylindrical coffee pot, by Robt. Timbrell and Joseph Bell, 1714, 9½in. high, gross 30oz. (Christie's)
$14,520 £8,800

A French coffee pot of ovoid form, the spout terminating in a ram's head, Paris, circa 1825, 24cm. high, 15.5oz. (Phillips) $1,137 £650

A George III cylindrical coffee biggin, stand and lamp, by J. Wakelin and R. Garrard, 1798, 11in. high, 28oz. (Christie's) $1,452 £880

A George III beaded pear-shaped coffee pot on spreading circular foot, with fluting and rococo flowers and foliage, 12¼ in. high, 25.5oz. (Christie's) $1,748 £935

A George II tapering cylindrical coffee pot, by Daniel Piers, 1754, 9in. high, gross 22oz. (Christie's) $2,450 £1,485

A 1960's silver coffee pot and hot water jug, by H. Brown, Birmingham hall-marks for 1963, 29cm. high, 40oz.12dwt. gross weight. (Christie's)
$902 £550

A Queen Anne plain tapering cylindrical coffee pot, by T. Holland, 1710, 10½in. high, gross 29oz. (Christie's)
$8,910 £4,950

A George I plain tapering cylindrical coffee pot, by Thomas Partis, Newcastle, 1725, 9in. high, gross 22oz. (Christie's) $5,702 £3,520

A George I small tapering cylindrical coffee pot, by Wm. Darker, 1724, 7¼in. high, gross 14oz.2dwt. (Christie's) $3,920 £2,420

A George II Irish tapering cylindrical coffee pot, on moulded circular foot, Dublin, circa 1740. 9in. high, 31ozs. (Christie's)
$4,114 £2,200

CREAM JUGS

A Georgian silver baluster cream jug on three shaped legs, London, 1748, 3½in. tall, 2oz. (J. M. Welch & Son)
$410 £270

A cream pitcher, urn-shaped, by Isaac Woodcock, Maryland, circa 1790-1810, 6¾in. high, 5oz. (Christie's)
$3,300 £1,995

A George II silver creamer, London, 1756, 3½in. tall. (J. M. Welch & Son)
$247 £150

CRUETS

A shaped oblong bright cut cruet on shell feet, fitted with seven cut glass condiment bottles, 9½in. (Christie's)
$198 £121

A five-part division Warwick cruet (2 oil bottles missing), by Samuel Wood, London, 1757, 46oz., 27.5cm. high. (Wellington Salerooms)
$2,856 £1,700

A George III Sheffield Plate oval cruet, the base on shell panel feet, circa 1785. (Woolley & Wallis)
$561 £340

A Victorian cruet frame, by Robert Garrard, 1839, 5¾in. wide, the frame 22oz.10dwt. (Christie's) $4,719 £2,890

A French 19th century oblong oil and vinegar stand on ball feet, 8¼in. high. (Christie's)
$316 £198

A Victorian condiment cruet, by James Dixon of Sheffield. (Woolley & Wallis)
$396 £240

CUPS

A Charles II plain tumbler cup, by Robert Williamson, York, 1669, 3½in. diam., 3oz.13dwt. (Christie's) $4,900 £2,970

A George III silver gilt fox mask stirrup cup, by Thomas Pitts, 1771, 5½in. long, 5oz. 13dwt. (Christie's) $4,174 £2,530

A Kalo sterling silver tumbler, Chicago, Illinois, 1914-18, 3.5/8in. high, approx. 3½ troy oz. (Robt. W. Skinner Inc.) $75 £40

A George III silver gilt two handled cup and cover, on spreading circular foot, by Rebecca Emes and Edward Barnard, 1817, London, 11½in. high, 66ozs. (Christie's) $8,228 £4,400

A silver gilt replica of the Norton Cup In The Fishmonger's Company, dated 1925, by Gerrard and Co Ltd., 1918, 14in. high, 49ozs. (Christie's) $1,645 £880

A George II two-handled cup and cover on circular moulded foot, by John White, 1728, 12½in. high, 82oz. (Christie's) $9,075 £5,500

The Richmond Race Cup, 1764: a George III silver gilt two-handled cup and cover, designed by Robert Adam; by D. Smith and Robert Sharp, 1764, 19in. high, 142oz. (Christie's) $106,920 £66,000

A 19th century Continental silver betrothal cup in the form of Queen Elizabeth I, 20cm. high. (Henry Spencer & Sons) $525 £300

A George III silver gilt two handled cup and cover on spreading circular foot, by John Emes, 1798, 13in. high, 36ozs. (Christie's) $3,702 £1,980

CUPS

A cup and cover in the early 17th century style, the gold plaque engraved 'The Manchester Cup 1924', 1923, 15ct., in fitted case, 17¼in. high, 54oz. (Christie's) $35,640 £19,800

Part of a set of six beakers and two footed cups, by John Targee, N.Y., 1809-14, beakers 3¾in. high, footed cups 5½in. high, 48oz. (Christie's) $7,700 £4,656

A George III two-handled partly-fluted cup and cover, by Andrew Fogelberg and Stephen Gilbert, 1789, 18¼in. high, 104oz. (Christie's) $6,237 £3,850

A presentation loving cup, by Dominick & Haff, Newark, for J. E. Caldwell & Co., 1895, in original mahogany box, 11½in. high, 82oz. (Christie's) $9,900 £5,985

A William IV silver stirrup cup, cast and chased as a fox mask, by C. G. Gordon, London, 1833, 6½in. long, 12oz. (Christie's) $8,250 £4,836

A German white metal large three-handled cup and cover, by J. H. Werner, circa 1905, 26½in. high, 10kg. (Christie's) $8,910 £4,950

The Richmond Race Cup, 1768: a George III silver gilt two-handled cup and cover, by D. Smith and R. Sharp, 1768, 17¼in. high, 112oz.17dwt. (Christie's) $16,929 £10,450

A George I Irish plain inverted pear-shaped two-handled cup, by Anthony Stanley, Dublin, 1715, 9½in. high, 62oz. (Christie's) $4,537 £2,750

A Victorian silver gilt cup, by Alfred Clark, in the manner of J. H. Hunt, 19in. high, London, 1879. (Woolley & Wallis) $1,567 £950

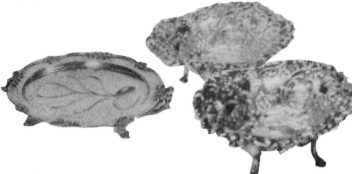

A mid Victorian Sheffield plated oval venison dish, two-handled and with gravy channels and well, 26in. long. (Lalonde Fine Art) $1,188 £720

A pair of Edwardian bon-bon dishes, Chester, 1901, 172gr. total. (Henry Spencer & Sons) $245 £140

One of a set of three George III oval meat dishes, by Wm. Bennett, London, 1807, 67oz. (Woolley & Wallis) $2,062 £1,250

One of a pair of George I large plain circular basins, by David Willaume, 1726, 15in. diam., 112oz. (Christie's) $24,410 £15,400

One of a pair of George I shell-shaped butter dishes, 1726, maker's mark perhaps IE a coronet above, a crescent below, 9oz.17dwt. (Christie's) $5,445 £3,300

One of a set of twelve plates, by Redlich & Co., New York, circa 1900, 9¾in. diam., 160oz. (Christie's) $5,280 £3,192

A tureen with domed cover, by Black, Starr & Frost, New York, circa 1900, 9½in. high, 14in. wide overall, 73oz.10dwt. (Christie's) $3,520 £2,128

Two of a set of four George III octagonal entree dishes, covers and handles, by Robert Sharp, 1788, 10½in. long, 155oz. (Christie's) $12,474 £7,700

Early 20th century plated bacon dish of oval form complete with revolving lid. (G. A. Key) $231 £140

DISHES

A Joel F. Hewes sterling silver hand-raised, footed candy dish, circa 1908, 6in. diam., approx. 10 troy oz. (Robt. W. Skinner Inc.) $400 £238

A late Victorian oval dish, by Gilbert Marks, 1899-1900, 15in. long, 30oz. (Christie's) $3,085 £1,870

An enamelled sterling silver and glass jam dish and spoon, by Mary P. Winlock, 4.5/8in. diam., approx. 5 troy oz. (Robt. W. Skinner Inc.) $500 £297

One of a set of six Charles II shell-shaped dishes, by S. Hood, 1675, 4¾in. wide, 10oz.7dwt. (Christie's) $57,024 £35,200

A George IV shaped oval meat dish with gadrooned, shell and foliage border, by Philip Rundell, 1821, 19¾in. long, 74oz. (Christie's) $6,897 £4,180

A shell-shaped bonbonniere on triple ball feet, Sheffield, 1910, 6½in. long, 6oz. (Hy. Duke & Son) $270 £150

A late Victorian dish, by Walker & Hall, Sheffield, 1898, 24cm. diam., 330gr. (Henry Spencer & Sons) $297 £170

One of a pair of Victorian dessert stands, by J. S. Hunt, 1857, 7½in. high, 72oz. (Christie's) $3,168 £1,760

One of a pair of Georgian silver gilt oval dishes, by William Pitts, London, 1817, 45oz., 10in. diam. (Wellington Salerooms) $3,192 £1,900

FLATWARE

A Charles II Puritan spoon, by Jeremy Johnson, 1662. (Christie's) $2,087 £1,265

An Elizabeth I apostle spoon, with fig-shaped bowl and tapering hexagonal stem, by Wm. Cawdell, 1599, 7in. long. (Christie's) $1,425 £880

A William III dog-nose spoon, by Richard Wilcocks, Exeter, 1701, 7½in. long. (Christie's) $801 £495

An Elizabeth I seal top spoon with partly fluted baluster top, by Wm. Rawnson, York, 1589. (Christie's) $1,542 £935

A set of four parcel gilt serving pieces, by Tiffany & Co., circa 1880-85, ladle 13½in. long, 18oz.10dwt. (Christie's) $9,350 £5,653

Part of an International Co. partial sterling silver flatware service, Meriden, Conn., circa 1934, consisting of 53 pieces, weight approx. 110 troy oz. (Robt. W. Skinner Inc.) $1,200 £648

Part of a Georg Jensen 36-piece 'Acorn' pattern table service, designed by Johan Rohde. (Christie's) $3,066 £1,870

Part of a 146-piece flatware service, by Tiffany & Co., New York, 1878-1900, in the original fitted oak box, 230oz. excluding knives. (Christie's) $7,700 £4,655

FLATWARE

A pair of grape shears, by Tiffany & Co., circa 1880-85, of shaped scissor-form, 8in. long, 5oz. (Christie's)　　　　$4,400 £2,660

A caddy spoon with hammered fig-shaped bowl and stylised flower handle set at centre with a cornelian boss, 1921. (Phillips)
$665 £380

A Charles II trefid spoon, the stem surmounted with the cast figure of a prancing greyhound and ring attachment, by Thomas Cory, 1684. (Phillips)　　　　　　　$1,137 £650

A Charles II slip top spoon, engraved with initials HS, by Jeremy Johnson, 1664. (Christie's)　　　　　　　$1,415 £858

Three of seven parcel gilt condiment servers, by Tiffany & Co., circa 1880-85, serving spoon 9½in. long, sauce ladles each approx. 7in. long, 13oz. (Christie's) $6,050 £3,657

Part of a 113-piece Victorian Queen's pattern table service by George Adams, 1869, 1870, 1872, soup ladle, 1902, 284oz. (Christie's)
$12,705 £7,700

Part of a 140-piece mixed metal flatware service, by Tiffany & Co., 1880-85, dinner fork, 8.1/8in. long, ladel 13in. long, 201oz. 10dwt. excluding knives. (Christie's)
$99,000 £59,855

Part of a 24-piece set of parcel gilt dessert knives and forks, by Tiffany & Co., circa 1880-85, knives 8¼in. long, 48oz.10dwt. (Christie's)　　　　　　$4,950 £2,992

An American silver wine goblet, a footed beaker and a cann, the first by Robert & Wm. Wilson, Phila., the second by W. W. Hannah, Hudson, New York, the third circa 1850. (Christie's) $770 £451

Two late 19th century Chinese Colonial silver wine goblets, struck with maker's mark WF and an ideogram, 7½in. and 7.5/8in. high, 20oz.10dwt. (Christie's) $935 £548

An American silver wine goblet, by Samuel Kirk, Baltimore, circa 1840, 6.1/8in. high, and a beaker 4½in. high, 118oz.10dwt. (Christie's) $1,045 £612

A Victorian silver gilt goblet, by George Angell, 1863, 16.3cm. high. (Lawrence Fine Art) $781 £418

Two American silver wine goblets, by W. Adams, New York, circa 1825, 5.7/8in. and 6.7/8in. high, 15oz.10dwt. (Christie's) $715 £419

A George III silver wine goblet, by Robert Hennell, 1778, 6.3/8in. high. (Christie's) $605 £354

One of two American silver wine goblets, by C. Bard & Son, one 5¾in. high, the other 6¼in. high, 9oz.10dwt. (Christie's) $660 £386

A pair of George III Irish silver wine goblets, by Joseph Jackson, Dublin, 1801, 6½in. high, 12oz. (Christie's) $2,750 £1,612

Mid 19th century Chinese Colonial silver wine goblet, by Khecheong, 6¼in. high, 9oz. (Christie's) $1,210 £709

INKSTANDS

A Victorian shaped oval inkstand, by Thomas Smily, fully marked 1859, 28.2cm. long, 15oz. (Lawrence Fine Art)
$1,398 £748

A George III silver-gilt circular inkstand, with scroll handle and three quill holders, by Robert Garrard, 1817, 5in. wide, 14ozs. (Christie's)
$8,832 £4,800

A shaped rectangular inkstand, the cut glass bottles with shaped circular silver caps, Sheffield, 1905, maker's mark WM&S, 27.6cm. long, 20.8oz. (Lawrence Fine Art)
$905 £484

A Victorian silver-mounted gadrooned heart-shaped tortoiseshell ink stand with loop handle, William Comyns, London 1889, 4¾in. long. (Christie's) $539 £308

An Elkington electrotype circular inkstand commemorating the Great Exhibtion of 1851 pattern, 9in. diam. (Woolley & Wallis)
$330 £200

A late Victorian shaped oblong inkstand on hoof feet, fitted with two silver topped cut-glass square inkwells, W. G. & J. L., London 1898, 10¾in. wide., 33oz. (Christie's)
$1,828 £1,045

A silver desk stand fitted with two glass and silver topped bottles, Chester, 1913, 15oz. (J. M. Welch & Son)
$516 £340

A large Victorian shaped oblong inkstand on leaf-capped claw feet with two cylindrical ink pots, Messrs Barnard, London 1868, 11in. 33oz. free. (Christie's)
$2,262 £1,210

An 18th century Victorian gadrooned rounded oblong inkstand, on curved legs, Goldsmiths & Silversmiths Co. Ltd., London 1899, 8¾in., 22oz. free. (Christie's) $929 £528

JUGS

A pitcher of baluster form, by Samuel Kirk, Baltimore, assay marks for 1824, 8¼in. high, 25oz.10dwt. (Christie's) $2,090 £1,263

A 19th century embossed and worked silver wine jug with four silver pictorial panels, Sheffield, 1857. (J. M. Welch & Son) $1,968 £1,200

One of a pair of William IV plain pear-shaped wine jugs, by Paul Storr, 1835, 7¾in. high, 30oz. (Christie's) $6,237 £3,850

A George IV silver gilt wine ewer, in the style of Francois Briot, by Wm. Eaton, 1827, 11½in. high, 37oz. (Christie's) $2,541 £1,540

A Queen Anne silver baluster hot water jug with scrolled thumb-piece, London, 1707, 23oz. (Dacre, Son & Hartley) $1,722 £1,050

A George III vase-shaped hot-water jug, by Andrew Fogelberg and Stephen Gilbert, 1782, 12¼in. high, 24oz. (Christie's) $2,178 £1,210

Early 20th century Arthur Stone sterling silver water pitcher, Gardner, Mass., 9in. high, 31 troy oz. (Robt. W. Skinner Inc.) $2,000 £1,081

A George III helmet-shaped milk jug, probably by Benjamin Mordecai or Benjamin Mountigue, London, 1790, 6¼in. high, 3¾oz. (Dreweatt Neate) $355 £190

A George II plain oval pear-shaped shaving jug, by Paul Crespin, 1749, 7¾in. high, 18oz.15dwt. (Christie's) $8,553 £5,280

MISCELLANEOUS

A George III silver gilt oval basin, 1764, and Victorian ewer, with the makers mark, the basin 13¼in. long, the ewer 8¾in. high, 50oz. (Christie's) $6,897 £4,180

An Old Sheffield plate cruciform mirror plateau, in five sections, circa 1830, 49¾in. long. (Christie's) $7,623 £4,620

Edwardian novelty desk clip and pen brush in the form of a muzzled bear, Birmingham, 1908. (Prudential Fine Art) $462 £280

A Georg Jensen tazza, stamped marks 264B GJ 925 S and London import marks for 1928, 30.5cm. high, 1.701kg. (Christie's) $5,772 £3,520

A Victorian cast model of a whippet, after Jiji by Jules-Pierre Mene, Sheffield, circa 1860, maker's mark WB, 6¼in. high overall. (Christie's) $1,815 £1,100

A late 19th century English electrotype shield with scenes from John Bunyan's 'Pilgrim's Progress', electroformed from the original by L. Morel-Ladeuil by Elkington & Co. (Christie's) $2,388 £1,430

Late 19th century Continental silver plated decanting cradle, in the form of a field gun, overall length 15in. (Christie's) $990 £580

Pair of Spanish Colonial silver spurs, 8½in. long, rhondell diam. 2¾in. (Robt. W. Skinner Inc.) $800 £449

A George III ivory biscuit barrel with Old Sheffield plate Greek key pattern base and hinged cover, 4½in. high. (Hy. Duke & Son) $576 £320

An American silver bottle cradle by the Gorham Co., 1890, oval with gadrooned borders, 13½in. long. (Christie's) $1,760 £1,031

A William IV silver barrel spigot, by Wm. Wheatcroft, London, 1830, 6¼in. long, 16oz.10dwt. (Christie's) $880 £515

A Victorian cast whistle formed as the head of a dog, by Samson Mordan, London, 1886, 2½in. long. (Christie's) $739 £462

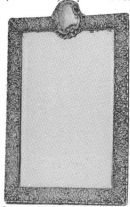

A late 19th century English electrotype shield with scenes from Milton's 'Paradise Lost', electroformed by Elkington & Co., Birmingham, 1887. (Christie's) $2,388 £1,430

A Continental silver metal figure of a curly haired youth, on black marble plinth, 29.5cm. high, and another group of a younger child, 30cm. high. (Phillips) $1,385 £850

A large easel mirror with bevelled rectangular plate in ornamental trellis and scroll, Chester, 1898, makers J.D. and W.D., 19 x 12½in. (Graves Son & Pilcher) $716 £400

A circular, gilt lined love token box, probably French, 2½in. diam. (Christie's) $492 £308

A George III plain vase-shaped argyle, by John Wakelin and Wm. Taylor, circa 1780, 8¼in. high, gross 16oz.13dwt. (Christie's) $1,247 £770

A Victorian shaped dressing table mirror with easel support, by William Comyns, London, 1893, 10¾in. high. (Christie's) $616 £385

MISCELLANEOUS

A strainer with ring handle, by John Brevoort, N.Y., 1742-75, 3½in. diam., 1oz.10dwt. (Christie's) $1,540 £931

Mid 19th century Dutch table bell with fluted handle, 5¾in. high. (Christie's) $616 £385

A German parcel gilt ewer and basin, by Johann Mittnacht, Augsburg, circa 1690, 24in. long, and 13in. high, 84oz. (Christie's)
$32,076 £19,800

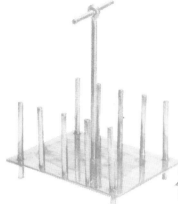

A Hukin & Heath electro-plated toast rack, designed by C. Dresser, 5¼in. high. (Christie's) $2,316 £1,430

A George III Scottish silver two-handled punch strainer, by Robt. Gray & Sons, Edinburgh, 1811, 11¾in. long, 8oz. (Christie's) $3,520 £2,063

A Tiffany sterling silver sealing wax set, N.Y., circa 1891-1902, 8½in. sq., wt. approx. 20 troy oz. (Robt. W. Skinner Inc.)
$800 £432

Late 19th century Victorian silver plated three-bottle decanter stand, by Martin Hall & Co., 13½in. high. (Christie's) $495 £290

A George III two-bottle stand, by William Eaton, 1815, 22.4cm. high, 19oz. (Lawrence Fine Art)
$863 £462

A 19th century American loud-hailer of trumpet shape, 52cm. high, circa 1850, 23oz. (Phillips) $3,675 £2,100

MUGS

A George III gilt-lined tapering mug with moulded rim and bracket handle, London 1806, 2½in., (Christie's)
$426 £228

A George II plain baluster mug on a spreading circular foot, Fuller White, London 1748, 4¼in., 9.5oz. (Christie's)
$623 £330

A good 19th century Chinese Export mug of tapering shape, by Cutshing of Canton, circa 1870, 11cm. high, 8.5ozs. (Phillips)
$748 £400

A Victorian gilt-lined tapering christening mug with moulded rim and loop handle, Robert Hennell, London 1878, 3¾in. high. (Christie's) $325 £176

A Victorian gilt-lined baluster christening mug on spreading circular foot, engraved with a monogram and date, circa 1891, 4in. high. (Christie's)
$400 £220

A George III mug, probably by Thomas Ollivant, 1804, 15.2cm. high, 23.4oz. (Lawrence Fine Art)
$1.069 £572

MUSTARDS

A French mustard pot with clear glass liner, Paris, circa 1825, 3.5oz. (Phillips)
$367 £210

A George III mustard pot, by Samuel Wheatley, 1816, 9.2cm. high. (Lawrence Fine Art)
$534 £286

An early Victorian pierced drum mustard pot, fitted with a blue glass liner, by Charles Fox, London, 1838, 4in. high. (Christie's)
$422 £264

POMANDERS

Early 18th century German silver pear-shaped pomander in three threaded sections, 2.5/8in. high. (Christie's)
$798 £484

A silver pomander with eight compartments, circa 1700, 2in. high. (Christie's)
$4,452 £2,420

Early 18th century German silver pomander with entwined foliage stem, 2in. high. (Christie's) $272 £165

Early 18th century silver gilt pomander of threaded acorn shape, 2½in. high. (Christie's)
$1,052 £638

A silver gilt pomander, the six-hinged segments engraved with flowers and foliate sprays, circa 1600, probably German, 1¾in. high. (Christie's)
$4,950 £2,750

Early 18th century German silver pear-shaped pomander with perforated interior, 2½in. high. (Christie's)
$816 £495

PORRINGERS

A James II plain circular two-handled porringer and cover, 1685, maker's mark PM, star above and below, 5in. high, 11oz.19dwt. (Christie's)
$5,808 £3,520

An important Commonwealth two handled porringer, cover and stand, by Arthur Mainwaring, 1657, salver 13in. diam. porringer 5¼in, 44ozs 4dwts. (Christie's)
$47,311 £25,300

An early Charles II two-handled porringer and cover, on three cast gilt spread scallop feet, circa 1670, 23ozs. (Phillips)
$74,800 £40,000

SALTS

A pair of Adam style boat-shaped salts, by Robert and Samuel Hennell, London, 1803, 6oz. (Hy. Duke & Son) $648 £360

One of a set four George III salts, by Thos. Robins, London, 1819, 2¾in. diam., 18oz. (Hobbs & Chambers) $742 £450

A Victorian drum mustard pot and a pair of oval salt cellars, by Henry Wilkinson & Co., Sheffield, 1851 and 1853, mustard pot 2¾in. high. (Christie's) $457 £286

Pair of late Victorian salt cellars by Hunt & Roskell Ltd., 1901, 6½in. high, 34oz. (Christie's) $9,504 £5,280

An Austro-Hungarian 19th century double shell plated salt made from cut white and clear glass painted with polychrome flowers, 5½in. high. (Christie's) $228 £143

Pair of Victorian peppers, with detachable heads, by Frederick Edmonds of Johnson, Sons & Edmonds, 6cm. high. (Lawrence Fine Art) $1,131 £605

A set of four George III style Edwardian silver salts, London, 1909, with matching spoons, 43oz. (Hetheringtons Nationwide) $1,023 £620

A pair of knife rests and open salts, by Tiffany & Co., 1878-91, also a set of four butter plates, each approx. 3in. wide, 13oz. (Christie's)
$3,080 £1,862

Two of a set of four Victorian gilt lined shell salt cellars with four matching spoons, in a fitted case, Sheffield 1872 and 1873. (Christie's) $427 £264

SAUCEBOATS

A fine pair of George II
style shaped oval sauceboats
and ladles, by D. & J. Welby,
1959 and 1960, 7¾in. long,
41oz. (Christie's)
$2,904 £1,760

Pair of Edwardian silver
sauceboats of Georgian style,
London 1905, 6¼in. wide, 17oz.
(Hobbs & Chambers) $608 £380

Pair of Victorian fluted shaped
sauceboats, by John S. Hunt,
1846, 7¾in. long, 36oz.
(Christie's) $7,128 £3,960

SNUFF BOXES

A William IV silver-gilt castle-
top snuff box, chased in high
relief witha view of 'Abbotsford House', 8 x 4.5cm, by
Joseph Willmore, Birmingham,
1832, 4.25ozs. (Phillips)
$1,159 £620

Late 19th century French
silver and gold snuff box,
maker's initials JL, Paris,
3½in. long. (Christie's)
$1,452 £880

A George IV rectangular
silver gilt snuff box, London,
1823, maker's mark TP
possibly for Thos. Peacock
or Thos. P. Prothero, in red
leather case, 3¼in. long.
(Christie's) $1,179 £715

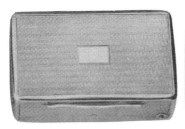

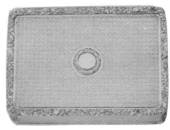

A George III silver gilt musical
snuff box, playing two tunes,
by S. Pemberton, Birmingham,
1816, with key, 3¼in. long.
(Christie's) $1,452 £880

A George III oblong silver
gilt snuff box, by Thomas
Phipps, James Phipps II and
E. Robinson II, London, 1815,
2¾in. long. (Christie's)
$1,452 £880

A George III silver gilt snuff
box, by Daniel Hockly,
London, 1816, 3¼in. long.
(Christie's) $998 £605

TANKARDS

A George I plain tapering cylindrical tankard on moulded rim foot, with scroll handle, by William Fawdrey, 1716, 7½in. high, 32ozs. (Christie's) $5,348 £2,860

A William III tapering cylindrical tankard, on reeded rim foot, by John Edwards, 1699, 8in. high, 39ozs. (Christie's) $13,987 £7,480

A Victorian cylindrical tankard and cover, by John Figg, 1839, 12¼in. high, 45oz. (Christie's) $6,237 £3,850

A George II baluster tankard, by Thomas Cooke II and Richard Gurney, 1752, 19.8cm. high, 31oz. (Lawrence Fine Art) $3,394 £1,815

A George I flagon, maker's mark of Richard Bayley overstriking another, 1717, 29.5cm. high, 40.5oz. (Lawrence Fine Art) $1,748 £935

A silver mounted leather 'blackjack', by Gorham Manuf. Co., Providence, circa 1905, 7½in. high. (Christie's) $330 £199

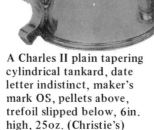

A George III tapering cylindrical tankard, by Solomon Hougham, 1792, 7½in. high, 27oz. (Christie's) $1,996 £1,210

A Charles II plain tapering cylindrical tankard, date letter indistinct, maker's mark OS, pellets above, trefoil slipped below, 6in. high, 25oz. (Christie's) $7,484 £4,620

A Queen Anne plain tapering cylindrical tankard, by Timothy Ley, 1710, 6in. high, 21oz. (Christie's) $5,082 £3,080

TANKARDS

A Danish cylindrical peg tankard on three crowned lion and ball feet, by Peder Brock, Randers, circa 1753, 8½in. high, 40oz. (Christie's) $4,633 £2,860

A silver mounted serpentine tankard and cover, circa 1670, maker's mark only struck three times, IC a star below, 5½in. high. (Christie's) $1,815 £1,100

An early 18th century Norwegian peg tankard, with ball and claw feet, by Anders Nielsen Borg, Trondheim, probably 1723, 16cm. high, 15.5ozs. (Phillips) $9,350 £5,000

A plain tapering cylindrical tankard, the body probably by K. Mangy, Hull, circa 1700, the cover by H. Brind, London, 1750, 6½in. high, 19oz. (Christie's) $1,782 £1,100

A Queen Anne plain cylindrical tankard and cover, on moulded foot, by Adam Billon, Cork, circa 1710, 7¾in. high, 21ozs. (Christie's) $6,171 £3,300

A large George II baluster tankard, by William Soame, 1758, 26cm. high overall, 44.5oz. (Phillips) $6,650 £3,800

A German large tapering flagon, by Korner & Proll, Berlin, late 19th century, 15¼in. high, 3330gr. (Christie's) $5,142 £2,750

A repousse tankard, by Tiffany & Co., N.Y. finished March 10, 1893, for the World's Columbian Exposition, Chicago, 1893, 10in. high, 52oz. 10dwt. (Christie's) $28,600 £17,291

A George III partly-fluted pear-shaped tankard, by James Barber, York, 1812, 9in. high, 38oz. (Christie's) $3,564 £2,200

TEA & COFFEE SETS

A three-piece tea service, by Shreve, Stanwood & Co., Boston, 1860-69, each globular, on four cast lion's paw feet with acanthus leaf joins, teapot 7in. high, 57oz. (Christie's)
$935 £565

A bullet-shaped silver teapot, matching milk jug and sugar bowl, London, 1930, approx. 30 oz. (J. M. Welch & Son) $571 £340

A three-piece tea service, by Garrett Eoff, New York, circa 1825, comprising a teapot, a covered sugar bowl, and a cream pitcher, each vase-shaped on a circular foot, gross weight 59oz.10dwt. (Christie's)
$1,760 £1,064

A Regency oval boat-shape three-piece tea service by Joseph Angel, London, 1818. (Woolley & Wallis) $1,254 £760

TEA & COFFEE SETS

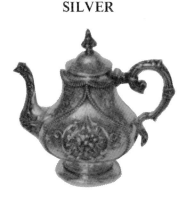

Victorian silver three-piece tea service having engraved and repousse decoration, maker JA, 46 troy oz., London 1875/77. (Giles Haywood) $820 £500

A three-piece tea service, by Gorham Manuf. Co., Providence, 1880-82, comprising a teapot with a bail handle wrapped in rattan, a cream pitcher and an open sugar bowl, teapot 6in. high. (Christie's) $2,090 £1,263

A three-piece demitasse service, by Tiffany & Co., New York, 1878-91, comprising a coffee pot, a cream pitcher, and an open sugar bowl, coffee pot 7.5/8in. high, gross weight 23oz. 10dwt. (Christie's) $15,400 £9,310

A vase-shaped tea and coffee service, by Mappin & Webb, 1903, 1912 and 1913, gross 173oz. (Christie's) $10,890 £6,050

SILVER

A Victorian three-piece tea service, all with leaf capped harp handles and on conforming pedestal bases, by Robert Harper, 1873, 21.5cm. height of teapot, 50.5oz. (Lawrence Fine Art) $1,769 £936

A five-piece tea service and tray, by Tiffany & Co., New York, circa 1881, comprising a coffee pot, a covered sugar bowl, a cream pitcher, a waste bowl and a large two-handled tray, coffee pot 8½in. high, tray 27¼in. long, gross weight 306oz. (Christie's) $41,800 £24,272

A George IV pear-shaped tea and coffee service, each on four mask, shell and scroll feet and chased overall with scrolls, foliage and shells, 1825, maker's mark IW, height of coffee pot 7½in., 98oz. (Christie's) $4,537 £2,750

A Victorian three-piece silver tea service comprising pumpkin-shaped teapot with embossed scroll decoration, 11½in. wide, and matching sugar basin and cream jug, Edinburgh, 1842, 65oz.10dwt. (Dacre, Son & Hartley) $1,485 £900

A Victorian tea and coffee service, comprising pear-shaped teapot, coffee pot, hot water jug, sugar basin and cream jug, on a two-handled shaped oval tray, by Elkington & Co., Birmingham 1897 and 1898, the tray 24¾in. long, gross 234oz. (Christie's) $10,890 £6,600

A five-piece tea and coffee service, by George B. Sharp for Bailey & Co., Phila., circa 1848-50, comprising a kettle on stand, a coffee pot, a teapot, a covered cream pitcher and a covered sugar bowl, coffee pot 15¼in. high, 231oz.10dwt. (Christie's) $19,800 £11,971

TEA CADDIES

A George III cube shaped tea caddy, with hinged flat cover, by John Vere and William Lutwyche, 1767, 3¾in. high, 15ozs. 13dwts. (Christie's) $5,759 £3,080

A George III oval tea caddy with central hinge, two covers and plain divider, by Henry Chawner, 1788, 7in. high, 15oz.10dwt. (Christie's) $3,811 £2,310

One of a pair of George I plain octagonal tea caddies, by S. Pantin, 1715, 4½in. high, 25oz. (Christie's) $9,801 £6,050

A George II plain octagonal tea caddy, Exeter, 1730, 4in. high, and another similar. (Christie's) $3,366 £1,870

A set of George II plain vase-shaped tea caddies and circular sugar bowl and cover, by Samuel Taylor, 1752, in oval satinwood box, circa 1790, 28oz. (Christie's) $8,167 £4,950

A Queen Anne octagonal tea caddy, by Thos. Ash, 1711, the base struck twice with the maker's mark of J. Farnell, 5in. high, 8oz.17dwt. (Christie's) $2,376 £1,320

A George III oval serpentine side tea caddy, 5.5in. high, by Thos. Satchell, London, 1791. (Woolley & Wallis) $3,135 £1,900

A George III Sheffield Plate oval tea caddy, the hinged cover with a Dutch drop handle, 4in. high. (Woolley & Wallis) $676 £410

A George III shaped tea caddy, with hinged domed cover and urn-shaped finial, by Henry Chawner, circa 1792. 5½in. high, 10ozs. 18dwts. (Christie's) $3,085 £1,650

TEA KETTLES

A Victorian compressed large tea kettle chased with flowers and foliage, complete with stand, 18¼in. overall. (Christie's) $610 £330

A William IV melon-shaped tea kettle, stand and lamp, engraved with a coat-of-arms and crest by Paul Storr, 1835, gross 68oz. (Christie's) $5,445 £3,300

A Victorian style part-fluted compressed tea kettle with a burner, probably George Fox, London 1912, 11½in., 45oz. (Christie's) $1,017 £550

Late 19th century silver plated kettle on stand with spirit burner. (Brown & Merry) $582 £320

A George III plain oval tea-kettle, stand and burner, by Edward Fernell, 1789, 13¼in. high, gross 68oz. (Christie's) $3,960 £2,200

A George III plain tapering cylindrical tea kettle, stand and lamp, by Chas. Wright, 1780, the stand and lamp, 1782, 15in. high overall, gross 56oz. (Christie's) $2,722   £1,650

A Victorian swing-handle com-pressed tea kettle engraved with scrolling foliage, with a burner, 13¾in. high. (Christie's) $591 £352

A Victorian inverted pear-shaped tea kettle, stand and lamp, by Harris Bros., 1896, gross 63oz. (Christie's) $1,425 £880

A Victorian circular kettle on stand, the underframe with a spirit heater, maker's mark two bells, 16.5in. high. (Woolley & Wallis) $693 £420

TEAPOTS

A George III teapot and cover, by John and Henry Lias, London, 1819, 6½in. high, 22oz. (Hy. Duke & Son) $414 £230

A George III rectangular section teapot on four ball feet with hinged lid, London, 1789, approx. 18oz. (Peter Wilson) $598 £340

A George II Scottish bullet shaped teapot, on circular moulded foot, by William Aytoun, Edinburgh, 1743, 20ozs. (Christie's) $2,879 £1,540

A William IV plain circular teapot, by Paul Storr, 1831, 7in. high, 31oz. (Christie's) $2,138 £1,320

A silver repousse teapot, probably Boston, circa 1835, 9½in. high, approx. 39 troy oz. (Robt. W. Skinner Inc.) $425 £265

A George IV inverted pear-shaped teapot and coffee pot, by John Bridge, 1823, height of coffee pot 8in., gross 48oz. (Christie's) $1,692 £1,045

A Georgian silver teapot with gadrooned rim, Exeter, 1814 or 1834, 22.3oz. (Dee & Atkinson) $421 £260

A William IV circular compressed melon panel teapot, by Wm. Burwash, London, 1837. (Woolley & Wallis) $462 £280

TEAPOTS

A George III Irish oval pointed end teapot with domed cover and ebonised handle, by Peter Wills, Cork, circa 1790, 20½oz. gross. (Dreweatt Neate) $1,402 £750

A George III shaped oval teapot and stand, by Robert and David Hennell, 1795, 7¼in. high, gross 20oz. (Christie's) $3,207 £1,980

A teapot, pyriform, with a high domed cover, marked 'HM', N.Y., 1715-25, 5¾in. high, gross weight 16oz.10dwt. (Christie's) $41,800 £25,272

An early Victorian circular teapot, by Reilly & Storer, London, 1839, 23.5oz. all in. (Woolley & Wallis) $495 £300

A W. M. Hutton & Sons electroplated teapot and hot-water jug, designed by H. Stabler, 15.7cm. high. (Christie's) $336 £220

A teapot, urn-shaped, the conical cover with a pineapple finial, by Charles Westphal, Phila., circa 1790-1800, 11in. high, gross weight 25oz. (Christie's) $8,250 £4,987

George III bullet-shaped teapot with baluster finial, by Francis Crump, London, 1769. (Reeds Rains) $417 £250

A George I Scottish plain circular teapot, by Charles Blair, Edinburgh, 1722, 5¼in. high, gross 20oz.10dwt. (Christie's) $4,989 £3,080

TRAYS & SALVERS

A silver footed salver having fancy border, London, 1912, 15in. diam., 46 troy oz. (Giles Haywood)$861 £525

A large shaped silver salver on four cabriole legs and ball-and-claw feet, Sheffield, 1934, 14in. diam., 45oz. (J. M. Welch & Son) $759 £460

A George II Scottish shaped circular salver on three hoof feet, by Robert Lowe, Edin., 1751, 8¾in. diam., 16oz.7dwt. (Christie's) $726 £440

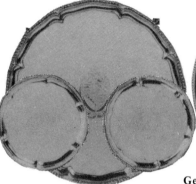

George III Irish shaped circular salver on four hoof feet, by John Nicolson, Cork, circa 1785, 16¼in. diam. (Christie's) $2,406 £1,375

A George III shaped circular salver and a pair of matching smaller salvers, by John Carter, 1772, 14¼in. and 7in. diam., 65oz. (Christie's) $5,263 £3,190

George III salver, circular with raised beaded border, maker possibly John Crouch, London, 1772, 14½in. diam., 44oz. (Hobbs & Chambers) $957 £580

A plain George II large shaped circular salver, by Robert Abercrombie, 1734, 18in. diam., 73oz. (Christie's) $8,553 £5,280

A silver footed two-handled tray with rope edge, Birmingham, 1930, 21 x 13in., 56 troy oz. (Giles Haywood) $754 £460

An inlaid waiter with an everted brim, on four cast feet, by Tiffany & Co., 1878-91, 9½in. diam., gross weight 10oz. (Christie's) $19,800 £11,971

TRAYS & SALVERS

A George III plain circular salver on slightly curved feet, by John Crouch and Thos. Hannam, 1785, 15¾in. diam., 48oz. (Christie's) $2,851 £1,760

A Victorian octafoil-shaped tray with beaded handles and border, London, 1874. (Reeds Rains) $4,175 £2,500

A George III shaped circular salver, by John Carter, 1773, 15in. diam., 52oz. (Christie's) $5,702 £3,520

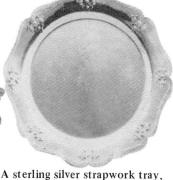

A George II shaped square salver, by Lewis Pantin I, 1735, 12½in. wide, 52oz. (Christie's) $9,801 £6,050

Silver salver on three feet, London, 1876, 25oz. (Brown & Merry) $800 £440

A sterling silver strapwork tray, signed Shreve & Co. San Francisco Sterling, circa 1918, 12½in. diam., 26 troy oz. (Robt. W. Skinner Inc.) $700 £378

A Victorian shaped circular presentation salver, by William Hunter, 1872, 41cm. diam., 56.4oz. (Lawrence Fine Art) $1,563 £836

A silver footed salver having fancy border, Sheffield, 1934, 12in. diam., 27 troy oz. (Giles Haywood) $492 £300

Late 19th century silver mounted shibayama inlaid lacquer tray, signed Yasuaki, 24cm. diam. (Christie's) $2,805 £1,650

A George III two handled soup tureen and cover on four scroll feet, by John Parker and Edward Wakelin, 1769, 16½in. long, 91ozs. (Christie's) $14,399 £7,700

A pair of George IV two handled circular soup tureens and covers, engraved by John Bridge, circa 1825, 12in. diam. 322ozs. (Christie's) $57,596 £30,800

One of a pair of George III two-handled sauce tureens and covers, engraved with a coat of arms and crests, by Joseph William Story and William Elliott, circa 1810, 10in. long. (Christie's) $6,376 £3,410

George IV two-handled oval soup-tureen and cover on four acanthus foliage and paw feet, by John Craddock and William Reid, 1823, width 16½in. 155 ozs. . (Christie's) $17,480 £9,500

A George III two handled circular soup tureen and cover, on spreading circular foot, by Paul Storr, 1803, 12in. high, 113ozs. (Christie's) $22,627 £12,100

An Old Sheffield plate moulded oval two-handled soup tureen and cover with scrolling foliate handle, on shell feet, Blagden, Hodgson & Co., circa 1820, 14¼in. high. (Christie's) $1,006 £572

One of a set of four George III two-handled oval sauce tureens and covers, by Robt. Sharp, 1788, 6in. high, 125oz. (Christie's) $3,564 £2,200

A pair of George IV two handled oval sauce tureens and covers, each on four cast lion's paw and foliage feet, Paul Storr, 1821, 8½in. long, 68ozs. (Christie's) $19,541 £10,450

One of a pair of George IV two-handled oblong sauce tureens and covers, by J. Angell, 1825, 72oz. (Christie's) $3,029 £1,870

URNS

A George III vase-shaped two-handled tea urn, by John Denziloe, 1784, 21¼in. high, gross 106oz. (Christie's) $3,294 £2,310

A tea urn, by Eoff & Shepherd for Ball, Black & Co., N.Y., 1839-51, 18in. high, 15in. wide, 112oz.10dwt. (Christie's) $3,520 £2,128

A fine George III two handled vase shaped tea urn, on four foliate scroll bracket feet, with a coat-of-arms and a crest, by Andrew Fogelberg, 1773, 20½in. high, 107ozs. (Christie's) $10,285 £5,500

Silver sugar urn, by Joseph Lownes, Phila., 1758-1820, 10in. high. (Robt. W. Skinner Inc.) $1,700 £955

An Art Deco chromium plated tea urn of tapering form, 42cm. high, stamped 'REG 849217'. (Phillips) $832 £520

An English Georgian Sheffield cannonball samovar, circa 1803. (Du Mouchelles) $300 £167

A 19th century plated samovar of globular form with lion ring handles, on four ball feet, 14in. high. (G.A. Key) $141 £75

An 1820 Sheffield samovar, by D. G. Holy & Co, with claw feet. (Du Mouchelles) $2,775 £1,500

An English Sheffield Russian style samovar, on square plinth, with bracket feet. (Du Mouchelles) $200 £111

VASES

An Art Nouveau baluster vase chased with lilies of the valley, the base impressed with a date 1896, 7¼in., 14.75oz. (Christie's) $519 £275

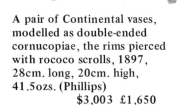

A pair of Continental vases, modelled as double-ended cornucopiae, the rims pierced with rococo scrolls, 1897, 28cm. long, 20cm. high, 41.5ozs. (Phillips)
$3,003 £1,650

A George III silver gilt two-handled sugar vase, by Paul Storr, 1815, weight overall 21.5ozs. (Phillips)
$9,100 £5,000

An urn-shaped vase, by Ball, Black & Co., N.Y., 1851-76, 9½in. high, 6oz.10dwt. (Christie's) $528 £319

A pair of Georg Jensen vases, stamped marks Dessin G J 925.S Georg Jensen 107A, 13.2cm. high, 332.5gr. (Christie's) $631 £385

A bud vase, the body inlaid in copper and niello with butterflies and cherry blos-soms, by Tiffany & Co., 1872-91, 5in. high, 3oz.10dwt. (Christie's) $3,080 £1,862

Late 19th century shaped octagonal silver vase and cover with eight oval lacquer panels, signed Haruaki, 46cm. high. (Christie's)
$20,570 £12,100

Hallmarked silver posy holder, with blue glass liner, Sheffield, 1904. (G. A. Key) $140 £80

An ovoid vase, by Tiffany & Co., N.Y., 1878-90, 6.5/8in. high, 14oz. (Christie's)
$7,150 £4,322

VINAIGRETTES

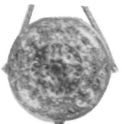

A silver gilt engine turned vinaigrette, by Nathaniel Mills, Birmingham, 1825, 1¾in. long. (Christie's) $580 £352

An attractive 19th century gold and champleve enamel vinaigrette, circa 1840. (Phillips) $328 £200

A Victorian oblong silver-gilt castle-top vinaigrette, with a view of a large church, Yapp & Woodward, Birmingham 1844. (Christie's) $544 £330

A George III articulated fish vinaigrette, 7.25cm. long, by Samuel Pemberton, Birmingham 1817. (Phillips) $598 £320

An attractive late Victorian vinaigrette, the cover set with turquoise and incised with a name in Persian script, by William Summers, 1888. (Phillips) $147 £90

A large silver gilt castletop vinaigrette, the hinged cover chased with a view of Warwick Castle, by Nathaniel Mills, Birmingham, 1839, 1¾in. long. (Christie's) $1,452 £880

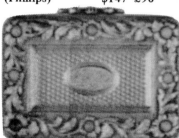

An early 19th century gold engine-turned rectangular vinaigrette, 3 x 2.2cm unmarked, circa 1830. (Phillips) $935 £500

A Victorian shaped oval gilt-lined vinaigrette, the lid depicting a river scene with tree-lined banks and buildings, Nathaniel Mills, Birmingham 1846, 1½in. (Christie's) $471 £286

A silver gilt vinaigrette, the cover repousse and chased with four pheasants in a wooded landscape, by Ledsam, Vale & Wheeler, Birmingham, 1829, 1¾in. long. (Christie's) $1,089 £660

A parcel gilt vinaigrette, the cover repousse and chased with a man in 17th century dress, by Nathaniel Mills, Birmingham, 1835(?), 1¾in. long. (Christie's) $907 £550

A small oblong gold vinaigrette, the cover with a winged putto holding a butterfly. (Christie's) $1,416 £770

A silver gilt vinaigrette with engine turned sides and base, London, 1829, maker's initials A.D. possibly for Allen Dominy, 1.5/8in. long. (Christie's) $635 £385

WINE COOLERS

An Old Sheffield plate tapering two-handled wine cooler
on rococo shell and scroll
feet with detachable liner, unmarked circa 1810, 10in. high.
(Christie's) $503 £286

An oval two-handled wine
cistern, in the Queen Anne
style, Britannia Standard,
maker's mark RR, 24in. long,
239oz. (Christie's)
        $21,384 £13,200

A Victorian silver plated ice
bucket, by Elkington & Co.,
circa 1880, 8½in. high,
together with three other ice
buckets. (Christie's)
        $1,100 £644

One of a pair of plated wine
coolers or jardinieres modelled
as sacks with moulded rims
and rope-twist ties, each with
two ring handles, 9in. high.
(Christie's) $460 £253

A pair of Sheffield plated
wine coolers, engraved with a
shield of arms, 24cm. high.
(Lawrence Fine Art)
        $2,005 £1,050

An Elkington plate wine
cooler and stand, stamped
Cunard White Star, 18¼in.
high. (Christie's)
        $702 £418

One of a pair of Old Sheffield
two-handled partly fluted
campana-shaped wine coolers,
circa 1820, 8¼in. high.
(Christie's) $3,385 £2,090

An Old Sheffield plate gadrooned two-handled compressed vase-shaped wine cooler on
a rising circular foot, 9¼in.
high. (Christie's) $619 £352

One of a pair of wine coolers
with lion mask drop ring side
handles, detachable rims and
tinned liners, 22.5cm. diam.,
circa 1775. (Phillips)
        $3,675 £2,100

WINE FUNNELS

A George III part-fluted wine funnel with curved spigot and reeded rim, maker's initials I.C., London, 1811, 4¾in. long, 5.75oz. (Christie's)
$712 £440

A George III silver wine funnel, by N. Middleton, London, 1805, 4½in. long, 3oz. (Christie's)
$2,970 £1,741

A George III Provincial silver wine funnel, by Richard Richardson, Chester, 4½in. long, 2oz. (Christie's)
$1,650 £967

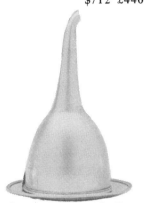

A George III Scottish silver wine funnel, circa 1800, 6.1/8in. long, the stand part-marked for Edinburgh, 1809, maker's mark GMH, 4¼in. diam., 5oz. (Christie's)
$880 £515

A George IV silver wine funnel, by John James Keith, London, 1828, 6¼in. long, 4oz. (Christie's) $1,540 £902

A Victorian silver wine funnel, by A. & J. Savory, London, 1854, 5½in. long, 3oz. (Christie's) $1,375 £806

A George III Scottish silver wine funnel, maker's mark WA, probably for Wm. Auld, Edinburgh, 1813, 5in. long, 4oz.10dwt. (Christie's)
$1,100 £644

Early 19th century Chinese Export silver wine funnel, by Sunshing, Canton, 5¾in. long, 4oz. (Christie's)
$3,520 £2,063

A George III Irish silver wine funnel, maker's mark AG, probably for Andrew Goodwin, circa 1768, 4¼in. long, the stand by Wm. Bond, 1798, 3½in. diam., 3oz. (Christie's)
$935 £548

A George III cast openwork wine label with a reclining satyr beside a barrel, by Phipps & Robinson, probably 1817. (Phillips)
$210   £120

One of a pair of George IV Irish oval wine labels, by James Scott, Dublin, circa 1825. (Phillips) $560 £320

A Victorian Provincial escutcheon wine label, possibly by Thomas Wheatley of Newcastle, circa 1850. (Phillips) $113 £65

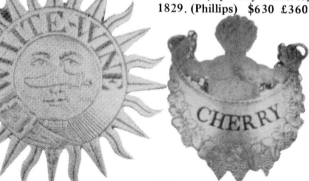

A pair of George III wine labels of shell and fruiting vine design, by Richard Turner, 1819. (Phillips) $402 £230

A Victorian silver bottle ticket for Sherry, in the form of a bat, English or Indian Colonial, circa 1880, 4¼in. wide. (Christie's) $880 £515

A George IV armorial wine label of openwork ribbed disc form, by Riley & Storer, 1829. (Phillips) $630 £360

A set of four Victorian wine labels, each engraved with a crest, by Rawlings & Sumner, London, 1859 and 1860. (Christie's) $281 £176

One of a matched set of four George III armorial wine labels, modelled as a sun with twenty-four rays, by John Rich, 1792. (Phillips)
$1,487 £850

A George III wine label modelled as a putto, by Peter, Anne and William Bateman, 1799. (Phillips) $1,435 £820

A George II Provincial wine label, formed as two putti, by Isaac Cookson, Newcastle, circa 1750. (Phillips) $367 £210

A George III Provincial rectangular thread-edge wine label, by Hampston & Prince, York, 1784/5. (Phillips)
$122 £70

A Victorian wine label of fruiting vine and leafy scroll design, circa 1840. (Phillips)
$210 £120

WINE TASTERS

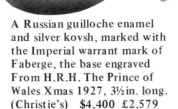

A Russian silver gilt and champleve enamel wine taster, probably Moscow, circa 1900, maker's mark KA, 3.7/8in. diam. (Christie's) $1,760 £1,031

A Russian guilloche enamel and silver kovsh, marked with the Imperial warrant mark of Faberge, the base engraved From H.R.H. The Prince of Wales Xmas 1927, 3½in. long. (Christie's) $4,400 £2,579

A Charles II two handled circular wine taster, punched with bunches of grapes, 1675, 3¾in. diam. (Christie's) $2,057 £1,100

A Louis XVI silver wine taster, Provincial, circa 1780, maker's mark PF over P crowned, 4in. long, 1oz.10dwt. (Christie's) $880 £515

A George III silver wine taster, maker's mark apparently that of Joseph Steward II, London, 1764, 4.1/8in. diam., 2oz. (Christie's) $9,350 £5,480

A Louis XVI silver wine taster, Provincial, circa 1780, possibly Angers, 3.5/8in. long, 1oz. (Christie's) $880 £515

A Louis XVI silver wine taster, maker's mark TN, cockerel between, Reims, 1781-89, 4in. long, 1oz.15dwt. (Christie's) $1,870 £1,069

An Austrian silver parcel gilt wine taster, Vienna, 1676, maker's mark FV, also struck with later control marks, 5½in. long, 3oz. (Christie's) $1,980 £1,160

A Louis XV silver wine taster, possibly by Chas. Despots, with the charge and discharge of A. Leschaudel, 4½in. long. (Christie's) $1,045 £612

A George IV silver wine taster, London, 1828, maker's mark IH, probably for Joseph Hodgson, 4½in. diam., 1oz. 10dwt. (Christie's) $1,045 £612

A Louis XVI silver wine taster, Provincial, circa 1780, with stylised snake handle, 4in. long, 1oz.5dwt. (Christie's) $880 £515

A Russian shaded enamel and silver gilt kovsh, marked the 11th Artel, St. Petersburg, 1908-17, 4½in. long. (Christie's) $2,200 £1,289

An 18th century white jade snuff bottle carved as an aubergine. (Christie's) $1,815 £1,100

A 19th century hair crystal snuff bottle with heavy black tourmaline needle inclusions and some iridescence. (Christie's) $726 £440

An amber snuff bottle carved as a finger citrus, mid Qing Dynasty. (Christie's) $1,089 £660

Late 19th century Lac Burgaute snuff bottle of flattened ovoid form, probably Japanese. (Christie's) $998 £605

Late 18th/early 19th century chalcedony agate snuff bottle, the translucent stone with honey-toned inclusions. (Christie's) $1,815 £1,100

An inside-painted glass snuff bottle, by Zhou Leyuan, signed and dated mid Autumn 1890. (Christie's) $5,445 £3,300

A glass overlay snuff bottle, the opaque blue ground with pink overlay, mid Qing Dynasty. (Christie's) $2,268 £1,375

Late 18th/19th century Baltic amber snuff bottle carved as a gourd. (Christie's) $1,452 £880

A two-colour glass overlay seal-type snuff bottle of baluster form, Yangzhou School. (Christie's) $816 £495

A 19th century brown stone snuff bottle carved as a peach. (Christie's) $907 £550

A chalcedony agate snuff bottle carved as a goldfish, the even stone varying from pale creamy colour to golden tones. (Christie's) $726 £440

An 18th century white brown-skinned jade snuff bottle carved as a double gourd. (Christie's) $1,815 £1,100

Late 18th/early 19th century yellow celadon brown-skinned jade snuff bottle with lion mask ring handles. (Christie's) $3,448 £2,090

Pair of 19th century red lacquer snuff bottles of pilgrim flask form. (Christie's) $1,179 £715

A 19th century moulded famille rose snuff bottle shaped as a cicada, (Christie's) $2,359 £1,430

Late 18th/early 19th century snuff bottle, the snowstorm ground with red overlay. (Christie's) $1,361 £825

A hornbill snuff bottle carved from the tip of the beak, late Qing Dynasty. (Christie's) $816 £495

A stained ivory snuff bottle of baluster shape, late Qing Dynasty. (Christie's) $816 £495

A 19th century nine-colour glass overlay snuff bottle. (Christie's) $544 £330

Late 18th/early 19th century embellished celadon jade snuff bottle, with fitted wood stand. (Christie's) $907 £550

An 18th century black and white jade snuff bottle, Suzhou School. (Christie's) $50,820 £30,800

Late 18th/early 19th century glass overlay snuff bottle of flattened spherical form. (Christie's) $871 £528

A carved white jade snuff bottle, both faces carved in low relief depicting a seated Pharaoh surrounded by simulated hieroglyphics, late Qing Dynasty. (Christie's) $1,179 £715

A two-colour glass overlay snuff bottle, the opaque white ground with black and caramel overlay. (Christie's) $1,815 £1,100

A rock crystal snuff bottle of rounded rectangular form, mid Qing Dynasty. (Christie's) $2,722 £1,650

A glass overlay seal-type snuff bottle of ovoid shape, Yangzhou School. (Christie's) $3,630 £2,200

A mottled glass snuff bottle of ovoid form, mid Qing Dynasty. (Christie's) $635 £385

An 18th century white jade snuff bottle, Suzhou School, the even stone with minor inclusions. (Christie's) $3,630 £2,200

Mid 19th century famille rose snuff bottle of pilgrim flask form, Qianlong six-character mark. (Christie's) $3,448 £2,090

A 19th century Baltic amber snuff bottle of rounded rectangular form. (Christie's) $1,815 £1,100

A 19th century embellished copper snuff bottle of flattened baluster form, Qianlong four-character seal mark. (Christie's) $1,542 £935

An inside-painted and carved rock crystal snuff bottle, signed Ye Zhongsan and dated 1933. (Christie's) $1,179 £715

An inside-painted rock crystal snuff bottle with flaring sides by Ye Zhongsan, signed and dated 1916. (Christie's) $2,722 £1,650

Late 18th/early 19th century pink glass snuff bottle, the rim with jewel festoons. (Christie's) $11,797 £7,150

A 19th century aquamarine snuff bottle, the translucent pale bluish stone of gem-like colour with minor cloudy inclusions. (Christie's) $3,448 £2,090

An enamelled copper European subject snuff bottle of bulbous pear shape, blue enamel Qianlong four-character mark and of the period. (Christie's) $23,595 £14,300

A conglomerate agate snuff bottle, the stone of varied brown and ochre tones with striations of wood-grain patterns, mid Qing Dynasty. (Christie's) $2,722 £1,650

An inside-painted smoky crystal snuff bottle, probably by Ye Zhongsan, signed and dated 1925. (Christie's) $834 £506

An 18th century chalcedony agate snuff bottle, the surface carved in relief with three carp interlocked with a goldfish. (Christie's) $3,267 £1,980

An important and rare Famille Rose gilt-copper enamel snuff bottle, an oval panel inset with a European lady, 18th/19th century. (Christie's) $36,300 £22,000

A chalcedony agate snuff bottle, Suzhou School, the stone highly translucent. (Christie's) $27,225 £16,500

A 19th century moulded and reticulated porcelain snuff bottle, seal mark. (Christie's) $816 £495

Late 18th/early 19th century chloromelanite snuff bottle, the stone of dark spinach tone with emerald-green mottling. (Christie's) $3,630 £2,200

A 19th century banded agate snuff bottle, the translucent stone with attractive bold opaque ochre, white and brown striations. (Christie's) $635 £383

Late 18th/early 19th century glass overlay snuff bottle, the oviform body with a bubble-glass ground with blue overlay. (Christie's) $1,815 £1,100

A pale apple and emerald-green jade snuff bottle, late Qing Dynasty, wood stand. (Christie's) $544 £330

Early/mid 19th century embellished pale celadon jade snuff bottle, fitted wood stand. (Christie's) $1,452 £880

An 18th century glass snuff bottle of spherical shape, probably Beijing workshops. (Christie's) $2,722 £1,650

A coral snuff bottle of ovoid form, carved in relief with a profusion of jars, vases and pots, mid Qing Dynasty. (Christie's) $3,630 £2,200

Late 18th/early 19th century glass overlay snuff bottle, the dense snowstorm ground with blue overlay. (Christie's) $453 £275

Late 18th/early 19th century shadow agate snuff bottle of ovoid form, the body well hollowed. (Christie's) $2,178 £1,320

Late 18th/early 19th century shadow agate snuff bottle, well hollowed. (Christie's) $4,356 £2,640

Early 19th century large white jade snuff bottle, signed Zigang. (Christie's) $1,270 £770

An inside-painted glass portrait snuff bottle, by Ma Shaoxuan, signed and dated Winter 1909. (Christie's) $18,150 £11,000

High Wheel Robot, clockwork mechanism, moveable legs, with visible rotating wheels, sparks in chest, with box, by Yoshiya (mk. 4), Japanese, 1960's, 25cm. high. (Christie's) $770   £412

Planet Robot, battery operated with remote control, rotating antenna on top, with box, by Yoshiya, Japanese, 1950's, 23cm. high. (Christie's) $949 £508

Television Spaceman, battery operated, moveable arms and legs, rotating eyes, screen in chest revealing a space scene, by Alps, Japanese, 1950's, 38.5cm. high. (Christie's) $949 £508

Attacking Martian, battery operated, moveable legs, chest opens to reveal flashing guns, with box, by Horikawa (mk. 6), Japanese, 1960's, 23cm. high. (Christie's)$1,009 £540

Sparky Robot, clockwork mechanism, moveable legs and sparking eyes, with box, by Yoshiya, Japanese, 1950's, 19.5cm. high. (Christie's) $562 £301

Answer-Game, battery operated immobile, executes simple mathematics, flashing eyes, by Ichida (mk. 3), Japanese, 1960's, 35.5cm. high. (Christie's) $2,494 £1,334

Gear Robot, battery operated, moveable legs with coloured wheel rotating chest and flashing head, possibly by Horikawa, Japanese, 1960's, 22.5cm. high. (Christie's) $622 £333

Busy Cart Robot, battery operated, pushing and lifting a wheelbarrow, with box, by Horikawa (mk. 6), Japanese, 1960's/1970's, 30cm. high. (Christie's) $1,187 £635

Ultraman, clockwork mechanism, moveable arms and legs, with box, by Bullmark (mk. 5), Japanese, 1960's, 23cm. high. (Christie's) $355 £190

Sparky Jim, battery operated with remote control, moveable legs and flashing eyes, Japanese, 1950's, 19.5cm. high. (Christie's)$1,247 £667

Nando, the mechanism activated by air pressure through remote control, moveable legs and head, with box, by Opset, Italian, circa 1948, 13cm. high. (Christie's)$2,197 £1,175

Astoman, clockwork mechanism, moveable arms and legs, by Nomura (mk. 1), Japanese, 1960's, 23.5cm. high. (Christie's)$1,067 £571

Space Explorer, battery operated box transforms into Robot, revealing '3-D' television screen, with box, by Yonezawa (mk. 2), Japanese, 1960's, 29.5cm. high. (Christie's) $2,434 £1,302

Mr. Robot, clockwork mechanism and battery activated, with box, by Alps, Japanese, 1950's, 20cm. high. (Christie's) $1,602 £857

Dyno Robot, battery operated, moveable legs, opening mask to reveal a flashing red dinosaur's head, with box, by Horikawa, Japanese, 1960's, 28.5cm. high. (Christie's) $770 £412

Confectionary Dispenser, battery operated, with coinslot, transparent chest showing sweets, Italian, late 1960's, 139cm. high. (Christie's) $2,257 £1,207

Giant Robot, battery operated, moveable legs, chest opening to reveal flashing gun, possibly by Horikawa, Japanese, 1960's, 41cm. high. (Christie's) $1,187 £635

Talking Robot, battery powered, mobile, speaks four different messages, with box, by Yonezawa (mk. 2), Japanese, 1950's, 28cm. high. (Christie's) $1,542 £825

A Royal Aubusson silk and wool tapestry, depicting The Pageant of Man's Redemption, circa 1784. (Christie's) $44,000 £25,142

Late 16th century Brussels silk and wool garden tapestry based on the courtship of Vertumnus and Pomona, 11ft.1in. x 12ft. 8in. (Christie's) $74,800 £42,742

Early 18th century Flemish tapestry with a traveller and two companions beneath trees, 8ft.8in. x 5ft.8in. (Christie's)$5,874 £3,300

Late 16th century Brussels tapestry woven in wools and silks with King Numitor, 10ft. x 12ft.8in. (Christie's) $31,328 £17,600

Mid 17th century Brussels tapestry woven with polychrome silk, wool and metallic threads depicting Moses at the rock, 13ft. 6in. x 15ft.2in. (Christie's)$29,370 £16,500

Late 16th century Brussels silk and wool garden tapestry. (Christie's)
$57,200 £32,683

A Mortlake tapestry depicting Diogenes seated, teaching the Academy of Plato, 3.15 x 2.87m. (Phillips) $7,380 £4,500

Mid 19th century Aubusson tapestry woven in silks and wools with Louis XIV and his army in a landscape defeating the Spanish, 6ft. x 7ft.8in. (Christie's) $4,895 £2,750

A 17th century Brussels mythological tapestry depicting a banquet with Dionysus and Ceres, 3.85 x 2.62m. (Phillips)
          $5,904 £3,600

Mid 16th century Flemish feuille de choux tapestry woven with a parrot and other birds, a snail and dragonfly amid flower-heads, Enghien, 11ft.10in. x 12ft.8in. (Christie's) $43,076 £24,200

A Mortlake tapestry depicting Diogenes lying beside his bath tub with two followers, 3.23 x 2.65m. (Phillips) $7,380 £4,500

A wall tapestry depicting Georgian woodland hunting scene, 70 x 100in. (J. M. Welch & Son) $456 £300

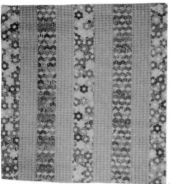

A 19th century patchwork coverlet worked in plain and printed cottons, 2.80 x 2.60m. (Phillips) $291 £180

A late 18th century oval silk-work picture depicting a country lass gathering wheat-sheafs in her apron, 34 x 28cm. (Phillips) $806 £480

A late 18th century Benares cover of red silk gauze woven in gold thread with a central shaped medallion, 1.08 x 1.14m. (Phillips) $297 £180

A 19th century Chinese coverlet of crimson silk, lined and fringed, 2.32 x 2.14m. (Phillips) $288 £160

A shaped panel of 19th century Chinese silk, the blue ground embroidered with coloured silks in pekin knot and satin stitch, 2.08m. high, joined. (Phillips) $648 £400

A late 18th century embroider-ed picture, the ivory silk ground worked mainly in satin stitches, 65 x 70.50cm. (Phillips) $604 £360

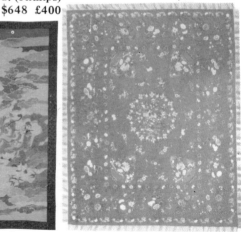

A silk embroidered picture, Mass., 1807, worked in silk yarns on ivory silk satin ground fabric, 8 x 8½in. (Robt. W. Skinner Inc.) $2,200 £1,333

A late 19th century Japanese wall hanging of K'o-ssu woven in pastel coloured silks and gold thread, 3.04 x 1.80m. (Phillips) $3,240 £2,000

An Oriental panel, the fuchsia ground worked in coloured silk threads with butterflies, flowers and Oriental figures, 2.60 x 2.40m. (Phillips) $972 £540

TEXTILES

A 17th century Turkish bocha, the linen ground embroidered in shades of red, blue, yellow and green silks, 1.10 x 1.04m. (Phillips) $1,260 £750

A pair of 19th century oval silkwork pictures, the ivory silk ground embroidered in black and cream silks with lakeside scenes, 11cm. high. (Phillips) $436 £260

An 18th century Anatolian embroidered panel, work in silk on beige silk fabric, 45 x 38in. (Robt. W. Skinner Inc.) $1,300 £787

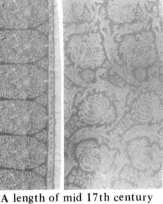

One of a pair of crewelwork curtains, one signed Mary Fincher 1703, 65 x 86in., another pair 41 x 52in. and two pelmets. (Christie's) $2,887 £1,650

An early 18th century Kashmir shawl of crimson pashmina, 2.40 x 1.26m. (Phillips) $1,848 £1,100

A length of mid 17th century Italian brocade woven in crimson and yellow silk, 2.12m. x 53cm., and a fragment similar. (Phillips) $324 £180

A mid 18th century gros et petit point arched firescreen panel worked in coloured wools with a garden scene of musicians, 87.50 x 67cm. (Phillips) $806 £480

An early 18th century needlework picture embroidered with coloured wools and silks in mainly tent stitch, 24 x 21cm. (Phillips) $1,512 £900

A 19th century Rescht cover of red worsted decorated with multi-coloured insertions and applique, 2.24 x 1.45m., fringed, lined. (Phillips) $672 £400

A needlework picture worked in polychrome silk threads on a natural ground, by Lois Burnham, Mass., 1775, 15¾ x 22in. (Christie's) $2,420 £1,463

A 19th century Japanese wall hanging, worked in applied floss silk and cord mainly in pastel shades, 2.5m. x 90cm. (Phillips) $324 £180

A mid 19th century Kashmir shawl, having a central medallion of fawn pashmina, 1.98m. square, reversible. (Phillips) $4,704 £2,800

A rectangular needlework cushion with summer flowers on a brown ground, 18in. wide. (Christie's) $311 £176

A needlework picture worked in petit-point, circa 1660, 13½ x 17in. (Christie's) $9,625 £5,500

Two of four panels from an embroidered screen, worked in coloured silks with various scenes, mid 18th century, two panels 51 x 16in., the other two 56 x 16in. (Christie's) $731 £418

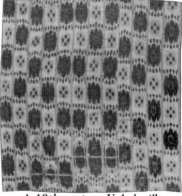

An early 19th century needlework picture of A Map of England & Wales, 49 x 44cm. (Phillips) $436 £260

A mid 17th century stumpwork picture, the ivory silk ground embroidered in coloured silks with mainly French knot, needlepoint and satin stitches, 55 x 58cm. (Phillips) $5,208 £3,100

A 19th century Uzbek silk ikat cover designed with bold red and yellow guhl motifs and green stripes, 1.55m. square, lined. (Phillips) $672 £400

Needlework picture, 'Mary Anne Rowe's Work, Reading, 1834', Penn., silk yarns on canvas, 18 x 22½in. (Robt. W. Skinner Inc.) $15,000 £8,426

A rectangular cushion worked with silver thread and crimson velvet, 18in. wide. (Christie's) $292 £165

'Borboleta de Noite', by Genaro de Carvalho, a gros point needlework picture embroidered in brilliant wools and signed Genaro, 1.05 x 1.22m. (Phillips) $100 £60

A Chinese coverlet of black silk embroidered in couched gold thread and coloured silks, 1.74m. square, lined. (Phillips) $1,134 £700

A mid 19th century needlework picture by Ann Wright, designed with a tablet showing 'The Given Chap. of Exodus', The Ten Commandments, Moses and Aaron, 46.50 x 31.50cm. (Phillips) $1,596 £950

A rectangular cushion worked with metal thread strapwork and foliage on a green silk velvet ground, 26in. (Christie's) $233 £132

An early 18th century English linen coverlet worked in coloured silks and applied silver thread with embroidered and applique motifs, 2.33m. square, (Phillips) $5,208 £3,100

A late 17th century stumpwork picture, the ivory silk ground embroidered mainly in green and brown silks and metal thread in needlepoint, 24 x 39cm. (Phillips) $1,440 £800

A mid 19th century Japanese fukusa, of blue silk with embroidered, applied and couched silks in pastel shades, 78 x 66cm. (Phillips) $745 £460

White Star Line Triple-Screw R.M.S. Olympic and Titanic 45,000 tons each, The Largest Steamers in the World, a colour postcard from R. Phillips to Mr. Wm. Squires, 4 Northfield Cottages, Ilfracombe, Devonshire, postmarked Queenstown 5.45pm 11 April. (Onslow's) $3,260 £2,000

White Star Royal Mail Steamer Titanic, artist drawn, pre-sinking colour postcard, postmarked 1st August 1912, State Series, Liverpool. (Onslow's) $228 £140

A contemporary watercolour drawing of R.M.S. Titanic Leaving Southampton April 12th 1912 Sunk April 15th 1912, signed J. Nicholson, in oval satin mount, 13 x 24cm. (Onslow's) $195 £120

 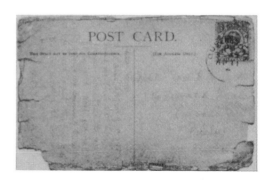

White Star Line Olympic and Titanic Smoke Room, a monochrome postcard to Master Tom Richmond, 14 Lennox Road, Crookston, Paisley, Lothian, postmarked Queenstown 3.45pm 11 April. (Onslow's) $2,445 £1,500

'The Iceberg', a contemporary bromide photograph with ink inscription, 'Iceberg taken by Capt. Wood S.S. Etonian 12 April 1912 in 41° 56N 49° 51W S.S. Titanic Struck 14 April and sank in three hours', 200 x 255mm. (Onslow's) $374 £230

Launch of White Star Royal Mail Triple-Screw Steamer Titanic at Belfast, Wednesday, 31 May 1911, at 12.15pm, a printed card admission ticket in two portions, each numbered 1246, overall size 84 x 136mm. (Onslow's)
$1,793 £1,100

A typed letter to Mr R Penny from W. T. Stead, dated 9 April 1912, on The Review of Reviews writing paper. (Onslow's)
$1,467 £900

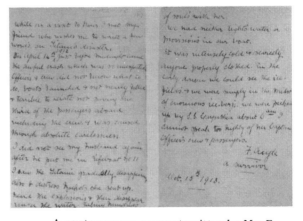

A contemporary account written by Mrs F. Angle of the disaster dated 15 October 1913, on two sheets. (Onslow's)
$978 £600

S.S. Titanic, the cast brass nameplate from Lifeboat No. 12, 322mm. long x 39mm. wide. (Onslow's) $9,128 £5,600

Titanic Leaving Southampton, glossy mono-chrome postcard, published by Nautical Photo Agency, N.W.7. (Onslow's)
$228 £140

'Unterseeboot', a painted metal submarine, by Bing, circa 1902, 17¾in. long. (Christie's) $998 £605

A tin toy car, modelled as two-seater Model A with leather wheels and painted details, 6in. high, 6in. wide, 20in. long. (Christie's) $154 £86

Tipp Co., clockwork lithographed bomber bi-plane TC-1029, wing span 36.5cm., 25.5cm. long, key, lacking pilot, three bombs. (Phillips) $537 £300

A Gunda-Werke lithograph tinplate motorcycle and sidecar with clockwork mechanism, 6½in. long, circa 1920, and a tinplate monkey moneybox. (Christie's) $1,361 £825

Lesney Massey Harris 745D tractor. (Hobbs & Chambers) $210 £120

'Echo', EPL 725, an early printed and painted tinplate motorcyclist with clockwork mechanism operating a metal painted spoked wheel, by Lehmann, circa 1910, 8¾in. long. (Christie's) $2,904 £1,760

Biplane No. 24, with clockwork mechansim, Deutsche Lufthansa markings, wingspan 20¼in. long, by Tipp, circa 1939. (Christie's) $653 £396

A boxed set of six green and cream Tipper lorries with drivers. (Phillips) $358 £200

'Mac 700', a printed and painted tinplate motorbike and rider with clockwork mechanism, causing the rider to hop on and off, 7¼in. long, by Arnold, W. Germany, circa 1955. (Christie's) $471 £286

An Ingap four-door limousine with clockwork mechanism, driving rear axle and operating front head lamps, 11¼in. long, circa 1930. (Christie's) $635 £385

Pre-war tinplate model of a two-seater tourer car, 9½in. long, and a cardboard model of a 'Daily Mail' pre-war aircraft. (Reeds Rains) $50 £30

'Strato Clipper', a printed and painted tinplate four-engine airliner with battery mechanism, by Gama, circa 1956, wingspan 20in. (Christie's) $172 £104

Six turned polychrome Ring Toss Game figures, New England, late 19th century, 14½in. high. (Robt. W. Skinner Inc.)
                                   $3,250 £1,825

Set 2052, Anti-Aircraft Unit with AA gun, searchlight and instruments and operating crew of eight men, in original box, 1959 Britain's. (Phillips) $1,072 £650

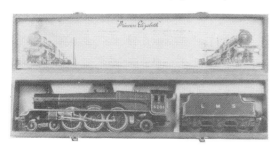

Hornby, 3.R.E. Princess Elizabeth and tender, boxed. (Phillips) $1,969 £1,100

A Schuco 6080 Elektro-Construction tinplate fire engine, in original box, circa 1955. (Osmond Tricks) $412 £250

A German clockwork flying car, 19.5cm., and a Hungarian open tourer in blue, 26cm. (Phillips) $125 £70

Britain's set of Indian Army Cavalry, one bugler and four troopers at the gallop, bearing swords (one sword missing), on original card but no box. (James Norwich Auctions)
$159 £90

Vertunni original paint, Louis XV of France, with his wife, mistress, mother, two Royal Guards and a gentleman. (Phillips) $264 £160

Pelham Puppets, Mickey Mouse and Minnie Mouse. (Phillips) $107 £60

Corgi 803 The Beatles Yellow Submarine, with the four famous members of the band, open hatches and revolving periscopes, in original box. (Christie's) $108 £66

A constructor Racing Car, probably French, with battery operated remote control, 29cm. long. (Phillips) $250 £140

Britain's Set No. 2, The Royal Horse Guards, one officer and four troopers, at the trot, bearing swords (one sword missing), box torn but with label intact. (James Norwich Auctions) $132 £75

'Cadillac', a printed and painted tinplate car, with friction-drive mechanism, rubber tyred wheels and tinted windows, by Ichiko, circa 1967, 28in. long. (Christie's) $651 £395

Britain's Farm, horse-drawn milk float with milkman and two churns, No. 131F, in original box. (Milkman has broken neck.) (James Norwich Auctions) $84 £48

A Harlequin set of nine Steiff skittles, circa 1908, on circular wooden bases. (Lawrence Fine Art) $9,615 £4,840

Dinky Guy 'Spratts' van, no. 514, boxed. (Hobbs & Chambers) $350 £200

A painted wood Noah's Ark on wheels, with opening roof, door and windows, German, circa 1890, 31in. long. (Christie's) $338 £209

Britain's Farm, single-horse plough with ploughman, No. 4/8, in original box. (James Norwich Auctions) $115 £65

A 2in. scale model of a Garrett 'undertype three-way tipper, live-steam wagon, 30in. long. (Anderson & Garland) $1,805 £1,020

Late 19th century Folk Art painted and carved mechanised wooden model of five bearded men at work, America, base 18½in. long. (Robt. W. Skinner Inc.) $1,200 £714

A plush covered lion cub, 9in. long, circa 1925 with Steiff button. (Christie's) $146 £88

Roger Berdou original 54mm. mounted figure entitled 'Garde Imperiale Tartares Lithuaniens Trompette 1812', signed R.B. (Phillips) $297 £180

A German clockwork Drummer Boy dressed as a soldier in busby, 28cm. high. (Phillips) $116 £65

Jigsaw Puzzle, John Wallis's chronological Tables of English History for the Instruction of Youth, 1788, one piece missing. (James Norwich Auctions) $212 £120

A musical teddy bear with swivelling head operated via his tail, 43cm. high. (David Lay) $360 £200

A live steam, spirit fired tinplate vertical steam engine, by Bing, circa 1928, 12½in. high, in original box. (Christie's) $160 £99

German made, a tinplate sentry box with 120mm. Sentry of the Foot Guards, in original box, 1890. (Phillips) $429 £260

Y 11 series 2, 1912 Packard Landaulet, in original box. (James Norwich Auctions) $23 £15

A carved and painted wooden paddle boat, 26in. long. (Christie's) $462 £260

Lehmann, early flywheel driven 'Africa', EP2 No. 170. (Phillips) $447 £250

A Falk tinplate painted clockwork battleship, HMS Invincible, 37cm. long. (Phillips) $751 £420

Tut-Tut or A Run In A Motor Card, A New and Exciting Game, with forty-eight cards depicting an Edwardian open tourer, contained in original box. (Onslow's) $112 £70

A Lehmann 'Lo and Li' tinplate toy. (Hobbs Parker) $1,674 £1,040

Y5 series 1, 1929 4½ litre Le Mans Bentley, in original box. (James Norwich Auctions) $49 £32

Marx, Walt Disney's Donald Duck Duet, boxed. (Phillips) $396 £240

A 70mm. scale figure of the Colonel-in-Chief, the Welsh Guards, with painted legend 'South Africa 1947' on the base, in original box, Britain's. (Phillips) $1,980 £1,200

A clockwork fur covered giraffe with clown rider, 31cm. high, and an HK, Fipps, clockwork nodding puppy. (Phillips) $90 £55

745

Early 20th century miniature Eskimo model of dogsled and team, wooden sled, and four rabbit skin covered papier mache dogs, sled 12.3/8in. long. (Robt. W. Skinner Inc.)
$475 £287

Late 19th century Wilkins cast iron trolley, 'Broadway Car Line 712', 12in. long. (Robt. W. Skinner Inc.) $2,000 £1,212

Hess, clockwork flywheel driven open tourer, 1920's, 23.5cm. long, pressed wheel version. (Phillips) $358 £220

Britains Bluebird, in original box. (James Norwich Auctions) $248 £160

Dinky pre-war set No. 50, 'Ships of the British Navy', together with five other warships and 'Famous Liners'. (Christie's) $267 £165

Dinky Supertoys, 919 Guy van, advertising 'Golden Shred', in original paintwork, with golly, in original box. (Christie's) $712 £440

Corgi, Gift Set No. 23, Chipperfields Circus Models, in original presentation box. (Christie's) $427 £264

JEP: No. 3, clockwork streamline speedboat painted in pale blue and cream with driver, 36cm. long. (Phillips) $81 £50

Dinky Supertoy, No. 514C Guy van, advertising 'Weetabix', in original paintwork and box. (Christie's) $463 £286

A painted tinplate river paddle steamer with clockwork mechanism, 11in. long, by Uebelacker, Nuremberg, circa 1902. (Christie's) $801 £495

A Fleischmann No. 855 oil tanker, a painted tinplate model, 26in. long, circa 1936. (Christie's) $855 £528

A Schuco Ingenico electric remote control car 5311/56, and a Carreto 5330 trailer, in original boxes. (Christie's) $338 £209

A clockwork German cow finished in brown and cream, the mechanism causing the animal to walk and nod, 18.5cm. long. (Phillips) $163 £100

Spot-On, set No. 260, The Royal Presentation Set, in original box. (Christie's) $388 £209

Dinky Supertoys, 514B Guy Van, advertising 'Lyons Swiss Rolls', in original paintwork and box. (Christie's) $570 £352

Large display box Set 93, containing Coldstream Guards with mounted officer, four pioneers, thirteen-piece band, two officers, twelve marching, twelve running, two trumpeters, six troopers and fifteen normal troopers, 1938, Britain's. (Phillips) $11,550 £7,000

Tyrannosaurus Rex and Triceratops. (Phillips) $214 £130

Late 19th century boxed Marklin wind-up train set, sold by F.A.O. Schwartz, New York. (Robt. W. Skinner Inc.) $2,100 £1,272

Fleischmann tinplate clockwork model of a two-funelled ocean liner, 10½in. long. (Prudential Fine Art) $247 £150

Mettoy, a large four-door Saloon finished in bright lime-green with cream lining, the interior with chaffeur at the wheel, in box, 35cm. long. (Phillips) $132 £80

SH-Japanese battery operated Space Station, boxed. (Phillips) $440 £270

Marx, Armoured Floating Tank Transporter, boxed. (Phillips) $74 £45

An early 20th century doll's house, paper covered to simulate brickwork, 88cm. high. (Osmond Tricks) $542 £290

A German post-war clockwork Boxing Match, boxed (no lid). (Phillips) $115 £70

Tekno, Mercedes Tuborg Pilsner Delivery lorry, boxed. (Phillips) $99 £60

A battery-operated four-door Cadillac State Service Car, boxed, 49cm. long. (Phillips) $363 £220

'The Game of Motoring', by Chad Valley, circa 1908, with original box. (Christie's) $169 £104

A model of a horse-drawn cart by Benefink & Co. (Lots Road Chelsea Auction Galleries) $643 £390

A painted wood Noah's Ark, by Erzegebirge, Germany, circa 1870, 23¾in. long, approx. 205 animals. (Christie's) $1,514 £935

Karl Bub, clockwork Atom Rocket Ship, boxed. (Phillips) $181 £110

A mixed collection of 15 lead models, including soldiers, cowboys and red indians, Spanish warship blowing up, two men-of-war, etc., circa early 1920's. (James Norwich Auctions) $34 £22

A collection of 38 French soldiers and Zouaves, including ski troops and one mule, made in France, circa 1940. (James Norwich Auctions) $108 £70

TM, battery operated Supersonic Moon Ship, boxed. (Phillips) $181 £110

Set 68, 2nd Bombay Native Infantry, First Version, in original unmarked early printer's type box, 1896. (Phillips) $1,072 £650

An English leaping clock-work hare. (Phillips) $75 £45

Spot-On, 265 Tonibell Ice Cream van, with server, in original box. (Christie's) $71 £44

'Bulky Mule, The Stubborn Donkey', EPL 425, by Lehmann, circa 1920, 7½in. long. (Christie's) $178 £110

'Our New Clergyman', a stained and carved wood, metal and tinplate preacher, probably by F. Martin, circa 1890, 10½in. high. (Christie's) $2,494 £1,540

Marx, clockwork Moon Mullins and Kayo hand car, 1935, boxed. (Phillips) $244 £150

'The Juba Dancers', carved and stained wood mechanical toy, by Ives, U.S.A., circa 1874, 10in. high. (Christie's) $463 £286

A golden plush covered teddy bear with pronounced hump, pointed snout and with Steiff button in ear, 29in. high. (Christie's) $4,719 £2,860

A printed paper on wood doll's house, by Lines Bros., 43in. wide. (Christie's) $1,542 £935

A golden plush covered teddy bear with boot button eyes, cut muzzle, hump and elongated limbs, with Steiff button in left ear, 19in. high. (Christie's) $871 £528

A honey plush covered pull-along bear on metal wheels, 6in. high, circa 1908, probably Steiff. (Christie's) $471 £286

Spot-On, 271 Express Dairy van, with driver and milk crates, in original box. (Christie's) $35 £22

A small German clockwork leaping Kangaroo. (Phillips) $75 £45

Linemar, battery operated Bubble Blowing Popeye. (Phillips) $391 £240

Two wooden rod puppets with painted faces. (Worsfolds) $164 £100

Marx, clockwork Hi-Yo-The Lone Ranger, boxed. (Phillips) $146 £90

A clockwork somersaulting teddy bear dressing in gold felt jacket, blue trouser and white vest, by Bing of Nuremberg, 9in. high. (Christie's) $943 £572

A painted wooden doll's box-type town house of three bays and three storeys, 25in. high. (Christie's) $544 £330

A golden plush covered teddy bear in the form of a child's muff, 15in. high. (Christie's) $290 £176

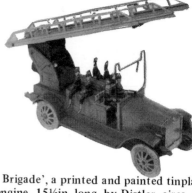

Spot-On cars, including No. 256 Jaguar Police car, two No. 215 blue Daimler SP 250 and No. 191/1 Sunbeam Alpine Hardtop, all in original boxes. (Christie's) $231 £143

'Fire Brigade', a printed and painted tinplate fire engine, 15½in. long, by Distler, circa 1936. (Christie's) $463 £286

An early Marklin gauge 1 mainline station, hand-enamelled, fitted for candle lighting, circa 1903. (Christie's) $1,069 £660

Royal Horse Artillery at the halt, Service Dress with peak caps, khaki uniform, Set 318, in original box, Britain's. (Phillips) $10,725 £6,500

A collection of Britains and other makers World War I soldiers and some trees, circa 1920. (James Norwich Auctions) $77 £50

The Three Bears, a set of miniature all bisque teddy bears jointed at shoulder and hip wearing original crochet clothes, 2¼in.-1¼in. high. (Christie's) $635 £385

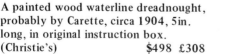

A painted wood waterline dreadnought, probably by Carette, circa 1904, 5in. long, in original instruction box. (Christie's) $498 £308

A Bing repainted three-funnel liner with clockwork mechanism, 14¾in. long, circa 1925. (Christie's) $635 £385

Britains Royal Air Force, set 2011, twenty-two pieces. (Robt. W. Skinner Inc.)
$300 £181

A Jacobean style wood and composition doll's house of four bays and two storeys, 27in. wide. (Christie's) $635 £385

Bing, English market clockwork tramcar of 'O' gauge proportions, 18.5cm. long. (Phillips) $717 £440

Three officers mounted on galloping chargers and two armed Africans riding on a camel, circa early 1920's. (James Norwich Auctions)
$31 £20

A Schuco-Varianto 3010 Motorway, in original box, US Zone W. Germany, circa 1955. (Christie's) $196 £121

The Buddy 'L', a painted metal push-along model T Ford Coupe, 10½in. long, U.S.A., circa 1924. (Christie's) $498 £308

Minic pre-war No. 30M 'Minic Transport' Artic, in original paintwork, with transfers, petrol can and white rubber tyres. (Christie's)
$89 £55

Royal Horse Artillery at the gallop in steel helmets, Set 1339, in original box, 1940 Britain's (Phillips) $11,550 £7,000

A Daimler Sedanca motor car, in the original box. (Geering & Colyer) $576 £320

Nurnberger Blechspielwarenfabrik, clockwork novelty toy in the form of a circus elephant with roller ball shute, 1950, 24cm. high. (Phillips) $125 £70

A searchlight lorry with adjustable electric search-light, in the original box. (Geering & Colyer) $342 £190

Early 19th century rooster squeak toy, moulded papier mache body on coiled wire legs, 5in. high. (Robt. W. Skinner Inc.) $225 £133

An early 20th century two-storeyed doll's house, facade 20 x 18in., depth 12in. (James Norwich Auctions) $448 £280

A gold plush teddy bear, with metal Steiff disc in left ear, German, circa 1907, 25in. high. (Hobbs & Chambers) $3,200 £2,000

A Le Praxinoscope optical toy with shade and ten picture strips, by Emile Reynaud, drum with sellers label. (Christie's) $221 £132

A 20th century wooden rocking horse, painted black, leather bridle and saddle and mounted on a boat-shaped rocker base, 6ft.7in. long. (Lawrence Fine Art)$469 £264

An early Lehmann automobile 'Tut Tut', EPL marque, circa 1910, 6¾in. long. (James Norwich Auctions) $566 £320

TOYS

Dinky 28/3a Hornby Trains Delivery Van, finished in red, advertising 'Hornby Trains British and Guaranteed', in gold decals. (Christie's) $363 £220

A carved wooden paddle toy, modelled as a peacock, 9½in. high. (Christie's) $175 £100

Gunthermann, post-war tramcar finished in orange, cream and pale yellow. (Phillips) $143 £80

A German printed tinplate musical cathedral, printed marks DRGM, Made in Germany, 17.5cm. high. (David Lay) $126 £70

An early gold plush tumbling teddy bear, the body of wood and cardboard, containing a key-wind mechanism, 9in. high. (Lawrence Fine Art) $97 £55

A German made tinplate sentry box with 60mm. mounted sentry of The Royal Horse Guards, in original box, 1890. (Phillips) $544 £330

German straw-filled teddy bear with hump back, pad feet, long nose and button eyes, 11in. high. (Giles Haywood) $311 £190

An early Lehmann, EPL marque, 'Paddy riding his pig to market', with clockwork mechanism, circa 1910, 5½in. long. (James Norwich Auctions) $566 £320

A Doll & Co. printed and painted carousel with a handcranked clockwork mechanism, 11½in. long, circa 1914, (Christie's) $508 £308

1955 Citroen Light 15 four-door saloon, Reg. No. WFX 436, Chassis No. 657720, 1,911 c.c., 56 b.h.p. (Christie's) $8,217 £4,950

1967 Morgan plus four open Sportscar, Reg. No. PUV 316F, Chassis/Engine Nos. not known, engine, Triumph TR4, 2,138 c.c., 104 b.h.p. (Christie's) $5,478 £3,300

1974 Alfa-Romeo 2000 Spider Veloce 2 + 2 open Sportscar, coachwork by Pininfarina, Reg. No. GLT 87N, Chassis No. 247/0730, Engine No. AROS 12/519285, 1,962 c.c., 131 b.h.p. (Christie's) $6,938 £4,180

1957 Ford Thunderbird Sports two-seater with hard and soft tops, Reg. No. KRV 1P, Chassis No. D7FH 302275, 352 cu. ins. (5,769 c.c.), 130 b.h.p. (Christie's) $19,602 £12,100

1935 Bentley 3½-litre four-door Sports saloon, coachwork by Hooper, Reg. No. BLE 714, Chassis No. B40CR, Engine No. U2 BH, 3,669 c.c., 105 b.h.p. (Christie's) $23,166 £14,300

1938 Rolls-Royce Phantom III two-door fixed head Coupe, coachwork by Hooper, Reg. No. 11 DPW, Chassis No. 3CM173, Engine No. P98N, 7,340 c.c., 50.7 h.p. (Christie's) $98,010 £60,500

1930 Austin Seven open two-seater, Reg. No. PG 5934, Chassis No. 105171, Engine No. 105002, 747 cc., 7.8 h.p., right-hand drive. (Christie's) $4,455 £2,750

1957 Mercedes-Benz 300SL two-seat Roadster, Reg. No. CSU 418, Chassis No. 7500143, Engine No. 198042, 2,996 c.c., 215 b.h.p. (Christie's) $76,692 £46,200

1949 Aston Martin DB1 open Sports two-seater, coachwork by Swallow, Reg. No. MKE 836, Chassis No. AMC 49/8, Engine No. LB6B/50/630, 2,580 c.c., (Christie's) $31,042 £18,700

1932 Mercedes-Benz 170 four-door saloon, Reg. No. GP 6387, Chassis No. U88418, Engine No. 88418, 1,692 c.c., 32 b.h.p. (Christie's) $7,669 £4,620

1937 MG VA four-seat drophead Coupe, coachwork by Tickford, Reg. No. COR 331, Chassis No. VA 0850, Engine No. TPBG 1099, 1,549 c.c., 55 b.h.p. (Christie's) $16,929 £10,450

1930 Rolls-Royce Phantom II Sedanca De Ville, coachwork by Barker, Reg. No. USV 694, Chassis No. 202 GN, Engine No. J65, 7.7-litre, 40/50 h.p. (Christie's) $94,952 £57,200

1937 Mercedes-Benz 540K Supercharged Cabriolet B, coachwork by Daimler-Benz, Sindelfingen, Reg. No. Not registered in U.K., Chassis No. 154119, 5,401 c.c., 115 b.h.p. (Christie's) $182,600 £110,000

1954 Jaguar XK 120 Roadster To Rally Specification, Reg. No. RJH 400, Chassis No. S661165, Engine No. F2111/85, 3,442 c.c., 160 b.h.p. (Christie's) $63,910 £38,500

1956 Bentley S1 four-door Sports saloon, Reg. No. JTL 717, Chassis No. B80 CK, Engine No. BC40, 3,887 c.c. (Christie's) $12,830 £7,920

1952 Aston Martin DB2 two-seat Sports saloon, Reg. No. NGO 655, Chassis No. LML/50/218, 2,580 c.c., 107 b.h.p. in standard tune. (Christie's) $12,474 £7,700

Leyland 36 H.P. platform lorry, circa 1920, Reg. No. UV 6025, Engine No. 26860, (Christie's) $8,217 £4,950

1959 Jaguar XK150 fixed head Coupe, Reg. No. 499 KBH, Chassis No. 8247620-W, Engine No. V6429-8, 3,442 c.c., 210 b.h.p. (Christie's) $15,147 £9,350

1899 De Dion-Bouton D1 3½ H.P. Vis-A-Vis, Reg. No. PM 643, Chassis No. 73, Engine No. 228, 400 c.c.. (Christie's) $24,057 £14,850

1926 Austin Seven Chummy two-door open tourer, Reg. No. PN 2231, Chassis No. 17973, Engine No. 7H2 TIA 38AF2, 747 c.c., 11 b.h.p. (Christie's) $7,669 £4,620

1921 Hillman 11 'Peace Model' two-seat drop-head Coupe with dickey, Reg. No. BY 3898, Chassis No. 1686, Engine No. 1686, 1,580 c.c., 10.4 b.h.p. (Christie's) $17,529 £10,560

1946 Rover Twelve four-door saloon, Reg. No. LSV 897, Chassis No. BA1372, Engine No. N/A, 1,496 c.c., 12 h.p. (Christie's) $2,739 £1,650

1954 Mercedes-Benz 300 SL two-seat Gull-wing Coupe, Reg. No. KVE 886F, Chassis No. 1980404500122, Engine No. 198980, Bosch fuel injection, 2,996 c.c., 215 b.h.p. (Christie's) $151,470 £93,500

Leyland ¾ ton chassis/cab, circa 1923, Reg. No. DY 4227, Chassis/Engine No. 13662, 30/36 h.p. (Christie's) $7,304 £4,400

1947 MG 1¼-litre Y-type four-door Sports saloon, Reg. No. MG 7180, Chassis No. YO297, Engine No. XPAG SC10051, 1,250 c.c., 46 b.h.p. (Christie's) $5,478 £3,300

1930 Lea-Francis P type 12/40 drophead Coupe with dickey, coachwork by Cross & Ellis, Reg. No. KX 4497, Chassis No. 13953, Engine No. 9982, 1,496 c.c., 40 b.h.p. (Christie's) $13,365 £8,250

1962 Mercedes-Benz 300 SL Roadster, Reg. No. Not Registered in the U.K., Chassis No. 1980421000298, Engine No. 19898010003022, Bosch fuel injection, 2,996 c.c., 215 b.h.p. (Christie's) $101,574 £62,700

1929 Austin Seven 'Top Hat' two-door saloon, Reg. No. KR 1019, Chassis Nos. 102226, Engine No. 84995, 747.5 c.c., 11 b.h.p. (Christie's) $10,225 £6,160

1968 ISO Grifo A3L 2 + 2 Sports Coupe, Not Registered in U.K., Chassis No. 820 202, Engine No. 1067Y0323HT, 5,359 c.c., 350 b.h.p. (Christie's) $17,820 £11,000

1955 Triumph TR2 two-seat Sportscar, Reg. No. RXV 318, Chassis No. TS 7707, Engine No. TS 8003, 1,991 c.c., 90 b.h.p. (Christie's) $7,304 £4,400

1953 Alvis-Healey G-type 3-litre convertible Sports 2/3 seater, Reg. No. NXR 829, Chassis No. G518, Engine No. 25318, 2,993 c.c. (Christie's) $10,956 £6,600

1931 Rolls-Royce 20/25 Doctor's Coupe, coachwork by Windover, Reg. No. GP 5803, Chassis No. GO510, Engine No. D9E, 3.7-litres, 20/25 h.p. (Christie's) $60,588 £37,400

1968 Aston Martin DB6 Superleggera Grand touring four-seater, Reg. No. SKK 714G, Chassis No. DB6L/L001R, Engine No. 400/406, 3,996 c.c., 282 b.h.p. (Christie's) $17,820 £11,000

1953 Jaguar XK120 Special Equipment two-seat Roadster, Reg. No. IRXB 240 (USA), Chassis No. S673307, Engine No. W6896-85, 3,442 c.c., 160 b.h.p. (Christie's) $24,057 £14,850

1963 Chevrolet Corvette Stingray 'Split-Window' Sports Coupe, Reg. No. ABK 747A, Chassis No. 30837S102721, 327 cu. ins. (5,350 c.c.). (Christie's) $28,512 £17,600

1927 Austin Seven four-seat Chummy tourer, Reg. No. WW 753, Chassis No. A4-2041, Engine No. 33977, 747 c.c., 7.8 h.p. (Christie's) $5,346 £3,300

1938 Daimler Light Straight Eight four-door Sports saloon, coachwork by Charlesworth, Reg. No. RN6265, Chassis No. 4770, Engine No. 88611, 3,421 c.c., 26 h.p. (Christie's) $24,651 £14,850

1956 Jaguar XK 140 two-door fixed head Sports Coupe, Reg. No. SDA 898, Chassis No. 804705, Engine No. 67855-8, 3,442 c.c., 190 b.h.p. (Christie's) $16,251 £9,790

1948 Rolls-Royce Silver Wraith Sedanca De Ville, coachwork by H. J. Mulliner, Reg. No. Not registered in U.K., Chassis No. WYA 32, Engine No. W197A, 4,256 c.c., approx. 125 b.h.p. (Christie's) $19,173 £11,550

1960 MGA 1600 two-seat Sports Coupe, Reg. No. YLT 629, Chassis No. CHD 82813, Engine No. 16JEUL 11195, 1,588 c.c. (Christie's) $4,747 £2,860

1950 MG TD Midget 2 + 2 seat Sportscar, Reg. No. KSM 567, Chassis No. TO TD 0509, Engine No. XPAG/TD/867, 1,250 c.c., 54 b.h.p. (Christie's) $10,225 £6,160

1949 HRG Sports two-seater, Reg. No. KYD 103, Chassis No. S96, Engine No. 7160986, 2,088 c.c., 90 b.h.p. (Christie's) $15,147 £9,350

1953 MG TF Midget two-seat Sportscar, Reg. No. OGN 866, Chassis No. HDA 261736, Engine No. XPAG/TF/30443, 1,250 c.c., 57 b.h.p. (Christie's) $18,260 £11,000

1923 Daimler CK 2/3 ton dropside lorry, Reg. No. BK 8749, Chassis No. CK 4269, Engine No. 46315, 22 h.p. (Christie's) $12,782 £7,700

1956 Bentley S1 Continental two-door drop-head Coupe, coachwork by Park Ward, Reg. No. PLG 123, Chassis No. BC 77 BG, Engine No. BA 76128 UE 3764. (Christie's)
$94,446 £58,300

1925 Dodge 24 H.P. four-seat tourer, Reg. No. YR 9579, Chassis No. A324590, Engine No. A396282, 3,478 c.c., 23.8 h.p. (Christie's)
$14,256 £8,800

1931 Lagonda 14/60 Low Chassis 2-litre Tourer, Reg. No. GN 4840, Chassis No. OH 9825, Engine No. OH 1574, 1,955 c.c., (Christie's)
$40,172 £26,950

1932 Austin Seven two-door saloon, Reg. No. KJ 5917, Chassis No. 15490, Engine No. M152369, 747 c.c., 7.8 h.p. (Christie's)
$4,455 £2,750

1982 De Lorean DMC 12 Gullwing Sports Coupe, Reg. No. C 441 FKE, Chassis No. 11761, Engine No. 7979, 2,850 c.c., 130 b.h.p. (Christie's)
$21,912 £13,200

1926/1932 Sentinel DG4 steam waggon, Reg. No. OD 1572, Chassis No. 8666, 120 b.h.p. (Christie's)
$42,454 £25,575

1948 Lago-Talbot Record T26 two-door Cabriolet, coachwork by Chapron, Reg. No. 3351 XC 77, Chassis No. 100060, 4,482 c.c., 170 b.h.p. (Christie's)
$40,172 £24,200

1938 Rolls-Royce 25/30 drophead Coupe, coachwork based on Vanden Plas design, Reg. No. BGG 759, Chassis No. U259, Engine No. GGR 23, 4,257 c.c.. (Christie's)
$44,737 £26,950

Dickens, B.R. Blackpool Gay and Bright Day and Night, quad royal. (Onslow's)
$352 £220

Frank Newbould, L.N.E.R. Isle of Walcheren Holland, quad royal. (Onslow's)
$272 £170

Tom Purvis, L.N.E.R. Yorkshire Moors, quad royal. (Onslow's)
$640 £400

Sir D. Y. Cameron, LMS Stirling, The Best Way Series No. 50, quad royal. (Onslow's)
$240 £150

Kenneth Shoesmith, Cowes Week & Yacht Racing In The Solent, pub. by Southern Railway, quad royal, 1933. (Onslow's) $704 £440

Norman Wilkinson, LMS Garston The LMS Merseyside Port, quad royal. (Onslow's)
$480 £300

Norman Wilkinson, LMS The Firth of Clyde, The Best Way Series No. 68, quad royal, 1925. (Onslow's) $256 £160

L.N.E.R. Scarborough, 1932, by Austin Cooper, quad royal, 40 x 50in. (Onslow's)
$573 £370

Ateo, Southern Railway, The Joys of North Cornwall and North Devon by 'Atlantic Coast Express', quad royal, 1929. (Onslow's) $704 £440

Maurice Greiffenhagen, LMS Carlisle The Gateway to Scotland, R.A. Series No. 2, quad royal. (Onslow's)
$368 £230

Leslie Carr, Navy Week Visit The Dockyards, Chatham, Portsmouth, Devonport, quad royal, 1930. (Onslow's)
$304 £190

Frank Mason, Famous Rivers of Commerce, The Humber, pub. by L.N.E.R., quad royal, 40 x 50in. (Onslow's)
$64 £40

Cambridge Architecture
Elizabethan, by Fred Taylor,
published by L.N.E.R.,
double royal, 40 x 25in.
(Onslow's) $124 £80

L.M.S. See The Peak District,
by S. R. Wyatt, double royal,
40 x 25in. (Onslow's)
                $248 £160

L.N.E.R. The Flying Scotsman's Cocktail Bar . . ., by
Maurice Beck, double royal,
40 x 25in. (Onslow's)
            $2,170 £1,400

L.M.S. Travel to Ireland By
The Stranraer-Larne Route
. . ., by Norman Wilkinson,
double royal, 40 x 25in.
(Onslow's) $279 £180

London - United - Electric
Tramways District Railway,
on two sheets, 50 x 40in.
(Onslow's) $201 £130

L.M.S. Bournemouth For
Health and Pleasure, Travel
By The 'Pines' Express . . .,
by G. D. Tidmarsh, double
royal, 40 x 25in. (Onslow's)
                $217 £140

L.N.E.R. Then — and Now
600 Golf Courses . . ., by
A. R. Thomson, double
royal, 40 x 25in. (Onslow's)
                $434 £280

Factories on L.N.E.R. Lines
Are on the Right Lines, by
Austin Cooper, double
royal, 40 x 25in. (Onslow's)
                $558 £360

B.R. East Coast Havens,
Norfolk, Sailing Trawlers
Leaving Gorleston, by F.
H. Mason, quad royal, 40
x 25in. (Onslow's) $124 £80

Poster by Alec Fraser, G.W.R.
Cheap Fares Fast Trains and
Steamers to Southern Ireland
It's Lakes and Landscapes,
double royal. (Onslow's)
$436 £260

Poster by Leonard Padden,
S.R. Swanage, Dorset, For
Sunshine And Health, double
royal, 1931. (Onslow's)
$67 £40

G.W.R. Barry, 1930, by
Lindsay Cable, double royal,
40 x 25in. (Onslow's)
$170 £110

B.R. Littlehampton for
Sands and Sunshine, 1950,
by Allinson, double royal,
40 x 25in. (Onslow's)
$147 £95

Poster S. & D.J.R. Attractive
Half-Day Excursions to Poole
and Bournemouth Sept. 1934,
letterpress, double royal .
(Onslow's) $30 £18

L.N.E.R. Sandringham Hotel,
Hunstanton, by Gordon
Nichol, double royal, 40 x
25in. (Onslow's) $310 £200

L.N.E.R. Fraserburgh . . .,
by H. G. Gawthorn, double
royal, 40 x 25in. (Onslow's)
$418 £270

L.N.E.R. Wages of Signalmen
for 1 year £1,837,647, Going
On All The Time, by Austin
Cooper, double royal, 40 x
25in. (Onslow's) $325 £210

L.N.E.R. Then — and Now,
'The Flying Scotsman' . . .,
by A. R. Thomson, double
royal, 40 x 25in. (Onslow's)
$511 £330

The Royal Mail Line to South America . . ., by Kenneth Shoesmith. (Onslow's)
$589 £380

H. G. Gawthorn, Power & Progress On The L.N.E.R., quad royal, 40 x 50in. (Onslow's) $672 £420

Cunard, Europe - America, Berengaria, by Odin Rosenvinge. (Onslow's)
$775 £500

United States Lines, S.S. Leviathan . . ., by R. S. Pike Dorland. (Onslow's)
$480 £310

S.R. Winter in the Southern Sunshine and Warmth of Bournemouth . . ., quad royal, 40 x 50in. (Onslow's)
$434 £280

Angrave, Great Western Railway South Wales For Bracing Holidays, double royal, 40 x 25in. (Onslow's) $400 £250

SEE BRITAIN FIRST ON SHELL

ROYAL STATION HOTEL YORK

Frank Sherwin, B.R. Windsor, double royal. (Onslow's)
$48 £30

Shillingford Bridge, Oxfordshire, See Britain First On Shell, No. 282, 30 x 45in. (Onslow's) $248 £160

Gordon Nicoll, Royal Station Hotel, York, double royal, 40 x 25in. (Onslow's)
$416 £260

Anchor Line, Glasgow &
New York via Londonderry,
by Kennth Shoesmith.
(Onslow's) $527 £340

Austin Cooper, Cruden Bay By East
Coast Route, quad royal, 40 x 50in.
(Onslow's) $1,056 £660

White Star to Canada, There's
Nothing Better, Cabin Lounge,
S.S. Laurentic, by Gordon
Nichol. (Onslow's) $449 £290

Frank Newbould, L.N.E.R.
Ripon, double royal.
(Onslow's) $120 £75

Robert Bartlett, Scotland By 'The
Night Scotsman', pub. by L.N.E.R.,
quad royal, 40 x 50in. (Onslow's)
                   $2,400 £1,500

Norman Wilkinson, Isle of
Man for Holidays, The Isle
of Man Steam Packet Co.
Ltd., double royal.
(Onslow's) $128 £80

Penaga, Great Southern &
Western Railway, The
Liverpool Overhead Electric
Railway, double royal.
(Onslow's) $368 £230

L.N.E.R. Harrogate, by Frank
Newbould, quad royal, 40 x
50in. (Onslow's) $325 £210

E. McKnight Kauffer, Orient
Line to Australia and Back
£140 First Class, double
royal. (Onslow's) $736 £460

The Royal Mail Line For Luxurious Travel To South America, by E. Hamilton, (Onslow's) $186 £120

E. E. Wise, Bridge of Allan Stirlingshire, The Caledonian Railway, on linen, 40 x 29in. (Onslow's) $192 £120

Walter Spradbery, L.N.E.R. Ely, double royal. (Onslow's) $80 £50

Webber, Winter Sports Expresses, pub. by Southern Railway, double royal, 1934. (Onslow's) $192 £120

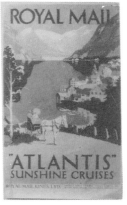

Padden, Royal Mail 'Atlantis' Sunshine Cruises, double royal. (Onslow's) $80 £50

Freiwirth, L.N.E.R. Up To Scotland From King's Cross, double royal. (Onslow's) $320 £200

Charles Pears, London & Isle of Wight in 40 minutes Daily Services, pub. by Southern Railway, double royal, 1935. (Onslow's) $512 £320

William McDowell, Southern Railway The New 'Golden Arrow' Pullman With Special Boat Service from May 15, double royal, 1929. (Onslow's) $704 £440

T. D. Kerr, Golfing in Southern England and On The Continent Southern Railway, double royal, 1932. (Onslow's) $384 £240

Rio De Janeiro, By Royal
Mail To South America, by
Kenneth Shoesmith.
(Onslow's) $372 £240

White Star Line, Liverpool
to Australia via Capetown.
(Onslow's) $356 £230

Alfred Lambart, L.N.E.R.
Dunbar, double royal.
(Onslow's) $384 £240

P-S-N-C To South America,
by Kenneth Shoesmith.
(Onslow's) $341 £220

Edwin Hubert, Pacific Line
Bermuda Tours 'Within The
Empire', double royal.
(Onslow's) $80 £50

Gordon Nicoll, North British
Station Hotel, Edinburgh,
double royal, 40 x 25in.
(Onslow's) $336 £210

Harry Hudson Rodmell,
Cruises from Liverpool to
The Scottish Firths & Fjords
Travel LMS to Liverpool,
double royal. (Onslow's)
                $160 £100

William McDowell, LMS
Express & Cunard Liner,
The Highest Standard of
Comfort in Rail and Ocean
Travel, double royal.
(Onslow's) $2,240 £1,400

Penaga, Great Southern &
Western Railway Paris In
London, on linen, double
royal. (Onslow's)
                $736 £460

Sheet copper weathervane, America, late 19th century, silhouette of a cannon, 24in. wide. (Robt. W. Skinner Inc.) $750 £414

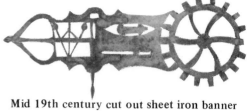

Mid 19th century cut out sheet iron banner weathervane, Lafayette, Rhode Island, 50in. long. (Robt. W. Skinner Inc.)
$2,500 £1,562

Late 19th century moulded copper and zinc running horse weathervane, 'Smuggler', America, 46in. high, 31in. long. (Robt. W. Skinner Inc.) $1,200 £674

Copper bull weathervane, America, late 19th century, full-bodied figure standing bull, 18½in. high. (Robt. W. Skinner Inc.)
$750 £414

Cast iron horse weathervane, Rochester, New Hampshire, late 19th century, full bodied figure of a prancing horse, 36in. wide. (Robt. W. Skinner Inc.)
$11,000 £6,077

Mid 19th century moulded copper and zinc leaping stag weathervane, New England, 27in. high, 30in. long. (Robt. W. Skinner Inc.)
$5,500 £3,089

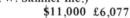

A large sheet iron horse weathervane, long. (Christie's) $550 £310

A 19th century moulded copper and zinc trotting horse weathervane, America, 23¼in. high, 34in. long. (Robt. W. Skinner Inc.)
$3,400 £1,910

Rare fire hose wagon weathervane, Mass., last quarter 19th century, full-bodied figure of copper horse pulling copper and iron hose wagon. (Robt. W. Skinner. Inc.) $55,000 £30,386

Early 20th century copper train weathervane, America, 60in. long, 12½in. high. (Robt. W. Skinner Inc.) $11,000 £6,547

Sheet iron train weathervane, America, late 19th/early 20th century, silhouette of Locomotive and tender on railroad track, 22in. long. (Robt. W. Skinner Inc.) $650 £359

Late 19th century copper and zinc quill weathervane, New England, with traces of gold leaf, 25½in. high, 24½in. long. (Robt. W. Skinner Inc.) $1,800 £1,011

Late 19th century gilded copper leaping stag weathervane with zinc head, 30in. long, mounted on display stand. (Robt. W. Skinner Inc.) $4,100 £2,440

A trumpeting angel silhouette weathervane, constructed of sheet iron, supported by wrought-iron strapping, New England, circa 1800, 59in. long. (Robt. W. Skinner Inc.) $40,000 £23,809

Mid 19th century copper telescope weathervane, New England, 62in. high, 49in. long. (Robt. W. Skinner Inc.) $4,500 £2,528

Late 19th century copper horse and trainer weathervane, America, traces of gold leaf under yellow ochre paint, 29in. long. (Robt. W. Skinner Inc.) $4,000 £2,380

1 bottle Chateau Haut-Brion—Vintage 1899, Pessac, Graves, 1er cru classe, Recorked by Whitwham & Co., 1979, excellent neck level and deep colour, label soiled. (Christie's) $902 £545

Two bottles of Chateau Haut-Brion—Vintage 1906, Pessac, Graves, 1er cru classe, one recorked by Whitwham & Co., 1980, top-shoulder level, excellent deep colour and good labels. (Christie's) $572 £345

1 bottle Chateau Lafite—Vintage 1858, Pauillac, 1er cru classe, Recorked by Whitwham & Co., 1980, with a neck level and deep colour. (Christie's) $2,420 £1,463

1 magnum Chateau Mouton-Rothschild—Vintage 1878, Pauillac, 1er cru classe, Recorked by Whitwham & Co., 1980, neck level and deep colour, label soiled. (Christie's) $2,860 £1,729

1 double magnum Chateau Lafite—Vintage 1865, Pauillac, 1er cru classe, with deep colour and level in the neck, with Christie's slip label. (Christie's) $17,050 £10,308

1 bottle Chateau d'Yquem—Vintage 1921, Sauternes, 1er grand cru classe, top-shoulder level and deep amber gold colour. (Christie's) $902 £545

1 bottle Chateau Mouton-Rothschild—Vintage 1899, Pauillac, 1er cru classe, Chateau-embossed capsule, neck level and deep colour. (Christie's) $902 £545

Six bottles of Barolo Riserva—Vintage 1947, Piedmont, Giacomo Borgogno & Figli. (Christie's) $858 £518

1 bottle Chateau Lafite-Vintage 1888, Pauillac, 1er cru classe, Recorked by Whitwham & Co., 1980, and with neck level. (Christie's) $792 £478

1 bottle Chateau Lafite—Vintage 1945, Pauillac, 1er cru classe, neck level. (Christie's) $682 £412

Two bottles of Chateau d'Yquem—Vintage 1940, Sauternes, 1er grand cru classe, excellent honey gold colour, neck level, labels slightly stained. (Christie's)
$1,012 £611

1 bottle Chateau Latour—Vintage 1874, Pauillac, 1er cru classe, Recorked by Whitwham & Co., 1982, excellent colour.(Christie's)
$1,485   £897

1 jeroboam Chateau Lafite—Vintage 1949, Pauillac, 1 er cru classe, with a neck level, deep colour, and pristine label. (Christie's) $2,420 £1,418

1 double magnum Chateau Petrus—Vintage 1953, Pomerol, neck level and pristine label. (Christie's)
$3,630 £2,194

1 bottle, with original cork attached, Chateau Mouton-Rothschild—Vintage 1888, Pauillac, 1er cru classe, Recorked by Whitwham & Co., 1980, level in neck. (Christie's) $682 £412

1 bottle Chateau Petrus—Vintage 1945, Pomerol, excellent top-shoulder level, label slightly tattered and soiled. (Christie's)
$1,650 £997

Three bottles of Chateau Cheval-Blanc—Vintage 1929, Saint-Emilion, 1er grand cru ciasse (A), two recorked by Whitwham & Co., 1982. (Christie's) $1,045 £631

1 jeroboam, in original case, Chateau Mouton-Rothschild—Vintage 1929, Pauillac, 1er cru classe, high-shoulder level, garnet colour and pristine label. (Christie's)
$8,800 £5,320

1 bottle Chateau Mouton—Vintage 1870, Pauillac, 1er cru classe, Bordeaux-bottled, neck level, deep garnet colour, clean label . (Christie's) $2,530 £1,529

Two bottles of Romanee-Conti—Vintage 1919, Recorked by Whitwham & Co., level only 1in.-1½in. below corks, deep colour. (Christie's) $1,265   £764

1 bottle Chateau Lafite Blanc—Vintage 1934, Pauillac, top-shoulder level and honey gold colour, excellent label, slightly soiled. (Christie's) $682 £412

1 bottle Romanee-Conti—Vintage 1924, Domaine de la Romanee-Conti, excellent level only 1½in. below cork, deep colour maturing at rim. (Christie's) $605 £365

Three magnums of Clos des Lambrays—Vintage 1947, Cote de Nuits, Heritiers Cosson, levels very high, only 1in.-2in. below corks. (Christie's) $682 £412

1 bottle Chateau Mouton-Rothschild—Vintage 1874, Pauillac, 1er cru classe, Chateau-embossed capsule, neck level, deep colour and pristine labels. (Christie's) $1,320 £798

1 bottle Chateau Margaux—Vintage 1888, Margaux, 1er cru classe, Recorked by Whitwham & Co., 1981, with neck level, original cork attached to neck of bottle. (Christie's) $418 £252

Two bottles of Romanee-Conti—Vintage 1934, Domaine de la Romanee-Conti, excellent level on 1in.-2in. below corks, deep colour to rim, labels slightly soiled. (Christie's) $902 £545

1 bottle Les Gaudichots—Vintage 1929, Domaine de la Romanee-Conti, excellent level only 1in. below cork, deep colour, label soiled. (Christie's) $572 £345

1 bottle Chateau Latour-Vintage 1896, Pauillac, 1er cru classe , Recorked by Whitwham & Co., 1981, neck level and deep colour, label soiled and worn. (Christie's) $462 £279

Two bottles of La Tache—Vintage 1945, Domaine de la Romanee-Conti, levels only 1½in.-2in. below corks, deep colour, labels slightly soiled. (Christie's) $1,045 £631

1 bottle Beaulieu Vineyard Napa Valley Cabernet Sauvignon—Vintage 1961, Private Reserve, Georges de Latour. (Christie's) $137 £83

1 bottle Chateau Petrus—Vintage 1943, Pomerol, top-shoulder level, label slightly soiled, resealed capsules. (Christie's) $550 £332

Three bottles, neck level, Chateau Cheval-Blanc—Vintage 1947, Saint-Emilion, 1er grand cru classe (A), top-shoulder levels and deep colour. (Christie's) $1,540 £931

1 bottle Chateau d'Yquem—Vintage 1928, Sauterns, 1er grand cru classe, top-shoulder levels and honey gold colour. (Christie's) $682 £412

1 magnum, neck level, Chateau Haut-Brion—Vintage 1947, Pessac, Graves, 1er cru classe, label with minor stains and soil. (Christie's) $792 £478

Two bottles of Chateau d'Yquem—Vintage 1937, Sauternes, 1er grand cru classe, top-shoulder levels and medium honey gold colour. (Christie's) $1,155 £698

1 magnum Chateau Lafite-Vintage 1869, Pauillac, 1er cru classe, excellent mid-shoulder level. (Christie's) $3,740 £2,261

A 19th century boxwood wrist-rest, unsigned, 5.5cm. long. (Christie's) $880 £550

A walnut carving of a horse-drover and horse pulling a section of tree, carved by A. L. B. Huggler, circa 1900, plinth 34in. x 8½in. (Prudential Fine Art) $1,541 £940

Early 19th century carved dark wood mask of Hannya, 5.8cm. high. (Christie's) $281 £176

Carved oak fire surround and overmantel, 5ft. long, 4ft 4ft. high. (Giles Haywood) $451 £275

A Maori wood fish hook, 12cm. high, and another two 9cm. and 10cm. high. (Phillips) $196 £120

One of a pair of giltwood jardinieres with overhanging reeded lips, 11in. wide. (Christie's) $1,837 £1,100

A 19th century lacquered wood mask of Ayagiri, 4.6cm. high. (Christie's) $1,487 £880

A Netherlandish oak panel carved in relief with the Adoration of the Magi, 17th/18th century, 71 x 81cm. (Phillips) $2,934 £1,800

One of a pair of Italian carved pine girandoles, 27½in. high. (Christie's) $2,204 £1,320

WOOD

Late 19th/early 20th century, Continental wood window display, probably French, in the form of a cask-rack, 22½in. high. (Christie's)
$1,760   £1,031

Two African wood carvings, Benin, an incised double bell, 4in. high, and a standing figure holding serpent, 6in. high. (Robt. W. Skinner Inc.)
$1,200   £727

Early 20th century primitive carved eagle, American, the body carved from a single block of pine, 21in. long. (Robt. W. Skinner Inc.)
$375   £234

A Gustav Stickley round slat-sided waste basket, no. 94, circa 1907, 14in. diam. (Robt. W. Skinner Inc.) $1,200 £714

A pair of Chinese painted carved wooden figures, late 18th/early 19th century, the gentleman 46¼in. high, the lady 21¼in. high. (Christie's) $17,820 £11,000

A mahogany octagonal waste paper basket with tapering fretwork sides and bracket feet, 11½in. wide. (Christie's) $4,329 £2,640

A Chinese carved hardwood figure of a sage with inset ivory eyes and teeth, 17in. high. (Dacre, Son & Hartley)
$147 £90

A large shaped rectangular framed wooden panel, unsigned, Meiji period, 82 x 60cm. (Christie's) $2,805 £1,650

A 16th century Flemish oak relief carved group of a moustachioed soldier and his female companion, 42cm. high. (Phillips)
$5,542 £3,400

Early 19th century George III mahogany wine tray, with twenty-two square divisions in two sizes, 18in. long. (Christie's) $1,210 £709

A Maori wood feather box of oval form, the lid carved with a tiki figure at each end, 45cm. long. (Phillips) $738 £450

Early 19th century George III mahogany bottle carrier, 15½in. by 14¼in. (Christie's) $1,210 £709

One of a pair of giltwood wall brackets of rococo design, 13½in. high. (Christie's) $4,989 £3,080

A late 16th century poly-chromed and carved lime-wood relief panel of a bearded saint, possibly St. Christopher, 37cm. high. (Phillips) $652 £400

One of a pair of George III giltwood and composition wall brackets, 16½in. high. (Christie's) $8,910 £5,500

An 18th century German carved boxwood group of the Madonna and Child, 19cm. high. (Phillips) $2,037 £1,250

A pair of Chinese carved hardwood figures of laughing boy musicians, 15½in. high. (Dacre, Son & Hartley) $164 £100

A Shaker miniature lidded pail with strap handle and two fingers, 2.3/8in. high. (Christie's) $550 £332

A treen barrel-form tobacco canister, the lift-off cover set with a wine bottle and two glasses, 7in. high. (Christie's) $330 £193

A wooden group of miniature human and animal figures, platform 5 x 9in. (Robt. W. Skinner Inc.) $360 £225

An ancient Egyptian wood carving of a rower, 6½in. high. (Robt. W. Skinner Inc.) $275 £166

A carved hardwood Indian figure of a man with feathered head-dress, 18½in. high. (Dacre, Son & Hartley) $65 £40

Two late 19th century Noh masks of Ko-Omote and Obeshimi, 22cm. long. (Christie's) $1,408 £880

An Easter Island wood carving of male ribbed figure, 'Moai Kavakava', 14in. long. (Robt. W. Skinner Inc.) $2,600 £1,575

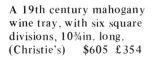

A 19th century mahogany wine tray, with six square divisions, 10¾in. long. (Christie's) $605 £354

A 16th/17th century carved and polychromed limewood group of the Madonna and Child, 52cm. high. (Phillips) $1,630 £1,000

A Mission oak magazine/wood carrier, circa 1910, 18in. high, 15¼in. wide. (Robt. W. Skinner Inc.) $450 £267

A scene from Tam O'Shanter, 'The Beginning of the Evening', wood carving by Gerrard Robinson, 13 x 14in. (Anderson & Garland) $1,026 £580

A well carved figure of the head of a man, 30in. long. (Christie's) $1,478 £880

One of two 19th century painted burlwood bowls, oval, 12in. wide, the second circular, 13in. diam. (Christie's) $352 £198

A painted cherrywood and gesso group of a couple dancing, 'Tango', 36in. high, by Elie Nadelman. (Christie's)$2,860,000 £1,597,882

A 19th century Japanese carved hardwood okimono of humorous deity, 5½in. high. (Hobbs & Chambers) $264 £160

An ebony and oval panelled shaped jelly mould, 6in high. (Woolley & Wallis) $66 £40

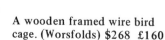

A carved and painted ship's head figure, modelled as a partially clad mermaid, 38in. high. (Christie's) $1,320 £744

A wooden framed wire bird cage. (Worsfolds) $268 £160

A 19th century carved and polychrome allegorical figure, America, 52in. high. (Robt. W. Skinner Inc.) $5,500 £3,089

Early 19th century carved and polychrome figurehead, New England, 23in. high. (Robt. W. Skinner Inc.) $3,500 £1,966

One of three 19th century burlwood bowls, each circular with moulded rim, two 13in. diam., the third 8in. diam. (Christie's) $935 £527

A Dutch mahogany birdcage, the stepped front with four compartments, late 18th century, 41in. wide. (Christie's) $30,525 £16,500

Late 19th century painted wooden sled, America, 48½in. long, 12in. wide. (Robt. W. Skinner Inc.) $1,600 £898

A Portuguese or Spanish carved walnut panel, 'The Adoration of the Magi', circa 1600. (Woolley & Wallis) $759 £460

Late 19th/early 20th century carved and painted wooden hanging clock shelf, possibly Virginia, 21½in. high, 14¾in. wide. (Christie's) $495 £279

A carved and painted wooden spoonrack, 22½in. high, 9in. wide. (Christie's) $352 £198

A stylised figure of a carved wooden horse, America, 23in. high, 23in. long. (Robt. W. Skinner Inc.) $1,200 £674

A 20th century carved wooden tobacconist figure, America, overall height 77½in. (Robt. W. Skinner Inc.) $2,500 £1,404

A Regency rosewood tazza with moulded ring-turned bowl, 10¼in. wide. (Christie's) $484 £275

Early 20th century Summer Yellow Legs carving, G. Shaw, Chatham, Mass., 5in. high, 9in. long. (Robt. W. Skinner Inc.) $1,100 £617

Late 18th century carved burl bowl, with carrying handles, America, 22½in. diam. (Robt. W. Skinner Inc.) $1,600 £952

Early 20th century standing male figure, 28in. high. (Robt. W. Skinner Inc.) $300 £168

Small carousel stander, mounted as a rocking horse, circa 1900, 27in. high, 29in. long. (Robt. W. Skinner. Inc.) $1,500 £892

Late 19th century 'Factory Girl' large painted sled, America, 3ft.8½in. long, 19in. wide. (Robt. W. Skinner Inc.) $3,200 £1,904

An Egyptian Anthropoid wood mask, 18cm. high, Ptolemaic Period. (Phillips) $254 £140

A 19th century American carved wood butter stamp, depicting a standing pig on grass, and a cylindrical cover, top 5¾in. diam. (Christie's) $264 £148

A 19th century American carved wood butter stamp, 4¼in. diam. (Christie's) $242 £136

A 19th century Swiss carved wood life-size model of a brown bear, 3ft.9in. long, 2ft.6in. high. (Capes Dunn) $7,697 £4,300

A 19th century painted and carved pine eagle, possibly taken from the stern of a ship, America, 28in. long. (Robt. W. Skinner Inc.) $1,900 £1,130

A Continental carved oak relief wall plaque, 32in. high, 44in. wide. (J. M. Welch & Son) $638 £380

A painted wooden caricature figure of Charlie Chaplin, by Betterway, Vienna, 52cm. high, circa 1930. (Phillips) $272 £170

A 19th century American large polychrome woven splint market basket, 19in. wide. (Christie's) $286 £161

Late 19th century carved and painted black figure of a male acrobat, possibly Italy, 31in. high. (Robt. W. Skinner Inc.) $2,900 £1,726

Late 19th century painted wooden architectural model, America, 32in. long, 33in. high. (Robt. W. Skinner Inc.) $575 £342

Early 19th century carved wooden dove, American, 10¾in. high. (Robt. W. Skinner Inc.) $350 £208

One of five carved wood butter stamps with turned handles, 4½in. diam. (Christie's) $198 £111

One of two carved wooden friction toys, the first modelled as a bird, the second as a grasshopper, 8in. and 8½in. long respectively. (Christie's) $275 £155

A polychrome woven splint lunch basket, probably Maine, 12in. high, 15in. long, 7½in. wide. (Christie's) $132 £74

A miniature Canada goose, by A. Elmer Crowell, Mass., original paint. (Robt. W. Skinner Inc.) $1,000 £595

A painted wood caricature figure of Douglas Fairbanks, Snr., by Betterway, Vienna, 51cm. high, circa 1930. (Phillips) $320 £200

A Charles X period carved walnut cradle on foliate scroll dolphin supports. (Phillips) $7,000 £4,000

Late 18th century carved hard pine spoon rack with chip carved decoration, New Jersey, 21in. high. (Robt. W. Skinner Inc.) $1,800 £1,071

A nickel and wood decanting cradle, on oval ebonised base, overall length 14in. (Christie's) $880 £515

A pair of late 19th century Italian limewood figures, Apollo and Peace, after Jacopo Sansovino, 94in. high, including wood pedestals. (Christie's) $33,000 £18,857

A 19th century crimping machine of Thomas Clark type. (David Lay) $187 £105

INDEX

Abbotsford House 703
Abbott, Thos. 510
Abercrombie, Robert 714
Abraham & Isaac 228
Absolon 518
Abuja 193
Academy 161
Academy of Plato 733
Ace of Spades 66
Acorn 692
Act of Parliament 319
Actaeon 137
Adam, Robert 688
Adams, George 693
Adams Jnr., George 133
Adams, W. 694
Adams-Acton, John 575
Adirondack 383
Admiral Fitzroy 133
Adoration of the Magi 776, 781
Advertising Signs 66-68
Adze Head 588
Aeolian Grand 634
Aero-Club 598
Africa 215, 745
African Hunter 149
After a German Retreat 644
Agra 658, 664
Agricola, G. 134
Aikuchi Tanto 118, 119
Aird & Thomson 296
Aitken, Mary 209
Ak & Cie 630
Akira 563
Albert 538
Albert, C. J. 246
Alboni, Maritta 268
Alcock & Co., Sam 253
Alcoso 85
Aldani, 639
Aldred & Son 325
Aldworth, Sam. 291
Alert 590
Alexeieff 651
Alfa-Romeo 756
Algarkirk & Yarmouth
   Vauxhall 650
Alken, Henry 134
Allchin 594
Alleine, Johnathan 678
Allinson 765
Aloncle 264
Alpine Artillery 96
Alps 730, 731
Alvis-Healey 760
Amadio, J. 133
Amadio & Son, F. 130
Amagatsu 623

Amati, Dom Nicolo 611
America 215
American China 172-177
American Civil War 92, 96
American Indian Art 69-73
American Mercantile Co. 605
American Waltham Watch Co. 321
Amish 159, 649
Amor 339
Amourette 604
Anatolian Panel 735
Anatolian Yastik 658
Anchises & Aeneas 229
Anchor Line 767
Anderlee, Josephius Servatius 336
Anderson & Sons Ltd., Wm. 75
Andrieu, B. 614, 618
Andrieu, F. 618
Ang-Ak-China 70
Angeil George 694
Angell, Joseph 706, 716
Angle, Mrs F. 739
Angrave 766
Anhua 248
Annesley, George 545
Annual Sweepstakes 599
Anrakusai 625
Ansonia Clock Co. 314
Answer-Game 730
Anti-Aircraft Unit 741
Anti-Laria Sparkling Wine 67
Antide-Janvier 310
Aphrodite 572
Apollino 572
Apollo 606
Apollo Belvedere 573
Apollo & Daphne 573
Apollo & Peace 784
Appetizer, The 66
Apres La Lecture 138
Apres Vous Sire 618
Apsley Pellatt 531
Arabian Nights 647
Arapaho 69, 72
Arcade 284
Arcangioli, Lorenzo 612
Archambo, Peter 670
Archbutt, J. & W. E. 554
Archduke Charles 614
Archer 598
Archer, H. W. 91
Arches 641-643, 646, 647
Architectural Model 783
'Ard of 'Earing 204
Ardley & Son, A. 428
Argyle, Silver 698
Argyll & Sutherland Highlanders,
   The 83

Argyll & Sutherland Highlanders, The
   7th Vol. Btn. 78
Argy-Rousseau, Gabriel 536, 537, 540,
   567
Aria 657
Aristophanes 281
Aristotle 309
Arita 178, 179
Armada Chest 561
Armentieres 319
Armida 194
Armoires & Wardrobes 504, 505
Arms & Armour 74-125
Armstrong & Bros., F. 315
Arnold 741
Arnold, J. R. 322
Aro 139
Artel, 11th 723
Artillery 595
Arts & Crafts 184, 302, 312, 315, 332,
   349, 356, 367, 421, 470, 504, 521,
   566, 567, 674, 675
Asahina Saburo 623
Ash, Joseph 674
Ash, Thos. 710
Ashbee, C. R. 567
Astbury 282
Astoman 731
Aston Martin 757, 760
Asquith 206
At the Fair 640
Ateo 763
Athena 150
Atlanta 591
Atlantes 333
Atlantic Coast Express 763
Atlantis Sunshine Cruiser 768
Ato 308
Atom Rocket Ship 749
Attacking Martian 730
Attu 585
Au But 145
Aubusson 665, 733
Aubusson, Louis Philippe 664
Auld, Wm. 721
Aura Argenta Linear 173
Austin, Josiah 673
Austin, R. 283
Austin Seven 756, 760, 762
Australia & Back, To 767
Australia, Bank of NSW 629
Australian Paratroopers 86
Austria 260
Auto Unions 603
Autograph Letters & Documents 126-128
   614, 615, 619
Automatons 129
Avelli, Francesco Xanto 231

Avery & Son,W. 552
Avus 603
Awataguchi 621
Ayagiri 776
Ayrshire Yeomanry, The 80
Aytoun, William 712

Babcock, A. 634
Baby Carriage 585
Baccarat 163, 524-529, 533
Bacchante 572
Bacchantes 538
Bacchus 277, 524, 574
Bacheller, Irving 136
Baddeley, J. 679
Badges 78-83
Bagshaw & Sons, John 492
Baihosai 622
Bailey & Co. 709
Bailey, Henrietta 175
Bailey, David 655, 656
Baird, A.H. 555
Bakelite 339
Baker T.K. 110
Bakewell, James 280
Baldock, E. H. 465
Baldwin, Gordon 210, 211
Ball, Black & Co. 717, 718
Ball, Wm. 238
Ballads & Poems 136
Ballantine, Robt. 165
Ballantyne, J. 619
Bank of Australasia 628
Banks, B. 610
Barbados 628
Barbedienne, F. 616
Barber, Benj. 314
Barber, James 705
Barbier, George 644
Barboleta De Noite 737
B.A.R.C. 599
Bard & Son, C. 694
Barker 757
Barlow, Florence 209
Barlow, Hannah 204, 207
Barnard Bros. 677
Barnard, Edward 684, 688
Barnard, Messrs. 695
Barnsley Sidney 354
Barolo Riserva 772
Barometers 130-133
Barovier & Toso 540
Barr, Flight & Barr 186, 284
Barranti, P. 573
Barraud & Lunds 320
Barre, A. 138
Barrel Organ 607
Barrel Pianos 635
Barrel Spigot, Silver 698
Barrett-Danes, Ruth 190, 191
Barrow, J. 304
Barry 765
Bartlett, Robert 767
Bartolini 572
Barye 147
Barye, Alfred 139, 142
Barye, Antoine Louis 144
Basket Carrier 250
Basket, Splint 783, 784
Baskets 547
Baskets, Silver 670, 671
Bassett-Lowke 136, 591, 593
Bat Dancer 146
Bateman, H.M. 596
Bateman, Peter, Anne & William 722
Batt, Mike 655
Bautte & Co, J. FS. 323
Bavarian Dragoons 96
Baxter 186, 198, 199, 284
Bayley & Blew 160
Bayley, Richard 704
Bayonet 84-86
Be Up To Date 598
Beaded New Shape 265
Beakers, Glass 510
Beatien Yazz 71
Beatles, The 128, 656
Beatles Yellow Submarine, The 742
Beatonson Wind Shields 602
Beaulieu Vineyard 775
Beautiful Duchess, The 221
Bebe Endormi 143

Bebe Premier Pas 345
Beck, Maurice 764
Beck, Richard 299
Becker & Co., F.E. 552
Bedfordshire & Hertfordshire Regt.,
    The 78
Beds 352, 353
Bee Gees 657
Beggar's Petition, The 666
Beginning of the Evening 780
Behrens, Peter 630
Beijing 729
Beilby 543
Beliers 536
Belga, Vander Elst 67
Bell I. J. 682
Bell, John W. 173
Bell, Joseph 685
Bell, Silver 699
Belleek 188
Bellew, G. 134
Belsize Motor Vehicles 600
Benares Cover 734
Benefink & Co. 749
Benin Wood Carvings 777
Bennett, Murrle 568
Bennett, Wm. 690
Bennington 275, 276
Bentley 596, 600, 756, 757, 762
Bentwood Box 162
Benzoni, G.M. 575
Berdou, Roger 744
Bergama 662
Bergdoll, Adam 218
Berge, H. 518, 525, 534
Bergen, Henry 193, 273
Bergman 137
Berlin 180, 181
Berliner 605, 608
Berliner, E. 604
Bermuda Tours 769
Berne 613
Bersaglieri 91
Berthoz, J. 616
Bertin, Jean-Baptiste 544
Bestiary Form 191
Best Way Series, The 763
Betterway 783, 784
Bettini 606
Betts 553
Beware of Trains 651
BFK Rives 644
Bianconi, Fulvio 539-541
Biddell 289
Bidjar 664
Biedermeier 438, 441
Biggs, D. 204, 205
Billerica 176
Billon, Adam 705
Bing 592, 593, 740, 744, 751-753
Biplane 740
Birch 211
Bird 290, 304
Bird Cage 780, 781
Birds in Branches 270
Birnkrug 216
Biscuit Barrel 697
Bishamon & Kichigo-Ten 261
Bisonte 647
Bisstrom, J.N. 574
Bisto Kids 342
Bizarre 197
Black Cat 66
Black Christmas 647
Black Forest 303, 312
Black Starr & Frost 312, 690
Black Tulips 640
Black Watch 75, 80
Blackmar, Abby 136
Blackamoor 572
Blackmore, Richard D. 135
Blackpool, Gay & Bright 763
Blagden, Hodgson & Co. 716
Blair, Charles 713
Blair, J. 133
Blanc Pere & Fils 325
Blard, E. 563
Blatt, J. 132
Blazuiere, P. 154
Blerzy, Veuve 544
Bleu Persan 186
Blocks 546-549
Blondes Have More Fun 655
Bloor Derby 202

Blower, G. 208
Blue For You 655
Bluebird 746
Blunderbuss 106
Boehm, Joseph E. 139
Boetia 277
Bohea & Green 268
Bohemian Glass 510, 511, 513, 517,
    520, 522, 533
Bohm, H. 316
Bohm, Hermann 681
Boker 84
Boloardo, Dr. 242
Bolviller 297
Bombay Native Infantry 749
Bonbon Nierre 194
Bond & Sons, Wm. 305
Bond, W. 106
Bond, Wm. 721
Bonham, John 657
Bonheur, Isidore 141
Bonheur, Rosa 143
Bonnet Dancer 71
Bontems 129
Book of Devotions 134
Bookcases 354-358
Bookprinter, Anne Marie 258
Books 134-136, 619
Boots 669
Bordjalou Kazak 663
Borg, Anders Nielsen 705
Borgogno & Figli 772
Bosch 759
Boson, John 428
Bott, Thomas 284
Bottger 217, 219, 272
Bottle Carrier 778
Bottle Cradle, Silver 698
Bottles, Glass 510, 547
Boucher 145,180
Boucher, F. 135, 639
Boulanger 264
Boullemier, A. 249
Boulton & Co. Matthew 677
Boulton, M. 146, 312, 682
Bouraine, A. 138
Bournemouth for Health.. 764
Bovet 322
Bovinet, E. 614
Bow 182, 183
Bowie Knife 87
Bowls, Glass 511, 512
Bowly, Devereux 291
Boxes & Caddies 154-163, 584, 586,
    589, 615, 616, 698
Boxes, Silver 674, 675
Boxing Match 748
Boxwell, A. 678
Boy George 655
Boy on a Seahorse 206
Boy with Turban 205
Boyasha Sonjiro 620
B.P. 600, 603
B.P.I. 655
B.R. 763-766
Bracing Holidays 766
Bracket Clocks 289-293
Braddock, Anna 667
Bradford & Teale 605
Bradford Riley Bros. Ltd 136
Bradford, Thos. 301
Bradley & Hubbard 570
Bradley, R. 475
Bradley, Will A. 135
Bramah Lock 509
Bramham Moor, The 593
Brander & Potts 111
Brandt, Bill 632
Brandt, Edgar 309
Braque, George 643
Brass & Copper 332-335
Breguet 320, 324, 331
Breguet & Fils 323
Bremond, B.A. 605
Bretby 189
Brevoort, John 699
Bright, Ellen 269
Bridge, John 712, 716
Bridge of Allan 768
Brighton Pavilion 397
Brighton Works 652
Brind, H. 705
Briot, Francois 696
Bristol 201

Bristol Hot Wells 349
Britain's 741-743, 746, 752, 753
Britannia 608
British Admirals 679
British China 184-191
Broad, A. 590
Broadway Car Line 746
Broadwood & Sons, John 634
Brock, Peder 705
Brocot, Achille 294, 309
Brooklands 596, 598, 603
Broom, Gerald 653
Bronze 137-151, 614-617
Brown, Errol 656
Brown, H. 686
Brown-Haired Clown 205
Brown, Jane 633
Browne, Sam 342
Browning 113
Browning, Robert 135
Bruant, Aristide 645
Bruguier, Chas. 675
Brunswick 216
Brussels Lace 340, 350
Brussels Tapestry 732, 733
B.S.A. 112
Buaku 563
Bub, Karl 749
Bubble Blowing Popeye 751
Bucherer 323
Buckets 152, 153, 546, 548, 549, 778
Budding 110
Buddy 'L', The 753
Buffet Tirelire 607
Bugak 624
Bugatti 598, 602, 603
Bugatti, Carlo 499
Buhre, Paul 295
Bule Mana 70
Bulky Mule 750
Bull, The 275
Bull Dog Bank 595
Bull Dog with Union Jack 209
Bullock, George 371, 378, 436, 448,
    452, 453, 464, 481, 560
Bullmark 730
Bummers Cap 96
Bundeseigentum 168, 169
Bundeswehr 165
Bunyan, John 697
Bureau Bookcases 359-361
Bureau de la Gendarmerie 615
Bureaux 362-366
Burnham, Lois 736
Burrell 594
Burrows & Co. 135
Burslem 208
Burton, E.E. 570
Burwash, Wm. 684, 712
Bushu Ju Masakata 122
Busy Cart Robot 730
Butler, Frank 204
Butter Stamp 782, 783
Button 547
B.V.R.B. 499

Cabernet Sauvignon 775
Cabin to Canada 767
Cabinets 367-371
Cable, Lindsay 765
Cabrier, Chas. 302
Cabriolet 762
Caddies & Boxes 154-163, 584, 586,
    589, 615, 616, 698
Cadillac 743, 748
Cadogan 258
Cafe, John 678
Cafe, Wm. 679
Cain & Abel 230
Caire, A. 276
Caledonian Railway 652, 768
Calderwood, Robert 672
Caldesi 633
Caldwell & Co., J.E. 320, 689
Callendar 559
Callot 218
Cambridge Architecture 764

Cameo Glass 511, 512, 515, 521, 522,
    530, 531, 534-536, 539, 541, 571
Cameras 164-169
Cameron, Sir D.Y. 763
Canada Goose 784
Canada Rifles, The 78
Candelabra, Silver 676, 677
Candlesticks, Glass 513
Candlesticks, Malachite 586
Candlesticks, Silver 678, 679
Canova 572, 573
Canterbury Tales 640
Canterburys 372, 373
Canton 192
Capacity-Mobility 651
Capela, Antonio 612
Capelle 262
Capt, Henry 320
Caracciola 600
Carcassi, Lorenzo & Tommaso 610
Card & Tea Tables 456-461
Cardew 193, 210, 211, 274
Cardew, Michael 193, 210, 211
Cardew, Seth 193, 274
Cardwell 137
Carette 752
Carlisle, The Gateway.. 763
Carlton 187
Carlton House 494, 496, 498
Carnarvon, Lord 221
Carousel Stander 782
Carpeaux, Jean-Baptiste 147, 277, 574,
    586, 587
Carpenter 310
Carpenter & Westley 555
Carr, Leslie 763
Carreto 747
Carriage Clocks 294-297, 614
Carrier-Belleuse, A. 139, 263, 572
Carter, John 714, 715
Carter Paterson & Co. 594
Cartier 327, 329
Cartonnier 163
Carvalho, Genaro de 737
Carved Brown Bear 783
Cary 131
Cascades 69
Cash, Mary Ann 667
Cask-Rack 777
Castel Durante 226
Castelli 226-231
Casters, Silver 680
Castrol 596
Cat. of Optical Lantern Slides 136
Cat. Parts for Rolls-Royce 136
Catalani, Angelica 574
Cater, W. 90
Catlinite 73
Cato 309
Cattle Culture 596
Caucasian Carpet 660
Caucasian Kilim 665
Caucasian Warrior 349
Caudebec 537
Caughley 185, 186, 191
Cauman, R. 333
Causard Horloger du Roy 318
Cavalry 106-108, 110, 111, 116-121
Cavell, Edith 126
Cawdell, Wm. 692
Celestina 606
Centre Tables 462-465
Centrepieces, Silver 681
Cephalus 194
Ceremonial Dancers 71
Cezanne, P. 647
Chad Valley 343, 749
Chagall, Marc 641-643, 647
Chalon, L. 148
Chamberlains 185, 284
Chamberlayne 93
Chambersticks, Silver 682
Champaigne, P. 644
Chandeliers 170, 171
Chang 208
Chanot, F.W. 613
Chanot, G.A. 609, 610
Chaplin, Charlie 783
Chapron 762
Chapuisaine 264
Charder 515
Charles II 128
Charlesworth 761
Charlet, N.T. 618

Charlier, Jacques 639
Charpentier 533
Chasselat, Pierre 636
Chasseurs 617
Chateau Cheval-Blanc 773, 775
Chateau D'Yquem 772, 773, 775
Chateau Haut-Brion 772, 775
Chateau Lafite 772-775
Chateau Lafite Blanc 774
Chateau Latour 773, 775
Chateau Margaux 774
Chateau Mouton Rothschild 772-774
Chateau Petrus 773, 775
Chateaux de Montargis 264
Chaucer, Geoffrey 640
Chaudet, Denis-Antoine 141
Chawner, Henry 710
Chaye, Germain 545
Cheap Fares, Fast Trains 765
Cheik Arabe de Caire 149
Chelsea 194, 195
Chelsea Ewer 285
Chelsea Keramic Art Works 173, 177
Cherokee 72
Chesne, Claudius du 293
Chests of Drawers 400-405
Chests on Chests 406, 407
Chests on Stands 408, 409
Cheval Mourant 648
Cheval Turc 147
Chevrolet Corvette Stingray 760
Cheyenne 72
Chiffoniers 410
Chikanobu 648
China 172-288
Chinese 196
Chiparus, D. 138
Chippendale Laboratory 605
Chippendale, Thos. 385, 393, 413, 487,
    578, 581
Chipperfields Circus 746
Chivers, F.H. 198
Chocktaw 72
Chocolate Pots, Silver 682
Chopard 330
Choshu Hagi Ju Kawaji 124
Choshu Hagi Ju Tomotsune 124
Choshu Ju Masasada 118
Chosu Ju Masaasada 125
Christ en Croix 646
Christ, Jacob 173
Christian, D. 521
Christofle 681
Chronometro Gondolo 322
Chryselephantine 139
Chuban Yoko-E 648
Chummy 758, 760
Churchill, Sir Winston 126, 127, 197
Cigarette Cases, Silver 683
Cinderella 268
Cinque Ports Artillery Vols., The 81
Circuit des Ardennes 600
Cirque 641
Cistercian 188
Citroen 756
City of Glasgow Bomber Squadron 78
Clarence 251
Claret Jugs, Silver 683
Clark, Alfred 689
Claughton Class Lord Rathmore 653
Clayton 594
Clayton, J. 86
Cleff, Ewald 120
Cleopatra 150
Clichy 524-529
Cliff, Clarice 197
Clifton 172, 175
Clock Sets 298
Clock Shelf 781
Clocks & Watches 289-331
Cloisello 191
Cloisonne 252
Clos des Lambrays 774
Clown 205, 208
Co-operative Doll Co. 342
Coalport 198, 199
Coasters, Lacquered 589
Coasters, Silver 684
Cobb, John 470
Coca-Cola 68
Cocks & Bettridge 339
Coffee Pots, Silver 685, 686
Coffers & Trunks 500-503
Coffre a Bijoux 158

Coldstream Guards, The 82, 120, 747
Cole, Benjamin 555
Cole, Rufus 161
Cole, Thos. 308, 317
Coleman, W.S. 249
Collin-Mezin, Ch.J.B. 609, 613
Collins, Phil 656
Colman's Starch 68
Colombo, Ambrogio 617
Colonial Mfg. Co. 302
Colonna 227
Colosseum 586
Colston, Rich. 303
Colt 109
Columbia 590, 608
Combe, William 134, 135
Comerford, John 637
Coming of Spring, The 206
Commedia Dell'arte 246, 247, 278
Commelin 264
Commissar for Education 126
Commode Chests 412, 413
Commodes & Pot Cupboards 411
Comolera, P. 249
Compisizione Piume 514
Complete Angler, The 135
Composition 643
Compound 592, 593
Compur 167
Comyns, Richard 676
Comyns, Wm. 675, 695, 698
Con Brio 143
Concert 608
Concho 69
Condliff 310
Conelly, Henry 459
Confectionary Dispenser 731
Connaught Rangers Regt., The 88th 78
Connolly Land 596
Conran, Terence 392
Console Tables 466, 467
Constantaras Freres 322
Constantinidis, Joanna 273, 274
Contaflex 167
Conway, General 202
Cooke & Sons, T. 558
Cooke, J. 303
Cooke, Richard 677
Cooke II, Thomas 704
Cooke Troughton & Simms Ltd. 555
Cookson, Isaac 682, 722
Cooper, Austin 763-765, 767
Cooper's Hammer Head 546
Cope & Collinson 504
Copeland 199
Copeland & Garrett 199
Coper, Hans 200, 256, 257
Coppel, Alex. 118, 121
Copper & Brass 332-335
Coq Nain 596, 603
Coqs et Plumes 539
Coquette 204
Cordier 148
Cordier, Charles-Henri-Joseph 149
Coralene 531
Corgi 742, 746
Coronation Doll 346
Corkscrews 336-339
Corner Cupboards 414, 415
Cornillet 617
Cornwall Railway 650
Cork Glass Co. 511
Corti, A. 131
Cory & Son Ltd., William 552
Cory, Thomas 693
Cossack 111
Costume 340, 341
Cote de Nuits 774
Cotswold School 426
Cottingham, Miss Elizabeth 637
Cotton, C. 135
Couches & Settees 436-441
Courtauld, Samuel 679
Courtesan 247
Count Bruhl's Tailor 243
Coup des Voitures Legeres 601
Courtecuisse & Cie, V. 316
Countie Pallatine 584
County Palatine 585
Coutts & Findlater Ltd. 378
Couvoisier & Comp'e 324
Cove, Sidney 279
Cowden & Wilcox 274, 276
Cowes Week 763
Coyne, Sallie E. 258

Craddock, John 716
Craig, H.B. 173
Crake! 646
Craven, Edwin 553
Cream Jugs, Silver 687
Creighton 303
Crespin, Paul 696
Cries of London 247
Cripps, Wm. 676
Cris de Paris 246
Croisy 253, 254
Crook, Russell G. 274
Croome, Capt. & Mrs. Wm. 638
Crosby, F. Gordon 602
Cross & Ellis 759
Cross of Lorraine 538-540
Crouch, John 714, 715
Crowell, A. Elmer 784
Cruden Bay 767
Cruets, Silver 687
Cruises to Scottish Fjords 769
Crump, Francis 685, 713
Crystal Palace 587
Cuirassiers 74, 92
Culotte de Satin Rouge 648
Cummings, Capt. John 636
Cunard 136
Cunard, Europe-America 766
Cunard White Star 720
Cupid 141, 194, 198, 244, 247, 254,
   533
Cupboards 416, 417
Cups, Silver 688, 689
Currey, F.E. 632
Curtis, Lemuel 319
Curtius, Marcus 231
Cuthbert, R. 611
Cutshing 700

Da Vinci 510
Daggers 84-87
Dai Nippon 139
Dai Nippon Setsuzan 261
Daily Mail 741
Daimler 752, 754, 761
Daimler-Benz 757
Daisy's Influence 136
Dakon 220
Dali, Salvador 441
Dalila 138
Dallmeyer 166
Dalou, Aime-Jules 141, 143, 144, 149
Daly, Matt 258
Danaides 541
Daniel, H. & R. 184, 186
Daniell & Sons 252
Dannhoffer 278
Danseuses 147
Daoist Immortals 213
Daphne et Chloe 643
Dardanelles 628
Darker, Wm. 686
Dart Freres 255
Daruma 620, 625, 626
Darwin, Charles 632
Daum 511, 512, 530, 536-540, 571
Davenports 418-419
'Davenport' Sewing Machine 418
David 614
David, J-L 308
Davidson 589
Davies, M. 207
Davis & Co., S. 418
Davis, Harry 284
Davis, Josiah 284
Daw, G.H. 115
DB6 Superleggera 760
De Dion-Bouton 758
De Grave & Co. 554, 556
De Grineau, Bryan 653
De Lorean 762
De Wancker Tot Loo 307
Deans Rag Book Co., Ltd 344
Death & A Maiden 139
Death of Achilles 231
Death of a Roman Warrior 280
Death of the Lion Queen 269
Death, The 283
Debucourt, P.L. 618
Decanter Stand, Silver 699
Decanters 514

Decanting Cradle 697, 784
Decauville, A.C. 309
Declaration of Independence 668
Dedham 172, 175, 177
Degue 571
Dejardin, J. 294
Delicia 197
Delight 209
Delvaux, Paul 643
Delft 201, 238
Demand, Carlo 600
Demarcay, Mme, la Baronne Cecile 587
Deming, Edwin Willard 634
Dent 295
Denziloe, John 717
Der Monatlich-Herausgegeben 134
Der Steinstosser 138
Derazey, H. 613
Derby 184, 188, 202, 203, 270
Derbyshire Regt., The 95
Deruta 226-229
Derval 619
Desdemona 656
Desk Clip, Silver 697
Desks & Writing Tables 494-499
Despots, Chas. 723
Desprez 262
Detected 253
Devisme 111
Devon Militia, The 1st 78
Devonmoor 591
Deutsche Lufthansa 740
Diana 148, 195, 315
Dickens 763
Dickens, C. 134,135
Dickens' Ware 206
Dine, Jim 648
Dinky 743, 746, 747, 755
Dining Chairs 374-383
Dining Tables 468, 469
Diogenes 733
Dionysus & Ceres 733
Dire Straits 657
Dirk 84-87
Dishes, Glass 515
Dishes, Silver 690, 691
Display Cabinets 420, 421
Disney, Walt 645, 745
Dispute in the Temple 230
Distler 752
Ditisheim, Paul 323
Dives & Lazarus 532
Dix, Otto 642
Dixey, G. & C. 133
Dixon, James 687
Dixon & Sons, James 88, 679
Dixon & Son 631
Dixon, W.S. 134
Dr. Wall 283
Dr. Syntax 188
Dragon in Compartments 240
Dragons in Compartments 284
Dragoon Guards, The 90, 120
Dragoon Regt., The 25th 118
Dragoons, The 8th 636
Drake 205
Drawing Cover 283
Dreher 244
Dresden 217, 220
Dresden Scroll 249
Dresser, C. 699
Dressers 422, 423
Dressing Tables 470, 471
Drew, E. 674
Drew, S.S. 674
Drew & Sons, J. 674
Dring & Fage 131
Drinking Sets 516
Drocourt 294, 295, 297
Dromard, L. 163
Drop Leaf Tables 472
Drouot, Edouard 139, 145
Drummer Boy 744
Dryburgh Abbey 198
Doctor's Coupe 760
Documents & Autograph Letters
   126-128
Dodge 762
Dodson, Richard 202
Dog Begging 207
Doig, James 292
Doll & Co. 755
Dollond 556
Dolls 342-347
Dombey & Son 134

Dominick & Haff 689
Dominion of Canada 628
Dominy, Allen 719
Donald Duck Duet 745
Donatello 175
Donegal Service, The 185
Don't Stop The Dance 655
Donzel 351
Dorn, Marion 659
Dorotheenthal 217
Dorset, Lionel, 1st Duke of 638
Dorsetshire Regt, The 94
Doughty, M. 425
Doulton 204-209
Doxa 597
Du Louier 319
Dubois, Lucien 322
Dubois, Paul 139
Duchesse du Barry 262
Duckham's Oils 66
Duckworth, Ruth 275
Ducommun Girod 607
Dudley Watch Co. 325
Duesbury & Co., Wm. 202, 203
Dugdale, James 602
Duke of Cambridge's Lancers, The 17th 79
Duke of Cornwall's Light Infantry, The 78
Duke of Edinburgh's Own Vol. Rifles, The 81
Duke of Gloucester Service, The 285
Duke of Northumberland 381
Duke of Westminster 369
Duke, Richard 612
Dumb Organist 605
Dumb Waiters 424
Dunbar 769
Dunlap 404
Dunlap, Major 406
Dupaquier 278
Dupont, J. 633
Durand, G. 499
Durand, Victor 512
Durer, Albrecht 640
Duret 149
Durham Light Infantry, The 82
Dutch Hearts 648
Dutton, Mattw. & Thos. 319
Duvelleroy, J. 350
Duvivier 288
Dyno Robot 731

Earthenware 210, 211
East Anatolian 660
East Caucasian 665
East Coast Havens 764
East Fence 631
Easter Island Carving 779
Eastern Woodlands Indian 340
Eastman Kodak Co. 166
Eastwood 394
Easy Chair 384-389
Eaton, Wm. 676, 696, 699
Eavestaff 635
Eberlein, J.F. 244
Echo 740
Edison 606
Edison Amerola 604
Edison Bell Commercial 605
Edison Diamond Disc 605
Edison Fireside 606
Edison Home 608
Edmonds, Frederick 702
Edward VII 142, 347
Edwards, John 704
Egg Cups 619
Egypt & Sinai 632
Egyptian Priestess 141
Eickhorn 85, 117, 118
Eijusai Masayoshi 625
Elbow Chairs 390-399
Eldorado 645
Elements 183
Eley 561
Elkington 140, 514, 695, 720
Elkington & Co. 673, 680, 684, 697, 698, 709, 720
Ellice, Rt. Hon. Edward 637
Elliott, William 716

Ellis, Harvey 430, 433, 496
Ellis, Joel 342
Elssler, Fanny 138
Elton 521, 534, 535
Ely 768
Emes, John 688
Emes, Rebecca 684, 688
E.M.G. 605
Emperor of Russia 198
Enamel 348, 349
Encrier 616
Enfield 111, 112, 115
Engleheart, George 636, 638
Engleheart, John Cox Dillman 636
English Dance of Death,The 134
Entering The Enemies Camp 179
Entwhistle, John 655
Eoff, Garrett 706
Eoff & Shepherd 717
Epstein, Brian 128
E.R.A. 599
Erfurt 217
Ermanox 166
Ernemann-Werke 166
Eros 277, 574
Erotic Figure 150, 270
Erzegebirge 749
Eskimo 73
Eskimo Model 746
Etruria 279
Eug Delatre 644
Eureka 315
Europa & The Bull 147
European China 212
European Watch & Clock Co. 329
Evans 264
Evans, J. 590
Eve 349
Evening with J.B. Gough, An 136
Everitz 85
Ewer & Basin, Silver 697, 699
Express & Cunard Liner 769
Express Dairy 751
Expression of Emotions 632

Faberge 723
Factories on L.N.E.R. Lines.. 764
Factory Girl 782
Faenza 226
Faguays, Le 140
Faience 207, 216-218
Fairbanks Snr., Douglas 784
Fairground Organ 607
Fairyland Lustre 279-281
Falk 745
Famille Rose 212, 728
Famille Verte 235
Famous Liners 746
Famous Orator, A 136
Famous Rivers of Commerce 763
Fanfare de Dragons 617
Fans 350, 351
Fantasque 197
Far East, The 632
Farnell, J. 710
Farnese Hercules 180
Farmer's Boy 209
Fasces 91
Favrile 570
Fawdrey, William 704
Fazy, Ph. 323
Felixmuller, Conrad 645
Femme de L'Artiste 643
Fender Telecaster 656
Fenton, H. 204, 205, 208, 209
Fereghan 662
Fernell, Edward 711
Ferrat 215
Ferry, Bryan 655
Field Artillery Regt., The 10th 92
Field Service Fighting Knife 86
Field, W. 132
Fifeshire Rifle Vol. Corps., The 1st 81
Figg, John 704
Finch, Raymond 273
Fincher, Mary 735
Finlay, Hugh & John 377
Finnigans Ltd. 289
Fipps, Hk. 745
Fire Brigade 752
Fire Buckets 152, 153

Fire Surround 776
Firemarks 586
Firmin 82
Firth of Clyde, The 763
Fischer & Toller 154
Fisher Ltd., S. 315
Flameng, F. 617
Flasks 88
Flatman, Thomas 636, 638
Flatware, Silver 692, 693
Fleischmann 747, 748
Flemish Tapestry 732, 733
Fletcher, John 299
Fletcher & Sons 130
Flight, Barr & Barr 285, 287
Flight into Egypt 229
Flora 572
Floriform 515
Florsheim 216
Flower 640
Flower Seller, The 129
Flower Seller's Children, The 208
Flying Fox 593
Flying Scotsman, The 764, 765
Flying Scotsman's Cocktail Bar 764
Fogelberg, Andrew 689, 696, 717
Folding Lady 338
Foley 184, 187
Folk Art 744
Folkestone Pier & Lift Co. 668
Fondu, Pierre 273
Fontana, Orazio 226, 227
Foot Artist 633
Foot, Maria 267
Ford Thunderbird 756
Forest, J. 556
Forster, Wm. 610
Forsyth, Gordon 239
Fossin, Jean-Baptiste 545
Foster, Samuel 304
Foujita, Tsuguji 646
Fountain 585, 587
Four Quarters of the Globe 203
Four Seasons 137
Fowke Sc., T. 144
Fowler, L.N. 269
Fox, Charles James 314
Fox, Chas. 683, 700
Fox, George 711
Frampton, Sir George 148
Franck, B. et ses fils 91
Francois I 138
Franke & Heidecke 167
Frankenthal 216-219
Frankfurt 217
Franklin, James 683
Franz Ferdinand, Archduke 128
Fraser 553
Fraser, Alec 765
Fraserburgh 765
Fraser's Highlanders, The 71st 81
Frauenkopf 245
Frederick The Great 615
Freedom Box 544, 545
Freeman, A. 425
Freiwirth 768
Fremiet 139, 145
French China 214, 215
French Cuirassiers 615
French Dragoons 91, 93
French Royal Exchange 313, 317
Fringilla or Tales in Verse 135
Frink, Dame Elizabeth 640
Frith, Francis 632
Frodsham 293, 312, 322
Fromanteel 305
Fry's Cocoa 68
Fuchi-Kashira 89
Fukurokuju 620
Fuller, Charles Francis 575
Fulper 172, 177
Furniture 352-509
Furstenberg 216, 219

Gaab 545
Gagliano, G. 611
Gagliano, Johannes 612
Gaina, C. 132
Gaines 380
Gallant & A Mops 244
Galle 511, 534, 535, 538, 539, 541

Gallopin & Co., L. 320
Gama 741
Gama Sennin 621
Gamages 592
Game of Motoring, The 749
Games Tables & Workboxes 492, 493
Gamy 601
Gan, Alexei 642
Gannazzi 673
Ganshoshi Nagatsune 89
Garde du Corps, The 116
Garde Imperiale Tartares.. 744
Garde Infantry Regt. The 116
Gardner, Thomas 292
Garrard 79
Garrard, Robert 677, 682, 686, 687, 695
Garrett 743
Garston, The LMS Port 763
Gaskin, Arthur 566
Gasnier 308
Gate Leg Tables 473
Gate, Simon 537
Gawthorn, H.G. 651, 765, 766
Gaze Meubles, E.G. 386
Gear Robot 730
Gebruder 347
Geelen, Johannes van 337
General Purpose Traction Engine 594
Genie 617
George III 198
George V 126, 127, 151
George The Fifth 593
George VI & Queen Elizabeth 632
Georgiana, Duchess of Devonshire 221
Geracimov, A.M. 294
Germaine, Sir John 637
German China 216-220
Gerold 603
Gerrard & Co., Ltd. 688
Geryk 559
Geschutzt 148
Gewa 612
Geyger, E.M. 140
Giambologna 138
Giant Robot 731
Gibralt, R. 628
Gibson, Richard 637, 638
Gilbert, Sir Alfred 140
Gilbert, Stephen 689, 696
Giles, James 287, 530, 531, 533
Gille L'Aine 316
Gillinder 528
Gillows 374, 379, 411, 419, 462, 471, 485, 499
Gimson, Ernest 408
Girandoles 776
Girardon 144
Girl & Boy 214
Girl Seated at Desk VII 640
Girl With Riding Crop 142
Given Chap. of Exodus 737
Gladenbeck u Sohn, H. 140
Gladys 208
Glandebeck, Oscar 141
Glandino, Betty 273
Glasgow Herald, The 584
Glasgow & New York 767
Glass 510-543
Glenister, William 612
Globuscope 166
G N R 592, 650
Goblets, Glass 517-520
Goblets, Silver 694
Goddard, Christo 307
Goddard-Townsend School 353
Godefroy, J. 616
Godfrey, Benjamin 670, 672
Goebel, William 347
Gogyoku 564
Going into Action 197
Going on all the Time 765
Gold 544, 545
Golden Marenghi 607
Golden Shred 746
Goldscheider 220
Goldschmid, J. 559
Goldsmiths & Silversmiths Co. Ltd 314, 695
Golf at Gleneagles 584
Golfing in Southern England 768
Goncharova, N. 644
Goodwin, Andrew 721
Goodwin, James 673
Goole Steam Shipping 650
Gordine, Dora 139

Gordon, C.G. 689
Gordon Highlanders, The 77, 79
Gorham Manuf. Co. 258, 672, 673, 681, 682, 698, 704, 707
Goshu Hino Yoshihisa 113
Goss 221, 253
Goss, Florence 221
Gothick 298
Goto Ichijo 119
Gott, Joseph 573, 574
Gouda 212
Gouel, Jean 682
Gould, Chr. 299, 305
Gould, James 679
Graham, Wm. 321
Grainger 283, 285, 288
Grainger, Lee & Co. 287
Graminis, A. 229
Gramophone Co, The 604
Gramophone & Typewriter Ltd 608
Gramophones 604-608, 634
Grand Prix 600-603
Grand Theodolite 558
Grande Chartreuse A Grenoble 264
Granges, David des 637
Granny 205
Grant 303
Grape Gatherers 251
Grath, A. 147
Graves 772, 775
Gray, B. 292
Gray & Sons, Robt. 699
Gray, T. 391
Great Eastern Railway 593
Great Eastern Ry., The 651
Great Exhibition 695
Great Lakes 71, 73
Great Southern & Western Ry. 767, 769
Greatbatch, Wm. 268
Greb, Nan 150,151
Green, J. 640, 641, 644
Green Jackets Brigade, The 79
Green, James 637
Greenaway, Kate 279
Greene 114
Greeton, Cha. 290
Gregg, Rich'd 289
Gregory, J. 591
Gregson 325
Greiffenhagen, Maurice 763
Grenades 547
Grenadier Guards 74, 75
Grenouille 596
Gretton, Cha. 291
Grey Voice 211
Griffin & George Ltd. 559
Griffin & Tatlock Ltd. 553
Grimaldi, William 639
Grover & Baker 552
Gruber, Jacques 532
Grue 226, 229, 231
Grueby 172, 174-177, 476
Gruen 326
Guadagnini, Johannes Baptista 613
Guan 248
Guanyin 589
Guardian Vessel 190
Gui 535
Guild Brown 655
Guild of Handicrafts, Ltd. 567
Gulliford 131
Gullwing Coupe 759, 762
Gun Ramrod 549
Gunda-Werke 740
Gunthermann 755
Gurney, Richard 704
Guy Van 743, 746, 747
Guyerde 308
GWR 593, 652, 653, 765, 766
Gyokiukendo San 565
Gyokumin 551, 585
Gyokuzan 625
Gypsy Caravan 588

Habaner Ware 218
Hadley 283
Hadley, James 185, 186, 190
Hadley, Sarah 666
Haile, Thomas Samuel 272, 276
Hair Peace 657
Hairdresser, The 214
Hakuo 626
Hakuzan 261
Halbakt 646
Halbig 345

Hale, W. 286
Half Day Excursions 765
Hall 114
Hall & Co., Martin 699
Hall of One Hundred Boys 179
Hall, Pierre Adolph 638
Hall's Distemper 67
Hall's Patent 558
Halls, Sina 666
Ham, G. 602
Hamadan 659
Hamano Noriyuki 122
Hamilton, E. 768
Hamilton, J. 685
Hamilton, Richard 647
Hampston & Prince 722
Hancock, C.F. 677
Hancock, Sampson 188, 202
Handcraft 353, 489
Handel 570
Handwerck, Max 342
Hanley, Sam 302
Hannah, W.W. 694
Hannam, Thos. 715
Hannong, Joseph Adam 216
Hannong, Paul 217
Hannya 776
Hardy, W.G. 632
Harlequin 183
Harlequinade 206
Harmonia 604
Harper, Robert 708
Harper's Ferry 114
Harpokrates 151
Harpsichord 635
Harradine, L. 204-209
Harris Bros. 711
Harris, Charles Stuart 678
Harris & Son, Thos. 552
Harris Ltd., Philip 556
Harris, W. 556
Harrogate 767
Harrow Rifles 93
Haruaki 718
Harunobu 648
Harushige 627
Harvey, W.J. 111
Hasselblad 166
Hastings Co. 469
Hatchard, Anne 210
Haughton, Wm. 305
Hausmalerei 247
Hawick up Home 650
Hawksley, G. & J.W. 88
Hawthorndean 198
Heal & Son 352, 478
Heath 602
Heath & Middleton 521
Heath Robinson, W. 596
Heath, Thomas 558
Hebe 343
Hebe & Eagle of Jupiter 145
Hebe & Mercury 142
Hebrard, A.A. 144
Heckel, Erich 643
Heer 164
Heidosmat 167
Heise, C.F. 673
Hel, J. 609
Helene 254
Helleu, Paul Cesar 645
Helmets 90-96, 615
Hemingway, Ernest 633
Henard, Charles 638
Henderson, Ewan 273
Hendrix, Jimi 656
Henk, M. 204, 205
Hennell, Robert 670, 671, 680, 684, 694, 700
Hennell, Robert & David 713
Hennell, Robert & Samuel 702
Hepple & Co. 586
Hepting 302
Herakles 149
Herbert & Co., S. 684
Hercules 138
Herder, R. 116
Hereke 661
Herez 662
Heritage-Henredon Furniture Co. 426
Heriz 658, 659, 663, 664
Herold, C.F. 241, 246
Herring, Jos. 300
Hess 746
Hess, Rudolf 127
Heubach 345, 347

Heubach-Koppelsdorf 342, 346
Hewes, Joel F. 691
Hi-Yo-The Lone Ranger 751
Hidekatsu 89
Hideyoshi 624
Higgs Y Diego Evans 290
High Wheel Robot 730
Highest Standard of Comfort 769
Highland Light Infantry, The 80, 94
Highlanders, The 74th 79
Hikoshichi 624
Hill, H.L. 613
Hill, Joseph 613
Hill & Sons, W.E. 609, 610
Hillman 758
Himmler, Heinrich 127
Hirado 621
Hirschfield, Nathaniel J. 259
H.M.S. Aurora 590
H.M.S. Centurion 332
H.M.S. Circe 590
H.M.S. Invincible 546-549, 745
H.M.S. Nelson 591
H.M.S. Rattlesnake 590
HMV 607, 608
Hoadley, Silas 306, 307
Hochst 216, 218, 219
Hockende 643
Hockly, Daniel 703
Hockney, David 640, 641, 644
Hodges, Nathaniel 290
Hodgkinson 648
Hodgson, Joseph 723
Hododa 565
Hoffmann, Josef 670
Hogarth 589
Hojitsu 623
Holdcroft 185
Holland, T. 686
Holme 137
Holmes 301
Holmes, H. & A. 602
Holy & Co., D.G. 717
Holy Water Stoup 230, 231
Home Office 126
Homer 281, 643
Homi 624
Homolka, Ferd. August 613
Hong Kong & Shanghai 629
Hood, S. 691
Hooper 756
Hope 182
Hopi 70-73
Horatii 308
Horikawa 730, 731
Hornby 592, 593, 741, 755
Hornby Trains Delivery Van 755
Horner, Chas. 674
Horoldt, J.G. 241, 245
Hot Chocolate 656
Hotei 627
Houden 277
Hougham, Solomon 704
Houghton's Ltd. 167
Howard & Sons 386
HRG 761
H.R.H. Duke of Kent 311
H.R.H. Prince of Wales 723
Hubert, Edwin 769
Hudgell, Regt. Sgt. Major 77
Hudson River Valley 482
Huggler, A.L.B. 776
Hughes, Capt. James 637
Hughes, Wm. 291
Hukin & Heath 521, 699
Hull's Royal Club 336
Humber 600
Humber, The 763
Humphrey, George 585
Humphrey, Ozias 638
Hunt, J.H. 689
Hunt, John S. 677, 685, 691, 703
Hunt & Roskell 311, 317, 566, 702
Hunter, William 715
Huny 262
Hussards 617
Hussars, The 92, 96, 121, 637
Hutton, John 532
Hutton & Sons Ltd., W. 675
Hutton & Sons, W.M. 713
Hyde, Henry 671
Hymen 643

Icart, Louis 645, 646
Iceberg, The 739

Ich Zeichnend 645
Ichida 730
Ichiko 743
Icons 585, 587
Ihagee Exakta 164
Ikat 341
Ile Saint-Louis 642
Ilford/Kennedy Instruments 167
I'm Left -- 656
Imari 222-225, 240, 278, 286, 287, 622
Imperial Austrian Dragoons 95
Imperial Austrian Navy, The 80
Imperial Austro-Hungarian 82
Imperial Bavarian Infantry 121
Imperial German Artillery 116
Imperial German Hussars, The 95
Imperial German Navy 117, 119, 120, 121
Imperial German Prussian Cavalry 116
Imperial Turkish W
Imperial Turkish Prussian Cavalry
Imperial Turkish Empire Air Force, The 80
Imperial Wurttemberg Cavalry 118
Improved Phantasmagoria 555
Indian Army Cavalry 742
Indian Boy 260
Indian Ware 172, 175
Infantry Regt., The 87th 93
Ingap 741
Ingenico 747
Ingles, D.N. 598
Inkstand 162, 616
Inkstands, Silver 695
Inkwell 588
Inniskilling Dragoons, 6th 633
Inniskilling Regt., The 27th 81
Ino 574
Inros 550, 551
Inseparables 310
Instruments 552-559
Intarsio 184, 187
Intermediate Monarch 607
International Co. 692
International Watch Co. 328
I.O.M. Steam Packet Co. 767
I.P. & Co. 679
Ireland, Northern Bank 629
Irish Mails, The 653
Iron & Steel 560, 561
Isabey, Jean Baptiste 616, 619, 639
Ishiguro Masayoshi 89
Isle of Man for Holidays 767
Isle of Walcheren 763
ISO Grifo 760
Italian Brocade 735
Italian China 226-231
Ives 750
Ivory 562-565, 614, 615

Jackemann, A. 295
Jackson, Joseph 694
Jackson, Michael 65, 657
Jackson, William & Cyril 639
Jacobs, Isaac 515
Jade Carving 588, 589
Jaeger 329
Jagd 533
Jaguar 757, 758, 760, 761
Jaguar Police Car 752
Jahn, Louis 252
Jambiya 86, 87
Japanese China 232-234
Japy 323
Jarge 204, 209
Jarvie 151
Jarvis, Thos 532
Jay, Henry 609
Jean, Philip 636, 637
Jelly Mould 780
Jensen, Georg 673, 677, 692, 697, 718
Jep 746
Jersey Mercantile Union 629
Jervis 177
Jeunefille 572
Jewellery 566-569
Jewish Bn. Royal Fusiliers, The 81
Jewitt, Georgiana 253
Jiji 697
Joan of Arc 139
Jockey 205
Johns & Co. 117
John's Children 656
Johnson 305
Johnson, Jeremy 692, 693

Johnson, Samuel 209
Johnson, Sons & Edmonds 702
Johnson, Thos. 674
Johnston, Peter 639
Johnstone & Jeanes 419
Join The R.A.C. 599
Jokasai 550
Joli & Chenevard 544
Jolly, Pickman 185
Jones, A.E. 673
Jones, Florrie 207
Jones, George 185, 188, 191
Jones, George G. 672
Jorrocks's Jaunts & Jollities 134
Joseph & the Midianites 226
Josephine 618
Journal of Ceylon 632
Joyce, Richard 190
Joys of North Cornwall 763
Judgement of Paris 229
Jugs, Glass 521
Jugs, Silver 696
Jumeau 129
Jumeau Medaille D'or Paris 346
Jump 294
Junior Car Club 596
Jurgensen, Jules 321, 322
Jurojin 624
Justice 183, 202
Justice, Faith, Hope & Charity 532
Jutta 346

Kachina 70-73
Kaendler 182
Kaga 232
Kageaki 125
Kaigyokusai 627
Kajikawa 550, 551
Kakiemon 178, 179, 183, 194, 232-234, 235, 286
Kalo 688
Kammer & Reinhardt 608
Kandler, J.J. 242, 245-247
Kane, Michael 523
Kangxi 196, 235
Kano 432
Kanshosai 550
Kap Kap 588
Karabagh Kilim 663, 665
Karashishi 622, 625
Karasu Tengu 588
Karsh Yousuf 633
Kas 504, 505
Kashan 660, 661, 664
Kashmir Shawl 735, 736
Kashu Ju Morisada 560
Katana 118
Katar 86
Kataro Shirayamadani 174
Kathleen 206
Kathleen Mavourneen 585
Katsuchika 123
Kauba, C. 148
Kauffman 415
Kauffman, A. 181
Kayserzinn 630
Kazak 658, 659, 661, 664
Kazak Karatchoph 659
Kedeasian, Souepile 666
Keirincx 370
Keith, John James 721
Kelim 658
Keller, Miss Lydia Emeline 649
Kelvin Bottomley & Baird Ltd 558
Kempthorne Pattern 286
Kendell & Co., J. 384
Kendo 621
Kennedy, James 544, 545
Kennedy School 611
Kensington Gore 252
Kent, John 304
Kerr 107
Kestner 345
Khecheong 694
Khlebnikov, Velimir 644
Kidney, William 671
King Arthur 575
King Charles II 128
King Class James I 653
King, David 672
King Francois I 138
King George V 126, 127, 151
King Numitor 732
King of the Road 603
King Otto of the Hellenes 340

King's Bodyguard for Scotland 117
King's Dragoon Guards, The 1st 93
King's Liverpool Regt, The 83
King's Own Norfolk Imperial Yeomanry,
    The 93
King's Own Norfolk Yeomanry, The 77
King's Regt., The 4th Bn. 95
Kinkozan 232, 233
Kipp, Karl 335
Kirchner, Ernest Ludwig 646
Kirk & Son, Samuel 672
Kirk Braddon Cross 221
Kirk, Samuel 694, 696
Kirk, Thos. 574
Kirman 661, 664
Kirkman, Jacob & Abraham 635
Kitaoji Rosanjin 272, 274
Kitchener, Lord 342
Kitsune 562
Klaftenburger, J. 297, 312
Klaxon 599
Kleininger, J. 559
Klikitat 69
Klinger, Gottfried 242
Klingert, Gustav 683
Kneehole Desks 425-428
Kneller, Sir Godfrey 638
Knight, Laura 640
Knollys, Sir Francis 520
Knubley 109
K'o-ssu 341, 734
Ko-Imari 223, 224
Ko-omote 623
Ko-omote & Obeshimi 779
Kobako 630
Kodama 623
Koehn, Ed. 320
Koen, J.J. 336
Koharu & Jihei 645
Kollwitz, Kathe 642
Kolping 84
Komo Metal Paste 66
Konagkend 661
Kondo Mitsuyasu 89
Koopman, E.B. 166
Korner & Proll 705
Korniloff 212
Kosai Moritoshi 623
Kovats 147
Kozan 562
KPM 180, 181, 241-243
Kramer, Jacob 647
Kriegsmarine 553
Kruchenykh, Alexei 644
Kruger 187
Kruger, Paul 595
Kruse, Kathe 347
Kruse, Katy 347
Kuba 661, 662
Kuchler, Rudolf 145
Kunichika 648
Kunisada 648
Kupplerin 642
Kuya 622
Kylin 284
Kyo 626
Kyo-satsuma 261
Kyoto School 621, 623
Kyusai 622

L. & N.W. Railway 653
L. & Y. Ry., Victoria Station 651
L'Accolade 144
L'Allumage Moderne 597
L'Avarice 644
L'Empereur, en Petit Costume 619
L'Envie 644
L'Espiegle 277, 586
L'Estrange, Gen. G.G. Carlton 575
L'Imperatrice en Petit Costume 619
L'Italienne 641
L'Odyssee 643
L'Orgeuil 644
La Baigneuse 149
La Colere 644
La Dame au Parasol 223
La Danse a la Campagne 640
La Fontaine 255
La Jardiniere 214
La Juive D'Alger 149
La Gourmandise 644
La Liseuse 139
La Luxure 644
La Paresse 644
La Reine de Saba 643

La Tache 775
Labour & Victory 136
Lac Burgaute 724
Lachartroulle, Vincent 341
Lachenal 215
Ladd, William F. 325
Ladder Scale 556
Ladell, Kezi 666
Lady Jester, The 208
Lady of the Georgian Period 207
Lady's Legs 337, 339
Lagarde 314
Lago-Talbot Record 762
Lagonda 762
Lalique 171, 310, 512, 516, 522, 523,
    531, 534-541, 596-599
Lambart, A. 653, 769
Lambe 589
Lambert, Leopold 129
Lambeth 201, 206, 209
Lambourn Valley Railway 651
Lamm 180
Lamps 570, 571
Lan Ts'ai Ho 182
Lancashire Rifle Vols., The 6th 80
Lancaster & Son, J. 167
Lancaster, Charles 112
Lancers, The 21st 82, 83
Land Locked Salmon, A 642
Landulphus, Carolus F. 610
Languedoc 536
Langyao 235
Lantern Clocks 299
Lap Desk 162
Large Tables 474, 475
Larionov, Mikhail 644
Last Ride, The 135
Last Supper, The 510
Latona 197
Latour, Georges de 775
Laub-und-Bandelwerk 517
Laudato 228
Lauderdale, 2nd Earl & Duke of 638
Laughing Boy 175
Launch of S.S. Titanic 739
Laundy, J. 554
Laupua (?), S. 618
Lautrec, Henri de Toulouse 645
Lawrence of Arabia 128
Lazzarini, Ferro 541
L.B.S.C.R. 651
Le Bel Jnr. 262
Le Corbusier 437
Le Divan 646
Le Faguays 140
Le Figurines et Masques 534
Le Jockey 645
Le Mans Bentley 745
Le Mesurier 657
Le Nid 253, 254
Le Panhard 600, 601
Le Paysan 642
Le Praxinoscope 754
Le Printemps 277
Le Roy 297, 315
Le Songe 646
Le Sport & Le Tourisme Automobile
    599
Le Verre Francais 570
Lea-Francis 759
Lea, Philip 585
Leach 236, 237
Leach, Bernard 236, 237
Leach, Janet 237
Leach, John 236
Leaping Deer 236
Leclerc, J.N. 611
Lecoultre, Eugene 322
Lecoultre, Jaeger 327
Led Zeppelin 657
Ledsam, Vale & Wheeler 719
Leeds 188
Leete, A. 596
Lefevre, Robert 617
Lefranc 298
Lehmann 740, 745, 750, 754, 755
Lehrmittelwerke 554
Leica 164-169
Leithner, W. 114
Leitz 164-169
Lejeune, Pierre F. 219
Lenci 344
Lennon, John 657
Lens, Gernard 636
Lepeltier 317

Leroy 249
Les Gaudichots 774
Les Graveurs Modernes 645
Les Joueurs de Cartes 647
Les Maitres de L'Affiche 641
Leschaudel, A. 723
Lesney 740
Lewis, R. 285
Ley, Timothy 704
Leyland 758, 759
Leyuan, Zhou 724
Lhote 674
Lias, John & Henry 712
Liberty & Co. 253, 630, 631
Lichtenstein, Roy 646
Life of Napoleon Bonaparte 619
Light Cavalry 120
Light, E.W. 207
Lilley & Son 555
Limbert 420, 442, 443, 446, 483
Limoges 215, 348, 349
Lincoln, Abraham 396
Lincoln, Elizabeth N. 259
Lindbergh, Charles A. 330
Linderby, Wm. 319
Linderman, Clara C. 258
Linedon 616
Linemar 751
Lines Bros. 750
Lingee, C.L. 616
Lingley, Annie 174
Linthorpe 211
Linton, James 633
Lip Sofa 441
Lion Engineering Co. 594
Liqueur Set 163
Lissitsky, El 642
Lit en Bateau 353
Lithyalin 537
Little No Shirt 71
Littlehampton, Sand & Sunshine 765
Littlejohns 653
Live Aid 655, 656
Liverpool 238
Liverpool & Manchester Ry. 650
Liverpool Overhead Elec. Ry. 767
Liverpool to Australia 769
Lizinka, Mme. Aimee Zoe 638
Lloyd, Philip 303
Lloyd, T. 188
LMS 593, 650-653, 763, 764, 769
LNER 593, 651-653, 763-769
LNWR 592, 593
Lo & Li 745
Lock, Edward 317
Loetz 540
London 201
London by Sleeper 651
London & Birmingham Rys. 650
London & Brighton Ry. Co. 668
London & I.O.W. 768
London United Elec. Tramways 764
Longcase Clocks 300-307
Longines 321, 328, 329
Longman Lukey & Co. 634
Longton Hall 184, 186, 188, 190
Loof 289
Loose Rein 134
Lord Rodney 190
Lord's Prayer, The 510
Lorenzl 148
Loud-Hailer, Silver 699
Louis XIV 151
Louis Philippe 148
Love Abandoned 575
Love Found 575
Lowboys 429
Lowe, Robert 714
Lowestoft 239
Lowestoft Express 652
Lownes, Joseph 717
Longhurst 607
Lt. Dragoons 616
Lucas 66, 603
Lucci, G. 609
Lucci, Giuseppe 612
Luck, J.F. 218, 219
Ludwigsburg 219
Luff, Wm.H. 609
Luftwaffen 164, 165, 169
Luggage in Advance 653
Luminant 166
Lunacharski, Anatoli V. 126
Lunceschloss 118
Lund & Blockley 296

Lundberg, J. 574
Luneville 214
Ludwig 657
Lustre 239
Lutwyche, William 670, 671, 710
Luxurious Travel 768
Lynn 512, 514, 533, 543
Lyons Swiss Roll 747
Lys 512

Ma Shaoxuan 729
'Mac 700' 741
Macclesfield 393
Machin, Arnold 280
Mackennal, Sir Bertram 148
Mackintosh, Charles Rennie 532
Madonna & Child 567, 778, 779
Madonna Di San Sisto 181
Madonna, The 228
Magazine/Wood Carrier 779
Magic Lanterns 136
Mahal 663
Mahantongo Valley 352, 414
Maharishi Yogi 128
Mahr, W. 308
Maiden Immortal 588
Mainwaring, Arthur 701
Maisley, Robt. 303
Maitland, John 638
Makepeace, John 425
Malachite Jug 586
Malacreda, G.L. 545
Malacrida 131
Malaya 629
Malayir 660, 661
Malby & Son 554, 557
Malfrey Pot 279
Malmaison 616
Man on the Moon 657
Manchester Cup, The 689
Mangy, K. 705
Mannerbildnis 643
Manners & Sons 290
Mannlicher Schoenauer 112
Mansfield 481
Mansion House Dwarfs 188, 270
Mantel Clocks 308-317
Manticha 132
Maori Comb 588
Maori Fish Hook 776
Map of England & Wales 736
Maple & Co. Ltd. 306, 357, 498
Mappin & Webb 583, 707
Maps 584, 585
Marble 572-575
Marc, HRR. 311
Marc, Hy. 129, 316
Marcantonio, Sforza di 229
Margaine, Francois-Arsene 294-297
Margot 604
Marie-Jose 646
Marklin 592, 593, 747, 752
Marks, Gilbert 691
Marquetz 149
Marquis, The 246
Marr, J. 306
Marseilles 215
Marshall, John 300
Martele 681, 682
Martie, F. 314
Martin Bros. 239
Martin, F. 750
Martinez, Richard 71
Martini 67
Martins Pecheurs 538
Martinware 239
Marx 745, 748, 750, 751
Mary Queen of Scots 216, 532
Masakatsu 624
Masakazu 621
Masanaga 125
Masanao 623
Masanori 620
Masatomi 119
Masatoshi 621, 627
Masatsugu 627
Masayuki 563
Mask 588
Mason, F.H. 764
Mason, Frank 763
Mason, Miles 240
Masonic 280, 322, 510
Mason's 240
Massey Harris 740
Matchless 67

Matisse, Henri 646, 648
Matsuda Sukenaga 620
Matthews Stanley 127
Maurer, Iohan 292
Mauritius 629
Mauser 108
Maw & Co. 187
Max Handwerck 342
May, John 305
May, Phil 603
Mayakovsky, Vladimir 642
Mayblossom 254
Maynard 114
Mays, Raymond 599
Mazawattee Tea 68
McBean, Angus 633
McCabe, James 316
McCartney, Paul 655
McCorquodale Studio 650
McDowell, William 768, 769
McHugh & Co., Joseph P. 374
McKnight Kauffer, Edward 665, 767
Med. Electric Telegraph 668
Medallion 614, 618
Medals 97-105
Medici 254
Medici, Lorenzo de 566
Meeter, Pieter 675
Mehlhorn 243
Meinelt, C. 278
Meisel, G. 180
Meissen 241-247
Melas 663
Melchior, Johann P. 218, 219
Meli, Salvatore 462
Mellon, Eric James 276
Melloni 553
Melodia 605
Memiller (?), A. 143
Mene, P.J. 138,140
Mene, P.J. 138, 140, 142, 144-147,
149, 697
Menier 269
Mercantile Bank of India 629
Mercedes 600, 602, 748
Mercedes Benz 599, 756, 757, 759
Mercer, Thomas 554
Mercury & Hebe 142
Mereaud 264
Merle, Jean-Marie 615
Merrimac 177
Mesurier, Robin Le 657
Metropolitan, Police 83
Metropolitan Railway 651
Mettoy 748
Meyer, F.F. 247
Meyer, J. J. 212
Meylan, C.H. 325
MG. 757, 759, 761
MGA 761
Micaud 263
Michelin 597
Mickey & Minnie Mouse 742
Middleton, N. 721
Mide Ghost Lodge Menominee 72
Mide-Wiwim 73
Midget 761
Midinette 207
Mignon 346
Mikado, The 204
Mildner, Johann 533
Milk Sold Here 269
Milkmaid Brand Milk 66
Mille Miglia 603
Miller & Co. 317
Mills, John 406
Mills, Nathaniel 719
Millville 523, 524, 526
Milne, Monsieur R.O. 462
Milton 698
Mimi 645
Minerva 214, 253, 309
Mine-Sweepers 645
Ming 150, 248
Miniature Piano Box 160
Miniatures 576
Minic 753
Minic Transport Artic 753
Ministere De La Guerre 615
Minolla, J. 130
Minotaure Caressant Une Femme 647
Minton 249-252
Mirror Plateau 697
Mirrors 577-583, 616, 698
Mirrors 577-583, 616, 698
Mirskontsa (World Backwards) 644

Miscellaneous, Silver 697-699
Miss England 591
Mission 352, 353, 420, 447, 478, 779
Mitchel, A. 585
Mitsu 261
MItsuhiro 562, 622, 625, 626
Mitsumasa 123, 620
Mitsutoshi 626
Mittnacht, Johann 699
Moai Kavakava 779
Moaven Al-Tajar 661
Model Ships 590, 591
Model T Ford 753
Model Trains 592, 593
Models 594
Moderno 144
Modigliani, A. 641
Mogul 593
Moigniez, J. 148
Moliere, J.B.P. 135
Molins, H. 141
Momillon, X 523
Monatlich-Herausgegeben, Der 134
Money Banks 595
Money for Nothing 657
Monkey Match Pot 251
Monobrar 167
Mons Meg 652
Monsters 66
Montaut, E. 597, 600, 601
Monte Carlo Rally 598
Montelupo 227
Montgomery, Sir Bernard L. 128
Montval 646, 647
Monty 206
Moon Mullins & Kayo 750
Moorcroft 253
Moorcroft, Walter 253
Moorcroft, Wm. 253
Moore, Frederick 206
Moore, Henry 640, 641, 647
Moore, Wm. 487
Mordan, Sampson 531
Mordan, Samson 698
Mordecai, Benjamin 696
Moreau, F. 173
Morel-Ladeuil, L. 697
Morey, M. 276
Morgan 756
Morice, Sir Wm. 128
Morin, Jean 644
Moritoshi 626
Morris 391, 398
Morris & Co. 462
Morris, R. J. 253
Morris, Robt. 668
Mortimer, John 677
Mortlake 733
Mortlock's 253
Mosaic Panel 586
Mosenthal Brothers 628
Moses 732
Moses & Aaron 737
Moso 621
Mother of God, The 587
Motocycles Comiot 647
Motoring Items 596-603
Motorist, The 653
Motschmann 343
Mount Washington 525, 526
Mountigue, Benjamin 696
Moustiers 215
Movado 320, 327, 331
Mr 592
M.R. 653
Mr. Punch 588
Mr. Robot 731
M.T.V. 657
Mucha, Alphonse 348
Mucha, Alphonse Maria 642
Mueller, Otto 648
Mugs, Silver 700
Muhr, J. 142
Muller 293
Muller Freres 571
Mulliner, H. J. 761
Mummified Hawk 586
Munehisa 565
Munenori 122
Munster 250
Murataya 645
Murillo 180, 278
Murray, James 315, 321
Murray, John 632
Musashino Koki 166
Muses 182, 183

Musical Boxes & Polyphones 604-608
Musical Instruments 609-613
Musical Mantel Clock 604
Musique De Hussards 617
Musique De La Garde Rep. 617
Muss, Charles 199
Mussolini, Benito 126
My Darling 596
Mycock, W. S. 239
Mystery of Edwin Drood, The 135

Nadelman, Elie 780
N.A.G. 596
Nagamasa 122
Nagatsugu 122
Nagayasu 621
Namban 118
Nando 731
Nanking 196
Naohiro 584
Naomitsu 622
Napier Motors 597
Naples 228, 229
Napoleonic Memorabilia 129, 184, 262,
    268, 320, 575, 614-619, 675
Nardin, Joseph 305
Nardin, Ulysse 321
Narrien 555
Nasatoshi 620
Nash I, Thos. 684
Nast 254
National Benzole 601
Nautical Photo Agency 739
Navajo 69, 71-73
Navy Week, Visit the Dockyards 763
Nazarene Style 349
Nazi 94, 117, 118
Neal, David 216
Nectar Tea 68
Negerrevue 644
Nelson 504
Neptune 183, 252, 540
Nesch, Rolf 644
Netsuke 620-627
Neubauer 600
Nevers 186
Neville, R. 591
Nevinson, C.R.W. 644
New Dancers 183
New Illustrated Catalogue 136
New Land 106
New Sculpture 148
Newbould, Frank 652, 763, 767
Newcastle 542
Newcomb 175
Newman & Guardia Sibyl 166
Nez Perce 70, 71
Nichol, Gordon 765-767, 769
Nicholas I 212
Nichols, Maria Longworth 259
Nicholson, J. 738
Nicolas, Sir H. 135
Nicolson, John 714
Nicole Freres 605
Niderviller 214
Nielsen, Harald 677
Night Fever 657
Nikkosai 550
Nikolaiev, Mitri 683
Njers, Ljerka 210
Noah's Ark 734, 749
Nock, H. 110
Noel R. 614, 617
Noh Masks 779
Nomura 731
Non-Such 515
Norrenberg 558
Norris, Charlotte 347
North American Indian 204
N. American Land Co. 668
North Berwick 652
North British Railway 650
North British, Station Hotel 769
North Eastern Railway 653
Northcote, Hannah 670
Northumberland Fusiliers, The 83, 91
Norton Cup/Fishmonger's Co. 688
Norton, Eardley 291
Norton, J. & E. 275, 276
Norwich General 586
Noseda, J. & P. 130
Notables De A France 614
Nothing Takes the Place of Leather 596
Notman 633
Novello, Ivor 655
Now the King. . 647

Nu 643
Nuremberg Hausmaler 217
Nurnberger Blechspielwarenfabric 754
Nutting, Henry 670
Nymphenburg 217-219

Occasional Tables 476-483
Oesterr, Waffenfabr. Ges. Steyr 112
Oeuvres 135
Of Two Squares 642
Ogawa Munekata 564
Ogden's Plug 68
Ohara Mitsuhiro 626
Ojibwa 72, 73
Old King Cole 205, 209
Old Mission Kopperkraft 571
Olfers, L. 337
Ollivant, Thomas 700
Omega 326
Omori 624
Omori Eishu 89
Omphale 140
On N'Passe Pas 618
One Metre 590
One of the Forty 207
Ono, Yoko 657
Onondaga Metal Shop 334
Opa Mu Nu 71
Operaphone 634
Opset 731
Oram, Anne 667
Oran 539
Orendi 665
Organ 634
Organette 604-606
Orient Line 767
Orrefors 537
Ortelli, A. 130
Otafuku 624
Otoman 626
Otto, F. 260
Our New Clergyman 750
Ovchinnikov 585
Ovum 68
Owen, Will 342
Ozier 181

Packard Landaulet 744
Pacific Line 769
Padden, Leonard 765, 768
Paddy & Pig 755
Paeonies & Fresias 640
Pageant of Man's Redemption 732
Pail 778
Paillard 608
Paillet 674
Palais Des Tuileries 617
Palekh School 585
Palmer, Jane 637
Palmerston, Lord 221
Panon 169
Pantin, S. 710
Pantin I, Lewis 715
Pantin I, Simon 680
Pantolone 216
Paper Money 628, 629
Papercut Picture 585
Paperweights 524-529, 617
Papua 590
Paradise Lost 698
Parfum Des Fleurs 646
Parian 253
Paris 254, 255
Paris Exhibition 263
Paris in London 769
Parker Hale 113
Parker, John 716
Parks, Jno. 299
Park Ward 762
Parnell 558
Parlourmaid 632
Parsons & Co. John 679
Partis, Thomas 686
Partis, Wm. 685
Pascal 557
Pascault, J. 262
Pashier, Edwd. 318
Pastorelli, J. 131
Patanazzi 228
Pattison 113
Pauillac 772-775
Paxman 609
Payne 292, 312, 313
Peace Model 758
Peacock 567
Peacock Thos. 703

Peale, James 636
Pears, Charles 650, 768
Pearson, D. 425
Peep Egg 587
Pelham Puppets 742
Pellerin & Co. 617
Pellipario, Nicola 231
Pemberton, S. 703, 719
Pembroke Tables 476, 484, 485
Penaga 767, 769
Penalva 227
Penet, L. 349
Penthesilia 138
Penny, Mr. R. 739
Pepys 355
Pepys, Samuel 128
Perche 598
Percier, Charles 619
Percy Tenantry 88
Perdult (?), T. 618
Perepedil 662
Perigal 289
Perkins, Roger 275
Perseus & The Three Graces 532
Persistence 590
Personnages Masques et Femme Oiseau
    646
Pesaro 229
Pessac 772, 775
Peter Pan 148
Peters & Co. H. 604
Petersburg Press 647, 648
Petit, Jacob 214, 254, 255, 311
Pewter 630, 631
Pfhol 522
Pharaoh's Daughter 575
Philippe & Co., Patek 311, 320, 322-328,
    330, 331
Phillips, R. 738
Phillips, R. H. 591
Phipp's Diamond Ale 68
Phipps II, James 703
Phipps & Robinson 722
Phipps, Thomas 703
Phoenix Park 603
Phonogram Ltd., 655
Phonograph 604-606, 608
Photographs 632, 633, 739
Phrenology Bust 269
Phyfe, Duncan 441, 467
Piano Orchestrion 604
Pianos 634, 635
Picard China Co. 173
Picasso, Pablo 646-648
Picking 652
Picture Frame 586
Pidduck & Sons 552
Piedmont 772
Pierotti 347
Piercing Spike 548
Pierray, Claude 609
Piers, Daniel 686
Pigment Barrel 548
Piguet. Audemars 328, 330
Pike Dorland, R.S. 766
Pilgrim's Progress 697
Pilgrim Vase 249
Pilkington 190, 239
Pilkington, Col. 95
Pilleau, Peze 685
Pima 72
Pina, Alfredo 572
Pines Express, The 764
Pink Room 381
Pininfarina 756
Pioneer Battalion 90
Pipe Case 587
Piptuka 71
Pisan Bridge Festival 91
Pistols 106-111
Pistor, Edward 291
Pitts, Thomas 681, 688
Pitts, Wm. 670, 691
Place, George 637
Plail Bros. 392, 393
Plail &Co. 454
Plains 69, 71-73
Planet Robot 730
Plateau 69
Plath, C. 553
Player's Drumhead Cigarettes 67
Plenty 190, 215
Plimer, Andrew 637, 639
Plummer, Michael 670, 671
Plummer, William 684
Plymouth 189

Pocketbook 589
Policeman & Woman 212
Poli, Flavio 536, 541
Polydor Ltd. 657
Polyphon 606-608
Polyphones & Musical Boxes 604-608
Pomanders, Silver 701
Pomerol 773, 775
Pomo 69, 70, 72
Poole Pottery 210, 275
Pope, F.C. 205
Porga 269
Porringers, Silver 701
Porter, P.W. 114
Porter, Raymond Averill 334
Portrait De Jeune Femme 644
Portrait Miniatures 618, 619, 636-639
Port Sunlight 653
Portland Vase 279
Portobello 184, 187
Post Savings Bank 595
Postcards, Titanic 738, 739
Posters 584, 585
Possible 73
Pot Cupboards & Commodes 411
Potted Daffodils 641
Potter, Beatrix 151
Potter & Co. Albert H. 321
Powell, James 517, 518, 535, 536
Power & Progress 766
Powhoge 70
Pratt 187-189, 269
Pratts 596
Preiss, F. 140, 143, 146, 308
Preissler, I. 219
Presley, Elvis 655-657
Presto, The 166
Presto Pocket Camera Primer 166
Presentation of Ribbons 214
Pressnitz, F. F. Meyer Von 247
Prevost, J. J. 545
Primavera 215
Prince Albert 185, 572
Prince Consort 140
Prince of Wales 144
Prince of Wales Leinster Regt., The 77
Princess Elizabeth 741
Princess Feather 649
Prints 640-648
Prior, Geo. 323
Private Reserve 775
Pro Dva Kvadrata 642
Procris 194
Prometheus 618
Prothero Thos. P. 703
Prussian Jager Zu Pferd 93
Prussian Reservist Artillery 96
P.S.N.C. To South America 769
Psyche 572
Ptolemaic Period 782
Pug 203
Pugin, A.W.N. 385, 465, 481
Pulchinella 217, 246, 278
Pullman's Palace Car Co. 668
Purvis, Tom 763
Pustelli, Franz Anton 219
Pyne, G. 609, 610
Pyx 158

Qashqai Kilim 662
Qianlong 213, 727
Qoia 72
Quah Ah 70, 71
Quail Pattern, The 183
Quaint 439
Quare, Dan. 291, 293
Queen Adelaide 638
Queen Alexandra 347
Queen Charlotte 198
Queen Elizabeth I 688
Queen Mary 127
Queen of the Amazons 138
Queen Victoria 198, 253
Queen's Jubilee, The 651
Queen's Own Cameron Highlanders 90
Quilts 649

Railway Tickets 654
Railways Wanted Board 651
Railwayana 650-654
Rain Cloud 192
Rakan 622
Rakan Nakasaina Sonja 627
Raleigh, Sir Walter 526
Rampillon 540
Raphael 181, 567

R.A. Series 763
Rawlings & Sumner 722
Rawlings, C. 154
Rawnson, Wm. 692
Ray, Daniel 306
Rebecca 209
Reclining Figure Point 647
Reclining Figures 640
Reconnaissance Corps, The 82
Record Cabinet 605
Red Ashay 599
Redcar 652
Redfern, Sarah 666
Redgate Table Waters 68
Redlich & Co. 690
Redline 597
Redware 172-176
Reed, Andrew 307
Reed, Olga Geneva 259
Regina 301, 606
Reid, William 716
Reilly & Storer 713, 722
Reinicke, P. 242-244, 247
Reliefzierrat 180
Remington 113
Renaldo 194
Renault 601
Renders, Louis 216
Renoir, Pierre-Auguste 640, 643
Rescht Cover 735
Restoration 255
Reveller, The 241
Reverie 642
Review of Reviews, The 739
Reymong, Pierre 348
Reynaud, Emile 754
Reynolds, Sir J. 532
Rhead, Frederick 187
Ribault 619
Rich, John 722
Richard, Keith 657
Richardson, Charlotte 667
Richardson, Richard 721
Richmond, Master Tom 738
Richmond Race Cup, The 688, 689
Richter, Adolph 173
Rie, Lucie 256, 257
Riedinger, P. 276
Rifle Brigade, The 79
Rifles 112-115
Rimbault, Stepn. 292
Rinaldi, G. 586
Rinehart, Wm. 573
RingToss Game 741
Rio de Janeiro 769
Ripol 87
Ripon 767
Rittreck 166
Rizzi 133
R.M.S. Edinburgh Castle 591
R.M.S. Lancastria 136
R.M.S. Olympic & Titanic 738
Road to Calvary, The 519
Robartes, Lord 650
Robert & Slater 684
Roberts, N. 286
Robertson, Wm. 320
Robins, John 671
Robins, Thos. 702
Robinson 633
Robinson II, E. 703
Robinson & Cleaver 188
Robinson, D. 300
Robinson, Gerrard 780
Robot 731
Rochishin 627
Rock 'n' Roll 655-657
Rockingham 258
Rodanet, A. H. 297
Rodmell, Harry Hudson 769
Rodney, Lord 190
Roger, Rhoda 666
Rogovin, I. 644
Rohde, Johan 692
Rohlfs, Charles 446
Rolex 326-331
Rolleiflex 167
Rolling Stones, The 657
Rolls, Hon. C. S. 598
Rolls-Royce 599, 756, 757, 760-762
Romanee-Conti 774, 775
Romanelli, Pasquale 575
Rombrich, J. C. 219
Romer, Emick 679
Romer, John 679
Rookwood 174, 258, 259

Roosevelt, F.D. 127
Rosel Von Rosenhof, A. 134
Rosen, Anton 680
Rosenberg, A. 127
Rosenvinge, Odin 766
Roshi 620
Rosi, L. 566
Ross 552, 559
Ross, Donald 488
Ross-shire Buffs, The 78th Regt. 87
Rothebusch, Frederick 259
Rotunda 156
Roualt, Georges 646
Round & Sons Ltd., John 678
Rouolle, L.C. 617
Rouse, J. 198
Rover 600, 758
Rover Patent, The 167
Rowe 132
Rowe, Mary Anne 737
Rowlandson 134
Rowntree's Pastilles 66
Royal Air Force 753
Royal Arms 522
Royal Army Medical Corps., The 95
Royal Artillery, The 83, 96
Royal Aubusson 732
Royal Co. of Archers, The 117
Royal Corps of Signals, The 95
Royal Dublin Fusiliers, The 78
Royal Dux 260
Royal Engineers, The 94
Royal Fusiliers, The 79
Royal Fusiliers City of London Regt.,
  The 82
Royal Garter 268
Royal Guards 742
Royal Guelphic Order, The 80
Royal Highlanders, The 80
Royal Horse Artillery, The 76, 82, 752,
  753
Royal Horse Guards, The 96, 121, 742,
  755
Royal Lancastrian 239
Royal Madras Fusiliers, The 102nd. 81
Royal Mail Line 766, 768, 769
Royal Navy 120
Royal Presentation Set, The 747
Royal Scots, The 92, 94
Royal Inniskilling Dragoons Guards, The
  5th. 83
Royal Irish Auto. Club 603
Royal Irish Regt. 76
Royal Irish Rifles, The 82
Royal Regt. 74
Royal Regt. of Artillery, The 76
Royal Warwickshire Regt., The 77, 95
Royal Welsh Fusiliers, The 80, 91
Royalist 201
Roycroft 335, 477
Roycrofters 135, 136
Rubens 180, 181
Rubino, E. 141
Rude 145
Rue 638
Rue De Seine 641, 644
Ruffier Noel 617
Rugs 658-665
Rumsey, P. 590, 591
Run in a Motor Card, A 745
Rundell, Philip 691
Running Antelope 71
Rush, James Blomfield 271
Rushworth & Son, T. 578
Russell, Ed. 319
Russian Dancer 140
Rye Cannon Ball 221
Ryujin 621
Ryuo (Ittosai) 122
Ryuraku 563
Ryushin 565

Sabrina 283
Sadakatsu 124
Sadler, T. 199
Sagittarius 140
Sailing Trawlers 764
Saint Emilion 773, 775
St. Christopher 523, 778
St. Francis 229
St. George 146
St. George & The Dragon 145, 266
St. Ives 210, 211, 272, 273
St. James' Palace 136
St. Jerome 640
St. John 230, 567

St. Joseph 524
St. Louis 522, 524-529, 535
St. Roman 585
St. Stephen 532
Saito 137
Saku 145
Salazar, Fiona 210
Sales, Jon. 302
Salomon 610
Salts, Silver 702
Salvers & Trays, Silver 714, 715
Samplers 666, 667
Samson 214
Sand Glass 546, 549
Sanderson, Henry 290
Sandringham Hotel 765
Sandwich 528
Sannino, Vincenzo 612
Sansho 620
Sansovino, Jacopo 784
Santa Barbara 229
Saskia 643
Satchell, Thos. 710
Sator, G. 219
Satsuma 234, 261, 570
Satterlee, G. A. 276
Saturday Evening Girls 174-176
Sauceboats, Silver 703
Sauternes 772, 773, 775
Savona 227, 231
Savory, A. & J. 721
Saxony Cavalry 120, 121
Saxton, Christopher 585
Scaramouche 278
Scarborough 763
Scarpa, Carlo 538
Scent Bottles 530, 531
Scheidt, George Anton 675
Schiestedt, Schrader von 219
Schindler, P.E. 242
Schleissner & Sons, J. D. 677
Schmit, Georg 323
Schneider 515
Schneider Xenar 167
Schoelcher 254
Schuco 741, 747, 753
Schwartz, F.A.O. 747
Schwarzlot 219, 511
Sciacca 231
Scipio 565
Scofield, John 676
Sconces 587
Scotcher & Son, C. 604
Scotland, Night Scotsman 767
Scott 311
Scott, James 722
Scott, Sir Walter 619
Scottish Rifles, The 4th Vol. Bn. 83
Screens 430-432
Scrubbing Brush 547
Scuffle 271
Sculpture 230
S. & D.J. R. 765
Sealing Wax Set, Silver 699
Seaman's Boot 547
Seated Rabbit 207
Second time, The 655
Second Yorkshire North Riding Regt.,
 The 81
Secretaire Bookcases 434, 435
Secretaires 433
Secretary of State 128
Sedan Chair 584, 589
Sedan Clock 614
Seddon & Moss 300
See Britain First Shell 766
See The Peak District 764
Segrave, Sir Henry 591
Seguso 536
Seguso, Archimede 514, 540
Seiryu 587
Seiya Zo 137, 145
Sekonic Microlite 168
Sentinel 762
Sentry of The Foot Guards 744
S.E.R. 652
Serapi 658
Setsubun 626
Settees & Couches 436-441
Settle, J. & T. 678
Seuter 217
Seuter, B. 246
Seven Years War 348
Sevres 262-264, 295, 313, 462, 498, 618
Sewan Kazak 665
SFBJ 347

S. & H. 344
Shaker 161, 376, 377, 411, 417, 475, 778
Shakespeare's House 221
Shalako Mana 73
Shannon 427
Share Certificates 668
Sharp, George B. 709
Sharp, R. 674, 688-690, 716
Shaw, G. 782
Shaw, T. E. 128
Shaw, Thos. 300
Shawsheen 176
Sheffield Simplex 601
Shell 67
Shell Oil 601
Shell Picture 587
Shelley 189, 191
Shellubricate 598
Sheppard, E. W. D. 594
Sheraton, Thos. 471
Sherratt, Obadiah 266, 267
Sherwin, Frank 766
Shillingford Bridge 766
Shinsoku 119
Ship's Figurehead 780, 781
Ships of the British Navy 746
Shirayamadani, K. 259
Shirvan 658, 660-662
Shiraz 660, 665
Shizuhisa 564
Shoe Buckles 546, 548
Shoe Last 546
Shoes 548, 669
Shoesmith, K. 653, 763, 766 767, 769
Shoji Hamada 272, 274, 275
Shojo 626
Shokasai 551
Shoki-Imari 222
Shoki & Oni 620
Shoko 624, 627
Shoko Co. 169
Shop-O'-The-Crafters 494, 577
Short Snorter 127
Shoulao 248
Shreve & Co. 715
Shreve, Stanwood & Co. 706
Shuck, A. 284
Shugetsu 624
Shuho Yamakawa 641
Siamese Cat 205
Sicilian 228, 230, 231
Side Tables 486-489
Sideboards 442-445
Siebe Gorman Co. Ltd. 334
Siegwart, Hugo 138
Silhouette 588, 589
Silver 670-723
Silver Wraith Sedanca de Ville 761
Silvy 633
Simon & Halbig 346
Sims, George R. 136
Singer Sewing Machines 67
Singing Bird 156, 161, 313
Siot Decauville 145
Sioux 69, 73
Sirens & Conche Shell 260
Sissons, W. & G. 683
Sitwell, Edith 633
Sitzendorf 216, 220
Six Figurines et Masques 534
Skinner's Horse 76
Sled 584, 781, 782
Smart , John 637, 639
Smily, Thomas 695
Smith 285, 596
Smith, B. & J. 682, 685
Smith, D. 674, 688, 689
Smith, Sidney 289
Smith, Tate, Hoult & Tate 684
Smuggler 770
Smuts 204
Snelling, Jams. 291
Snuff Bottles 724-729
Snuff Boxes 619
Snuff Boxes, Silver 703
Snow White 645
Snow White & The Seven Dwarfs 343
Snowman 190
Soame, William 705
Societe Des Bronzes De Paris 138
Sofa Tables 490, 491
Sogo No goro 623
Soko 623
Solomon Island Ornament 588
Solon, L. 249, 252
Somalvico & Co, Joseph 132, 133

Somersetshire Light Infantry, The 94
Somin 588
Songoku 622
Sonni, Jack 657
Sosui 624
Soten Style 89
Sotiau 309
Soumac 659, 660, 663
S. Devon, Cornwall Rys. 650
South African Statesman 187
South Staffordshire 348, 349
South Wales 766
Southern Railway 763, 765, 766, 768
S. R. Golden Arrow 653, 768
S. R. Swanage, Dorset 765
Southern Rhodesia 628
Southey 221
Southill 370
Space Explorer 731
Space Station 748
Space Toys 730, 731
Spackman, Wm. 685
Sparky Jim 731
Sparky Robot 730
Special Boat Service 768
Speede, John 584
Spelzini 130
Spencer 569
Spinets 634, 635
Spirit Barrel 549
Spirit of the Wind 597, 599
Spode 265
Spodes New Stone 265
Spooner, F. W. 502
Spoonrack 781, 784
Spot-On 747, 750-752
Spradbery, Walter 768
Spratts Van 743
Spring 189
Spurs, Silver 697
Squires, Mr. Wm. 738
S. S. Etonian 739
S. S. Laurentic 767
S. S. Leviathan 766
S. S. Talacre 591
S. S. Titanic, Lifeboat Nameplate 739
Stabler, H. 713
Stabler, Harold & Phoebe 275
Stadler, J. E. 245
Staffordshire 266-271, 282
Stained Glass 532
Stands 446-449
Stanley, Anthony 689
Star of Bethlehem 649
Starkies 595
State Series 738
Status Quo 655
Stead, W. T. 739
Stearns, Thomas 541
Steel & Iron 560, 561
Steiff 743, 744, 750, 754
Steiner, Jules Nicholas 345
Steinlen, T. A. 647
Steinway 634, 635
Stephanus 263
Stephenson 650
Steuben 170, 512
Stevens 592
Stevens, Betsey 667
Stevens Co., J. & E. 595
Stevens, J. & E. 595
Steward II, Joseph 723
Stewart, Cal. 605
Stewart, Rod 655
Steyr 112
Stickley Bros. 334, 439, 444, 449
Stickley, Gustav 335, 352, 354, 356, 357,
 377, 382, 390, 391, 393, 394, 396-
 398, 400, 401, 404, 426, 430, 431,
 433, 436-438, 440, 443, 445, 447,
 450, 451, 453, 469, 472, 476, 479,
 482, 483, 495-497, 502, 505, 571,
 577, 579, 777
Stickley, L. & J. G. 304, 353, 354, 356,
 394, 447, 448, 452, 478, 489, 495
Stinton, H. 283, 287
Stinton, J. 288
Stinton, Jas. 285, 288
Stinton, John 283, 287
Stirling, The Best Way 763
Stirn, C. P. 167
Stockton & Darlington Ry. 650
Stollwerck Bros. 595
Stone, Anna 667
Stone, Arthur 332, 673, 696
Stoneware 272-276, 548

Stools 450-453
Storr & Mortimer 566
Storr, Paul 671, 685, 696, 711, 712, 716, 718
Story, Joseph William 716
Story of a Passion, The 136
Stourbridge 536
Stowell, M. Louise 585
Strainer, Silver 699
Stratford & Midland Ry. 651
Strato Clipper 741
Strauss, Richard 127
Street & Co., R. W. 558
Streeter & Co. 292
Strigel, Geo. Phi. 323
Stripp, M. 510
Stuart Major 594
Stubborn Donkey, The 750
Stubbs, Thos. 302
Stuffed Birds 584
Stump Speaker 595
Styles, Susannah 667
Sublime Harmony 604, 608
Success to Queen Caroline 189
Suites 454, 455
Summer Yellow Legs 782
Summers, Gerald 381
Summers, William 719
Sun Label 656
Sunbeam Alpine 752
Sung 206
Sunlight 68
Sunshing 721
Supernal 591
Supersonic Moon Ship 749
Supertoys 746, 747
Surtees, R. S. 134
Suruga Takayoshi 123
Susannah 574
Suss, Gerr 307
Sutherland Tables 473
Sutton, Fred 208
Suzhou School 726-728
Suzuribako 155, 157-159
Svenska Express 166
Swallow 757
Swansea 188
Sweet & Twenty 208
Sweet Violets 536
Swingewood 518, 520
Swint, J. 438
Sword Dancer 151
Swords 116-121
Symphonion 604

Tables 456-499
Tables of English History . . 744
Tabriz 659
Tadahisa 625
Tairyusai Sokan 119
Takaramono 625
Talking Robot 731
Tallis's Railway Map 650
Tam O' Shanter 780
Tameteka 625
Tammany Bank 595
Tango 780
Tank Transporter 748
Tankards, Silver 704, 705
Tantalus 159
Tap Dancer, The 584
Tapestries 732, 733
Tapies, Antonio 632
Targee, John 689
Taroni & Co., Leoni 131
Tasse D'Amitie 181
Tatham 107
Tatham, Henry Jnr. 108
Tatlin, V. 644
Tatsuke Takamasu 550
Taylor III, Isaac 588
Taylor, Fred 764
Taylor, John 639
Taylor, Samuel 710
Taylor, Wm. 698
Taylor's Depository 68
Tazza, Silver 697
Tazza, Wood 782
Tchalenko, Janice 273
Tea Caddies, Silver 710
Tea & Card Tables 456-461
Tea & Coffee Sets, Silver 706-709
Tea Kettles, Silver 711
Teapots, Silver 712, 713
Teco 173, 176
Tekkai Sennin 623

Tekke 660
Tekno 748
Television Spaceman 730
Temple Press 598
Temptation of Adam 231
Ten Commandments 737
Teniers 254
Tenkodo Hidekuni 123
Tenn, Svenskt 630
Terchi, Bartholomeo 227
Terracotta 277
Terras, R. 309
Terry & Sons, E. 312
Tete De Belier 597
Tete De Coq 597
Tete De Mort 644
Texier Nicolas 318
Textiles 734-737
Thames Police 645
Theatre Stamford 585
Theed, W. 572, 573, 575
Thelsitor 269
Then & Now, Flying Scotsman 765
Then & Now, 600 Golf Courses 764
Theodor, Carl 217, 219
Theroude 129
Theseus & The Minotaur 142
Thevenet 262, 263
Thibouville Lamy & Co., J. 606
Thomas Clock Co., Seth 315
Thomese, Albert De 680
Thomson, A. R. 764, 765
Thorens 634
Thorley's Poultry Spice 68
Thornton & Co., Ltd. 603
Thorpe, Dorothy 522
Three Balls (?) 640
Three Bears, The 752
Three Midgets 632
Three Reclining Figures 641
Thwaites, Aynsth. & Jono. 293
Tickford 757
Tidmarsh, G. D. 764
Tiffany & Co. 324, 325, 515, 530, 570, 571, 672, 676, 692, 693, 699, 702, 705, 707, 708, 714, 718
Till, Thomas 250
Timbrell, Robt. 682, 685
Tinworth, George 206
Tipp Co. 740
Tipper 740
Titanic Memorabilia 738, 739
Tizer 66
Tlingit 70
TM 749
Toast Rack, Silver 699
Tobacco Box 587
Tobacco Canister 779
Tobacco Pattern 213
Tobacco Pouch 584, 585
Tobacconist Figure 781
Toddy, Jimmy 71
Toft, Charles 214
Toiler, The 206
Tojo 550
Toleware 589
Tomlinson 303
Tomohisa 89
Tomotada 624
Tompion 293
Tonibell Ice Cream Van 750
Tonita Pena 70, 71
Top Hat 759
Topsy 70
Torch Dancer 140
Torento 106
Toshinaga 551
Tososei 623
Toumanova As La Sylphide 633
Tourist Trophy, 1906. 602
Tournheim-Tourneau, Henry K. 331
Tour(s) of Doctor Syntax, The 135
Tower of London 208
Townsend, E. 185
Townshend, Pete 656
Toys 740-755
Track Records 656
Trafalgar, Battle of 504
Transitional 356, 380, 496
Transport 756-762
Transvaal Moneybox 595
Travel Posters 763-769
Travel to Ireland 764
Trays & Salvers, Silver 714, 715
Tree of Life 160

Tregent 292, 293, 312
Trembley Rose 188, 190
Tremelo 608
Tribunal 139
Triceratops 747
Trick Dog 595
Triumph 756, 760
Troubetskoy, Paolo 146
Troughton & Simms 130, 556, 559
Trousse 87
Trunks & Coffers 500-503
Trusty Servant, The 221
Tsubas 122-125
Tuborg Pilsner 748
Tudric 630, 631
Tulip Painter 239
Tumblers, Glass 533
Tunn, James 290
Tunon, Carlo 611
Tureens, Silver 716
Turell, Wm. 678
Turkish Bocha 735
Turner, Richard 722
Turner, Thos. 115
Turtle & Chipmunk 645
Tuscan 226
Tustin, Charles 210
Tustin, Sidney 210
Tutankhamen 589
Tut-Tut 745, 754
Tyrannosaurus Rex 747

Udall & Ballou 671
Uebelacker 747
Uhlan Regt., The 77, 91, 93, 94
Ultraman 730
Uncle Sam 564
Undress Hat 587
United States Lines 766
United States & Spain 595
Unione Militare 91
Universal 330
Universal Autograph Coll. Club 656
Unterseeboot 740
Up to Scotland 768
Urbino 226-228, 230, 231
Urns 159
Urns, Silver 717
U.S.M.C. Stiletto 87
Utamaro 644, 645
Ute Reservation 72
Uzbek Silk Ikat 736

Vacheron & Constantin 320, 321, 324, 326, 327, 329, 331
Valentien, Albert R. 259
Valentien, Anna Marie 259
Valkyrie Rider 148
Valva 536
Van Briggle 176
Van de Velde, Henry 662
Van Dyke 511
Van Gogh, V. 642
Van Houten's Cocoa 68
Vanden Plas 762
Varianto Motorway 753
Vase Aux Ombelles 538
Vases, Glass 534-541
Vases, Silver 718
Vaso A. Canne 537
Vaucher Fils 608
Vauthier 614
Vauxhall 601
Vedar 517, 519
Vela, F. 616
Velicogna 128
Venetian 226
Venice 226
Venini 514, 537-541
Veno's Cough Cure 68
Venus 149
Venus Africaine 148
Venus & Cupid 573
Venus De' Medici 575
Vere, John 670, 671, 710
Vernon & Co., Ltd., T. 136
Vertical Vessel 210
Vertumnus & Pomona 732
Vertunni 742
Vest Camera 167
Vestal Virgin 181
Vesuvius 229
Vetro A Granulari 538
Vetro Pesante Inciso 514
Veuve Perrin 215
Vicar & Moses 189

Vicarino & Co., Gay 317
Vickery, J. C. 338
Victoire 597
Victor Emmanuel, King 126
Victoria 528
Victory 230
Vienna 278
Vieyres & Repignon 315
Villanis, E. 138, 140
Villon, Jaques 641, 642, 644, 647
Vinaigrettes, Silver 719
Vincent, Alfred 611
Vincent, Edward 680
Vincenti 318
Viner 315
Viners 672
Violettes 541
Virgin & St. John 144
Virginia Cigarettes 66
Vitesse 599
Vittory & Dannelli 132
Vladimirskaya 587
Vollard 647
Voltaire 529
Volunteer Artillery 95
Volunteer Medical Staff Corps., The 80
Vom Bergwerck XII Bucher 134
Vorticist Figure 647
Voyage of the Nations 139
Voysey, C. A. 499
Vuillaume, N. 609
Vyse, Charles 275

Waddington 640
Waddington Prints Ltd., Leslie 640
Wadsworth, Edward 645
Wages of Signalmen 765
Wagner 278
Wake, T. 590
Wakelin, Edward 716
Wakelin, J. 686, 698
Wakizashi 118, 119
Waldo, Daniel 153
Walker & Hall 691
Wall Clocks 318, 319
Wall Lights 584
Wall, Dr. 283
Wallis, John 744
Wallwork, Alan 272
Walter, Almeric 518, 525, 528, 534
Walton 269, 470, 504
Walton, George 532
Walton, I. 135
Walzenkrug 217
Wandering Minstrel 204
Wandering Musicians 218
Ward & Co., Ltd., A. 596
Ward, John 274, 275
Ward, Robt. 299
Wardrobes & Armoires 504, 505
Warhol, Andy 640
Warings 471
Warner, C. 307
Warwick 687
Warwick Castle 719
Washington 527
Washstands 506
Waste Paper Baskets 777
Watch Stand 586
Watches 320-325
Watches & Clocks 289-331
Water Carrier 153
Watkins & Hill 555
Watkins, F. 131
Watson & Son 554, 557
Watt 111
Wattenumalerei 243
Waveney Steam 668
W. D. & H. O. Wills Ltd. 599
Weathervanes 770, 771
Webb 530
Webb & Sons, Thomas 534
Webb, Wm. 300
Webber 768
Webster, William 308
Wedding Album 657
Wedgwood 268, 279-281
Wedgwood & Bentley 280, 281
Weetabix 746
Weimar Republic German Cavalry 116
Weiss 557, 559
Weisweiler 480, 481
Welby, D. & J. 703
Welch, Vic 653
Weller, Louwelsa 177
Weller, Sicard 173

Wellington 250, 253
Welsh Antiquities 221
Welsh Guards, Col. in Chief 745
Wemyss 187, 190
Wenford Bridge 193, 210, 274
Werner, J. H. 689
Werro, J. 613
Wesley, John 271
West Pans 191
West Yorkshire Regt., The 81
Westerwald 216, 272-274
Westley Richards 114, 115
Westminster 289, 301
Westphal, Charles 713
Wetherell, Harriot 666
Weyersberg, Gebr. 121
Weyersberg Kirschbaum 120
Weymouth Vol. Artillery 637
Whatnots 507
Wheatcroft, Wm. 698
Wheatley, Samuel 700
Wheatley, Thomas 722
Wheeler, & Wilson 418
Whieldon 271, 281, 282
Whistle, Silver 698
Whistler, J. A. McNeill 645
Whitcombe, Eliz. Matilda 666
Whitley Bay 653
White Star Line 738, 739, 767, 769
White, Fuller 700
White-haired Clown 208
White, John 688
White, Wm. 204
Whitehead, Edw. 302
Whittington 301
Whittington, Dick 208
Whitwham & Co. 772-775
Who, The 655, 656
Wilcocks, Richard 692
Wilcox, Harriet E. 259
Wild II, Hans J. 245
Wilde, Kim 655
Wilding, Dorothy 632
Wien 220
Wiener Werkstatte 670
Wilkes, John 202
Wilkins 746
Wilkins, Geo. 293
Wilkinson 197
Wilkinson & Co., Henry 683, 702
Wilkinson Sword Co., Ltd. 75, 86, 121
Wilkinson, Henry 120, 678
Wilkinson, Norman 642 763, 764, 767
Wilkom, C. G. 413
Will's Star Cigarettes 599
Willaume, David 690
Willebrand, Johan 553
Williams 301
Williamson 338
Williamson, Robert 688
Williamson, Thos. 682
Willmore, Joseph 703
Willmore, Thos. 336
Willow 279
Wills, Peter 713
Wilmot, J. 683
Wilmshurst 299
Wilson, Ino. 319
Wilson, J. J. 132
Wilson, Robert & Wm. 694
Wimshurst 556
Winchcombe Pottery 193, 210, 211, 273
Winchell, Hannah 666
Winchester 115
Windler, J. M. 134
Windmills, J. 291, 306
Windover 760
Windsor 766
Windsor Castle 136
Wine 772-775
Wine Coolers 508, 509
Wine Coolers, Silver 720
Wine Funnels, Silver 721
Wine Glasses 542, 543
Wine Labels, Silver 722
Wine Tasters, Silver 723
Wine Tray 778, 779
Winlock, Mary P. 691
Winter Dancers 70
Winter in the Southern Sunshine 766
Winter Sports Expresses 768
Wise, E. E. 768
Wise, Jno. 300
Withers, E. 611
Witteman, Charles R. 594
W.K.C. 84, 116, 117

WMF 516, 578, 579, 581, 630, 631, 681
WMF Secessionist 581
Wogdon & Barton 110
Wolfe In Wien, Carl 310
Wolffe, Madame 645
Wolfsohn 217, 220
Wolseley 76
Wombles, The 655
Wood 776-784
Wood, Capt. 739
Wood, David 304
Wood, E. G. 136
Wood, Ralph 187, 189, 266, 267
Wood, Samuel 687
Woodcock, Isaac 687
Wooden Plate 549
Wooden Toys 784
Woodlands Indian 341
Woolwork Picture 588
Wooton Desk Co. 495
Worcester 283-288
Workboxes & Games Tables 492, 493
World's Columbian Exposition 705
Wortley Montagu, Lady Mary 287
Wright 481
Wright, Ann 737
Wright, Chas. 711
Wright, Frank L. 426, 488
Wright, Michael 601
Wright, Tho. 552
Wrigley, G. 591
Wrist Rest 776
Wristwatches 326-331
Writing Set 589
Writing Slope 161, 163
Writing Tables & Desks 494-499
Wucai 248
Wurttemberg Cavalry 118
Wurttemberg Infantry 96
Wyatt, S. R. 764

Xhrouet 264

Y5 Series 745
YII Series 744
Yabu Meizan 233
Yamabushi 623, 627
Yamaguchiya Tobei 644
Yangzhou School 724, 726
Yanyan 235
Yapp & Woodward 719
Yasuaki 623, 715
Yasumasa 89, 625
Yasuyuki 550
Yingqing 236, 237
Yixing 196
Ye Zhongsan 727, 728
Yeomanry Cavalry 107, 108
Yomud Asmalyk 662
Yonezawa 731
Yonge, G. & W. 296
Yongzheng 196
Yorkshire 184, 185
Yorkshire Moors 763
Yoshiharu 621
Yoshihide 622
Yoshijuro Urishibawa 640
Yoshimasa 622
Yoshiya 730
Young, Samuel 302
Young, & Co., J. 392
Young Christ, The 181
Young Girl & Frog 150
Young Miss Nightingale 207
Younge & Co., S. C. 679, 684
Your Girlfriend 656
Yuhuchunping 196
Yukimoyoi 641
Yung Cheng 213
Yuramosuke 625

Zack Bruno 142
Zampa 604
Zanzibar 628, 629
Zapf, 180, 181
Zeiss Tessar 166, 167
Zeppelin 78
Zia 71
Zigang 729
Zinke, Christian Frederick 639
Zither Marmonique Piccolo 608
Zouaves 749
Zuni 174, 568, 569
Zwei Madchen 648
Zwei Schwatzende Frauen 642
Zwischengoldglas 510, 533